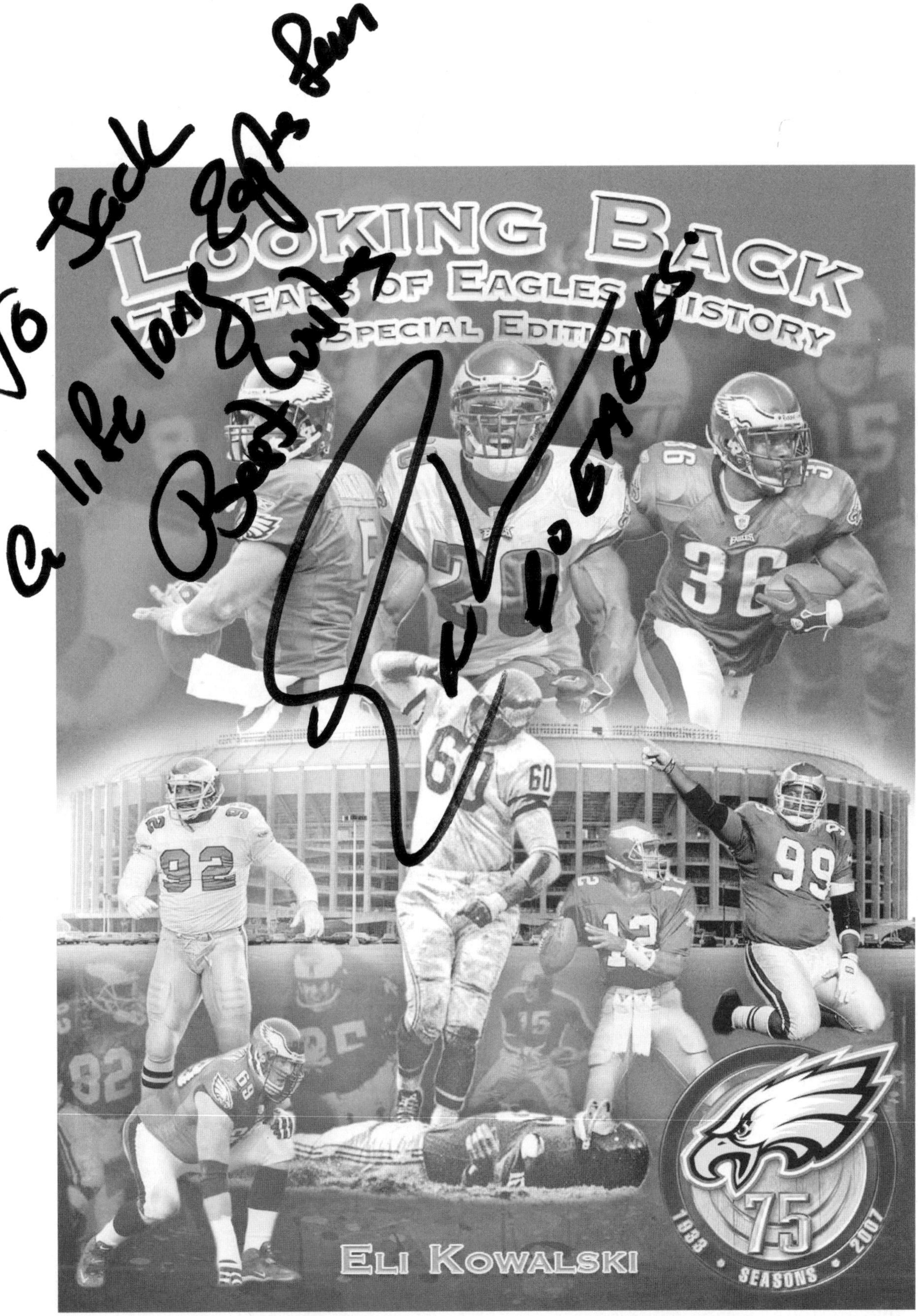
LOOKING BACK
75 YEARS OF EAGLES HISTORY
SPECIAL EDITION
ELI KOWALSKI
75
1933 • SEASONS • 2007
To Jack
a life long Eagles fan
Best Wishes

Looking Back 75 years of Eagles History: Special Edition

First Published 2008
Printed in the United States of America

ISBN: 978-0-615-21091-9

Library of Congress Control Number: 2008905338

Cover Designed by Bright Imaging
Digital Composition by Sean Miller

In support of the Eagles "Go Green" commitment and initiative, this book was printed using recyclable paper.

The following individuals and organizations generously gave permission to reproduce photographs and images in this book: The Philadelphia Eagles; Philadelphia Newspapers, LLC; Maple Leaf Productions; Bob Carroll and Sports Illustrated/Time Inc.

The photo's used on the front cover courtesy of The Philadelphia Eagles, (from left to right top portion), #5 Donovan McNabb, #20 Brian Dawkins, #36 Brian Westbrook, Veterans Memorial Stadium, (left to right bottom portion), #82 Mike Quick, #92 Reggie White, #69 Jon Runyan, #25 Tommy McDonald, #60 Chuck Bednarik, #12 Randall Cunningham and #99 Jerome Brown.

The photo's used on the back cover courtesy of The Philadelphia Eagles, Terry Bradshaw with Head Coach Andy Reid.

This book is published with permission granted by The Philadelphia Eagles.

Publisher
Sports Challenge Network
Philadelphia, PA 19102
www.sportschallengenetwork.com
email: elik@sportschallengenetwork.com

Dedication

This book is dedicated to my father, Peter Kowalski, who passed away in July 2007 while I was completing this book. My dad, a man who knew and enjoyed sports who was loved deeply by his family and the countless friends who had the privilege to know him.

I also dedicate this book, to the hundreds of thousands of loyal Eagles fans who over the years bleed Eagles green. This book is for you!

Acknowledgements

I feel fortunate as a fan to been able to compile Looking Back 75 years of Eagles History: Special Edition, the official history of the Philadelphia Eagles. I would like to express my sincere gratitude to the following individuals for their enormous contributions to this book:

First, to the following in the Eagles organization: Mark Donovan, senior vice president of the Eagles, who believed in this book project and me; Mike Malo, director of marketing for the Eagles; Bob Kent, internet/publications manager; and Ryan Hughes, Ed Mahan, Joe Lobolito, Tom Briglia, Drew Hallowell and Rob Babik who were so helpful in assisting me with images and material necessary to relive the Eagles history over the past 75 years. To my good friend, Jim Gallagher, retired Eagles public relations director and member of the Eagles Honor Roll, for his wisdom and for introducing me to some of the great former Eagles players; his memories of the Eagles are priceless.

I want to thank the staff members at the Philadelphia Inquirer and Philadelphia Daily News for their incredible patience and hard work in pulling all the various sports pages for me.

I would also like to thank the many local sportscasters and writers who shared with me some of their fondest Eagles memories, such as Ray Didinger, Michael Barkann, Lou Tilley, Jody McDonald, Don Tollefson, Bill Campbell, Vinnie "the crumb", and Steve Sabol.

Many thanks go out to both current and former Eagles players who shared with me their fondest memories as players. They include Chuck Bednarik, Tom Brookshier, Pete Retzlaff, Tommy McDonald, Garry Cobb (who was instrumental in assisting me with player interviews), Randall Cunningham, Brian Dawkins, Billy Ray Barnes, Jon Runyan, Bill Mackrides, David Akers, William Thomas, Sheldon Brown, Harold Carmichael, Fred Barnett, Mike Quick, Hugh Douglas, Ed Khayat, Vaughn Hebron, Bill Bergey, Vince Papale, Ike Reese, Ron Jaworski, Vai Sikahema, Jeremiah Trotter, Brian Westbrook, and Donovan McNabb.

Thanks to the various die-hard Eagles fans who shared their memories with me, including Ryan Hughes "SWOOP," Shaun Young, Tom Murphy ("Green Man"), Gary Discount, John Spitzkopf, Adam Poppel, Ray ("the Midas Man"), Larry Kagel, Steve Odabashian, Carl Henderson, Saul Braverman, Jerry D'Addesi, Jim Murray, Brian "Shifty" Schiff, and Neil Tobin.

To my family, Wendy, Zack and Josh, great Eagles fans, for their patience, support and understanding during this entire process.

- Eli Kowalski

PREFACE

My goal in compiling this book was to look back at the Eagles' 75 years of professional football. I hope to provide you, the reader, an entertaining and informative compilation of Eagles information, along with a statistical chronicle of the franchise. There has never before been a book with such a comprehensive collection of actual vintage sports pages from both the Philadelphia Inquirer and Philadelphia Daily News newspapers, spanning the past 75 years. I want Eagles fans to relive game memories by looking back at these sports pages.

I have incorporated chapters that will help you reminisce. You will be able to look at the stats for every season played during the past 75 years, see where all the training camps were held, and view a pictorial history of the evolution of the various Eagles uniforms. Also included are all retired jerseys numbers and, in chronological order, every jersey number worn and the corresponding players who wore them over the past 75 years. You will be able to look back on all the head coaches, owners, Eagles in the Hall of Fame, the Eagles Honor Roll; review all the Monday Night Football games in which the Eagles played; see all the Eagles that graced the front cover of Sports Illustrated; look at the first draft selections per year; and find your favorite player in the all-time players roster.

What really made this an interesting project was contacting former and current Eagles players to get their views and hear some of their fondest memories as an Eagles player. I also spoke with many local sportscasters and writers who covered the Eagles over the past 75 years, and of course the fans as well, about their memories. Mixed in with the memories are some defining moments in Eagles history.

Enjoy looking back at the past 75 years of Eagles history.

CONTENTS

1930's

Decade in Review

1933
Pennsylvania's move to repeal its Blue Laws – which prohibit numerous Sunday activities, including pro sporting events – paves the way for Philadelphia and Pittsburgh to enter the NFL.

The Frankford Yellowjackets franchise, which folded two years earlier, is awarded to a syndicate headed by Bert Bell and Lud Wray for $2,500. The club is christened the "Eagles" in honor of the symbol of the National Recovery Act established by Franklin Roosevelt during the Depression. After holding training camp in Atlantic City, the Eagles first play on October 15 vs. the NY Giants. Their home opener is three days later at the Baker Bowl vs. the Portsmouth Spartans.

1935
Though only a reserve halfback, Edwin "Alabama" Pitts, a former star on the Sing Sing Prison Gridiron team, becomes a fan favorite in his one season with the Eagles.

1936
With an additional investment of $4,000, Bert Bell becomes sole owner of the Eagles.

Bell's proposal for equalizing the distribution of talent throughout the league - the annual college draft - is implemented and, with the first selection overall, Philadelphia selects Heisman Trophy winning halfback Jay Berwanger. His rights, however, are traded to Chicago and Swede Hanson leads the club in rushing for a fourth straight year.

The Eagles move to a new home, leaving the Baker Bowl (Broad & Huntington Sts.) for Municipal Stadium. Located in South Philadelphia on what in the 1990s would become the site of the First Union Center (home of the 76ers and Flyers), Municipal Stadium hosts Eagles games for the remainder of the decade.

A trade with Chicago brings end Bill Hewitt, a future Hall of Famer, to the Eagles.

1939
Philadelphia drafts another Heisman Trophy winner, 5-7, 151-pound, quarterback Davey O'Brien, who reportedly signs a deal that includes a percentage of the gate. As a rookie, O'Brien sets an NFL record and earns all-pro honors with 1,324 passing yards.

On October 22, the Eagles earn a place in history by playing in the first televised pro football game. NBC broadcasts the game against the Brooklyn Dodgers to the 1,000 TV sets in existence in Brooklyn.

Frankford Yellowjackets

Eagles Owner Bert Bell was present when Pennsylvania repealed its Blue Laws

Alabama Pitts signs contract with coach Lud Wray

Swede Hanson

Jay Berwanger

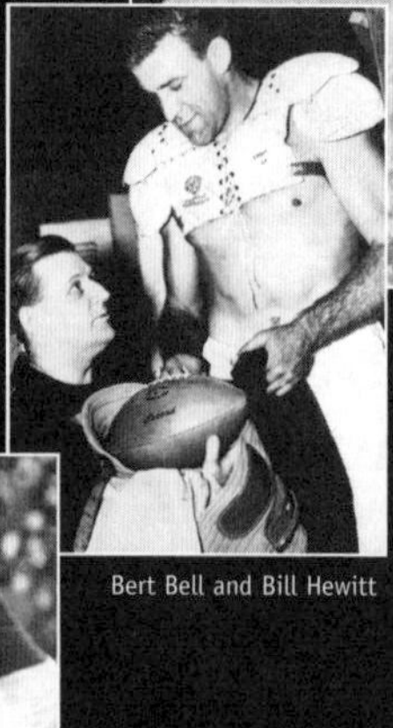

Bert Bell and Bill Hewitt

Box Seats at the Baker Bowl

Davey O'Brien

1930's

Decade Win-Loss Record:
18-55-3

Home Field:
Baker Bowl 1933-35; Temple Stadium 1934-35; Municipal Stadium 1936-39

Playoff Appearances:
None

Championships:
None

Head Coaches:
Lud Wray 1933-35 (9-21-1),
Bert Bell 1936-1939 (9-34-2)

Hall of Fame Inductees:
Bert Bell, Bill Hewitt

Award Winners:
None

All Pro:
Swede Hanson 1933-34,
Joe Carter 1935-36 and 1938, Ed Manske 1935,
Bill Hewitt 1937-38, Davey O'Brien 1939

All-Star Game Selections:
Joe Carter 1938-39, Davey O'Brien 1939

First Game of the Decade:
October 15, 1933 crushing loss to New York Giants 56-0

Last Game of the Decade:
December 3, 1939 loss to Cleveland Rams 35-13

Largest Margin of Victory:
November 6, 1934 vs. Cincinnati Reds 64-0

Largest Margin of Defeat:
October 16, 1933 vs. New York Giants 56-0

Eagle Firsts of the Decade:

First Touchdown
35-yard touchdown pass from Roger Kirkman to Swede Hanson on October 29, 1933 vs. Green Bay

First Safety
by George Kenneally on October 29, 1933 vs. Green Bay

First Field Goal
Guy Turnbow kicked a 20-yard field goal on November 12, 1933 vs. Chicago Bears

First Win
November 15, 1933 vs. Cincinnati Reds, 6-0

First Shutout
17-0 over the Pirates in Pittsburgh on September 26, 1934

First Draft Pick
Jay Berwanger in 1936

1933

RECORD: 3-5-1, 4TH IN NFL EAST
HEAD COACH: LUD WRAY

SCHEDULE

REGULAR SEASON

Wk. 5	Oct 15	L	56-0	at New York Giants
Wk. 6	Oct 18	L	25-0	vs Portsmouth Spartans
Wk. 7	Oct 29	L	35-9	at Green Bay Packers
Wk. 8	Nov 5	W	6-0	at Cincinnati Reds
Wk. 9	Nov 12	T	3-3	vs Chicago Bears
Wk. 10	Nov 19	W	25-6	vs Pittsburgh Pirates
Wk. 11	Nov 26	W	20-3	vs Cincinnati Reds
Wk. 12	Dec 3	L	10-0	vs Green Bay Packers
Wk. 13	Dec 10	L	20-14	vs New York Giants

After the Frankford Yellow Jackets folded, a syndicate headed by Bert Bell and Lud Wray paid $25,000 for the franchise for the purpose of placing a NFL team in Philadelphia. The club was christened "Eagles" in honor of the symbol of the New Deal's National Recovery Act. On October 15, the Eagles made their debut, with Lud Wray holding the coaching reigns, in New York by getting slaughtered by the Giants 56-0. A week later they did not do much better in their debut before the home fans of Philly, being shut out by the Portsmouth Spartans 25-0. After losing to the Packers in Green Bay the Eagles finally won their first game on November 5 by beating the Cincinnati Reds 6-0 at the Baker Bowl. The Eagles would go on to finish their inaugural season with a 3-5-1 record.

1933 PHILADELPHIA EAGLES STATS

Passing	Comp	Att	Comp %	Yds	Y/Att	TD	Int	Rating
Red Davis	2	6	33.3	62	10.33	1	3	72.9
Jack Roberts	4	10	40.0	97	9.70	1	3	69.6
Nick Prisco	0	2	0.0	0	0.00	0	0	39.6
Red Kirkman	22	73	30.1	354	4.85	2	13	17.0
Reb Russell	8	32	25.0	0	0.00	0	2	13.5
Dick Thornton	2	13	15.4	52	4.00	0	4	4.2
Swede Hanson	7	28	25.0	50	1.79	0	4	0.0
Jodie Whire	1	5	20.0	10	2.00	0	2	0.0
Harry O'Boyle	0	2	0.0	0	0.00	0	1	0.0
Les Woodruff	0	1	0.0	0	0.00	0	1	0.0
Rick Lackman	0	1	0.0	0	0.00	0	1	0.0

Rushing	Rush	Yds	Avg	TD
Swede Hanson	133	475	3.6	3
Jack Roberts	91	261	2.9	1
Reb Russell	32	96	3.0	0
Les Woodruff	22	74	3.4	1
Rick Lackman	17	59	3.5	0
Red Davis	15	57	3.8	1
Red Kirkman	22	43	2.0	0
Jodie Whire	8	14	1.8	0
Dick Thornton	5	14	2.8	0
Nick Prisco	7	6	0.9	0
Harry O'Boyle	2	4	2.0	0

Interceptions	Int	Yds	Avg	TD
Swede Hanson	3	0	0.0	0
Jack Roberts	2	0	0.0	0
Ray Smith	2	0	0.0	0
Rick Lackman	1	0	0.0	0
Lipski	1	0	0.0	0
Reb Russell	1	0	0.0	0
Les Woodruff	1	0	0.0	1

Kicking	PAT Made	PAT Att	PAT %	FG Made	FG Att	FG %	Pts
Joe Carter	1	1	100	0	0	0.0	13
Reb Russell	0	1	0	0	0	0.0	12
Red Davis	3	5	60	0	0	0.0	9
Red Kirkman	2	3	67	0	0	0.0	8

Receiving	Rec	Yds	Avg	TD
Swede Hanson	10	186	18.6	1
Joe Carter	5	109	21.8	2
Red Kirkman	4	84	21.0	1
Red Davis	4	50	12.5	0
Les Woodruff	3	57	19.0	0
George Kenneally	2	37	18.5	0
Dick Thornton	2	14	7.0	0
Nick Prisco	2	7	3.5	0
Dick Fencl	1	20	20.0	0
Porter Lainhart	1	20	20.0	0
Jodie Whire	1	15	15.0	0
Ev Rowan	1	12	12.0	0
Nip Felber	1	8	8.0	0
Jack Roberts	1	6	6.0	0
Larry Steinbach	1	5	5.0	0

Punting	Punts	Yds	Avg	Blocked
Davey O'Brien	6	246	41.0	0
Elmer Kolberg	10	401	40.1	0
Joe Bukant	15	568	37.9	0
Franny Murray	30	1098	36.6	0
John Cole	10	336	33.6	0
Foster Watkins	2	45	22.5	0

1933

SPORTS The Philadelphia Inquirer SPORTS

PHILADELPHIA, MONDAY MORNING, OCTOBER 16, 1933

RAPHAEL TAKES PHILA. LOOP CROWN

GRID GIANTS DRILL EAGLES, 56-0

QUAKERS DISSATISFIED; CHANGES LOOM

The Old Sport's Musings

IF YOU CAN'T BOOST DON'T KNOCK

DISTINCT BULL MOVEMENT IN PHILADELPHIA DISTRICT FOOTBALL OVER WEEK-END, WITH TEMPLE, PENN, LA SALLE, DREXEL AND P. M. C. DECLARING DIVIDENDS; SERIOUS SLUMP IN VILLANOVA WILDCAT, WHICH CLOSES AT LOW

THERE was a distinct bull movement in Philadelphia District Football over the week-end. Penn, Drexel, La Salle and P. M. C. all made substantial advances in brisk trading during the afternoon session on Saturday, while Temple closed strong on Friday night, making a gain of 21 points and going through its high for the year.

The movement upward, however, was not general throughout the local list. Villanova suffered a technical setback, closing weak, 2 under par, while Swarthmore and Haverford each surrendered 6 points before heavy pounding from Gettysburg and Susquehanna, respectively.

Where is That Scoring Punch?

When a Smart Team Blunders

Drexel-LaSalle in Notable Wins

NEWMAN HERO FOR N. Y. TEAM AS BIRDS FALL

Former Michigan Star Flips Pass After Pass to Crush Lud Wray's Gridmen in League Debut

Eagle Moleskinners No Match for Coogan's Bluff Clan as Steady Stream of Touchdowns Makes Tilt One-sided

Newman's Aim Unerring

Continued on Page 14, Column 7

Yep, Still Playing Ball—and He's Safe at Third

After a long, vigorous and strenuous campaign of six months ball playing the curtain finally fell on the Philadelphia League yesterday when Raphael defeated South Phillies in the final game for the title. Here is Maitland, of Raphael, sliding into third in the sixth frame of the settle. He beat Logan's throw to Brakefield, the former handling Holstein's slow infield grounder on which Maitland reached third by a smart dash from second.

TABBUTT HURLS 7-HIT GAME TO CAPTURE TITLE

Holds South Phillies Runless After Opening Inning and Raphael Takes Game and Crown

Error by Black Foozles Double Play, Then Logan Follows With Fumble to Settle Tilt in Fourth Frame

Continued on Page 14, Column 5

ST. CHARLES ELEVEN BEATS SUN VILLAGE ON 1ST PERIOD PASS

Joe Regan Tosses to Tony Dekovitch for Lone Score of Battle

Bywood Hornets Push Over Tally to Sting Tinicum

Clearview Eleven Wins 27th Straight

PENN STARTS DRIVE FOR INDIANS TODAY

Mentors to Meet and Hear Miller's Report on Next Foe; "Engle Brilliant, But Isn't He Always?" Fox; Stofko, Soph Tackle, Pleases Coach

Fox Approves Stofko

Continued on Page 14, Column 8

Cycling Knights of Old Revive Yesteryear's Stunts

Bike Game Slipping

Continued on Page 14, Column 6

HAGEN'S BRILLIANCY EARNS PRO GOLFERS "ALL-EVEN" VERDICT

Detroit Ace and Smith Rally to Draw With Brinke and Gunn

By GEORGE HINGSTON

Both Snare Birdies

Continued on Page 14, Column 3

Coach Defends Tactics of Cats Against Bisons

October 16, 1933 - Eagles First Game; 56-0 loss to NY Giants

1934

RECORD: 4-7-1, 3RD IN NFL EAST
HEAD COACH: LUD WRAY

Schedule

Regular Season

Wk. 2	Sep 16	L	19-6	at Green Bay Packers
Wk. 4	Sep 26	W	17-0	at Pittsburgh Pirates
Wk. 5	Oct 7	L	9-7	vs Pittsburgh Pirates
Wk. 6	Oct 14	L	10-0	vs Detroit Lions
Wk. 7	Oct 21	L	6-0	at Boston Redskins
Wk. 8	Oct 28	L	17-0	at New York Giants
Wk. 9	Nov 6	W	64-0	vs Cincinnati Reds
Wk. 10	Nov 11	L	10-7	vs Brooklyn Dodgers
Wk. 11	Nov 18	L	14-7	vs Boston Redskins
Wk. 12	Nov 25	W	13-0	at Brooklyn Dodgers
Wk. 14	Dec 2	W	6-0	vs New York Giants

The Eagles continued to struggle in their second season, losing five of their first six games and going on to finish with a 4-7 record. Amazingly the Eagles four wins of the season were all shutouts. They defeated, in order, Pittsburgh 17-0, Cincinnati 64-0 (this was their only win at Temple Stadium), Brooklyn 13-0, and the NY Giants 6-0 in the final game of the season.

1934 Philadelphia Eagles Stats

Passing	Comp	Att	Comp %	Yds	Y/Att	TD	Int	Rating
Dan Barnhart	1	1	100.0	4	4.00	1	0	122.9
Reds Weiner	3	6	50.0	40	6.67	2	0	111.1
Jim Leonard	2	10	20.0	29	2.90	0	0	39.6
Ed Matesic	20	60	33.3	278	4.63	2	5	25.6
Swede Ellstrom	3	14	21.4	40	2.86	1	5	23.8
Red Kirkman	7	23	30.4	38	1.65	1	2	18.2
Swede Hanson	4	12	33.3	28	2.33	0	2	2.8
Ed Storm	8	30	26.7	97	3.23	0	6	1.0
Jack Knapper	0	7	0.0	0	0.00	0	3	0.0

Rushing	Rush	Yds	Avg	TD
Swede Hanson	146	805	5.5	7
Swede Ellstrom	72	287	4.0	1
Ed Storm	81	281	3.5	2
Jim Leonard	55	207	3.8	1
Ed Matesic	63	181	2.9	0
Reds Weiner	9	37	4.1	0
Jack Roberts	10	28	2.8	0
Jack Knapper	10	19	1.9	0
Red Kirkman	6	12	2.0	0
Rick Lackman	4	9	2.3	0
George Kavel	2	5	2.5	0
Joe Pilconis	1	5	5.0	0
Lorne Johnson	1	0	0.0	0

Kicking	PAT Made	PAT Att	PAT %	FG Made	FG Att	FG %	Pts
Swede Hanson	2	2	100	0	0	0.0	50
Jim Leonard	5	7	71	0	0	0.0	11
Red Kirkman	5	7	71	0	0	0.0	11
Reds Weiner	3	4	75	1	2	50.0	6

Receiving	Rec	Yds	Avg	TD
Joe Carter	16	238	14.9	4
Red Kirkman	8	114	14.3	1
Ed Storm	5	34	6.8	0
Swede Hanson	5	22	4.4	0
Rick Lackman	4	83	20.8	0
Ed Matesic	3	38	12.7	1
Jim Leonard	3	7	2.3	0
Swede Ellstrom	1	18	18.0	0
George Kenneally	1	12	12.0	0
Bob Gonya	1	4	4.0	1
Joe Pilconis	1	3	3.0	0

Interceptions	Int	Yds	Avg	TD
Swede Hanson	4	0	0.0	1
John Lipski	2	0	0.0	0
Diddie Willson	2	0	0.0	0
Chuck Hajek	1	0	0.0	0
Jack Knapper	1	0	0.0	0
Ed Matesic	1	0	0.0	0
Joe Pilconis	1	0	0.0	0
Reds Weiner	1	0	0.0	0

1934

SPORTS The Philadelphia Inquirer SPORTS

PUBLIC LEDGER

PHILADELPHIA, WEDNESDAY MORNING, NOVEMBER 7, 1934

abcdef 19

W. PHILLY NIPS CENTRAL, NEARS TITLE

NATIONAL MAGNATES WANT HEYDLER BACK

EAGLES BURY REDS UNDER 64-0 DELUGE

The Old Sport's Musings

FORTY thousand dollars is a lot of money! But if I were Branch Rickey, I would not only give the Deans the forty thousand they demand for their next season's services in the pitching box, but I would also thank my stars that I was fortunate enough to have two such men on my ball club.

SPEEDBOYS TOP FOE ON AERIAL, STUDENTS MIX

Free-for-All Between Rival Rooters Starts on Field at Finish and Continues Outside Park

West Philly, Sure of Tie for Public High Title, Can Clinch Laurels Next Week; Harrison Takes Pass to Score

By FRED BYROD

Continued on Page 22, Column 6

West Philadelphia Stops Central's Thrust

John Nojunas, Central fullback, was stopped without gain by West Philadelphia on the play pictured above, "snapped" in the first quarter of the Public High League gridiron tilt before 7000 yesterday at the Phillies' ball park. Jimmy Rocks, Speedboy centre, made the tackle. West Philadelphia won, 6-0.

BIRDS SOAR TO NEW LOOP SCORING MARK AS CINCY FADES OUT

Hanson and Carter Contribute Three Touchdowns Each as Wraymen Swamp Reds With 10 Six-Pointers in One-Sided Grid Fray at Temple Stadium; Eagles Leave Cellar

By STAN BAUMGARTNER

Record Score

Continued on Page 21, Column 1

EFFORTS TO "DRAFT HEYDLER" TO BE MADE; WILL HAVE DEANS IN LINE, SAYS BREADON

National League Owners Unable to Find Successor to Veteran Executive

Want Him to Fill Out His Present Term as League Head

They Want Him - Will be Fair

JOHN A. HEYDLER

SAMUEL BREADON

Card Owner Predicts That Famous Brothers Will Be Easy to Sign

Always Fair With Other Stars, Will Be With Deans, Says Breadon

Continued on Page 21, Column 7

EAGLES OPEN SEASON AGAINST PROVIDENCE

Cricket Club Yellows Beat Bala Maids in Hockey Fuss

By DORA LURIE

Continued on Page 22, Column 5

Continued on Page 21, Column 3

Chicago Cards Down Dodger Gridmen, 21-0

Pannonia, Standard Land Victories in Jewish Loop

Cochrane Wants Al Simmons

November 7, 1934 - Largest Shutout Win; 64-0 against Cincinnati Reds

1935

RECORD: 2-9, 5TH IN NFL EAST
HEAD COACH: LUD WRAY

Schedule

Regular Season

Wk. 1	Sep 13	L	17-7	vs Pittsburgh Pirates
Wk. 2	Sep 20	L	35-0	at Detroit Lions
Wk. 5	Oct 9	W	17-6	at Pittsburgh Pirates
Wk. 5	Oct 13	L	39-0	vs Chicago Bears
Wk. 7	Oct 27	L	17-6	at Brooklyn Dodgers
Wk. 8	Nov 3	W	7-6	at Boston Redskins
Wk. 8	Nov 5	L	3-0	vs Brooklyn Dodgers
Wk. 9	Nov 10	L	12-3	at Chicago Cardinals
Wk. 11	Nov 24	L	10-0	at New York Giants
Wk. 12	Dec 1	L	21-14	vs New York Giants
Wk. 13	Dec 8	L	13-6	vs Green Bay Packers

The Eagles kept on struggling, finishing with a horrid 2-9 record. Their two wins came on the road, defeating Pittsburgh 17-6 and Boston 7-6. General Manager Bert Bell proposed an annual college draft to balance the talent in the league. The proposal was adopted on May 19, 1935, for the upcoming 1936 season. An unusual signing occurred when the Eagles signed Alabama Pitts upon his release from Sing Sing Prison. Following the '35 season Bert Bell bought out Lud Wray and became the team's sole owner.

1935 Philadelphia Eagles Stats

Passing	Comp	Att	Comp %	Yds	Y/Att	TD	Int	Rating
Swede Hanson	1	1	100.0	23	23.00	0	0	118.8
Red Kirkman	1	1	100.0	1	1.00	1	0	118.8
Ed Storm	15	44	34.1	372	8.45	3	10	48.9
Irv Kupcinet	1	5	20.0	6	1.20	0	0	39.6
Steve Banas	0	2	0.0	0	0.00	0	0	39.6
Ed Matesic	15	64	23.4	284	4.44	2	13	16.4
Jim Leonard	11	32	34.4	119	3.72	0	3	7.2
Bob Rowe	1	11	9.1	6	0.55	0	2	0.0
Mike Sebastian	0	4	0.0	0	0.00	0	1	0.0

Rushing	Rush	Yds	Avg	TD
Swede Hanson	77	209	2.7	0
Izzy Weinstock	58	176	3.0	0
Jim Leonard	74	171	2.3	1
Ed Storm	84	164	2.0	0
Ed Matesic	50	138	2.8	1
Mike Sebastian	17	76	4.5	0
Rick Lackman	22	56	2.5	0
Bob Rowe	7	21	3.0	0
Joe Carter	7	19	2.7	0
Stumpy Thomason	3	14	4.7	0
Eggs Manske	3	9	3.0	0
Steve Banas	5	3	0.6	0
Bill Brian	1	2	2.0	0
George Kenneally	3	-4	-1.3	0

Receiving	Rec	Yds	Avg	TD
Joe Carter	11	260	23.6	2
Eggs Manske	9	205	22.8	4
Izzy Weinstock	8	107	13.4	0
Rick Lackman	5	49	9.8	0
Swede Hanson	4	82	20.5	0
Ed Storm	3	44	14.7	0
Alabama Pitts	2	21	10.5	0
Mike Sebastian	1	19	19.0	0
Burle Robison	1	18	18.0	0
Glenn Campbell	1	2	2.0	0

Kicking	PAT Made	PAT Att	PAT %	FG Made	FG Att	FG %	Pts
Hank Reese	4	6	67	1	0	0.0	7
Bud Jorgensen	1	1	100	0	0	0.0	4
Red Kirkman	1	1	100	0	0	0.0	1

1933 • 75 SEASONS • 2007

1935

German Soccermen Defeat Scots-Americans to Grab Sixth Straight Win

SPORTS **The Philadelphia Inquirer** SPORTS

PUBLIC LEDGER

PHILADELPHIA, MONDAY MORNING, OCTOBER 14, 1935 — abcde 13

CHI BEARS CRUSH EAGLES, 39-0

PETILLO WINS, SETS WORLD RECORD

THE OLD SPORT'S MUSINGS

IF YOU CAN'T BOOST DON'T KNOCK

PENN OWES HUMILIATING DEFEAT TO WEAKNESS IN FUNDAMENTALS: QUAKER TACKLING AND BLOCKING ATROCIOUS; TEMPLE AND VILLANOVA IMPRESSIVE IN WEEK-END TRIUMPHS: ALBRIGHT HAS WHAT IT TAKES

TIME may soften but can never erase the chagrin of those who follow the football fortunes of Penn as they slowly and sadly melted away from Franklin Field after seeing the Quakers blotted out by Yale, 31 to 20.

It is idle to say that here was a game that Penn should have won because the Red and Blue once held a lead of 20 to 6. Had the Quakers led 200 to 6, with unlimited time to play, the Bulldogs would have overtaken them, as Harman's pupils were performing in that second half.

Football teams can be pounded into submission by powerful opponents; when two fairly evenly matched gridiron forces clash one well-conceived and beautifully executed play may decide the issue—but when a team that musters the individual strength of Penn yields a total of 229 yards in four plays FOR FOUR TOUCHDOWNS, something is radically wrong.

Something is radically wrong with Penn and that something was evident to everyone who witnessed the downfall of the Quakers against Yale. They are not versed in the fundamentals; there was no finality about their tackling; their blocking was atrocious and their defense was without elasticity.

Three of Yale's five touchdowns were scored on long runs developed from the same type of play—a reverse which feinted at the long side of Penn's line and then struck at the short side. In each case the ball carrier got loose to score without a Penn tackler having a fair shot at the runner.

Rare is the football team that is not occasionally caught out of position, drawn in, by a perfectly executed deception play—but when eleven men are repeatedly deceived by the same play something should be done about it.

Quaker Blocking Without Finality

NO TEAM can get anywhere without blocking—the type of blocking that puts a potential tackler definitely out of the play. Simply hitting a defensive player does not suffice; he must be definitely cut down, rendered totally impotent.

Against Yale, Penn repeatedly got the ball carrier away behind a cloud of interference. But the blockers either failed entirely to take their men out or made such a half-way job of their assignment that the Eli tacklers sifted through to nail the Quaker runner before he could cut in and cross the line of scrimmage.

The Red and Blue blockers never seemed to have their heads up, particularly in the second half. On one occasion three Quaker interferers "ganged-up" on a single Bulldog. They put their man out of the play all right, but they left their ball carrier an easy victim for two other Eli tacklers who almost ruined him.

It was pitiful to see plays well conceived by Coach Harman and his assistants fail because of the running interferers' failure to play heads-up football. It was even more pitiful to see eleven Penn defensive players repeatedly deceived and drawn out of position.

Incidentally, the Old Sport does not aim to discount Yale's courageous, efficient and versatile play. Yale's strength was not Penn's weakness. The Bulldogs played hard and alert football. They did not lose heart when trailing, 20 to 6, against a team that had the greater power. Instead they went into "high" and in the end capitalized their superior speed and gridiron sense to win the football game.

No review of what happened on Franklin Field Saturday would be complete without mention of one individual—Train, a Bulldog end. This young man spent most of the afternoon in Penn's backfield and he contributed an all-around performance that should recommend him to those who pick All-American teams.

Nourishing Week-end for Locals

WITH the exception of Penn, Haverford and Swarthmore, teams in this sector spent a profitable week-end. Haverford lost a close one to Susquehanna, 19 to 16, while the Little Quakers bent the knee to Washington College, 13 to 6.

In a nocturnal combat on Friday night the Temple Owls broke the winning streak of Vanderbilt, 6 to 3, after trailing until the final quarter. It is significant to note that Kosko, who is giving Dave Smukler a hard fight for the fullback post, was chiefly instrumental in scoring the winning touchdown.

Villanova gave another exhibition of snappy, well-organized football by blotting out the Thundering Herd of Bucknell, 25 to 0. The Wildcats have not yielded a point this season and, in Raimo and Kotys, have uncovered two offensive backs who must be ranked among the best of the year thus far.

Salutations to La Salle, which regained its winning stride at the expense of Ursinus, 18 to 0. After going through the season of 1934 undefeated, and getting off on the right foot this year, the La Salles were smothered by Catholic U. Many teams would have slowed down under the circumstances, but not this aggregation of fighters.

One of the surprises of the day was the 12 to 0 defeat inflicted on the West Chester Teachers by P. M. C. Victorious over Rutgers and North Carolina, the Teachers were favored to defeat the Cadets, who had succumbed to Villanova and Bucknell. But Timm's pupils bounded back after three scoreless periods against West Chester, marched 44 yards for a touchdown and then added another by intercepting a forward pass.

One of the outstanding developments of the week-end on the gridiron was the number of missed points after touchdown. One point would have decided the Drexel-Juniata fuss, which ended in a tie. Accurate kicking seems to be a lost art.

St. Joseph's, developing steadily, scored a convincing triumph over St. Francis', 26 to 6, rounding out a satisfactory day for most of our local teams.

Little Albright Serves Notice

EASILY the most impressive victory scored by an up-State team was Albright's astonishing conquest of Lafayette, 38 to 0. Coach Munn has put together a team that flings a challenge to any minor college in the East—a team that served notice of its power by putting the convincer on Georgetown and then smothered Lafayette.

F. and M. and Lehigh, two other gridiron powers this year, came through with little trouble—the Roses trouncing Moravian, 26 to 0, and Lehigh bouncing Dickinson, 26 to 0.

Penn State, however, had plenty of trouble getting by Western Maryland, tucking the game away by the margin of a safety in the first period. Western Maryland made a determined drive in the final quarter, but Coach Bob Higgins had sufficient and efficient replacements to balk the Green Terrors.

P. L.

POLLOCK STAR AS CHI ELEVEN BATTERS BIRDS

22,000 See Second-Period Onslaught Roll Up 27 Points in Phils' Park Combat

Ex-Northeast and P. M. C. Hero Scores Three Touchdowns; Pitts' Ramble Gives Philly Rooters Only Thrill

By STAN BAUMGARTNER

A flaming redhead, not the famous phantom Red Grange, but our own Reds Pollock, former Northeast High and P. M. C. star, another will-o-wisp in mole-skins came back yesterday in alien regalia to lead the Chicago Bears to a convincing 39-0 triumph over the Eagles before 22,000 stunned fans at the Phillies ball park.

Darting here and there like an enraged rattler, ripping and tearing, sinking his fangs into the Eagle line and whipping his mighty body around the flanks, Pollock crossed the local goal line three times and amassed 18 of his team's 39 points.

In all, the Bears tallied six touchdowns and Manders place-kicked for three additional points.

Four of these touchdowns were scored in a furious second period after the Bears had been frustrated in two goal line drives in the initial session. This display of power gave the victors a 27-0 lead at the half and in the final they contented themselves with a touchdown in each of the third and fourth quarters.

Pollock launched his devastating attack and raced to his first six-pointer three minutes after the second session got under way on a loose-hipped drive of 15 yards through the centre of the line, bone crushing two Eagles and cleverly sidestepping the secondary defense on his way to the final ribbon.

This was the spark that ignited the fury of the Bear attack and in less than 12 minutes they scored 20 more points against the helpless and hapless and completely bewildered local eleven.

Before the quarter was over Pollock made two more drives of five and eight yards for touchdowns and Molesworth tossed a 20-yard forward pass to Johnsos for another six-pointer.

It was all over except for the matter of adding up the Bears' points when the second half got under way and the Chicagoans took pity on the Wraymen, contenting themselves with scoring only two more touchdowns in the final 30 minutes.

Eagles Feeble Birds

The first of these came in the third period when Kawal, Bear centre, intercepted an Eagle pass on the Eagles' own 13-yard line and rushed over the final ribbon. The second and final touchdown of the half was made in the fourth quarter when the Bears marched 95 yards for a score—Ronzani ending the advance with a five-yard sweep around left end.

The Eagles were pitiful. They gave an exhibition of general all-around inefficiency that would have made

Continued on Page 15, Column 6

Gangway for Petillo - - - Orendorf Cracks Up

Kelly Petillo, winner of the most recent Indianapolis Speed classic, won the feature event at Langhorne yesterday and set a world mark for the 100-mile grind on a one-mile track. Top shows Petillo left, roaring on his way at the 60-mile mark. Lower pictures the wreckage of Vern Orendorf's racing car. Directly in front of the pits, he blew a tire during the "century" test, skidded and crashed into the rail. Fortunately, neither Orendorf nor his mechanic was injured.

CLIFTON GRIDMEN UPSET PASSYUNK IN AERIAL BATTLE

All Touchdowns Result of Passes as Delaware Countians Triumph

By FRED BYROD

Clifton Heights continued its unchecked march through the semi-pro gridiron ranks by bumping Passyunk Square from the undefeated list, score 14 to 6, before a crowd of 6000 yesterday on Kent Field, Clifton Heights.

Trailing almost all the way, Passyunk Square, nevertheless, fought stubbornly for the full 60 minutes and didn't concede defeat until the Clifton clan turned an intercepted pass into its second touchdown, a few minutes before the final whistle.

Clifton Heights tallied in the second quarter on a nine-yard forward pass, Cy McFadden to Tony Dekovitch, and added the extra point on a perfect placement kick by Captain Norbert "Gus" Werner.

Great line play by Clifton's guards—Werner and Bernie Bradley—checked the visitors on the ground, but Passyunk in turn struck overhead to tally on a sensational pass from Tony Lapolla to Dave James covering 25 yards.

Extra Point Try Fails

Louie Dell, little Clifton halfback, batted down Lapolla's pass, intended for James, on the extra point try and Clifton was still ahead, but it took a 17-yard run following an intercepted pass by Jim Cleary to clinch the conquest for the Delaware countians.

Neither team could get anywhere in the first quarter, but opportunity knocked for Clifton Heights at the beginning of the second period when a Passyunk Square player was detected clipping from behind as C. McFadden punted to the visitors' four-yard line. This violation gave the homesters a first down on the four.

But the defense of the South Philadelphians was unyielding. 2

Continued on Page 15, Column 7

HOOSIER HERO HANDY WINNER AT LANGHORNE

Indianapolis Victor Lowers Mark for "Century" on One-mile Track Before 18,000

Winn Finishes Second and Roberts Third; Winnai and Paulowski Injured Slightly in Mishap; Fowler Also Crashes

By PERRY LEWIS

Kelly Petillo came to town seeking the vindication for his indifferent showing on the Langhorne Speedway early in the season and he left for his home in Indianapolis last night with vindication and a number of other important things, not the least of which was a world record for 100 miles of auto racing on a one-mile track.

Meeting the challenge of Billy Winn and other noted pilots, the Indianapolis winner sped around the Langhorne track 100 times in 65.17.13. This bettered the old mark of 69.53.8 established at Langhorne by the late Frank Farmer several years ago.

The young Italian speed king, of course, won the century event with ease, although he was led over the first 24 miles by little Billy Winn, who finished second. Third place went to Floyd Roberts, a California driver.

Fred Winnai Crashes

Although there were four accidents during the time trials and the race proper, no one was seriously injured. The most serious mishap of the day was when Fred Winnai skidded and turned over directly in front of the stands. Both Freddy, a local favorite, and Johnny Paulowski, his mechanic, were taken to the Bristol Hospital. There it was found that Freddy had fractured eight ribs, cut lip, leg sprains and a bruised hip.

His mechanic, who was thrown clear when the car turned over, suffered laceration of the hip and nose.

After being treated for his injuries Paulowski was discharged, but Winnai remained in the hospital.

Ken Fowler, Paterson, N. J., went through the outer rail in making his time trial and, although his car was wrecked, he was uninjured. The veteran pilot, Chet Gardner, another Californian, threw a tire coming into the stretch, but kept his car under control. The detached tire rolled along the track in front of other speeding cars, but the pilots managed to avoid it.

Orendorf Averts Trouble

Undoubtedly the finest exhibition of emergency driving was given by Vern Orendorf, of Florida, who blew a tire directly in front of the pits, went into a bad skid which turned him completely around and crashed into the rail. Neither Orendorf nor his mechanic was even scratched.

After the luckless Paulowski had been patched up at the hospital following his accident, he returned to the track and was standing inside the rail in one of the pits when Orendorf skidded. He tried to leap clear of the swerving car and succeeded, but was showered with hot

Continued on Page 14, Column 2

TALLY BY ALTEMOSE GIVES GERMANS GAME

Inside Left Ace Scores in Opening Half to Give Philadelphians Victory Over Scots-Americans and Sixth Straight Conquest of Season

By GEORGE BUTZ

Displaying a power-house attack the German-Americans sent the league-leading Scots-Americans down the toboggan for their first American League defeat yesterday before the largest crowd ever to view a game at the Tabor Field. The score was 1-0.

Flashing a drive from the start to the final whistle, the Germans rang up their sixth straight victory and atoned for their lone loss reverse by the Scots recently in Newark.

The only goal of the game was netted by Charlie (Chic) Altemose, lanky speedster from up-State, who played the game to the hilt at the Germans' inside left post.

Altemose's goal came after 25 minutes of the first half and was ably assisted by Ray Richards, blond right-winger from Nanticoke, Pa. Richards swung one over from right wing and Altemose beat Goalie George Davis, who ventured out from his post and spilled in an [illegible]

The Lineup

[illegible]

[illegible] Richards touch from wing [illegible] to Nemchik, the German [illegible]

This was the fourth straight game in which Altemose has scored a goal.

Scotsmen's Rush Fails

In the second half the Scotsmen were out for a goal at any cost but

Continued on Page 14, Column 1

WENTZ OLNEY TRIPS DIGGERS RIVAL, 2-0, IN SEASON'S OPENER

Tigers Tally Safety in Second Quarter to Win Initial Tussle

Prying off the lid of another lengthy gridiron campaign, Wentz Olney captured its initial win by the margin of a safety over the Diggers eleven as "Tobe" Tyler's newly named Tigers failed to live up to their advance notice when their highly heralded offensive required the good fortune of a second period break that allowed the Orange and Black to jump off with the 2 to 0 [illegible] at Front and Chew sts. before a large opening day crowd yesterday afternoon. In the other game of a bargain bill the Olney Aces downed Penllyn 30-0.

Wentz Olney with a coterie of former collegiate greats headed by Sam Levin and Claire Lyons, presented a mighty dusty moleskin machine which will need plenty of polishing if it expects to mow down the opposition with the same ease as the 1934 aggregation.

The Tigers presented virtually a new line-up with two holdovers from last season as the keystones of the front and back lines—the veterans Joe Snyder at centre, and Wee Willie Totser at quarterback. Irish Rogan also saw service last season in the guard post which he held down yesterday.

To this small group has been added Levin, erstwhile Ursinus linesman, who played such a prominent role in the Bears' 7-6 defeat of Penn last year. In the backfield Lyons, a former member of the Colgate eleven which went undefeated two years ago, will more than likely become the spearhead of the Wentz attack which should function in the future.

Lesser lights in the Tiger cast included Sam Rubin, all-scholastic guard from Germantown High, and Dick Cahill, of Roman Catholic High fame.

But with all these outstanding forces mobilized into one offensive unit, Wentz Olney could not dent the Diggers' forward wall and had to be satisfied with an automatic safety for the two-point edge of triumph.

The opportunity came late in the

Continued on Page 15, Column 8

RUNYAN CAPTURES LOUISVILLE OPEN

AUDUBON COUNTRY CLUB, Louisville, Ky., Oct. 13 (A. P.)—Blasting a sub par 70 on the final 18, diminutive Paul Runyan, White Plains, N. Y., professional, overhauled the early leader, Alvin Krueger, Beloit, Wis., to win the $5000 Louisville Open Golf tournament here today.

His 72-hole total was 283, one under par.

Runyan, starting today's play two strokes behind, tabbed a 37, two over par, on the out nine of the afternoon round. He settled down to business on the backstretch, however, to can four birdies for a 33, three under regulation figures.

Second place went to Harry Cooper, who turned in the best performance of the day with a 69 on the afternoon round. He was out in 33 and back in 36 and needed pars on the last three holes to catch Runyan. His drive on the 16th, however, found the trap just in front of a heel-print which prevented a chance of distance. He wound up with a 6 on this hole and his chances were gone.

Vic Ghezzi, Deal, N. J., shot two rounds today of 72 and 70 to wind up in third place with 287. Tied for fourth were Bill Kaiser, Louisville; Kreuger, Frank Walsh, Chi-

Continued on Page 15, Column 7

KEN STRONG GLEAMS AS GIANTS TRIUMPH

NEW YORK, Oct. 13 (A. P.)—Two points a minute was Ken Strong's average today as the New York Giants defeated the Brooklyn Dodgers 10 to 7, in a National Pro Football League game before 30,000 spectators at the Polo Grounds.

The former New York University All-American fullback tore around the greenpersied Dodgers' right end for 24 yards for a touchdown and kicked the placement for the extra point in the first period. All told the touchdowns required only six plays. A few seconds later he came out a pile-up limping badly, and left the game.

[illegible]

Cards Seek Third Baseman, Martin Back to Outfield

ST. LOUIS, Oct. 13 (A. P.)—Among the deals the St. Louis Cardinals may swing this winter, look for one that will bring a third baseman to the dethroned National League champions.

That won't mean the benching next season of Pepper Martin, but it will mean the return of the Wild Horse of the Osage to his first love—the outfield.

President Sam Breadon, who, by the way, can't see anyone but the Cardinals on top of the heap next year, said he believed his team would be greatly strengthened by the shift.

"I believe right field is Martin's position," he explained. "He has the speed and the arm and it won't take him long to regain his outfield sights. It's my opinion also that he will be a more consistent hitter as an outfielder than as a third baseman. He plays so hard that he wears himself out in the infield where he is constantly on the jump."

With Martin in right, Terry Moore in centre and Joe Medwick in left, Breadon said he would have "a 1936 combination that should rank with the best the game has ever seen."

It is possible that Charles Gelbert, who frequently replaced Martin at third this past season, may be at the hot corner regularly when the next campaign starts.

However, while Gelbert has recovered fully from the shotgun wound in his left leg which threatened to wreck his baseball career several years ago, there is some doubt about his ability to play day in and day out through a schedule of 154 games. For that reason the Cardinals would like to obtain a young Pie Traynor, leaving Gelbert as a reserve.

KUNES BLASTS PAR IN PRACTICE ROUND

OKLAHOMA CITY, Oct. 13 (A. P.)—Gene Kunes, Canadian Open champion, blasted out a sub par 34 for the first nine of the twin hills links in practice today to serve notice that he was a contender in the National Professional Golfers Association tourney opening Thursday.

He did not do so well on the back side, devoting most of his time to position plays.

"This course is plenty tough," commented the 26-year-old Kunes, whose home is in Norristown, Pa.

Practice scoring honors, however, went to Gene Sarazen, and Bill Malcolm of West Orange, N. J., [illegible]ing out and a sub par 34 coming in. Both carded 70s. Each took a 36 go-[illegible]

Arrivals today included Russell Stonehouse, of Indianapolis, who played with Kunes; Al Houghton, of Virginia Beach, Va.; William Whalen, of West Hartford, Conn.; Mike Seamah, of Paterson, N. J., and Graham Reid, of Farmington, Conn.

Paul Runyan plans to come here from the Louisville open, which ended today, to defend his PGA title.

October 14, 1935 - Second shutout loss of over 35 points in the season, 39-0 to Chicago Bears; Eagles had four shutout losses in 1935

1936

RECORD: 1-11, 5TH IN NFL EAST
HEAD COACH: BERT BELL

SCHEDULE

REGULAR SEASON

Wk. 1	Sep 13	W	10-7	vs New York Giants
Wk. 2	Sep 20	L	26-3	vs Boston Redskins
Wk. 3	Sep 27	L	17-0	vs Chicago Bears
Wk. 4	Oct 4	L	18-0	at Brooklyn Dodgers
Wk. 5	Oct 11	L	23-0	vs Detroit Lions
Wk. 6	Oct 14	L	17-0	at Pittsburgh Pirates
Wk. 7	Oct 18	L	17-7	at Boston Redskins
Wk. 8	Oct 25	L	21-17	at New York Giants
Wk. 9	Nov 5	L	6-0	vs Pittsburgh Pirates (at Johnstown, PA)
Wk. 10	Nov 8	L	13-0	at Chicago Cardinals
Wk. 11	Nov 22	L	28-7	vs Chicago Bears
Wk. 12	Nov 29	L	13-7	vs Brooklyn Dodgers

Bert Bell was now the sole owner of the Eagles and also took over as head coach, though he did not have any more success than Lud Wray on the field, losing six games by shutouts. His only win occurred in the second game of the season against the NY Giants, winning 10-7 at home. Then the Eagles hit an all-time low, losing the next 10 games. The 1936 season was their worst season on record, as the Eagles scored only 51 points and finished with an awful record of 1-11. Also, in the very first draft the Eagles had the first pick and they selected QB Jay Berwanger, who recently had won the first Heisman Trophy. However, Berwanger had no intention of ever playing pro-football so he never signed.

1936 PHILADELPHIA EAGLES STATS

Passing	Comp	Att	Comp %	Yds	Y/Att	TD	Int	Rating
Dave Smukler	21	68	30.9	345	5.07	3	6	26.9
Jim Leonard	2	6	33.3	45	7.50	0	2	21.5
John Kusko	6	27	22.2	108	4.00	0	8	4.2
Reds Bassman	1	3	33.3	3	1.00	0	1	2.8
Don Jackson	7	35	20.0	80	2.29	0	11	0.0
Stumpy Thomason	1	10	10.0	11	1.10	0	3	0.0
Walt Masters	1	6	16.7	11	1.83	0	1	0.0
Swede Hanson	0	15	0.0	0	0.00	0	4	0.0

Rushing	Rush	Yds	Avg	TD
Swede Hanson	119	359	3.0	1
Stumpy Thomason	109	333	3.1	0
Dave Smukler	99	321	3.2	0
John Kusko	49	209	4.3	1
Don Jackson	46	76	1.7	0
Jim Leonard	33	72	2.2	0
Reds Bassman	4	19	4.8	0
Walt Masters	7	18	2.6	0
Glenn Frey	7	8	1.1	0

Receiving	Rec	Yds	Avg	TD
Eggs Manske	17	325	19.1	0
Jim Leonard	5	46	9.2	1
Joe Pilconis	4	51	12.8	1
Joe Carter	4	42	10.5	1
Glenn Frey	3	65	21.7	0
Swede Hanson	3	33	11.0	0
Reds Bassman	2	38	19.0	0
George Mulligan	1	3	3.0	0

Kicking	PAT Made	PAT Att	PAT %	FG Made	FG Att	FG %	Pts
Hank Reese	3	3	100	2	0	0.0	9
Stumpy Thomason	1	1	100	0	0	0.0	7
Dave Smukler	2	2	100	1	0	0.0	5

Platt Meets Lehman in One of Four National Amateur Headliners Tod

SPORTS — The Philadelphia Inquirer PUBLIC LEDGER — SPORTS

PHILADELPHIA, MONDAY MORNING, SEPTEMBER 14, 1936 — abdef 17

64,417 WATCH GIANTS-CARDS SPLIT

EAGLES WIN OPENING GRID TILT, 10-7

This Giant Started to Go Places, But Got Nowhere

In the first period of yesterday's gridiron struggle at the Stadium between the Philadelphia Eagles and New York Giants, Elvin (Kink) Richards, New York, hopefully started around the Birds' right end. He was doing very nicely when nailed from behind by an Eagle tackler, who trapped his right leg. Richards is seen carrying the ball and "13." Eagles won the game, 10-7.

THE OLD SPORT'S MUSINGS

IF YOU CAN'T BOOST DON'T KNOCK

DEATH OF BOB GUNNIS REMOVES FROM WORLD OF SPORT A MAN OF STERLING QUALITIES WHO COMBINED BUSINESS ACUMEN WITH LOFTY BUSINESS PRINCIPLES

ON MY way to the office yesterday I met two heart-broken men of middle age walking slowly and somewhat aimlessly along arm-in-arm. The eyes of both were moist, their faces drawn and haggard, their usually erect shoulders drooping.

One of them was Bill Gunnis, the other Herman Taylor, and they had just come from a hospital room in which lay the still form of Robert H. (Bobby) Gunnis—beloved brother to one, life-long friend and partner to the other.

There are thousands who will share their grief when the death of Bobby Gunnis becomes generally known this morning. Bob was a man of many friendships. To know him was to admire his fine qualities as a man; to know him well was to love him as a true friend and brother.

The writer's friendship with Bobby Gunnis extended over a period of 30 years, during which time Bob was a manager of fighters and, later, member of Philadelphia's most successful firm engaged in the promotion field. As a chronicler of sports we were frequently in contact.

Familiar with the deals that he made as a manager and later as a promoter in association with Herman Taylor, the writer asserts, without fear of contradiction, that Bob never broke his word. One did not need a contract to be assured that Bob would go through with his part of a bargain. His promise was his bond.

Gunnis and Taylor went into partnership in 1918 and since then have handled millions of dollars. They never bothered with a contract for neither considered such a document necessary.

Interested in All Sports

ALTHOUGH Bob's business was boxing, he was interested in all forms of sport, particularly football and basketball. He seldom missed a gridiron or floor struggle in which Penn was a participant and he was a fimiliar figure at outstanding scholastic events.

The business of promoting boxing is a precarious one and those who follow it must take the bitter with the sweet, the disappointments with the triumphs, the downs with the ups. Neither Bob nor his partner escaped dismal periods when they went into the "red," but they always came up with a smile and cleared decks for another venture that they hoped would prove more fortunate.

On many occasions the writer talked with Bob on mornings following shows that had lost thousands. I saw him very frequently during the dark days of 1929 when his personal fortune was shrinking. But the only time I ever saw Bob completely downhearted and totally discouraged was last year when Penn played Navy on Franklin Field.

Bob's son, "Young Bill," was out there warming up with the Penn team, and for days there had been jubilation on the Quaker campus over the return of Bill Gunnis to form following a knee injury. The pride of the father, seated high up in the stands, made his face beam as he watched that stalwart son run through signals, and he trembled with excitement as the teams lined up for the kickoff.

Young Bill Gunnis was "hot" that day; the coaches knew it, the players knew it, the father knew it, and the spectators in the stands had been told about it in the press. Fifty thousand pairs of eyes were focussed upon Right Guard Gunnis as Penn kicked off.

The Blow That Hurt Bob Most

YOUNG BILL came tearing down the field like an avalanche, and with one of his teammates, hit the ball-carrier with one of those thunderous tackles that swell football casualty lists. Two teammates assisted Bill from the field, through for the season, and high up in the stands Bob, robust as he was, seemed to shrivel up and two tears trickled down his kindly face.

Bob was a sick man then, the disease that caused his death early yesterday already having him in its insidious grip. But this man, powerful in his muscular strength, still more powerful in his stout heart, was a hard man to down.

Always ailing and suffering most of the time, Bob insisted upon carrying on the business affairs of his firm. Day after day he came to his office when he should have been in bed, and when his desk chair was empty, visitors knew that Bob had again been forced to retire to a hospital for treatment.

Up to within a few days ago he went over details of the approaching Louis-Ettore fight with his partner and had a clear grasp of the situation. Bob knew that he would not see this bout, but he did hope to hear about what promises to be his firm's greatest triumph, and that he won't seems to be a cruel stroke of fate.

"The evil that men do lives after them:
"The good is oft interred with their bones."

So wrote Shakespeare, and I have often thought that, in this case, the Bard of Avon was wrong. More often we are wont to extol the dead and forget the evil they have done. But in the case of Bob Gunnis it makes no difference. He did no evil that will live after him, and his good works, his many little-known charities, survive him.

Feller's Remarkable Feats

ONE of the most remarkable individual feats in the history of baseball was spun yesterday at Cleveland by a 17-year-old boy, Bob Feller, who, pitching for Cleveland, fanned 17 of the Athletics, which smashes the American League record and ties the National League mark established by Dizzy Dean three years ago.

This was not the first time that an Athletics team has been the victims of a record strike-out performance. Twenty-eight years ago one of Connie Mack's teams was baggied by Rube Waddell, who threw the ball past the bewildered batsmen for 16 strikeouts, which stood as an American League record until Feller went crazy yesterday.

Waddell's performance was an act of vengeance. The year before Connie had become fed up with Rube's antics and "sold him down the river" to St. Louis. Waddell was no red-hot with the Browns until St. Louis came here for a series with Rube's old teammates.

There was an amused smile on Waddell's face when he stepped on the hill, a smile that was returned by his former pals—until the big fellow started to throw baseballs past them with blistering speed. He continued to smile, but the batsmen became very serious indeed.

Feller may flatten out, one can never tell, but just now he seems destined to become one of the greatest pitchers of all time—possibly to rank with Mathewson, Johnson, Brown, Alexander and Waddell.

P. L.

OTT'S HOMERS AID N. Y. WIN; DIZ SAVES 2D

Dean, Pitching for 3d Time in Two Days, Relieves Parmelee to Hold 'Cap; Mize Socks Homer

By ALAN GOULD

NEW YORK, Sept. 13 (A. P.)—Amid the tumult and the roar of the mightiest crowd ever to witness a National League baseball game, an overflow crowd of 64,417 that packed the Polo Grounds to the rafters, the league-leading New York Giants split a spectacular double-header today with their foremost challengers, the St. Louis Cardinals.

Rushing to the rescue of the faltering Roy Parmelee in the eighth inning of the final game, the great Dizzy Dean saved an even break for the crippled "Gas House Gang" after the Giants had pinned their ears back with an 8-4 victory in the opener, with the aid of two homers by Mel Ott.

Dizzy Saves Final

Dean, pitching in his third game in two straight days, turned back the home team with the tying run on second base in each of the last two innings. His brilliant relief job protected a one-run margin, clinched a 4-3 decision for the Cardinals that was due mainly to Johnny Mize's homer with two on, and kept alive what's left of the furious pennant battle.

Fighting hard for a double triumph that would have all but ended lingering doubt about the championship outcome, the Giants nevertheless preserved their lead of 3½ games over the Cardinals, with the last game of the series due tomorrow. Meanwhile the Chicago Cubs, by dividing two games in Brooklyn, remained five behind, in third place. The Giants now have 14 games left to play, the Cards 13 and the Cubs 12.

A four-run blast against Southpaw Al Smith in the third inning gave the Cardinals command of the after-piece. It was capped by Mize's circuit clout into the right field stands after basehits by Terry

Continued on Page 19, Column 2

American Standings

Yesterday's Results

Cleveland, 5; Athletics, 2. (First game).
Cleveland, 5; Athletics, 4. (Second game).
New York, 10; St. Louis, 7. (First game).
New York, 13; St. Louis, 1 (second game)
Boston, 7; Detroit, 4.
Washington - Chicago (postponed, rain).

How They Stand

	W.	L.	P.C.	G.B.
New York	93	48	.664	..
Chicago	78	64	.543	17½
Washington	75	66	.532	19
Detroit	74	68	.521	20½
Cleveland	74	68	.521	20½
Boston	72	71	.503	23
St. Louis	51	88	.367	41½
Athletics	49	93	.345	45½

G. B.—Games Behind.

Today's Games and Pitchers

Washington at Chicago (2 games—Newsom and Appleton vs. Lyons and Kennedy).
Boston at Detroit (Wilson or Henry vs. Bridges).
(Only games scheduled).

JORGENS WINS 'CAP AFTER PHILS WALK PLANK IN STARTER

Pirates Pummel Sivess in Opener, 5-3; Errors Aid Wilsons Score, 4-3

By JAMES C. ISAMINGER

Before about 7000 men and women, the Phillies and Pirates halved a snappy double bill here yesterday. The Phillies took the final combat, 4 to 3, after dropping the opening tilt, 5 to 3.

Nothing was at stake for either team, but the combatants battled as fiercely as if they were in the pennant fight and held spectators to the finish.

A Pirate uprising in the eighth inning swept Pete Sivess to defeat in the first game. Lefthander Ralph Birkofer, who relieved Big Jim Weaver, was the official winner.

Jorgens Wins Second

Orville Jorgens' powerful flinging and a damaging Pittsburgh boot by Shortstop Arky Vaughan enabled the resident band to square things by taking the second game. Mace Brown was the loser.

Chuck Klein unloosed Homer No. 23 in the first game with a pal aboard, but this coup could not avert defeat. "Klein hits homer, but Phillies lose" is still a standing headline.

Third Baseman Pinky Whitney was the victim of an odd accident. In the ninth inning of the first game while at bat, a foul hit him in the eye and he had to retire.

Bucky Walters had to go in and finish his bat. He was in the tough spot of two strikes and one ball. Blanton got over another strike and the game ended.

Whitney was unable to qualify for the second game. As a result, Lou

Continued on Page 19, Column 4

Dickey Speaking—Yanks in 5 Games

LITTLE ROCK, Ark., Sept. 13 (A. P.)—Bill Dickey, catcher for the New York Yankees, returned to his home town for a few days rest yesterday and predicted the American League champions would "take the World Series in about five games.

Dickey, injured slightly several days ago when struck on the finger by a foul ball, said he would rejoin the Yanks on their final Western trip. He left here tonight on a two-day fishing trip.

REESE'S FIELD GOAL DEFEATS N. Y. GIANTS

Bird Booter Shoots Ball Over Bar From Ten-yard Line to Win Game Tied Up at 7-7; Winners Score on Remarkable Forward Lateral

By STAN BAUMGARTNER

Electrifying 20,000 hysterical fans with one of the greatest upsets ever achieved in professional football, Bert Bell's Eagles defeated the famed New York Giants at the Municipal Stadium yesterday by the score of 10-7.

Both teams scored a touchdown, the Eagles crossing the New York goal line late in the first period, while the Giants took the ball over the local final yard stripe in the early part of the fourth period, to tie the score.

Then, with the count deadlocked at 7-7, Hank Reese booted a placement goal a few minutes later to give the Philadelphians their well-deserved and astonishing triumph.

From the very first play it was a thrilling, tingling struggle with the Eagles stunning the huge throng with the sturdiness of their defense, and then thrilling it to the core with one of the most spectacular touchdown plays ever seen on a local gridiron.

This play in itself was a football game. It came late in the first period, with the Eagles on their own 48-yard line. The ball was snapped back to Smukler, who quickly faded 15 yards behind the line of scrimmage, turned and tossed the ball to Manske, who caught it on the Giants' 28-yard line.

There the blond end man of the Eagles found himself hemmed in by four Giant tacklers. As they closed in about him like giant claws there did not seem an avenue of escape. But, quick as a flash, he made a complete pivot, left his foe riveted to the ground, and shot toward the side lines.

By this time other Giant tacklers thundered in upon him. Again he seemed at the end of the trail. But with a lightning-like stroke of genius the blond spiraled a lateral pass to Joe Carter, captain and end, 20 yards away. Carter snuggled the pigskin to his jersey on the dead run and raced over the goal line unmolested.

Twenty thousand hysterical rooters arose as one man and gave the three principals involved, as well as the entire team, a mighty ovation.

With the cheers still ringing in his ears, Smukler booted the ball

Continued on Page 20, Column 5

High Flying!

New York Gts.	Positions.	Phila. Eagles
Singer	Left end	Manske
Morgan	Left tackle	Buss
Karlan	Left guard	Zizak
Hein	Center	Kresse
Dell Isola	Right guard	McPherson
Lewis	Right tackle	MacMurdo
Anderson	Right end	Carter
Danowski	Quarterback	Leonard
Burnett	Left halfback	Hanson
Richards	Right halfback	Smukler
Shaffer	Fullback	Thomason

Giants	0	0	0	7—7
Eagles	7	0	0	3—10

Referee—T. T. Haskell, Buffalo. Umpire—C. J. Carty, Philadelphia. Head linesman—Stan Baumgartner, Philadelphia. Field judge—C. G. Eckles, Upper Darby. Touchdowns—Carter, Burnett. Points after touchdown—Smukler (placement), Manton (placement). Field goal—Reese (placement). Substitutions—Giants, Mitchell for Singer, Corzine for Shaffer, Grant for Lewis, Leemans for Richards, Manton for Leemans, Richards for Manton, Owen for Dell Isola, Tarrant for Anderson, Andrews for Tarrant, Dell Isola for Owen, Owen for Dell Isola, Manton for Leemans, Richards for Manton, Davis for Karlan, Jones for Dell Isola, Krause for Burnett, Tarrant for Anderson. Eagles, Frey for Thomason, Russell for Zizak, Brian for MacMurdo, Pivarnick for Russell, Russell for Zizak, MacMurdo for Buss, Kusko for Smukler, [illegible] for Manske, Thomason for Kusko, [illegible] for McPherson.

Surprise to Alice Marble

Could Hardly Believe Herself Champion; Would Meet Miss Jacobs Again

By ALICE MARBLE

AS TOLD TO MURRAY GOODMAN

NEW YORK, Sept. 13 (U. S.)—I am very happy to be called queen of America's tennis courts, but I must admit I was surprised to find myself winning the national women's singles championship.

I cannot exactly explain the reason for my surprise, but at the end of the match in which I defeated Helen Jacobs yesterday, I could hardly believe that I was the new champion. It may be that in the last two sets I had the match more or less my own way, but I will say right now that Helen gave me one of the hardest matches I have ever had.

Yes, she played as hard as I have ever seen her play—as hard a game as she played when she defeated me in a match about two weeks ago. I would like to, and probably will, play Miss Jacobs again next year, just to attempt to prove that my victory over her yesterday was not one of those "fluke" affairs.

I think it was my forehand and service which bothered the defending champion. I have been practicing steadily and naturally improved my game. I was "on edge" for that match and possibly Helen did not expect the stern opposition she received.

My plans for the future are rather indefinite, but I can say now that at no time will I consider offers to turn professional.

I am leaving for the Coast on Tuesday to compete in the Pacific Coast tournament. I haven't heard that Helen Wills Moody plans to compete in that tournament, but I hope she does because I would love to play against her.

Yes, I hope to go to Wimbledon next summer, but as yet I don't know what I'll do. I'm too happy right now over winning the title I have sought since 1932 that I can't spend too much time in planning.

National Ratings

Yesterday's Results

First Games

Pittsburgh, 5; Phillies, 3.
New York, 8; St. Louis, 4.
Cincinnati, 2; Boston, 1.
Brooklyn, 6; Chicago, 3.

Second Games

Phillies, 4; Pittsburgh, 3.
St. Louis, 4; New York, 3.
Boston, 6; Cincinnati, 1.
Chicago, 9; Brooklyn, 7.

How They Stand

	W.	L.	P.C.	G.B.
New York	84	56	.600	..
St. Louis	81	60	.574	3½
Chicago	80	62	.563	5
Pittsburgh	75	66	.532	9½
Cincinnati	70	71	.496	14½
Boston	64	75	.460	19½
Brooklyn	59	81	.421	25
Phillies	49	91	.350	35

G. B.—Games behind.

Today's Games and Pitchers

Pittsburgh at Philadelphia (2 games—Johnson and Benge vs. Lucas and Swift).
St. Louis at New York (J. Dean vs. Hubbell).
Cincinnati at Boston (Derringer vs. Chaplin).
Chicago at Brooklyn (Henshaw vs. Mungo).

210 ON FIRING LINE AT GARDEN CITY FOR 40TH LINKS CLASSIC

Platt-Lehman, Haas-Mayo, Fischer-Meister, Leslie-Lynch Feature Today

GARDEN CITY, N. Y., Sept. 13 (A. P.)—The famed Garden City course was shaved and stretched to the fences today in preparation for the 40th National Amateur golf championship, which starts tomorrow.

There are 210 players, including eight former champions and 19 foreign stars, competing for the crown abdicated by Lawson Little, now a professional. Forty-six players drew byes in the first round, the others will meet tomorrow in 82 matches.

The field will be reduced to 128 after tomorrow's play. One 18-hole round Tuesday, two 18-hole rounds Wednesday, and two more on Thursday, will reduce the field to the semi-finalists. Semi-finals Friday and finals Saturday will be over the 36-hole route.

Four Outstanding Matches

There are four outstanding matches in the first round. Paul Leslie, New Orleans, the Western amateur champion, plays Joe Lynch, Canton, Mass., semi-finalist last year; Johnny Fischer, Cincinnati, meets Eddie Meister, Cleveland; Fred Haas, New Orleans, the Canadian amateur champion, plays Charlie Mayo, Jr., Long Beach, L. I., Long Island amateur champion; and J. Wood Platt, Philadelphia, tackles Johnny Lehman, Chicago district champion.

Both favorites, Albert "Scotty" Campbell, Seattle and Johnny Goodman, Omaha, play in the first round. Campbell against Forrest Thompson, Landover, Md., and

Continued on Page 18, Column 4

ROOKIE FELLER WHIFFS 17 A'S; TRIBE SNARES 2

Cleveland Youth Betters Waddell's 1908 Loop Mark and Equals Diz Dean's 1933 Record

CLEVELAND, Sept. 13.—Bob Feller, 17-year-old schoolboy who learned to pitch a "hard one" by throwing rocks at targets on his father's farm in Van Meter, Iowa, stenciled his named in major league baseball archives today by striking out 17 Athletics in the first game of today's double-header between the Mackmen and the Cleveland Indians.

The Tribe won, 5 to 2, behind the youngster's sensational two-hit pitching and then annexed the nightcap, 5 to 4.

The tall, loose-jointed boy hurler, who gained national fame by whiffing 15 St. Louis Browns in a game last month, established a new American League record with his 17 strikeouts. The previous mark was 16, set by Rube Waddell in 1908. He also tied the modern major league record held by Dizzy Dean, of the St. Louis Cardinals, who breezed 17 Cubs in 1933.

Every Philadelphia batter with the exception of Pinch-hitter Moss went down swinging at least once as Feller blazed his fast ball down the alley. Luby fanned three times, Puccinelli, Johnson, Higgins, Hayes and Gumpert twice each and Finney, Moses, Dean and Peters once each.

The rookie star was in trouble throughout the game, despite his record strikeout crop, but exhibited the courage of a veteran in the tight spots and managed to get out of every hole with the exception of one.

Feller Passes Nine

Nine Athletics walked, one was hit and seven stole bases, but two passes, a single by Chubby Dean and a double steal gave the Mackmen their only tallies in the third inning.

Randall Gumpert, 18-year-old Philadelphia right-hander who limited the Chicago White Sox to two hits several weeks ago, held the In-

Continued on Page 20, Column 2

Perry May Turn Pro, But Not Now

DETROIT, Mich., Sept. 13 (U. S.)—Fred Perry, British tennis star, who won the American singles championship yesterday at Forest Hills, may turn professional eventually, "but not now," he declared here today in commenting on rumors that he was about to desert the amateur ranks.

He was asked: "Are you going to turn professional?"

Perry replied: "Everybody asks that question. I've got so I just ignore it. I may turn professional in time, but not now."

September 14, 1936 - Only win of the '36 season happened in the first game; 10-7 vs. NY Giants. Hank Reese kicks the game winning field goal

1937

RECORD: 2-8-1, 5TH IN NFL EAST
HEAD COACH: BERT BELL

SCHEDULE

REGULAR SEASON

Wk. 1	Sep 5	L	27-14	at Pittsburgh Pirates
Wk. 2	Sep 10	L	13-7	vs Brooklyn Dodgers
Wk. 3	Sep 21	L	21-3	vs Cleveland Rams
Wk. 4	Sep 26	T	6-6	vs Chicago Cardinals
Wk. 5	Oct 3	L	16-7	vs New York Giants
Wk. 6	Oct 10	W	14-0	at Washington Redskins
Wk. 7	Oct 17	L	21-0	at New York Giants
Wk. 8	Oct 24	L	10-7	vs Washington Redskins
Wk. 9	Oct 31	L	16-7	at Pittsburgh Pirates
Wk. 10	Nov 7	W	14-10	at Brooklyn Dodgers
Wk. 11	Nov 14	L	37-7	at Green Bay Packers (at Milwaukee, WI)

The Eagles signed the last NFL player not to wear a helmet, Bill Hewitt. After losing their first three games, the Eagles snap a 14-game losing streak spread over two seasons by tying the Chicago Cardinals 6-6 at Municipal Stadium. In week five, they lost to the NY Giants 16-7, then they finally got a win by stunning the eventual NFL Champion Redskins 14-0 in Washington. The Eagles would go on to finish with a 2-8-1 record.

1937 PHILADELPHIA EAGLES STATS

Passing	Comp	Att	Comp %	Yds	Y/Att	TD	Int	Rating
Dave Smukler	42	118	35.6	432	3.66	5	14	21.5
Rabbit Keen	1	5	20.0	86	17.20	1	0	118.8
Swede Hanson	0	2	0.0	0	0.00	0	0	39.6
Glenn Frey	0	1	0.0	0	0.00	0	0	39.6
Winnie Baze	0	3	0.0	0	0.00	0	0	39.6
Emmett Mortell	18	71	25.4	320	4.51	2	8	15.7
John Kusko	2	7	28.6	11	1.57	0	2	0.0

Rushing	Rush	Yds	Avg	TD
Emmett Mortell	100	312	3.1	0
Dave Smukler	92	247	2.7	1
Rabbit Keen	34	154	4.5	0
Swede Hanson	18	59	3.3	1
Bob Masters	9	32	3.6	0
John Kusko	17	27	1.6	0
Joe Pilconis	2	21	10.5	0
Winnie Baze	3	14	4.7	0
Glenn Frey	5	11	2.2	0
Jay Arnold	5	7	1.4	0

Receiving	Rec	Yds	Avg	TD
Bill Hewitt	16	197	12.3	5
Joe Carter	15	282	18.8	3
Jay Arnold	8	142	17.8	0
Joe Pilconis	6	59	9.8	0
Rabbit Keen	5	45	9.0	0
Bob Masters	4	60	15.0	0
Glenn Frey	4	19	4.8	0
John Kusko	2	47	23.5	0
Winnie Baze	1	2	2.0	0
Emmett Mortell	1	0	0.0	0
Dave Smukler	1	-4	-4.0	0

Kicking	PAT Made	PAT Att	PAT %	FG Made	FG Att	FG %	Pts
Dave Smukler	8	9	89	1	0	0.0	17
Hank Reese	3	3	100	0	0	0.0	3

1937

SPORTS **The Philadelphia Inquirer** SPORTS

PHILADELPHIA, MONDAY MORNING, NOVEMBER 15, 1937

The Old Sport's Musings

The Sport Light

By GRANTLAND RICE

Mr. and Mrs. Golf Fan Have a Look at John Montague

Part of the gallery of 10,000 that rampaged over the course of the Fresh Meadow Country Club, at Flushing, L. I., yesterday to see John Montague play in an exhibition match is pictured above watching golf's Paul Bunyan hit one of his tremendous drives. Babe Ruth leans on his club at the right. The spectators swarmed on the ninth green, forcing abandonment of the match. Montague and his partner, Sylva Annenberg, trailed Ruth and Babe Didrikson at the time.

GALLERY STOPS MONTY'S LINKS MATCH AT N.Y.

Unruly Mob of 10,000 Halts Play With Miss Annenberg and John Trailing

Green Bay Packers Beat Phila. Eagle Eleven, 37-7

MILWAUKEE, Wis., Nov. 14.—Philadelphia's Eagles closed their disastrous National Pro League football season here this afternoon by taking a 37 to 7 walloping from the fast-stepping Green Bay Packers, defending champions, as 15,000 fans watched.

The Packers, riding the crest of a six-game winning streak, which saw them come from nowhere in the race to a commanding position in the battle to retain their title, were again invincible. When their ground game stalled they took to the air with devastating effect, and when the air game failed they pounded the ground defense into submission.

The Eagles pet offensive maneuver for the day was a pass, Smukler to Carter, and it was the latter who scored the Eagles' only touchdown late in the game when he took a 48-yard pass from Keen on the Bays' 35, and ran away from Herber for a total gain of 84 yards. It was the most brilliant play of the game.

SPECTACULAR PLAY

Superiority on the ground helped the Packers materially. They picked up 193 yards on rushing to the Eagles' 35 and made 243 yards on passes to the Eagles' 162. All told the Eagles tried 28 aerials and completed nine against the Packers' 19 attempts and 11 completions.

It was a grand offensive show all the way, and the Eagles, although smothered in the final count, helped to make it so with some beautifully executed plays. Keen was the most effective Eagle runner, but it was the passes of Smukler that caused the Bays the most concern.

HINKLE KICKS FIELD GOAL

Green Bay utilized the air-lanes to put their scoring machinery in motion shortly after the game started. After an exchange of punts, the Packers got the ball on the Eagles' 36 and reeled off two first downs on line plays. Then Bob Monnett passed to Eddie Jankowski over the goal line for a touchdown and Engebretsen missed the try for the extra point.

Early in the second period the Eagles stopped a Packer drive and Clark Hinkle dropped back to the 24 and kicked a field goal to make the score 9 to 0.

Later in the quarter Hinkle set up another Packer touchdown with a 60-yard dash to the Philadelphian's 21. Again the champions went into the air, two passes from Arnold Herber to Don Hutson, putting the ball in the end zone. Hinkle converted to make it, 16 to 0, at half-time.

The Eagles braced and showed their best defense in the third period, but the Packers resumed scoring in the final period, adding 21 points more. A short pass, Herber to Bernard Scherer, end, was converted into the third touchdown when the latter

Continued on Page 21, Column 1

GERMAN-AMERICANS UPSET SCOT RIVALS FOR 2D LEAGUE WIN

By GEORGE BUTZ

Top-Ranking Teams Hold Places Over Weekend

By ALAN GOULD

Nativity Passers Beat St. Josaphat

Nativity scored its second Catholic League victory yesterday afternoon by sending St. Josaphat's, of Manayunk, down to a 33 to 24 defeat, before a crowded hall at Belgrade and Madison sts. The victory gave Nativity the league lead.

Nativity proved the better all-around club. The Manayunkers staged a fast rally at the start of the second period, but Nativity flashed a last five-minute rally that gained the victory.

Barney Konieczny was the star for Nativity. He was in every play, intercepting passes, following up missed shots to convert into double deckers and guarding his opposing forward closely. Barney batted in three goals and whipped in two others from the side of the court.

Nativity Reserves defeated St. Josaphat's reserves, 45 to 17.

Dominick McGinley, Nativity's No. 1 rooter, tossed up the first ball. Jimmy McMonigle, who has been made manager this season and also plays on the team, was presented with a floral horseshoe, from the Nativity Catholic Club.

Santa Clara Beats St. Mary's

Detroit Gridmen Rout Giants For 17-0 Triumph

By DREW MIDDLETON

California Poloists Beat Mexicans, 13-11

Nolan Scores a Touchdown for St. Joseph's

John Nolan (see arrow) plunged through the Southeast Catholic line from the five-yard line for the St. Joseph's touchdown shown above. Nolan's brilliant work helped St. Joseph's score an easy victory in the Catholic High League grid battle yesterday at the Phillies' Park.

St. Joseph's Team Brushes Aside So. Catholic, 31-0

By FRANK O'GARA

BREAK LOOMS OVER AMATEUR ELECTION

Phillips-McDonald Win at Pinehurst

November 15, 1937 - Last game of a horrible season (winning only two games) losing 37-7 to Green Bay

1938

RECORD: 5-6, 4TH IN NFL EAST
HEAD COACH: BERT BELL

Schedule

Regular Season

Wk. 2	Sep 11	L	26-23	vs Washington Redskins
Wk. 3	Sep 16	W	27-7	at Pittsburgh Pirates (at Buffalo, NY)
Wk. 4	Sep 25	W	14-10	vs New York Giants
Wk. 5	Oct 2	L	28-6	vs Chicago Bears
Wk. 7	Oct 16	L	17-7	at New York Giants
Wk. 8	Oct 23	L	20-14	at Washington Redskins
Wk. 9	Oct 26	W	7-0	at Chicago Cardinals (at Erie, PA)
Wk. 10	Nov 6	L	10-7	vs Brooklyn Dodgers
Wk. 11	Nov 13	L	32-14	at Brooklyn Dodgers
Wk. 12	Nov 20	W	14-7	at Pittsburgh Pirates (at Charleston, WV)
Wk. 14	Dec 4	W	21-7	at Detroit Lions

The Eagles showed signs of improvement, playing solid football at times on the way to a 5-6 record, which was bolstered by two straight wins to close the season. They defeated Pittsburgh 14-7 and Detroit 21-7. The Eagle training camp was moved to West Chester State Teachers College.

1938 Philadelphia Eagles Stats

Passing	Comp	Att	Comp %	Yds	Y/Att	TD	Int	Rating
Dave Smukler	42	102	41.2	524	5.14	7	8	48.0
Joe Bukant	1	1	100.0	14	14.00	0	0	118.8
Emmett Mortell	12	57	21.1	201	3.53	6	7	37.3
Dick Riffle	9	31	29.0	178	5.74	2	4	32.9

Rushing	Rush	Yds	Avg	TD
Dave Smukler	96	313	3.3	1
Emmett Mortell	110	296	2.7	0
Dick Riffle	65	227	3.5	1
Joe Bukant	48	119	2.5	0
Jay Arnold	19	22	1.2	0
Woody Dow	4	20	5.0	0
Rabbit Keen	3	10	3.3	0
John Cole	1	4	4.0	0

Receiving	Rec	Yds	Avg	TD
Joe Carter	27	386	14.3	7
Bill Hewitt	18	237	13.2	4
Jay Arnold	6	74	12.3	2
Red Ramsey	5	122	24.4	1
Woody Dow	5	88	17.6	1
John Cole	2	9	4.5	0
Bob Pylman	1	1	1.0	0

Punting	Punts	Yds	Avg	Blocked
Dick Riffle	17	683	40.2	0

Kicking	PAT Made	PAT Att	PAT %	FG Made	FG Att	FG %	Pts
Joe Carter	1	1	100	0	0	0.0	13
Jay Arnold	3	3	100	0	1	0.0	27
Dave Smukler	6	6	100	0	2	0.0	18
Hank Reese	10	13	77	1	6	16.7	13

SPORTS **The Philadelphia Inquirer** SPORTS

PHILADELPHIA, SATURDAY MORNING, SEPTEMBER 17, 1938 abdef 19

LAVENGRO SURPRISES AT HAVRE

Eagles, West Chester Win

Flashing Down Havre Stretch

Photo by Larry Keighley, Inquirer Photographer

Lavengro, with Johnny Gilbert up, responded gamely in the stretch and defeated Sun Egret (on rail), ridden by Al Shelhamer, for a photo finish victory in the Susquehanna Handicap, feature of the opening card at Havre de Grace yesterday.

The Old Sport's Musings

One week ago today there appeared in this column a piece concerning the 1888 Penn football team that played and won three games on successive days — Wesleyan on Thursday, Nov. 29; Johns Hopkins, Nov. 30 and Navy, Dec. 1. The game with the Middies inaugurated what has become one of football's traditional series.

Since then the Old Sport has received a number of letters suggesting that possibly only two or three Penn players saw action in all three games. Thanks to a communication from Louis de Pui (Bucky) Vail, one of the four surviving players of the 1888 Penn team, the writer is in a position to state that such was not the case.

Of the Quaker team that opposed Wesleyan, only four players were missing when Penn lined up against Hopkins. They were Wagenhurst, left end; Cash, right tackle; Church, quarterback, and Colladay, halfback. Cash was back on Saturday to play against Navy.

ELIGIBILITY?

Apparently, they paid slight attention to eligibility rules 50 years ago. Quoting from Mr. Vail's letter in this connection:

"We were short four regulars in the Hopkins game, and, in addition, Hopkins played Jesse Riggs, of Princeton, at guard; Lewis, of Princeton, at fullback, and Paul Dashiell, who had graduated from Hopkins and was not in the university, at one of the halves."

Commenting on a report of the game published in a Baltimore newspaper the morning following the game, in which it was written that Penn far outweighed Hopkins, Mr. Vail has this to say:

"We did not outweigh Johns Hopkins by an average of 25 points or anything approaching it. Riggs was a 190-pound guard, Lewis was as heavy as Hill, one of our halfbacks. Dashiell outweighed both of them, and in those days I weighed 132."

TAYLOR NAVY STAR

With the 50th anniversary of the Penn-Navy series approaching, it is interesting to read some of Mr. Vail's recollections of that first game of 88, which the Quakers won, 20 to 9.

"Pennsylvania scored four touchdowns in the first half," he writes. "The Navy did not score until, with only about five minutes remaining of the second half, Ford, fullback, was replaced by Taylor, who came on the field wearing a blue flannel shirt and white duck trousers.

"He made a touchdown from which he missed the goal, and followed this up a short time later with a field goal, giving Navy its nine points (at that period a touchdown counted four points and a field goal five). Taylor's was a fine exhibition, particularly by a substitute, and I believe he afterward became Admiral Taylor, of the Construction Department.

'SOME POND'

"In justice to Pennsylvania, it is only fair to say that not only did the team break training on Thursday night following the Wesleyan game, but was playing its third game in three days, and after making 20 points in the first half, was coasting along. The boys were dead on their feet.

"An amusing incident of that game, played a half-century ago, comes to memory. The playing field was along the Chesapeake beyond what is now the location of Bancroft Hall.

"However that may be, the ball was punted out of bounds and was rolling toward the bay when Tommy Holmes, our captain, yelled:

"'Don't let the ball go in the pond, boys!'

"'Some pond,' a Middie retorted."

THE MARK OF A CHAMPION

It is easy to be what is called in sport a "front runner." When one is leading a single opponent or the pack he can concentrate on the business of maintaining his advantage, but when the going suddenly becomes rough and disaster threatens, the pretender collapses.

John Henry Lewis was well out ahead of Jimmy Adamick last Thursday night at the Arena. At the end of eight rounds the light-heavyweight champion was so far in the lead that only a knockout could deprive him of victory.

Suddenly the tide turned. For two rounds Adamick bounced Lewis all over the ring and had him groggy on several occasions. It was then that John Henry proved himself a champion indeed when a lesser fighter would have succumbed. Raked with murderous punches, his body weakened, but, his wits clear and his heart stout, Lewis not only stayed on his feet, but furnished an exhibition of defensive work that marked him a real champion who knows what to do when the going becomes rocky.

P. L.

How They Stand In American Loop

Yesterday's Results

New York, 6; Detroit, 4.
Boston, 2; Cleveland, 1.
A's-Chicago, postponed, wet grounds.
Washington-St. Louis, postponed, bad weather.

HOW THEY STAND

	W.	L.	Pct.	G.B.
New York	94	43	.686	.. —
Boston	79	58	.577	15
Cleveland	77	60	.562	17
Detroit	72	66	.522	22½
Washington	68	70	.493	26½
Chicago	56	75	.427	35
Athletics	50	87	.365	44
St. Louis	47	84	.359	44

G.B.—Games back of leader.

Today's Schedule and Pitchers

Athletics at Chicago (2 games) (Nelson and Henninger vs Lyons and Gabler).
New York at Detroit (Pearson vs. Benton)
Boston at Cleveland (Wilson vs. Humphries)
Washington at St. Louis (2 games) (Monteagudo and Krakauskas vs. Van Atta and Bildilli).

FAVORITE NOSE BEHIND WINNER IN OPENING DAY FEATURE EVENT

Sun Egret Second, Masked General 3d In Susquehanna 'Cap Before 7500 Fans

By JOHN WEBSTER

HAVRE DE GRACE, Md., Sept. 16.—In a pulse-strumming finish that required the camera's decision, Norman W. Church's mad-charging Lavengro got up in the final jump to score a nose victory over the favored Sun Egret in the six-furlong Susquehanna Handicap, featured event of the inaugural program at the Harford track this afternoon.

A length off the runner-up was Masked General, from Donald Ross' Brandywine Stable, to save third money by a length and a half from W. J. Hirsch's Mosawtre, who finished fourth in the field of 10 speedy sprinters.

Only lightly backed by the opening day crowd of 7500, which had sent the A. C. Compton entry of Sun Egret and Clingendaal into favoritism, the winner, a big, black gelded son of Diavolo, paid $15.30 for a straight bet. Place and show prices were $6.80 and $4.30.

Capable Johnny Gilbert broke on top with Lavengro, took back when he was outrun by the early-footed Sun Egret, but remained in second place and always within a length of the white Compton silks. Into the stretch, and Sun Egret, winner of 11 races this season, was still on top. But whip as he would, Jockey Al Shelhamer, on the people's choice, couldn't shake off Lavengro.

Inside the final furlong, Gilbert lashed at Lavengro, and the husky charger closed with determination on the outside. He crept up slowly but steadily. His nose edged past the driving Sun Egret right on the wire.

Lavengro, who picked up 114 pounds, finished out the three-quarters of a mile in 1.12 1-5, and earned $1650 for his owner, a well-known turfman from California.

NEDAYR 3D AT START

Behind Mosawtre, the order of the finish was Gustave Ring's Lady Maryland, Willis Sharpe Kilmer's Arlington classic winner, Nedayr, Milldale Stable's Mower, Clingendaal, F. C. Murray's Clocks and W. L. Brann's Challephen.

Nedayr was prominent in the early running, when he lay third, but he began to shorten stride around the bend, and dropped back into the dust clouds. Masked General, the medium of a heavy play from the Delaware squires, moved into contention at the half-mile pole, and finished stoutly in the third slot, although unable to menace the leaders. Mosawtre, a rank outsider today, came through with his usual late speed, but had to be satisfied with fourth place. The others never figured.

Leaden-footed favorites were the only disappointing note for the horse players on a beautiful September day. The sun broke through the gray clouds shortly after first post-time, and smiled down benignly upon the pretty Havre de Grace plant, spic and span in early autumn glory and a few coats of new paint. But those short-priced horses wouldn't stand up, and Sun Egret's defeat was the fourth in a row for the public choices.

Pharabelle made every post a winner in her first trip to the post

Continued on Page 20, Column 1

The Sport Light

By GRANTLAND RICE

OAKMONT, Pa., Sept. 16.—Elmsford, N. Y. and Pasadena, Calif., pleasant hamlets 3000 miles apart, send their favorite golfing sons into action Saturday to battle for the amateur championship of the United States.

In Elmsford's corner, we have 23-year-old Willie Turnesa, the only amateur survival of seven golfing brothers, who is pitted against Pat Abbott, public links champion in 1936. One of the two will take over the gleaming coronet which Johnny Goodman gave up when Dick Chapman stopped him in the quarter-final whirl.

Turnesa, the stylist of the field, an extremely fine swinger, came to his big chance by stopping Ed Kingsley, the hard-scrapping entry from Magna, Utah.

Pat Abbott, trailed by his pal from Pasadena, Ellsworth Vines, ran down Dick Chapman of Greenwich, Conn., 5 and 4.

TURNESA FAVORED TO WIN

As a result of these proceedings, the Atlantic and the Pacific cross swords or exchange thrusts in a final test where Willie Turnesa will start as the favored entry, due largely to his greater power over a long course that is still soft.

Turnesa, in his semi-final match, had a 75 in the forenoon round against Kingsley, and Willie had a 77 when his match against the Utah challenger came to an end.

Pat Abbott was moving along at a 79 clip all day, which indicates that neither entry was flirting extensively with Oakmont's rugged par of 72. They label 475-yard holes par 4 and 255-yard holes par 3, so you can make a slight guess as to what par means over this extended landscape, softened up by recent rains.

Turnesa is 23—Abbott is 25. Willie is a stocky, well built youth, while Abbott is a thin young fellow with a displacement around 135 pounds. The Western challenger has to make up in deadly accuracy and a fine short game for his lack of length.

Turnesa, for several years, has been one of the best shot-makers in amateur ranks. An extremely quiet, modest type, he has lacked what some philosopher called "the killer instinct," or the grim determination to cut his way through.

ABBOTT PRAISED BY VINES

Abbott is another quiet type, with a magnificent capacity to concentrate.

"He is one of the greatest concentrators I have ever seen in any sport," Ellsworth Vines told me. "He isn't strong and he isn't long, but he never loses his head or makes a foolish mistake. The only thought in his head is the next shot he has to play - - - and just how he should play it.

Dick Chapman, the Connecticut entry, stuck with the slender Californian for the better part of the first round. But Chapman's short game began to crumble up as the match moved along. He had been swift poison on the somewhat baffling Oakmont greens until this match, and he was up against a master putter with a smooth, even stroke.

Abbott led 4 up on the forenoon and advanced this lead when Chapman topped his drive off the tee to start the afternoon parade. Abbott was 6 up when they passed the 27th hole. Here Chapman rallied gamely and won the next two holes to remain 4 down as they faced the long 622-yard twelfth.

After Chapman's counter-attack, Abbott promptly closed the door by inserting a fine birdie 3 on the fourteenth green, after Chapman had missed his try.

TOUGH GOING FOR TURNESA

Willie Turnesa had a trifle more trouble against Ed Kingsley, who at times was just as tough as the Utah copper he inspects.

Turnesa was 3 up in the morning round. But Kingsley insisted on sticking along, using a peculiar stance with both feet pointing in almost opposite directions.

Kingsley made his best counter-attack when he cut Turnesa's lead from 3 holes to 1 as they came to the long trek needed to reach the twelfth green. Here Turnesa blew his second shot, but came back with a fine 3 iron shot from 150 yards away. Kingsley's third caught a trap and left him 2 down.

The decisive shot of the match took place at the 175-yard thirteenth. Turnesa's iron hit the green and bounded over. "It is an almost impossible shot," Ed Dudley of Philadelphia, said. "Willie has only one foot of space to hit over this high mound to a fast, down-sloping green." But Willie hit the foot of space and stopped his ball two feet from the cup to close out the show.

PITTSBURGH SPLITS WITH BOSTON BEES

BOSTON, Sept. 16 (A. P.).—Pittsburgh's jittery Pirates, following the example of the other contenders, marked time in the drive for the National League pennant today by splitting a double-header with the Boston Bees.

Johnny Rizzo's 20th homer of the season enabled the Pirates to win the opening game, 7-6, in 11 innings. But a three-run rally in the ninth earned the Bees the nightcap, 6-4.

The Pirates maintained their three-game lead over the second place Chicago Cubs, whose game with the fourth-place Giants was postponed. The third-place Reds remained stationary by dividing a twin bill with the Phillies.

Rizzo hit the first ball pitched to him in the 11th by Deacon Danny MacFayden over the left field wall to decide the heart-stirring opener, during which the Bees came from behind with two consecutive three-run bursts to gain a 6-4 lead in the seventh.

The Pirates, whose too-careful fielding indicated acute nervousness, tied the score in the eighth when Pinch-hitter Heinie Manush tripled between singles by Pep Young and Paul Waner.

Rizzo's decisive homer was the first he has made in Boston. During the season he has belted baseballs out of every other park in his loop, including both Philadelphia plants.

Mace Brown, veteran relief pitcher who has participated in 45 games,

Continued on Page 21, Column 8

No Middleweight Title For Apostoli or Corbett

PROVIDENCE, R. I., Sept. 16 (A. P.).—The National Boxing Association will not recognize as middleweight champion the winner of the Fred Apostoli-Young Corbett, III, bout, scheduled by Mike Jacobs for Nov. 18 at New York, Secretary Edward C. Foster said today.

"Al Hostak won the middleweight championship when he knocked out Freddie Steele," Foster said, "and the next champion will be the man who beats Hostak, and no one else."

Willie Turnesa, Pat Abbott Gain Finals in U. S. Amateur Tourney

By FRITZ HOWELL

OAKMONT, Pa., Sept. 16 (A. P.).—Willie Turnesa, New York, and B. Patrick Abbott, California, landed in the finals of the National Amateur Golf Championship today over the Oakmont C. C. links, the latter completing the longest non-stop flight ever made by a freshman in the annual fairway frolic.

As the two long shots from the Atlantic and Pacific Coasts jammed their way into the title scrap here in Western Pennsylvania's hills, they rounded out the picture of the 1938 simon pure show as the biggest upset tourney in 42 years.

Seven Walker Cup players, defending champion Johnny Goodman and a host of former titleholders fell during the week's firing, but the two long shots survived battles with heavy rains, high winds and more noted foes to take their seats at the entrance to the throne room where one of them will be crowned king in tomorrow's 36-hole finals.

TURNESA BEATS KINGSLEY

Turnesa, member of the exclusive Briar Hills Golf and Country Club of Briar Cliff Manor, N. Y., and brother of six golf professionals, defeated Edwin Kingsley, 23-year-old ore sampler from Magna, Utah, by a 4 and 3 margin in today's 36-hole semi-finals.

Abbott, a stock company actor who aspires to a spot in the films but who succeeded only in "making" the news reels as he won the 1936 National Public Links title, had a tougher chore. He faced Dick Chapman, Greenwich, Conn., who yesterday eliminated Champion Goodman in the tourney's most startling upset, but the machine-like Californian took care of the Easterner by a 5 and 4 margin, most of it gained on the morning 18 under the impetus of nine one-putt greens.

Should Abbott grab the coveted crown in tomorrow's grand finale, he would turn a trick that hasn't

Continued on Page 21, Column 3

HANK SLAMS 51ST AS DETROIT LOSES

DETROIT, Sept. 16 (A. P.).—Hank Greenberg's 51st homer of the year, a blow that put him even with Babe Ruth's record 1927 pace, wasn't enough today and the New York Yankees whipped the Tigers, 6 to 4, to move within two games of clinching the American League pennant.

The Yanks used the winning combination of home-run power and Lefty Gomez to chalk up the decision. Joe Gordon and Frankie Crosetti provided the walloping in a big second inning, their homers netting four runs. Staked to that lead, Gomez coasted up with his 17th victory of the year, although he was tagged for 11 hits.

Big Hank's round-trip clout came in the fourth inning, with the bags empty. The game was the Tigers' 138th of the year. Ruth hit his 51st in the Yanks' 138th contest in '27 the year he set the all-time high of 60 for one season.

The Tigers sent three pitchers to the wars, but the starter, George Gill, gave up the winning margin. Even "Boots" Poffenberger, the right-hander who thinks like a left-hander, was given a chance to show his stuff, coming in as relief in the eighth, for his first appearance since being recalled from double-A class.

Red Rolfe's triple and an infield out gave the Yanks their first run in the opening frame. Then Gordon hit his 23d homer of the year, with a mate aboard, in the second, and Cro-

Continued on Page 21, Column 6

How They Stand In National Loop

YESTERDAY'S RESULTS

Cincinnati 2, Phillies 0 (first).
Phillies 2, Cincinnati 1 (second).
Pittsburgh 7, Boston 6 (first, 11 innings).
Boston 5, Pittsburgh 4 (second).
St. Louis 4, Brooklyn 1 (first).
St. Louis 5, Brooklyn 4 (second).
Chicago - New York, postponed, threatening weather.

HOW THEY STAND

	W.	L.	P.C.	G.B.
Pittsburgh	79	57	.581	—
Chicago	76	60	.559	3
Cincinnati	76	62	.551	4
New York	75	62	.547	4½
Boston	69	68	.504	10½
St. Louis	67	72	.482	13½
Brooklyn	62	75	.453	17½
Phillies	44	92	.324	35

G. B.—Games back of leader.

Today's Schedule and Pitchers

Cincinnati at Philadelphia (Vander Meer vs. Johnson)
Chicago at New York (2 games) (Lee and Bryant vs. Wittig and Lohrman)
Pittsburgh at Boston (Klinger vs. Shoffner)
St. Louis at Brooklyn (P. Dean vs. Tamulis)

WEST CHESTER TOPS P. M. C. BY 27-14

By FRED BYROD

WEST CHESTER, Pa., Sept. 16.—The fortunes of football ran hot and cold, but mostly hot, for West Chester Teachers in the East's first intercollegiate gridiron battle here tonight.

Four aerial thrusts, following three recovered fumbles and a blocked kick gave West Chester a 27 to 14 victory over Pennsylvania Military College before a crowd of 12,600, sitting under star-peckled skies. The luck was not all one sided, for West Chester fumbles likewise paved the way for both of the P. M. C. touchdowns.

But the Cadets, although they outgained the winners in first downs 16 to 5, were badly outplayed after they had fought the Teachers to a 7-7 standstill in the first half.

THROW SCORING PASSES

Jimmy Ward and Jack Harris each threw a pair of scoring passes for the winners. Bill Stratton caught two of them, while Arthur Farley and Tommy Gauntlett each snared one. Bob Nye place-kicked three extra points.

For P. M. C., Vince Hartnett and Willie Piff lugged the leather on the two touchdown plays and Frank Hartzell place-kicked the extra points.

It was one of those bull in the china shop games, just one break after another. P. M. C. fumbled six times, partly because of bad passing from centre and didn't recover any.

Continued on Page 21, Column 1

EAGLES WIN EASILY OVER PIRATES, 27-7

BUFFALO, N. Y., Sept. 16.—Showing a relentless first half attack and unusually alert defense, Bert Bell's Philadelphia Eagles trounced the Pittsburgh Pirates before more than 22,000 persons as National Pro League football returned to Buffalo here at Civic Stadium tonight after an absence of more than a decade and a half.

Even the presence of the famed Byron "Whizzer" White, $15,000 All-American contribution to the Bold Buccaneers from Colorado, couldn't keep the Quaker City combination from notching their first league conquest of the current campaign, a 27 to 7 victory that gives the Philadelphians an even break for the two title tilts waged so far this year.

In fact, errors by White and the astuteness of Eagle defenders against the offensive threat of the Whizzer played a prominent part in the Eagles' one-sided triumph. Not that White was a washout; far from it.

GETS OFF NICE RUNS

He got off to a couple of nice runs, returned punts fearlessly and for good distances, but the Bellmen were in such form that the Pirates weren't in the ball game at any time.

Jay Arnold, most-improved performer of the Eagles—a fair rookie of last year and a star this season—was the big noise in his team's success. Arnold dug in for three touchdowns, two of them on intercepted passes and a third by taking a long aerial. He was the standout for the Birds.

Dick Riffle, sensational rookie and Little All-American from Albright, was only a bit less sensational than Arnold. Riffle did most of the successful throwing for the Eagles, got off some booming punts and provided the game's biggest thrill, a 45-yard sprint for the winners' fourth tally.

Joe Carter, veteran end, added to his prestige as the leading pass-receiver in the National League. He converted two tries for extra points on placement kicks, Hank Reese another.

Reese essayed a 45-yard field goal but his placement boot was just an

Continued on Page 21, Column 4

Rose Hofkin Wins Net Title Again

Playing her usual steady game, Rose Hofkin retained the Huntingdon Valley Country Club women's clay court tennis title yesterday by brushing aside Frederika Bancroft, 16-year-old Wilmington schoolgirl, in the final round. The scores were, 7-5, 6-1.

Miss Hofkin, 26-year-old southpaw, gained a 5-2 lead in the first set, but was held to a standstill by her younger opponent who dashed to the net for volleyed points. At 5-5 Miss Hofkin's deadly steadiness again proved the deciding factor as she pocketed the 13th and 14th games to take the opener.

Running up a 4-0 lead in the second Miss Hofkin dropped the fifth game on service and then won the next pair for 6-1 and match conquest.

World Series Opens Oct. 5 In National League City

By SID FEDER

NEW YORK, Sept. 16 (A. P.).—Commissioner Kenesaw M. Landis got together with the interested parties today and laid plans to start the 1938 World Series in the home of the National League winner Wednesday, Oct. 5, but pending the outcome of the hot senior circuit pennant fight many of the details were left up in the air.

With the Pittsburgh Pirates, Chicago Cubs, Cincinnati Reds and New York Giants all still very much in the thick of the National League race, the commissioner had to consider the possibility of a tie, as well as a necessary "break" for traveling in the event the Cubs win the flag.

So, in his conference with the presidents of both circuits, the representatives of the four National League clubs and the New York Yankees, who are just about "in" with their third straight American League flag, the commissioner settled it this way:

If there is no tie, the first two games will be played in the National League city Oct. 5 and 6, the next three, including the week-end contests—which naturally will draw the larger crowds—in the 70,000-capacity Yankee Stadium, and the last two, if necessary, back in the National League park.

If the Cubs win, there will be an "off day" Friday for traveling, and

Continued on Page 21, Column 5

Budge and Wood Advance to Semi-Round In U. S. Tennis Play; Mrs. Fabyan Wins

By BILL BONI

FOREST HILLS, N. Y., Sept. 16 (A. P.).—Only two nations still were represented at the end of today's fast-paced program that brought the men's and women's national singles tennis championships down to the semi-final stage.

The United States has three survivors in each division and Australia one in each. Tomorrow, Defending Champion Don Budge will face Sidney Wood, of New York, and Gene Mako, Budge's doubles partner, will play John Bromwich, of Australia. In the women's matches it will be Alice Marble against Mrs. Sarah Palfrey Fabyan and Dorothy May Bundy against Nancy Wynne, of Australia.

Budge, Wood, Miss Marble and Mrs. Fabyan came through to the next-to-last round this afternoon, each with a masterpiece of its creator's individual art.

Budge completely overpowered Harry Hopman, wiry little Australian Davis Cup captain, 6-3, 6-1, 6-3; Wood defeated Bitsy Grant, 6-2, 6-3, 6-2; Miss Marble turned on the steam to crush England's beautiful southpaw, Kay Stammers, 6-0, 6-0, after a fumbling first set, and Mrs. Fabyan, winner of the last two U. S. doubles titles with Miss Marble, upset Jadwiga Jedrzejowska, of Poland, husky 1937 runner-up and top-seeded invader, 6-1, 6-4.

Budge was on top of Hopman all the way. When the big California redhead is on his game he doesn't hit any shot without a definite purpose. He belts drives down first one sideline and then the other to get his man on the run, and then, just to cross him up, drops a soft shot barely over the net or sends his opponent digging futilely back to the spot he'd just left.

It was that way against Hopman. The veteran internationalist's experience didn't help him get his racquet on a ball that went whistling by. The only time the Australian

Continued on Page 21, Column 3

Pennant Race At a Glance

By Associated Press

The Pittsburgh Pirates, splitting a double-header with Boston, remained three games in front of the idle Chicago Cubs in the National League race yesterday, although the nightcap defeat for the Bucs left the Cubs only three games down on the all-important losing side. Cincinnati, breaking even with the Phillies, continued to trail the Cubs by a game and to lead the fourth-place Giants by half a game.

The Yankees whipped Detroit to climb within two wins of clinching the American League pennant. Cleveland, by losing to Boston, was eliminated from a final mathematical chance at the flag. The Indians now are 17 games behind, with only 15 to play.

The picture:

NATIONAL LEAGUE

Club.	W.	L.	Pc.	G.B.	T.P.
Pittsburgh	79	57	.581	—	18
Chicago	76	60	.559	3	18
Cincinnati	76	62	.551	4	16
New York	75	62	.547	4½	17

AMERICAN LEAGUE

Club.	W.	L.	Pc.	G.B.	T.P.
New York	94	43	.686	—	15
Boston	79	58	.577	15	17
Cleveland	77	60	.562	17	15

1938

September 17, 1938 - First win of five for the season defeating Pittsburgh 27-7; game played in Buffalo, NY

1939

RECORD: 1-9-1, T-4TH IN NFL EAST
HEAD COACH: BERT BELL

SCHEDULE

REGULAR SEASON

Wk. 2	Sep 17	L	7-0	vs Washington Redskins
Wk. 3	Sep 24	L	13-3	vs New York Giants
Wk. 4	Oct 1	T	0-0	vs Brooklyn Dodgers
Wk. 6	Oct 15	L	27-10	at New York Giants
Wk. 7	Oct 22	L	23-14	at Brooklyn Dodgers
Wk. 9	Nov 5	L	7-6	at Washington Redskins
Wk. 10	Nov 12	L	23-16	vs Green Bay Packers
Wk. 11	Nov 19	L	27-14	at Chicago Bears
Wk. 12	Nov 23	W	17-14	vs Pittsburgh Pirates
Wk. 12	Nov 26	L	24-12	at Pittsburgh Pirates
Wk. 13	Dec 3	L	35-13	at Cleveland Rams (at Colorado Springs, CO)

Davey O'Brien, an All-American QB, signed with the Eagles for a reported $12,000 per year salary and a percentage of the gate. O'Brien played in every game and set an NFL passing yardage record with 1,324 yards. Despite the success of O'Brien, the Eagles could only muster a 1-9-1 record; their only win was on Thanksgiving Day against Pittsburgh, 17-14. However the Eagles would make history that year. On October 22nd, the Eagles played in the first televised NFL game and fell to the host Brooklyn Dodgers, 23-14. Allan "Skip" Walz broadcast the game for WNBC from Ebbetts field to the approximately 1,000 TV sets then in Brooklyn.

1939 PHILADELPHIA EAGLES STATS

Passing	Comp	Att	Comp %	Yds	Y/Att	TD	Int	Rating
Davey O'Brien	99	201	49.3	1324	6.59	6	17	45.3
Joe Bukant	10	1	1000.0	0	0.00	0	0	79.2
Emmett Mortell	12	41	29.3	134	3.27	1	0	48.8
Dave Smukler	7	20	35.0	56	2.80	0	4	4.2
Dick Riffle	1	4	25.0	2	0.50	0	1	0.0

Rushing	Rush	Yds	Avg	TD
Dave Smukler	45	218	4.8	0
Franny Murray	49	137	2.8	1
Joe Bukant	59	136	2.3	3
Emmett Mortell	37	88	2.4	0
Dick Riffle	18	61	3.4	0
Drew Ellis	1	6	6.0	0
Joe Carter	1	4	4.0	0
Jay Arnold	8	1	0.1	0
Bill Hewitt	1	1	1.0	0
Chuck Newton	1	0	0.0	0
Woody Dow	1	-7	-7.0	0
Davey O'Brien	108	-14	-0.1	1

Kicking	PAT Made	PAT Att	PAT %	FG Made	FG Att	FG %	Pts
Joe Carter	1	1	100	0	0	0.0	13
Franny Murray	8	12	67	2	4	50.0	26
Hank Reese	1	1	100	2	4	50.0	7

Receiving	Rec	Yds	Avg	TD
Red Ramsey	31	359	11.6	1
Joe Carter	24	292	12.2	2
Bill Hewitt	15	243	16.2	1
Jay Arnold	13	207	15.9	1
Franny Murray	13	144	11.1	1
Chuck Newton	9	123	13.7	1
Dick Riffle	6	57	9.5	0
Woody Dow	5	58	11.6	0
Elmer Kolberg	3	33	11.0	0

Punting	Punts	Yds	Avg	Blocked
Joe Bukant	1	54	54.0	0
Dave Smukler	10	483	48.3	0
Jay Arnold	1	42	42.0	0
Davey O'Brien	3	120	40.0	0
Emmett Mortell	23	907	39.4	0
Franny Murray	33	1220	37.0	0
Dick Riffle	14	479	34.2	0

EAGLES WIN ON O'BRIEN'S PASS, 17 TO 14

The Philadelphia Inquirer

PHILADELPHIA, FRIDAY MORNING, NOVEMBER 24, 1939 abdefg 27

Strictly Sports

Penna.-New York Pact Ideal, But Will It Work?

Empire State Boxing Commission's Previous Nullification Recalled

Cy Peterman, regular conductor of Strictly Sports, is ill and unable to write his column here. Until his recovery, the column will be written by other members of The Inquirer sports staff.

By PERRY LEWIS

LEON L. RAINS, chairman of the Pennsylvania Athletic Commission, did a fine job when he consummated a working agreement between the governing body he heads and the New York State Boxing Commission. Undoubtedly he is right when he asserts that the arrangement will prove a boon to the ring sport in both States—but at this point the writer edges in with an "if."

Any coalition that strengthens governing bodies whose common aim is to keep a sport clean is desirable. This working agreement between the Pennsylvania and New York commissions will fulfill the optimistic forecast of Chairman Rains—if it works. It is plain that a working agreement that fails to work is useless, and it is history that other such agreements between these two commissions have held only so long as it served the purposes of the New York board to concur.

This hand-in-hand stuff is not new business. Away back yonder the headmen of boxing in Pennsylvania and New York agreed to work together. They were still working together in 1927 when, with the featherweight championship vacant, Benny Bass was matched to fight Red Chapman at our Municipal Stadium. The Pennsylvania body voted to recognize the winner as champion, and the Boxing Fathers of Broadway concurred—until Benny defeated Red in ten sensational rounds.

* * *

THEN the New York body did a complete about-face in the interests of Tony Canzoneri, a great favorite with the late Professor William Muldoon, then chairman of the Empire State commission. Bass was not champion and wouldn't be recognized as anything more than a contender until he had defeated Canzoneri, Muldoon and his associates ruled.

By a curious coincidence, Tex Rickard was right on the spot with his hands full of contracts for a Bass-Canzoneri bout to be held in Madison Square Garden. Tex was quick on the trigger that way; he seemed to sense what action the New York Commission would take.

Phil Glassman, then manager of Bass, was wise enough to realize he was on one of those "or else" spots, and having great confidence in Bass, signed on the dotted line. How Benny lost the decision and the title to Tony after suffering a broken collarbone when knocked down in an early round, is pugilistic history.

The name of Benny Bass does not appear on the New York Commission's record of featherweight champions. But here in Pennsylvania, Bass was boss of the class from Sept. 12, 1927, when he brushed Chapman aside, until Feb. 10, 1928, the date of his defeat by Canzoneri. As Ben later won the junior lightweight title, he is among the ring aristocrats who have held championships in two divisions.

* * *

GETTING back to working agreements: This one had failed to work, but the breach was healed in 1928; then the commissions again decided to become one big happy family. But it was only an armistice, for in 1932 the New York commissioners, in order to oblige a pet performer, refused to see eye-to-eye with the Pennsylvania board.

Stanley Poreda had broken a contract to box George Godfrey here, and was suspended. He was still under suspension when matched with Ernie Schaaf by a New York promoter; the Broadway solons said it would be all right with them.

A spirited protest was registered by Harry Farrell, then chairman of the Pennsylvania Commission, but to no avail. The working agreement was no longer working insofar as the New York group was concerned. There was nothing that Farrell and his colleagues could do about it except to sever relations in as dignified a manner as possible.

For the good of boxing in New York, as well as in Pennsylvania, it is to be hoped that this latest renewal of an old working agreement, can be made to click. It won't work unless the letter of the agreement is observed by both commissions. There will, of course, be differences of opinion; that is inevitable. But if Chairman Phelan is as diplomatic as Chairman Rains always has been, any serious friction is unlikely—and boxing patrons will reap the benefits of a wise amalgamation.

* * *

BOXERS and managers who take a powder after contracting to box in Pennsylvania should certainly be unwelcome in New York, and vise versa. Ringmen who give an unsatisfactory performance in New York are not wanted in Pennsylvania, and record another vise versa.

It is taken for granted, of course, that in any warfare between promoters bidding for the same fight or for the services of a certain fighter, neither commission will declare itself in. Any such developments come under the head of regular promotion business and, as such, is beyond the scope of commission business. Any effort by a promoter to use either commission as a whip must, of necessity, be frowned upon.

If this working agreement is observed to its logical conclusion it follows that any fighter, manager or promoter who defies or vilifies one commission, defies and vilifies the other. So far as the Old Sport knows, this has never occurred in Pennsylvania, but it has in New York.

Success to the amalgamation! It's a fine idea anyhow.

Holiday Football Scores

College

LOCAL

LaSalle, 20; P. M. C., 0.
Lincoln (Pa.), 14; Howard (Wash.) 7.
Penn (150), 12; Lafayette (150), 8.

STATE

Franklin & Marshall, 40; Ursinus, 0.
Gettysburg, 40; Dickinson, 7.
Lock Haven Teachers, 19; Shippensburg Teachers, 0.

EAST

Catholic University, 35; Long Island University, 14.
Army Jayvees, 46; Dartmouth Jayvees, 14.
Wyoming Seminary, 32; Manhattan Frosh, 0.
Princeton (150), 0; Rutgers (150), 0.

MID-WEST

Western Reserve, 18; Case, 0.
Cincinnati, 13; Miami (Ohio) 0.
Washington (St. Louis), 32; Missouri School of Mines, 0.
Wayne, 7; Kalamazoo Teachers (Mich.), 6.
Baldwin-Wallace, 22; Ohio Wesleyan, 7.
John Carroll, 25; Akron, 6.
Toledo, 20; Xavier (Cin.), 0.
Illinois Wesleyan, 6; Bradley, 0.
Springfield Teachers, 25; Hastings, 21.
William Jewell, 20; Missouri Central, 7.
Kemper M. I., 18; Moberly J. C., 7.
Wentworth, 7; Ila J. C., 7.

SOUTH AND SOUTHWEST

Loyola (N. O.), 13; Springhill, 7.
Marshall, 47; West Virginia Wesleyan, 13.
Syracuse, 10; Maryland, 7.
William & Mary, 7; Richmond, 0.
V. M. I., 19; V. P. I., 14.
Citadel, 24; Erskine, 0.
Statesboro Teachers, 7; Armstrong Teachers, 0.
Missouri Valley, 8; Warrensburg

Continued on Page 30, Column 8

O'BRIEN DISCOURAGES COMPETITION FOR HIS PASSING LAURELS

Not only did Davey O'Brien pass his Eagles to a sensational 17-14 triumph over the Pittsburgh Pirates yesterday, but he saw to it that no one else stole his aerial thunder. Here he is about to rush in and spear a pass that is bouncing off the finger tips of Sam Boyd, Pirate end. Lou Tomasetti, 1939 Inquirer A. A. All-Star player, threw the pass. Davey returned it to the Eagles 25-yard line. Two other Eagles—Murray (11) and Dow (14)—also are seeking to intercept the heave.

Burrs Beaten By W. Phila.

Sigholtz Kicks Goal To Beat W. Catholic Before 12,000 Fans

By FRANK O'GARA

Bob Sigholtz, a titan in size and performance, booted West Philadelphia into a thrilling 9-7 victory over West Catholic yesterday with but two minutes of their 19th annual neighborhood high school game remaining, before 12,000 at Shibe Park.

Trailing at 6-7 and in possession of the ball due to one of the breaks in which the game abounded, West Philly used the same method that had given it victory last year, when Sigholtz, 210-pound tackler, kicked a perfect placement from the 16-yard line. In the 1938 battle, Len Zaroff's toe provided the margin of a 3-0 triumph.

Sigholtz was no one-play hero; he personally forced the break that led up to his winning effort.

BAD GUESS ON BOOT

The crucial events started with Gil "Babe" Gekoski's boot to West Catholic's safety, Charlie McCreesh. The later played it smartly by ignoring it and taking no chance on a fumble. But it was a bad guess. The ball bounded 15 yards further to West Catholic's nine.

On one of the ensuing running plays, Tom Curley, the Burr punter, had his wrist hurt, as the clawing Speedboy defense tried to wrest the ball from his hand. He had the wrist taped, went back to kick on third down, but had trouble in adjusting the ball. Sigholtz rushed in, hurried

Continued on Page 29, Column 6

Catholic University Gains 8th Victory

NEW YORK, Nov. 23 (A. P.).—The power which carried Catholic University to its most successful season in years today beat back a deceptive Long Island University eleven, as the Cardinals scored their eighth triumph in nine starts, 35-14, at Ebbets Field. The Black Birds, completing their first gridiron campaign after a seven-year layoff, suffered their third setback against five victories.

Catholic indicated its supremacy in the opening minutes of the game when a 82-yard drive culminated in a touchdown by Henry Brosick on an eight yard sweep around end. Included in the parade was a pass play, immediately preceding the tally, which covered 44-yards from Henry Sachon to Albert Norris.

Catholic U.	Pos.	Long Island U.
[illegible]	Left end	King
[illegible]	Left tackle	[illegible]
[illegible]	Left guard	[illegible]
White	Centre	[illegible]
[illegible]	Right guard	Callahan
C. Pirro	Right tackle	[illegible]
[illegible]	Right end	[illegible]
Norris	Quarterback	Perugino
[illegible]	Left halfback	[illegible]
Brosick	Right halfback	Millman
[illegible]	Fullback	[illegible]

Catholic U. — 7 7 14 7—35
Long Island U. — 0 7 0 7—14

[illegible]

Girard Estate Loses

Harry Cafry place-kicked the extra point to give the South Philly Panthers a 7-6 victory over Girard Estate at Front and Mifflin sts.

Girard Estate — 0 0 0 6—6
S. P. Panthers — 0 0 7 0—7

[illegible]

12th in Row For San Jose

'Pop' Warner's Team Beats Fresno State

FRESNO, Calif., Nov. 23 (A. P.).—Unbeaten San Jose State College, employing the finest football technique developed by the master tactician Glenn "Pop" Warner, boomed into the national gridiron picture today with a 42 to 7 victory over previously undefeated Fresno State College.

Earlier this season Amos Alonzo Stagg, 77-year-old dean of coaches, described the San Jose team as the "perfect coached Warner squad." It lived up to that praise today.

It was San Jose's twelfth win of the season and the most conclusive. Thus far the Spartans have amassed 312 points, meanwhile permitting opponents 29.

South Catholic Ties Southern

By EDWARD J. KLEIN

Stymied on offense after the opening period, Southern High's football team staved off five thrusts in the last three quarters by Southeast Catholic High's victory-lean eleven yesterday to hold the Pirates even, 0 to 0, before 10,000 at the old Phillies' Park.

Not since 1935 has Southeast Catholic whipped Southern in their six-year-old rivalry for South Philadelphia's scholastic football championship. The gold-and-purple-jerseyed Pirates had won one and lost four in the annual rivalry prior to yesterday's stalemate.

Led by the passing and plunging of Ed Shanahan and Hugh Jeffers, Southeast Catholic reached Southern's 20 five times, passing that spot on three occasions. In the second period, the Pirates drove to the one, then went to the 18 and 15 on marches in the fourth quarter.

The Pirates' golden scoring chance came, by all odds, in the second sea-

Continued on Page 28, Column 5

California Gridder Dies of Injuries

PASADENA, Calif., Nov. 23 (A. P.). Paul Becker, 247-pound centre on the California Institute of Technology football team, died today, 24 hours after his skull was fractured in a Cal-Tech game with La Verne College.

Imprints of shoe cleats were found on his head. He was injured in a pile-up of players in the third quarter of the game, which Cal-Tech won, 13-7.

La Salle Jars P. M. C., 20-0

Explorers Score In Three Periods; 5000 Watch Game

By JAMES C. ISAMINGER

Pennsylvania Military College lost its Turkey Day football battle to La Salle College, 20 to 0, at Chester yesterday but they added a new note to college football by staging a football game on horseback to entertain a crowd of 5000 between halves.

Two teams of five men each, all polo players, staged Col. Frank K. Hyatt's version of horseback football. They were mounted on polo ponies and their horsemanship was subjected to a severe test because there are no rules or traditions on horseback football and everything went.

The combatants passed the ball to each other and when it fell to the turf, a player had the privilege of dismounting and then getting astride his pony again. Spectators often saw riderless mounts galloping to the sidelines.

To score a rider had to toss the ball over the cross bar as he raced toward the posts. The West team beat East, 3 to 2. Onlookers seemed to enjoy the novelty and applauded the riders.

CADETS OUTCLASSED

In the football game played afoot, Marty Brill's Explorers outclassed the Cadets from the start. They had more power in their attack, punted better and played a sounder all around game.

The nearest the Cadets could get to scoring was in the ebbing moments of the second period when they uncorked their one and only burst of power and had the ball on LaSalle's 13 yard stripe when the half ended.

The Explorers ripped off three

Continued on Page 28, Column 4

Report Maryland Coach to Resign

WASHINGTON, Nov 23 (A. P.).—Coach Frank M. Dobson, of Maryland University's football team, one of the best known mentors in this area, will resign his post tomorrow, authoritative sources said tonight.

Dobson came to Maryland in 1936 from Richmond University. During his first three years at Maryland his teams won 21 games, tied two, and lost nine. In the last two years, they lost 14 and won four.

Two years ago a school restriction limited athletic scholarship assistance to boys who came from Maryland schools, forbidding help to out-of-State athletes.

Dobson closed his coaching career today when his team lost to Syracuse, 10 to 7.

Rumors this fall have had it that Dobson was to be succeeded at Maryland by Coach Dick Harlow, of Harvard. Harlow, however, has denied them.

Late Aerial Beats Pirates

Bill Hewitt Catches Forward in Last Minute, Laterals to Arnold for Deciding Score as 20,000 Look On

Statistics

First downs	8	7
Net yards rushing	40	129
Yards passing	201	138
Passes attempted	24	21
Passes completed	9	8
Passes intercepted by	8	1
Number of punts	7	5
Average distance	35	28
Punts returned	3	4
Yardage returned	30	27
Fumbles	5	1

Pittsburgh — 0 0 0 14—14
Eagles — 0 7 3 7—17

THE LINEUP

Eagles.	Positions.	Pittsburgh.
Ramsey	Left end	Boyd
Ellis	Left tackle	Campbell
Schmidt	Left guard	Midler
Harper	Centre	Marne
Cuppoletti	Right guard	Kakasic
Wolfe	Right tackle	Nicolai
Carter	Right end	Sortet
O'Brien	Quarterback	Bond
Arnold	Left halfback	McCullough
Murray	Right halfback	Tomasetti
Dow	Fullback	Brumbaugh

Officials: Referee, Wilmer Crowell; umpire, Ronald Kinney; head linesman, Stan Baumgartner; field judge, Hinkey Haines. Time of periods, 15 minutes.

Touchdowns — Carter, Arnold, Brumbaugh, Platukis. Points after touchdowns—Murray 2 (placements); Nicolai 2 (placements). Field goal—Murray. Substitutions: Eagles—ends, Hewitt, Kolberg; tackles, Fyman, Somers; guards, Kolling, Hughes, White; backs, Bukant, Riffle. Pittsburgh—ends, Platukis; tackle, Karp; guard, Doyle; backs, Johnston, McDonough.

By PERRY LEWIS

The magic arm of little Davey O'Brien accounted for another gridiron upheaval yesterday when his last-minute pass went for a 66-yard touchdown to give Philadelphia Eagles a 17-14 victory over the Pittsburgh Pirates before 20,000 at Municipal Stadium.

The midget sharpshooter rifled one of the longest passes he has ever thrown in this last-ditch attempt, and the speeding end, Bill Hewitt, pulled it in on the Pittsburgh 28. As he was hit, Hewitt lateralled to Jay Arnold, and the maneuver fooled the Pirates to such an extent that the latter romped easily to the winning touchdown.

No more sensational adieu to Philadelphia football ever could have been made by Hewitt, who is giving up the sport after eight years in pro ranks. And no more glorious way could be found to end the home season of a year which previously had not yielded a triumph.

O'Brien was no less sensational than he has been in his previous two games, in which he broke league records for passing. Previous to his payoff touchdown he tossed a magnificent pass to Captain Joe Carter, who covered the remaining distance for a 65-yard score.

PREVIOUS O'BRIEN SCORE

In between Davey's great touchdown heaves, Franny Murray inserted a vital three-pointer on a field goal from the 31-yard line. In the final analysis, this boot provided the margin of victory. Franny also kicked both points after touchdown.

Coming in the third period, Murray's boot gave the Birds a 10-0 lead. But then the Pirates got busy, driving 30 yards for a touchdown, climaxed by Boyd Brumbaugh's four-yard plunge. When Armand Niccolai added the extra point, the Eagles' margin was shaved to 10-7.

As the minutes passed it look very much as though this score would be the payoff. Once the Eagles were in scoring position by virtue of a 37-yard run from scrimmage by O'Brien, but eventually the Pirates took the ball on downs on their own 30. A few

Continued on Page 29, Column 1

Frankford Beats N. Catholic, 18-6

Frankford High worked up a powerful offensive to overthrow North Catholic High, 18-6, in their 12th annual football battle yesterday at Large and Wakeling sts.

A crowd of 10,000 was treated to two touchdowns by Vince Galcone, Frankford's quarterback, one a thrilling 67-yard jaunt. These scores put the Pioneers ahead, 12-0, by the middle of the third quarter. Then after End Cliff Kaupp tallied North Catholic's touchdown on a forward late in that period, Frankford returned with a crashing attack in the fourth quarter to go 65 yards to a score, Joe Nejman crossing the goal line.

N. CATHOLIC STILL LEADS

The outcome of this game made the series record stand seven victories in favor of North Catholic, four on the Frankford side and one contest drawn.

After the struggle had gone in North Catholic's favor in the first period with the Falcons reaching the opposing six, from where Frank Giraffa had failed in a placement kick attempt, Frankford gained the upper hand in the second quarter.

The Pioneers were put on the path to victory by Ray Gurzynski, the same husky back who had tallied the only touchdown in Frankford's last triumph over North Catholic in 1937.

Gurzynski touched off the advance by intercepting Captain Bob Miller's

Continued on Page 28, Column 5

Spiegal Rally Overcomes Tony Saraullo

By JOHN WEBSTER

Tommy Spiegal won the fight, but he must have been thankful many times that his State lightweight championship wasn't at stake in the Cambria ring yesterday afternoon.

For Tony Saraullo, a downtown kid who served his fistic apprenticeship in The Inquirer A. A. tournaments, waged an amazing battle against the Uniontown, Pa., veteran and narrowly lost the holiday feature duel after 10 rounds of violent slamming.

As it was, trim, dark-haired Saraullo, who beamed 135¼ pounds so that Spiegal's newly won title was not on the block, took the decision of Referee Irving Kutcher, but lost when the judges, Eddie Loughran and Harry Lasky, voted for Spiegal who [illegible] a modest 133¼.

FINISHED STRONG

Loughran scored six rounds for the Czechoslovakian Hebrew, gave three to Saraullo, and called one even. With Lasky it was 4-3-3, while the referee made it 5-3-2 in favor of the skilled, sharp hitting South Philadelphian.

On my score sheet, they were even in rounds at five apiece, but Spiegal's strong finish in the tenth when he hammered Saraullo from bell to bell gave him a faint edge over the boy from the prelims.

Yet, if Spiegal won the fight, Saraullo won the fans—the whole corporal's guard. Tony's unexpectedly strong showing against the limping Latruper who recently dethroned Bob Montgomery in the same ring had them screaming all along the route.

Moving nimbly and mixing sharp

Continued on Page 28, Column 3

Bowl Test Won By Sourdoughs

JUNEAU, Alaska, Nov. 23 (A. P.).—An ambulance, Red Cross nurses and doctors were on the sidelines today as the continent's "Bowl" season got under way.

The Alaska Sourdoughs football team defeated the Baranoff Bears 6 to 0, in the first Gold Bowl game.

Only one player was injured. He was Quarterback Jim Mailer, of the Bears, who suffered a broken ankle. He was well taken care of by the medical corps which was on hand because the cinder-strewn playing field was frozen into a rough sandpaper complexion.

Mrs. Robert Bender, daughter of Territorial Governor John Troy, dedicated the charity game as an annual affair by breaking a bottle of champagne on the goal posts.

Max Lewis, who said he played at various schools in the States, boomed over for the score shortly before the end of the first half. He is the son of Victor A. Lewis, sculptor whose Sourdough bronze is one of Seattle's better known monuments.

More than 60 players, the majority of whom were former gridders in the States, made up the two teams.

Lake View Scores

Harry Cantrell climaxed a 65-yard touchdown drive in the last period by plunging over to score as Lake View defeated the Haverford gridders in their Thanksgiving Day game at Ardmore.

First Setback For Richmond

RICHMOND, Va., Nov. 23 (A. P.).—William and Mary's surprising Indians scored their second upset within a week by trouncing the previously undefeated University of Richmond football team, 7 to 0, before 12,000 spectators today.

The winning touchdown came in the third period to climax a march of 80 yards. Jimmy Howard, sophomore back, went over from the six-inch mark.

Richmond.	Positions.	W. and M.
[illegible]	Left end	[illegible]
[illegible]	Left tackle	[illegible]
[illegible]	Left guard	Ramsey
[illegible]	Centre	W. Goodlow
[illegible]	Right guard	[illegible]
[illegible]	Right tackle	[illegible]
[illegible]	Right end	[illegible]
[illegible]	Quarterback	[illegible]
[illegible]	Left halfback	[illegible]
[illegible]	Right halfback	[illegible]
[illegible]	Fullback	Howard

[illegible]

Collingdale Turns Back Darby,

Illustrated on Page 30

After waiting 12 years, Collingdale High finally turned back its most important Suburban Conference rival, Darby, before a vociferous crowd of 12,000 at Darby yesterday morning. The score was 19-6. After the hard-fought battle was over, tear gas was needed to disperse the overwrought supporters of both teams.

(For Details of Riot see Page 1 story.)

Dave McKeag, Darby quarterback, suffered a serious neck injury early in the first period and was rushed to the Fitzgerald-Mercy Hospital.

Collingdale just about clinched the decision early in the second period when it scored two touchdowns in rapid succession. Warren Moxley's pass was blocked and taken in the air by Bud Palmer who raced 45 yards to the first six-pointer. Then, Moxley, back to punt, received a bad pass from centre, Bob Vickery blocked the kick and ran 20 yards to score.

Darby then counted when Johnny Greer ran five yards with Moxley's 20-yard pass. Collingdale, with Al Carlin and Paul Hart carrying the ball, drove 98 yards to a last period touchdown. Jack Thompson dove over from the one-yard line and Captain Al Reichenback placekicked the extra point.

Collingdale	Position	Darby
W. Hershey	Left end	Greer
Lytle	Left tackle	Colbert
Vickery	Left guard	D'Antonio
Tully	Centre	[illegible]
Feathers	Right guard	[illegible]
[illegible]	Right tackle	[illegible]
Palmer	Right end	[illegible]
Thompson	Quarterback	McKeag
R. Hershey	Left halfback	[illegible]
Reichenbach (c)	Right halfback	[illegible]
Carlin	Fullback	Moxley

Collingdale — 0 12 0 7—19
Darby — 0 6 0 0—6

[illegible]

November 24, 1939 - First and only win of the '39 season; also last win of the decade was played against Pittsburgh 17-14 ourchases a 50 percent share of the Eagles from Bert Bell.

Don Looney sets an Eagles' single-game record that will survive into the next century, catching 14 passes on December 1 at Washington.

1941

Bell and Rooney swap franchises with Pittsburgh's Alexis Thompson who, upon arriving in Philadelphia, hires Earl "Greasy" Neale as the Eagles' new head coach.

The Eagles leave Municipal Stadium for Shibe Park at 21st St. & Lehigh Ave.

A December 7 game vs. the Redskins in the nation's capital is overshadowed by the Japanese attack on Pearl Harbor. Although most fans are unaware of what has just happened in Hawaii, the stadium's public address announcer urges officials of the armed forces to report to their offices.

1943

As World War II brings change to the map in Europe and the Pacific, so, too, would it alter the NFL landscape. A manpower shortage leads to a one-year merger of Steelers and Eagles players, who play the 1943 campaign as the "Steagles," splitting their "home" schedule between Philadelphia and Pittsburgh.

The NFL issues a league-wide mandate: all players are required to wear helmets.

1944

The Eagles draft future Hall of Fame halfback Steve Van Buren and, after 11 seasons without a winning record, the club's fortunes begin to rise. A dominant force, Van Buren will lead the league in rushing yards and TDs four times from '45-'49.

1946

Bert Bell, former Eagles coach and owner, is elected commissioner of the NFL, whose headquarters were then located in Bala Cynwyd, PA.

1947

The Eagles shut out Pittsburgh, 28-0, in their first post-season game and earn the first of three straight appearances in the NFL Championship Game. The Birds subsequently fall, however, to the host Chicago Cardinals, 28-21, at frozen Comiskey Park. The home team dons sneakers from the outset, rather than cleats, in order to get better traction.

1948

The Eagles return to the Championship Game and win their firs NFL title, defeating the Chicago Cardinals, 7-0, in a snowstorm at Shibe Park. The start of the game is delayed 30 minutes while crews, including the players, remove the snow-covered tarp from the field. Steve Van Buren scores the game's only TD.

1949

Alexis Thompson sells the club to a group of 100 buyers led by James Clark and Frank McNamee. Known as the "100 Brothers," each pays roughly $3,000 for an equal share of the franchise.

The Eagles draft All-America center/linebacker - and future Hall of Famer - Chuck Bednarik.

The Eagles reach the NFL Championship Game for the third consecutive year and top the Rams, 14-0, to earn their second straight crown. Playing in torrential rain at the LA Coliseum, Steve Van Buren runs for 196 yards, Pete Pihos hauls in a TD pass, and Leo Skladany returns a blocked punt for a score. Never before, nor since, has a NFL team posted consecutive shutouts in championship play.

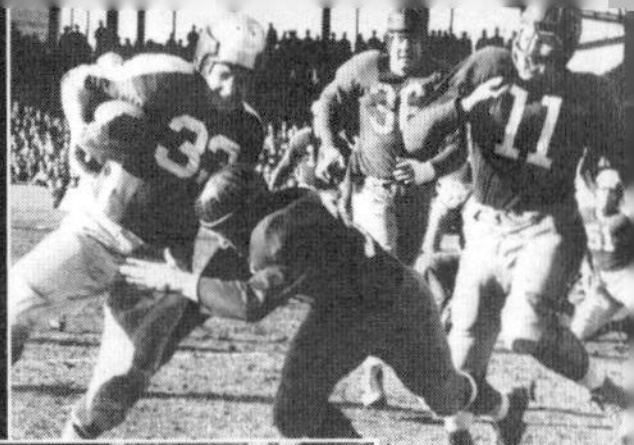

Eagles Vs. Redskins December 7, 1941

The 1943 "Steagle

Eagles Owner Alexis Thompson(left) with GM Al Ennis

Steve Van Buren

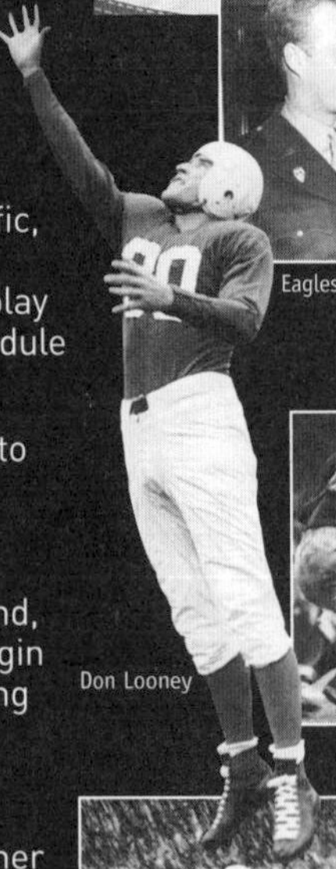

Don Looney

1947 Championship Game

Crews remove snow from Shibe Park before 1948 Title Game

As was the case during the '47 and '49 championship games, the weather also was a factor in the 1948 Title Game.

Leo Skladany blocks a Rams' pun in 1949 Championship Game

Pete Pihos

Welcome Home
WORLD CHAMPIONS
PHILA. EAGLES

The Mayor of Philadelphia welcomes home the 1949 Champions

1940's

40s Decade in Review

Decade Win-Loss Record:
58-47-5, (3-1 postseason record)

Home Field:
1940-49 Shibe Park, 1941 and 1947 Municipal Stadium

Playoff Appearances:
1947, 1948 and 1949

Championships:
Divisional Championship 1947 (NFL East),
1948 (NFL East) and 1949 (NFL East)
NFL Championship Games 1947, 1948, 1949
NFL Champions 1948, 1949

Head Coaches:
1940 Bert Bell (1-10); 1941-49 Greasy Neale (67-45-7) (3-1 postseason record);
1943 Walt Kiesling as the Steagles (5-4-1)

Hall of Fame Inductees:
Chuck Bednarik, Bert Bell, Bill Hewitt, Greasy Neale, Pete Pihos, Steve Van Buren, Alex Wojciechowicz

Award Winners:
Greasy Neale, Coach of the Year 1948

All Pro:
Dick Bassi 1940, Don Looney 1940, Davey O'Brien 1940, Dick Humbert 1941, Phil Ragazzo 1941, Bob Suffridge 1941, Tommy Thompson 1942 and 1948-49, Jack Hinkle 1943, Eberle Schultz 1943, Vic Sears 1943 and 1945, Ernie Steele 1943, Leroy Zimmerman 1943-44, Steve Van Buren 1944-49, Al Wistert 1944-49, Bruno Banducci 1945, Jack Ferrante 1945 and 1949, Augie Lio 1946, Pete Pihos 1947-49, Bucko Kilroy 1948-49, Joe Muha 1948, Cliff Patton 1949

All-Star Game Selections:
Dick Bassi 1940, Don Looney 1940, Dick Humbert 1941, Enio Conti 1942, Tommy Thompson 1942, Bosh Pritchard 1942

First Game of the Decade:
September 15, 1940 lost to Green Bay 27-20

Last Game of the Decade:
December11, 1949 defeated NY Giants 17-3

Largest Margin of Victory:
October 10, 1948 vs. NY Giants 45-0,
October 17, 1948 vs. Washington Redskins 45-0,
November 14, 1948 vs. Boston Yanks 45-0

Largest Margin of Defeat:
November 30, 1941 vs. Chicago Bears 49-14

Eagle Firsts of the Decade:

First Game at Shibe Park,
September 28, 1940, loss to NY Giants

First Winning Season –
1943, 5-4-1 as Steagles

First 300-Yard Passing Game –
Davey O'Brien completed 33 of 60 passes totaling 316 yards in a losing effort against the Washington Redskins, December 1, 1940

First 200-Yard Rushing Game –
Steve Van Buren rushed 27 times gaining 205 yards in a win over the Pittsburgh Steelers, November 27, 1949

First 100 points scored –
Steve Van Buren scored 110 points during the 1945 season

First 20 Touchdown Passes –
Tommy Thompson threw 25 touchdown passes in the 1948 season

First Postseason Game –
Shut out Pittsburgh Steelers 21-0 in their first playoff game on December 21, 1947

1940

RECORD: 1-10, 5TH IN NFL EAST
HEAD COACH: BERT BELL

SCHEDULE

REGULAR SEASON

Wk. 2	Sep 15	L	27-20	at Green Bay Packers
Wk. 3	Sep 22	L	21-13	at Cleveland Rams
Wk. 4	Sep 28	L	20-14	vs New York Giants
Wk. 5	Oct 4	L	30-17	at Brooklyn Dodgers
Wk. 6	Oct 13	L	17-7	at New York Giants
Wk. 7	Oct 20	L	34-17	vs Washington Redskins
Wk. 8	Oct 26	L	21-7	vs Brooklyn Dodgers
Wk. 10	Nov 10	L	7-3	at Pittsburgh Pirates
Wk. 11	Nov 17	L	21-0	vs Detroit Lions
Wk. 13	Nov 28	W	7-0	vs Pittsburgh Pirates
Wk. 13	Dec 1	L	13-6	at Washington Redskins

After selling the Pittsburgh Steelers to Alexis Thompson, Art Rooney bought a half interest in the Eagles, who move their games to Shibe Park (later known as Connie Mack Stadium). However, the Eagles would limp along again, finishing with an awful 1-10 record. Following the season Rooney, along with Eagles co-founder Bert Bell, swapped franchises with Thompson. Bell, who also departed his post as Eagles coach, would one day go on to be commissioner of the NFL. The struggling Eagles won only one game that season, against Pittsburgh 7-0, thus ending a nine-game losing streak. One positive note was that Don Looney's 58 receptions set a new club record that stood for many years.

1940 PHILADELPHIA EAGLES STATS

Passing	Comp	Att	Comp %	Yds	Y/Att	TD	Int	Rating
Davey O'Brien	124	277	44.8	1290	4.66	5	17	39.2
Foster Watkins	28	85	32.9	565	6.65	1	3	46.4

Rushing	Rush	Yds	Avg	TD
Dick Riffle	81	238	2.9	4
Elmer Hackney	32	101	3.2	1
Frank Emmons	29	77	2.7	1
John Cole	26	75	2.9	0
Joe Bukant	18	50	2.8	1
Franny Murray	8	7	0.9	0
Theodore Schmitt	1	6	6.0	0
Jay Arnold	39	0	0.0	7
Les McDonald	2	-2	-1.0	0
Joe Carter	1	-3	-3.0	0
Don Looney	2	-4	-2.0	0
Foster Watkins	14	-76	-5.4	0
Davey O'Brien	100	-180	-1.8	1

Receiving	Rec	Yds	Avg	TD
Jay Arnold	145	0	0.0	0
Don Looney	58	707	12.2	4
Red Ramsey	17	143	8.4	0
Les McDonald	14	289	20.6	0
Joe Carter	12	201	16.8	0
Franny Murray	12	125	10.4	0
Joe Wendlick	8	67	8.4	0
Dick Riffle	8	58	7.3	1
Elmer Kolberg	6	43	7.2	0
Frank Emmons	3	19	6.3	1
John Cole	2	11	5.5	0
Elmer Hackney	2	4	2.0	0
Chuck Newton	1	22	22.0	0
Joe Bukant	1	13	13.0	0
Theodore Schmitt	1	8	8.0	0

Punting	Punts	Yds	Avg	Blocked
Davey O'Brien	6	246	41.0	0
Elmer Kolberg	10	401	40.1	0
Joe Bukant	15	568	37.9	0
Franny Murray	30	1098	36.6	0
John Cole	10	336	33.6	0
Foster Watkins	2	45	22.5	0

Kicking	PAT Made	PAT Att	PAT %	FG Made	FG Att	FG %	Pts
Joe Carter	1	1	100	0	0	0.0	13
George Somers	1	1	100	2	9	22.2	7
Franny Murray	6	8	75	0	1	0.0	6
John Cole	3	4	75	1	1	100.0	6
Foster Watkins	2	2	100	0	0	0.0	2

Interceptions	Int	Yds	Avg	TD
Davey O'Brien	4	92	23.0	0
Franny Murray	2	10	5.0	0
Elmer Kolberg	1	15	15.0	0
Chuck Newton	1	12	12.0	0
Joe Bukant	1	10	10.0	0
Red Ramsey	1	5	5.0	0
Jay Arnold	1	4	4.0	0
Chuck Cherundolo	1	0	0.0	0

THE PHILADELPHIA INQUIRER, FRIDAY MORNING, NOVEMBER 29, 1940

St. Joseph's Easily Beats Catholic High

Hawklets Roll to 20 to 0 Triumph Over Cahill Foe

FOOTBALL FAREWELL: DAVEY O'BRIEN'S LAST STAND WITH EAGLES HERE; F. B. I. NEXT STOP

Running around the ends, whacking at the tackles and passing to out-stretched receivers came to an end for Davey O'Brien, the Eagles' little gridder, yesterday as the Birds won their first game of the season by defeating the Pittsburgh Steelers, 7 to 0, at Shibe Park. Photo shows O'Brien off on a typical end run in the second quarter, with Teammate Carter acting as interference. O'Brien definitely rings down the curtain on his pro football career Sunday when he and his Eagle mates tackle the Redskins in Washington. Only about 5000 saw the gam e.

Younger Brothers Follow Family Traits in Ring Event

William Saraullo, Bill Ettore, Herb Carter, Bob Wilson and Angelo Sfrisi Seek Fame In Inquirer A. A. Diamond Belt Tourney

By JOHN WEBSTER

While no brother battlers in previous Inquirer A. A. tournaments have ever threatened to eclipse the fame of Romulus and Remus, there are nevertheless several youngsters in this fifth Diamond Belt and Middle Atlantic Amateur Boxing Championships who hope to duplicate the deeds of noted elder brothers.

Two of these lads are to have their second try at tournament thumping, having been eliminated early in last season's classic. Undaunted by a single setback, these tight-lipped lads are more determined than ever to make the grade this year.

SARAULLO, ETTORE RETURN

TWO SFRISIS TO FIGHT

BROTHER AL WAS STAR

MANY BOUTS CARDED

TOURNEY STARTS MONDAY

South Catholic Ties Southern

CATHOLIC THREATENS

Eagles Beat Pittsburgh Steelers, 7-0, As 5000 Fans Bid Farewell to O'Brien

By PERRY LEWIS

Continued From First Sports Page

ELUDES SECONDARY

Statistics

THE LINEUP

STEELERS THREATEN

West Catholic Defeats W. Phila.

Continued From First Sports Page

Abington Held To 0-0 Tie

Continued From First Sports Page

Upper Darby Rolls Over Haverford, 19-6

Collingdale High Upsets Darby

Glen-Nor Stays Unbeaten; Swamps Yeadon High, 26-0

Speedboys Tie Owls

Prospect Park Jars Ridley Park

St. Teresa Wins Out

1940

November 29, 1940 - Eagles only win for the season was a 7-0 shutout versus Pittsburgh

1941

RECORD: 2-8-1, 4TH IN NFL EAST
HEAD COACH: GREASY NEALE

SCHEDULE

REGULAR SEASON

Wk. 2	Sep 13	L	24-0	vs New York Giants
Wk. 3	Sep 21	W	10-7	at Pittsburgh Steelers
Wk. 4	Sep 27	L	24-13	vs Brooklyn Dodgers
Wk. 6	Oct 12	L	16-0	at New York Giants
Wk. 7	Oct 19	L	21-17	vs Washington Redskins
Wk. 8	Oct 26	W	21-14	vs Chicago Cardinals
Wk. 9	Nov 2	L	15-6	at Brooklyn Dodgers
Wk. 10	Nov 9	T	7-7	vs Pittsburgh Steelers
Wk. 11	Nov 16	L	21-17	at Detroit Lions
Wk. 13	Nov 30	L	49-14	vs Chicago Bears
Wk. 14	Dec 7	L	20-14	at Washington Redskins

Bell and Rooney swapped franchises with Thompson. The new owner hired Earl (Greasy) Neale as the new head coach of the Eagles. With Neale as head coach the Eagles continued to struggle, posting a 2-8-1 record (with wins over Pittsburgh 10-7 and Chicago 21-14), while returning to play in Municipal Stadium for one season.

1941 PHILADELPHIA EAGLES STATS

Passing	Comp	Att	Comp %	Yds	Y/Att	TD	Int	Rating
Tommy Thompson	86	162	53.1	959	5.92	8	14	51.4
Foster Watkins	6	10	60.0	62	6.20	1	0	111.3
Dan DeSantis	3	7	42.9	78	11.14	1	1	84.2
Wes McAfee	1	4	25.0	4	1.00	0	0	39.6
Len Barnum	19	55	34.5	260	4.73	0	10	11.0
Jim Castiglia	0	7	0.0	0	0.00	0	1	0.0
Nick Basca	0	4	0.0	0	0.00	0	1	0.0

Rushing	Rush	Yds	Avg	TD
Jim Castiglia	60	183	3.1	4
Dan DeSantis	45	125	2.8	0
Terry Fox	21	97	4.6	0
Jack Banta	27	92	3.4	1
Mort Landsberg	23	69	3.0	0
Sam Bartholomew	21	69	3.3	0
Len Barnum	35	64	1.8	0
Fred Gloden	22	55	2.5	0
Nick Basca	15	44	2.9	1
Lou Tomasetti	10	37	3.7	0
Foster Watkins	15	11	0.7	0
Wes McAfee	9	6	0.7	0
Lou Ghecas	2	0	0.0	0
Enio Conti	1	-1	-1.0	0
Tommy Thompson	54	-2	-0.0	0

Punting	Punts	Yds	Avg	Blocked
Jack Banta	9	412	45.8	0
Len Barnum	41	1788	43.6	0
Tommy Thompson	1	43	43.0	0
Nick Basca	10	348	34.8	0
Wes McAfee	1	32	32.0	0
Dan DeSantis	7	206	29.4	0

Receiving	Rec	Yds	Avg	TD
Dick Humbert	29	332	11.4	2
Bob Krieger	19	240	12.6	2
Hank Piro	10	141	14.1	1
Terry Fox	6	71	11.8	0
Lou Tomasetti	5	54	10.8	1
John Shonk	5	52	10.4	0
Mort Landsberg	5	51	10.2	0
Larry Cabrelli	4	90	22.5	1
Dan DeSantis	4	53	13.3	0
Foster Watkins	4	36	9.0	0
Tommy Thompson	4	30	7.5	1
Jim Castiglia	4	24	6.0	0
Wes McAfee	3	30	10.0	1
Sam Bartholomew	3	15	5.0	0
Nick Basca	2	45	22.5	0
Jack Banta	2	42	21.0	0
Jack Ferrante	2	22	11.0	0
Fred Gloden	2	13	6.5	0
Len Barnum	1	11	11.0	0
Kirk Hershey	1	11	11.0	0

Kicking	PAT Made	PAT Att	PAT %	FG Made	FG Att	FG %	Pts
Nick Basca	9	9	100	1	2	50.0	18
Len Barnum	2	2	100	2	6	33.3	8
Wes McAfee	2	2	100	0	0	0.0	8
Dan DeSantis	1	1	100	0	0	0.0	1

1941

Eagles Check Cardinals' Rally to Win, 21-14

Strictly Sports

Penn's Fresh Grid Power Suggests a Victory Cycle

Championship Class Instilled Spirit Spreads to Spark Lowest Subs

By CY PETERMAN

PENN has won another football game, its fourth in succession, this by the biggest margin of all after the natural letdown from sweeping Harvard, Yale and Princeton. But we're not going to talk about that.

It was sufficient to tabulate eight touchdowns of varying length and execution Saturday evening, enough to keep straight a score of 55-6 against battling but overpowered Maryland. Penn was expected to win handily, but not as easily as it did.

We prefer to look at these four victories at the half-way mark from another angle, overlooked to date in the year to year survey of American football. It has to do with dynasties.

We are beginning to suspect Pennsylvania has entered that ascending arc of winning teams, inside whose spinning orbit Red and Blue adherents, like many another alumni group, may rotate dizzily not only from triumph to triumph, but perhaps for a number of seasons.

Let us look back a moment. Do you remember Princeton under Fritz Crisler? Or Yale of the Clint Frank-Larry Kelly era? Or mighty Colgate, and Dartmouth, and before them the Army teams of Ralph Sasse and Davidson? They weren't only good for a year—they rolled on until a grid dynasty ended.

• • •

MOST recent case is that of Cornell.

Beaten for the Ivy League championship by the Bicentennial Red and Blue in a contest which left little to choose between them, the Big Red is by no means a past number. Look at what they did to Andy Kerr's Red Raiders Saturday, note the new and spectacular kids coming to prominence on this, the fourth week of the schedule.

This isn't peculiar to the East where we mention only a few outstanding cases; Temple, under Warner, with big Dave Smukler was pretty hot; Villanova, under Clipper Smith, ripped its rivals wide apart. The saga of Pittsburgh, under Jock Sutherland, is the more impressive in retrospect as the dehided Panther struggles desperately to score a touchdown, let alone a victory in its current, deflated state.

We could go on and on, naming Michigan of the early 1930's, Minnesota under Bierman, Duke under Wade—football dynasties which didn't produce a winner for one year, but rolled on from season to season.

Let's look around and see what's happened.

The Texas Aggies without Big John Kimbrough contrived to flatten Baylor with its Jack Wilson playing, 48 to 0. Stanford, minus many a Rose Bowler, ended Washington's last hopes, while both Michigan and Minnesota are doing rather well without either Tom Harmon or Franck.

All of which suggests there is more to putting out a winner than crying over graduations.

• • •

PENN lost 15 lettermen from last year's championship team, including its No. 1 back for many seasons, Frank Reagan. But with only five winners from that squad as a nucleus, Coach George Munger and his staff have evolved a team which wins more impressively thus far than the 1940 eleven. Is that food for thought or are we looking at the wrong scoreboard?

Here, we believe, is the answer: Building a winner at college football is more than assembling a flock of good boys. Of course the material comes in mighty handy as one goes along, but it's a great deal tougher to get them rolling to the first good season than to continue that success afterward.

As a soured old scout once remarked in the training camp stand at St. Petersburg, "Those dam' Yankees; I swear I could round up a dozen high school kids, put 'em in New York uniforms and come near to lickin' any team in the league. There's just something about playing with 'em—with the team that had Ruth, Gehrig, Lazzeri and that crowd—which seems to make mediocre guys great."

What we're trying to point, is that once they've hit the peak, no matter how many graduations or other losses in personnel, the championship squad is hard to haul off its pedestal. And that's one reason Penn is smashing along so smoothly while everyone stands with mouths agape.

Penn is in the victory vortex, its kids filled with confidence and high faith in their abilities, buoyed by a spirit which doesn't expire over night. How else can we explain the brilliant play, the flawless passing from centre, the keen defense on passes not only of second-stringer Bill Mostertz, but of Walt Weismiller, the No. 3 pivot?

When they handed Ray Frick his degree, Penn lost such a leader and centre it looked practically dismal when he vacated. But along came Don Bitler, quiet and unassuming, to play a remarkable game. Then he was hurt and a kid who played junior varsity was placed in service. He did the job as well as his predecessor. And lo, when he went out there was Weismiller carrying on in A-1 fashion.

• • •

THAT'S what we have long called the quality of "class." Class is a shining armor available only to those who have utter faith they can handle the situation, go in with complete poise and do so. It makes first stringers out of the lowest subs, sends Walt Motsons careening 93 yards through broken fields for startling touchdowns, while equally surprising lads perform blocks even the Bicentennial beauties didn't surpass.

When we watch Pennsylvania's concentrated interference sweeping down the field, making a swath for the ball carriers only a blind cripple couldn't follow, when we follow Bert Stiff's smashing gains, we understand the value of mutual confidence between squad and coaches.

Big Jack Cohen, Al Brechka, Mort Shickman, good-natured Walter Moeling, and those hard-hitting ends, Kuczynski and Nelson, plus the 25 others who went in as replacements, are playing the same sprightly ball that is winning at Stanford, Michigan, Cornell, and Texas A. and M., where things were also supposed to be in recession. Penn may not win all the time, but they are hard to take any time.

Far from being envious or displeased, the rest of the Ivy Leaguers should applaud. Cornell came up off the floor. Army is rising while Navy has almost neared the crest.

So if Penn is in the victory cycle, let's quit acting surprised and join the cheers. With a couple more robust winners maybe the sniffing critics will concede the Ivy League is more than mellow traditions "and a good song ringing clear."

The Philadelphia Inquirer

PHILADELPHIA, MONDAY MORNING, OCTOBER 27, 1941 abdefgh 23

La Salle Conquers Canisius, 7-0

Bynon Scores For Explorers In 3d Period

Forwards Pave Way for La Salle Victory in Buffalo

Special to The Inquirer

BUFFALO, N. Y., Oct. 28.—Bill Bynon, senior triple-threat from Kingston, played the hero's role again here today, when La Salle College scored its third football victory of the season by defeating Canisius, 7 to 0.

A crowd of 10,000 saw the veteran repeat his brilliant performance of 1939, when he led a fourth-quarter drive to upset an unbeaten, unscored-upon Canisius eleven, 14 to 3. Today Bynon's winning surge came in the third quarter.

CANISIUS TRIES AIR

Jim Henry's Explorers from Philadelphia had staved off two aerial attacks in the first half to turn back the Griffins. Tom Colella, Canisius passing star, took to the air when his team couldn't gain on the ground. Twice the Griffs sped to the Explorer 17, to be turned back on downs and again when Tom McCarthy, a handy individual, intercepted a pass.

Leo Bonder, who was at quarterback in place of injured Captain Deschak, started the La Salle attack rolling soon after the second half had gotten under way. He fielded Colella's quick kick on the third bound, reversed and came back 25 to the Explorer 43.

CONLEY TUMBLES

Ed Conley made a terrific grab of Bynon's pass, tumbling to snatch a low pitch, and going down on the Canisius 33. On third down Bynon tossed a long flat pass across the field to Bonder, who was dragged down on the 20.

Bynon picked up five, then saw McCarthy gain another three. On third down Bynon went the remaining 12 yards, cutting inside left tackle and going straight across the double stripe. He added the point for good measure.

MONTERO BRILLIANT

Canisius never had a chance on the ground against the rugged Ex-

Continued on Page 25, Column 3

Passes Win For St. Mary's Over Loyola

LOS ANGELES, Oct. 26 (A. P.)—Little Loyola University's gallant football team played the role of giant killer for half a football game today but had to yield to the seasoned St. Mary's Gaels in a bruising clash before a capacity crowd of 18,500.

Loyola stunned the Gaels and delighted its backers with two touchdowns in the first quarter, but Halfback Johnny Podesto went to work and pitched three perfect strikes and the awakened Gaels went on to a 20-13 triumph to give St. Mary's its sixth consecutive win over the under-manned Lions.

Coach Marty Brill's Loyolans stopped the Gael running attack cold but the Red eleven couldn't stop passing Podesto nor match St. Mary's superior reserve strength.

Penn Bankers 2d In Pistol Shoot

Pennsylvania Company Bankers finished second to the New York Police in an All-Eastern States Pistol and Revolver shoot yesterday at Port Washington, N. Y. The Boston Police came in third.

The Quaker team totaled 1193 to New York's 1194. Shooting for the Pennsylvania team were William Belmont, with 299; Robert Sturm, 299; Melvin Pierce, 298, and Salvadore Bartletti, 297. Boston's total was 1187.

Canadian Draft May Take Hockey Players

NEW YORK, Oct. 26 (A. P.)—President Maurice Podoloff told a meeting of the American Hockey League tonight that rulings by divisional boards in Canada in determining whether players of military age should be given permission to play in the United States this winter may cost the league "anywhere from 15 to 18 players."

The league, swelled to 10 teams this season with the addition of Washington, opens its season Oct. 29 with games at Cleveland, Philadelphia and New Haven.

The all-star game for the benefit of indigent hockey players will be played in Cleveland Feb. 3. Selection of players will be made at a hockey writers dinner in New York Dec. 13.

EAGLES BREAK UP CHICAGO CARDINALS' PASS IN END ZONE
Nick Basca (No. 47) deflects heave intended for Chicago's John Hall.

W. Catholic Beats South

West Catholic High side-stepped another stumbling block on the way to a successful defense of its Catholic League crown with a 13-0 victory over South Catholic High yesterday before an overflow crowd of 9000 at Pinesey Stadium, 54th st. and City Line.

The victory enables the Burrs, unbeaten in four league starts, to remain in a deadlock with Roman Catholic for first place.

WILLIS IS ACE

John Willis, the only returning regular from the championship backfield, scored all the West Catholic points with a pair of touchdowns, one each in the first and fourth periods, and a conversion from placement.

The Burrs were hard pressed for the win and only managed to strike inside Pirate territory twice, but on

Continued on Page 24, Column 1

Temple, Penn Among 5 Unbeaten, Untied

By FRED BYROD

While their week-end triumphs were overshadowed by more startling developments on other gridirons Pennsylvania and Temple, two of the East's five remaining major all-victory teams, ran up impressive scoring totals.

Temple's 131 points for five games is tops among the undefeated untied quintet—of which the others are Fordham, Duquesne and Army—and second in the East to the 138 amassed by twice-whipped Boston College, the Owls' rival Saturday at Boston.

PENN'S AVERAGE HIGHEST

Penn has banked 125 points in four times out, however, and thus boasts the East's highest game average—31.25, against Boston College's 27.6 and Temple's 26.2.

Villanova, which faces another tartar in Duquesne Saturday at Pittsburgh, was toppled from the perfect list Friday by Manhattan, while Navy, this Saturday's Franklin Field visitor, was elbowed out by Harvard's unpredictable team, which held the Tars to a 0-0 stalemate.

TOP SURPRISE

Harvard's draw with Navy was indubitably the most surprising event of the day in the East, and from a tactical viewpoint, it was gained chiefly by the "offensive" defense given the Crimson by Coach Dick Harlow.

Last year Harvard befuddled Penn on Franklin Field with its "looping" defense. Saturday at Cambridge the Crimson used at least six different defensive alignments against the Middies, changing them so fast that

Continued on Page 24, Column 6

73,391 Sell-Out For Penn-Navy

A complete sell-out for the Penn-Navy football game on Franklin Field this Saturday was announced yesterday by H. Jamison Swarts, director of athletics at the University of Pennsylvania. Navy officials telephoned here that their block of tickets were sold, while mail orders completed the sale at the university. The total disposal is 73,391 tickets.

Unbeaten, Untied

Scoring records of the East's five major undefeated, untied college football teams:

	G.	Pts.	Opp. Pts.
Temple	5	131	43
Duquesne	5	111	23
Penn	4	125	19
Fordham	4	95	38
Army	4	70	33

Kaplan 7-5 Choice to Beat Padlo in Arena Ring Tonight

By JOHN WEBSTER

Freed from the hardships of weight-making, Mike Kaplan moves back into the fiery furnace of fisticuffs tonight and battles Philadelphia's newest aspirant for major ring honors, Mayon Padlo, in the 10-round final bout at the Arena.

Kaplan, Boston's crack candidate for the welterweight title, was rated a 7-5 choice over Padlo last night. However, there seemed a fair possibility that strong backing for the paralyzing Pole of Grays Ferry would whittle the price practically to even money by fight time in Herman Taylor's ring.

LOST TO STANDOUT STAR

This is Kaplan's first bout since he finished runner-up to Blastin' Bob Montgomery in a spectacular punching duel here in September. In that match, the boyish Bay Stater not only was weakened by shucking off pounds but also was pitted against outstanding opposition—the Bobcat's perhaps the greatest fighter today in those parts of the world in which they still fight with fists.

MATTER OF DOUBT

Prior to that defeat, Mike had lost only twice in his fighting career, and had beaten not only Fritzie Zivic former 147-pound champion, but Freddie Cochrane, the current head man, as well. The 23-year-old Boston Hebrew boxes like a young master and hits with jarring force. Further-

Continued on Page 24, Column 3

Catholic Tops St. John's, 6-0

A fourth down pass from Jim Priel to John Conlon in the opening minutes of play provided the touchdown that enabled Roman Catholic's undefeated eleven to maintain a first-place tie with West Catholic in the Catholic League race, the Cahillites defeating St. John's, 6-0, yesterday at the Seville and Pechin sts. field before 2500 fans.

Roman Catholic had only this one golden opportunity shortly after the kickoff when a poor St. John's kick rolled out of bounds on the St. John's 30.

Four running plays carried for a first on the 18. Four more running plays, with Priel in the leading role, gained another first on the eight and the stage was set.

ST. JOHN'S FIGHTS HARD

St. John's fought hard and yielded only two yards in three plays, but

Continued on Page 24, Column 4

Rookie Tallies Twice

Castiglia Star In Eagles' 2d Triumph

By PERRY LEWIS

Perhaps the Eagles found a tonic in the brisk autumn air yesterday afternoon at Shibe Park, but whatever it was that provided the inspiration our Birds didn't miss as they scored their second victory of the National Football League season at the expense of the Chicago Cardinals, 21 to 14, as 12,683 watched.

Greasy Neale's pupils played heads-up, smart football as they rushed the ball into pay-off territory early in the second period, forward-passed it over a few minutes later for a second score, and then harvested a third touchdown shortly after the second half got under way by virtue of a combination of ground plays and forward passes. The extra points were harvested after each of these three touchdowns.

CLEMENT SPURS CARDS

The Cardinals were trailing, 21-0, midway of third period, and their case appeared hopeless. They had been deprived of the ball three times in the first half when in scoring position and did not seem destined to go anywhere against the hard-fighting Eagles.

Then a youth known as Johnny Clement, who played his college football at S. M. U. and is a freshman pro, came into the game for the Cardinals, and some disagreeable things happened to the Eagles. Clement passed the ball with precision and carried it with power as he sparked the Cards to a pair of touchdowns.

BACK IN BALL GAME

Conversions made after both of these trips across the Eagles' goal line and with eight minutes still to go, Chicago was back in the ball game. And those Cards came very close at least to overtaking the Eagles when Clement passed and rushed the ball down to the Eagles' 14, where it was first down.

But the Birds were not going to let this one slip through their fingers, and they eventually took the ball on downs on their own five after three

Continued on Page 25, Column 6

Parker Stars, Giants Lose To Brooklyn

BROOKLYN, Oct. 26 (A. P.)—Ace Parker regained his old form today for the first time this year, and as a result the Brooklyn Dodgers downed the New York Giants, 16-13, to hand the New Yorkers their first defeat of the National Football League campaign.

The league's most valuable player of 1940, hampered until now by an ailing leg, passed for one touchdown, pitched and ran 35 yards to put the ball in position for an important field goal and finally dashed 60 yards to set up the winning tally for the entertainment of a highly partisan crowd of 28,675 customers.

PARKER NO. 1 HERO

All afternoon the former Duke All-American was the particular white-haired lad on the ball field, despite

Continued on Page 25, Column 5

St. Carthage Retains Grid League Lead

St. Carthage retained its lead in the Cobbs Creek Division of the Fairmount Park League by swamping the Tigers, 25-0, at 65th and Catherine sts. yesterday afternoon.

St. Cyril subdued the Arrows, 18-0, and Valmar whipped the Senators by the same score on the same field.

Bobbie Stratton and Nick Welsh each scored two tallies for the St. Carthage eleven. Welsh converted for one extra point.

Flop Last Week, Kimbrough Stars as Yanks Win, 31-14

NEW YORK, Oct. 26 (A. P.)—John Kimbrough, a colossal flop in his debut last week, earned his first professional football bravos from 13,666 New York fans today.

"Jarrin' Jawn" battered the Buffalo Tigers for 56 minutes, carrying the ball 19 times for 84 yards, and led the second-place Americans to a 31 to 14 triumph at the Yankee Stadium.

Kimbrough scored the Americans' first touchdown on three rushes from the Tiger four after Andy Karpus had fumbled Bill Hutchinson's 67-yard punt on the Buffalo nine. Shortly before the end of the quarter, Hutchinson sped 40 yards for the Americans' second touchdown.

The Tigers scored twice in the third quarter. They went 76 yards on 16 plays after the kickoff, with Merle Osborne bucking over from the one. Osborne crossed from the same point five minutes later after a Tiger parade of 77 yards in seven plays.

Kimbrough contributed 20 yards to an American advance of 71 yards in the final period, leading to the New Yorkers' last touchdown, which was scored on Hutchinson's two-yard pass to Al Owen in the end zone.

New York	14	10	0	7	—31
Buffalo	0	0	14	0	—14

[illegible]

October 27, 1941 - One of only two wins for the entire '41 season, 21-14 against the Chicago Cardinals

1942

RECORD: 2-9, 5TH IN NFL EAST
HEAD COACH: GREASY NEALE

SCHEDULE

REGULAR SEASON

Wk. 1	Sep 13	W	24-14	at Pittsburgh Steelers
Wk. 2	Sep 20	L	24-14	at Cleveland Rams (at Akron, OH)
Wk. 3	Sep 27	L	35-14	vs Brooklyn Dodgers (at Buffalo, NY)
Wk. 4	Oct 4	L	14-10	vs Washington Redskins
Wk. 5	Oct 11	L	35-17	at New York Giants
Wk. 6	Oct 18	L	14-0	vs Pittsburgh Steelers
Wk. 7	Oct 25	L	45-14	at Chicago Bears
Wk. 8	Nov 1	L	30-27	at Washington Redskins
Wk. 9	Nov 8	L	14-0	vs New York Giants
Wk. 10	Nov 15	W	14-7	at Brooklyn Dodgers
Wk. 12	Nov 29	L	7-0	vs Green Bay Packers

After moving back to Shibe Park full time, the Eagles continued to be one of the worst teams in the NFL, posting a wretched 2-9 record. They won their first game against Pittsburgh 24-14, but then flew to an eight game losing streak until finally they defeated Brooklyn 14-7. In the final game of the season they lost to Green Bay 7-0, which landed them in last place, again.

1942 PHILADELPHIA EAGLES STATS

Passing	Comp	Att	Comp %	Yds	Y/Att	TD	Int	Rating
Tommy Thompson	95	203	46.8	1410	6.95	8	16	50.3
Billy Jefferson	0	1	0.0	0	0.00	0	0	39.6
Len Barnum	1	9	11.1	6	0.67	0	1	0.0

Rushing	Rush	Yds	Avg	TD
Bob Davis	43	207	4.8	2
Bosh Pritchard	35	193	5.5	0
Ted Williams	50	183	3.7	2
Ernie Steele	24	124	5.2	0
Lou Tomasetti	45	102	2.3	0
Dick Erdlitz	21	69	3.3	1
Len Barnum	30	64	2.1	0
Billy Jefferson	11	57	5.2	0
Bert Johnson	27	54	2.0	0
Jack Stackpool	15	47	3.1	0
Irv Hall	8	14	1.8	0
Fred Meyer	2	13	6.5	0
Bob Masters	1	3	3.0	0
Len Supulski	1	1	1.0	0
John Binotto	1	-10	-10.0	0
Tommy Thompson	92	-32	-0.3	1

Punting	Punts	Yds	Avg	Blocked
Billy Jefferson	1	50	50.0	0
Len Barnum	50	2106	42.1	0
Irv Hall	1	36	36.0	0
Bosh Pritchard	17	595	35.0	0
Ernie Steele	2	61	30.5	0

Kicking	PAT Made	PAT Att	PAT %	FG Made	FG Att	FG %	Pts
Len Barnum	7	8	88	3	7	42.9	16
Dick Erdlitz	8	8	100	0	0	0.0	14
Ernie Steele	1	1	100	0	0	0.0	13
Ed Kasky	0	0	0.	0	1	0.0	0

Receiving	Rec	Yds	Avg	TD
Fred Meyer	16	324	20.3	1
Larry Cabrelli	15	229	15.3	1
Bert Johnson	9	123	13.7	2
Ted Williams	9	58	6.4	0
Len Supulski	8	149	18.6	1
Ernie Steele	7	114	16.3	1
Bob Davis	6	93	15.5	1
Dick Erdlitz	5	78	15.6	0
Bob Priestly	4	47	11.8	0
Bill Combs	4	44	11.0	1
Lou Tomasetti	4	22	5.5	0
Len Barnum	3	54	18.0	0
Jack Stackpool	2	59	29.5	0
Irv Hall	2	18	9.0	0
Bosh Pritchard	2	4	2.0	0

Interceptions	Int	Yds	Avg	TD
Tommy Thompson	4	28	7.0	0
Bosh Pritchard	3	23	7.7	0
Ernie Steele	2	49	24.5	0
Bob Davis	2	35	17.5	0
Lou Tomasetti	1	23	23.0	0
Len Barnum	1	11	11.0	0
Ken Hayden	1	5	5.0	0
Len Supulski	1	5	5.0	0
Dick Erdlitz	1	0	0.0	0
Woody Gerber	1	0	0.0	0
Ray Graves	1	0	0.0	0

1942

St. Joseph's Wins, 7-0; Villanova Loses, 9-0

The Philadelphia Inquirer

PHILADELPHIA, MONDAY MORNING, NOVEMBER 16, 1942 abdefgh 23

Strictly Sports

State, Not Penn, Beat Penn in So-Called Upset

Lion Defenders, Notably Cenci, Made Rival Quarterbacks Look Bad

By LEO RIORDAN

YEARS BACK when Pennsylvania lost, rooters often insisted that the Quakers had defeated themselves. You would have thought the Penn footballers just lolled around in Cleopatra poses and allowed the opposition to score without hindrance. This narrow-minded viewpoint got a killing jolt in 1936. A great Quaker team was on Yale's one-yard line, first down, less than a minute before halftime—and didn't score. Yale went on to win, 7-0.

The howl went up immediately; Penn's quarterbacking was lame-brained. The next week the Quakers scored early and held five times at their goal line to beat Princeton, 7-0. Rooters rightfully toasted a grand, fighting defense. Nobody complained about poor Princeton quarterbacking. That would have been silly, for the great Ken Sandbach was calling them for the Tigers. As a sophomore Ken had quarterbacked Princeton to a one-defeat season; as a junior to an unbeaten record; as a senior against Penn in 1936, he should have been at his peak—and was.

JOE COLONE

• • •

Quarterbacking rides with success. Abraham Lincoln, the quarterback of America's destiny, spoke for all signal callers one day. As a young lawyer he entered court with two cases. In the morning he took one side of the law and won. That afternoon he took the opposite side before the same judge. The judge pointed out the contradiction and Lincoln replied, "Your honor, I thought I was right this morning, but I know I'm right this afternoon." And Abe won that one, too.

• • •

This is by way of backing into Penn's second defeat in as many Saturdays which saw it out-gaining and outplaying but not outscoring Annapolis and Penn State. Now, to keep the record straight, State has a solid, hard-hitting, keenly coached, high-purpose team. Usually a team's job is to stop the opponent's scoring star; Penn's task was to block out State's defensive star, 225-pound, six-foot Quarterback Aldo Cenci, who proved a tank-trap all day and wasn't flattened once.

The Quaker players likened him to "Mr. Five by Five," in the clever song. This gentleman stands five feet and is as wide as he is high. But where Mr. Five-by-Five has several sets of chins, Mr. Cenci has several sets of chests, all oak. Now, no one man ever wins a game, but you would have to do some heavy research to find a Nittany Lion who messed up Penn's offense more than did clever Quarterback Cenci, backing up a State line that, tackle to tackle, was flint-hard.

Of course, the town is saying that Coach George Munger's men had four real scoring targets against Navy without hitting and four more against State — reaching the Lions' 6, 12, 2 and 4-yard line — without scoring until Coach Bob Higgins' team led, 13-0. Then and only then, with less than three minutes left, did the once-crunching Penn powerhouse score—too late.

• • •

The defeat by Annapolis was explained on the Navy's superb combativeness and conditioning. The State setback is a ditto, although the angle may seem stale. For while the Navy defeated Penn, the Lions deflated Penn. This two-game record of one touchdown on nine marches is not the mark of a great team. All hands now realize that the difference between the once-beaten 1941 team and the thrice-beaten 1942 squad (largely the same players a year older) was the shrewd climax quarterbacking of the now Ensign Gene Davis—not top-flight team strength.

Fans want to know why Lee Roy Pietz' kick was blocked at his 35, to set up State's early touchdown by Earl Brown. The fault did not lie with Pietz, 19-year-old soph starting his first game. Ken Schoonover, State's bristling left tackle, took advantage of the fourth-down-and-13-to-go situation, knowing Pietz could not fake and run again.

• • •

A play preceding the blocked kick tipped off Penn's fatal weakness. Dick Martin, an emergency quarterback who took over the post at Fall camp and who suffered from unkind comparisons to the great three-year-star Davis, was mixing his plays well. Dick had just pulled Penn out of a hole at its 25, where it was trapped on kicks by Joe Colone, 18-year-old Lion freshman fullback. Dick had called a fake kick and Pietz whisked 20 yards to State's 45. It became third and one at State's 46; Martin had his team rolling.

The truly great 1940 Quaker team paced by Frank Reagan, now a Marine lieutenant, had faced third-down-and-15 to go spots three times against Cornell in the storied 22-20 victory. Three times it got those hard yards. This Penn team was asked to get only one. It was guilty of holding and penalized 15 yards back to its 39. Thus it was third down and 16 to go. All right, a kick was indicated with the score 0-0 and the wind against Penn, but Martin thought he saw the hole he wanted. He sent Pietz through again, but Lee got only three. The fatal fourth-down number was up and Schoonover knocked it down and the game went tumbling.

• • •

You can also question the judgment of [illegible] Motson, sub quarterback, who missed camp drills because of an appendectomy. He ordered a kick at State's 39 on fourth and one midway through the final period with State ahead, 13-0. With some 5 minutes left, he had fourth and 6 at State's 39, tried for first and failed. Yet it was off this this second move that Penn scored directly. If Penn were a great team, it would have secured that one yard for Martin and those six yards for Motson. And both men would today have been considered clever quarterbacks—it's that simple.

We prefer to take up the cry that echoes through the Nittany Mountains today — the huzzah for Coach Bob Higgins and two guys named Joe — Halfback Larry Joe and Fullback Joe Colone. Not merely because Larry Joe raced 36 yards on three sprints to score the doubly fatal second touchdown—after he had streaked 45 for a score the officials voided—but also for his equally vital defensive stops. When Bob Odell broke away in the second period, Larry Joe nailed him; when Bill Miller got off for 24 yards in that same quarter, Larry Joe stopped him, and in the fourth period, this 19-year-old freshman stopped Jackie Welsh, who has run through the best teams on Penn's 1940-41-42 schedules.

• • •

State beat Penn; Penn didn't beat Penn. That in a sentence is the death sentence of the Quakers' high 1941 hopes that saw them rated No. 8 nationally after they jolted Army, 19-0.

From here, Penn doesn't have a great team, but it does have a coach with a touch of greatness. "Taking our players apart, you can't say one of them played poorly; all went better than they did against Navy," Munger insists, "and that's why I blame myself." That's greatness in this book.

Fairman Seeks Strong Team For Batesville in Tourney

By JOHN WEBSTER

Boisterous, red-haired Harold Fairman has been an almost silent worker this season as he set about the task of building his Batesville A. A. team to formidable proportion for the rapidly-approaching fist-storms in The Inquirer A. A. Tournament.

Since this sturdy, often pugnacious manager generally doesn't stop talking from the close of his outdoor amateur season in Haddonfield until Diamond Belting is well underway, the Philadelphians are disposed to regard this restraint as, well, at least ominous. They know Batesville will be tough, perhaps tougher.

Known as Mr. South Jersey in amateur ring circles, Mr. Fairman feels it is only right that he should have a lien on every young ringman to come up in that territory. It makes him very unhappy when a Philadelphia manager reaches over the Delaware, and plucks a prospect from his domain.

This might explain the unprecedented calm in the Batesville precincts as usually blustering Harold schools his fistic pupils for the wars. His well-appointed gym, located in the Milner Hotel, Second and Penn

Continued on Page 24, Column 1

LA SALLE HIGH MISSES THIS EARLY CHANCE TO SCORE AGAINST ST. JOSEPH'S

Bob Fitzmyer, St. Joseph's centre (No. 21) thrust aside this pass as LaSalle's Pete Villari stood with waiting arms on the threshold of a touchdown.

Americans Prevail, Top Soccer League

By GEORGE BUTZ

Philadelphia's Americans booted themselves into first place in the American League soccer race yesterday afternoon by outscoring the Kearny (N. J.) Celtics, 5-1, before 2000 fans at the Cambria Stadium, Kensington and Torresdale aves. With Brookhattan idle in New York, the defending champions encountered little opposition from the New Jersey Irishmen.

It was the Philadelphians' fifth triumph in a row. Although victory gave the Americans the lead, it was costly because they lost the services of sharpshooting Davey Dick, who suffered a badly wrenched left ankle.

CELTICS WEAKENED

Kearny's booters fought in vain to turn the tide after trailing, 2-0, at half time, but they lacked the finish to their goal attacks. With Fergus Hunter, a sub goalie, between the nets, the Celtics were weakened defensively from the start, but that did not detract from the Philadelphians' splendid passing and goal shooting. George (Beefy) Davis, ace goal-tender, did not accompany the Celtics here because of his warplant job.

The winners' scoring was led by Curt Weller, former Reading Americans' centre forward, who went into action in the second half in place of Ted Swieconek, U. S. Coast Guardsman. Weller was in the match only a few minutes when he netted the first of his two goals. Single tallies were registered by Jim Reid, Swieconek and Dick.

Charlie (Chappie) Sheppell, Celtic winger, saved his team from a coat of whitewash. He scored midway in the final half on a fast breakaway play.

AMERICANS SCORE EARLY

Although the Irishmen led in corner kicks, 3-2, they never had a chance against the co-ordinated attack of the Americans. From the outset the superior team play and accurate passing of the Americans asserted itself.

The champions scored on a beautiful swing pass combination with Dick on the scoring end and Werner Meith supplying the set-up shot. Meith lofted the ball to the right of the Celts' net, and Dick timed a cross-angled liner nicely into the far corner.

A few minutes later, Swieconek came through with a 20-yard drive that Goalie Hunter fumbled and let drop back into the network.

After the intermission, the Philly

Continued on Page 25, Column 7

West Catholic Jars St. John's

West Catholic High kept in the running for the Catholic League football championship by driving to a 6-0 victory over a stubborn St. John's High eleven yesterday at Seville and Pechin sts.

This fourth league triumph for the unbeaten but thrice tied Burrs, who are deadlocked for the lead with St. Joseph's High, came about on a 39-yard march in the second quarter with Leo Dillon getting the touchdown on a smash from the 1-yard line.

BACICA STARS

A spectacular play some minutes before prepared the ground for this successful attack. Sam Bacica, who played great ball all the way for West Catholic, intercepted Bill Ryan's forward pass and ran 67 yards down the field to St. John's 3, where he was tackled from behind by Dan Jones.

Here St. John's put on the day's finest defensive stand when it wrested the ball away from West Catholic on downs a scant 6 inches from the goal line. Dillon was held without gain on the first play. Bill Gross

Continued on Page 25, Column 6

St. Joseph's Jolts La Salle

By KEN HAY

Slugging and the ejection of Charles Schaefer, La Salle High's star, from the game proved only an aftermath in an exciting third period that saw Harry Doyle, St. Joseph's halfback, skirt right end for four yards to give St. Joseph's a 7-0 victory in their Catholic League game at McCarthy Stadium, 20th st. and Olney ave.

A crowd of 12,000 was on hand for LaSalle's Homecoming Day celebration only to see the Little Explorers lose. Between the halves, alumni of LaSalle High dedicated a service flag to the 316 graduates now in the Nation's Armed Forces.

FR. KNABLES BLESSES FLAG

The St. Joseph's band and the Yearsley American Legion Bugle and Drums Corps formed a "V" as Father E. Ward Knabels, director of athletics at St. James High, Chester, blessed the flag. Brother Emilien James, F. C. S., delivered an address and Brother Clement, F. C. S., accepted the flag from John McCann, president of the LaSalle Alumni Association.

With the victory the Hawklets eliminated La Salle from the Catholic League race and maintained a deadlock with West Catholic, defending champions, for the league lead. A victory over Roman Catholic next Sunday at Finneswy Field, 54th st. and City Line, remains the lone barrier to the outright winning of the crown by St. Joseph's.

Doyle, Jack Small and Jack Welsh were the spearheads of a varied attack in which the Hawklets traversed over the ground and soared through the air for 60 yards after the second-half kickoff.

On a punt by La Salle immediately

Continued on Page 25, Column 6

Eagles Stop Losing; Beat Dodgers, 14-7

By FRANK O'GARA

Inquirer Sports Reporter

BROOKLYN, N. Y., Nov. 15.—Perhaps it shouldn't happen even to the Dodgers but it did today when the downtrodden Philadelphia Eagles picked on the Brooklyns for a 14-7 football feast to break a two-month, eight-game fast.

Only the personal friends of the players, augmented by the recuperating coach, Earl (Greasy) Neale, saw the Birds score their first National Football League triumph since thumping Pittsburgh in the opening game on Sept. 13. Greasy, the only articulate member of a cheerless gathering of 3858, bordered on another heart attack such as he suffered a week ago in Philadelphia while his assistant, Honest John Kellison, ran the team from the bench.

WELL-EARNED WIN

However unexpected in view of the eight straight previous reverses, the triumph was richly deserved. The Eagles drove to their scores with finesse, and for the first time this season showed a tight pass defense. It was this factor that stymied the losers throughout the game.

After outplaying the Dodgers by a convincing but unproductive margin, the Birds broke loose for the first score midway of the third period, yielded a tying touchdown early in the final quarter, then drove back relentlessly to push over the winning counters.

DRIVE 83 YARDS

An 83-yard assault was necessary for the first score, but Bosh Pritchard's sparkling scampers and Tommy Thompson's perfect peg to End Fred Meyer ate up the yardage in large chunks.

The apple was on the alien 41 when Thompson unleased his vital chuck, leading it perfectly to the speeding Meyer. He pulled it in on the 15, was smacked down on the 10, but struggled to his feet and twisted to the five before being snowed under.

Then Pritchard, the V. M. I. rookie, lunged to the one-foot line after apparently being trapped for a loss.

PUZZLING RULING

One of the peculiar occurrences of pro football saved a touchdown on the next play. Thompson sneaked across as a horn sounded on the play. Head Linesman Larry Conover signalled a touchdown, but without any manual explanation, Referee Sam Weiss disallowed it. On the next try, however, Rookie

Continued on Page 25, Column 3

Magnolia Rally Tops Zuni A. A.

Exploding a fourth-period attack which produced two touchdowns, Magnolia ended Zuni's unbeaten streak yesterday, by downing the defending champions, 13-10, in an Eastern Conference game at Church and Tacony sts. It was the first defeat since 1939 for Zuni, pace-setters of the league race.

Shamrocks defeated Lloyd A. C., of Chester, 13-7, in another Conference fray at 26th and Mifflin sts. Shamrocks and Magnolia are tied for second place.

FORTH TOSSES FOR SCORES

Frankie Forth and Danny O'Donnell, a top notch forward passing team, saved the day for Magnolia. Porth threw two scoring aerials to O'Donnell and each covered 25 yards in a wild and thrilling finish.

The Mags needed this sensational rally to overhaul Zuni, who fashioned 10 points in the third period when Ted Lau kicked a field goal, also an extra point, and Ray Cochran stabbed across for a touchdown. This margin seemed a good bet to hold, but the tide quickly turned.

Shamrocks and Lloyd staged a

Continued on Page 25, Column 5

Early Drive Decides

Titans Score, Trap Postus For Safety

By PERRY LEWIS

Inquirer Sports Reporter

DETROIT, Mich., Nov. 15.—Detroit's Titans clicked in one period this afternoon, Villanova clicked in no period; and so the Wildcats of Philadelphia's Main Line lost their second game of the season to a collegiate rival, 9 to 0.

Each of Detroit's points, as a matter of fact, all points, were scored in the first quarter—a safety, a touchdown and an extra point after touchdown. Thereafter the embattled teams merely went through the motions of a game that was as bleak as the weather, which was plenty bleak. If you are skeptical you were not in Detroit today—and were certainly not one of the 11,000 spectators who stuck it out to the finish.

SCORED IN HURRY

One could record the first period of this ballgame and then call it a day, without shirking. Detroit scored its points in a hurry, and then folded up; Villanova folded up without scoring at all—and remained in a tangle until the final whistle.

It was early in the game when Al Postus dropped back into Villanova's end zone to kick following an intercepted forward pass. The Wildcat line failed to hold and the Titans' tackle, John Hart, filtered through to drop Postus before he could get his foot into the ball. A safety and two points for Detroit while the spectators were still looking for their seats.

PUNTS AGAINST BLASTS

The Detroit touchdown came a few minutes later and it was very abrupt. Postus, kicking against a strong wind, punted out of bounds on Villanova's 30. Then, with Tom Seffner and Elmer Madarik, ace Titan backs, lugging the leather, Detroit crossed the Wildcat goal line on seven plays.

It was Seffner who scored the touchdown on a slash off tackle from the 4-yard line. This play climaxed a sustained power attack that appeared to bend the Wildcat line from end to end, and was the only worthwhile march of the game. Hart harvested the extra point and Detroit was out in front, 9 to 0.

Nothing much happened thereafter, certainly not from a Villanova angle. The Wildcats simply could not get started and remained impotent right up to the finish. Once Art Alois, freshman centre, intercepted a forward pass in the second period and appeared to be in the clear with a blocker ahead of him, when Madarik slipped in from nowhere and dropped Art on Detroit's 38. The 'Cats moved no further and eventually surrendered the ball on downs.

'CATS RARELY THREATEN

Thus was Villanova's most potent scoring gesture given the brushoff by an alert group of Titans. Thereafter Wildcats never threatened, although just before the close of the first half they penetrated to De-

Continued on Page 24, Column 6

42,787 See Bears Sink Packers, 38-7

CHICAGO, Nov. 15 (A. P.).—The mighty Chicago Bears virtually assured themselves of the Western Division championship of the National Football League today by smashing the Green Bay Packers at will for a 38 to 7 triumph before a sell-out crowd of 42,787.

Rolling to their 21st consecutive victory—15th in league competition—the Bears scored in the first two and a half minutes of the opening quarter on a recovered fumble, twice in the second and once in each of the last two periods. The Packers were unable to get started until the final quarter when Cecil Isbell strung out five aerials to Don Hutson, the last for seven yards and a touchdown to cap off a 77-yard march.

COMPLETE 17 PASSES

In all, Isbell completed 17 of [illegible]4 passes for a total of 161 yards. Hutson's catch for a touchdown boosted to 14 the number he has snatched for scores this season. He also placekicked his 26th extra point for a total output of 110 points in eight games.

The Packers outgained the Bears in first downs, 14-12, making a dozen of them by passing. They picked up only 43 yards by rushing, but the Bears yielded 118 more on penalties.

RECOVERS FUMBLE

Before the largest gathering of the pro season had settled down, Bulldog Turner, Bears' alert centre,

Continued on Page 25, Column 2

U. S. G. A. Slates New Treasurer

NEW YORK, Nov. 13 (U. P.).—The United States Golf Association will propose only one change in personnel of the officers and executive committee for 1943 at the annual meeting here Jan. 9, it was announced today.

Daniel A. Freeman, Jr., of New York, has been nominated as treasurer succeeding John P. Riddell, Jr., also of New York. Otherwise, the administration, headed by George W. Blossom, Jr., of Lake Forest, Ill., as president, will remain intact.

The other officers are Morton G. Bogue of Great Neck, N. Y., and Charles W. Littlefield of Montclair, N. J., vice-presidents; Frank M. Hardt of Ardmore, Pa., secretary, and James H. Douglas, Jr., of Lake Bluff, Ill., general counsel.

Don't Look Now, But--

Jack O'Brien and the Long Count

MR. CHARLEY McCROSSEN, a little man with a long memory, harkens back to 1902 to recall a feud obituary stories missed last week in recounting the career of Philadelphia Jack O'Brien, whose funeral is to be held this morning. One of Jack's most persistent rivals was a bag-punching expert, the late Charley McKeever, who had moved to Philadelphia from Bridgeport. For some reason McKeever never thought very highly of O'Brien, and when the latter went to England, he followed him. O'Brien's three-round victory over McKeever in England—the result of a foul—didn't improve feeling between them, and when O'Brien returned to Philadelphia, McKeever followed by the next boat. They were matched again at the old Washington Sporting Club, and in the third round McKeever tagged O'Brien flush on the jaw. O'Brien went down, but McKeever, instead of standing back, continued raining punches on him. The late Billy Rocap, the referee, was so busy pulling McKeever away that fully a minute passed, McCrossen declares, before the count even started. . . . "And they say Dave Barry gave Gene Tunney a long count with Dempsey in Chicago," McCrossen comments. . . . O'Brien, like Tunney, finally got up—and outpointed McKeever the rest of the way, winning after six rounds. . . . O'Brien and McKeever met three more times, with Jack gaining two more newspaper decisions and scoring one first-round knockout.

MEN IN SERVICE — Walter Welham, erstwhile Southern High three-sport star, who is now a Navy doctor on duty in the Pacific, has just been promoted to lieutenant commander, according to Marty Williams, Broadwood handball expert. . . . Leo Hoffman, another ex-Southern athlete, is an Army lieutenant at the Quartermaster's, Al Rosen reports. . . . Edward Fernberger, 1941 Penn freshman football centre and son of Psychology Professor Dr. Samuel Fernberger, is in the 591st Technical Squadron School, Flight B 571, Kessler Field, Miss., Joe Lebrum informs. . . Bernie Jennings, former Catholic League and K. of C. bowler, is in the Army.

BOWLING BRIEFS — On the sidelines since mid-summer, Bill Ward, national K. of C. all-events champion, hopes to return to the wooden ways in January. . . Dykes' K. of C. Auto Clubbers—Harry Frederick, Gene Fleming, John Kolbmann, Marty Luff and Charley Rupertus—twice have beaten the Holy Saviour's South Jersey Catholic League champions, but Paul Kelly and his teammates are seeking a third match. . . Six Philadelphia teams will compete in the finals of the 185-class Tri-State doubles tournament at Hudson Saturday—John Gallagher-Bill Milne, Jack Coulter-Dave Paxson, Tony Dubano - Charles Parker, T. W. Huft-J. J. Baker, J. Crocian-R. O. Orms and Sam Bretzian-Charles Egner.

COLLEGIANS—Penn Centre Don Bitler's father played basketball for Penn State. Bill Brady, Herb Cooper, John Donaldson and Sam Ellis, of Penn's grid squad, are sons of men who went to Penn.

ART MORROW

St. James Beats Malvern Prep

A 55-yard runback of a kick by Buck Haley spotlighted the play as St. James High, of Chester, eleven trounced Malvern Prep, 40-0, at Chester yesterday afternoon.

The Bulldogs registered a touchdown in the first period and gained momentum as the game progressed, with Enright, basketball star of last year, leading the attack with two touchdowns in the third quarter. St. James tallied twice in the second session and added three more in the final session.

November 16, 1942 - In what was the lowest attended game, 3.858 watched the Eagles defeat the Brooklyn Dodgers 14-7

1943

RECORD: 5-4-1, 3RD IN NFL EAST
HEAD COACH: GREASY NEALE & WALT KIESLING

SCHEDULE

REGULAR SEASON

Wk. 3	Oct 2	W	17-0	vs Brooklyn Dodgers (at Philadelphia, PA)
Wk. 4	Oct 9	W	28-14	vs New York Giants (at Philadelphia, PA)
Wk. 5	Oct 17	L	48-21	at Chicago Bears
Wk. 6	Oct 24	L	42-14	at New York Giants
Wk. 7	Oct 31	W	34-13	vs Chicago Cardinals (at Pittsburgh, PA)
Wk. 8	Nov 7	T	14-14	vs Washington Redskins (at Philadelphia, PA)
Wk. 9	Nov 14	L	13-7	at Brooklyn Dodgers
Wk. 10	Nov 21	W	35-34	vs Detroit Lions (at Pittsburgh, PA)
Wk. 11	Nov 28	W	27-14	at Washington Redskins
Wk. 12	Dec 5	L	38-28	vs Green Bay Packers (at Philadelphia, PA)

With a shortage of players due to World War II, the Eagles merged with the Pittsburgh Steelers, and become the Phil-Pitt Steagles, with both teams' coaches (Walt Kiesling and Greasy Neale) splitting duties. The Steagles would actually play competitive football, posting a solid 5-4-1 record and their first winning season for the franchise. Another Eagles record occurred while defeating the Giants 28-14; the Eagles fumbled a record ten times. Following the season Eagles owner Alex Thompson dissolved the merger.

1943 PHILADELPHIA EAGLES STATS

Passing	Comp	Att	Comp %	Yds	Y/Att	TD	Int	Rating
Roy Zimmerman	43	124	34.7	846	6.82	9	17	44.0
Allie Sherman	16	37	43.2	208	5.62	2	1	68.3
Johnny Butler	6	13	46.2	84	6.46	0	1	35.4
Ernie Steele	0	1	0.0	0	0.00	0	1	0.0

Rushing	Rush	Yds	Avg	TD
Jack Hinkle	116	571	4.9	3
Ernie Steele	85	409	4.8	4
Johnny Butler	87	362	4.2	3
Bob Thurbon	71	291	4.1	5
Charlie Gauer	12	69	5.8	0
Ben Kish	22	50	2.3	0
Ted Laux	9	23	2.6	0
Tony Bova	1	11	11.0	0
Bob Masters	2	6	3.0	0
Steve Sader	3	5	1.7	0
Dean Steward	1	-6	-6.0	0
Allie Sherman	17	-20	-1.2	0
Roy Zimmerman	33	-41	-1.2	1

Punting	Punts	Yds	Avg	Blocked
Dean Steward	2	84	42.0	0
Ben Kish	1	42	42.0	0
Johnny Butler	11	407	37.0	0
Roy Zimmerman	44	1521	34.6	0
Jack Hinkle	4	78	19.5	0

Kicking	PAT Made	PAT Att	PAT %	FG Made	FG Att	FG %	Pts
Roy Zimmerman	26	28	93	1	6	16.7	35
Ted Laux	2	2	100	0	0	0.0	2
Gordon Paschka	2	2	100	0	0	0.0	2

Receiving	Rec	Yds	Avg	TD
Tony Bova	17	419	24.6	5
Larry Cabrelli	12	199	16.6	1
Ernie Steele	9	168	18.7	2
Ben Kish	8	67	8.4	1
Bob Thurbon	6	100	16.7	1
Johnny Butler	3	63	21.0	0
Tom Miller	3	60	20.0	1
Bill Hewitt	2	22	11.0	0
Ted Laux	2	19	9.5	0
Charlie Gauer	2	18	9.0	0
Jack Hinkle	1	3	3.0	0

Interceptions	Int	Yds	Avg	TD
Ben Kish	5	114	22.8	1
Roy Zimmerman	5	19	3.8	0
Jack Hinkle	4	98	24.5	0
Larry Cabrelli	1	24	24.0	1
Ted Laux	1	24	24.0	0
Ray Graves	1	15	15.0	0
Al Wukits	1	7	7.0	0
Bob Thurbon	1	3	3.0	0
Enio Conti	1	0	0.0	0
Charlie Gauer	1	0	0.0	0
Tom Miller	1	0	0.0	0

1950's

50s Decade in Review

Decade Win-Loss Record:
51-64-5

Home Field:
Shibe Park 1950-57, Franklin Field 1958-59

Playoff Appearances:
None

Championships:
None

Head Coaches:
Greasy Neale 1950 (6-6); Bo McMillian 1951 (2-0); Wayne Milner 1951 (2-8); Jim Trimble 1952-55 (25-20-3); Hugh Devore 1956-67 (7-16-1); Buck Shaw 1958-59 (9-14-1)

Hall of Fame Inductees:
Chuck Bednarik, Sony Jurgensen, Tommy McDonald, Pete Pihos, Norm Van Brocklin, Steve Van Buren, Alex Wojciechowicz

Award Winners:
Bobby Walston, Rookie of the Year 1951

All Pro:
Chuck Bednarik 1950-57; Bucko Kilroy 1950-54; Joe Muha 1950; Pete Pihos 1950 and 1952-55; Vic Sears 1950 and 1952; Steve Van Buren 1950; Al Wistert 1950-51; Vic Lindskog 1951; Bobby Walston 1951; Lum Snyder 1952-55; Bobby Thomason 1953; Norm Willey 1953-55; Frank Wydo 1953; Wayne Robinson 1955; Tom Scott 1955-56; Pete Retzlaff 1958; Tom Brookshier 1959; Tommy McDonald 1959

Pro Bowl Selections:
Walter Barnes 1951; Chuck Bednarik 1951-55 and 1957-58; John Green 1951; Pete Pihos 1951-56; Al Wistert 1951; Russ Craft 1952-53; Mike Jarmoluk 1952; Bucko Kilroy 1953-55; Ken Farragut 1954; Lum Snyder 1954-55; Bobby Thomason 1954 and 1956-57; Adrian Burk 1955-56; Wayne Robinson 1955-56; Norm Willey 1955-56;Jim Weatherall 1956-57; Buck Lansford 1957; Billy Ray Barnes 1958-59; Jerry Norton 1958-59; Tommy McDonald 1959; Pete Retzlaff 1959; Norm Van Brocklin 1959

First Game of the Decade:
September 16, 1950 in a loss to the Cleveland Browns 35-10

Last Game of the Decade:
December 13, 1959 losing to the Cleveland Browns 28-21

Largest Margin of Victory:
October 25, 1953 vs. Chicago Cardinals 56-17

Largest Margin of Defeat:
October 19, 1952 vs. Cleveland Browns 49-7

Eagle Firsts of the Decade:

First African-American Eagles – In 1952, Ralph Goldston and Don Stevens were draft selections.

First Pro Bowlers – In 1950, Piggy Barnes, Chuck Bednarik, John Green, Pete Pihos, and Al Wistert took part in the first Prow Bowl game.

First 400 Yards Passing – On November 8, 1953, Bobby Thomason completed two of44 passes for437 yards in a win over the New York Giants 30-7.

First 200 Yards Passing – On December 7, 1952, Bud Grant caught 11 passes for 203 yards in a win over the Dallas Texans 38-21.

First 1,000-Yard Receiving – in 1953, Pete Pihos gained 1,049 yards.

First 90-Yard Pass Play – On November 14, 1954, Tommy McDonald caught Norm Van Brocklin's pass for a 91-yard touchdown in a win over the New York Giants 27-24.

First Game at Franklin Field – On September 28, 1958 in a loss to the Washington Redskins 24-14.

1950

RECORD: 6-6, T-3RD IN AFC
HEAD COACH: GREASY NEALE

Schedule

Regular Season

Wk. 1	Sep 16	L	35-10	vs Cleveland Browns
Wk. 2	Sep 24	W	45-7	at Chicago Cardinals
Wk. 4	Oct 7	W	56-20	vs Los Angeles Rams
Wk. 5	Oct 15	W	24-14	at Baltimore Colts
Wk. 6	Oct 22	W	17-10	at Pittsburgh Steelers
Wk. 7	Oct 29	W	35-3	vs Washington Redskins
Wk. 8	Nov 5	L	9-7	vs Pittsburgh Steelers
Wk. 9	Nov 12	W	33-0	at Washington Redskins
Wk. 10	Nov 19	L	14-10	vs Chicago Cardinals
Wk. 11	Nov 26	L	7-3	at New York Giants
Wk. 12	Dec 3	L	13-7	at Cleveland Browns
Wk. 13	Dec 10	L	9-7	vs New York Giants

The two-time NFL champs lost their home opener 35-10 to Cleveland. After playing solid football for most of the season the Eagles went into a sudden tailspin, falling out of competition with a season ending four-game losing streak that ended their season with a disappointing 6-6 record. Following the season Coach Greasy Neale was fired. Bo McMillan replaced him.

1950 Philadelphia Eagles Stats

Passing	Comp	Att	Comp %	Yds	Y/Att	TD	Int	Rating
Tommy Thompson	107	239	44.8	1608	6.73	11	22	44.4
Bill Mackrides	14	46	30.4	228	4.96	4	6	37.5

Rushing	Rush	Yds	Avg	TD
Frank Ziegler	172	733	4.3	1
Steve Van Buren	188	629	3.3	4
Toy Ledbetter	67	320	4.8	1
Jim Parmer	60	203	3.4	7
Jack Myers	29	159	5.5	0
Bill Mackrides	21	82	3.9	0
Frank Reagan	3	55	18.3	0
Russ Craft	8	52	6.5	0
Clyde Scott	13	46	3.5	0
Tommy Thompson	15	34	2.3	0
Pat McHugh	4	14	3.5	0
Joe Sutton	1	1	1.0	0

Receiving	Rec	Yds	Avg	TD
Pete Pihos	38	447	11.8	6
Jack Ferrante	35	588	16.8	3
Frank Ziegler	13	216	16.6	2
Jack Myers	12	204	17.0	0
Neill Armstrong	8	124	15.5	1
Jim Parmer	6	103	17.2	2
Toy Ledbetter	4	81	20.3	2
Steve Van Buren	2	34	17.0	0
Billy Hix	2	25	12.5	0
Russ Craft	1	14	14.0	0

Punting	Punts	Yds	Avg	Blocked
Frank Reagan	54	2270	42.0	0
Joe Muha	2	48	24.0	0

Kicking	PAT Made	PAT Att	PAT %	FG Made	FG Att	FG %	Pts
Cliff Patton	32	33	97	8	17	47.1	56
Joe Muha	0	0	0	0	5	0.0	6

Interceptions	Int	Yds	Avg	TD
Joe Sutton	8	67	8.4	0
Frank Reagan	4	132	33.0	1
Pat McHugh	4	34	8.5	0
Neill Armstrong	3	4	1.3	0
Russ Craft	2	61	30.5	0
Joe Muha	2	40	20.0	1
Norm Willey	1	41	41.0	1
Chuck Bednarik	1	9	9.0	0
Alex Wojciechowicz	1	4	4.0	0

California	14	Purdue	28	Princeton	34	Army	41	Cornell	26	Michigan	27	Oklahoma	34	Nebraska	32	Maryland	34
Penn	7	Notre Dame	14	Rutgers	28	Penn St.	7	Syracuse	7	Dartmouth	7	Texas Ag	28	Minnesota	26	Mich. St.	7

68,098 See Yanks Beat Phillies, 5-2, to Sweep Series

SPORTS BASEBALL **The Philadelphia Inquirer** RACING MAIL ORDER
PUBLIC LEDGER
An Independent Newspaper for All the People
SUNDAY MORNING, OCTOBER 8, 1950 g S

Purdue Snaps Notre Dame Streak

Sports Results

College

FOOTBALL

PHILADELPHIA DISTRICT

California 14	Penn 7
Delaware 32	P. M. C. 20
Drexel 13	Gettysburg 7
Haverford 20	Ursinus 12
National Aggies 6	N. Y. Aggies 6
Princeton 34	Rutgers 28
Washington (Md.) 32	Swarthmore 0
West Chester 26	Cortland 0

STATE

Army 41	Penn State 7
Albright 20	Moravian 12
Boston U. 21	Duquesne 7
Bridgeport 25	Wilkes College 13
Carnegie Tech 24	Bethany 3
Case 25	W. & J. 7
E. Stroudsburg 14	Mansfield 0
F. & M. 7	Dickinson 0
Geneva 33	Grove City 0
Hartwick 20	Juniata 15
Indiana STC 20	California STC 0
J. Hopkins 34	Susquehanna 0
Kutztown 35	Glassboro STC 13
Lehigh 27	Bucknell 6
Lock Haven 28	Millersville 7
Morgan State 42	Lincoln U. 13
Muhlenberg 20	Lebanon Valley 13
Oberlin 14	Allegheny 10
Ohio State 41	Pitt 7
Scranton 20	Lafayette 7
Shippensburg 13	Shepherd 7
Slippery Rock 39	Edinboro 7
Thiel 20	Westminster 7

EAST

IVY LEAGUE

Columbia 28*	Harvard 7

Standings of the Teams

	W.	L.	P.C.
Yale	1	0	1.000
Columbia	1	0	1.000
Penn	0	0	.000
Princeton	0	0	.000
Cornell	0	0	.000
Dartmouth	0	0	.000
Harvard	0	1	.000
Brown	0	1	.000

OTHER EAST

Alfred 7	Clarkson 6
Amherst 14	Champlain 0
Am. Intl. 44	Loyola (Montreal) 13
Catholic U. 32	Bridgewater 0
Colgate 47	W. Reserve 6
Colby 47	C.C.N.Y. 6
Connecticut 20	Ohio Wesleyan 14
Cornell 26	Syracuse 7
Holy Cross 41	Brown 21
Lowell Textile 7	Mass. Maritime 0
Maine 15	Vermont 7
Michigan 27	Dartmouth 7
Middlebury 21	Hamilton 6
Mississippi 54	Boston College 0
N. Hampshire 27	Rhode Island 14
Niagara 27	Buffalo 13
Northeastern 6	Tufts 0
Northwestern 22	Navy 0
N.Y.U. 6	U.S.M.M.A. 6
St. Lawrence 20	Hobart 13
St. Michael's 44	Norwich 7
Springfield 27	Bates 0
Trenton T. 13	New Britain T. 0
Trinity 41	U.S.C.G.A. 0
Tulsa 21	Georgetown 7
Union 20	R.P.I. 0
Wagner 20	Hofstra 19
Wesleyan 14	Bowdoin 7
Williams 23	Rochester 0
Worcester 21	Massachusetts 20
Yale 21	Fordham 14

MIDWEST

WESTERN CONFERENCE

Indiana 20	Iowa 7
Wisconsin 7	Illinois 6

Standings of the Teams

	W.	L.	P.C.
Wisconsin	1	0	1.000
Indiana	1	0	1.000
Michigan	0	0	.000
Minnesota	0	0	.000
Northwestern	0	0	.000
Ohio State	0	0	.000
Purdue	0	0	.000
Illinois	0	1	.000
Iowa	0	1	.000

BIG 7 CONFERENCE

Kansas 27	Colorado U 21

Standings of the Teams

	W.	L.	P.C.
Iowa State	1	0	1.000
Kansas	1	0	1.000
Colorado U.	1	2	.333
Missouri	0	0	.000
Nebraska	0	0	.000
Oklahoma	0	0	.000
Kansas State	0	1	.000

MOUNTAIN STATES CONFERENCE

Utah 28 (tie)	Brigham Young 28
Wyoming 34	Colorado A.&M. 0

OTHER MIDWEST

Adams State 14	W. New Mexico 14
Alma 7	Adrian 0
Baldwin Wallace 33	Akron 6
Ball State 27	Depauw 13
Bowling Green 20	Bradley 14
Carleton 21	Grinnell 19
Cincinnati 28	Louisville 20
Colo. College 21	Colo. Mines 12
Concordia 7	Wisconsin Tech 7
Denison 26	Otterbein 0
Hanover 6	Indiana Central 0
Hillsdale 7	Albion 7
Ill. North Central 52	Elmhurst 0
Illinois Normal 14	Cent. Mich. 13
Iowa State 26	Iowa STC 8
John Carroll 48	Kent State 7
Kenyon 13	Wooster 13
Knox 33	St. Lawrence 7
Loras 52	Upper Iowa 6
Manchester 20	Franklin 12
Marquette 46	Kansas 6
Maryland 34	Michigan State 7
Millikan 20	Augustana 0
Minot T. 2	Jamestown 0
Mission House 34	Aurora 6
Missouri Mines 14	Maryville 0
Nebraska Wesleyan 19	Kearney 12
Notre Dame "B" 13	Purdue "B" 6
Nebraska 32	Minnesota 26
Ohio U. 21	Butler 14

Continued on Page 8, Column 7

Irish Beaten First Time In 40 Games

Soph Samuels Stars in Upset

Illustrated on Page 5

By CHARLES CHAMBERLAIN

SOUTH BEND, Ind., Oct. 7 (AP).—Purdue today ended Notre Dame's reign of terror on the gridiron which had gone unchecked through 39 games without defeat, the greatest record in modern college football.

The sophomore-dominated Boilermakers buried the Irish, 28-14, in a stunning upset that shocked the Notre Dame campus and left 56,748 fans shaking their heads in disbelief.

IRISH OUTPLAYED

It was no fluke. Purdue, a 20-point underdog, outplayed the Irish in every category—including an overpowering fighting spirit and confidence.

The Boilermakers lashed to a 21-0 halftime lead. Notre Dame had cut it to 21-14 by the outset of the fourth period.

But the rally, unleashed as a drizzle slicked the field, only pumped more fire into Purdue. The pent-up wrecking crew came right back to score on a 56-yard pass play, sophomore Dale Samuels to Mike Maccioli, and slam the door in Notre Dame's face.

LAST LOSS IN 1945

The Notre Dame giant died without its seven-league boots on. Missing was its vaunted aerial attack and pulverizing running that had geared the gridiron goliath through four seasons without a setback.

The last time the Irish were beaten was 39-7 by the Great Lakes Naval Training Station team on Dec. 1, 1945. Since then 37 teams folded before them.

Two others, Army with a 0-0 deadlock in 1946 and Southern California with a 14-14 standstill in 1948, came close to victory but that was all.

It was Notre Dame's first loss at

Continued on Page 16, Column 1

(Acme Telephoto)

GENE WOODLING SCORES YANKS' INITIAL RUN IN 1ST INNING

New York outfielder tallies easily from second base on Yogi Berra's single at Yankee Stadium in fourth game of World Series. Phils' catcher, Andy Seminick, after taking throw, makes sure Yogi doesn't try to go to second on peg. The umpire is Charley Berry. Yanks won, 5-2, to win Series in four straight games. (Other pictures on Page 5.)

Kids Get Two in 9th After 2 Outs As Woodling Drops Seminick's Fly

Reynolds Relieves Ford, Fans Lopata With Two on Base For Final Out; N. Y. Chases Miller, Tallies 3 Off Konstanty

By STAN BAUMGARTNER

Inquirer Sports Reporter

NEW YORK, Oct. 7.—The Fightin' Phillies, who won the acclaim of the sports world when they captured Philadelphia's first National League pennant in 35 years, today became the 13th team since 1921 to bow before the New York Yankees in the World Series.

The biggest crowd of baseball's 47th fall classic—68,098—watched Ed (Whitey) Ford, 21-year-old rookie southpaw, and veteran Allie Reynolds, who faced only one batter, pitch the Yankees to a 5-2 victory over the Whiz Kids at Yankee Stadium as the Bombers swept the best-of-seven Series in four games. It was the sixth time in 17 tries that New York's American League pennant winners have won the world championship by 4-0. They were the last club to do it, too—in 1939 against the Cincinnati Reds.

30TH FOR AMERICAN LEAGUE

The Yankees' championship clincher came on the heels of three one-run triumphs—1-0, 2-1 and 3-2, in that order. Victory gave the American League its 30th world title in 47 Series with the National. And, for the Bombers, the sweep was added to their four-game romps of 1927, 1928, 1932, 1938 and 1939.

Defeat was the Phillies' eighth straight in Series competition, for the 1915 club—their first and only other flag winner—lost the final four contests with the Boston Red Sox.

But, even in defeat, they upheld their name of Fightin' Phillies. Faced with a 5-0 setback and their second shutout of the Series as they came to bat in the ninth inning, they staged a rally which netted two runs, and they had the tying run at the plate when pinch hitter Stan Lopata struck out.

FAILURE IN PINCHES

It was the final rap of frustration in a Series marked by frustrations, bad breaks and failure of the Whiz Kids' key hitters to come through when men were on base.

Starting with Wednesday's first game at Shibe Park against Vic Raschi and then against Reynolds on Thursday, Ed Lopat yesterday and Ford today, the Phillies time and again were in a position where one hit—the softest sort of single—would have turned the tide. But that all-important safety did not materialize.

Today, as the Whiz Kids faced the bleak tableau of four straight setbacks, the impotence of their attack was even more painful. In the first inning, they had runners on second and third with one out. In the fourth, they had men on first and third, again with one away. But on each occasion they failed to come through.

WOODLING DROPS FLY

Yet, in the ninth, they showed the spark that had carried them to the championship over clubs that were as good if not better than the Yankees.

Willie Jones opened the final frame with a whistling drive to left-center for a single, and Del Ennis was hit with a pitched ball. Dick Sisler forced Ennis on a grounder to second baseman Gerry Coleman and Gran Hamner struck out, but Andy Seminick hit a tremendous fly to left field. Gene Woodling caught the ball after a long run, then dropped it for an error. Jones and Ken Johnson, who ran for Sisler, raced over the plate.

Seminick, hobbling on an injured leg, made it only to first and was relieved by pinch runner Jack Mayo.

GOLIAT KEEPS RALLY ALIVE

The crowd, rooting loudly for the Phils all afternoon, stopped moving toward the exits. They sensed a rally, a dramatic uprising that might tie the score, perhaps even bring the

Continued on Page 4, Column 7

Official Series Box Score

FOURTH GAME

PHILLIES (N. L.)

	*B.Av.	ab.	r.	h.	2b.	3b.	hr.	tb.	rbi.	sb.	sh.	o.	a.	e.
Waitkus, 1b	.267	3	0	1	0	0	0	1	0	0	0	9	0	0
Ashburn, cf	.176	4	0	0	0	0	0	0	0	0	0	3	0	0
Jones, 3b	.286	4	1	2	1	0	0	3	0	0	0	0	4	0
Ennis, rf	.143	3	0	1	0	0	0	1	0	0	0	1	0	0
Sisler, lf	.059	4	0	0	0	0	0	0	0	0	0	2	0	0
b-K. Johnson	.000	0	1	0	0	0	0	0	0	0	0	0	0	0
Hamner, ss	.429	4	0	1	0	0	0	1	0	0	0	2	2	0
Seminick, c	.182	4	0	0	0	0	0	0	0	0	0	3	1	0
d-Mayo	.000	0	0	0	0	0	0	0	0	0	0	0	0	0
Goliat, 2b	.214	4	0	1	0	0	0	1	0	0	0	4	4	1
Miller, p	(0-1)	0	0	0	0	0	0	0	0	0	0	0	0	0
Konstanty, p	(0-1)	2	0	1	0	0	0	1	0	0	0	0	1	0
a-Caballero	.000	1	0	0	0	0	0	0	0	0	0	0	0	0
Roberts, p	(0-1)	0	0	0	0	0	0	0	0	0	0	0	0	0
c-Lopata	.000	1	0	0	0	0	0	0	0	0	0	0	0	0
Totals		34	2	7	1	0	0	8	0	0	0	24	12	1

NEW YORK YANKEES (A. L.)

	*B.Av.	ab.	r.	h.	2b.	3b.	hr.	tb.	rbi.	sb.	sh.	o.	a.	e.
Woodling, lf	.429	4	1	2	0	0	0	2	0	0	0	4	0	1
Rizzuto, ss	.143	4	0	0	0	0	0	0	0	0	0	2	4	0
Berra, c	.200	4	2	2	0	0	1	5	2	0	0	10	0	0
DiMaggio, cf	.308	3	1	2	1	0	0	3	1	0	0	1	0	0
Mize, 1b	.133	3	0	1	0	0	0	1	0	0	0	5	1	0
Hopp, 1b	.000	1	0	0	0	0	0	0	0	0	0	1	1	0
Brown, 3b	.333	3	1	1	0	1	0	3	1	0	0	0	1	1
W. Johnson, 3b	.000	1	0	0	0	0	0	0	0	0	0	0	0	0
Bauer, rf	.133	3	0	0	0	0	0	0	1	0	0	1	0	0
Coleman, 2b	.286	3	0	0	0	0	0	0	0	0	0	2	3	0
Ford, p	(1-0)	3	0	0	0	0	0	0	0	0	0	1	0	0
Reynolds, p	(0-0)	0	0	0	0	0	0	0	0	0	0	0	0	0
Totals		32	5	8	1	1	1	14	5	0	0	27	10	2

a-Fanned for Konstanty in 8th. b-Ran for Sisler in 9th. c-Fanned for Roberts in 9th. d-Ran for Seminick in 9th.

PHILLIES	0	0	0	0	0	0	0	0	2	—2
NEW YORK YANKEES	2	0	0	0	0	3	0	0	x	—5

Jones and K. Johnson scored in 9th on Woodling's error.

Double play—Mize and Berra; Coleman, Rizzuto and Mize. Left on base—Phillies, 7; New York Yankees, 4. Base on balls—Ford, 1 (Waitkus). Strikeouts—Ford, 7 (Sisler, Ashburn, Goliat, Jones, Hamner 2, Caballero); Konstanty, 3 (Ford 2, DiMaggio); Reynolds, 1 (Lopata). Hits and runs off—Miller, 2 hits, 2 runs, in 1-3 inning; Konstanty, 5 hits, 3 runs, in 6 2-3; Roberts, 1 hit, 0 runs, in 1; Ford, 7 hits, 2 runs, in 8 2-3; Reynolds, 0 hits, 0 runs, in 1-3. Hit by pitcher—By Konstanty (DiMaggio); by Ford (Ennis). Wild pitch—Miller. Winner—Ford. Loser—Miller. Umpires—Berry (A.L.) plate; Conlan (N.L.) 1b; McGowan (A.L.) 2b; Boggess (N.L.) 3b; McKinley (A.L.) lf; Barlick (N.L.) rf. Attendance—68,098. Time—2:05.

*Batting average for Series.

Army Routs Penn State

WEST POINT, Oct. 7 (AP).—Sparked by Bobby Blaik's flashy passing, Army's football team today handed Penn State a 41-7 trimming before 26,252 in Michie Stadium.

Uncertain on offense at the outset and hampered by numerous penalties, Army caught fire and turned in two sensational scoring plays at the finish to turn a tough game into a rout.

STATE STOPPED TWICE

Army twice stopped the Nittany Lions close to the goal in the first quarter. Coach Earl Blaik's son threw two touchdown passes to Dan Foldberg in the second period.

Army rolled up two more touchdowns in the third quarter with Gil Stephenson and Gene Filipski scoring, but its attack still wasn't consistent. While the Cadets got together for two long marches, the second featured by Al Pollard's 34-yard run, they were turned back near the goal on another occasion and kept getting in trouble through repeated rules infractions.

ARMY DRAWS PENALTIES

They virtually gave Penn State its touchdown, drawing two 15-yard penalties after a fumbled punt had

Continued on Page 8, Column 7

California Victor As Penn Rally Fails

Illustrated on Page 7

By MORT BERRY

Inquirer Sports Reporter

BERKELEY, Calif., Oct. 7.—If defeat can be glorious, Pennsylvania lost in that manner today when it extended a shockingly powerful California football team to a 14-7 score in the presence of 64,000 surprised onlookers.

Virtually driven back beyond the Mississippi by the relentless Golden Bear machine in the first half, Pennsylvania rebounded with the same brilliance it exhibited in overtaking Virginia, 21-7, last week at Franklin Field.

But a 14-0 first-half lead by a team that had swept 26 straight regular-season rivals since an early 1947 loss was too huge for Penn to overcome as it wound up on the short end for the fourth time in the four-game intersectional series that got under way in 1925.

Nevertheless, Penn proved it possesses one of its best second-half teams. Limited to 31 ground yards and seven in the air during the course of a first half in which the Golden Bears moved tank-fashion over 222 yards of terrain, Penn dominated action from the moment play was resumed.

PENN STOPPED ON SEVEN

The gallant Red and Blue thrust first to the seven. Checked there, the resourceful single-wing pupils of Coach George Munger, came back all the way from their 31 the next time they got the ball.

Actually the 14-play touchdown march was longer than 69 yards for Penn had to overcome a 15-yard penalty. The loss was offset by tailback Red Bagnell's 22-yard pass to Warren Horton. And fittingly, Bagnell, the inspirational leader, was the player to tally. He did a neat hip weave over the last 12 yards after thrusting outside his right tackle on a delayed buck.

The touchdown run on which guard Dave Hovey blasted safety man Carl Van Heuit out of the picture was the longest land gain by the Red and Blue.

California, on the other hand, had

Continued on Page 7, Column 3

Eagles Vanquish Rams, 56-20

By FRANK O'GARA

The Los Angeles Rams, whose hapless fate it is under the new National Football League setup to be the "natural rival" of the Philadelphia Eagles, once again proved a 14-karat "natural" for our champions last night.

The powerful, but Eagle-jinxed Coast club surrendered this one in ungracious fashion, 56-20, for its worst walloping in history after a wild whirligig of action that included a kickoff runback for a 103-yard touchdown by the victors' Russ Craft.

RUN IS TOP THRILL

The exploit of the stocky little speedster, only two yards less than the all-time NFL record, provided the top thrill of the cool evening to a paying crowd of 24,134 at Municipal Stadium, but the many other spectacular plays so satiated the audience that many left long before the Eagles had rolled up their highest total since 1934.

Only the 105-yard gallop under similar circumstances by the Chi-

Continued on Page 8, Column 3

Oklahoma Beats Texas Aggies

NORMAN, Okla., Oct. 7 (AP).—A desperate passing attack covering 65 yards and capped by a four-yard touchdown run by Leon Heath with 37 seconds remaining pulled Oklahoma past the Texas Aggies, 34-28, here today.

The last-minute victory extended Oklahoma's winning string, the longest in major college football, to 23 games.

A crowd of 40,000 watched the aerial drive that started with one minute and 44 seconds left and the Sooners behind 28-27.

HEATH SCORES 3 TIMES

The touchdown was the third of the day for Heath, who is the only returning starter from last year's Sugar Bowl champions. The Sooners' last defeat was to Santa Clara 17-20 the first game of the 1948 season.

The game appeared all but over and a few persons made for the exit after Claude Arnold passed to Billy Vessels for a 32-yard touchdown with 3½ minutes remaining and Jim Weatherall failed to make the kick

Continued on Page 8, Column 4

Tough Day For the Irish

NEW YORK, Oct. 7 (UP).—It was a tough day for the Irish!

The Irish of Notre Dame went down to their first defeat in five seasons at the hands of Purdue.

Noor, sensational Irish-bred horse, wound up eating dust behind Hill Prince in the $50,000 Jockey Club gold cup race.

And Ireland lost to England in an international football match.

Title for Yanks Is 13th Out of 17

YANKEE STADIUM, New York, Oct. 7 (AP).—Today's World Series victory by the New York Yankees over the Phillies was . . .

The sixth time the Yankees have won the world championship in four straight games.

The 13th World Series victory in 17 attempts.

The second consecutive world championship for the Yankees.

Series Runs Set Record Low Despite Yanks' Final Splurge

By ART MORROW

Inquirer Sports Reporter

NEW YORK, Oct. 7.—The National Leaguers' worst fears were realized today when the pent-up power of the Yankees exploded in the faces of the Phillies for the final and most decisive victory of the brief 1950 World Series.

Even so, the score was only 5-2, and baseball's 47th October classic wound up as the lowest run-producer of them all. The Yanks' 1-0, 2-1, 3-2 and today's 5-2 triumphs added up to a grand total of just 16 runs, two less than the Athletics and New York Giants amassed away back in 1905.

5 SHUTOUTS IN ROW

At least, the Phillies recorded more runs—thanks to the two unearned tallies in the finale—than the three completed by the A's in that sad sequence of two generations ago. However, Chief Bender, of the Athletics, did best Iron Man McGinnity in one of 1905's five successive shutouts, three scored by the Giants' late, great Christy Mathewson.

This was the seventh World Series completed in the minimum of four games, and the sixth swept by the Yankees. They squelched the Pittsburgh Pirates in 1927, the St. Louis Cardinals in 1928, the Chicago Cubs in 1932 and 1938 and the Cincinnati Reds in 1939. Boston's "Miracle Braves" stunned the A's in similar fashion in 1914.

THE SCRIPT IS ALTERED

The grand sequence of 1950 did not go exactly according to script. Experts had forecast the Yankee triumph, but not the manner of its achievement. Most unbiased observers felt that the American League champions packed too much punch for the Phillies, and yet, until this afternoon, they had to squirm and

Continued on Page 4, Column 3

Facts, Figures On World Series

Yesterday's Results

N. Y. Yankees, 5; Phillies, 2.

Final Standing of the Teams

	W.	L.	P.C.
New York (A.L.)	4	0	1.000
Phillies (N.L.)	0	4	.000

First Game

											R.	H.	E.
Yanks	0	0	0	1	0	0	0	0	0	—1		5	0
Phils	0	0	0	0	0	0	0	0	0	—0		2	1

Batteries—Raschi and Berra, New York; Konstanty, Meyer (9) and Seminick, Phils.

Second Game

												R.	H.	E.
Yanks	0	1	0	0	0	0	0	0	0	1	—2		10	0
Phils	0	0	0	0	1	0	0	0	0	0	—1		7	0

Batteries—Reynolds and Berra, New York; Roberts and Seminick, Silvestri (8), Lopata (10), Phils.

Third Game

											R.	H.	E.
Phils	0	0	0	0	0	1	1	0	0	—2		10	2
Yanks	0	0	1	0	0	0	0	1	1	—3		7	0

Batteries—Heintzelman, Konstanty (8), Meyer (9) and Seminick, Phils; Lopat, Ferrick (9) and Berra, New York.

Fourth Game

											R.	H.	E.
Phils	0	0	0	0	0	0	0	0	2	—2		7	1
Yanks	2	0	0	0	0	3	0	0	x	—5		8	1

Batteries—Miller, Konstanty (1), Roberts (8) and Seminick, Phils; Ford, Reynolds (9) and Berra, New York.

Yesterday's Attendance, Receipts
Attendance—68,098.
Receipts—$312,355.04.
Commissioner's share—$47,003.26.
Players' share—$159,811.07.
Clubs' and Leagues' share—106,540.71.

Four-Day Figures
Attendance—196,009.
Receipts—$953,669.03.
Commissioner's share—$143,050.35.
Players' share—$486,371.21.
Clubs' and Leagues' share—$324,247.47.

Eagle River, I Will Finish In Dead Heat at Camden

Illustrated on Page 9

Race Charts and Results on Page 9

By TEDDY COX

Mrs. Helen S. Reineman's Eagle River, an invader from Chicago, and Jaclyn Stable's I Will, a veteran who at one time was a high-ranking star, provided abundant thrills yesterday before 18,547 when they finished in a dead heat in the $10,000 Princeton Handicap at Garden State Park, Camden.

Not by any means disgraced in the wide-open six furlongs dash was Brookfield's game Iatan, a slight choice at 5-1 in the field of 15. He set a blistering pace and then held on courageously to take the show, only a head in back of the two leaders. Fourth honors went to William Ziegler, Jr.'s Leading Home.

Time for the distance was 1:10 1-5, three-fifths of a second away from the track record. Logan Batcheller, who gained his start on the Windy City circuit, was astride Eagle River, while the Eastern sensation, Joe Culmone, showed a brilliant effort aboard I Will.

Eagle River had displayed sparkling speed in his initial outing of

Continued on Page 9, Column 1

Colgate Wins, 47-6, After Nine Losses

HAMILTON, N. Y., Oct. 7 (AP).—Colgate, which had been looking for a football victory since the 1949 opener, beat Western Reserve, 47-6, today.

The Red Raiders had dropped nine straight since beating Buffalo, 32-0.

Alan Egler scored two touchdowns and had a third called back when an 80-yard dash was nullified by a penalty. A 22-yard dash by Bob Schirmer, a 51-yard sprint by Armand Allaire, a Stratton to Wylie pass and a close-up buck by Al Simmons accounted for the other scores. The losers' only tally came on a 79-yard march in the first quarter.

Hill Prince Beats Noor for Gold Cup

NEW YORK, Oct. 7 (UP).—C. T. Chenery's Hill Prince, the "runningest" horse in the land, sent Irish-bred Noor down to his third straight defeat today in the $50,000 Jockey Club gold cup.

Streaking around Belmont Park's wide turns as if somebody had given him a hot-foot, the Prince from Virginia cakewalked home four lengths in front of Noor. It was another seven lengths back to the third finisher, Mrs. Walter M. Jeffords' Adile, while A. E. Masters' Titien 2d wound up fourth. C. V. Whitney's Dooly, the only other starter, was pulled up before reaching the end of the two-mile run.

"HORSE OF THE YEAR"

Hill Prince was hailed as the king of the three-year olds when he won the recent Jerome handicap. And today's victory virtually assured him honors as "horse of the year."

Noor, four-time conqueror of Citation, was expected to give Hill Prince a run for the money. Instead,

Continued on Page 9, Column 5

Jim Konstanty Says:

Trouble With Control Costly As Yankees Scored 3 in 6th

By Jim Konstanty

Phillies Pitcher

NEW YORK, Oct. 7.

I NEVER thought they'd do it. The Yankees are a good ball club but they aren't so much the better team that they should beat us four straight. Of one thing I'm sure. Even though they won four straight, they didn't outclass us. We don't have to hang our heads. We might have won every game, and particularly the second and third ones. But we just didn't come up with the clutch hit in any game and they did. That's baseball.

I had a bad inning today and that didn't help us any. The Yanks scored three runs off me in the sixth inning and one of them was a homer by Yogi Berra.

I don't know what happened to me in that inning. It was the only time in the game I had trouble with my control. And in addition to Berra's hit, Joe DiMaggio lined sev-

Continued on Page 4, Column 6

Justice Won't Play Any Pro Football

CHAPEL HILL, N. C., Oct. 7 (AP).—All-America football player Charlie Justice said today he won't play pro ball with the Washington Redskins or anybody else.

He had just returned from a trip to Washington and an interview with George Preston Marshall, owner of the Redskins. He said Marshall made him an attractive offer but "I realized that I really did not want to play professional football."

Blew Chances For Runs—Sawyer

By HANK LITTLEHALES

Inquirer Sports Reporter

NEW YORK, Oct. 7.—Eddie Sawyer, a fellow who can take it without wincing, walked straight to the New York Yankees' dressing room after the fourth and final game of the 1950 World Series today.

There the genial manager of the Phillies shook hands with Casey Stengel, twinkle-eyed pilot of the triumphant Yanks, and extended congratulations to all Yankee players within reach.

SURPRISED AT BATTLE

"You have a fine ball club, Eddie," said smiling Stengel. "No kidding, I was surprised you gave us such a hard battle all the way. The way everybody was talking before the series, I thought we would beat you easier than we did."

Sawyer, who undoubtedly would have traded these kind words for

Continued on Page 4, Column 1

LaBeach Runs 100 Meters In 0:10.1; Betters Mark

GUAYAQUIL, Ecuador, Oct. 7 (AP).—Lloyd LaBeach, Panama, bettered the accepted world record for the 100-meter dash today when he ran the distance in 0:10.1 in the Bolivarian Games.

The accepted mark is 0:10.2 held jointly by LaBeach, Jesse Owens and Harold Davis. Meet officials said they would submit the mark for international recognition.

1950

October 8, 1950
Eagles defeat Los Angeles in a romp, 56-20

1951

RECORD: 4-8, 5TH IN AFC
HEAD COACH: BO McMILLIAN & WAYNE MILLNER

Schedule

Regular Season

Wk. 1	Sep 30	W	17-14	at Chicago Cardinals
Wk. 2	Oct 6	W	21-14	vs San Francisco 49ers
Wk. 3	Oct 14	L	37-24	at Green Bay Packers
Wk. 4	Oct 21	L	26-24	at New York Giants
Wk. 5	Oct 28	L	27-23	vs Washington Redskins
Wk. 6	Nov 4	W	34-13	at Pittsburgh Steelers
Wk. 7	Nov 11	L	20-17	at Cleveland Browns
Wk. 8	Nov 18	L	28-10	vs Detroit Lions
Wk. 9	Nov 25	L	17-13	vs Pittsburgh Steelers
Wk. 10	Dec 2	W	35-21	at Washington Redskins
Wk. 11	Dec 9	L	23-7	vs New York Giants
Wk. 12	Dec 16	L	24-9	vs Cleveland Browns

The Eagles won their first two games under Coach Bo McMillan. However, the new coach was forced to resign after becoming ill. Under his replacement Wayne Millner the Eagles would struggle, winning just two of their remaining ten games on the way to a 4-8 record.

1951 Philadelphia Eagles Stats

Passing	Comp	Att	Comp %	Yds	Y/Att	TD	Int	Rating
Adrian Burk	92	218	42.2	1329	6.10	14	23	44.5
Bill Mackrides	23	54	42.6	333	6.17	3	5	43.2
Johnny Rauch	5	12	41.7	51	4.25	0	1	19.8

Rushing	Rush	Yds	Avg	TD
Frank Ziegler	113	418	3.7	2
Steve Van Buren	112	327	2.9	6
Jim Parmer	92	316	3.4	2
Clyde Scott	45	161	3.6	1
Al Pollard	24	119	5.0	0
Dan Sandifer	35	113	3.2	1
Ebert Van Buren	16	60	3.8	0
Johnny Rauch	6	21	3.5	0
Adrian Burk	28	12	0.4	1
Bill Mackrides	7	9	1.3	0
Bosh Pritchard	31	6	0.2	0

Interceptions	Int	Yds	Avg	TD
Frank Reagan	4	60	15.0	0
Neill Armstrong	4	18	4.5	0
Pete Pihos	2	30	15.0	0
Joe Sutton	2	8	4.0	0
Russ Craft	1	32	32.0	1
Dan Sandifer	1	28	28.0	0
Ebert Van Buren	1	23	23.0	0
Pat McHugh	1	19	19.0	0
Mike Jarmoluk	1	9	9.0	0

Receiving	Rec	Yds	Avg	TD
Pete Pihos	35	536	15.3	5
Bobby Walston	31	512	16.5	8
Jim Parmer	13	80	6.2	0
Clyde Scott	10	212	21.2	3
Bosh Pritchard	8	103	12.9	0
Frank Ziegler	8	59	7.4	0
Steve Van Buren	4	28	7.0	0
Red O'Quinn	3	58	19.3	0
Neill Armstrong	3	44	14.7	0
Al Pollard	3	17	5.7	0
Dan Sandifer	2	36	18.0	1
Vic Lindskog	0	21	0.0	0
John Magee	0	7	0.0	0

Punting	Punts	Yds	Avg	Blocked
Adrian Burk	67	2646	39.5	0
Frank Reagan	10	367	36.7	0

Kicking	PAT Made	PAT Att	PAT %	FG Made	FG Att	FG %	Pts
Bobby Walston	28	31	90	6	1	600.0	94

Football Reflections

Princeton's Ace Trumps Penn; Villanova Soaring

By Leo Riordan
Inquirer Executive Sports Editor

APPROPRIATELY enough, a new type of rubber football was used experimentally in the LSU-Georgia Tech game Saturday. The way the sport is acting up this year, you need a rubber ball to absorb the extra quota of crazy bounces. Repeat crazy bounces.

ED BELL

Eagan Wins Langhorne Title Race

Marriott Second In Stock Event

(AP Wirephoto)

EAGLES' CLYDE SCOTT RUNS INTO TRAFFIC JAM OF PACKERS

Eagles' speedboy is hemmed in by Green Bay players after gaining six yards in first quarter yesterday at Green Bay. Identifiable Packers include (left to right) Abner Wimberly, Rebel Steiner and Dick Wildung. Packers won, 37-24.

Packers Hand Eagles 1st NFL Loss, 37-24

Green Bay Rolls After 10-10 Tie In Third Period; Fumbles Ruin Birds

By FRANK O'GARA
Inquirer Sports Reporter

GREEN BAY, Wis., Oct. 14.—The Philadelphia Eagles were knocked out of their league lead and almost out of their sox by the bone-crushing power of the Green Bay Packers today in a 37-24 battle that delighted 18,489 partisans at City Stadium.

The Quaker City athletes, who appeared sluggish most of the time against the charged-up Packers, didn't come as close to the victors as the scoreboard suggests, but they were the victims of a disheartening succession of bad breaks.

TIED IN 3D QUARTER

Outplayed through the first half they nevertheless gained a 7-7 intermission tie and pulled up to 10-10 after four minutes of the third quarter. But they couldn't keep the volatile end Bob Mann bottled up or check the blasts of Billy Grimes.

Trailing, 10-24, with about eight minutes left and on the verge of a score that would bring them into contention, they saw Bill Summerhays pick off an Adrian Burk pass and gallop 88 yards to score. They might just as well have called the game at that point.

Mann, speedy, tricky end, was the principal malefactor in spoiling the debut of Wayne Millner as acting head coach in place of the hospitalized Alvin (Bo) McMillin. He latched onto three scoring passes—five and 30-yarders from Bobby Thomason, and a 46-yarder from Tobin Rote. Thomason also flipped to end Carlton Elliott for a six-yard touchdown and Fred Cone kicked a 20-yard field goal.

PIHOS SCORES ON PASS

The Eagles struck first with only 2:22 left in the half when Bill Mackrides passed to end Pete Pihos for 24 yards, got into another tie on end Bobby Walston's 27-yard field goal, later cut the lead to 31-17 on Dan Sandifer's one-yard plunge, and completed the day's scoring on Frank Ziegler's two-yard smash.

The Eagles spent the first 27 minutes backed up near their goal, either in possession of the ball or defending against scoring chances. In succession, they held on their 11, fumbled away and held on the one, and lost the ball again on the eight when the ball was clawed out of Clyde Scott's hands on the ground on the eight.

On the next play Rote was smacked solidly and the ball flew out of his grasp. But, unfortunately, the officials didn't allow this as a bobble and, encouraged by this break, the Packers finally struck on Thomason's five-yarder to Mann.

EAGLES KEPT IN HOLE

Still in the hole, by such breaks as Cone's 40-yard field goal try that was so awry that it went out of bounds on the five, the Eagles finally got a chance when end Bud Grant recovered Rote's bobble on the enemy 24, whereupon Mackrides wafted to Pihos, who took it in full flight on the 12 and raced across.

The Eagles drew two roughness penalties that put the Packers in position for a pair of touchdowns. Despite Mann's spotlighted play and the scoring strikes of the passers, it was right-half Billy Grimes' stellar all-around running that enabled the Packers to keep driving.

Mackrides passed extremely well for the losers and would have had a better mark had not a few good ones been dropped. Making his debut, end John (Red) O'Quinn

Continued on Page 26, Column 6

South Tops North; West, Roman, St. Joseph's Win

By JOHN DELL

North Catholic's high hopes of a third straight football championship in the Catholic League were ground down beneath the feet of John McDonnell yesterday. The South halfback made a fine, dodging run after taking a short pass from Lou Solari to complete a 29-yard touchdown maneuver, which sent North to its second defeat in three league games. The score was 7-0.

WEST HOLDS LEAD

SCORES AFTER BLOCKED PUNT

Continued on Page 26, Column 1

Unbeaten Giants Rally in 4th to Top Cards; Rams Upset Lions; Bears, Browns Triumph

By HANK LITTLEHALES

A 14-point rally in the fourth quarter gave the New York Giants a 28-17 triumph over the Chicago Cardinals yesterday at the Polo Grounds and left Steve Owen's well-balanced machine the only unbeaten entry in the 12-club National Football League.

The Giants' late surge was typical of final-period action throughout the circuit, except for Washington's 45-0 pasting by the champion Cleveland Browns, but the rallies came too late in all other instances. Five teams now share the National Conference lead, with the Giants pacing the American division.

Just as Philadelphia's Eagles chalked up 14 meaningless markers in the fourth stanza at Green Bay, Pittsburgh found two late touchdowns insufficient to avert a 28-24 loss to San Francisco.

YANKS SCARE BEARS

Detroit menaced Los Angeles with a fourth-period TD, but suffered its first setback, 27-21, while the New York Yanks scared the daylights out of Chicago's Bears by striking for 21 points in three minutes before accepting a 24-21 setback.

TUNNELL GAINS 181 YARDS

52,997 SEE LIONS LOSE

Continued on Page 26, Column 4

10 Autos Pile Up In Flames in Race

Continued From First Page

CAR CATCHES FIRE

CAR FLIPS INTO SKID

LIST OF VICTIMS

Sports Results

College

FOOTBALL

School

FOOTBALL

Professional

FOOTBALL

NATIONAL LEAGUE

ICE HOCKEY

SOCCER

EXHIBITION BASKETBALL

Independent

FOOTBALL

Continued on Page 27, Column 3

Babe Zaharias Wins Fourth Texas Open

FORT WORTH, Tex., Oct. 14 (UP).—Babe Didrikson Zaharias won her fourth women's Texas Open golf title at River Crest Country Club today with an 8 and 7 victory over defending champion Betty Jameson, Indio, Calif.

Santa Clara Winner Over Loyola, 20-16

Stranahan Triumphs in Willard Golf

FORT SMITH, Ark., Oct. 14 (AP).—Frank Stranahan, Toledo, won the Willard Memorial amateur golf tournament today, defeating George Bigham, Oklahoma A. & M., 3 and 2.

Campanella's All-Stars Beat Hodges' Team, 4-1

MAYS TO TAKE PHYSICAL

Caps Win 2d in Row

Pete Fleming Wins Ozark Golf Title

Americans Top New York, 3-0

Olympians Beat Royals

Donahue Wins Title

Rate Princeton, Villanova, Cornell Best in the East

Princeton Star Out for Season

18,792 See NL Stars Beat AL Aces in Denver

Missouri Halfback Suffers Concussion

LIONS HOST TO MICH. STATE

BENNERS PACES SMU

Continued on Page 26, Column 3

Red Smith's next "Views of Sport" column will appear in The Inquirer tomorrow.

(AP Wirephoto)

WHOOPS, DEAR, WATCH THAT HOLDING

The Pi Beta Phis ran "perfect" interference for halfback Lou Laidlaw (right) in annual Powder Bowl game between Ohio University sorority teams yesterday at Athens, O., and beat Alpha Xi Deltas, 12-0. Pi Phi at left (holding opponent's arm) is taking slight liberty with rules.

1951

October 15, 1951 - Eagles lose to Green Bay giving up the largest number of points for the season, 37-24

1952

RECORD: 7-5, T-2ND AFC
HEAD COACH: JIM TRIMBLE

Schedule

Regular Season

Wk. 1	Sep 28	W	31-25	at Pittsburgh Steelers
Wk. 2	Oct 4	L	31-7	vs New York Giants
Wk. 3	Oct 12	W	26-21	vs Pittsburgh Steelers
Wk. 4	Oct 19	L	49-7	vs Cleveland Browns
Wk. 5	Oct 26	W	14-10	at New York Giants
Wk. 6	Nov 2	L	12-10	at Green Bay Packers (at Milwaukee, WI)
Wk. 7	Nov 9	W	38-20	vs Washington Redskins
Wk. 8	Nov 16	W	10-7	vs Chicago Cardinals
Wk. 9	Nov 23	W	28-20	at Cleveland Browns
Wk. 10	Nov 30	L	28-22	at Chicago Cardinals
Wk. 11	Dec 7	W	38-21	vs Dallas Texans
Wk. 12	Dec 14	L	27-21	at Washington Redskins

When Jim Trimble took over the coaching reigns the Eagles went back to playing solid football, landing in second place with a 7-5 record. The Eagles signed their first African-American players, halfbacks Ralph Goldston and Don Stevens.

1952 Philadelphia Eagles Stats

Passing	Comp	Att	Comp %	Yds	Y/Att	TD	Int	Rating
Bobby Thomason	95	212	44.8	1334	6.29	8	9	60.5
Adrian Burk	37	82	45.1	561	6.84	4	5	59.0
Fred Enke	22	67	32.8	377	5.63	1	5	26.8

Rushing	Rush	Yds	Avg	TD
John Huzvar	105	349	3.3	2
Ralph Goldston	65	210	3.2	3
John Brewer	50	188	3.8	2
Al Pollard	55	186	3.4	1
Frank Ziegler	67	172	2.6	2
Don Stevens	33	95	2.9	0
Bobby Thomason	17	88	5.2	0
Adrian Burk	7	28	4.0	0
Fred Enke	14	25	1.8	0
Jim Parmer	12	23	1.9	0
Bob Stringer	2	5	2.5	0
Ebert Van Buren	7	1	0.1	0

Interceptions	Int	Yds	Avg	TD
Bibbles Bawel	8	121	15.1	0
Joe Sutton	3	54	18.0	0
Mike Jarmoluk	2	48	24.0	1
Chuck Bednarik	2	14	7.0	0
Russ Craft	1	32	32.0	1
Vic Sears	1	9	9.0	1
Bob Stringer	1	9	9.0	0
Clyde Scott	1	0	0.0	0
Norm Willey	1	0	0.0	0
Neil Ferris	0	3	0.0	0

Receiving	Rec	Yds	Avg	TD
Bud Grant	56	997	17.8	7
Bobby Walston	26	469	18.0	3
Don Stevens	13	174	13.4	0
John Huzvar	13	37	2.8	0
Pete Pihos	12	219	18.3	1
Frank Ziegler	8	120	15.0	2
Al Pollard	8	59	7.4	0
John Brewer	5	19	3.8	0
Ebert Van Buren	4	73	18.3	0
Bibbles Bawel	2	60	30.0	0
Fred Enke	2	19	9.5	0
Ralph Goldston	2	12	6.0	0
Jim Parmer	2	10	5.0	0
Bob Stringer	1	4	4.0	0

Punting	Punts	Yds	Avg	Blocked
Adrian Burk	83	3335	40.2	0

Kicking	PAT Made	PAT Att	PAT %	FG Made	FG Att	FG %	Pts
Bobby Walston	31	31	100	11	20	55.0	82

1952

THE PHILADELPHIA INQUIRER, MONDAY MORNING, DECEMBER 8, 1952 · 31

Football on Television

Unlimited TV Called Aid to Learning Sports

Majors Approve 2-Loop Waivers, Adopt Bonus Rule

Big Leagues Put Ban On 24-Hour Recall Of Optioned Players

Eagles Beat Texans, 38-21, Take Undisputed 2d Place; Browns Win, 10-0, Retain One-Game Lead Over Birds

Cleveland Tops Cards, Clinches Tie for Conf. Title

A Texan from Dallas "bulldozed" a rampaging "steer" in the Eagles' backfield when Jim Lansford tackled the Birds' Al Pollard after a seven-yard gain in the first quarter yesterday at Shibe Park. John Petitbon (23), Dallas, and Frank Ziegler (41), Eagles, are others in foreground. Eagles won the National Football League game, 38-21.

Grant Catches 11 Passes, Sets 2 Club Marks

By FRANK O'GARA

Harry (Bud) Grant, the Eagles' extraordinary end, enjoyed the most successful pass-snatching afternoon a member of that organization has experienced in its 20-year history and also erased the club's seasonal record for aerial yardage yesterday before 18,376 at Shibe Park to add a fillip to the Philadelphians' 38-21 conquest of the homeless, hapless Dallas Texans.

The triumph, which accrued far easier than it sounds, kept the Eagles within striking distance of Cleveland for the divisional championship of the National Football League with the final games coming up next week. The Birds (7-4) took over sole tenancy of second place as New York bowed, and can do no worse than end up in a tie for second.

TIE CAN RESULT

Should New York (6-5) beat Cleveland (8-3) Sunday and the Eagles get by Washington (3-8) at the Capital, there will be a playoff at Shibe Park Dec. 21.

Grant, the slick wingman from Minnesota, who developed his guile further by playing pro basketball for two seasons with the Minneapolis Lakers, was a show in himself as he grabbed 11 aerials for 203 yards and two touchdowns. Both TDs and most of the passes he grabbed were [illegible] by Bobby Thomason.

BREAKS SEASON MARK

That yardage exploit erased his own mark of 186 yards, set last week against the Cardinals and belatedly recognized as a club standard. And on his first reception of the afternoon—a 41-yard touchdown—he zoomed past the 766 yards with which Pete Pihos had set an Eagles season record in 1948. Subsequent catches boosted his total to 941 on 52 completions—a tidy average of 18.1 yards.

His other touchdown came when he lost defenders and waited as lonely as a hermit for the 23-yard peg into the end zone. In order, his receptions during the afternoon were for the following yardage: 41-10-7-44-11-23-13-23-9-15-7. This is the wingman, 6-03 and 200 pounds, reputedly the fleetest player on the team, who chafed all last season while playing a bang-up defensive game as Gordon Soltau, his sub at Minnesota, was making headlines for San Francisco as a pass-catcher.

Although the outcome and the Texans' 10th defeat in 11 games was decided early when the Eagles collected on their first three chances for a 17-0 lead, the game was much more interesting than many a tight battle. Among other features, it produced four of the screwiest plays of the year, to wit:

SEARS SCORES

With the ball on the Dallas 43, Bob Celeri went back on fourth down, ostensibly to punt. The pass from center flew over his head and after retrieving it, he scurried around, dodging tacklers. Captain Mike Jarmoluk finally plastered him on the Dallas 7, and as he was going down, he flipped out a perfect "lateral"—straight at tackle Vic Sears, who romped 9 to score. It was Vic's first TD in 12 years with the Birds.

Encouraged by this success as a ball-carrier, Sears, 6-03 and 230, took a subsequent kickoff, "sped" into the clear and went 45 to the enemy 30.

Then Al Pollard, who continued to show belated power and speed in ball-carrying, was trapped after taking a handoff from Adrian Burk and proceeded to toss a two-handed pass back to Burk for a six-yard gain and credit as a forward pass.

STRANGEST PLAY AT END

But the strangest play was reserved for the game's final seconds. Bubbles Bawel [illegible] a pass [illegible] and after [illegible] around [illegible], slipped a lateral to Ebert Van Buren. The stellar defensive back in turn lateraled to Neill Ferris, whereupon Bawel came around and accepted a lateral from him on the four and raced 35 yards—almost going the distance.

The Eagles scoring went this way: A 41-yard march with John Huzvar barreling over from the 5. A 70-yard drive on which Huzvar rammed

Continued on Page 35, Column 2

Meyer Is 'Serious' After Heart Attack

PHOENIX, Ariz., Dec. 7 (AP)—Bill Meyer, 60, recently released as manager of the Pittsburgh Pirates, suffered a heart attack in his Adams Hotel room today and was rushed to Memorial Hospital.

The hospital reported his condition as "serious but not critical."

Meyer recently ended a five-year contract as manager of the Pirates.

Warriors Shaded, 94-92, By Royals' Strong Surge

Redskins Blast Giants' Title Bid

NEW YORK, Dec. 7 (AP)—Eddie Le Baron threw four touchdown passes, three to Hugh Taylor, as the lowly Washington Redskins whipped the New York Giants, 21-17, and wrecked any chance the Polo Grounders had for championship...

Lions Rout Bears, 45-21, To Near Title Tie; Box Ace

DETROIT, Dec. 7 (AP)—End Cloyce Box triggered the Detroit Lions to within shooting distance of a pro football championship by grabbing two over-the-shoulder touchdown passes within a 96-second span of the first period today, and from there the Lions went on to trounce the Chicago Bears, 45-21, before 50,410.

In all, Box caught three touchdown passes from quarterback Bobby Layne, who had one of his greatest days. Layne's Lions thus...

Americans Win, Lead League

Rams Roll, 45-27, Over Green Bay

College Basketball Roundup

Indiana Victim of Upset; La Salle, Kansas State Win

Sports Results

Nats' Rally in 4th, Top Hawks, 71-67

Pistons Down Knicks As Meineke Scores 27

15 Finished Unbeaten, Untied

Rangers, Canadiens Tie

Wings, Bruins Tie, 1-1

Notre Dame Plans Commercial Television Station

December 8, 1952 - Eagles rout the Dallas Texans, 38-21
Bud Grant catches 11 passes for 203 yards and scores two touchdowns

1953

RECORD: 7-4-1, 2ND IN NFL EAST
HEAD COACH: JIM TRIMBLE

Schedule

Regular Season

Wk. 1	Sep 27	L	31-21	at San Francisco 49ers
Wk. 2	Oct 2	T	21-21	vs Washington Redskins
Wk. 3	Oct 10	L	37-13	at Cleveland Browns
Wk. 4	Oct 17	W	23-7	vs Pittsburgh Steelers
Wk. 5	Oct 25	W	56-17	at Chicago Bears
Wk. 6	Nov 1	W	35-7	at Pittsburgh Steelers
Wk. 7	Nov 8	W	30-7	vs New York Giants
Wk. 8	Nov 15	W	45-14	vs Baltimore Colts
Wk. 9	Nov 21	W	38-0	vs Chicago Cardinals
Wk. 10	Nov 29	L	37-28	at New York Giants
Wk. 11	Dec 6	L	10-0	at Washington Redskins
Wk. 12	Dec 13	W	42-27	vs Cleveland Browns

Bobby Thomason and Adrian Burk combined to pass for a league-high 3,089 yards, while Pete Pihos caught 63 passes for 1,049 yards and 10 touchdowns to lead the league. Rookie defenseman Tom Brookshier led the team with eight interceptions while Chuck Bednarik returned an interception for a touchdown against Baltimore. The Eagles finish in second place again with a 7-4-1 record, while snapping the Cleveland Browns 11-game winning streak with 42-27 win in the season finale.

1953 Philadelphia Eagles Stats

Passing	Comp	Att	Comp %	Yds	Y/Att	TD	Int	Rating
Bobby Thomason	162	304	53.3	2462	8.10	21	20	75.8
Adrian Burk	56	119	47.1	788	6.62	4	9	48.6
Frank Ziegler	0	1	0.0	0	0.00	0	0	39.6
Bob Gambold	6	14	42.9	107	7.64	0	2	30.1

Rushing	Rush	Yds	Avg	TD
Don Johnson	83	439	5.3	5
Jerry Williams	61	345	5.7	3
Frank Ziegler	83	320	3.9	5
Jim Parmer	38	158	4.2	2
Hal Giancanelli	44	131	3.0	1
Toy Ledbetter	41	120	2.9	1
John Brewer	17	85	5.0	1
Adrian Burk	8	54	6.8	3
Al Pollard	23	44	1.9	0
Bobby Thomason	9	23	2.6	1
Bob Stringer	1	5	5.0	0
Bob Gambold	2	-2	-1.0	0

Receiving	Rec	Yds	Avg	TD
Pete Pihos	63	1049	16.7	10
Bobby Walston	41	750	18.3	5
Jerry Williams	31	438	14.1	1
Hal Giancanelli	20	346	17.3	5
Frank Ziegler	15	211	14.1	0
Jim Parmer	14	89	6.4	0
Toy Ledbetter	13	137	10.5	2
Don Johnson	12	227	18.9	2
Al Pollard	7	33	4.7	0
John Brewer	4	43	10.8	0
Bob Schnelker	4	34	8.5	0

Punting	Punts	Yds	Avg	Blocked
Adrian Burk	41	1765	43.0	0
Chuck Bednarik	12	483	40.3	0

Kicking	PAT Made	PAT Att	PAT %	FG Made	FG Att	FG %	Pts
Bobby Walston	45	48	94	4	13	30.8	87
Al Pollard	1	1	100	0	2	0.0	1

Interceptions	Int	Yds	Avg	TD
Tom Brookshier	8	41	5.1	0
Chuck Bednarik	6	116	19.3	1
Russ Craft	4	46	11.5	0
Bob Hudson	3	74	24.7	0
Ebert Van Buren	1	13	13.0	0
Bob Stringer	1	7	7.0	0
Mike Jarmoluk	1	2	2.0	0

1953

Jim Christy still is on his back in mid-air after carrying North Catholic's John Lauch over goal line on four-yard touchdown jaunt with seven-yard pass from his brother Dick in first period yesterday at Connie Mack Stadium. In foreground is North's Ray Banas. St. James won, 9-0, over North, snapped city champion Falcons' unbeaten string at 17 games and gave undefeated St. James the Catholic League lead.

St. James Turns Back North, 9-0

17-Game Streak Of Falcons Ends; D. Christy Star

By HAL FREEMAN

Solid St. James, as up for the big game as any team could be, yesterday ended city champion North Catholic's undefeated string at 17 games with a rousing 9-0 football victory before 20,502 at Connie Mack Stadium.

Turning a fumble into a first-period aerial score, then adding Tom Delone's 28-yard field goal in the succeeding session, unbeaten St. James moved into undisputed possession of first place in the Catholic League and became the favorite to win the championship for the first time since entering the league 10 seasons ago.

SOUTH, ROMAN WIN

Continued on Page 25, Column 3

Reflections

Penn Spirit, Gambles, Tradition Upset Navy

By LEO RIORDAN
Inquirer Executive Sports Editor

T. TRUXTUN HARE, four-time (1897-'8-'9-'00) Penn All-America guard, stood in White Training House Saturday in the happy haze that followed the 9-6 upset over Navy. Hare is a legend and the players glowed when he said: "I can recall no victory that tops this . . . it is in our great tradition." Since Hare has been following Penn football 60 years, this was no casual pop-off after a victory with 59 seconds to go.

Seeking parallel fiction finishes on Franklin Field, the gathering naturally mentioned the 1912 Michigan game. Michigan led, 21-0, in the first half; Penn won, 27-21, in the last minute. Reaching back, Hare recalled the 1899 Michigan game won by his team, 11-10, in the last minute. There memories halted.

In 1899 five yards was first down. "It was all simpler," Hare smiled. "Comparing football then and now . . . is, well, like checkers against chess."

• • •

Mrs. Hare revealed that they had attended the Princeton-Navy game with Rear Adm. John H. (Babe) Brown, Jr., and watched the 65-7 carnage. "Frankly, I expected the game here to be appalling," Hare admitted, "but still no Pennsylvania man ever misses the Navy game."

• • •

John Lavin nailed nine passes for what may be a Penn record and racked them up on defense. Castle broke up a Navy screen pass by eluding three men and tossing the ball-carrier for a six-yard loss in a clutch.

• • •

Jack Shanafelt went 60 superb minutes again at tackle, little John (Mighty Mouse) Cannon, 59 at guard. Stew Haggerty was great. They were typical. Regulars became stars, and subs suddenly played like regulars.

Grandstand quarterbacks questioned Gramigna's judgment in calling Varaitis so much on the TD drive—eight of the last nine plays. But Varaitis, who had impressed pro scouts in the first half with his blocking and tackling, was as durable as Frank Reagan in the famed 22-20 victory over Cornell. These two games will be bracketed in Penn legend.

It was obvious in 1940 that Reagan would carry and you didn't have to be occult Saturday to know it was Varaitis or nothing.

In victory, Feiver's misfortune will be forgotten. But, for the book, how can you criticize a soph without spring practice in this year of new rules and confusion? From here he has done remarkably well under unfair conditions.

• • •

Statistics mean little. One of Robinson's heartbreaks before the oomph finish was being the victim of a pass interference ruling that gave Navy 30 yards—and it netted only 40 in the air all day.

Statistics show that Penn had the ball on 81 plays; Navy on 45. Of Penn's plays, 55 were single wing (it also threw in one surprise winged T play and also a double wing formation).

Critics of single wing admit it permits you to keep the ball, citing the adage that they can't score if you have the ball. But Navy did. It was weird and wonderful. Penn escaped without injury and now faces a "relaxing" Saturday at Michigan.

Kelly Wins Pair In Mexico City; Miller Is Victor

MEXICO CITY, Oct. 25 (AP).—John B. Kelly, Jr., U. S. national single sculls champion from Vesper Boat Club, Philadelphia, today helped lower the Mexican senior doubles sculls record in the Mexican National Rowing Championships.

Kelly and his boatmate, Tom McCreesh, Penn AC, Philadelphia, won in 4:25 2-5 for the 1200 meters, erasing the record of 1:27 2-5. Anatares BC, Mexico City, was second.

ROW IN CANAL

They rowed on the main canal in the famed floating gardens of Xochimilco, long a tourist resort. The flower sellers canoes and restaurant boats were cleared off to provide a course and the flower-decked tourist boats formed a floating gallery.

Hogan Cards 72 'Against' Britons

Giants Boom to Victory On Rhodes' Grand Slam

NAGOYA, Japan, Oct. 25 (AP).—After trailing by six runs, the New York Giants boomed back on a grand slam homer by Jim Rhodes and downed the professional Nagoya Dragons, 9-6, for their seventh victory in Japan.

Leahy Reported In Good Condition

SOUTH BEND, Ind., Oct. 25 (AP).—Frank Leahy, Notre Dame coach, who collapsed in the Irish dressing room between halves of his team's 27-14 football victory over Georgia Tech, was reported in good condition today.

Doctors in St. Joseph Hospital, where Leahy was taken, said he suffered an acute attack of virus enteritis, commonly known as intestinal influenza, but the illness was not regarded as serious.

A hospital spokesman said Leahy would remain there for observation for several days and could receive visits from members of his family. The coach spent a restful night

Browns Capture 5th NFL Victory, Trip Giants, 7-0

NEW YORK, Oct. 25 (AP).—A New York penalty on Cleveland's missed fourth-down field goal attempt set up the winning touchdown today as the unbeaten and untied Browns stormed to their fifth National Football League triumph with a hard-earned 7-0 victory over the New York Giants.

A crowd of 20,773 braved a steady all-day rain that drenched the Polo Grounds field and made playing conditions almost impossible. The soggy terrain made running a hardship and cut passing to a minimum.

The lone touchdown came after 2:46 of the second quarter. The Browns, who had dominated the play in the first period but were unable to score, climaxed a 28-yard drive to the giant 11. On fourth down, Lou Groza, the field goal ace, attempted his specialty from the 18. The kick went wide but an official detected a Giant offside and Cleveland was awarded a first down on the six.

GRAHAM SCORES

After Billy Reynolds sloshed to the four, Otto Graham sneaked over for the touchdown. Groza added the extra point.

The victory not only enabled the Browns to solidify their firm grip on the top run of the Eastern Conference, but enabled them to even their overall series with the Giants at four victories each. The Giants had been the only team to hold an edge over the Browns since they entered the league in 1950.

The loss was the fourth for the Giants in five starts this season. Their only victory came over the Chicago Cardinals last week.

The Giants, unable to penetrate Cleveland territory in the first half, made several futile fourth-quarter bids.

GIANTS' BIDS STOPPED

Twice in the final five minutes they drove deep into the enemy territory and each time Cleveland intercepted a pass by Chuck Conerly.

A 37-yard pass play from Conerly to Ray Pelfrey gave the Giants a first down on Cleveland's 31, but Ken Gorgal intercepted Conerly's long pass on the goal line and ran it back to the 20.

Four plays later the Giants again got the ball and stormed back to Cleveland's 28 on a 27-yard heave from Conerly to Rote.

After Sonny Grandelius picked up two yards, Conerly attempted another pass. He was hit hard by tackle Derrel Palmer and dropped the ball. Cleveland end Lenny Ford caught the ball in midair and ran it back to the Browns' 32. The Giants never got the ball again.

CLEVELAND BROWNS

NEW YORK GIANTS

Cleveland Browns	0	7	0	0	—7
New York Giants	0	0	0	0	—0

CLEVELAND SCORING: Touchdown—Graham. Extra point—Groza.

STATISTICS

Sports Results

Professional

FOOTBALL

NATIONAL LEAGUE

EAGLES	56	Chicago Cards	17
Cleveland	7	New York	0
Baltimore	27	Washington	17
Detroit	14	San Francisco	10
Los Angeles	38	Chicago Bears	24

CANADIAN BIG FOUR LEAGUE

SOCCER

ICE HOCKEY

BASKETBALL

School

FOOTBALL

CATHOLIC LEAGUE

Continued on Page 25, Column 6

Eagles Smother Cards, 56-17, Set 2 Club Marks on Passes

By ART MORROW
Inquirer Sports Reporter

CHICAGO, Oct. 25.—Chicago's downtrodden Cardinals had the impudence to score first at Comiskey Park today, and the Eagles wreaked a horrible vengeance. Jim Trimble's inspired Philadelphians, growing more ferocious with every period, rolled to a 56-17 victory as 22,060 looked on in amazement.

It was the worst defeat in history for the Cardinals, a charter member of the National Football League, and a new modern victory margin for the Eagles. The triumph was even more decisive than the Eagles' 56-20 frolic with the Los Angeles Rams in 1950, and the defeat more flattening than Chicago's 55-24 setback by the Green Bay Packers in 1942.

7 LONG DRIVES

The Eagles seemed insatiable. They scored in almost every conceivable manner: they tallied thrice on passes, two thrown by Bobby Thomason and one by Adrian Burk; four times on line cracks after sustained drives, and once on what was officially ruled a fumble in the end zone. They had continuous marches of 67, 56, 61, 89, 68, 77, and 64 yards for touchdowns, with Bob Walston place-kicking every extra point.

Thomason, a starter for the first time in the Trimble T-with-flanker, accounted for 239 yards alone with his passes, and Burk pitched 127 more. As a result, the Eagles gained no less than 528 yards—

Continued on Page 25, Column 1

Chicago Cardinal halfback Charley Trippi appears to be standing on the head of Eagles fullback Bob Stringer after catching touchdown pass from Jim Root yesterday in Chicago. This score was scant solace to Cardinals as Eagles breezed to 56-17 triumph in National Football League. (AP Wirephoto)

49,546 See Rams Jar Bears, 38-24

LOS ANGELES, Oct. 25 (UP).—Norman Van Brocklin, Los Angeles Rams, won a quarterback passing duel with George Blanda, Chicago Bears, today, 38-24, but only with an able assist from brilliant runs by Deacon Dan Towler and Skeet Quinlan.

Van Brocklin and the Bears' big pivot man both pitched or set up all touchdowns and field goals. They chalked up a total of 657 yards gained with aerials before a crowd of 49,546.

RAMS SHARE LEAD

54,862 Watch Lions Trip 49ers on Layne's Passing

SAN FRANCISCO, Oct. 25 (AP).—Texas' Bobby Layne threw two long bull's-eye passes for touchdowns today to lead the defending champion Detroit Lions to a 14-10 victory over the San Francisco 49ers in their crucial National Football League game before 54,862, the largest crowd of the season here.

Layne quarterbacked the Lions from a 0-10 deficit to a victory that kept them tied with Los Angeles atop the Western Division.

The defeat knocked the 49ers out of a share of the leadership.

CLINE, DIBBLE TALLY

PACED BY 'ORPHAN'

Continued on Page 25, Column 5

46 Grid Teams Still Unbeaten

NEW YORK, Oct. 25 (AP).—Little Peru (Neb.) State Teachers today headed a list of 46 undefeated, untied college football teams around the country. It is the only team with seven triumphs.

Boston College Wallops Xavier

Piedmont League To Stay in Business

RICHMOND, Va., Oct. 25 (AP).—Piedmont League directors reaffirmed today they "definitely" plan to stay in business in 1954.

Football Roundup: Purdue's Upset of MSC Boosts Notre Dame Status

NEW YORK, Oct. 25 (AP).

PURDUE'S 6-0 upset of Michigan State may have cleared the way for Notre Dame's return to the national championship status from which those same Boilermakers had knocked them in 1950.

While Notre Dame, currently the Nation's top team, overpowered fourth-rated Georgia Tech, 27-14, to end a 31-game unbeaten string for the Engineers, Purdue was snapping a 28-game victory streak for the Spartans, ranked No. 2 before the contest.

Ironically, Notre Dame's principal competitor in the national title race was stopped by the squad that had ended Irish supremacy of 1948-49 with a 28-14 victory early in 1950. It also had severed the longest modern undefeated record at 39.

Ironically, too, it was a student who had transferred from Michigan State, Dan Pobojewski, whose touchdown beclouded Spartan hopes for a Big Ten title in their first year as an active member.

Maryland, seemingly growing in stature each week, enhanced its No. 3 position with a 30-0 defeat of Miami Friday night. The Terps' biggest foe appears to be a schedule which offers less of a challenge than does Notre Dame's.

• • •

MICHIGAN STATE and Georgia Tech were not alone Saturday as disaster or close calls rocked most of the top-ranking elevens, leaving only the Irish, Maryland, Baylor, West Virginia, Utah and Mississippi Southern among the major unbeaten, untied schools.

Paul Giel's masterful performance and an unyielding defense enabled Minnesota to hand Michigan, No. 5, its first setback of the season, 22-0. The game marked the 50th anniversary of the Little Brown Jug and the Gophers' first triumph in the series since Bill Garnaas' field goal gave them a 16-14 edge in 1942.

By the margin of a deflected conversion attempt, Baylor, No. 6, nudged Texas A & M, 14-13, in the battle of the day in the Southwest. Merrill Green's 51-yard scoring run with 36 seconds remaining in the game brought ninth-place Oklahoma a 27-20 victory over Colorado. Illinois, No. 7 and current leader in the Big Ten, had to hustle to turn back Syracuse, 20-13.

Eighth-ranked West Virginia had an easier time, running over Virginia Military, 52-20.

Southern California, No. 11, and UCLA, No. 12, continued to hurtle toward their late-November meeting with Pacific Coast Conference victories. The Trojans whacked California's title bid, 32-20, while the Bruins, resuming their winning ways after a 21-20 loss to Stanford, blasted Washington State, 44-7. But Stanford emerged atop the PCC standings with a 13-7 triumph over Washington.

• • •

WELL-BALANCED attacks and an emphasis on fundamentals were the major factors in the day's big games.

Notre Dame's raw power enabled the Irish to march 80 yards with the opening kickoff, most of it through the middle of the Georgia Tech line, for the margin of a 7-0 halftime lead. Fullback Neil Worden blasted the final 14 yards on three straight drives.

With Coach Frank Leahy on his way to a hospital following a muscular spasm attack at the half the Irish gave up a tieing score in the third period, then unleashed the power again.

A pass from brilliant quarterback Ralph Guglielmi to halfback Joe Heap and a fumble recovery by tackle Art Hunter made it 21-7. Tech closed the gap on a 53-yard pass play from freshman quarterback Wade Mitchell to halfback Billy Teas. But All-America Johnny Lattner helped celebrate his 21st birthday by crunching the

Continued on Page 26, Column 3

October 26, 1953 - Eagles handed the Chicago Cardinals their worst defeat in team history by the score 56-17

1954

RECORD: 7-4-1, 2ND IN NFL EAST
HEAD COACH: JIM TRIMBLE

Schedule

Regular Season

Wk. 1	Sep 26	W	28-10	vs Cleveland Browns
Wk. 2	Oct 3	W	35-16	at Chicago Cardinals
Wk. 3	Oct 9	W	24-22	vs Pittsburgh Steelers
Wk. 4	Oct 17	W	49-21	at Washington Redskins
Wk. 5	Oct 23	L	17-7	at Pittsburgh Steelers
Wk. 6	Oct 30	L	37-14	vs Green Bay Packers
Wk. 7	Nov 7	W	30-14	vs Chicago Cardinals
Wk. 8	Nov 14	L	27-14	at New York Giants
Wk. 9	Nov 21	L	6-0	at Cleveland Browns
Wk. 10	Nov 28	W	41-33	vs Washington Redskins
Wk. 11	Dec 5	T	13-13	at Detroit Lions
Wk. 12	Dec 12	W	29-14	vs New York Giants

After winning their first four games, the Eagles continued to be one of the NFL's strongest teams, finishing with a 7-4-1 record, to finish in second place for the third season in a row. Leading the Eagles success was punter Bobby Watson who led the NFL with 114 points and seta club record by scoring 25 points in a single game (3 touchdowns and 7 extra points) against Washington 49-21.

1954 Philadelphia Eagles Stats

Passing	Comp	Att	Comp %	Yds	Y/Att	TD	Int	Rating
Adrian Burk	123	231	53.2	1740	7.53	23	17	80.4
Bobby Thomason	83	170	48.8	1242	7.31	10	13	61.0

Rushing	Rush	Yds	Avg	TD
Jim Parmer	119	408	3.4	0
Toy Ledbetter	81	241	3.0	1
Jerry Williams	47	183	3.9	1
Neil Worden	58	128	2.2	1
Dom Moselle	29	114	3.9	1
Hal Giancanelli	33	47	1.4	0
Bobby Thomason	10	45	4.5	0
Adrian Burk	15	18	1.2	0
Don Johnson	7	16	2.3	0
Pete Pihos	1	-1	-1.0	0
Jerry Norton	1	-3	-3.0	0

Receiving	Rec	Yds	Avg	TD
Pete Pihos	60	872	14.5	10
Jerry Williams	44	668	15.2	3
Bobby Walston	31	581	18.7	11
Dom Moselle	17	242	14.2	2
Toy Ledbetter	15	192	12.8	3
Hal Giancanelli	14	195	13.9	4
Jim Parmer	12	40	3.3	0
Neil Worden	7	63	9.0	0
Don Luft	3	59	19.7	0
Norm Willey	2	50	25.0	0
Don Johnson	1	20	20.0	0

Punting	Punts	Yds	Avg	Blocked
Adrian Burk	73	2918	40.0	0

Interceptions	Int	Yds	Avg	TD
Bob Hudson	8	89	11.1	0
Jerry Norton	5	110	22.0	1
Wayne Robinson	4	41	10.3	0
Bucko Kilroy	4	29	7.3	0
Harry Dowda	2	34	17.0	0
Roy Barni	2	0	0.0	0
Jess Richardson	1	10	10.0	0
Chuck Bednarik	1	9	9.0	0
Ed Sharkey	1	4	4.0	0

Kicking	PAT Made	PAT Att	PAT %	FG Made	FG Att	FG %	Pts
Bobby Walston	36	39	92	4	10	40.0	114

Eight Buy Stock of Connie, Earle; Keep A's Here

Group to Invest Four Million, Hire Top Gen. Manager, Pilot

By ART MORROW

Continued From First Page

—the eight newcomers and Roy Mack.

"As far as we're concerned, the nine men that we have named are the corporation," said Rosenberg, spokesman for the group. "Each is on an equal footing. If any of them disposes of part of his holdings—to a reputable person, of course—we would consider it none of the corporation's business."

SEVEN-HOUR MEETING

Rosenberg's Food Fair assistant and public relations man . . . Jules Schwartz, for 25 years a statistician at Penn football games . . . helped him draft the following written statement issued after the new group had huddled more than seven hours on the fifth floor of the building at 16th and Chestnut:

"Roy Mack today announced that his father, Connie Mack, his brother, Earle, and he have sold control of the Philadelphia Athletics to a group of eight well-known Philadelphia businessmen.

"Roy Mack stated: 'I have notified William Harridge, president of the American League, that we have agreed to sell to this fine group of civic-minded Philadelphia businessmen. I have requested League approval. Our lawyers are now meeting and are drafting the necessary legal documents. I am very, very happy to be able to keep the A's in Philadelphia. That has always been my goal.'

INVEST $4,000,000

"Rosenberg declared: 'We are investing approximately $4,000,000 to keep the A's in Philadelphia. The first action of the new group was a unanimous vote naming Mr. Connie Mack as our Honorary President. Officers and directors of the reorganized club will be elected at the organizational meeting to be held in Philadelphia this week after completion of the legal details of the sale.'

"The new owners jubilantly expressed their confidence that Philadelphia is a great baseball city and their determination, through a comprehensive rebuilding program, to bring the best available baseball brains and talent into the organization."

Numerous others attended the meeting, including Roy Mack's son, Connie, 3d. David Torrence, an accountant, hustled all through the luxurious suite, but perhaps the ones who had most to say—if you couldn't guess—were, half a dozen lawyers.

POLICE STAND GUARD

These included Sylvan M. Cohen, of Cohen and Cohen, who had been counseling the group since its inception; Samuel A. Goldberg, of Wolf, Block, Schorr and Solis-Cohen, representing Sley and Liebman; Samuel A. Blank, representing Rosenberg; Alfred L. Luongo, Earle Mack's attorney, and two counselors of the club itself, J. Channing Ellery and Frank Schilpp, of Rambo and Mair.

Throughout the day three policemen stood guard at the glass-paneled doors on Chestnut st.—not so much because they didn't trust the syndicate members in sight of the Brown Brothers Harriman and Co. vaults that could be seen through a passage-way left open by building improvements, but rather to keep interlopers out.

When the police arrived shortly before 1 o'clock, not without some screaming of sirens, there was a gathering of the curious outside.

FLOOD OF MESSAGES

"Have they made the deal yet?" several passers-by stopped to inquire.

Late last night the Western Union reported a flood of congratulatory messages from all over the country, addressed to Roy Mack.

Roy sat in on the lengthy deliberations, which—for most of those present—ran through lunch as well as dinner. The deal was set by the time Mr. Mack and Earle arrived.

'FEEL GOOD'—C. MACK

"I have been waiting for this news all day," smiled the venerable Mr. Mack, who spent 79 years in professional baseball as catcher, manager and club executive. "Now I feel very good. I was sick at the thought that the club might leave Philadelphia."

Mr. Mack plans to set up a trust fund for his daughters with the money he received.

Earle, vice president, secretary and general manager of the A's after serving from 1925 through early '49 as assistant manager, almost split his jowls, so wide was his grin.

"The Athletics never would have left Philadelphia," he confided. "If this deal had been turned down, we'd have kicked up an awful fuss. Most of these fellows are all my good friends."

EARLE TO ADVISE

In a subsequent huddle between the press and the new owners — mostly devoted to the acrobatics of photographers crawling over the big table for close-up shots—someone asked Earle what he planned to do now.

Earle has devoted his whole life to baseball, and the wrench of leaving the game stirred a ripple of pain.

"The A's always will be my team," he said. "I'll hang around awhile to help them. I'll probably have to advise these fellows a little on players."

Said Rosenberg, pleasantly surprised: "We'll take that advice."

HAPPY FOR FATHER

"I'm happy for my father," said Connie Mack, 3d. "This is what he has been fighting for— to keep the Athletics in Philadelphia."

Although it was announced that the new group had entered into no binding commitments, it is believed Roy Mack, the executive vice-president and treasurer, will remain with the club—probably as the only paid elective officer. The others, it was hinted, will serve without pay.

NOT READY YET

"We are not ready to discuss our board of directors or administrative officers," Rosenberg said, parrying a question—but somewhat later, in what he described as "not a slip", the food chain executive referred to "our president — Arthur Gallagher."

"I'm happy and proud to be associated with this group," said the old East Falls oarsman, one of 13 children. "I only hope that Philadelphia will come out and see the new A's."

Rosenberg explained that anything he said would be subject to American League approval: "And besides," he added, "whatever we decided in the way of organization

Continued on Page 29, Column 2

Sketches of 8 New Stockholders in A's

Sketches of the eight new principal stockholders in the Athletics:

JOHN P. CRISCONI, 59, president of automobile agency, rose from newsboy at 13 to big business. He is president of the Greater Philadelphia Magazine and New Jersey Manufacturers Magazine.

He and his wife, Inez, are parents of two sons, Walter, 36, and John Jr., 33, and a daughter, Jeanette.

A member of the Penn AC and Whitemarsh CC, he has been active in the Order of the Sons of Italy and Boys Town of Italy. He has received the American Legion's commendation for his work in the veterans' hiring program, and has been active in many hospital and other charitable activities. He is on the Redevelopment Authority board.

BARNEY FISHER, Ardmore, automobile and oil company official in Ardmore was born in Lower Merion Dec. 8, 1888. He attended Lower Merion schools and is still active in athletic affairs at the high school. He is chairman of the finance committee of Lower Merion township.

For years he was a writer on various Philadelphia newspapers and also along the Main Line. Former president and long-time secretary of the Bala Golf Club, now president of the Bird Lovers Association of Lower Merion. Did some of the preliminary public relations for the new group.

Married to the former Charlotte LaRue. They have no children.

ARTHUR ANTHONY GALLAGHER, general manager E. A. Gallagher & Sons, a trucking firm. He was born July 5, 1918, in East Falls. Lives on Fishers rd., Bryn Mawr. As an oarsman, he won five National championships for Penn AC and Bachelors Barge Club. In the 1948 Olympics he and his partner, the late Joe Angyl, were semifinalists in doubles.

He is married to the former Marcella Daly, sister of Watten Daly, ex-Penn football star. They have four children, Meg, 4½, Arthur, Jr., 3; Lottie, 2 and Rita, 1.

Gallagher is treasurer of the Sandlot Sports Association, vice president of the Penn AC, director of the Philadelphia Visitors Bureau of the Chamber of Commerce, and a member of the Bala Golf Club, the Union League, and the Bachelors Buttons (Bachelors Barge).

THEODORE R. HANFF, 51, investment banker, was born near Columbia Park, the A's pre-Mack Stadium home, two years after Connie Mack brought the team here from Milwaukee. He has been an A's rooter all his life.

In his youth he was a sandlot player and still takes an active interest in athletics for boys through his association with the Police Athletic League.

The graduate of West Philadelphia High School formerly was president of the Burlington-Bristol Bridge Co., which operated both the span bearing its name and the Tacony-Palmyra Bridge. He also was a shareholder in the Ocean City Bridge Co., which operated the Beesley's Point Bridge across Great Egg Harbor Bay. For many years he was a bridge painting contractor.

A member of the Bankers Club of New York, he is married, but hasn't any children. He lives at 267 Trevor la., Cynwyd.

MORTON LIEBMAN, 25, of the B. E. Block Brothers department store, Norristown, has been a "minor" sports promoter for years. A semi-pro basketball team he backed claimed the independent championship of the Philadelphia district last season. His softball team competed in a National tournament and his baseball team formerly was in the defunct Main Line League.

A graduate of Overbrook High School and the Wharton School of the University of Pennsylvania, he is married and childless. He is a veteran of three years in the Air Force. He belongs to the American Legion and the Philmont Country Club.

JACK G. RENSEL, 35, vice president of a trailer company, is realizing a long-time ambition to get into the executive end of baseball. He is a director of Junior Baseball Federation and formerly was assistant public relations director with the Phillies.

The graduate of Simon Gratz High School and Temple University, has served as master of ceremonies at special programs at A's and Phillies' games.

He and his wife, Lillian R., are parents of two girls, Ellen Jill, 5, and Lynn Susan, 7 months.

In '941, Rensel wrote the lyrics to a song, "Blue Jay Jeanne," dedicated to the Phillies. During the Second World War he was a captain in the Army Air Force. He was special services officer in charge of athletics.

ARTHUR ROSENBERG, 44, vice president, director of sales and purchasing for Food Fair stores, is a great sports enthusiast. He also has been particularly interested in interscholastic wrestling because his son, Robert, was captain of the Lower Merion High School wrestling team last year. The son is now a freshman at Ohio State. Rosenberg's daughter, Sharon, is a junior at Penn.

In 1952, Rosenberg was the recipient of the National Torch of Hope, an award by the City of Hope, charitable organization which maintains a non-sectarian health center at Duarte, Calif.

He holds directorships in Every Woman's Magazine, North Eastern Hospital, the Golden Slipper Square Club and its camp, the Jefferson Hospital Building Fund and Green Valley Country Club.

He was born in New York City and lives at 7 Merion rd., Merion.

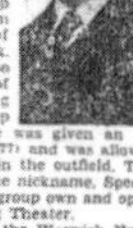

ISADORE (SPEED) SLEY, president of the Racquet Garage Corp. He was born in Chicago on Sept. 24, 1900 and was graduated from Mt. Carmel, Pa., High School.

For years he made a winter trip to Florida, timed to include a visit to the Athletics training camp and became an admirer of Connie Mack. He became so much a part of the spring training camp party that he was given an A's uniform (No. 77) and was allowed to shag flies in the outfield. This gained him the nickname, Speed.

He and his group own and operate the Viking Theater.

He lives at the Warwick Hotel. His son, Ronald Brewster Sley, 15, attends Hill School.

The new order is congratulated by the old as A's change hands in deal consummated yesterday. Arthur A. Gallagher, one of the eight new stockholders who is expected to become president of the club, is congratulated by 91-year-old Connie Mack, retiring president, while Roy Mack looks on. Connie will be honorary president, while Roy, who retained one-ninth of the team's stock, is expected to serve the club in an executive capacity. He had been executive vice president and served as general manager.

Burk's 7 TD Passes Tie Mark; Eagles Win

Rout Redskins; Birds Take 4th In Row, 49-21

WASHINGTON, D. C., Oct. 17—Rangy Adrian Burk, the soft spoken Texan who has had difficulty convincing Philadelphia fandom that he belongs with the game's elite, tied a National Football League record by hurling seven touchdown passes against the hapless Washington Redskins as the Eagles romped to their fourth straight victory, 49-21, before 22,051 in Griffith Stadium today.

The former Baylor star, who did his playing under Bobby Thomason's shadow the past two campaigns, set a new mark for an Eagles' player when he completed his fifth scoring pass in the third quarter and then tied the 11-year record held by Sid Luckman with two bull-eyes in the final period.

JUST 10 SECS. TO GO

He matched Luckman's feat with a three-yard heave to Pete Pihos for the final touchdown just 10 seconds before the game ended. He replaced Thomason, who had very little chance to see any action because of the Texan's brilliance, just one play before this climactic tally, coach Jim Trimble obviously wanting to give him a shot at the record.

Burk promptly set the stage for the score with a 10-yard toss to Jerry Williams that placed the ball on the three, and then didn't miss on his next chuck to Pihos.

Earlier Burk had found Pihos for scoring passes of 18 and 19 yards, and he also threw three times to Bobby Walston for scores on plays that covered 26, five and four yards. He pitched nine yards to Toy Ledbetter for the other six-pointer.

In all, Burk completed 19 of 27 passes for a total of 229 yards, as the Eagles enjoyed themselves immensely as they beat Washington for the first time in two years.

Pihos caught nine passes for 135 yards and three TDs.

If Burk's dazzling performance, coming on the heels of his last-ditch, game-saving touchdown

Continued on Page 29, Column 6

Sports Results

Professional

FOOTBALL

NATIONAL LEAGUE

EAGLES	49	Washington	21
San Francisco	31	Chicago Bears	24
Green Bay	35	Los Angeles	17
Pittsburgh	55	Cleveland	27
New York	31	Chicago Cardinals	17

Standings

Eastern Division	W	L	T	PC	Western Division	W	L	T	PC
EAGLES	4	0	0	1.000	Detroit	3	0	0	1.000
Pittsb'gh	3	1	0	.750	S.Fr'cisco	3	0	1	1.000
New York	3	1	0	.750	Chi. Bears	2	2	0	.500
Cleveland	1	2	0	.333	L.Angeles	1	2	1	.333
Chi.Cards	0	4	0	.000	Baltimore	1	3	0	.250
Wash'ton	0	4	0	.000	GreenBay	1	3	0	.250

School

FOOTBALL

CATHOLIC LEAGUE

LaSalle	19	Roman	0
North	19	St. Thomas More	13
South	20	West	0
St. James	35	St. Joseph's	7

Standings: [illegible]

OTHER GAMES

St. Matthew's	13	St. John's	6
St. Joseph's (Camden)	27	Holy Spirit	0
Prendergast	13	Lansdale Cath.	0

Independent

FOOTBALL

POP MILLER CONFERENCE

[illegible]

NORTHEAST COOPERATIVE LEAGUE

[illegible]

POP WARNER CONFERENCE

[illegible]

PHILA. COOPERATIVE LEAGUE

[illegible]

OTHER GAMES

[illegible]

Continued on Page 29, Column 3

Steelers Romp; Worst Loss for Browns, 55-27

PITTSBURGH, Oct. 17 (UP).—The Pittsburgh Steelers, led by a Jim Finks-to-Ray Mathews passing combination, today handed the Cleveland Browns their worst National Football League defeat, 55-27.

Wearing a protective mask, Finks fired three touchdown passes to Mathews and found fullback Fran Rogel for another score. Mathews scored another touchdown by rushing to set a Steeler individual touchdown record for a single game.

Rookie Johhny Lattner, Jerry Butler and Russ Craft each added single touchdowns to crown the Pittsburgh Steelers' inspired victory.

1ST in 9 TRIES

The previous record for the most humiliating defeat administered to the Browns was set last year by the Philadelphia Eagles with a 42-27 score.

It was the first time in nine meetings today that the Steelers were able to beat the Browns. Otto Graham and Lou Groza, who figured in all previous victories over the Steelers, could not do it today.

The Steelers twice intercepted Graham's passes for springboards to scores and another snag went immediately for a score.

Cleveland	14	6	0	7	—27
Pittsburgh	7	27	14	7	—55

CLEVELAND SCORING: Touchdowns—Reynolds, Jones, Lavelli 2. Conversions—Groza 3. PITTSBURGH SCORING: Touchdowns—Mathews 4, Rogel, Butler, Lattner, Craft. Conversions—Rost 7.

STATISTICS

	Steelers	Browns
First downs	[illegible]	[illegible]
Rushing yardage	[illegible]	167
Passing yardage	257	[illegible]
Passes completed	13 of 17	22 of 29
Passes intercepted	[illegible]	[illegible]
Punts	[illegible]	[illegible]
Punting average	41	40
Fumbles lost	[illegible]	[illegible]
Yards penalized	100	67

Rookie Ace in Victory

PROVIDENCE, R. I., Oct. 17 (AP). — Rookie Charles Hodges played a standout game in goal as the Providence Reds defeated the Springfield Indians, 5-2, tonight in an American League Hockey game.

Reflections

Penn Improves, Needs Drills on Fundamentals

By LEO RIORDAN

Inquirer Executive Sports Editor

THE Penn-George Washington game was drooping toward halftime Saturday when a pressbox wag asked: "Is it true that the Penn franchise will be transferred to Kansas City if the A's stay here?" This side-splitter came with Penn trailing, 0-20, and Temple down 0-20 to Bucknell—after Villanova had lost, 20-0 to Detroit U. Friday.

This peachy coincidence in scores led a keen analyst to inquire: "Can anyone give me a good reason why George Washington won't win by 40 or 50 to nothing?" All hands pooled the possibilities, but couldn't total up to one fairish reason.

Now it was a minute to go to the half, Penn's ball in GW territory. Custom demanded that Penn try some let-'er-rip-McGee passes into the end zone. Usually the would-be receiver makes a wild clutch at the ball like a guy whose hat has been whisked away by Hurricane Hazel, and that's that. But a few hopeful fans always say: "Boy, if he'd held onto that one!"

• • •

But, by golly, he did. Jim Castle, Penn's undiscourageable captain, made a Willie Mays catch on the two—and yelled time-out with the same breath. At that only 17 seconds were left on the clock. Yet Stan Chaplin got the TD. Had the clock run out, it would have been more typical of the luckless Penns this year.

• • •

That TD, to quote your favorite Space Cadet, was the blast-off for a rousing rally from 0-20 to 19-26 to the final 27-32.

Yet no matter how you tune it in, Penn is thoroughly unvictorious in four games. But even a man who predicted that Penn would be lucky to win three games this year—and now humbly asks permission to revise it downward to two games (without any in mind)—is ready to stand up and be counted on the claim that Coach Steve Sebo has a much-improved team.

Castle's chin-up, head-up feat keyed an even more improbable third-period feat. This was pictured in yesterday's Inquirer. It was another pass. GW's Arnie Tranen has two hands on the ball, Castle one—and rather tentatively. Just how Castle outwrestled Tranen and wound up on the ground with the ball is explainable only by the late Knute Rockne's inspirational cliche: "On a pass, the man who wants it most gets it."

This was Castle's peak day, and the team's this year. Between blunders it was pretty close to its potential—one strong eleven and perhaps three sound reserves. Sebo and staff worked themselves red-eyed readying for this game and the kids responded.

Walt Hynoski ran and passed well; Neil Hyland, who still lacks a radar sense due to inexperience gets better on every carry; Joe Callahan, a soph quarterback thrown in cold in big-time does incredibly well; Fred Dustin, Bob Kinlock and Howard Jackson stood out in the line. And all hands did better.

• • •

Yeah, but how come Penn is still unvictorious? Without spring practice, camp drills were cram sessions and Penn is still making first-game errors. The fumbles, offside penalties and poor blocking all reveal lack of time for fundamentals.

• • •

Critics could argue that Sebo tried to transplant a Fancy Dan offense from the Big Ten, where they get ready—with top talent—in the spring to Penn, bound by Ivy rules, but not playing Ivy teams. Maybe you could make a case that pouring 200 plays into kids in camp was over-optimistic, but Sebo was simply showing them the whole range, hoping to buoy their confidence and worry their rivals.

There never was any plan to have 200 plays ready for any one game, but only a manageable number, which would be thoroughly reviewed during each game week.

Realistically, Sebo cut back for W and M, Princeton and GW. He realizes that single wing (a sloppily-ballyhooed formation) is a worrisome mystery to pure T teams meeting only the T. So Penn ran more single wing Saturday. Besides, its 14 Wing T plays were virtually single wing in different dress. Usually the pass went through the T quarterback's legs to the deep back. And the blocking was single-winngish.

Every cut in plays has scraped up a little more time to review fundamentals. A day's practice is barely one hour, 40 minutes. Short-change defense drill and your rival will run wild; neglect offense drill and you'll stand still. Fail to shore up fundamentals and you can't block, tackle, run or pass. It all adds up to a jolly situation like budget balancing.

• • •

Like any coach in such a situation, Sebo had only one guess, and erred once or twice, so did the players. But when a coach can inspire and a team rally from 0-20, all hands rate respect. They are trying to redeem blunders of the previous university administration (as late as 1952) and they must love football to tackle the odds.

• • •

You sense in rival coaches an embarrassment, or maybe they're just scared that the dreamboat spring-practice ban reform will become general.

Rationally, you can't see how Penn can beat Navy Saturday. You couldn't last year either, but it won, 9-6. It will be a contest; this series is that way. Villanova will be the underdog Friday night against Houston at Municipal Stadium; so will Temple Saturday at Brown (conquerors of Princeton).

Outscored 306-82 by their 11 conquerors in 11 starts, our local Big Three may have to enter November before finding a victory. Some fun, eh, kid?

Eagles' end Bobby Walston takes a first-quarter pass from Adrian Burk as Harry Gilmer, Washington Redskins' halfback, makes a futile try at a block. Walston raced for a touchdown after grabbing ball at Washington. (AP Wirephoto)

Corbitt Takes First In AAU Marathon

DETROIT, Oct. 17—(UP)—Ted Corbitt, New York Pioneer Club, took first place today in a National AAU marathon race in suburban Dearborn with a time of 2:33.50 and the Boston AA won the open division team trophy.

Corbitt won the open division, finishing ahead of John DiComandrea, Boston AA, who took fourth in overall competition with 2:46.05.

Rodenberger Duo Wins Hatfield Race

HATFIELD, Pa., Oct. 17.—The team of Dick Rodenberger and Red Lesher was a winning one today in the 100-lap feature stock car race at the Hatfield speedway as the season closed before 4000.

The event was stopped in the 92d lap because Bill Ellis crashed into another racing car in the back stretch. Ellis was thrown out of his car and knocked out. Later, he was sent to North Penn Hospital where he was treated and released.

Bryan Triumphs in 100-Mile Race

SACRAMENTO, Calif., Oct. 17 (UP).—Jimmy Bryan, the Phoenix, Ariz., big car driver built like a fullback, won his second consecutive Sacramento 100-mile National AAA championship race today, winning as he pleased by taking the lead in the ninth lap and holding it all the way to the checkered flag before 10,000.

Bryan, who has cinched the AAA 1954 point championship, lapped every finishing car except second place Jack McGrath, Inglewood, Calif., who was three-quarters of a lap back. Bryan's time was 1:9.08, beating the record of 1:11.05 set by Freddie Agabashian, San Leandro, Calif., in 1949.

October 18, 1954 - Eagles QB Adrian Burk throws league-tying record of seven touchdown passes as the Eagles smothered Washington 49-21

1955

RECORD: 4-7-1, T-4TH IN NFL EAST
HEAD COACH: JIM TRIMBLE

Schedule

Regular Season

Wk. 1	Sep 24	W	27-17	vs New York Giants
Wk. 2	Oct 1	L	31-30	vs Washington Redskins
Wk. 3	Oct 8	L	21-17	at Cleveland Browns
Wk. 4	Oct 15	L	13-7	at Pittsburgh Steelers
Wk. 5	Oct 23	T	24-24	at Chicago Cardinals
Wk. 6	Oct 30	W	24-0	vs Pittsburgh Steelers
Wk. 7	Nov 6	L	34-21	at Washington Redskins
Wk. 8	Nov 13	W	33-17	vs Cleveland Browns
Wk. 9	Nov 20	L	31-7	at New York Giants
Wk. 10	Nov 27	L	23-21	vs Los Angeles Rams
Wk. 11	Dec 4	W	27-3	vs Chicago Cardinals
Wk. 12	Dec 11	L	17-10	at Chicago Bears

Pete Pihos again led all NFL pass receivers with 62 catches for 864 yards. However, the Eagles struggled to a meager 4-7-1 record. Eagles All-Pro tackle Bucko Kilroy started in 101st consecutive game against the Giants, then suffered a career-ending knee injury. Pete Pihos retired at the end of the season. In his nine-year career he managed to catch 373 receptions for 5,619 yards and 63 touchdowns. Hugh Devore replaced Jim Trimble as head coach following the season.

1955 Philadelphia Eagles Stats

Passing	Comp	Att	Comp %	Yds	Y/Att	TD	Int	Rating
Bobby Thomason	88	171	51.5	1337	7.82	10	7	80.0
Adrian Burk	110	228	48.2	1359	5.96	9	17	49.2
Jerry Norton	0	1	0.0	0	0.00	0	0	39.6

Rushing	Rush	Yds	Avg	TD
Hal Giancanelli	97	385	4.0	2
Rob Goode	76	274	3.6	0
Jerry Norton	36	144	4.0	1
Adrian Burk	36	132	3.7	2
Jim Parmer	34	129	3.8	1
Ted Wegert	26	120	4.6	2
Dick Bielski	28	67	2.4	1
Toy Ledbetter	21	48	2.3	0
Bobby Thomason	17	29	1.7	0
Don Johnson	3	1	0.3	0
Bobby Walston	1	-3	-3.0	0
Ralph Goldston	14	-7	-0.5	0

Receiving	Rec	Yds	Avg	TD
Pete Pihos	62	864	13.9	7
Bill Stribling	38	568	14.9	6
Bobby Walston	27	443	16.4	3
Hal Giancanelli	25	379	15.2	1
Jerry Norton	11	125	11.4	1
Rob Goode	10	137	13.7	0
Dick Bielski	8	48	6.0	0
Toy Ledbetter	7	88	12.6	1
Ted Wegert	3	17	5.7	0
Ralph Goldston	2	8	4.0	0
Bibbles Bawel	1	6	6.0	0
Jim Parmer	1	-4	-4.0	0

Punting	Punts	Yds	Avg	Blocked
Adrian Burk	61	2615	42.9	0

Interceptions	Int	Yds	Avg	TD
Bibbles Bawel	9	168	18.7	2
Bob Hudson	3	48	16.0	0
Chuck Bednarik	1	36	36.0	0
Eddie Bell	1	30	30.0	0
Wayne Robinson	1	20	20.0	0
Jerry Norton	1	0	0.0	0

Kicking	PAT Made	PAT Att	PAT %	FG Made	FG Att	FG %	Pts
Dick Bielski	23	24	96	9	23	39.1	56
Bobby Walston	6	7	86	2	3	66.7	30

30 abdefgh★ THE PHILADELPHIA INQUIRER, MONDAY MORNING, NOVEMBER 14, 1955

Trailing by 17, Eagles Rally to Trounce Browns, 33-17, Before Record 39,303

Cleveland's Otto Graham scores from the one in the first quarter as the Eagles' Norm Willey (right) tries to pry the ball out of his hands. The Birds' player with a headlock on Graham is unidentified.

Burk Passes To Stribling Bring 2 TDs

By HERB GOOD

After resembling a club that appeared destined to be chased right out of the park in the first 12 minutes the Eagles had a remarkable reversal of form yesterday. They blasted Cleveland's Browns into submission, 33-17, to the delight of a season record, turn-away crowd of 39,303 at Connie Mack Stadium. Police estimated more than 10,000 were denied admission.

Inspired by the dazzling play of quarterback Adrian Burk and end Bill Stribling, the Eagles overcame an early 0-17 deficit for their third and most satisfying victory of the year in a thrilling, action-packed battle.

END WINNING STREAK

The Birds weren't able to get the upper hand until the fourth quarter when they exploded for two touchdowns and a field goal within three minutes, 54 seconds to hand Cleveland its second defeat and end a five-game winning streak.

The Browns, now 6-2, retained first place in the NFL's Eastern Division despite the loss that helped keep alive the Eagles' slim chances of overtaking them and gave the Birds the satisfaction of breaking even with the champs for the fourth straight campaign.

BROWNS
Sept. 25—lost to Washington, 27-17.
Oct. 2—defeated San Francisco, 38-3.
Oct. 9—defeated EAGLES, 21-17.
Oct. 16—defeated Washington, 24-14.
Oct. 23—defeated Baltimore, 18-13.
Oct. 30—defeated Chicago Cards, 21-20.
Nov. 6—defeated New York, 24-14.
Nov. 13—lost to Eagles, 33-17.
Nov. 20—Pittsburgh.
Nov. 27—at New York.
Dec. 4—at Pittsburgh.
Dec. 11—Chicago Cards.

EAGLES
Sept. 24—defeated New York, 27-17.
Oct. 1—lost to Washington, 31-30.
Oct. 9—lost to Cleveland, 21-17.
Oct. 15—lost to Pittsburgh, 13-7.
Oct. 23—tied Chicago Cards, 24-24.
Oct. 30—defeated Pittsburgh, 24-0.
Nov. 6—lost to Washington, 34-21.
Nov. 13—defeated Cleveland, 33-17.
Nov. 20—at New York.
Nov. 27—Los Angeles.
Dec. 4—Chicago Cards.
Dec. 11—at Chicago Bears.

There were heroes galore among the Eagles as they decisively outplayed the Browns with furious, unrelenting, heads-up ball through the last three periods. But Burk and Stribling were just a bit more brilliant than the others with their finest performances of the season.

BAYLOR ACE SCORES

Burk, who directed the Eagles' for 60 minutes, fired touchdown passes of two and 21 yards to Stribling as he completed 12 of 28 aerials for 198 yards. The former Baylor ace scored in person on a one-yard plunge and he ran the ball smartly on five other occasions for a total of 3[illegible] yards as he kept Cleveland's defense off balance.

Burk, who thrilled the fans with scampers of 17 and 13 yards, stole the show from the fabulous Otto Graham, who had been the big noise in the 21-17 victory over the Eagles at Cleveland earlier in the season.

Graham completed only seven of 17 passes for 150 yards. But he teamed up with Ray Renfro on a 61-yard scoring pass and also scored on a one-yard plunge to account for Cleveland's 17-0 first-quarter lead after tackle Lou Groza kicked a 17-yard field goal. But thereafter Graham was kept under terrific pressure, especially by end Tom Scott.

FOUR SNAZZY CATCHES

In addition to scoring twice, Stribling, who was picked up as a free agent when discarded by the Giants, made four other snazzy catches to account for 123 yards.

He accounted for the season's most spectacular play here when he made a shoestring catch while almost falling on his face in the last minute of the first half. Somehow he managed to keep his balance after grabbing the ball far out in front of him and he raced about 25 yards on a 56-yard play before being tackled from behind on the Cleveland 10 by Ken Konz.

Unfortunately it went for naught as Burk was unable to get off a pass on the last play of the half, being smeared for a seven-yard loss by tackle Bob Gain.

BASK IN SPOTLIGHT

Also basking in the spotlight were:

Bibbles Bawel, who raced 40 snaky yards for a touchdown on one of his two pass interceptions; rookie Dick Bielski, who kicked field goals from the 23 and 40 and place-kicked three extra points.

Defensive halfback Bob Hudson, who not only blocked a kick to pave the way for Burk's TD, but who

Continued on Page 32, Column 4

The Eagles also provided their share of thrills in the game yesterday at Connie Mack Stadium. Here's Pete Pihos being tackled in air by Browns' Ray Renfro after catching a pass from Adrian Burk.

Bears Deadlock Rams for Lead, Win 5th Straight

Chicago Scores 24 In First 19 Minutes; 50,187 Watch Rout

CHICAGO, Nov. 13 (UP).—The Chicago Bears riddled the Los Angeles Rams with merciless efficiency today to rack up their fifth straight victory, 24-3, before 50,187 fans and move into a first place tie in the National Football League's Western Division.

The Rams came within 55 seconds of their first shutout in 91 games, extending back to Green Bay's 16-0 decision in the fourth game of the 1948 season. Then Les McFadin kicked a 41-yard field goal for the only Los Angeles points.

The Bears sealed the verdict in the opening 19 minutes, scoring all their points as quarterback Ed Brown hit on five of six passes for 154 yards, pitching touchdown passes to Harlon Hill for 84 yards and to Gene Schroeder for 35.

HOFFMAN RUNS 47

The other Bear touchdown was by Chick Jagade on a one-yard plunge after Jack Hoffman romped 47 yards to set up the marker. George Blanda, who converted after each Bear touchdown to run his consecutive streak to 133, kicked a 24-yard field goal for the other Chicago points.

The Bears' defensive and offensive platoons shared honors equally, despite the opening drive in which Chicago scored each of the first four times it had possession. The closest the Rams came to the Bear goal was the 22 in the fourth period when Andy Robustelli recovered Rick Casares' fumble.

But Norm Van Brocklin and Larry Morris lost 24 yards in two plays and the chance to score was gone. Both Van Brocklin and Bill Wade were largely unsuccessful in their passing. Van Brocklin connected on nine of 23 for 91 yards, but he had one intercepted and re-

Continued on Page 32, Column 3

Yanks Rout Stars; End Tour Unbeaten

TOKYO, Nov. 13 (AP).—The New York Yankees whipped the Japan All-Stars, 9-3, before 45,000 today to wind up their 16-game Japan tour without a defeat. They tied one game early in the series.

The Japanese made a fight of it for five innings, despite a pair of two-run homers by Yogi Berra and a bases-empty homer by third baseman Andy Carey.

The Yanks led, 5-3, going into the sixth and then the Japanese fell apart. They committed three errors and the alert Yankees scored four unearned runs before the inning was over.

Bob Grim, following Whitey Ford and Jim Konstanty to the mound, shut the Japanese out the rest of the game.

Reflections

Football in Ivy League Packs Glamor, Thrills

By LEO RIORDAN
Inquirer Executive Sports Editor

THE sample Ivy League script that Princeton and Yale used Saturday promises to be a nice thing in the nerve tonic concession around the official Ivy circuit starting next year. Anything that would keep fans' hearts from crowding their collars ought to sell faster than routine program, food and souvenir concessions. That's a tip for Pennsylvania's budget when it gets back to playing kids its own size in 1956.

ROYCE FLIPPIN

Saturday provided a second 1955 look at Princeton, pride of Delaware Valley, USA, a first view of a fine, if ill-starred, Yale squad and a preview of the 1956 Ivy round robin. A lot of things didn't make sense in picturesque Palmer Stadium, but traditional football seldom does. Some fans assumed that Yale's astonishing 14-12 victory over Army powered the 46,000 sellout. Actually, the game sold out a month earlier—before any one could rate either team or know whether Princeton Captain Royce Flippin could play. Traditional football sells on what has occasionally happened in the past, and gets glamorized in the retelling and could happen again! And, by George, it did!

Friday it figured Yale by two TDs, which you trimmed to one to allow for the strange chemical quality in a traditional rivalry. Saturday when Yale took the opening kickoff and made like an Apache war party, it loomed Eli by four. As you know, Princeton won by two, 13-0. This is sense?

Even the top memories of 30 years' football coverage offer no parallel to Flippin's game-turning role for derring-do or drama. Even today it makes no sense. A knee injury, the most mockingly unsolveable football injury, had sidelined him all season. The knee had buckled in one three-play appearance seven weeks earlier. Football is timing. Golfers need practice; footballers scrimmage, then game testing.

In all Flippin played a scant seven minutes Saturday in three successively more testing appearances. At first, Coach Charlie Caldwell was testing. Flippin was largely a decoy. He ran wide while Fullback Dick Martin clawed into the line; he slipped downfield for a surprise pass; he decoyed on a statue of liberty play; he quick-kicked. You could say the knee had held up—so far—when the big third period opening beckoned, after End Joseph DiRenzo nailed Yale's fumble on the Eli 22.

* * *

Now you had football thrills at the summit. **Princeton's stands chanted "Go, Flip, Go!" Alumni recalled his two soph TDs against Yale; his pass for a third; his three TDs last year—the final with 16 seconds left, to win it. But there was no chance for decoys when Princeton reached Yale's 5. One rip off tackle got perhaps a foot, and there was breath-holding until Flip rose from the pile. Then in one furious burst on the old familiar single wing tailback smash, Flip made it, and another legend went into the series and this was the exact play on which he had authored three TDs at Yale last year.**

* * *

Of course, it wasn't just Flippin, but Caldwell's poised, precision, slick single-wing attack, emotionally high for Yale with Flippin as catalyst. Coach Jordan Olivar showed a superbly coached, talented T team, but with less poise. Dean Loucks was a sharp quarter; Denny McGill and Al Ward slashing halves and Curt Coker a sturdy fullback. None graduates, and at least Yale has seen the last of Flippin, a jinx comparable to the Clint Frank-Larry Kelley Yale hex of the mid-1930s. Yale is the best team I've seen lose, 13-0, in a long time; Princeton is another Caldwell classic of single wing symmetry.

Penn, with typical try and lack of success, has cleared its last pre-Ivy obstacle course game. It lost, 40-0, to Army as the City Big Three all were blanked: Villanova, 6-0, by Detroit; Temple, 46-0, by Delaware, another Delaware Valley pride. Delaware is interested in a bid to either the Tangerine Bowl or the Sun Bowl, and rates one.

Penn looks to Cornell Thanksgiving Day as its Ivy takeoff-spot; Red Blaik is getting ready for Navy. It won't be easy. Penn's chances against Cornell seem a mite better by comparison. Unbeaten Drexel rolled over Coast Guard Academy, 27-7, and now has only PMC, beaten, 32-6, by Scranton. Haverford, now a favorite over Swarthmore, beat Susquehanna, 22-7, while the Garnet was clawed, 39-0, by unbeaten Juniata.

Skins Stall 49ers, 7-0, Trail Browns by Game

WASHINGTON, Nov. 13 (AP).—It was thievery in broad daylight today as the Washington Redskins beat the San Francisco 49ers, 7-0. One spectacular play by Washington's Gene Brito set up the winning touchdown as he batted the ball away from Y. A. Tittle and recovered on the San Francisco 33.

The score had been 0-0 up to that point late in the third period, with Washington's defensive squad keeping it so by four times holding the 49ers inside the Redskin 20. Brito, Volney Peters and J. D. Kimmel performed the bulk of the heroics.

GAME BEHIND BROWNS

The victory, achieved before 26,202 fans, moved the Redskins within a game of the Cleveland Browns in the National Football League's Eastern Division. Cleveland lost to Philadelphia, 33-17.

It was only the second time in the club's history that San Francisco was shut out and it was a rookie, Bert Zagers from Michigan State, who inflicted the scoring damage for Washington. He streaked 12 yards around his left end with less than two minutes left in the third quarter.

For the invading 49ers it was an afternoon of frustration. Twice the San Franciscans had touchdowns recalled because of penalties, one on a 68-yard pitch from Tittle to Billy Wilson and the other on a three-yard smack by Joe Arenas.

PASS HIT POST

And to add the final insult, the goal post cost San Francisco a touchdown. Tittle had Wilson all alone in the end zone midway through the second quarter, but his pass hit the post and fell to the ground.

Those four San Francisco scoring shots in the first half all were set up by Washington errors. Twice the 49ers recovered fumbles and twice 49er backs intercepted passes. The four thrusts died on the 17, 8, 3 and 13. Twice Gordie Soltau missed short field goal tries.

But while the 49ers dominated play in the first half, the Redskins were clearly the better team at the finish. In the last quarter they drove to the 49er 14 before penalties pushed them back. Later they got to the 11 before more penalties hurt them. Janowicz missed field goal tries from the 38 and 28.

San Francisco	0	0	0	0	— 0
Washington	0	0	7	0	— 7

WASHINGTON SCORING: Touchdown—Zagers (12, end run). PAT—Janowicz.

STATISTICS

	Wash'ton	San Fran
First downs	[illegible]	[illegible]
Rushing yardage	[illegible]	[illegible]
Passing yardage	[illegible]	[illegible]
Passes attempted	14 of 28	[illegible]
Passes intercepted by	[illegible]	[illegible]
Punts	[illegible]	[illegible]
Punting average	[illegible]	[illegible]
Fumbles lost	[illegible]	[illegible]
Yards penalized	[illegible]	[illegible]

Sports Results

Professional

FOOTBALL

NATIONAL LEAGUE

EAGLES 33		Cleveland 17
New York 17		Baltimore 7
Detroit 31		Pittsburgh 28
Chicago Bears 24		Los Angeles 3
Green Bay 31		Chicago Cards 14
Washington 7		San Francisco 0

EASTERN DIVISION	W.	L.	T.	Pct.	WESTERN DIVISION	W.	L.	T.	Pct.
Cleveland	6	2	0	.750	Chi. Bears	5	3	0	.625
Wash'n	5	3	0	.625	Los Ang.	5	3	0	.625
Pitt'h	4	4	0	.500	Balto.	4	4	0	.500
EAGLES	3	4	1	.429	Grn. Bay	4	4	0	.500
Chi. Cards	3	4	1	.429	San Fra.	3	5	0	.375
N. York	3	5	0	.375	Detroit	2	6	0	.250

THIS SUNDAY'S SCHEDULE: EAGLES at New York; Chicago Bears at Detroit; Los Angeles at Baltimore; Pittsburgh at Cleveland; San Francisco at Green Bay; Washington at Chicago Cards.

BASKETBALL

NATIONAL ASSOCIATION

[illegible]

ICE HOCKEY

AMERICAN LEAGUE

[illegible]

NATIONAL LEAGUE

[illegible]

EASTERN LEAGUE

[illegible]

INTERNATIONAL LEAGUE

[illegible]

SOCCER

AMERICAN LEAGUE

[illegible]

School

FOOTBALL

CATHOLIC LEAGUE

[illegible]

Independent

FOOTBALL

PENN-JERSEY LEAGUE

[illegible]

Continued on Page 31, Column 5

33,982 Watch Giants Turn Back Colts, 17-7

NEW YORK, Nov. 13 (UP).—The New York Giants put a tight rein on Alan (The Horse) Ameche and the rest of the Baltimore Colts today and rolled to a 17-7 victory that ruined the Colts' chance to move into a tie for the National Football League's Western Division lead.

The Giants ran up a 17-0 margin before quarterback George Shaw threw a 20-yard pass to end Jim Mutscheller with less than two minutes to go for Baltimore's only touchdown.

The Giants won on Ben Agajanian's 32-yard field goal, Alex Webster's two-yard plunge and Charley Conerly's 28-yard pass to end Ken MacAfee.

40 YARDS, 13 TRIES

Ameche, former Wisconsin All-America, entered the game leading the league in rushing with 667 yards but was able to pick up only 40 yards in 13 tries.

The Colts, who could have tied the Chicago Bears and Los Angeles Rams for first place if they had won, now have a 4-4 record. The Giants have a 3-5 mark in the Eastern Division.

Don Heinrich started at quarterback for the Giants, but the home club didn't start to move until eight-year veteran Conerly began calling signals in the second quarter.

Conerly's 30-yard screen pass to Kyle Rote and a penalty against the Colts for roughing Frank Gifford as he got off a pass helped the Giants score the only first-half points. Another Conerly pass to Rote put the ball on the Baltimore 25, but the Giants had to settle for Agajanian's field goal with 50 seconds left in the half.

The Giants moved 60 yards in six plays to clinch victory in the third period. Conerly's 20-yard pass to Rote put the ball on the Baltimore two and Webster plunged over from there.

Midway in the final quarter Conerly ended an 80-yard drive in eight plays with his pass to MacAfee in the end zone.

A crowd of 33,982—largest New York home crowd of the season—

Continued on Page 32, Column 7

Rote, Packers Rout Cardinals

GREEN BAY, Wis., Nov. 13 (UP).—Tobin Rote, returning to an old football axiom that the best defense is a good offense, passed, ran and quarterbacked the Green Bay Packers to a 31-14 victory over the Chicago Cardinals today.

The Cardinals, in one of their few bright spots, came close to a National Football League record when rookie back Ogden Compton from Hardin-Simmons threw from his own end zone to Dick Lane near midfield for a 98 yard pass-run touchdown.

It was the first meeting between the two teams since 1949 and the first Packers victory in eight games. The win in the home finale broke a three-game losing streak for Green Bay.

In the first half, Green Bay scored 24 points, had 16 first downs to two for the Cardinals, outrushed them, 132 to 27, and outpassed them, 125 to 48 yards. Until the last play of the half, when Ollie Matson hit Dick Brubaker with a 43-yard pass, Chicago had gained only 27 yards and made one first down.

TRIPPI IN GAME

Charlie Trippi made his first appearance for the Cardinals since being seriously injured in an exhibition game.

Rote, ably supported by the running of Howie Ferguson, Joe Johnson and Carmichael, accounted for four touchdowns passing and running. He completed 10 of 29 passes for 149 yards.

Washington's touchdown follow-

Continued on Page 32, Column 3

UCLA Loses Knox Until Rose Bowl

LOS ANGELES, Nov. 13 (AP).—The UCLA Bruins have lost their air arm via a broken leg.

Halfback Ronnie Knox, the publicized transfer from California, suffered the break in the opening moments against Washington yesterday. He can't run for an estimated five weeks, but the team physician says he should be ready in time for the Rose Bowl Jan. 2.

His loss will be felt keenly on Saturday in the Bruin's televised traditional cross-town battle with the University of Southern California since he constitutes virtually all of the team's passing attack. UCLA, beaten early in the season by Maryland, remains undefeated in Pacific Coast Conference play.

Tom Hopkins (52), LaSalle fullback, crowds past off-balance Bob Mastripolito, St. Thomas More fullback, on four-yard rush leading up to Catholic League champions' first touchdown in 22-0 victory. Defenders Jim DiSantis (25) and Gaspare Pellegrini (27) are moving in to stop play. Story on Page 32.

November 14, 1955 - Eagles explode for two touchdowns and a field goal within three minutes and 54 seconds to defeat Cleveland 33-17

1956

RECORD: 3-8-1, 6TH IN NFL EAST
HEAD COACH: HUGH DEVORE

SCHEDULE

REGULAR SEASON

Wk. 1	Sep 30	L	27-7	at Los Angeles Rams
Wk. 2	Oct 6	W	13-9	vs Washington Redskins
Wk. 3	Oct 14	W	35-21	at Pittsburgh Steelers
Wk. 4	Oct 21	L	20-6	vs Chicago Cardinals
Wk. 5	Oct 28	L	20-3	at New York Giants
Wk. 6	Nov 4	L	28-17	at Chicago Cardinals
Wk. 7	Nov 11	W	14-7	vs Pittsburgh Steelers
Wk. 8	Nov 18	L	16-0	vs Cleveland Browns
Wk. 9	Nov 25	T	10-10	vs San Francisco 49ers
Wk. 10	Dec 2	L	17-14	at Cleveland Browns
Wk. 11	Dec 9	L	19-17	at Washington Redskins
Wk. 12	Dec 15	L	21-7	vs New York Giants

The fans witnessed 17 players getting injured during the season, while losing another seven starters to retirement. The Eagles offense never took flight, as they struggled to score 143 points on the season while landing in last place with a terrible 3-8-1 record. Despite the struggles during the frustrating season, the Eagles defense continued to be one of the strongest in the league, allowing just 215 points.

1956 PHILADELPHIA EAGLES STATS

Passing	Comp	Att	Comp %	Yds	Y/Att	TD	Int	Rating
Bobby Thomason	82	164	50.0	1119	6.82	4	21	40.7
Don Schaefer	1	3	33.3	11	3.67	1	0	84.7
Adrian Burk	39	82	47.6	426	5.20	1	6	36.9

Rushing	Rush	Yds	Avg	TD
Ken Keller	112	433	3.9	4
Don Schaefer	102	320	3.1	2
Dick Bielski	52	162	3.1	1
Hal Giancanelli	42	148	3.5	1
Ted Wegert	47	127	2.7	1
Will Berzinski	15	72	4.8	0
Adrian Burk	17	61	3.6	0
Bobby Thomason	21	48	2.3	2
Bob Smith	9	8	0.9	0
Jim Parmer	1	-2	-2.0	0

Interceptions	Int	Yds	Avg	TD
Eddie Bell	4	61	15.3	1
Lee Riley	3	57	19.0	0
Jerry Norton	2	34	17.0	0
Chuck Bednarik	2	0	0.0	0
Bibbles Bawel	1	33	33.0	0
Tom Brookshier	1	31	31.0	0
Rocky Ryan	1	17	17.0	0
Tom Scott	1	12	12.0	0
Marion Campbell	1	1	1.0	0

Receiving	Rec	Yds	Avg	TD
Bobby Walston	39	590	15.1	3
Don Schaefer	13	117	9.0	0
Pete Retzlaff	12	159	13.3	0
Hank Burnine	10	208	20.8	2
John Bredice	10	146	14.6	1
Hal Giancanelli	10	104	10.4	0
Dick Bielski	8	63	7.9	0
Ken Keller	7	36	5.1	0
Ted Wegert	6	46	7.7	0
Will Berzinski	3	35	11.7	0
Bill Stribling	2	11	5.5	0
Rocky Ryan	1	31	31.0	0
Lee Riley	1	10	10.0	0

Punting	Punts	Yds	Avg	Blocked
Adrian Burk	68	2843	41.8	0

Kicking	PAT Made	PAT Att	PAT %	FG Made	FG Att	FG %	Pts
Bobby Walston	17	18	94	6	13	46.2	53
Dick Bielski	0	0	0	0	1	0.0	6

Yanks, Ford Win on Slaughter's 3-Run HR

The Philadelphia Inquirer
PUBLIC LEDGER
An Independent Newspaper for All the People
SUNDAY MORNING, OCTOBER 7, 1956
SPORTS SECTION

UP Telephoto

Here's the start of the play in ninth inning yesterday that stopped the Dodgers. Yankee outfielders Mickey Mantle (left) and Hank Bauer wait for Carl Furillo's drive (arrow) to bounce off the wall.

AP Wirephoto

Here, third baseman Andy Carey takes Billy Martin's relay from Bauer and puts it on the headfirst sliding Furillo trying to stretch his double into a triple. Ump Hank Soar calls Furillo, "Out!"

AP Wirephoto

Carey tumbles over the hatless Dodger who futilely clutches third base. The play, leading off the inning, is tops defensively in the Series thus far. It preserved the Yankees' slim two-run lead.

Brooks Lose, 5-3, Before 73,977 in 3d Series Game

By OSCAR FRALEY

NEW YORK, Oct. 6 (UP).—Forty-year-old Country Slaughter, an old pro who refuses to go down the other side of the baseball hill, came up with a three-run homer today that gave the New York Yankees a 5-3 victory and their first win over the Brooklyn Dodgers after two straight World Series defeats.

The Yankees had their backs tight against the Yankee Stadium wall—two games down and trailing 2-1—and were as gloomy as the cloudy skies above when the old warhorse, who earlier said, "I'd play on one leg to get into the Series," strode to the plate with two men on and two away in the sixth.

Mickey Mantle, the Yankees' home run hero, had failed them with a weak popup to first. But

Today's Batteries

Brooklyn: Erskine & Campanella.

New York: Sturdivant & Berra.

Slaughter, who came to the Yankees Aug. 26 and is fighting for a full Series share which would be welcomed with a new baby expected momentarily at home, didn't disappoint the roaring crowd of 73,977.

FORD VICTOR

Old Enos worked the count to 3 and 1 and, in the twilight of his career, reached back 10 years into the past for a blast that put the Yankees on top to stay. Slaughter had hit his last World Series homer in 1946, almost 10 years ago to the day.

Young Whitey Ford, first game loser at Ebbets Field, took it from there. He gave up one more run but fought his way out of a tough seventh inning jam, got a big break in the ninth and won his fourth World Series game by scattering eight hits.

The loser was lanky Roger Craig, who hadn't won a game since August—but might have today except for old Country's blast into the right field stands.

MARTIN HOMERS

The Yanks had tied it up once earlier, on a second inning homer by Billy Martin after the Dodgers jumped into the lead at the top of the second. The Brooks moved ahead by one in the sixth and—after Slaughter's big blow—scored once again in the seventh only to have it matched by the Yankees in the eighth.

Brooklyn, fighting to hang a third straight loss on the Yanks—a deficit from which no team in Series history ever has come back—jumped into the lead in the top of the second when ever dangerous Jackie Robinson walked on five pitches.

Big Gil Hodges, the hitting star of the first two games, lashed a single into the hole at short to move Robinson to second. Robinson took third when Carl Furillo flied to right and trotted casually home as Roy Campanella drove Hank Bauer back to the right field bullpen for the second out.

THREATS FAIL

The wire-tough Martin tied it up in the bottom of the inning when he put all of his 170 pounds into a 1-2 pitch to send the ball into the seats just inside the left field foul line.

Brooklyn made determined bids in the third and fifth. The first time Craig led off with a single, only his second safety of the year, but Ford got out of it with a double play. Then, in the fifth, Campanella opened with a single but, after Charley Neal struck out, Roy was thrown out on a missed bunt attempt by Craig.

The Yankees had threats going in those same innings when Slaughter singled with one out in the third but Martin hit into a double play, and in the fifth when Gil McDougald led off with a Texas League single to right, but Andy Carey struck out and Ford hit into a double play.

BAUER STARTS IT

Brooklyn charged in front in the sixth, 2-1, when Pee Wee Reese tripled to right center with one away, the ball skimming between Mantle and Bauer and rolling to the bleacher wall. Snider drilled a

Continued on Page 2, Column 7

Series Facts And Figures

STANDINGS

	W.	L.	P.C.
Brooklyn (NL) —	2	1	.667
New York (AL) —	1	2	.333

First Game, Oct. 3:
New York — 200 100 000— 3 9 1
Brooklyn — 023 100 00x— 6 9 0

Ford, Kucks (4), Morgan (6), Turley (8) & Berra, New York; Maglie & Campanella, Brooklyn.

Second Game, Oct. 5:
New York — 150 100 001— 8 12 2
Brooklyn — 061 220 02x—13 12 0

Larsen, Kucks (2), Byrne (2), Sturdivant (3), Morgan (3), Turley (5), McDermott (6) & Berra, New York; Newcombe, Roebuck (2), Bessent (3) & Campanella, Brooklyn.

Third Game, Oct. 6:
Brooklyn — 010 001 100— 3 8 1
New York — 010 003 01x— 5 8 1

Craig, Labine (7) & Campanella, Brooklyn; Ford & Berra, New York.

REMAINING SCHEDULE

Fourth game at Yankee Stadium today. Fifth game at Yankee Stadium, Monday, Oct. 8. Sixth game (if necessary) at Ebbets Field, Tuesday, Oct. 9. Seventh game (if necessary) at Ebbets Field, Wednesday, Oct. 10.

FINANCIAL FIGURES

Third Game

Attendance—73,977.
Net Receipts—$429,658.71.
Commissioner's Office Share—$65,948.81.
Players' Share—$224,225.94.
Clubs' and Leagues' Share—$149,483.96.

Three Game Totals

Attendance—144,673.
Net Receipts—$897,818.35.
Commissioner's Office Share—$134,672.76.
Players' Share—$475,887.36.
Clubs' and Leagues' Share—$305,258.22.

Penn Jars Dartmouth, 14-7

Penn line springs a mousetrap to open hole for Neil Hyland to carry ball four yards for Quakers' first touchdown against Dartmouth. Penn right tackle Frank Brody (73) has pulled, inducing Dartmouth's Wayne Kakela to come in and be trapped (to right of ball carrier) by Pete Keblish, the Penn left guard.

1st-Half Scores In Ivy Debut End Loss Skein at 19

By HERB GOOD

Ah, the Ivy League. It's wonderful!

Rub your eyes again, folks. Take a second look. That's really and truly the University of Pennsylvania up there in a first-place tie with Yale and Princeton.

The Penns finally threw off the shackles of defeat and despair by

Sequence pictures of Penn's winning touchdown pass and diagram of another vital play. Page 10.

turning all the pent-up energies of three frustrating seasons against a startled, unnerved Dartmouth College eleven for a clean-cut 14-7 victory to the astonished delight of 15,568 at Franklin Field yesterday.

A beautifully executed 25-yard pass from quarterback Rich Ross to end Dick Schafer late in the first half accounted for the decisive touchdown that got the Red and Blue away to a flying start in the

Continued on Page 10, Column 1

Play on Furillo Crucial Moment, Says Ole Case

By WILL GRIMSLEY

NEW YORK, Oct. 6 (AP).—After a much-needed let up in the Series pressure on the Bronx Bombers, through a 5-3 conquest of Brooklyn's Dodgers today, Ole Case Stengel, the New York nine's sage pilot, put his finger on a brilliant — Yankee — fielding play as the crucial effort of the game.

It was the play at the start of the ninth inning which caught the not-so artful Dodger Carl Furillo attempting to stretch an opening double into a three-base blow.

Furillo sent one of Whitey Ford's pitches into deep right center, then scurried to third like a frightened rabbit.

BAUER-MARTIN-CAREY

Rightfielder Hank Bauer retrieved the ball, shot it to Billy Martin at second, who relayed to Andy Carey at third for the "big out."

"Martin's relay was perfect," Stengel said. "It was an important play in this game."

Martin said Bauer's peg was also on the beam, and he couldn't have made the play without a perfect throw by the rightfielder.

None of the Yankees sought to second-guess Furillo, or Brooklyn's board of strategy, for attempting the gamble when two runs were needed to win the ball game.

"Remember," said Casey, "it

Continued on Page 6, Column 1

Temple Beats Muhlenberg on Rally by 19-14

By DAVE WILSON
Inquirer Reporter

ALLENTOWN, Pa., Oct. 6.—Temple University fought back for a touchdown with four minutes, nine seconds to go, after losing a 13-0 halftime edge, to defeat Muhlenberg College today, 19-14, and end a 10-game losing streak.

The Owls, who had not won since a 20-0 triumph over Scranton University, Nov. 12, 1954, spoiled Homecoming Day for 2000 Muhlenberg rooters. It also gave the Owls sweet revenge for a 7-6 loss last year.

Frank Fahey, who was slowly but surely assuming the role of the goat in this sixth renewal of a series started in 1900, shook off an attack of fumblitis that affected him three times just after the midway point of the fourth quarter to snatch the hero's mantle with a 38-yard pass play that turned a one-point defeat into a glorious triumph.

Temple did not have a monopoly in bobbles, for Muhlenberg fumbled right back to the Owls as they fought viciously down the stretch. On the last of these several exchanges, Lonnie Staton, Temple junior end, recovered a bobble by Bobby Lee, senior halfback from Wayne, Pa., on the Muhlenberg 35.

The recovery by the former Bartram High player set the stage

Continued on Page 4, Column 4

Football Scores

LOCAL

Drexel 13 .... Ursinus 7
Haverford 33 .... Wagner 7
Lafayette 28 .... Delaware 14
National Aggies 12 ... Wilson 12
New Britain 25 .. Trenton STC 14
New Haven 33 ... West Chester 7
PMC 28 .... Bridgeport 6
Swarthmore 13 .. Susquehanna 12
Temple 19 .... Muhlenberg 14

IVY LEAGUE

Penn 14 ...., Dartmouth 7
Princeton 39 .... Columbia 0
Yale 20 .... Brown 2

Standings

	W	L	Pts.		W	L	Pts.
PENN	1	0	2	Harvard	0	0	0
Princeton	1	0	2	Cornell	0	0	0
Yale	1	0	2	Dartmouth	0	1	0
Brown	1	1	2	Columbia	0	2	0

STATE

Army 14 .... Penn State 7
Brockport 12 .... Clarion 7
California 14 .... Pitt 0
Carnegie Tech 19 ... J. Hopkins 13
Cortland 6 .... Bloomsburg 3
E. Stroudsburg 13 Shippensburg 0
F & M 15 .... Dickinson 0
Geneva 7 ...(tie)... J. Carroll 7
Gettysburg 20 .... Albright 6
Ind. (Pa.) STC 14 Edinboro STC 6
Juniata 25 .... Moravian 0
Lehigh 25 .... Bucknell 6
Lock Haven 14 ..... Calif. STC 6
Lycoming 19 .. Lebanon Valley 0
Mansfield 20 ..... King's (Pa.) 12
Millersville 7 .... Kutztown 6
Montclair STC 14; Cheyney STC 6
W & J 14 ...(tie)... Allegheny 14
Westminster 60 ... Grove City 0
Wilkes 12 .... Ithaca 0

EAST

Alfred 53 .... Kings Point 6
Amherst 40 .... Union 27
Bethany 31 .... Thiel 6
Brandeis 13 .... American Int. 12
Connecticut 27 .... Rutgers 7
Delaware St. 46 Hampton Inst. 6
Glenville 21 .... Concord 7
Hamilton 47 .... RPI 0
Hobart 20 .... Rochester 0
Holy Cross 20 .... Colgate 6
Maine 14 .... Vermont 0
Maryland St. 28 ...... Hofstra 8
Navy 14 .... Cornell 0
N. Hampshire 13 Rhode Island 7
Norwich 20 ...... St. Lawrence 7
Springfield 26 ... Northeastern 0
Trinity 40 .... Bowdoin 13
Tufts 19 .... Harvard 13
Upsala 7 .... Bates 6
Wesleyan 19 .... USCGA 12

Continued on Page 7, Column 2

Eagles Erase 9-7 Deficit in Fourth As Thomason TD Tops 'Skins, 13-9

By GENE COURTNEY

The Eagles sent in two boys to do a man's job last night at Connie Mack Stadium—and they succeeded with the help of an old pro.

The old pro was quarterback Bobby Thomason, who scored the winning touchdown as the Eagles rallied to defeat the Washington Redskins, 13-9, for their first National Football League victory before 26,607 rain-drenched rooters.

The boys were rookies Ken Keller, from North Carolina, and Don Schaefer, from Notre Dame. Keller did the bulk of the groundwork for the Eagles in their home debut, carrying the ball 20 times for a total of 67 yards, while Schaefer picked up 40 in 14 attempts and racked up the Eagles' first touchdown in the second quarter.

Keller and Schaefer carried 34 of the Eagles' 40 ground plays and gained 107 of the teams' 108 total. Thomason, who kept his throwing arm under wraps in the first half, as the Eagles led, 7-6, opened up in the second to complete eight of 11 for 104 yards.

After a scoreless first period, when the teams battled on even terms, the Redskins took a 6-0 lead on an 81-yard march to a touchdown at 6:40. The Eagles' defensive unit, particularly Jim Weatherall, Tom Scott and Eddie Bell, was outstanding as it gave up each yard grudgingly.

However, the 'Skins' Leo Elter, former Villanovan; rookie Dick James, and fullback Dale Atkeson, who was never haunted by the cloistered confines of campus life, chewed up yardage, with Atkeson finally tallying from the 3.

The Eagles stormed back after Bell recovered quarterback Al Dorow's fumble on the Redskin 25. Keller and Schaefer then combined to carry the ball to the 7.

One yard short of a first down, coach Hugh Devore tried to send in his field-goal backfield. But Thomason & Company waved them back, and fans' boos turned to cheers as they anticipated a TD.

Thomason kept the ball for a one-yard sneak and a first down, and two plays later, Schaefer crashed two yards for his first touchdown in pro football.

Walston's kick was good, and the Eagles were ahead, 7-6.

The Redskins took the lead in the third period, however. Midway in the period, Washington was stalled and Dorow elected to try for a field goal. Fullback Sam Baker, recently returned from the Armed forces, came in to boot one

Continued on Page 7, Column 5

World Series Box Score

BROOKLYN DODGERS

	B.Av.	ab.	r.	h.	2b.	3b.	hr.	tb.	rbi.	o.	a.	e.
Gilliam, lf	.100	4	0	0	0	0	0	0	0	2	0	0
Reese, ss	.337	4	1	2	0	1	0	4	0	2	3	0
Snider, cf	.300	3	0	0	0	0	0	0	1	4	0	0
Robinson, 3b	.364	3	1	1	0	0	0	1	0	0	0	0
Hodges, 1b	.600	3	1	1	0	0	0	1	0	5	1	0
Furillo, rf	.417	4	0	2	1	0	0	3	0	1	0	0
Campanella, c	.200	3	0	1	0	0	0	1	1	7	0	0
Neal, 2b	.000	4	0	0	0	0	0	0	0	2	2	1
Craig, p	(0-1)	2	0	1	0	0	0	1	0	1	1	0
a-Jackson	.000	1	0	0	0	0	0	0	0	0	0	0
Labine, p	(0-0)	0	0	0	0	0	0	0	0	0	0	0
Totals		31	3	8	1	1	0	11	x2	24	7	1

NEW YORK YANKEES

	B.Av.	ab.	r.	h.	2b.	3b.	hr.	tb.	rbi.	o.	a.	e.
Bauer, rf	.286	4	1	1	0	0	0	1	0	2	1	0
Collins, 1b	.111	4	1	0	0	0	0	0	0	8	0	0
Mantle, cf	.272	4	0	1	0	0	0	1	0	2	0	0
Berra, c	.364	4	1	2	1	0	0	3	1	8	1	0
Slaughter, lf	.583	3	1	2	0	0	1	5	3	1	0	0
Martin, 2b	.273	4	1	1	0	0	1	4	1	1	3	0
McDougald, ss	.222	2	0	1	0	0	0	1	0	4	2	0
Carey, 3b	.167	3	0	0	0	0	0	0	0	1	5	1
Ford, p	(1-1)	3	0	0	0	0	0	0	0	0	0	0
Totals		31	5	8	1	0	2	15	5	27	12	1

a—Flied out for Craig in 7th.
x—Hodges scored on Carey's error in 7th.

BROOKLYN	0	1	0	0	0	1	1	0	0—3
NEW YORK	0	1	0	0	0	3	0	1	x—5

Sacrifice Flies—Campanella, Snider. Double Plays—Martin, McDougald and Collins; Craig, Reese and Hodges; Neal, Reese and Hodges. Left—Brooklyn, 5; New York, 4. Bases on Balls—Craig 1 (McDougald); Labine 1 (Slaughter); Ford 2 (Robinson, Hodges). Strike Out—Craig 4 (Carey 2, Ford, Bauer); Labine 2 (Carey, Ford); Ford 7 (Reese, Snider 3, Furillo, Neal, Campanella). Hits Off Craig, 7 in 6 innings; Labine 1 in 2. Runs and Earned Runs—Craig 4-4, Labine 1-0, Ford 3-2. Loser—Craig. Umpire—Boggess (NL), plate; Napp (AL), first base; Pinelli (NL), second base; Soar (AL), third base; Gorman (NL), left field line; Runge (AL), right field line. Time—2:17. Attendance—73,977.

Lions Beat Colts On Layne's Passes

BALTIMORE, Oct. 6 (AP).—Quarterback Bobby Layne's passes sailed through the mist as though directed by radar for two touchdowns tonight and led to a couple more for a 31-14 victory by the Detroit Lions over the Baltimore Colts.

The National Football League veterans' first three passes hit for 58 yards, the last going 11 yards over the goal to halfback Don McIlhenny. His next one found Dorne Bibble all alone for a 55-yard scoring play before the 42,622 fans, who had braved showers, barely settled down.

Detroit ——— 14 7 0 10—31
Baltimore ——— 7 0 7 0—14

DETROIT SCORING: Touchdowns—McIlhenny [illegible]

BALTIMORE SCORING: Touchdowns—[illegible]

Princeton Wins As Morris Stars

Special to The Inquirer

PRINCETON, N. J., Oct. 6.—Princeton's defending Ivy League champions, picked no better than third in most pre-season ratings, served notice of their power today by walloping Columbia, 39-0, in their 25th meeting before 16,000 fans at Palmer Stadium.

Princeton meets the University of Pennsylvania at Franklin Field next Saturday.

Led by junior tailback Tom Morris, who scored three touchdowns, the Tigers successfully opened their title defense by winning their 23d game in the series with the Lions. They scored at least once in every period and led at the half, 20-0.

19.6-YARD AVERAGE

Morris, a lanky six-foot-one, 177-pounder, was the outstanding back on the field as he averaged 19.6 yards in seven carries and completed a 20-yard pass.

The Tiger tailback opened the scoring in the first period by skirting three yards through left tackle for a touchdown. With 16 seconds remaining to the half, he added another tally by cutting 18 yards inside right end to the end zone.

Although Princeton coach Charlie Caldwell was alternating his tailbacks, Morris made the most of his appearances. Inserted again into the lineup at the start of the third period, the Columbia (O.) speedster capped off his performances with a brilliant 39-yard touchdown sprint around right end.

Columbia was hobbled through-

Continued on Page 6, Column 5

Arcaro Spilled At Paris Track

PARIS, Oct. 6 (UP).—Jockey Eddie Arcaro took a tumble today at the start of a race at Longchamps track. He was not injured.

Arcaro, getting in shape for tomorrow's $120,000 Prix Arc de Triomphe in which he will ride C. V. Whitney's Career Boy, was thrown by his nervous French mount, Montmajour, in a mile and one-half race, the length of tomorrow's classic.

Sam Boulmetis, who will be up on Whitney's Fisherman tomorrow, finished third on a French horse today at Longchamps.

Steelers Stopped, Browns Win, 14-10

PITTSBURGH, Oct. 6 (UP).—Fullback Ed (Mighty Mo) Modzelewski bolted up the middle in the final period for 14 yards and a touchdown that enabled the Cleveland Browns to defeat the Pittsburgh Steelers, 14-10, tonight. The Browns staved off a Steeler threat with a desperate goal line stand in the final minutes as 35,398 groaned.

Steelers ——— 0 10 0 0—10
Browns ——— 0 7 0 7—14

STEELER SCORING: [illegible]

BROWNS SCORING: Touchdowns—[illegible] Modzelewski (14, run). Conversions—Groza 2.

Slaughter Only Hopes His Hits 'Keep Dropping In'—So Do Yanks

AP Wirephoto

Old pro Enos Slaughter (left) and young pro Whitey Ford relax in Yankee dressing room after combining forces to keep team in Series contention.

By ALLEN LEWIS
Inquirer Reporter

NEW YORK, Oct. 6.—An old pappy guy of 40 and a comparative youngster of 27 saved the New York Yankees from fading almost completely out of this 53d World Series today at Yankee Stadium.

Enos Slaughter, the oldest regular in either major league who has been acting like a successful Ponce de Leon, clouted a three-run homer. Whitey Ford, a different pitcher in a different ball park, held back the Brooklyn Dodgers as the Yanks won, 5-3. Without these two, the Brooks would have a 3-0 lead and the Series would be all but over.

Slaughter, who played in his first World Series when Ford was in the eighth grade, met a Roger Craig pitch in the sixth inning with the Dodgers ahead, 2-1, sent it deep into the lower right field stands over the 344-foot mark and trotted home behind two teammates to the thunderous cheers of 73,977 fans.

FORD NOT AT BEST

Then, Ford, while not at his razor-sharp best, gave up no more than one hit an inning the rest of the way. Whitey thus gained revenge for his opening game, three-inning knockout in Brooklyn.

Slaughter, an amazing, bold, almost bald hustler who before today's game weighed exactly the same 188 as he did upon reporting to the St. Louis Cardinals in 1938,

Continued on Page 6, Column 1

1956

October 7, 1956
Eagles rallied to defeat the Redskins 13-9

1957

RECORD: 4-8, 5TH IN NFL EAST
HEAD COACH: HUGH DEVORE

Schedule

Regular Season

Wk. 1	Sep 29	L	17-13	at Los Angeles Rams
Wk. 2	Oct 5	L	24-20	vs New York Giants
Wk. 3	Oct 13	L	24-7	at Cleveland Browns
Wk. 4	Oct 20	W	17-7	vs Cleveland Browns
Wk. 5	Oct 27	L	6-0	at Pittsburgh Steelers
Wk. 6	Nov 3	W	38-21	at Chicago Cardinals
Wk. 7	Nov 10	L	27-16	vs Detroit Lions
Wk. 8	Nov 17	L	13-0	at New York Giants
Wk. 9	Nov 24	W	21-12	vs Washington Redskins
Wk. 10	Dec 1	W	7-6	vs Pittsburgh Steelers
Wk. 11	Dec 8	L	42-7	at Washington Redskins
Wk. 12	Dec 14	L	31-27	vs Chicago Cardinals

The Eagles continued to struggle, finishing with a 4-8 record. However, rookie quarterback Sonny Jurgensen played solid football all season, showing signs of brilliance at times. In their best college draft to date, the Eagles selected Billy Ray Barnes, Tommy McDonald, Clarence Peaks, and Sonny Jurgensen. Following the season Coach Hugh Devore was fired and replaced by Buck Shaw.

1957 Philadelphia Eagles Stats

Passing	Comp	Att	Comp %	Yds	Y/Att	TD	Int	Rating
Tommy McDonald	1	1	100.0	11	11.00	0	0	112.5
Clarence Peaks	2	3	66.7	56	18.67	0	1	70.1
Sonny Jurgensen	33	70	47.1	470	6.71	5	8	53.6
Bobby Thomason	46	92	50.0	630	6.85	4	10	47.2
Billy Barnes	0	1	0.0	0	0.00	0	0	39.6
Jerry Norton	0	1	0.0	0	0.00	0	0	39.6
Al Dorow	17	36	47.2	212	5.89	1	4	35.6

Rushing	Rush	Yds	Avg	TD
Billy Barnes	143	529	3.7	1
Clarence Peaks	125	495	4.0	1
Ken Keller	57	195	3.4	0
Neil Worden	42	133	3.2	0
Jerry Norton	2	73	36.5	0
Bobby Thomason	15	62	4.1	3
Al Dorow	17	52	3.1	2
Tommy McDonald	12	36	3.0	0
Bobby Walston	1	7	7.0	0
Sid Youngelman	0	3	0.0	0
Sonny Jurgensen	10	-3	-0.3	2

Receiving	Rec	Yds	Avg	TD
Billy Barnes	19	212	11.2	1
Bill Stribling	14	194	13.9	1
Bobby Walston	11	266	24.2	1
Clarence Peaks	11	99	9.0	0
Pete Retzlaff	10	120	12.0	0
Tommy McDonald	9	228	25.3	3
Dick Bielski	8	81	10.1	2
Hank Burnine	7	63	9.0	0
Rocky Ryan	4	91	22.8	2
Ken Keller	4	31	7.8	0
Neil Worden	1	3	3.0	0
Bob Gaona	1	-9	-9.0	0

Punting	Punts	Yds	Avg	Blocked
Jerry Norton	68	2798	41.1	0

Interceptions	Int	Yds	Avg	TD
Jerry Norton	4	155	38.8	1
Tom Brookshier	4	74	18.5	0
Jimmy Harris	3	99	33.0	1
Chuck Bednarik	3	51	17.0	0
Eddie Bell	2	38	19.0	0
Frank Wydo	1	25	25.0	0

Kicking	PAT Made	PAT Att	PAT %	FG Made	FG Att	FG %	Pts
Bobby Walston	20	21	95	9	12	75.0	53
Dick Bielski	0	0	0	0	2	0.0	12

28 abdefgh★ THE PHILADELPHIA INQUIRER, MONDAY MORNING, NOVEMBER 4, 1957

Thomason Stars as Eagles Smash Cards

QB Gets 2 TDs, Passes for 2 in 38-21 Triumph

CHICAGO, Nov. 3 (AP). — The Philadelphia Eagles scored 17 points in the first 10 minutes and rambled to a 38-21 victory over the Chicago Cardinals today to pull into a fourth-place tie in the Eastern Division of the National Football League before 18,718.

Two fumbles, an interception and the deadly passing of Bobby Thomason enabled the Eagles to jump into a quick lead. The Cardinals banged away with a touchdown in the second quarter and another in the third to pull within three points but the Eagles caught fire for three touchdowns in the final quarter and an easy victory.

SCREEN PASS HITS

Thomason tossed two touchdown passes in the first quarter but the key play of the game was in the fourth quarter.

With the Eagles leading 24-21 and a third-and-10 situation on their own 39, Thomason completed a screen pass to Bobby Walston who bounced off five would-be tacklers and carried to the Cardinal 25. An interference penalty moved the ball to the Cardinal one and Thomason sneaked over for the touchdown which put the game beyond reach.

Philadelphia's final touchdown came late in the fourth period when Frank Wydo intercepted a pass and ran 25 yards to the Cardinal 22. Several plays later Al Dorow passed to Rocky Ryan for the touchdown and Walston executed his fifth conversion giving him a total of 14 points.

McHAN HITS 16 OF 32

The Cardinals kept their hopes alive until the fourth quarter mainly on the passing of Lamar McHan who completed 16 of 32 passes for 265 yards.

Thomason completed eight passes in 15 attempts for 183 yards.

The Eagles made good use of Cardinal mistakes in racing to the 17-0 first quarter lead. Chicago took the opening kickoff and rapidly moved to the Eagle 24 where Ollie Matson fumbled.

Thomason hit Clarence Peaks with a pass good to the 47. Billy Barnes lost five. Thomason went back to pass, broke loose from a host of tacklers and fired a pass to Bill Stribling who took the ball on the Cardinal 45 and went all the way. Walston converted.

BELL RECOVERS

Philadelphia kicked off and on the second play from scrimmage, Jerry Norton intercepted a McHan pass on the Cardinal 35 and drove to the 18. Thomason stepped back and tossed a 21-yard touchdown pass to Walston.

Again the Eagles kicked off and on the second play from scrimmage, Matson again fumbled and Eddie Bell recovered on the 28. The Cards finally held and Walston booted a 26-yard field goal.

Chicago's only first-half score came early in the second quarter

Continued on Page 29, Column 1

RECORDS

EAGLES

Sept. 29—Lost to Los Angeles, 17-13.
Oct. 5—Lost to New York, 24-20.
Oct. 13—Lost to Cleveland, 24-7.
Oct. 20—Defeated Cleveland, 17-7.
Oct. 27—Lost to Pittsburgh, 6-0.
Nov. 3—Defeated Chicago Cards, 38-21.
Nov. 10—Detroit.
Nov. 17—At New York.
Nov. 24—Washington.
Dec. 1—Pittsburgh.
Dec. 8—At Washington.
Dec. 14—Chicago Cards.

CHICAGO CARDS

Sept. 29—Defeated San Francisco, 20-10.
Oct. 6—Lost to Washington, 37-14.
Oct. 13—Lost to Pittsburgh, 29-20.
Oct. 20—Defeated Washington, 44-14.
Oct. 27—Lost to Cleveland, 17-7.
Nov. 3—Lost to EAGLES, 38-21.
Nov. 10—At New York.
Nov. 24—New York.
Dec. 1—At Cleveland.
Dec. 8—Chicago Bears.
Dec. 14—At EAGLES.
Dec. 22—Pittsburgh.

UP Telephoto

Eagles are bigger and stronger birds than Cardinals, so it takes two of the latter to bring down one of the former, Clarence Peaks, yesterday at Chicago. Peaks helped Eagles to 38-21 victory by gaining eight of his 79 yards on this play.

Steelers, Morrall Jar Colts; Browns Edge 'Skins, 21-17

Baltimore Drops 3d in Row, 19-13

BALTIMORE, Nov. 3 (UP).—Earl Morrall threw two touchdown passes to Ray Mathews today as the Pittsburgh Steelers defeated the fading Baltimore Colts, 19-13, before 42,575 but Jack Butler was scarcely less a thorn in the losers' side.

Morrall passed the Colts dizzy for the best passing performance of the year in the National Football League. He picked up 270 yards in 18 completions out of 30 attempts. The previous best this year was by Y. A. Tittle of the San Francisco 49ers, who completed 16 of 26 for 268 yards against the Chicago Bears.

The Steelers made only 15 yards rushing.

Butler blocked Bert Rechichar's PAT attempt on Baltimore's first-period touchdown. Late in the first half, Butler stopped a Baltimore drive when he intercepted in his end zone a pass by George Shaw.

BUTLER INTERCEPTS AGAIN

And in the fourth period, when the Colts seemed to be catching fire for a come-from-behind drive, Butler intercepted a Johnny Unitas pass on the Baltimore 34.

The Colts now have dropped three games in a row after winning their first three games. The surprising Steelers are tied with the New York Giants, one game behind the Cleveland Browns, with a 4-2 record.

Baltimore	6	0	7	0	—13
Pittsburgh	0	7	7	5	—19

BALTIMORE SCORING: Touchdowns—Berry (5, pass from Unitas), Shaw (8, run). PAT—Rechichar.
PITTSBURGH SCORING: Touchdowns—Mathews 2 (48, pass-run from Morrall; 22, pass from Morrall). PAT—Glick 2. Field goal—Glick (16). Safety—McPeak (tackled in end zone).

STATISTICS

	Pittsburgh	Baltimore
First downs	12	17
Rushing yardage	15	168
Passing yardage	270	100
Passes	18 of 30	6 of 15
Passes intercepted by	4	1
Punts	7-41	5-[illegible]
Fumbles lost	0	0
Yards penalized	50	42

AP Wirephoto

Holy Cross' Jack Ringel leaps to grab last-period touchdown pass in front of Quantico's Tom Karnoscak yesterday at Worcester.

Cleveland Holds Division Lead

CLEVELAND, Nov. 3 (AP).—Cleveland's Browns mixed up a devastating ground and aerial attack for three long-drive touchdowns today to defeat the Washington Redskins, 21-17, before 52,936.

The victory gave the Browns a 5-1 record and undisputed leadership of the National League's Eastern Division at the season's halfway mark.

Ed LeBaron, the Redskin's league-leading passer, suffered a mild brain concussion in the second quarter and did not return.

LeBaron was injured when Cleveland's defensive ends, 258-pound Len Ford and 245-pound Bill Quinlan, broke through to throw him for an eight-yard loss on an attempted pass. The 165-pound LeBaron said following the game he had a headache, but "I feel pretty good. I'll probably have some X rays taken tomorrow."

BROWN GAINS 109

Jim Brown, Syracuse All-American, playing his first year of pro ball, joined quarterback Tom O'Connell as the Browns' big guns. Brown gained 109 yards in 21 tries, just 12 less than the entire Redskin rushing output. O'Connell completed eight of 12 passes for 122 yards.

Brown contributed two touchdowns as Cleveland moved 80 yards in 12 plays, 73 in 11, and 65 in 10, for its scores. In the second drive, 36 yards were eaten up by O'Connell's passes, mostly to end Darrell Brewster, who caught five for 103 yards. The final drive, a 65-yarder, was all on the ground.

The Redskins converted an intercepted pass into their first touchdown and a 56-yard punt return into the second after Sam Baker had booted a 10-yard field goal, 35 seconds before the first half ended.

Washington	0	10	7	0	—17
Cleveland	7	0	7	7	—21

WASHINGTON SCORING: Touchdowns—Sutton (2, run), Zagers (56, punt return). Field goal—Baker (10). PAT—Baker 2. CLEVELAND SCORING: Touchdowns—Brown 2 (4, 9, runs), O'Connell (1, plunge). PAT—Groza 3.

STATISTICS

	Redskins	Browns
First downs	12	21
Rushing yardage	106	231
Passing yardage	58	122
Passes completed	5-12	8-12
Passes intercepted	1	1
Punts	5-43	4-35
Fumbles lost	0	2
Yards penalized	15	30

Knicks Trounce Warriors After Celts Trip Nats

Special to The Inquirer

NEW YORK, Nov. 3 — The usually smooth-oiled Philadelphia Warriors' scoring machine clicked only spasmodically tonight and the New York Knickerbockers took advantage of this lapse to carve out an easy 123-105 victory in Madison Square Garden before 14,850.

In the opener, the unbeaten Boston Celtics scored 18 straight points in the second half to beat the Syracuse Nats, 113-95, for their fifth in a row.

JOHNSTON TALLIES 31

Only Neil Johnston gave the Knicks some fits, scoring 31 points, but his partner Paul Arizin was blanketed effectively by Mel Hutchins and tallied a mere 14 points. The Knicks, getting a lift out of Hutchins' torrid defensive play, took the lead near the end of the first period and maintained it thereafter.

The Warriors scored only 14 field goals on 55 tries in the opening half and threatened seriously but once in the latter. Then New York, with eight players scoring in double figures, broke open the game in the final session with a 21-6 scoring outburst to turn the contest into a runaway. The two-team, fourth-quarter total of 82 points was an NBA record.

The Warriors, who play the Knicks in Philadelphia Thursday, got a scare early in the third session when Arizin twisted his ankle going underneath and hobbled off the court. But Paul, his foot taped up, returned to action later in the session with no serious effects.

SHARMAN IN FIGHT

In the first game, the Celtics, still clobbering the rest of the league both with points and fists, had another brawl in this one. Bill Sharman, who capped the second-half drive with 18 points, mixed it up with Nats' player-coach Paul Seymour in a brief but busy scrap during the last period.

Bob Cousy, bedded with the flu the past couple of days, saw a little more than 12 minutes of action but passed well in the 18-0 spurt that put Boston ahead, 93-78, early in the final period to overcome a 78-75 deficit.

Warriors	19	25	24	37	—105
New York	22	30	26	45	—123

FIRST GAME

Syracuse	G	F	P	Boston	G	F	P
Harrison	2	1-1	5	Heinsohn	9	8-12	26
Schayes	7	7-8	21	Risen	2	0-1	4
Hopkins	9	5-5	23	Tsioropulos	4	2-3	10
Kerr	0	0-2	0	Russell	10	3-7	23
Lloyd	3	1-1	7	Nichols	1	0-0	2
Costello	4	3-5	11	Sharman	11	5-5	27
Bianchi	5	4-5	14	Ramsey	5	2-3	12
Hoiup	3	0-0	6	Phillip	1	0-1	2
Seymour	1	2-2	4	Jones	1	0-0	2
Palazzi	1	2-3	4	Cousy	2	1-1	5
Totals	37	21-28	95	Totals	46	21-28	113

Syracuse	27	32	19	17	— 95
Boston	26	33	24	32	—113

AP Wirephoto

A firm if illegal grip on the face mask of Billy Wilson, San Francisco end, is taken by Detroit's Yale Lary, who'll face Eagles here Sunday. Lions lost, 35-31.

49ers Conquer Lions, 35-31, in Last 11 Seconds

SAN FRANCISCO, Nov. 3 (AP). —Quarterback Y. A. Tittle, capping one of his greatest days with the San Francisco 49ers, hurled a 41-yard scoring pass to R. C. Owens with 11 seconds left to beat Detroit, 35-31, today.

It was the fifth scoring push engineered by the 30-year-old field general and came when the cause looked lost to the 49ers and most of the 59,702.

Detroit's Tobin Rote, with 1:20 to go, had just completed his fourth touchdown pass of the game. It appeared Detroit had won and gone into a tie with San Francisco for leadership in the National Football League's Western Conference.

SPECTACULAR CATCH

The seemingly victorious pass followed James Martin's recovery of Hugh McElhenny's fumble on the San Francisco eight-yard line. It proved insufficient.

Instead the lightning hit with Tittle's pass to rookie Owens, who leaped into the air over two Lion defenders for one of his most spectacular catches. That gave the 49ers a 5-1 conference record compared with 3-3 for the Lions and Baltimore.

This seesaw game saw Detroit lead 10-0, the 49ers build up a 28-10 advantage and then trail 31-28 before finally pulling it out.

Rote threw touchdown passes of 34, 31 and eight yards to end Jim Doran and another of 13 to Steve Junker. Bobby Layne kicked all four conversions and added a nine-yard field goal.

SCORES ON SNEAK

San Francisco's opening touchdown came on a nine-yard pass from Tittle to Clyde Conner in the second period. Y. A. personally added the second on a one-yard sneak in a drive abetted by two pass interference calls on Detroit. The second penalty gave the 49ers possession on the one-yard line.

The 49ers led 14-10 at the half. After the intermission, Tittle contributed a surprising 26-yard run to a 50-yard drive that Hugh McElhenny ended with a six-yard touchdown burst.

Tittle passes of 33 yards to Conner and 15 to fullback Gene Babb highlighted the fourth touchdown drive that went 67 yards. Babb tallied from a yard out.

Detroit	7	3	0	21	—31
San Francisco	0	14	7	14	—35

DETROIT SCORING — Touchdowns: Doran 3 (34, pass-run from Rote; 31, pass from Rote; 8, pass from Rote); Junker (13, pass from Rote). Field Goal: Layne (9). PAT—Layne, 4. SAN FRANCISCO SCORING—Touchdowns: Conner (9, pass from Tittle); Tittle (1-ft., sneak); McElhenny (6, run); Babb (1, plunge); Owens (41, pass from Tittle). PAT—Soltau 5.

STATISTICS

	Detroit	San Fran.
First Downs	22	26
Rushing Yardage	137	151
Passing Yardage	271	226
Passes Completed	20-35	21-38
Passes Intercepted by	1	0
Punts	3-39	3-46
Fumbles Lost	0	2
Yards Penalized	71	45

LaSalle Still Tops But North Soars

By LES RIBLER

Undefeated, untied LaSalle (6-0) quickly asserted its superiority over West (0-6) in the Catholic League yesterday by taking a 26-0 lead in the first 12 minutes to drub the victoryless Burrs, 39-0. It was LaSalle's fifth league success, but the hardest part of its schedule—Roman, St. James and North—is yet to come.

North (4-1-1) kept its chances of a second straight championship very much alive by dumping St. Thomas More, 19-6, behind league-leading scorer Greg Puckett, who broke away for three touchdowns to run his point total to 72. The win moved North into second place, ahead of idle Bishop Neumann (4-1).

St. James (2-2) all but eliminated previously unbeaten Roman (2-1-2) from title contention with a 13-6 upset at Chester, and Monsignor Bonner (2-3) halted a three-game losing streak by trouncing Father Judge, 26-6, in other league encounters.

In non-league play, Frank DiGiacomo scored two touchdowns and passed for a third in Gloucester Catholic's 18-6 win over St. Joseph's (Camden); unbeaten Salesianum (6-0) whitewashed St. Matthews (Conshohocken), 22-0, and Pius X (Bangor) overcame a 14-0 deficit to whip Mark Jarmoluk's Lansdale Catholic eleven (1-3), 26-14.

Speedy John Herrera, LaSalle's 5-5 whiz, racked up three of his team's touchdowns and added two placements to raise his season's output to 61, second only to North's Puckett. He didn't run often, but when he did it was for distance. He clicked off 43, on a

Continued on Page 31, Column 5

Sports Results

Professional

FOOTBALL

NATIONAL LEAGUE

EAGLES	38	Chicago Cards	21
Cleveland	21	Washington	17
Pittsburgh	19	Baltimore	13
New York	31	Green Bay	17
Chicago Bears	16	Los Angeles	10
San Francisco	35	Detroit	31

Standings

Eastern Division	W	L	Pct.	Western Division	W	L	Pct.
Cleveland	5	1	.833	San Fran'o	5	1	.833
New York	4	2	.667	Baltimore	3	3	.500
Pittsburgh	4	2	.667	Detroit	3	3	.500
EAGLES	2	4	.333	Los Ange'es	2	4	.333
Chi. Cards	2	4	.333	Green Bay	2	4	.333
Washington	2	4	.333	Chi. Bears	2	4	.333

THIS WEEK'S SCHEDULE: Sunday, November 10—EAGLES vs. Detroit, at Connie Mack Stadium, 2:05 P. M.; Baltimore at Washington; Green Bay at Chicago Bears; Pittsburgh at Cleveland; Chicago Cards at New York; San Francisco at Los Angeles.

BASKETBALL

NATIONAL ASSOCIATION

New York	123	WARRIORS	105
Boston	113	Syracuse	95
Detroit	94	Cincinnati	88

STANDINGS

Eastern Div.	W	L	Pct.	Western Div.	W	L	Pct.
Boston	5	0	1.000	Cincinnati	2	2	.500
New York	2	1	.667	Detroit	2	2	.500
WARRIORS	2	2	.500	St. Louis	2	3	.400
Syracuse	2	3	.400	Minneapolis	0	4	.000

ICE HOCKEY

NATIONAL LEAGUE

Boston	4	Detroit	0
New York	3	Chicago	2

STANDINGS

	W	L	T	Pt.		W	L	T	Pt.
Montreal	7	2	2	16	Boston	5	6	0	10
New York	7	4	1	15	Detroit	4	7	0	8
Chicago	4	5	2	10	Toronto	3	6	1	7

AMERICAN LEAGUE

Hershey	5	Buffalo	3
Providence	6	Cleveland	3
Springfield	3	(overtime tie) Rochester	3

Continued on Page 29, Column 4

Wings, Sawchuk Fall to Bruins, 4-0

BOSTON, Nov. 3 (AP). — Incited by the first local appearance of Detroit's Terry Sawchuk since he quit the Bruins last year, Boston defeated the Red Wings, 4-0, tonight to end strings of six losses and 135 scoreless minutes.

Sawchuk made 48 saves but could not avert the effects of such a barrage in the National Hockey League contest at the Garden.

Pass Interception Gains King's a Tie

LATROBE, Pa., Nov. 3 (AP).—John Ferguson intercepted a pass and rambled 75 yards in the final period today to help King's College play St. Vincent to a 26-26 tie.

The game completed one of St. Vincent's most successful seasons. The Bearcats won five, lost one and tied one, while King's College now has a record of one victory, four defeats and a tie.

Kings	0	7	6	13	— 26
St. Vincent	6	13	0	7	— 26

KINGS SCORING—Touchdowns: Sabeski (42, pass from Kovaly); German (45, pass interception); Schiavi (11, pass from Kovaly); Ferguson (75, pass interception). PAT—Ferguson 2.
ST. VINCENT SCORING—Touchdowns: Demalon (11, recovered fumble); Shalala 2 (16, pass interception; 38, pass from Sullivan); Scalena (23, run). PAT—Mastrean, Fox.

Rangers Win, Paille Saves 39

CHICAGO, Nov. 4 (AP).—Harry Howell's goal midway in the final period gave New York's high-flying Rangers a 3-2 National Hockey League victory over the Chicago Black Hawks at Chicago Stadium tonight, their third straight win.

Howell's goal decided a neck and neck game in which the score was tied twice after both teams fought through a scoreless opening period.

The New York win marked the second successive outstanding performance for goalie Marcel Paille who was called up from Providence yesterday to take over for the injured Lorne (Gump) Worsley. Paille stopped 39 shots and got a cheer from 14,814 fans when he weathered a last-minute barrage to preserve the victory.

Quantico Bows To Holy Cross

WORCESTER, Mass., Nov. 3 (AP). — Tom Greene triggered a 33-14 Holy Cross victory over the Quantico Marines today by firing three scoring passes and contributing two vital defensive saves.

The junior quarterback launched six-point aerials to Dave Stecchi for nine yards, Chuck Pacunas for five and Jack Ringel for 29.

Two pass interceptions, a fumble recovery, and two stone wall stands gave the Crusaders the ball leading to their tallies.

Quantico	0	7	0	7	—14
Holy Cross	13	0	7	13	—33

QUANTICO SCORING—Touchdowns: Lucas (11, pass-run from Wolff); Namak (4, pass from Broderick). PAT: Lucas, Trask.
HOLY CROSS SCORING—Touchdowns: Stecchi (9, pass from Greene), Pacunas (5, pass from Greene), Ringel 2 (5, run; 29, pass from Greene), Toland (18, pass-run from Komodzinski). PAT: Greene 2, Komodzinski.

TEAM STATISTICS

	Quantico	Holy Cross
First downs	11	11
Rushing yardage	81	118
Passing yardage	193	199
Passes	10-24	11-23
Passes intercepted by	2	3
Punts	6-31.6	7-35.1
Fumbles lost	1	0
Yards penalized	65	25

Piston Rally Tops Royals, 94-88

CINCINNATI, Nov. 3 (AP).—Detroit's Pistons swarmed from behind with a fourth-quarter surge tonight that handed Cincinnati's Royals their second straight National Basketball Assn. defeat, 94-88.

The Pistons, hot at the free throw line, took the lead, 88-86, when Harry Gallatin sank two one pointers with less than three minutes left in the game.

Two more good free throws by George Yardley — the game's leading scorer with 23 points—and four points by Chuck Noble kept the game out of Cincinnati reach.

Cincinnati	G	F-FT	P	Detroit	G	F-FT	P
Stokes	5	5-8	15	Thieben	0	0-0	0
Twyman	4	3-1	11	Gallatin	4	6-8	14
Paxson	2	2-6	6	Yardley	3	17-24	23
Piontek	1	0-0	2	Dukes	3	3-6	9
Nicholls	2	0-0	4	Clifton	7	3-4	17
Lavelleie	4	1-5	9	Houbregs	0	4-6	4
Regan	6	3-5	15	Noble	2	2-2	6
Marshall	5	2-3	12	Aiha	0	0-0	0
Duckett	6	2-2	14	McGuire	3	6-7	12
Paulson	0	0-0	0	Shue	4	1-3	9
Totals	35	18-32	88	Totals	26	42-60	94

Cincinnati	23	23	21	21	—88
Detroit	20	24	22	28	—94

Komets Edge Toledo

FORT WAYNE, Ind., Nov. 3 (AP).—The Fort Wayne Komets scored three goals in the third period tonight to overcome a two point deficit and defeat the Toledo Mercurys, 4-3, in an International Hockey League game. The victory broke a four game losing

Bears, in Rally, Top Rams, 16-10

LOS ANGELES, Nov. 3 (AP). —Rookie Jon Arnett of the Los Angeles Rams electrified a crowd of 80,456 when he returned the opening kickoff 98 yards for a touchdown but three field goals by George Blanda and a gift touchdown gave the Chicago Bears a 16-10 triumph today.

Arnett's dazzling performance came before most of the crowd had settled down. The favored Rams' 7-0 margin was shortlived. Halfback Dick Zucco picked up a loose ball fumbled by Tom Wilson of the Rams and ran untouched 43 yards to tie the score.

The Rams went in front again before the quarter ended when Paige Cothren booted a 29-yard field goal. That ended the Ram scoring for the afternoon.

Blanda kicked his first field goal from 29 yards out to tie the score in the second quarter and his second from 17 yards sent the Bears out in front and on to their second straight victory over Los Angeles, their only National Football League wins in six games. The third field goal by Blanda in the fourth quarter more than cinched the game and gave the Rams their fourth loss against two wins in the league.

Chicago	7	3	3	3	— 16
Los Angeles	10	0	0	0	— 10

CHICAGO SCORING—Touchdown: Zucco (43, run after fumble recovery). PAT—Blanda. Field Goals—Blanda 3 (29, 17, 22).
LOS ANGELES SCORING — Touchdown: Arnett (98, kickoff return). PAT—Cothren. Field goal—Cothren (29).

STATISTICS

	Bears	Rams
First downs	17	17
Rushing yardage	78	84
Passing yardage	147	[illegible]
Passes completed	14 of 29	16 of 35
Passes intercepted by	2	0

'Gibraltar' Giants Triumph

GREEN BAY, Wis., Nov. 3 (AP).—The defending champion New York Giants parlayed a 17-point second quarter and a Gibraltar-like goal line stand in the fourth period into a 31-17 National Football League victory over the Green Bay Packers today.

A sellout crowd of 32,070 at Green Bay's new City Stadium watched the Giants' defensive line hold for four downs on their own one to deprive the Packers of what could have tied the score 24-24, early in the final period.

Then, with only a minute and a half to go, Em Tunnell killed off the Packers' last chance by intercepting a pass by Babe Parilli and racing 52 yards for the Giants' insurance touchdown.

The Giants' first score came in the first quarter when Cliff Livingston charged through the Packer line and blocked a punt by Dick Deschaine. The ball rolled 10 yards into the end zone where Sam Huff fell on it for a touchdown. The Packers tied the score a minute later on a 77-yard pass play from Bart Starr to Billy Howton.

But the Giants rolled up 17 points in the second quarter on Ben Agajanian's 12-yard field goal, Frank Gifford's three-yard run and a three-yard pass from Charley Conerly to Ken MacAfee. Fred Cone's 39-yard field goal was the best the Packers could do, and they trailed at the half 24-10.

Don McIlhenny scampered 40 for a touchdown in the third to whittle the Giants' edge to seven points, but New York's defense took over and stopped Green Bay

Scoring

New York	7	17	0	7	—31
Green Bay	7	3	7	0	—17

NEW YORK SCORING: Touchdowns—Huff (recovered blocked punt in end zone), Gifford (3, run), MacAfee (3, pass from Conerly), Tunnell (52, run with intercepted pass). Field goal—Agajanian (12). PAT—Agajanian 4.
GREEN BAY SCORING: Touchdowns—Howton (77, pass-run from Starr), McIlhenny (40, run). Field goal—Cone (39). PAT—Cone 2.

STATISTICS

	Green Bay	New York
First downs	17	16
Rush yardage	228	175
Pass yardage	185	151
Passes completed	11-32	10-22
Passes intercepted by	1	3
Punts	5-33	5-45.4

November 4, 1957 - QB Bobby Thomason scores twice on quarterback sneaks and passes for two more touchdowns to defeat the Chicago Cardinals 38-21

1958

RECORD: 2-9-1, T-5TH IN NFL EAST
HEAD COACH: BUCK SHAW

Schedule

Regular Season

Wk. 1	Sep 28	L	24-14	vs Washington Redskins
Wk. 2	Oct 5	W	27-24	vs New York Giants
Wk. 3	Oct 12	L	24-3	at Pittsburgh Steelers
Wk. 4	Oct 19	L	30-24	vs San Francisco 49ers
Wk. 5	Oct 26	L	38-35	at Green Bay Packers
Wk. 6	Nov 2	T	21-21	at Chicago Cardinals
Wk. 7	Nov 9	L	31-24	vs Pittsburgh Steelers
Wk. 8	Nov 16	W	49-21	vs Chicago Cardinals
Wk. 9	Nov 23	L	28-14	at Cleveland Browns
Wk. 10	Nov 30	L	24-10	at New York Giants
Wk. 11	Dec 7	L	21-14	vs Cleveland Browns
Wk. 12	Dec 14	L	20-0	at Washington Redskins

To give the team a veteran quarterback, the Eagles acquired Norm Van Brocklin from the Los Angels Rams. In week two Van Brocklin threw a club record 91-yard touchdown pass to Tommy McDonald to defeat the Giants 27-24. After that game, the Eagles lost the next four games, then tied Chicago 21-21, lost to Pittsburgh, defeated Chicago, and lost their last four games. They struggled throughout the season and ended in last place with a 2-9-1 record. However, despite the struggles the Eagles would double attendance, moving to historic Franklin Field on the campus of Pennsylvania University.

1958 Philadelphia Eagles Stats

Passing	Comp	Att	Comp %	Yds	Y/Att	TD	Int	Rating
Norm Van Brocklin	198	374	52.9	2409	6.44	15	20	64.1
Billy Barnes	4	6	66.7	104	17.33	3	0	149.3
Sonny Jurgensen	12	22	54.5	259	11.77	0	1	77.7

Rushing	Rush	Yds	Avg	TD
Billy Barnes	156	551	3.5	7
Clarence Peaks	115	386	3.4	3
Billy Wells	24	92	3.8	1
Walt Kowalczyk	17	43	2.5	1
Brad Myers	9	23	2.6	0
Norm Van Brocklin	8	5	0.6	1
Sonny Jurgensen	1	1	1.0	0
Tommy McDonald	3	-4	-1.3	0
Pete Retzlaff	1	-4	-4.0	0

Receiving	Rec	Yds	Avg	TD
Pete Retzlaff	56	766	13.7	2
Billy Barnes	35	423	12.1	0
Tommy McDonald	29	603	20.8	9
Clarence Peaks	29	248	8.6	2
Dick Bielski	23	234	10.2	1
Bobby Walston	21	298	14.2	3
Walt Kowalczyk	8	72	9.0	0
Billy Wells	4	49	12.3	0
Brad Myers	4	25	6.3	0
Gene Mitcham	3	39	13.0	1
Andy Nacrelli	2	15	7.5	0

Punting	Punts	Yds	Avg	Blocked
Norm Van Brocklin	54	2225	41.2	0

Interceptions	Int	Yds	Avg	TD
Bob Pellegrini	4	90	22.5	0
Eddie Bell	2	33	16.5	0
Tom Scott	2	15	7.5	0
Rocky Ryan	1	38	38.0	0
Bob Hudson	1	15	15.0	0
Lee Riley	1	8	8.0	0
Bill Koman	1	5	5.0	0
Walt Kowalczyk	1	2	2.0	0
Tom Brookshier	1	0	0.0	0
Jerry Norton	1	0	0.0	0

Kicking	PAT Made	PAT Att	PAT %	FG Made	FG Att	FG %	Pts
Bobby Walston	31	31	100	6	14	42.9	67

Peaks Gets 4 TDs as Eagles Romp, 49-21

Cards Battered In Birds' Best Attack Since '54

By HERB GOOD

Snapping violently out of a five-week slump, the Eagles crushed the Chicago Cardinals, 49-21, with their most devastating all-around play of the season to the delight of 18,315 at Franklin Field yesterday.

Clarence Peaks scored four touchdowns and Walt Kowalczyk, Tommy McDonald, and Bobby Walston chipped in with one each as the Philadelphia pros exploded for their mightiest offensive effort since scoring the same number of points against Washington in 1954.

RECEIVERS HELP

Sharing the spotlight with this quartet were Norm Van Brocklin and Billy Barnes. The former riddled the Cards' defense with 19 completions in 29 attempts for 318 yards and two of the touchdowns. Barnes contributed 244 yards with his running, pass catching and two pass completions.

The strikes thrown by Van Brocklin, who came within two yards of equalling the best NFL individual passing performance of the season, were made all the more effective by the unusual spirited, hard-running of his receivers.

BREAK 7-7 TIE

Three touchdowns within a five and a half-minute stretch of the second period broke a 7-7 deadlock and gave the Eagles complete control of a lively battle, filled with long pass plays and thrilling runs.

The offense clicked so well that the Eagles outgained the visitors, 515 net yards to 321, surely the best possible answer for their troublesome pass defense.

Peaks scored all three of the rapid-fired TDs that sent the Cards reeling in the second period. He started the deluge by romping into the end zone on a 33-yard pass play that concluded an 80-yard drive.

Then he ploughed over from the one and the two on drives of 37 and 44, respectively. His second tally stemmed from a pass interception by Bill Koman and the third from a sparkling 35-yard punt return by McDonald, a brilliant performer throughout the cloudy, misty afternoon.

CAPS 80-YARD DRIVE

Peaks made his other TD from the one to conclude another 80-yard drive in the final minute of the third quarter. Kowalczyk also scored from the one at the end of a 60-yard drive that gave the Eagles a 7-0 first-quarter lead.

McDonald tallied on a 47-yard pass from Van Brocklin in the third quarter and Walston put the finishing touches to the rout by scoring on a 71-yard, pass-and-run dazzler, engineered by Barnes in the final period.

Barnes' pass, made on the run after taking a pitchout from Sonny Jurgenson, was one of four attempted after Van Brocklin was given a much deserved rest in the fourth quarter.

The only opportunity the Eagles muffed was in the early moments of the final period when they gave up the ball on downs on the 16 after Tom Scott intercepted a pass and ran 10 to the nine on the last play of the previous period.

MATSON HELD TO 32

The Eagles' defensive unit, spearheaded by Marion Campbell, Ed Meadows and Tom Brookshier, did such a good job that the ever-dangerous Ollie Matson was limited to a mere 32 yards rushing as the Cards were held to 105 yards on the ground.

Rushing tactics by the Eagles also made the passing of rookie M. C. Reynolds and Lamar McHan considerably less effective than in the 21-21 stalemate at Chicago two weeks ago.

However, McHan managed to fire a 10-yard pass to Joe Chil-

Continued on Page 27, Column 4

A view from the point of Chicago Cardinals' linebacker shows how Clarence Peaks mounted the line to move ball a yard for one of his four touchdowns.

Quarterback Norm Van Brocklin (11) watches after having made the handoff. Cardinal defenders include Jack Patera (61), Ed Culpepper (73), Ed Husmann (66).

Brown Clips Record, Browns Jolt 'Skins

WASHINGTON, Nov. 16 (UPI).—Jim Brown broke Steve Van Buren's 10-year National Football League rushing record today and led the Cleveland Browns to a 20-10 victory over the Washington Redskins. The big Cleveland fullback, needing 135 yards to tie Van Buren's mark of 1146 yards in a single season, made it with room to spare—152 yards in 27 carries. He also scored twice to come within one touchdown of matching another record — 18 TD's in a season — and would have done it except for 62-yard scoring run that was called back for clipping.

But Brown was not the only hero of Cleveland's hard-fought victory, which bounced the Browns back into sole possession of first place in the NFL's Eastern Conference before 32,372.

It was veteran Lou Groza who contributed what proved to be the winning points with a 25-yard field goal in the closing minutes, a boot that broke a 10-10 tie. Brown's final touchdown—a five-yard cruise around end—came after Cleveland intercepted a desperation Washington pass on the Tribe's 11 with seconds to play.

BROWNS' EARLY LEAD

Until the last five minutes, the underdog Redskins played the Browns to a standstill. They spotted Cleveland an early lead when Milt Plum caught them napping on the third play of the game with a 74-yard pass play to Preston Carpenter. That put the ball on the Washington six and four plays later Brown covered the last yard with a crunching smash off tackle.

Ralph Guglielmi put the 'Skins back in the game a few minutes later when he threw a 64-yard scoring strike to halfback Jim Podoley, and the Redskins went in front briefly on Sam Baker's 35-yard field goal in the second period. But the boot was only necessary because two plays earlier, Podoley dropped Guglielmi's perfect pass in the end zone for what would have been a certain TD.

Groza evened the count on a 10-yard field goal midway through the second quarter and the game stayed deadlocked in a bruising defensive battle until the Browns finally got a sustained drive going with nine minutes left to play.

Washington	7	3	0	0	—10
Cleveland	7	3	0	10	—20

WASHINGTON SCORING—Touchdown—Podoley (64, pass from Guglielmi). Field Goal—Baker (35). PAT—Baker.
CLEVELAND SCORING: Touchdowns—Brown, 2 (1, run; 5, run). Field Goals—Groza, 2 (10, 25). PAT—Groza, 2.

STATISTICS

	Washington	Cleveland
First Downs	[illegible]	[illegible]
Rushing Yardage	[illegible]	[illegible]
Passing Yardage	[illegible]	[illegible]
Passes	[illegible]	[illegible]
Passes Intercepted By	[illegible]	[illegible]
Punts	[illegible]	[illegible]
Fumbles Lost	[illegible]	[illegible]
Yards Penalized	[illegible]	[illegible]

AP Wirephoto

What happened? Well, it seems as if Ram halfback Jack Morris (right) has deflected a pass and Packer Max McGee (85) is about to catch the ball for a score. That's what happened. Story on page 27.

Steelers Upset Giants, 31-10, on Layne's Passes

PITTSBURGH, Nov. 16 (AP).—Quarterback Bobby Layne's pinpoint passing and some of the most aggressive line play ever turned in by a Pittsburgh team gave the Steelers a 31-10 victory over the New York Giants today in a National Football League game.

The upset, in which the Steelers registered their third consecutive victory by overcoming a 10-point deficit, was a severe blow to the Giants' hopes for the Eastern Conference title. The Giants had won three in a row until today, starting the drive three weeks ago by beating the Steelers, 17-6, at New York. They now trail Cleveland by one game.

30,030 SEE GAME

A crowd of 30,030 in balmy weather at Pitt Stadium saw Layne pass nine yards for one touchdown and set up another on a pass play which carried 68 yards. The veteran quarterback also scored two touchdowns on one-yard plunges.

Gary Glick, thanks to the aggressive play of his mates, scored for the Steelers as he picked up Frank Gifford's fumble and ran it back 36 yards.

GIFFORD SCORES

The Giants' lone touchdown came in the first period. Gifford plunged over for the score from three yards out, climaxing a 61-yard drive.

The Giants got their other three points on a 42-yard field goal by Pat Summerall in the second period. He missed two other field goal attempts.

Tom Miner accounted for seven Steeler points, kicking a 43-yard field goal and four conversions.

New York	7	3	0	0	—10
Pittsburgh	0	7	14	10	—31

NEW YORK SCORING: Touchdown—Gifford (3, plunge). PAT—Summerall. FG—Summerall (42).
PITTSBURGH SCORING: [illegible]

STATISTICS [illegible]

Continued on Page 28, Column 3

LaSalle Hits Top On 40-14 Victory

LaSalle High School, defending league and City champion, was assured of at least a first-place tie in the Catholic League race yesterday. The Little Explorers walloped Cardinal Dougherty, 40-14, to stand alone in the lead, after Monsignor Bonner lowered St. James to a second-place tie.

The Chester team's 21-12 upset by Bonner gave St. James and Bishop Neumann identical 6-2 records. LaSalle has a 7-1 mark. Each team plays nine league games.

Neumann stayed in the race by beating Father Judge, 18-8, while in other games, West Catholic defeated North, 28-13, and Roman downed St. Thomas More, 28-0.

GUARINI STARS

Howard Guarini had a field day in leading LaSalle. He scored the first touchdown from the one, passed for three others. His scoring throws all came in the 22-point second quarter, during which LaSalle iced the game.

First he hit Fred Shaughnessy from the 10, then he tossed from the 29 to Gerry Woltemate, who made a diving catch. Finally, he threw 40 yards to Tom McTear, who ran another 25 to complete a 65-yard play.

Joey Maxwell's 17-yard run and Tom Koss' four-yard end sweep accounted for other LaSalle TDs. Dougherty (2-5-1) tallied as John Grispon blocked a punt, recovered the ball and carried it five yards, with Dave Fecak running the last 10.

Ron Grillo's 44-yard run gave Bonner its upset of St. James. It was followed by Bill Grubb's two-point pass to Fran Welsh to give Bonner the lead for keeps, 14-6.

GRUBB'S SNEAK TIES

A run of similar distance by Vince Czyzewski had given St. James a 6-0 start, but Bonner tied on Grubb's one-yard sneak at the end of a 77-yard drive.

After Grillo scored, St. James closed the gap on Charley O'Hara's 45-yard run. But Bonner's lead (14-12) was preserved when Tony Dolcemore blocked Al Filoreto's pass try for two points.

Later, Charley Ricevuto ran

Continued on Page 28, Column 3

Sports Results

Professional

FOOTBALL

NATIONAL LEAGUE

EAGLES	49	Chicago Cards	21
Cleveland	20	Washington	10
Baltimore	17	Chicago Bears	0
Pittsburgh	31	New York	10
Los Angeles	20	Green Bay	7
Detroit	35	San Francisco	21

Standings

Eastern Conference	W	L	T	Pct.	Western Conference	W	L	T	Pct.
Cleveland	6	2	0	.750	Baltimore	7	1	0	.875
New York	5	3	0	.625	Chi. Bears	5	3	0	.625
Pittsburgh	4	4	0	.500	Los Angeles	5	3	0	.625
Washington	3	5	0	.375	Detroit	3	4	1	.429
EAGLES	2	5	1	.286	S. Francisco	3	5	0	.375
Chi. Cards	2	5	1	.286	Green Bay	1	6	1	.143

BASKETBALL

NATIONAL ASSOCIATION

New York 98 ... Minneapolis 90

Standings

Eastern Division	W	L	Pct.	Western Division	W	L	Pct.
New York	[illegible]	[illegible]	[illegible]	St. Louis	[illegible]	[illegible]	[illegible]
Syracuse	[illegible]	[illegible]	[illegible]	Detroit	[illegible]	[illegible]	[illegible]
Boston	[illegible]	[illegible]	[illegible]	Minneapolis	[illegible]	[illegible]	[illegible]
WARRIORS	[illegible]	[illegible]	[illegible]	Cincinnati	[illegible]	[illegible]	[illegible]

EASTERN LEAGUE

Wilkes-Barre 108 ... Hazleton 98

Standings [illegible]

ICE HOCKEY

EASTERN LEAGUE

Washington 6 ... Johnstown 5
New Haven 4 ... Charlotte 2

Standings [illegible]

NATIONAL LEAGUE

Chicago 3 ... Detroit 2
New York 2 ... Montreal 1
Toronto 4 (tie) ... Boston 4

Standings [illegible]

AMERICAN LEAGUE

Springfield 3 ... Buffalo 1
Rochester 5 ... Hershey 1
Cleveland 4 ... Providence 3

Standings [illegible]

SOCCER

AMERICAN LEAGUE

Ukrainian Nats 0 (tie) ... Fall River 0
Phila. Uhriks 5 ... Brookhattan 4

School

FOOTBALL

CATHOLIC LEAGUE

LaSalle 40 ... Dougherty 14
West 28 ... North 13
Neumann 18 ... Judge 8

Continued on Page 28, Column 5

Colts Win, 17-0, Over Bears to Near West Title

CHICAGO, Nov. 16 (AP).—The Baltimore Colts today combined the running of Alan Ameche and the passing of George Shaw with a great defense to hand the Chicago Bears a 17-0 shutout—their first in 149 National Football League games.

The last time the Bears were blanked was in 1946 by the New York Giants, 14-0.

The Colts, who crushed the Bears earlier this season, 51-38, took a stranglehold on the Western Conference lead with a 7-1 record, while the Bears' bid all but collapsed with their third defeat.

48,664 SEE GAME

At one stage of the game, which attracted Wrigley Field's largest crowd of the season—48,664—quarterback Shaw hit on nine passes in a row, including six straight in a 93-yard scoring surge at the outset of the second quarter.

During this drive, Shaw's aerials accounted for 79 yards and was capped by his seven-yard toss to Ray Berry, who made a diving catch in the end zone.

Later in the second period, the Colts scored their only other touchdown on Ameche's 4-yard smash that ended a 60-yard thrust in four plays. Shaw's 22-yard pass to Lenny Moore touched it off and a 32-yard pass interference infraction set up Ameche's TD from the four.

AMECHE GAINS 142

In all, Ameche hammered 142 yards in 26 carries and Shaw made good on 10 of 23 passes for 131. Steve Myhra booted two extra points and a 12-yard field goal in the last quarter.

In losing to the Colts for the fourth straight time, the Bears come closest to threatening a touchdown in the first quarter when they reached the 17 behind Willie Galimore's 17-yard bolt. But a field goal attempt by George Blanda failed.

Galimore again broke loose in the second period in returning a punt 66 yards to the Colt 33. After moving to the 22 they fumbled away the ball.

Colts	0	14	0	3	—17
Bears	0	0	0	0	— 0

COLTS SCORING: Touchdowns—Berry (7, pass from Shaw); Ameche (4, run). PAT—Myhra, 2. Field Goal—Myhra (12).

STATISTICS

	Colts	Bears
First Downs	14	[illegible]
Rushing Yardage	[illegible]	[illegible]
Passing Yardage	[illegible]	[illegible]
Passes	10-23	[illegible]
Passes Intercepted By	[illegible]	[illegible]
Punts	[illegible]	[illegible]
Fumbles Lost	[illegible]	[illegible]
Yards Penalized	[illegible]	[illegible]

Cards Win Two In Japan Finale

TOKYO, Nov. 16 (AP).—The St. Louis Cardinals (14-2) wound up their 16-game Japan tour today by handing the Japan All Stars a double drubbing, 8-2, 4-2.

More than 40,000 American and Japanese, including U. S. Ambassador Douglas MacArthur, 2d, saw the American team overtake the Japanese with a three-run seventh-inning rally to win the second game.

The Cards hammered out 13 hits in the first game, including two home runs by catcher Gene Green. They scored five runs on as many hits in the third inning to put the game on ice. Sad Sam Jones and Phil Paine limited the Japanese to five hits.

FIRST GAME

Cardinals [illegible]
Japan [illegible]
JONES, Paine (6) and Green. SUZUKI, Akiyama (4), Dobashi (5), Fujita (8) and Nomura. HR—Green (2), Nomura.

SECOND GAME

Cardinals [illegible]
Japan [illegible]
Jackson, Brosnan (4), Blaylock (7), Broglio (8) and Smith. Inao, SUGIURA (7), Ono (8), Aramaki (9) and Fujio, Nomura (7). HR—Boyer.

Ridings Dies at 51; Columbia Coach

NEW YORK, Nov. 16 (UPI).—Gordon Ridings, who guided Columbia's basketball team to three Eastern Intercollegiate League championships in five years, died early today of a heart attack. He was 51.

Mr. Ridings was head coach at Columbia from 1946 to 1952. His teams won a total of 94 games and lost 22 for an .810 percentage. He won the Eastern title in 1946-47 with a 15-5 mark, repeated in 1947-48 with a 21-3 record and won a third title in 1951-52 with a 22-1 mark.

Born Jan. 3, 1907, in Marquam, Oregon, Mr. Ridings was a baseball and basketball star at the University of Oregon.

He served as Lt. Commander in the Navy during the Second World War and was with the Fourth Fleet in Brazil.

Rocky Delayed, Ramblers Fret

By FRANK DOLSON

Sickness in Rocky Rukavina's family has delayed the little winger's return to the Ramblers and may, in fact, force him to remain at his Kapuskasing, Ont., home, the Inquirer learned last night.

The Ramblers had announced Monday that Rukavina, a holdout, had agreed to terms over the phone and would report soon. Rukavina had been suspended by the Ramblers for failure to report to camp.

"It's up to Rocky now," Rambler president-manager George Davis admitted. "I talked to him Friday night and thought he'd be on his way by now."

The 5-4½ winger was still in Kapuskasing last night, although unavailable for comment. His father didn't think Rocky would report.

"It's not a matter of salary terms, but family details that are holding him back," Davis emphasized. "I'll have to try to get hold of him tomorrow to see what I can do to help . . . It sure is a mess, but maybe something can still be worked out. We'll know better in a day or two."

Rambler player-coach Doug Adam refused comment except to say: "There'll be an official statement when we get to the bottom of this."

Davis indicated that word of Rukavina's suspension had not been sent to Kapuskasing through a mix-up in the Eastern Hockey League office. Because of that, Rocky has been playing for his home-town team, the Huskies. He even suffered a slight leg injury Saturday night, according to his father.

Chirp Signs

Edgar (Chirp) Brenchley, who resigned as coach and manager of the Ramblers last season, has signed as manager-coach of the Niagara Falls (Ont.) Rockets.

One of Brenchley's players is Alex Zubatiuk, a Rambler in 1957-58.

Amerks Beat Bears

ROCHESTER, N. Y., Nov. 16 (AP). — The Rochester Americans snapped a five-game losing streak by defeating the Hershey Bears, 5-1, in an American Hockey League game tonight.

Gedman Stars As Lions Win

DETROIT, Nov. 16 (UPI).—Gene Gedman, who hadn't thrown a pass all season, today fired one touchdown pass, set up another with a 30-yard toss and scored twice to lead the Detroit Lions to a 35-21 victory over the San Francisco 49ers before 54,523.

Gedman and quarterback Tobin Rote methodically picked apart the 49er pass defense, with Rote clicking for three touchdown passes for the second straight week.

The 49ers led briefly, 7-0, after recovering a fumble on the opening kickoff at the Detroit 28. But San Francisco didn't threaten again until the final period, when the Lions held a 28-7 margin.

Actually, the play that broke the 49ers' spirit came on Detroit's first play from scrimmage after San Francisco had scored. Rote handed off to Gedman, who fired a 36-yard pass to Cassady. The fleet Detroit halfback raced the remaining 45 yards.

The aroused Lions, avenging a last-period loss two weeks ago at San Francisco, came up with a crack passing attack which found rookie Jim Gibbons, Dave Middleton and Jim Doran making circus catches. Detroit three times came through on tough third-down situations and converted them into touchdowns.

Detroit	14	14	0	7	—35
San Francisco	7	0	0	14	—21

DETROIT SCORING: Touchdowns—Cassady (81, pass from Gedman); Gibbons (35, pass from Rote); Gedman 2 (2, run; 21, pass from Rote); Middleton (11, pass from Rote). PAT—Martin 5.
SAN FRANCISCO SCORING: Touchdowns—Perry 2 (1, plunge; 1, plunge); Conner (11, pass from Brodie). PAT—Soltau 3.

STATISTICS

	Detroit	San Francisco
First Downs	21	22
Rushing Yardage	[illegible]	[illegible]
Passing Yardage	[illegible]	[illegible]
Passes	[illegible]	[illegible]
Passes Intercepted By	[illegible]	[illegible]
Punts	[illegible]	4-41
Fumbles Lost	[illegible]	1
Yards Penalized	60	[illegible]

Blades Turn Back Clippers by 4-2

NEW HAVEN, Conn., Nov. 16 (AP).—The New Haven Blades defeated the Charlotte Clippers, 4-2, in an Eastern Hockey League game tonight before 3200 at the New Haven Arena.

Yvan Chasle, Don Davidson, Nick Donaleshen and Hugh Riopelle scored for the winners, who tied an early goal by Charlotte in the first period, added two more in the second and then split goals with the Clippers in the finale.

Herve Lalonde and Ken Murphy scored for Charlotte.

Presidents Win In Overtime, 6-5

JOHNSTOWN, Pa., Nov. 16 (AP).—Winger Wally Kullman pushed in a goal at 1:11 of a sudden-death overtime period today to give the Washington Presidents a 6-5 victory over the Johnstown Jets in an Eastern Hockey League game.

Steve Kuzma led the Washington scoring with two goals. Frank Kuzma, Bernie Bernaquez and Moose Lallo each contributed a goal for the winners.

Penn, Army Win With Haymakers

By JOHN DELL

In boxing parlance, it went something like this: Penn swung nothing but haymakers against Columbia; Villanova and Army were near even in the sparring, but Army also landed several roundhouse clouts; Temple, although overmatched again, gave a good account of itself, but Gettysburg caught it twice with its guard down.

Penn's 42-0 victory, the highest score in the five seasons under Steve Sebo, came on touchdown plays of 90, 87, 54, 41, 23 and 29 yards.

The 90-yarder, which enabled Penn to reach 42 for the first time since their 42-26 defeat of Dartmouth in 1950, was the longest pass play in Penn annals. George Koval threw it to Grev Munger, son of former coach George Munger. The 87-yard run by Fred Doelling was a modern Penn record for a run from scrimmage.

DAWKINS BRILLIANT

Villanova, despite Army's wide statistical advantage in maintaining its unbeaten mark with a 26-0 victory, had the stopper for almost every Army maneuver, except the long ones made by particularly brilliant Pete Dawkins. He scored three times, on an 80-yard punt return, a 46-yard pass play from Joe Caldwell and a six-yard run. Army drove from its own territory to Villanova's end zone only once, late in the game.

Similarly, Gettysburg marched from beyond the midfield stripe once against Temple. The Bullets' other two touchdowns in a 22-6 victory stemmed from recoveries of Temple fumbles 33 and 12 yards from the goal.

Penn, now winner of four straight Ivy League games, has a chance to finish tied for second place on a combination of results, including a Penn victory over Cornell, also 4-2 in the league, on Thanksgiving.

TITLE TILT SATURDAY

Princeton, a 50-14 victor over Yale, and Dartmouth, which beat Cornell, 32-15, meet Saturday at Princeton to decide the title. Princeton coach Dick Colman thinks his Tigers have an excellent chance of retaining their championship, because they "have momentum up."

Colman also denied charges by Yale's Jordan Olivar that Princeton deliberately ran up the score to where it matched the previous high made against Yale by Penn in 1940. Colman declared, "We had everybody and his brother in there, includ-

Continued on Page 28, Column 3

Musical Foes Run the Scale

A trumpet player ran a scale ranging from 25 to 50 yards to make three touchdowns and lead the Philadelphia Music Academy to a 26-12 victory over Curtis Institute in the "Melodey Bowl" football game yesterday at Merchantville, N. J.

The winners also scored on a 40-yard pass from a clarinetist to another trumpeter. The losers' heavy work was done by a tuba player, who raced 60 on an interception, and a trombonist, who passed 35 to a violinist.

The players on the seven-man teams (four linemen, three backs) played without music. Neither school had a band at the game.

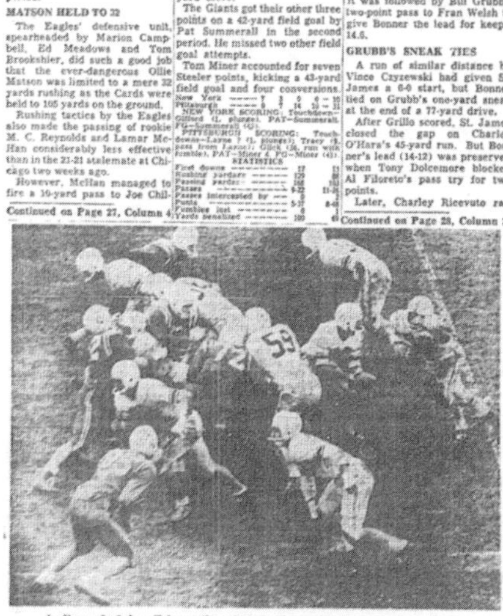

As lines clash in a T-formation play, St. James High quarterback Al Filoreto prepares to hand off ball to Ronald Rogers in second quarter of yesterday's game with Monsignor Bonner at Villanova Stadium. Bonner won, 21-12.

1958

November 17, 1958 - Clarence Peaks scores four touchdowns as the Eagles crush the Chicago Cardinals 49-21

1959

RECORD: 7-5, T-2ND IN NFL EAST
HEAD COACH: BUCK SHAW

Schedule

Regular Season

Wk. 1	Sep 27	L	24-14	at San Francisco 49ers
Wk. 2	Oct 4	W	49-21	vs New York Giants
Wk. 3	Oct 11	W	28-24	vs Pittsburgh Steelers
Wk. 4	Oct 18	L	24-7	at New York Giants
Wk. 5	Oct 25	W	28-24	at Chicago Cardinals (at Minneapolis, MN)
Wk. 6	Nov 1	W	30-23	vs Washington Redskins
Wk. 7	Nov 8	L	28-7	at Cleveland Browns
Wk. 8	Nov 15	W	27-17	vs Chicago Cardinals
Wk. 9	Nov 22	W	23-20	vs Los Angeles Rams
Wk. 10	Nov 29	L	31-0	at Pittsburgh Steelers
Wk. 11	Dec 6	W	34-14	at Washington Redskins
Wk. 12	Dec 13	L	28-21	vs Cleveland Browns

Quarterback Norm Van Brocklin became one of the league's top passers, hitting targets like Tommy McDonald (47 receptions for 846 yards and 10 touchdowns) and Pete Retzlaff (34 catches for 595 yards and one touchdown). Tragedy struck as NFL commissioner (and once Eagles owner) Bert Bell collapsed and died while watching the Eagles defeat Pittsburgh 28-24 at Franklin Field. The Eagles would finish the season with a 7-5 record and tied for second place with the Cleveland Browns.

1959 Philadelphia Eagles Stats

Passing	Comp	Att	Comp %	Yds	Y/Att	TD	Int	Rating
Norm Van Brocklin	191	340	56.2	2617	7.70	16	14	79.5
Sonny Jurgensen	3	5	60.0	27	5.40	1	0	114.2
Billy Barnes	0	7	0.0	0	0.00	0	2	0.0

Rushing	Rush	Yds	Avg	TD
Billy Barnes	181	687	3.8	7
Clarence Peaks	124	451	3.6	3
Theron Sapp	41	145	3.5	1
Walt Kowalczyk	26	37	1.4	0
Norm Van Brocklin	11	13	1.2	2
Bobby Walston	2	8	4.0	0
Joe Pagliei	2	-5	-2.5	0
Tommy McDonald	2	-10	-5.0	0
Pete Retzlaff	2	-11	-5.5	0

Receiving	Rec	Yds	Avg	TD
Tommy McDonald	47	846	18.0	10
Pete Retzlaff	34	595	17.5	1
Billy Barnes	32	314	9.8	2
Clarence Peaks	28	209	7.5	0
Bobby Walston	16	279	17.4	3
Dick Bielski	15	264	17.6	1
Walt Kowalczyk	9	33	3.7	0
Theron Sapp	6	47	7.8	0
Ken MacAfee	5	48	9.6	0
Joe Pagliei	2	9	4.5	0

Punting	Punts	Yds	Avg	Blocked
Joe Pagliei	1	45	45.0	0
Norm Van Brocklin	53	2263	42.7	0

Kicking	PAT Made	PAT Att	PAT %	FG Made	FG Att	FG %	Pts
Bobby Walston	33	34	97	0	1	0.0	51
Paige Cothren	1	1	100	8	18	44.4	25
Dick Bielski	0	0	0	0	5	0.0	6

Interceptions	Int	Yds	Avg	TD
Jimmy Carr	5	65	13.0	0
Bob Pellegrini	3	42	14.0	0
Art Powell	3	17	5.7	0
Tom Brookshier	3	13	4.3	0
Chuck Weber	2	8	4.0	0
Gene Johnson	1	22	22.0	0
Marion Campbell	1	0	0.0	0
Ed Khayat	1	0	0.0	0
Lee Riley	1	0	0.0	0

24 abdh★ THE PHILADELPHIA INQUIRER, MONDAY MORNING, OCTOBER 5, 1959

Record Crowd Plays Part in Dodger Win

Key Single Is Blamed On White Background

By ALLEN LEWIS
Inquirer Reporter

LOS ANGELES, Oct. 4.—For the first time in World Series history, the crowd may have been the deciding factor in victory or defeat Sunday. The greatest collection of baseball fans—92,294—in major league annals gathered in the huge, odd-sized Coliseum and their very presence influenced the Los Angeles Dodgers' 3-1 win over the Chicago White Sox.

In the infield and outfield and even behind the plate, players of both teams agreed it was extremely hard to follow the ball against the multitude of white shirts that formed the background in the third game of the Series.

Carl Furillo's ground single to center that scored the first two runs might well have been handled in a normal ball park with a normal background.

HIT LOOKED LIKE OUT

Furillo's key seventh - inning hit looked as if it could have been fielded when it left the bat—particularly since Sox shortstop Luis Aparicio is an accredited fielding magician.

"I can't see the ball come off the bat," the pleasant Venezuelan said in his locker cubicle after the game. "I got a pretty good jump on the ball but not like I would normally.

"If I had I would have been more in front of the ball. As it was I had to reach for it. I thought I was going to get it, but the ball hopped over my glove," he added with a shrug of his thin shoulders.

BOTHERED CARL, TOO

Furillo himself, a veteran of two seasons here, admitted that the tough background was the only thing he was worried about when he went up to the plate to bat for Don Demeter in the climax of a rather dull game.

"You know how it is here for most day games," the former Reading Rifle said. "We never have anyone sitting out in center field, and before I left the dugout I knew it was going to be tough to follow the ball from what our fellows had told me.

"One reason I took that first pitch—a curve ball—was because I wanted to find out how hard it was to see. Then he threw me a sinker and I hit it and that was that.

BIG HIT IN PLAYOFF

"But the big hit for me was the one the other day against the Braves (that helped win the game in the 12th inning). I'd have to say this was sort of an anti-climax," said Furillo, who added he hoped to play two more years and then retire — as a Dodger, if possible.

Dodger Manager Walter Alston, who it seems has smiled more in the past week than in the past three seasons combined, thought the background was a factor.

"I not only think it influenced this game," Alston said, "but I think it's going to continue to be a big factor with 92,000 at every game.

"I don't say it will always help us too much, though, because we hardly ever play any day games here. We only played about 12 here this season and then never had that many people. But I think we have the pitching to capitalize on it."

LOPEZ CAUTIOUS

Sox Manager Al Lopez, cautious because he doesn't want to make excuses for his club's defeat, said, "It's a park, a beautiful stadium," implying it wasn't a baseball park.

"I can't say how much the background or our unfamiliarity with it hurt us. It's hard to say."

If the Sox had rallied to pull out the victory in the eighth, when they trailed, 2-0, the "goat"

Continued on Page 28, Column 7

World Series Boxscore

CHICAGO WHITE SOX

	B.Av.	ab.	r.	h.	2b.	3b.	hr.	tb.	rbi.	o.	a.	e.
Aparicio, ss	.286	4	0	2	0	0	0	2	0	0	3	0
Fox, 2b	.333	4	0	3	0	0	0	3	0	3	6	0
Landis, cf	.333	5	0	1	0	0	0	1	0	2	0	0
Kluszewski, 1b	.455	3	1	1	0	0	0	1	0	11	1	0
Lollar, c	.364	4	0	2	0	0	0	2	0	5	1	0
Goodman, 3b	.500	3	0	2	0	0	0	2	0	1	1	0
c-Esposito, 3b	.000	0	0	0	0	0	0	0	0	0	0	0
Smith, lf	.273	4	0	0	0	0	0	0	0	0	0	0
Rivera, rf	.000	3	0	0	0	0	0	0	0	1	0	0
Donovan, p	(0-1)	3	0	1	0	0	0	1	0	1	1	0
Staley, p	(0-0)	0	0	0	0	0	0	0	0	0	0	0
d-Cash	.000	1	0	0	0	0	0	0	0	0	0	0
Totals		34	1	12	0	0	0	12	x-0	24	13	0

LOS ANGELES DODGERS

	B.Av.	ab.	r.	h.	2b.	3b.	hr.	tb.	rbi.	o.	a.	e.
Gilliam, 3b	.167	4	0	0	0	0	0	0	0	3	2	0
Neal, 2b	.462	4	1	2	1	0	0	3	1	3	2	0
Moon, rf	.182	4	0	0	0	0	0	0	0	1	0	0
Larker, lf	.111	2	1	0	0	0	0	0	0	1	0	0
Hodges, 1b	.300	2	0	1	0	0	0	1	0	6	1	0
Demeter, cf	.000	2	0	0	0	0	0	0	0	0	0	0
a-Furillo	.500	1	0	1	0	0	0	1	2	0	0	0
b-Fairly, cf	.000	0	0	0	0	0	0	0	0	0	0	0
Roseboro, c	.091	3	0	0	0	0	0	0	0	9	3	0
Wills, ss	.300	3	1	1	0	0	0	1	0	3	2	0
Drysdale, p	(1-0)	2	0	0	0	0	0	0	0	1	1	0
Sherry, p	(0-0)	0	0	0	0	0	0	0	0	0	0	0
Totals		27	3	5	1	0	0	6	3	27	11	0

x—Kluszewski scored on double play in 8th.
a—Singled for Demeter in 7th.
b—Ran for Furillo in 7th.
c—Ran for Goodman in 8th.
d—Struck out for Staley in 9th.

CHICAGO ———— 0 0 0 0 0 0 0 1 0—1
LOS ANGELES ———— 0 0 0 0 0 0 2 1 x—3

Base on Balls—Donovan—2 (Larker, Hodges); Drysdale—4 (Fox, Kluszewski, Rivera, Aparicio). Strike Outs—Donovan—5 (Larker, Wills, Drysdale (2), Hodges); Drysdale—5 (Aparicio, Smith, Landis (2), Donovan); Sherry—3 (Cash, Aparicio, Landis). Stolen Base—Landis. Sacrifice—Sherry. Double Play—Aparicio, Fox and Kluszewski; Roseboro and Neal; Gilliam, Neal and Hodges. Left—Chicago—11; Los Angeles—3.

	IP.	H.	R.	ER.
Donovan (L)	6⅓	2	2	2
Staley	1⅔	3	1	1
Drysdale (W)	7	11	1	1
(Faced 2 batters in 8th)				
Sherry	2	1	0	0

Hit by Pitcher—By Sherry (Goodman).
Umpires—Hurley (AL), Secory (NL), Summers (AL), Dascoli (NL), Dixon (NL), Rice (AL). Time—2:33. Attendance—92,294.

'Leetie' Bad Bounce Becomes Nightmare For Aparicio, Chisox

LOS ANGELES, Oct. 4 (AP).—A "leetle" bad bounce and a heroic pitcher who tired—that was the story in the glum White Sox dressing room. "If the ball stays down I have a chance to get it," said Sox shortstop Luis Aparicio of Carl Furillo's pinch single that broke up Sunday's third World Series game.

Furillo's shot bounded just out of Aparicio's reach into center field, scoring the first two Dodger runs in the seventh inning.

Venezuelan Aparicio, tabbed as one of the greatest shortstops ever to play in the American League, said:

"I got a good enough start on Furillo's ball, but it took a leetle bad bounce over my glove. The background is rough on fielders. You can't see the ball coming off the bat."

DONOVAN TIRING

Manager Al Lopez said he removed starter Dick Donovan in the game-turning seventh because he thought the big righthander was getting tired.

"No, I didn't ask him if he was tired," said Lopez. "I never ask a pitcher if he wants to come out of a game.

"I still think we have a helluva chance to win this Series. We haven't done anything easy all year. So it will probably be the same thing in this Series."

DICK ACTS BITTER

Donovan, who pitched magnificently through the first six innings, was crestfallen, perhaps a little bitter.

"No, I wasn't tired," he snapped. "Al didn't ask me. After all, he won the pennant and I guess he knew what he was doing."

The Go-Go Sox expressed admiration for Dodger catcher

Continued on Page 29, Column 5

World Series At a Glance

STANDINGS

	W.	L.	Pct.
Los Angeles	2	1	.667
Chicago	1	2	.333

FIRST GAME

At Chicago, Oct. 1
Los Angeles
0 0 0 0 0 0 0 0 0—0 8 3
Chicago
2 0 7 2 0 0 0 0 x—11 11 0

CRAIG, Churn (3), Labine (4), Koufax (5), Klippstein (7) and Roseboro; WYNN, Staley (8) and Lollar.
Home runs—Chicago, Kluszewski 2.

SECOND GAME

At Chicago, Oct. 2
Los Angeles
0 0 0 0 1 0 3 0 0—4 9 1
Chicago
2 0 0 0 0 0 0 1 0—3 8 0

PODRES, Sherry (7) and Roseboro; SHAW, Lown (7) and Lollar.
Home runs—Los Angeles, Neal 2, Essegian.

THIRD GAME

At Los Angeles, Oct. 4
Chicago — 0 0 0 0 0 0 0 1 0—1
Los Angeles 0 0 0 0 0 0 2 1 x—3

DONOVAN, Staley (7) and Lollar, Chicago; DRYSDALE, Sherry (8) and Roseboro, Los Angeles.

REMAINING GAMES

Fourth game, at Los Angeles, Monday, Oct. 5.
Fifth game, at Los Angeles, Tuesday, Oct. 6.
Sixth game, if necessary, at Chicago, Thursday, Oct. 8.
Seventh game, if necessary, at Chicago, Friday, Oct. 9.

THIRD GAME FINANCIAL FIGURES

Attendance	92,294
eceipts	$594,071.76
Players' share	$280,026.60
Commissioner's share	$82,360.76
Clubs and Leagues' share	$46,671.16

THREE-GAME TOTALS

Attendance	187,675
Total receipts	$917,472.03
Players' share	$611,096.86
Commissioner's share	$179,734.35
Clubs and Leagues' share	$267,164.61

Rangers Win, 4-2

ST. PAUL, Minn., Oct. 4 (AP).—The New York Rangers wound up their week-end exhibition series with the Winnipeg Warriors Sunday with a 4-2 victory.

Jim Rivera rides an invisible sled and the White Sox outfielder coasts toward second on an attempted steal in the second inning. Maury Wills covers.

AP Wirephotos

Wills jumps clear of Rivera after tagging him out. Dodgers won to lead World Series, 2-1.

Eagles Romp as McDonald Scores 4

By HERB GOOD

Lifted to startling heights by the tornado-like performance of speedy Tommy McDonald, the Eagles walloped the New York Giants to the astounding tune of 49-21 before 27,023 delighted sun-

Other National League Football Games Page 29

baked onlookers at Franklin Field Sunday.

McDonald, a jet-propelled 182-pounder who always has that vital extra burst in reserve, scored four big touchdowns as the Eagles rebounded with stunning violence from their opening-game loss at San Francisco to even their NFL ledger in their home debut.

Enjoying his greatest hours since coming here from the University of Oklahoma campus three years ago, McDonald scored on pass plays of 23, 55 and 19 yards and returned a punt 81 thrilling yards for the other tally.

Quarterback Norm Van Brocklin, who threw perfect strikes for McDonald's first two scores; rookie Theron Sapp and linebacker Chuck Weber, who fell on a fumble in the end zone, also made touchdowns as the Eagles handed the Giants their worst setback since the Cleveland Browns beat them, 63-14, in 1953.

It was the most one-sided Philadelphia conquest of the New Yorkers since a 45-0 romp in 1948. It was the second straight year Buck Shaw's

Picture on Page 30

charges upset the Giants here after losing their opening game.

The Giants, who overcame last year's loss to win the Eastern title, were never in this one although you'd never believe it by the statistics, which gave the invaders a 333-299 net yardage edge rushing and passing.

The Eagles grabbed an early 14-0 lead, led at halftime, 21-7, and skyrocketed their edge to 42-7 in the second half before the Giants were able to rally for two fourth-period TDs.

Rookie Art Powell, who contributed one of the key blocks on McDonald's punt-return TD in the closing minutes of the first half, provided one of the sunny day's big thrills when he returned the second-half kickoff 95 yards, probably the longest non-scoring such return in the league's history.

Powell had a clear path to the goal, but inside the five he tried to take an extra long stride and it threw him off balance. He stumbled and fell on the two. Assistant Coach Charley Gauer said later he thought Powell stepped in a hole at the same time the rookie lengthened his stride.

Powell had no regrets since Van Brocklin scored on a one-yard sneak three plays later.

But this was a McDonald story from start to finish, another superlative chapter in a career that seems destined to be one of the most glorious in Eagle history.

Although a marked man, McDonald caught six passes for 133 yards all told, and in addition to his spectacular punt return he

Continued on Page 30, Column 2

'Lucky to Win,' Alston Concedes

LOS ANGELES, Oct. 4 (UPI).—Walt Alston frankly conceded the White Sox out-played his Dodgers Sunday and made no secret that he felt "we were lucky to win."

"What else can you say when they get 12 hits and so many walks, and we get only five?" commented the soft-spoken Los Angeles skipper.

"Nope, I'm not going to make any predictions on how many games it will take us to win," he added. "A lot of things can happen yet."

For the most part, the Dodgers' dressing room was uncommonly quiet and one might have gotten the idea they had lost instead of won. Even Carl Furillo, whose two-run single in the seventh proved the key blow, wasn't shouting or carrying on.

'LITTLE SURPRISED'

"I thought that ball I hit was going through the infield," he said, "although I didn't spend too much time looking. I was a little surprised when they called on me to hit for (Don) Demeter. I figured they were going to use Duke (Snider)."

Alston made it clear there never was any doubt in his mind about picking Furillo.

"I needed someone up there who doesn't strike out," Alston explained. "Furillo was the perfect choice because he generally meets the ball. If I wanted the long ball, I would've gone for either (Chuck) Essegian or Snider."

DON'S NOT UPSET

Don Drysdale, who started for the Dodgers, pitched his way in and out of trouble, and gave way to Larry Sherry in the eighth, said he wasn't particularly upset over being yanked.

"Naturally, I would have liked to stay in the ball game," he said, "but he (Alston) came out and told me I had thrown a lot of balls and Sherry was warm. As long as we win, I don't care who wins it."

Charlie Neal was on third base when Furillo came through with his seventh-inning blow and he claimed he thought White Sox

Continued on Page 29, Column 5

Series Lineups

White Sox	Dodgers
11 Aparicio, ss	19 Gilliam, 3b
2 Fox, 2b	43 Neal, 2b
1 Landis, cf	9 Moon, rf
8 Klusz'ski 1b	5 Larker, lf
10 Lollar, c	14 Hodges, 1b
6 Goodm'n, ss	2 Demeter, cf
16 Smith, lf	44 Roseboro, c
5 Phillips, 3b	30 Wills, ss
24 Wynn, p	38 Craig, p

WHITE SOX—3 McAnany; 6 Goodman; 14 Esposito; 15 McBride; 17 Torgeson; 18 Latman; 19 Pierce; 20 Romano; 21 Staley; 22 Donovan; 26 Battey; 27 Lown; 29 Moore; 32 Cuccinello, coach; 34 Cooney, coach; 35 Shaw; 37 Berres, coach; 38 Cash; 39 Gutteridge, coach; 42 Lopez, manager; 49 Arias.

DODGERS—1 Reese, coach; 4 Snider; 6 Furillo; 7 Dressen, coach; 8 Fairly; 16 McDevitt; 20 Repulski; 22 Podres; 23 Zimmer; 24 Alston, manager; 29 Essegian; 31 Mulleavy, coach; 32 Koufax; 33 Becker, coach; 35 Klippstein; 40 Williams; 41 Labine; 45 Churn; 51 Sherry; 53 Drysdale; 58 Pignatano.

TELEVISION—WRCV, Channel 3, 4:45 P. M.; RADIO — WRCV, 1060, 4:45 P. M.

Celtics Defeat Lakers, 107-84

BOSTON, Oct. 4 (AP).—Boston outmaneuvered Minneapolis on a slippery floor Sunday night for a 107-84 National Basketball Association exhibition victory.

The Celtics, defending world champions, made it four straight over the Lakers in their 14-game exhibition tour minus Bob Cousy and Tommy Heinsohn. Cousy was out with the flu and Heinsohn was sidelined by water on the knee.

Rudy Larusso, former Dartmouth star and the No. 2 Minneapolis draft choice, was the game's high scorer with 21 points.

Dodgers 17-10 Series Pick

NEW YORK, Oct. 4 (UPI).—The Los Angeles Dodgers became a 17-10 pick to win the World Series after taking a 2-1 lead in games over the White Sox in Sunday's third game.

Monday's fourth game was rated an 11-10 pick 'em affair by New York odds-makers.

Haney Refuses New Pact, Quits As Braves' Pilot

LOS ANGELES, Oct. 4 (AP).—Fred Haney resigned Sunday night as manager of the Milwaukee Braves, of the National League.

Haney, who led the Braves to two pennants and one world championship in the 3½ years he handled the team, met with owner Lou Perini, president Joseph Cairns, vice president Birdie Tebbetts and general manager John McHale to discuss his future.

He was offered a one-year contract to return as Braves' manager but turned it down.

FAMILY COMES FIRST

Haney said he was perfectly happy with the Braves, but that he wanted to spend more time with his family.

"It is not fair to myself or to my family with whom I have not spent much time while managing," he said.

"Nothing whatsoever that happened during the past season influenced my decision," said Haney.

He obviously was referring to the fact that the Braves lost the National League pennant to the Los Angeles Dodgers in a playoff.

WANTS VACATION

"All the officials of the club have given me their 100 percent cooperation," he added. "Right now I have nothing on my mind except to take a vacation with Mrs. Haney."

The 63-year-old Haney replaced Charley Grimm as manager of the Braves on June 15, 1956. He previously had managed the Pittsburgh Pirates and the St. Louis Browns. He spent most of his playing career with the Detroit Tigers.

Haney won the pennant in '57 and beat the New York Yankees in seven games in the World series. He won the pennant in '58, but lost to the Yanks in seven games after winning three of the first four.

Dodgers Win, 3-1, On Hit by Furillo

By OSCAR FRALEY

Continued From First Page

in 88-degree heat. For those fans sunbathing without shirts and wearing every description of sun hat—constituted a crowd which broke the Series record of 86,288 at Cleveland in 1948 against the Braves. It wasn't the biggest, the Dodgers having drawn 93,103 for a Roy Campanella exhibition against the Yankees last May, but it must have been the loudest.

They roared, cheered and pleaded as the White Sox got three on with only one out in the first and then put three runners aboard in the second, but left two of them on base with the other going out stealing. In the third, the White Sox had two runners and again they died on the sacks.

Inning after inning they had their chances, but two were left aboard in the seventh and others were wiped out in double plays or by Roseboro's arm which threw out three men trying to steal.

There was one out in the seventh when Neal started the winning rally with the first hit since Hodges tapped the only previous Los Angeles hit in the second. Up to this point, Donovan had appeared invincible, not even giving up a walk.

Neal went to second as Wally Moon grounded out to Nellie Fox, but then Donovan wavered. He walked Norm Larker on four straight pitches and walked Gil Hodges on five pitches to fill the bases.

That was all for the big Irishman. Staley, the White Sox relief ace, came on—and so did Furillo.

Furillo, batting for Don Demeter, lashed the single which sent Neal and Larker barrelling across the plate with two big runs as Hodges held up at second. Staley got out of it when Roseboro lined to Fox to end the rally.

The White Sox roared back in a vain attempt to pull it out. Big Ted Kluszewski laced a single to left and went to second as Sherm Lollar followed with a single to right field which Wally Moon lost in the sun.

That was when Drysdale left.

Sherry caused a faint uproar among the few White Sox fans when he hit Billy Goodman on the right knee to fill the bases. But then he fed a double play ball to Al Smith which let Big Klu score with one run, but ended the threat by getting Jim Rivera on a pop to Roseboro.

The Dodgers got that one right back when Maury Wills led off the eighth with a single to right and Sherry sacrificed him to second. He went to third as Gilliam grounded out and scored on Neal's double off Sam Esposito's glove.

Staley kept Neal there as he got Moon to ground out—and then it was up to Sherry.

Young Larry didn't let the Dodgers down. He struck out pinch-hitter Norm Cash, sent a third strike whistling past Aparicio, allowed Fox a single—and then finished striking out the side by getting Landis.

Wynn, Craig Duel Again

Early Wynn and Roger Craig, the starting pitchers in last Thursday's World Series opener, again will face each other Monday in another battle of righthanders at the Coliseum.

Wynn, 22-10 during the regular season for the White Sox, beat Craig in the first game, 11-0, although forced to leave in the eighth inning when his elbow stiffened. Craig (11-5) was routed by the Sox in a seven-run third inning.

But He Has Faith

Furillo's Son Shuns Prayer

From Our Wire Services

LOS ANGELES, Oct. 4.

CARL FURILLO'S 10-year-old son, Butch, sat next to sports writer Dick Young in the Coliseum press box Sunday. When his dad came up to pinch hit, Young whispered to the youngster: "Say a prayer for your old man."

"I don't have to say a prayer," was the answer. "I know my pop. He'll get a hit!" (He did).

* * *

Nellie Fox broke out in fever blisters around the mouth and White Sox trainer Ed Froehlich applied medicine to soothe his lips. Looked like lipstick and he took a ribbing.

"I don't have to make any explanations," he laughed.

Continued on Page 28, Column 6

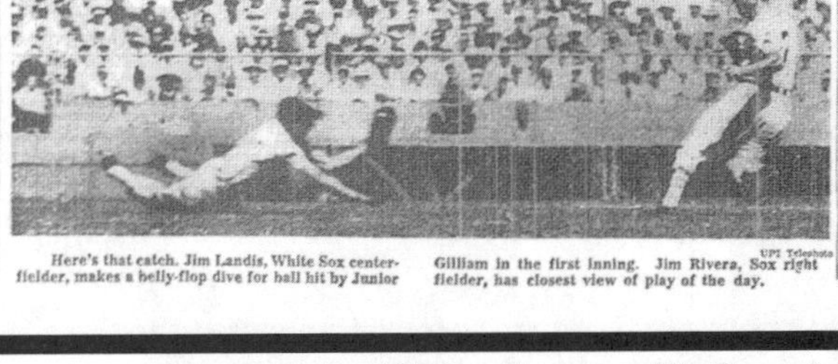

UPI Telephoto

Here's that catch. Jim Landis, White Sox centerfielder, makes a belly-flop dive for ball hit by Junior Gilliam in the first inning. Jim Rivera, Sox right fielder, has closest view of play of the day.

AP Wirephoto

The hit that won it bounds into the outfield, beyond White Sox shortstop Luis Aparicio. Nelson Fox (2) watches the ball, which Carl Furillo hit for a two-run single in the seventh inning.

1959

October 5, 1959 - Tommy McDonald scores four touchdowns as the Eagles soar pass the NY Giants 49-21

1960's Decade in Review

In a decade marked by social upheaval, the football landscape also changes markedly. While the American Football League begins play in 1960, more noteworthy that year is the ascent of Pete Rozelle to NFL Commissioner. Over the next three decades, Rozelle helps the NFL evolve into the most successful and popular league in pro sports. By 1966, with a merger on the horizon, the leagues agree to play the AFL-NFL World Championship Game, which becomes known as the Super Bowl.

1960

Philadelphia captures its third NFL title with a 17-13 win over Vince Lombardi's Green Bay Packers in front of 67,325 fans at Franklin Field. QB Norm Van Brocklin lofts a scoring strike to Tommy McDonald and Ted Dean sets up his own game-winning, 4th-quarter TD run with a 59-yard kickoff return. Basking in the glow of the championship, Van Brocklin and coach Buck Shaw soon announce their retirements.

Chuck Bednarik etches his name into NFL lore for his effort on a single play and for his effort on both sides of the ball. First, in a key win over the Giants, his tackle of Frank Gifford causes a fumble and renders the legendary halfback unconscious. Later, he plays the entire Championship Game at center and linebacker, earning the nickname, "the last of the 60-minute men."

Chuck Bednarik's legendary tackle of Frank Gifford

Head Coaches Buck Shaw and Vince Lombardi

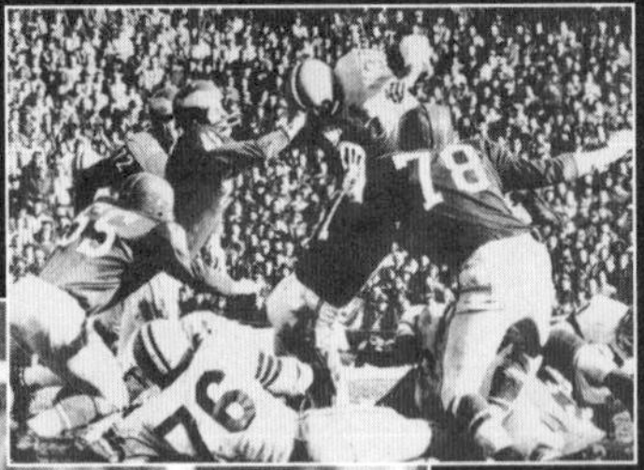

1961

Sonny Jurgensen takes over at quarterback and promptly leads the league and sets single-season Eagles records with 3,723 passing yards and 32 TD strikes. The yardage mark will stand for 26 years. The TD pass figure survives into the next century.

Flanker Tommy McDonald sets an Eagles record with 237 receiving yards in a game vs. the Giants. The record will last beyond the year 2000.

Sonny Jurgensen

1963

The Eagles' franchise changes hands when Washington, DC, real estate developer Jerry Wolman buys the club for $5.5 million.

Halfback Timmy Brown sets an NFL single-season record when he logs 2,436 all-purpose yards.

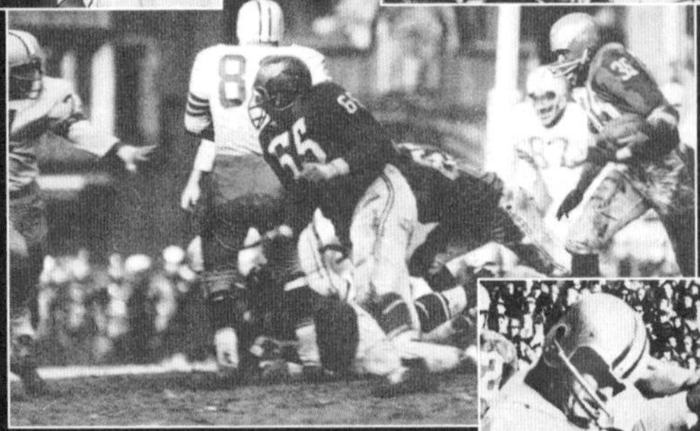

Ted Dean scores winning TD in 1960 Championship Game vs. Green Bay

Tom Brookshier halts Packer Jim Taylor

1965

The Eagles tie an NFL record with nine interceptions in a single game (at Pittsburgh on December 12). Three of the thefts were logged by Al Nettles, two by Joe Scarpati.

1966

Franklin Field is the place where a pair of Eagles set NFL records. Against Dallas on November 6, Timmy Brown becomes the first player in league history to return two kickoffs for scores in a single game. Five weeks later, Al Nelson sets the mark for the longest return of a missed field goal when he runs one back 100 yards for a TD vs. the Browns.

Record-setting return, Tim Brown (22, above at right)

1969

Ownership of the Eagles changes hands for the second time in the 1960s when Philadelphia trucking magnate Leonard Tose pays $16.1 million, a then-record price for a pro sports franchise.

1960's

Decade Win-Loss Record:
57-76-5; (1-0 postseason record)

Home Field:
Franklin Field 1960-69

Playoff Appearances:
None

Championships:
NFL Champion Game 1960
NFL Champions 1960

Head Coaches:
Buck Shaw 1960 (10-2), (1-0 postseason record);
Nick Skorich 1961-63 (15-24-3);
Joe Kuharich 1964-68 (28-41-1);
Jerry Williams 1969 (4-9-1)

Hall of Fame Inductees:
Chuck Bednarik, Bill Bradley, Tom Brookshier, Timmy Brown, Jim Gallagher (executive), Sonny Jurgensen, Tommy McDonald, Pete Retzlaff, Norm Van Brocklin

Award Winners:
Norm Van Brocklin, MVP 1960;
Buck Shaw, Coach of the Year 1960;
Pete Retzlaff, MVP 1965

All Pro:
Chuck Bednarik 1960-61; Tom Brookshier 1960; Don Burroughs 1960-62; Tommy McDonald 1960-62; Jess Richardson 1960; Norm Van Brocklin 1960; Maxie Baughan 1961 and 1964-65; Sonny Jurgensen 1961; Leo Sugar 1961; Tim Brown 1963 and 1965-66; Bob Brown 1964-68; Pete Retzlaff 1964-66; Jim Ringo 1964 and 1966; Tom Woodeschick 1968-69

Pro Bowl Selections:
Billy Ray Barnes 1960, Jess Richardson 1960, Maxie Baughan 1961-62 and 1964-66; Chuck Bednarik 1961; Tom Brookshier 1960-61; Marion Campbell 1960-61; Tommy McDonald 1960-63; Pete Retzlaff 1961 and 1964-65; Norm Van Brocklin 1960-61; Ted Dean 1962; Bobby Walston 1962; Sonny Jurgensen 1962; J.D. Smith 1962; Tim Brown 1963-64 and 1966; Sam Baker 1965 and 1969; Irv Cross 1965-66; Floyd Peters 1965-68; Jim Ringo 1965-66 and 1968; Bob Brown 1966-67; Norm Snead 1966; Tom Woodeschick 1969

First Game of the Decade:
September 25, 1960, loss to the Cleveland Browns 41-24

Last Game of the Decade:
December 21, 1969, loss to San Francisco 49ers 14-13

Largest Margin of Victory:
October 22, 1961, huge win over the Dallas Cowboys 43-7

Largest Margin of Defeat:
October 9, 1966, losing to the Dallas Cowboys 56-7

Eagle Firsts of the Decade:

First Hall of Fame Inductee - Bert Bell became a charter member of the Pro Football Hall of Fame in 1963

First 3,000-Yard Passer – Sonny Jurgensen threw 3,723 total yards in 1961

First 30 TD Passes – Sonny Jurgensen threw 32 touchdowns during the 1961 season

First 2 Kickoff Returns for Touch-downs in One Game – November 6, 1966, Tim Brown returned two kickoffs for touchdowns of 93 and 90 yards respectively

1960

RECORD: 10-2, 1ST IN NFL EAST
HEAD COACH: BUCK SHAW

Schedule

Regular Season

Wk. 3	Sep 25	L	41-24	vs Cleveland Browns
Wk. 4	Sep 30	W	27-25	at Dallas Cowboys
Wk. 5	Oct 9	W	31-27	vs St. Louis Cardinals
Wk. 6	Oct 16	W	28-10	vs Detroit Lions
Wk. 7	Oct 23	W	31-29	at Cleveland Browns
Wk. 9	Nov 6	W	34-7	vs Pittsburgh Steelers
Wk. 10	Nov 13	W	19-13	vs Washington Redskins
Wk. 11	Nov 20	W	17-10	at New York Giants
Wk. 12	Nov 27	W	31-23	vs New York Giants
Wk. 13	Dec 4	W	20-6	at St. Louis Cardinals
Wk. 14	Dec 11	L	27-21	at Pittsburgh Steelers
Wk. 15	Dec 18	W	38-28	at Washington Redskins

Post Season

League Championship

	Dec 26	W	17-13	vs Green Bay Packers

The Eagles started the season out on the wrong foot by losing their season opener at home to the Cleveland Browns 41-24. A week later the Eagles would barely beat the expansion Cowboys by a score of 27-25 in Dallas. However, from there the Eagles would soar, winning nine straight to capture the Eastern Division with a 10-2 record. Spurring on the Eagles was quarterback Norm Van Brocklin, who had a spectacular season by passing for 2,471 yards, and Chuck Bednarik, who played sixty minutes a game at center and linebacker. Bednarik made his presence felt in a big way in a 17-10 win over the Giants in New York on November 20, when he laid a ferocious hit on Frank Gifford that nearly ended the star wide receiver's career. In the NFL Championship Game at Franklin Field, the Eagles faced the Green Bay Packers. After holding a 10-6 lead throughout the third quarter, the Eagles suddenly found themselves trailing 13-10 when the Packers scored early in the fourth. However, Ted Dean would return the ensuing kickoff deep into Packers territory as the Eagles retook the lead 17-13 with 5:21 left in the game. The Packers would not go down quietly, driving deep into Eagles territory. However, Bednarik would save the game with a crushing tackle of Jim Taylor on the eight-yard line as time expired, clinching the Eagles third NFL Championship. Following the season both Coach Buck Shaw and quarterback Norm Van Brocklin retired.

1960 Philadelphia Eagles Stats

Passing	Comp	Att	Comp %	Yds	Y/Att	TD	Int	Rating
Norm Van Brocklin	153	284	53.9	2471	8.70	24	17	86.5
Sonny Jurgensen	24	44	54.5	486	11.05	5	1	122.0
Billy Barnes	0	3	0.0	0	0.00	0	2	0.0

Rushing	Rush	Yds	Avg	TD
Clarence Peaks	86	465	5.4	3
Billy Barnes	117	315	2.7	4
Ted Dean	113	304	2.7	0
Timmy Brown	9	35	3.9	2
Theron Sapp	9	20	2.2	0
Sonny Jurgensen	4	5	1.3	0
Pete Retzlaff	2	3	1.5	0
Norm Van Brocklin	11	-13	-1.2	0

Receiving	Rec	Yds	Avg	TD
Pete Retzlaff	46	826	18.0	5
Tommy McDonald	39	801	20.5	13
Bobby Walston	30	563	18.8	4
Billy Barnes	19	132	6.9	2
Ted Dean	15	218	14.5	3
Clarence Peaks	14	116	8.3	0
Timmy Brown	9	247	27.4	2
Dick Lucas	3	34	11.3	0
Theron Sapp	2	20	10.0	0

Punting	Punts	Yds	Avg	Blocked
Norm Van Brocklin	60	2585	43.1	0

Interceptions	Int	Yds	Avg	TD
Don Burroughs	9	124	13.8	0
Chuck Weber	6	48	8.0	0
Bobby Freeman	4	67	16.8	0
Maxie Baughan	3	50	16.7	0
Gene Johnson	3	34	11.3	0
Jimmy Carr	2	4	2.0	0
Chuck Bednarik	2	0	0.0	0
Tom Brookshier	1	14	14.0	0

Kicking	PAT Made	PAT Att	PAT %	FG Made	FG Att	FG %	Pts
Bobby Walston	39	40	98	14	20	70.0	105

THE WEATHER
U. S. Weather Bureau Forecast
Philadelphia and vicinity: Cloudy Tuesday morning, becoming fair by afternoon, and colder toward evening. High near 30, with wind northwesterly 10 to 20 miles an hour. Mostly fair Wednesday, with high near 30.
COMPLETE WEATHER DATA ON PAGE 20

The Philadelphia Inquirer

PUBLIC LEDGER

An Independent Newspaper for All the People

FINAL CITY EDITION

November Circulation: Daily, 611,270; Sunday, 1,031,427 — 132d Year — TUESDAY MORNING, DECEMBER 27, 1960 — WFIL 560 KC • WFIL-TV CH. 6 — FIVE CENTS

67,352 See Eagles Beat Packers for Title, 17-13

Dean's TD Decides As Losers Drive To Phila. 9 at End

By HERB GOOD

The Eagles became the undisputed champions of the professional football world Monday by outscrapping the young Green Bay Packers in a 17-13 thriller that kept a sellout crowd of 67,352 at Franklin Field in nerve-wracking suspense until the very last play.

The Eagles did it the hard way, following the pattern of their regular season play to the letter.

They allowed the Packers to get off to a 6-0 lead, overtook them at 7-6, then fell behind at 10-13 at the start of the fourth quarter before storming back to win on a five-yard end sweep by rookie Ted Dean with 9:40 left.

SPECTACULAR RUN

Dean, who turned the tide of the tense, hard-fought game with a spectacular 58-yard kickoff return, shared the spotlight with the ever brilliant Norm Van Brocklin and defensive standouts Chuck Bednarik, Tom Brookshier, Marion Campbell and Jim Carr as the Eagles rewarded

Page of Pictures on Page 29; Related Stories, Statistics and Additional Pictures on Pages 26, 27, 28 and 30.

Buck Shaw with his first NFL crown in his final season of a distinguished coaching career.

The defensive quartet was in the forefront, figuring in most of the big clutch plays, as the Eagles held on grimly after Dean's decisive tally and had the extreme satisfaction of holding the second-strongest NFL offense to a single touchdown.

HORNUNG HURT

The much-feared Paul Hornung, league scoring champion, and Jim Taylor, the loop's second leading ground gainer, weren't permitted to run wild and they were stopped dead when it counted. The former, who kicked early field goals from the 20 and 23 and who missed one from the 13 on the last play of the first half, received a shoulder injury on a Bednarik tackle in the middle of the third quarter and handled only kicking chores thereafter.

Highlighting the Eagles' toughness on defense in the clutch were their feats of holding for downs on the five after losing the ball on an interception on their first scrimmage play; of forcing the Packers to settle for a field goal when they gave the ball away on a fumble at the 22 several minutes later; and of taking the ball away on downs on the home 24 in the third period.

LATE SCORING BID

Even so, the Packers were able to give Eagle fans a bad time in the fading moments. In the last 75 seconds Bart Starr completed six passes during a desperation 56-yard drive that penetrated to the nine as the game ended.

This was the kind of frustration Green Bay had most of the sunny afternoon as the Western Conference champions outgained the Eagles, 401 net yards to 296 and had a 22-13 edge in first downs.

But while the Packers were doing all the hard work, the Eagles

Continued on Page 26, Column 4

Police and fans rush to help the Eagles' Tommy McDonald to his feet after he plowed into crowd along sidelines in scoring team's first touchdown on a second-quarter pass from Norm Van Brocklin.

Roaring Crowd Hails Eagles, Wild Melee Mars Jubilation

By JEROME S. CAHILL

Jubilant Philadelphians celebrated the return of the professional football championship with a mighty roar heard for blocks Monday at Franklin Field.

The roar came when an official's gun marked the end of a hair-raising 17-13 victory over the Green Bay Packers with the Western champs just nine yards from the goal of the hometown Eagles, Eastern titlists of the National Football League.

Marring the jubilation was a wild melee between some fans and police ringing the eastern end of the field. Snowballs and chunks of ice filled the air before the fracas ended after more than 15 minutes when the police forces left the area.

Down came the goal posts.

67,352 SPECTATORS

A total of 67,352 fans, including Mayor Richardson Dilworth and Gov. David L. Lawrence, were on their feet at the tense finale. The stands shook when the sharp report of the time-

Pictures and Related Story on Page 3

keeper's gun signaled Philadelphia's first NFL title since 1949.

"A wonderful game, a wonderful victory," Mayor Dilworth shouted.

"It was marvelous, simply marvelous," said Gov. Lawrence.

Versions of who was at fault for the melee differed.

Police Commissioner Albert N. Brown said it was a "holding action" directed against "a handful of people with a history of hoodlumism" and designed to give more orderly fans time to leave the field uninjured.

MANY FANS DISAGREE

Many fans couldn't see it the commissioner's way.

Some fans said they were angered by the presence of police between them and the goal posts, which have come down after every Eagle home victory except the Nov. 27 conquest of the New York Giants. After that game, the mere presence of police ringing the field preserved order.

Other spectators said there was general resentment at the way the bluecoats repulsed the first few tentative attempts to break through a waist-high rope barrier and police lines. In several cases, fans were picked up bodily and pitched back over the rope.

STRUCK IN FACE

At any rate, boos and snowballs soon filled the air, with some of the latter hitting home with remarkable accuracy. Scores of officers were hit in the face with snow or chunks of ice.

In what seemed to be retaliation, flying squads of policemen invaded the lower grandstands to go after their tormentors.

Brown indicated the objects of the flying squads were known troublemakers whose activities throughout the season in the east stands had been a source of danger to other spectators. A number of these were collared by police and escorted unceremoniously to the nearest exits.

Meanwhile, sorties against the rope barrier and the police line continued.

OTHERS SLIP THROUGH

One fan bounced into the rope at the 10-yard line and was turned back. He tried at the 15-yard line and was bounced back again, only to repeat his thrusts over and over until he was beyond midfield and out of contention.

Other groups of fans had more

Continued on Page 3, Column 5

Traffic Deaths At 464 in Nation; 15 in Pa., N. J.

Traffic deaths on the Nation's highways rose to 464 early Tuesday as motorists started home after the long holiday week-end.

In addition to the highway deaths, 76 persons were killed in fires, including five in Pennsylvania, and 77 lost their lives in other types of accidents. This brought the holiday grand total to 617.

493 A YEAR AGO

In a comparable 78-hour period a year ago, 493 persons were killed on the Nation's highways.

The death rate slackened in the waning hours of the Christmas weekend, and the National Safety Council said that if the trend continued, it would be the safest Christmas holiday since 1949. The three-day holiday traffic toll that year was 413.

BELOW ESTIMATE

A spokesman said the number of highway deaths would fall below the 510 estimated by the council prior to the 78-hour period that started at 6 P. M. Friday.

The all-time Christmas record is 609 deaths, set during the "Black Christmas" of 1955.

The National Safety Council estimated that the holiday had put virtually every one of the Nation's 74,000,000 cars on the road in a record-breaking national traffic jam. The council said an average of 350 persons could be expected to die in traffic accidents during a non-holiday 78-hour period in December.

DIES OF INJURIES

Eight highway fatalities, including one in Philadelphia, were reported in Pennsylvania. A Burlington youth was one of seven persons killed in auto accidents in New Jersey.

He was Wallace Rohlfing, Jr., 19, of Cottage ave., Edgewater Park, who died Monday in Burlington County Hospital, Burlington, from internal injuries he suffered Christmas Eve in a two-car accident.

California topped all States in the number of highway deaths, with 39. Texas was next with 34.

As the toll of traffic deaths quickened during the homeward rush, Howard Pyle, president of the NSC, appealed to every driver to "realize that traffic in the closing hours of the day is not only heavy but dangerous."

"It must be offset with a great patience and a constant regard for the safety and welfare of everyone on our streets and highways," he said.

Truman to Attend The Inauguration

NEW YORK, Dec. 26 (AP).—Former President Harry S. Truman said Monday he plans to attend the inauguration of President-elect John F. Kennedy.

Mr. Truman was asked during his morning walk whether Kennedy, who will wear a top hat for the ceremony, would be attired in the "right headgear." President Eisenhower wore a homburg.

"Yes, he will," Mr. Truman replied. "The other fellow didn't know what headgear to wear. It didn't make any difference. He got inaugurated anyway."

Cold Makes Return Visit

Cloudy and colder weather was predicted for Philadelphia Tuesday, accompanied by northwesterly winds 10 to 20 miles an hour, and gusty at times. A low of 28 was expected.

The drop in temperature was caused by a cold front that arrived from central Pennsylvania Monday night. Light showers began falling at 7:30 P. M.

A high near 30 was forecast for Tuesday with clear skies in the afternoon.

Belgian Forces Beefed Up for Walkout Crisis

BRUSSELS, Belgium, Dec. 26 (UPI). — A 6-day-old Socialist-led general strike that has paralyzed Belgium spawned an outburst of sabotage and street violence Monday and the Government began bringing home military technicians from NATO duty abroad to help cope with the crisis.

Some reservists were called to active service for strike duty.

SHOWDOWN EXPECTED

A showdown was expected Tuesday, first working day after Christmas, between the striking Socialist unions opposing the Government's new austerity program, and several Christian Socialist unions which have denounced the strike as "political."

The Socialists retaliated with a call for nonstrikers, especially in the Wallonia area of south Belgium, to join the walkout, which mushroomed through the rail, utility and postal services and spread to other channels of trade and commerce during the Christmas rush.

Police closed the Brussels-Namur rail line after an anonymous caller tipped them that it had been mined. However, no mines were found.

VIOLENCE REPORTED

At Mons, a gasoline-filled bottle was hurled into a cafe but did not ignite and caused no damage. A window of a labor newspaper office in Mons was smashed.

A locomotive was blocked at a switch near Mons, which had been wrecked by saboteurs. Some telephone lines were reported cut in the Mons area.

Police units were kept at maximum strength despite the holiday and paratroopers were alerted to guard rail centers.

Some reservists were called up

Continued on Page 2, Column 1

Massive Revamping Of Regulatory Bodies Is Urged on Kennedy

PALM BEACH, Fla., Dec. 26 (AP)—President-elect John F. Kennedy released a bristling report Monday night that said Federal regulatory agencies have been afflicted with outside pressure, political appointees and a lack of concern by Presidents Truman and Eisenhower.

The report, which recommends a massive shake-up and reorganization of the agencies, is the one-man product of James M. Landis, former Harvard Law School dean and former member or chairman of several of the agencies involved.

'FAIRY TALE' PROGRAMS

It speaks of "Alice-in-Wonderland procedures," of drifting and stalling, and of costly delays in getting the work done.

Kennedy is expected to use the report, which he praised, as the basis for action and recommendations of his own, which would require new legislation.

The report brings in Mr. Truman and Mr. Eisenhower unmistakably but not by name.

With relation to the awarding of overseas airline routes, it says "lobbying in its worst sense" has been prevalent since 1948 around mystery-shrouded approaches to the White House.

OUTSIDE INFLUENCES

It says there has been in the last two Administrations a notable lack of Presidential self-restaint in avoiding outside influence in this field.

Of regulatory agencies in general, the report says that for the last decade "the Executive appears to have had no real concern with their operation." The decade covers most of Mr. Eisen-

Landis Profile on Page 3

hower's Administration and two years of Mr. Truman's.

It was on assignment from Kennedy that Landis surveyed the agencies, picked out their faults, and proposed remedies. The Civil Aeronautics Board, which Landis once headed, and the Federal Power, Communications and Interstate Commerce Commissions were particular targets.

But Landis said nothing in the way of cures would work as long as key positions are filled on the basis of "political reward rather than competency."

'STEPPING STONES'

Landis said top administrators often appeared to be picked just to give them a "stepping stone" to a higher political or industrial job.

Kennedy appraised the report in his one-sentence statement:

"This is a most important and impressive analysis of the regulatory agencies which deserves the attention of the members of Congress as well as the agencies themselves."

CAB IS ASSAILED

Among other things, the report urges curbs on efforts to influence agencies—Kennedy has taken a similar stand—and says that:

1. One chief criticism of CAB is that the outcome of cases appears to be determined by "the intrusion of influences off the record." It recommends a freeze on existing air routes for a while.

2. FCC continues to use "Alice - in - Wonderland procedures" and there is a strong suspicion that radio-TV networks

Continued on Page 3, Column 1

Small Nuclear Bomb Detonated by French On Sahara Desert

From Our Wire Services

PARIS, Dec. 27 (Tuesday).—French scientists detonated a small nuclear device Tuesday at the atomic proving grounds in Reganne in the Sahara Desert in Southern Algeria, official sources reported. The device was exploded at 1 A. M. EST.

The test explosion, France's third at the testing ground, was described as "of small strength." The announcement said the explosion was a success.

1ST TEST IN FEBRUARY

France exploded her first atomic bomb at the Sahara testing base last Feb. 13. The bomb was said to be about three times the force of the U. S. bomb dropped on Hiroshima in 1945.

The second bomb, reportedly much smaller than the first, was set off on April 1, while Soviet Premier Nikita S. Khrushchev was paying an official visit to President Charles de Gaulle, prior to the ill-fated Summit Conference in May.

The Defense Ministry said of Tuesday's test blast:

"As planned in the first explosions, all security measures have been taken so that the fallout does not represent any danger to populations."

PROTEST BY AFRICANS

Several African nations have protested the French tests in the Sahara, contending that the African people were endangered by radioactivity. The French replied that all necessary safeguards were taken.

The testing site is 20 miles south of Reggane and about 1500 miles south of Oran, Algeria.

In Washington, there was no immediate official U. S. reaction to the news of the third atomic bomb explosion.

Washington reacted with obvious coolness when the first French atomic bomb was exploded last Feb. 13.

The State Department said at that time that the French feat was no surprise. There was no word of praise or congratulations from the State Department at that time and no comment by the White House.

VEHEMENT PROTESTS

The more vehement protests against French atomic explosions in the Sahara were made by Ghana, Guinea and Mali, the last two former French colonies.

Ghana's Premier, Kwame Nkrumah, sent notes of protest to President de Gaulle, warning him of dire consequences if the French went ahead with their planned tests.

'House of Prayer' Robbed of $50,000

LOS ANGELES, Dec. 26 (UPI). —Burglars stole $50,000 Sunday night from the "House of Prayer" mansion where Negro evangelist Charles Manuel (Sweet Daddy) Grace lived until his death last Jan. 12.

Walter McCullough, a bishop in the "House of Prayer" sect which Grace founded, said the cash, in a briefcase, was apparently taken from his second-story bedroom by someone who climbed silently through a window.

Grace's estate, estimated at as much as $12 million, has been involved in tax actions. The Federal Government claims the religious leader was $5,966,000 in arrears on income taxes and interest at the time of his death.

Girl, 10, Admits Slaying Father

CHARLOTTESVILLE, Va., Dec. 26 (AP).—A 10-year-old girl has admitted stabbing her father to death early Monday during a family argument, police said.

Oscar Mahanes, 40, was found dead at his home when police arrived shortly after 2:30 A. M.

Edith Dianne Mahanes told police she did not intend to stab her father. She said she intended only to frighten him with the knife, but she slipped, police said, and the 10-inch blade pierced his heart.

Of Special Interest Today

The bold colors and simplicity of the silhouette of the Oriental costume is influencing new cocktail costumes, pictured in full-color in the Fashion in Living Section.

Page 9

No Business Like Show Business

The glamorous doings of people in show business are reported by Louella Parsons, Herb Stein, Hy Gardner and Whitney Bolton in daily Best of Hollywood and Best of Broadway columns on the Feature Page.

Page 15

Historic Altar Destroyed in Fire

A Christmas night fire destroyed the historic altar of St. Mark's Lutheran Church in Oaklyn, N. J. A story on the fire, giving the origin of the 100-year-old altar, appears on

Page 25

New Test Asked For Goldfine

BOSTON, Dec. 26 (UPI).—United States Attorney Elliott Richardson said Monday he has filed a motion seeking re-examination of the competency of industrialist Bernard Goldfine to stand trial for income tax evasion.

The millionaire textile tycoon, whose gifts and payment of hotel bills for former Presidential aide Sherman Adams preceded Adams' resignation in 1958, was released Saturday from a Washington mental hospital into the custody of his son, Solomon, to recover mental peace in a familiar atmosphere.

Last October, Federal Judge George C. Sweeney had ordered Goldfine confined to the hospital. Sweeney ruled that the textile magnate was mentally incompetent to stand trial for evasion of nearly $800,000 in personal and corporate income taxes.

China Capitalizes on Science
Red Giant Leaps Forward

By EARL UBELL
Special to The Inquirer

NEW YORK, Dec. 26.—Communist China, the sleeping giant, is stirring. Science is awakening her 600 million people and may bring her to an industrial level close behind the United States and Russia within 20 years.

Thirteen scientists examined her physical science and engineering Monday and recorded a picture of amazing progress in the 10 years since the Communists took over.

"Do not be surprised," one of them said, "if the Chinese explode an atomic bomb or launch a rocket soon."

Each spoke at a special symposium on Chinese science at the opening sessions of the annual meeting of the American Association for the Advancement of Science, which continues through Saturday.

The secret behind Communist Chinese progress appears to lie, the scientists agreed, in their rapid training of new scientists. In geology alone, the Chinese have increased the number of geological workers 100 times since 1950—from 200 to 21,000.

However, it will be some time before the Communist scientists can contribute significantly to fundamental science, the experts said. Most of them have been put to work on practical projects. They are pushing Chinese industrial production and it's paying off.

Dr. Kung-ping Wang, Far East specialist of the United States Bureau of Mines, estimated that by 1970 China will increase her steel and iron production sixfold to become the world's third largest producer.

That's why, according to Dr. Edward C. T. Chao, of the United States Geological Survey, the Chinese have put such great emphasis on geology. They want the ores and have come up with great ore masses hidden in that 5-million-square-mile territory.

Dr. Chao said China has reported discoveries of large deposits of coal, iron and copper. Recent reports, he said, indicate they have the largest deposits in the world of molybdenum, a metal used to harden steel. New nickel lodes—unknown before 1950—have turned up.

Behind much of this stands the big scientific brother, the Soviet Union, which has not only sent hundreds of technicians to China, but has brought Chinese scientists to study in Russia.

One of the panel, Dr. Robert T. Beyer, a Brown University physicist, pointed out the extent to which the Chinese are involved with the Soviets.

"About one-third of the scientific papers originating at the Soviet nuclear research center at Dubna, near Moscow, have Chinese names attached to them," Dr. Beyer said.

If, as recently reported, the Russians withdrew or threatened to withdraw their technicians from China, Dr. Beyer said, it could be a heavy blow to China.

In chemistry, the Chinese have a "silk-purse-out-of-a-sow's-ear" philosophy, Dr. Arthur Yu, of the Thiokol Chemical Corp., said they are making nylon from castor oil, rayon from sugar cane, and cortisone, an anti-arthritic drug, from plants.

Other scientists on the panel reported great advances in road building, electronics and electric power.

Dr. T. C. Tsao, of Columbia University, made the prediction about an atomic bomb and a rocket launching.

Passengers Saved As Ships Collide

GALVESTON, Tex., Dec. 26 (AP).—Two foreign freighters collided about 12 miles off Galveston in a heavy fog Monday and a Coast Guard boat rescued passengers from one of the ships. No injuries were reported.

The ships involved were the Norwegian freighter Fernmore and the Greek ship Tharaos.

On the Air

WFIL-AM 560 On Your Dial
6:00 A. M.—Rise and Shine—Phil Sheridan
9:30 P. M.—J. J. Moran Show

WFIL-TV Channel 6
2:30 P. M.—Road to Realty
10:30 P. M.—Eyewitness
11:15 P. M.—Judy Garland, Gene Kelly in "The Pirate" on World's Best Movies.

WFIL-FM 102.1 mc.
4:00 P. M.—Spotlight

Television and Radio Listings on Pages 22 and 24.

In The Inquirer

Departments and Features

Amusements 10, 11, 12
Bridge 21
Business and Financial 13
Classified Ads 30 to 33
Comics 20, 21
Death Notices 24
Editorials 14
Obituaries 5, 6, 7
On the Lighter Side 18
Sports 26 to 30
Television and Radio 22, 23, 24
Women's News 9, 10

Feature Page — Page 15
John M. Cummings — Page 14
Red Smith — Page 27
Washington Background — Page 14
Your Legal Problems — Page 20
Complete Weather — Page 20

LOST AND FOUND

[illegible]

Other Lost & Found Page 30

December 27, 1960 - Eagles come from behind victory over the Green Bay Packers, 17-13 to win the NFL Championship. Coach Buck Shaw and Norm Van Brocklin retire after season

1961

RECORD: 10-4, 2ND IN NFL EAST
HEAD COACH: NICK SKORICH

SCHEDULE

REGULAR SEASON

Wk. 2	Sep 17	W	27-20	vs Cleveland Browns
Wk. 3	Sep 24	W	14-7	vs Washington Redskins
Wk. 4	Oct 1	L	30-27	vs St. Louis Cardinals
Wk. 5	Oct 8	W	21-16	vs Pittsburgh Steelers
Wk. 6	Oct 15	W	20-7	at St. Louis Cardinals
Wk. 7	Oct 22	W	43-7	at Dallas Cowboys
Wk. 8	Oct 29	W	27-24	at Washington Redskins
Wk. 9	Nov 5	W	16-14	vs Chicago Bears
Wk. 10	Nov 12	L	38-21	at New York Giants
Wk. 11	Nov 19	L	45-24	at Cleveland Browns
Wk. 12	Nov 26	W	35-13	vs Dallas Cowboys
Wk. 13	Dec 3	W	35-24	at Pittsburgh Steelers
Wk. 14	Dec 10	L	28-24	vs New York Giants
Wk. 15	Dec 17	W	27-24	at Detroit Lions

Nick Skorich was named the new head coach as Sonny Jurgensen took over as the starting quarterback. Jurgensen won seven of the first eight games and ended up with a record season, passing for 3,723 yards and connecting on 32 touchdown passes. However, the Eagles who finished with a 10-4 record and had to settle for second place after two costly losses to the New York Giants.

1961 PHILADELPHIA EAGLES STATS

Passing	Comp	Att	Comp %	Yds	Y/Att	TD	Int	Rating
Sonny Jurgensen	235	416	56.5	3723	8.95	32	24	88.1
King Hill	6	12	50.0	101	8.42	2	2	78.8
Clarence Peaks	0	1	0.0	0	0.00	0	0	39.6

Rushing	Rush	Yds	Avg	TD
Clarence Peaks	135	471	3.5	5
Timmy Brown	50	338	6.8	1
Ted Dean	66	321	4.9	2
Billy Barnes	92	309	3.4	1
Sonny Jurgensen	20	27	1.4	0
Theron Sapp	7	24	3.4	1
King Hill	2	9	4.5	0
Pete Retzlaff	1	8	8.0	0

Receiving	Rec	Yds	Avg	TD
Tommy McDonald	64	1144	17.9	13
Pete Retzlaff	50	769	15.4	8
Bobby Walston	34	569	16.7	2
Clarence Peaks	32	472	14.8	0
Ted Dean	21	335	16.0	1
Billy Barnes	15	194	12.9	3
Timmy Brown	14	264	18.9	2
Dick Lucas	8	67	8.4	5
Theron Sapp	3	10	3.3	0

Punting	Punts	Yds	Avg	Blocked
King Hill	55	2403	43.7	0

Kicking	PAT Made	PAT Att	PAT %	FG Made	FG Att	FG %	Pts
Bobby Walston	43	46	93	14	25	56.0	97

Interceptions	Int	Yds	Avg	TD
Don Burroughs	7	90	12.9	0
Irv Cross	2	36	18.0	0
Chuck Bednarik	2	33	16.5	0
Tom Brookshier	2	20	10.0	0
Jimmy Carr	2	20	10.0	0
Maxie Baughan	1	22	22.0	0
Chuck Weber	1	15	15.0	0
John Nocera	0	3	0.0	0

SPORTS — The Philadelphia Inquirer — MAIL ORDER
An Independent Newspaper for All the People
SPORTS SECTION — SUNDAY, MORNING, JANUARY 7, 1962 — PAGE ONE

Jurgensen Hurt as Lions Shock Eagles

UPI Telephoto
This is the play on which Sonny Jurgensen suffered a shoulder separation. Lions' Wayne Walker is hitting Sonny (No. 9) with jarring block while Yale Lary makes 66-yard run with intercepted pass.

By HERB GOOD
Inquirer Reporter

MIAMI, Jan. 6.—If Eastern pro coaches were embarrassed by what happened to the Giants at Green Bay, they'll be going into hiding after what happened to the Eagles in the National Football League's second Playoff Bowl Saturday afternoon.

The Detroit Lions, apparently stimulated by the memory of four successive losses to the Flock in the last two years, handed the Philadelphians a 38-10 shellacking before a shirt-sleeved crowd of 25,612 in the Orange Bowl and a National television audience.

In winning third-place honors for the second straight year, the Western Conference runnersup made the most of three interceptions and a recovered fumble as they jumped off to a quick 10-0 lead and increased it to 24-0 before the Eagles got their only points in the third quarter.

It wasn't much of a show for the crowd, which enjoyed only the 81-degree temperature, and especially was a bitter disappointment for some 500 Eagle fans who made the trip by chartered plane, train and automobile.

The Eagles, who had squeezed out a 27-24 last-second win over the Lions in the final regular-season game at Detroit to finish just a half-game behind Eastern champ New York, not only came out of the rather dull game with bruised pride, but with six cripples to boot.

All-league quarterback Sonny Jurgensen and offensive tackle J. D. Smith were so badly hurt that they'll miss the Pro Bowl game at Los Angeles next Sunday.

Jurgensen received a badly separated right shoulder early in the second period when he was blocked on an interception run by Yale Lary that led to Detroit's second TD. He watched the rest of the game from the sidelines with his arm in a cast. Dr. Mike Mandarino said an operation would be necessary Tuesday in Philadelphia.

Smith received a fracture of the right tibia, similar to the injury that put Tom Brookshier on the sidelines half the season. He was treated at Jackson Hospital.

Others hurt were linebacker John Nocera, who received a bad spike wound on his left hand, requiring six stitches, in the early minutes; defensive end Leo Sugar, sprained knee, and fullback Clarence Peaks, a pulled leg muscle.

It was just one of those bad days when nothing went right. The Eagles, who started the season the first week of July and who were completing the longest season ever for an NFL team, were flat to start with and, when the injuries started piling up, what little enthusiasm they might have had for the game soon evaporated.

Even so, the Eagles managed to outgain the Lions, 177 net yards to 151 in the air, but were outgained 180 net yards to 58 on the ground.

Jim Ninowski and Earl Morrall directed the rout for the Lions, each tossing two TD passes, two of which were caught

Continued on Page 5, Column 3

Fun in the Sun?

Jurgensen Expected To Be OK Next Year, Smith Career in Doubt

Special to The Inquirer

MIAMI, Jan. 6.—Although Sonny Jurgensen came out of the debacle with the Lions with the "worst shoulder separation" Dr. Mike Mandarino has ever seen, the Eagles' team physician insisted that the injury wouldn't harm the all-NFL quarterback's passing next season.

Dr. Mandarino said Sonny would be throwing the ball as sharp as ever next season. He predicted Sonny would be playing with the Eagles' basketball team within eight weeks after an operation Tuesday at the Hahnemann Hospital in Philadelphia.

The leg fracture received by tackle J. D. Smith looms more serious as far as his pro future is concerned. He may be in a cast as long as six months and he might not be ready to join the Eagles by the time they report to camp next July.

BREAK WORSE THAN BROOKSHIER'S

Smith has a compound fracture of the right tibia, lower on the leg than that received by Tom Brookshier in the Bears game, and this means it will take longer to heal, according to Dr. Mandarino. Smith had his leg set at Jackson Memorial Hospital and will remain there until Tuesday.

Jurgensen was hit hard by a shoulder block thrown by Detroit linebacker Wayne Walker as the Eagles' star was rushing to tackle Yale Lary on a runback of an interception. The collision tore two sets of ligaments in Jurgensen's shoulder and forced the clavicle several inches out of the shoulder.

Dr. Mandarino said future trouble with the shoulder would be avoided with the repairing of the ligaments Tuesday. Jurgensen, who completed eight of 17 passes for 62 yards, had his arm put in a cast immediately at the Orange Bowl and watched the second half from the sidelines.

Back at his hotel, Jurgensen was in obvious pain, although under sedation. He said it was the first serious injury he had ever had in football. Early in the season he had been bothered with an injured toe.

HE'LL MISS PRO BOWL GAME

Jurgensen, who threw 32 touchdown passes and gained more yardage in the air this season than any other NFL quarterback in history, was bitterly disappointed that the injury would keep him out of the Pro Bowl game. He would have been the starting East quarterback next Sunday. It was a similar blow to Smith who, like Jurgensen, had been selected for the Los Angeles classic for the first time.

The injuries will cost the two players $800 or $600, the winning and losing players' shares in the Pro Bowl.

Bobby Walston, Tommy McDonald, Ted Dean and Maxie Baughan, the other Eagles in the Pro Bowl, left for the West Coast by air immediately after the game.

—*HERB GOOD*

Temple Whips Scranton, 90-70, For 4th Straight

SCRANTON, Pa., Jan. 6—Temple led all the way Saturday night to rout the University of Scranton Royals, 90-70, before 1200 fans at the Scranton CYC.

The once-beaten Owls ran up an 8-0 lead in the early minutes as they streaked to their fourth straight victory and ninth of the year. Scranton's loss was the fifth in 10 games.

The Temple starters were in action only about 20 of the 40 minutes as Coach Harry Litwack cleared his bench and gave 13 players an opportunity to play.

GORDON GETS 19

All managed to score, with Russ Gordon leading the parade with 19. Bruce Drysdale hit for 18, three points under his average.

Drysdale, Earl Proctor, Gordon and Ed Devery got the Owls off to the 8-0 lead before Joe Barbuti finally hit for Scranton after 2:30 had elapsed.

The Owls went from there to a 19-4 lead after five minutes and prevailed 30-10 after 10 minutes. Litwack began substituting and the Royals managed to hold the Temple advantage to 20 points at halftime, 46-25, thanks to an eight-point spree near the end of the half.

BECOMES ROUT

At the start of the second half, the Temple regulars turned the game into a complete rout before Litwack waved in his scrubs. The count went to 70-38 before the shock troops took over.

The Owls hit on 44.7 percent of their shots from the field, making 38 of 85. Scranton was 33.3, with 21 of 63. Gordon hit on seven of 10 shots and led in rebounds with 13. Temple outrebounded Scranton, 59-53.

[illegible]

Halftime—Temple, 46-25

Ellen Gery Wins Harder Hall Golf

SEBRING, Fla., Jan. 6 (AP)—Ellen Gery, of Miami, won the sixth annual Harder Hall Women's Golf Tournament Saturday by two strokes in a nine-hole playoff with champion Marge Burns after both completed 54 holes in 236.

The rubber round was played in rain so intense it caused a delay after eight holes. Rain was still falling when they shot par 3s on the ninth. The winner used 38 strokes.

Miss Burns, Greensboro, N. C., missed a chance to win her fourth consecutive Harder Hall title in 54 holes when she got a bogey on No. 18 for 38-41—79. Miss Gery carded 41-38—79.

Jinny Dyson, Sugar Loaf, Pa., finished seventh with a 246 total.

Mississippi State Stays Unbeaten

STATE COLLEGE, Miss., Jan. 6 (AP).—Undefeated Mississippi State had a close call but remained one of the Nation's two basketball teams with perfect records by defeating Auburn, 51-48, Saturday night.

It was the 10th straight victory for the ninth-ranked defending Southeastern Conference champions, who stand with Ohio State in the unbeaten class. The game was the SEC opener for both schools.

Sophomore Doug Hutton sank a fall-away shot with six seconds to play to put State ahead, 50-48. The Maroons had stalled for three minutes following the fourth of four straight free throws by W. D. Stroud that tied the score.

W. Virginia Snaps Villanova's Streak; Penn, St. Joseph's Victors at Palestra

Referees Criticized By NYU

By FRANK DOLSON

It was a rough Saturday night for visiting coaches at the Palestra, but an enjoyable one for 4038 fans.

Princeton's Jack McCandless watched his defending Ivy League champions lose to Penn, 64-56, then had to rush to the hospital to check on the condition of his injured Capt. Al Kaemmerlen.

Then New York University's Lou Rossini saw his high-jumping sophomores lose a 59-55 thriller to St. Joseph's—and spent the next 15 minutes pacing up and down in front of his dressing room, battling successfully not to say anything he might regret later.

McCandless, the first-year coach who replaced the late Cappy Cappon, went home with a high regard for Penn high scorers Dave Robinson and John Wideman, and god news about Kaemmerlen, who survived a jolting collision with a mild concussion. Rossini went home full of admiration for St. Joseph's Jimmy Lynam and Tom Wynne—and bad thoughts about local officiating.

Penn-Princeton

Princeton, surprising Penn with a 1-2-2 zone, stayed in contention until the last two minutes despite scoring ace Pete Campbell's 2-for-17 shooting night and a freak accident that knocked out Capt. Al Kaemmerlen.

Kaemmerlen was carried off the court on a stretcher with 14:48 left and taken to University Hospital for observation. He was KO'd in a collision with Campbell after Penn's Sid Amira had heaved the ball high in the air over his head in an attempt to stop it from sailing out of bounds.

Kaemmerlen, Princeton's best rebounder, Campbell, and Penn's Robinson leaped for it as they converged from three directions. Campbell was knocked down but uninjured. Robinson was untouched and Kaemmerlen wound up flat on his back, unconscious.

THE LITTLE TAILOR

"I went up for the ball," said Robinson, "and the next thing I saw was the two of them on the ground, moaning. I thought Kaemmerlen was faking for a second, then I looked at his eyes and I knew he wasn't. I felt like

Continued on Pag. 6, Column 2

Anxious Al Kaemmerlen elbows Princeton mate Jim Day (30) out of way to grab rebound. Kaemmerlen was later KO'd in scramble for another rebound. Quakers are John Wideman (10) and J. D. Graham.

Fouls Hurt Wildcats in 88-82 Loss

By JOHN DELL
Inquirer Reporter

MORGANTOWN, W. Va., Jan. 6—The clock struck 12 for Philadelphia's Cinderella team Saturday night.

Coach Jack Kraft's Villanovans lost their first game after 12 straight victories, 88-82, in the valley between the human palisades at Mountaineer Field House, home of the University of West Virginia.

A sellout crowd of 6800 drowned out the cries of protest that Villanova's handful made against certain calls by officials.

"For a game this good, we should have had two top-flight officials. We didn't have them tonight," was Kraft's only comment.

FOULS HURT WILDCATS

Villanova was in the game nearly all the way against a team that has lost only twice in six seasons on its home court, even though the Wildcats were forced to sacrifice some of their aggressiveness after Wally Jones, Jim McMonagle and Jim O'Brien ran into early foul trouble.

All had three personals well before halftime and Jones was forced to the bench for six minutes to preserve his eligibility against the tallest team Villanova has met so far.

But with White scoring 28 points, Jones 19 and George Leftwich 18, Villanova, after holding the lead through most of the first half, trailed by only a point at intermission. The Wildcats were only four points behind with 1:26 left in a game in which the lead changed seven times and the score was tied five times.

FINALLY CATCH UP

Villanova took the lead on a White jump shot which severed the last tie, 59-59, with 12:31 left. White also added a foul but West Virginia came back on an overhead set shot by 6-6 Paul Miller and tap-in by Rod Thorn, 6-4 Mountaineer star who was game-high scorer with 29 points.

West Virginia stayed ahead after that, but Villanova never slipped entirely out of contention. With less than two minutes left, McMonagle was fouled and his right knee injured as White was sinking a short jump from the side. Kraft substituted Joe McGill, who made the most of the one-and-one award to McMonagle to reduce the Mountaineer lead to 82-78 with 1:47 left.

STOLEN PASS HURTS

McMonagle shortly afterward threw a cross-court pass that West Virginia's Jim McCormick intercepted in the backcourt. McCormick dribbled in for a field goal. Then Thorn drew two shots

Continued on Page 6, Column 4

Dietzel Signs Pact At Army for 5 Years

WEST POINT, N. Y., Jan. 6 (UPI).—Paul Dietzel, after an exhausting, day-long trip from Louisiana, signed a five-year contract late Saturday night as the new head coach of the Army football team.

The 37-year-old Dietzel, who gained his release as head coach at Louisiana State Friday although he had four years remaining on a five-year contract, arrived at the U. S. Military Academy about 10:20 P. M.

He signed to succeed Dale Hall as the Cadets' head coach at 11 P. M. in the quarters of Col. Emory S. Adams, Jr., the Academy's director of athletics.

Terms of the contract were not announced but it was learned Dietzel will be paid approximately $20,000 a year.

Originally, Dietzel was supposed to have signed at 4 P. M., but bad weather caused delay in his arrival.

FLIES TO WASHINGTON

Upon landing in Atlanta this morning from Baton Rouge, La., Dietzel learned that rain and fog had closed in the airport at New York. He then boarded a plane to Washington and made the remainder of the trip to New York by train.

The former LSU coach was met at the New York train terminal by Col. Red Reeder, Capt. Don Holleder and publicity director Joe Cahill, all of whom accompanied him on the 65-mile automobile trip to the Military Academy.

Dietzel said his first official order of business will be meeting his staff Sunday morning after which he will leave for Greenville, S. C., to serve as guest speaker at an Atlantic Coast Conference meeting on Monday.

Sports Results

Professional

FOOTBALL
RUNNERUP BOWL
Detroit 38 — EAGLES 10

ICE HOCKEY
NATIONAL LEAGUE
[illegible scores and standings]

AMERICAN LEAGUE
[illegible scores and standings]

EASTERN LEAGUE
[illegible scores and standings]

BASKETBALL
NATIONAL LEAGUE
[illegible scores and standings]

AMERICAN LEAGUE
[illegible scores]

Continued on Page 6, Column 6

StateComeback Tops Pitt, 74-62

PITTSBURGH, Jan. 6 (AP).—Penn State's basketball team scored 48 points in the second half Saturday night for a come-from-behind 74-62 victory over Pittsburgh.

The game was tied four times and the lead changed hands five times.

Pitt led 30-26 at the half, but the Nittany Lions closed the gap and with 12:36 remaining, John Mitchell hit on a jump shot that gave Penn State a 39-38 lead. State was never headed after that.

Gene Harris led the State with 19. Pitt's high scorer was Cal Sheffield with 13.

[illegible]

Halftime—Pitt, 30-26

Palestra Lineups

G, field goals; ST, shots tried; F, fouls made; FT, fouls tried; R, rebounds; A, assists; Per, personal fouls; Pts, points scored.

FIRST GAME

[illegible]

Halftime—Penn, 34-22. Officials—Jim Lennon and Phil Fox.

SECOND GAME

[illegible]

Halftime—NYU, 25-22. Officials—Jerry Bulls and Lou Bender.

Art Tokle Repeats At Bear Mountain

BEAR MOUNTAIN, N. Y., Jan. 6 (AP).—Art Tokle, veteran Brooklyn skier, won the Torger Tokle Memorial Ski Jump at Bear Mountain for the sixth straight year Saturday. He had leaps of 139 and 140 feet that netted 204 points.

It was the seventh time in the 17 years of the competition that Art Tokle won the award in the meeting named for his brother, who was killed in action while with the U. S. Forces in northern Italy during the Second World War.

Charley Scott Upsets Ortega in TV Match

By JACK CUDDY

NEW YORK, Jan. 6 (UPI).—Charley Scott of Philadelphia, a substitute in a substitute national TV fight, scored a mild upset Saturday night by left-hooking his way to a unanimous 10-round decision over welterweight contender Gaspar Ortega of Mexico at Madison Square Garden.

Ortega, the ninth-ranking welterweight contender, was favored at 6-5 for the 10-rounder.

Unrated Scott, who accepted the bout last Sunday, weighed 148½ pounds to Ortega's 148, and forced the action in most of the rounds.

NO KNOCKDOWNS

Because of his harder punching, he won the decisions on a rounds basis as follows: referee Harry Kessler, 6-3-1; judge Tony Castelano, 5-4-1 and judge Bill Recht, 6-1-3.

There were no knockdowns. Ortega's nose began bleeding in the fourth round and he suffered a nick at the outside corner of his left brow in the eighth.

Ortega, probably the world's busiest fighter, was competing for the 16th time in 12 months. He had 15 fights in the last 11 months of 1961. He went into the ring Saturday night with a string of three straight knockouts.

It seemed in some of the rounds that Ortega would be knocked out because of the bombing he took from the 25-year-old Scott's left hooks. Lanky Ortega's knees were buckled five times in the second round.

He was sent swaying into the ropes by a right and left hook to the head in the third, and was hanging on in the fifth. His knees were buckled by left hooks in the ninth and he was groggy at the bell.

The Detroit Tigers' personnel and problems are reviewed by Allen Lewis in the first of a mid-winter series on the major league baseball teams . . . . Page 4

West Chester Loses 1st Game

EAST ORANGE, N. J., Jan. 6 (AP).—Upsala converted four free throws down the stretch to nip West Chester (Pa.) State College, 77-75, in basketball Saturday night.

The setback was the first of the season for West Chester, which entered the game with a 6-0 record. Upsala is 3-7.

With the score tied at 73, Upsala's Bob Brandes was awarded two free throws and converted both. West Chester missed a field goal attempt and Upsala recovered the rebound. West Chester battled to get the ball back and in the process fouled Chuck Engler. He converted both shots.

Brandes finished with 21 points and Engler had 20 to pace Upsala. Dale Waters was high for the losers with 23.

Paul Walker Held For Grand Jury

RALEIGH, N. C., Jan. 6 (UPI).—New Yorker Paul Walker, accused of conspiring to bribe two North Carolina State basketball plays in 1960, waived preliminary hearing Saturday before Justice of the Peace H. A. Bland.

The 30-year-old Walker was bound over to Wake County Superior Court and returned to county jail in lieu of $25,000 bond.

District Solicitor Lester V. Chalmers said a bill of indictment naming Walker, a New York trucking official, will be presented Monday to the Wake County grand jury. The grand jury opens a regular term at that time.

January 7, 1961 - Eagles lose to the Detroit Lions, 38-10, in the Playoff Bowl.

1961

1962

RECORD: 3-10-1, 7TH IN NFL EAST
HEAD COACH: NICK SKORICH

Schedule

Regular Season

Wk. 2	Sep 16	L	27-21	vs St. Louis Cardinals
Wk. 3	Sep 23	L	29-13	vs New York Giants
Wk. 4	Sep 30	W	35-7	vs Cleveland Browns
Wk. 5	Oct 6	L	13-7	at Pittsburgh Steelers
Wk. 6	Oct 14	L	41-19	at Dallas Cowboys
Wk. 7	Oct 21	L	27-21	vs Washington Redskins
Wk. 8	Oct 28	L	31-21	at Minnesota Vikings
Wk. 9	Nov 4	T	14-14	at Cleveland Browns
Wk. 10	Nov 11	L	49-0	vs Green Bay Packers
Wk. 11	Nov 18	L	19-14	at New York Giants
Wk. 12	Nov 25	W	28-14	vs Dallas Cowboys
Wk. 13	Dec 2	W	37-14	at Washington Redskins
Wk. 14	Dec 9	L	26-17	vs Pittsburgh Steelers
Wk. 15	Dec 16	L	45-35	at St. Louis Cardinals

An unpredicted number of injuries hampered the Eagles all season as they crashed into last place with a disappointing 3-10-1 record. Tommy Mc-Donald passed for a touchdown to Tim Brown on a busted play as the Eagles defeated Washington 37-14. Following the season Chuck Bednarik, the last true two-way player, would retire at age 37, after 14 ferocious seasons.

1962 Philadelphia Eagles Stats

Passing	Comp	Att	Comp %	Yds	Y/Att	TD	Int	Rating
Sonny Jurgensen	196	366	53.6	3261	8.91	22	26	74.3
Tommy McDonald	1	1	100.0	10	10.00	1	0	147.9
King Hill	31	61	50.8	361	5.92	0	5	34.9

Rushing	Rush	Yds	Avg	TD
Timmy Brown	137	545	4.0	5
Clarence Peaks	137	447	3.3	3
Theron Sapp	23	53	2.3	2
Sonny Jurgensen	17	44	2.6	2
King Hill	4	40	10.0	1
Ralph Smith	1	13	13.0	0
Merrill Douglas	4	7	1.8	0
Hopalong Cassady	1	6	6.0	0

Receiving	Rec	Yds	Avg	TD
Tommy McDonald	58	1146	19.8	10
Timmy Brown	52	849	16.3	6
Clarence Peaks	39	347	8.9	0
Pete Retzlaff	30	584	19.5	3
Dick Lucas	19	236	12.4	1
Hopalong Cassady	14	188	13.4	2
Theron Sapp	6	80	13.3	0
Frank Budd	5	130	26.0	1
Bobby Walston	4	43	10.8	0
Ralph Smith	1	29	29.0	0

Punting	Punts	Yds	Avg	Blocked
King Hill	64	2747	42.9	0

Interceptions	Int	Yds	Avg	TD
Don Burroughs	7	96	13.7	0
Irv Cross	5	46	9.2	0
Ben Scotti	4	72	18.0	0
Jimmy Carr	3	59	19.7	0
Mike McClellan	3	2	0.7	0
Bob Harrison	2	14	7.0	0
Maxie Baughan	1	0	0.0	0
John Nocera	1	0	0.0	0

Kicking	PAT Made	PAT Att	PAT %	FG Made	FG Att	FG %	Pts
Bobby Walston	36	38	95	4	15	26.7	48
John Wittenborn	0	0	0	2	4	50.0	6

The Philadelphia Inquirer
33 MONDAY DECEMBER 3, 1962 h★

TODAY'S SPORTS

Also in this section . . .
Classified
Death Notices

Brown Runs 99, Eagles Rout 'Skins, 37-14

DOUGLAS (E)
HATCHER (R)
WITTENBORN (E)
SMITH, J. D. (E)
BROWN (E)
NOCERA (E)
MILLER (R)
1

Timmy Brown is off on 99-yard kickoff return for Eagles' first touchdown. With J. D. Smith and Merrill Douglas leading the way, Tim starts to cut at his 12 as John Nocera forces Ron Hatcher wide and John Wittenborn starts to block Allen Miller.

Timmy's 3-TD Burst Triggers Comeback

By HERB GOOD
Inquirer Reporter

WASHINGTON, D. C., Dec. 2.—It was a grand day of firsts for the Eagles as they exploded for their highest score this season while drubbing the Washington Redskins, 37-14, before 32,229 in sunny D. C. Stadium Sunday afternoon.

Tommy McDonald thew a touchdown pass, Frank Budd, former Villanova Olympian, scored a TD and John Wittenborn kicked a field goal, each an individual first as pros, as the Eagles gained their third victory.

Timmy Brown scored three touchdowns, one a 99-yard kickoff return.

EAGLES MOVE UP

In avenging an early-season 27-21 setback, the Eagles moved into undisputed possession of sixth place by handing the Redskins their fifth loss, third in a row and fifth in their last six games.

The reverse dropped the Redskins from third to fourth place in the National Football League's Eastern Division.

While McDonald, Budd and Wittenborn provided the unusual, Brown, Pete Retzlaff and Sonny Jurgensen made tremendous contributions as the Eagles overcame a 14-0 deficit in a wide-open game marked by long runs and big aerial bombs.

The slippery Brown, voted the outstanding Eagle by the Sports Writers Football Club last week, had one of his best days; Retzlaff scored one TD while catching eight passes for 135 yards in one of his finest efforts, and Jurgensen made another big climb on the comeback road by stealing the show from Washington's Norm Snead with 14 completions in just 19 attempts.

STAR ON DEFENSE

Also prominent in the victory were Maxie Baughan, who recovered two fumbles that led to touchdowns; rookie Mike McClellan, who also recovered a fumble and intercepted a pass; Jimmy Carr, who intercepted a pass and was the "glue man" in the secondary that was efficient when it counted, and tackle Riley Gunnels, who was his usual aggressive self.

After Snead got the Redskins off to a flying start by tossing short TD passes to Steve Junker and Dick James, it was the nimble-footed Brown who put the Eagles back in the game and fired their comeback with a 99-yard kickoff return for the first Philadelphia score.

It was his second scoring dash of that impressive distance this season, the first coming on the return of a missed field goal against the Cardinals in the opening game at Philadelphia.

This time he went all the way on the kickoff that followed Washington's second score, which came on the first play of the second quarter.

KEYS' BLOCK HELPS

Brown used his speed and shiftiness to break into the clear near the left sideline. Upon crossing midfield, he cut inside a screening block by Howard Keys on James to leave the last enemy at his heels.

Brown's second TD came on a spinning three-yard run on which he fell backward into the end zone on the ninth play of a 77-yard drive after the second-half

Continued on Page 34, Column 4

BALL

Eagles' passer Sonny Jurgensen, thrown for 19-yard loss in second quarter, complained that Redskin John Paluck illegally grabbed his face mask, as shown here. Officials brushed off complaint.

Giants Conquer Bears, 26-24, to Win Title in East

CHICAGO, Dec. 2 (AP).—The New York Giants clinched their second straight Eastern Conference title of the National Football League on Sunday by defeating the Chicago Bears, 26-24, on two touchdown passes by Y. A. Tittle and four field goals by Don Chandler.

The first meeting between the clubs since New York pasted the Bears, 47-7, in the 1956 championship game was a rough, hardplayed contest that kept an overflow Wrigley Field crowd of 49,043 alternating boos with cheers.

Several fist-swinging incidents charged up the battle. The only player ejected was the Bears' Ed O'Bradovich, who started punching Phil King in the third period. King was forced to the Giant bench to rest with an ice pack against his face.

O'Bradovich's flare-up cost the Bears a 15-yard penalty and set up Chandler's 37-yard field goal that pushed the Giants ahead, 23-17. Chandler, who booted a 26-yard field goal in the first quarter and a 47-yarder early in the third, added his fourth from 16 yards midway in the final period.

He also booted extra points after the two touchdowns to total 14 points.

5TH IN 7 YEARS

The triumph, assuring the Giants their fifth divisional crown in the last seven years, was their seventh straight. It gave them a 10-2 record with two games to play.

After Chandler's field goal put New York in front, 26-17, in the fourth, the Bears scored on a 59-yard drive capped by Bill Wade's 25-yard pass to Angelo Coia. Roger Leclerc converted for the third time. He also kicked a 31-yard field goal in the third.

It was Wade's second touchdown pass. He hit Johnny Morris in the corner for a 30-yard tally in the first period to end a 66-yard push in four plays.

The veteran Tittle hurled

Continued on Page 46, Column 3

Records

GIANTS LOG
Sept. 16—Lost to Browns, 17-7.
Sept. 23—Defeated EAGLES, 29-13.
Sept. 30—Defeated Steelers, 31-27.
Oct. 7—Defeated Cardinals, 31-14.
Oct. 14—Lost to Steelers, 20-7.
Oct. 21—Defeated Lions, 17-14.
Oct. 28—Defeated Redskins, 49-34.
Nov. 4—Defeated Cardinals, 31-28.
Nov. 11—Defeated Cowboys, 41-10.
Nov. 18—Defeated EAGLES, 19-14.
Nov. 25—Defeated Redskins, 42-24.
Dec. 2—Defeated Bears, 26-24.
Dec. 9—Browns.
Dec. 16—Cowboys.

BEARS LOG
Sept. 16—Defeated 49ers, 30-14.
Sept. 23—Defeated Rams, 27-23.
Sept. 30—Lost to Packers, 49-0.
Oct. 7—Defeated Vikings, 13-0.
Oct. 14—Lost to 49ers, 34-27.
Oct. 21—Defeated Colts, 35-15.
Oct. 28—Lost to Lions, 11-3.
Nov. 4—Lost to Packers, 38-7.
Nov. 11—Defeated Vikings, 31-30.
Nov. 18—Defeated Cowboys, 34-33.
Nov. 25—Defeated Colts, 57-0.
Dec. 2—Lost to Giants, 26-24.
Dec. 9—Rams.
Dec. 16—Lions.

Hornung Back, Packers Romp Over LA, 41-10

MILWAUKEE, Dec. 2 (UPI).—Green Bay's Paul Hornung made his long-awaited comeback Sunday and teamed with quarterback Bart Starr and fullback Jim Taylor to lead the Packers to a 41-10 victory over the Los Angeles Rams before 46,833.

Hornung, who hadn't seen extended action since an injury seven weeks ago, scored the Packers' first touchdown on a 30-yard pass from Starr and later took a 35-yard pass from Starr to set up Green Bay's second score.

Taylor scored twice to run his National Football League-leading total to 102 points. Starr also passed to Ron Kramer for four yards and a touchdown, and Jerry Kramer kicked 35 and 37 yard field goals as well as adding five extra points.

The Packers now need win only one of two games on the West Coast against the Rams and San Francisco to wrap up at least a tie for a third successive Western Division crown.

Hornung, who has played only briefly since Oct. 14, gained 27 yards in nine carries, caught two passes and threw one, which was intercepted.

He left the game limping in the third quarter.

Green Bay	10	14	3	14	—41
Los Angeles	3	0	0	7	—10

GB—Hornung, 30, pass from Starr (J. Kramer kick).
LA—FG, Villanueva, 11.
GB—FG, J. Kramer, 35.
GB—Taylor, 1, run (J. Kramer kick).
GB—R. Kramer, 4, pass from Starr (J. Kramer kick).
GB—FG, J. Kramer, 37.
GB—Taylor, 2, run (J. Kramer kick).
LA—Pass, 25, lateral from Gabriel (Villanueva kick).
GB—Gros, 15, run (J. Kramer kick).

STATISTICS

	L. A.	Gr. Bay
First downs	14	28
Rushing yardage	128	185
Passing yardage	[illegible]	258
Passes	18-38	16-24
Passes intercepted by	[illegible]	[illegible]
Punts	6-4[illegible]	3-45
Fumbles lost	[illegible]	[illegible]
Yards penalized	67	41

Records

PACKERS LOG
Sept. 16—Defeated Vikings, 34-7.
Sept. 23—Defeated Cardinals, 17-0.
Sept. 30—Defeated Bears, 49-0.
Oct. 7—Defeated Lions, 9-7.
Oct. 14—Defeated Vikings, 48-21.
Oct. 21—Defeated 49ers, 31-13.
Oct. 28—Defeated Colts, 17-6.
Nov. 4—Defeated Bears, 38-7.
Nov. 11—Defeated EAGLES, 49-0.
Nov. 18—Defeated Colts, 17-13.
Nov. 22—Lost to Lions, 26-14.
Dec. 2—Defeated Rams, 41-10.
Dec. 16—at Rams.

RAMS LOG
Sept. 16—Lost to Colts, 30-27.
Sept. 23—Lost to Bears, 27-23.
Sept. 30—Lost to Cowboys, 27-17.
Oct. 7—Lost to Redskins, 20-14.
Oct. 14—Lost to Lions, 13-10.
Oct. 21—Lost to Vikings, 38-14.
Oct. 28—Defeated 49ers, 28-14.
Nov. 4—Lost to Lions, 12-3.
Nov. 11—Lost to Colts, 14-2.
Nov. 18—Lost to 49ers, 24-17.
Nov. 25—Tied Vikings, 24-24.
Dec. 2—Lost to Packers, 41-10.
Dec. 9—at Bears.
Dec. 16—Packers.

Valley Forge Loses in Polo

Harley Williams scored six goals and Fred Fortungo five to lead the Oxford Royals, of Kelton, Pa., to a 14-7 indoor polo victory over Valley Forge Military Academy on Sunday at Wayne. The loss ended a 12-game winning streak by the Cadets.

Oxford		Valley Forge	
Fred Fortungo	1	Mike Tierney	
Sam Dixon	2	Mark Cunningham	
Harley Williams	3	Russ Rarkley	

Oxford	2	1	4	5	—14
Valley Forge	2	3	0	1	—7

Scoring—Oxford: Williams 6, Fortungo 5, Dixon 3. Valley Forge: Rarkley 3, Cunningham 2, Tierney 2.

Celtics Defeat Royals, 128-127

CINCINNATI, Dec. 2 (UPI).—The Boston Celtics cooled off the hot Cincinnati Royals Sunday night, coming from behind for a 128-127 overtime victory on the clutch shooting of Tom Heinsohn before 8719, the largest crowd of the local season.

Boston	G	F	P	Cincinnati	G	F	P
Heinsohn	10	2	22	Boozer	5	4	14
Sanders	6	4	16	Twyman	13	3	29
Russell	8	4	20	Embry	9	2	20
Cousy	4	6	14	Bockhorn	10	2	22
S. Jones	12	3	27	Robertson	11	7	29
Havlicek	0	1	1	Hawkins	3	2	8
K. C. Jones	3	1	7	Reed	1	0	2
Loveliette	2	2	6	Smith	0	3	3
Ramsey	4	4	12				
Swartz	0	3	3				
Totals	49	30	128	Totals	52	23	127

Boston	27	35	22	36	8—128
Cincinnati	32	31	34	23	7—127

FREE THROWS MISSED—BOSTON: Cousy, S. Jones, Ramsey 2, Russell 1, Sanders. CINCINNATI: Bockhorn, Boozer, Embry, Hawkins, Reed, Robertson, Twyman.

PERSONAL FOULS—BOSTON: Cousy 4, Havlicek 2, Heinsohn 4, K. C. Jones 1, S. Jones 1, Loveliette 2, Ramsey 2, Russell 3, Sanders 2, Swartz 2. CINCINNATI: Bockhorn 4, Boozer 2, Embry 2, Hawkins 5, Reed 4, Robertson 5, Smith 2, Twyman 4.

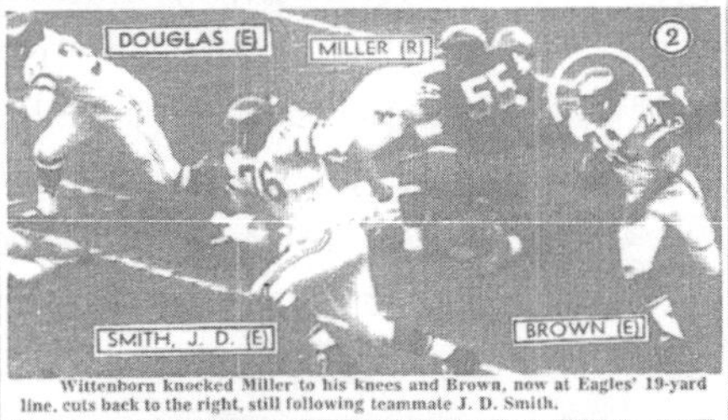
DOUGLAS (E)
MILLER (R)
SMITH, J. D. (E)
BROWN (E)
2

Wittenborn knocked Miller to his knees and Brown, now at Eagles' 19-yard line, cuts back to the right, still following teammate J. D. Smith.

DAVIDSON (R)
BROWN (E)
SMITH, J. D. (E)
3

J. D. Smith tried to block Washington's Ben Davidson at Eagles' 30. He couldn't knock him down but he knocked him off stride and Brown races by.

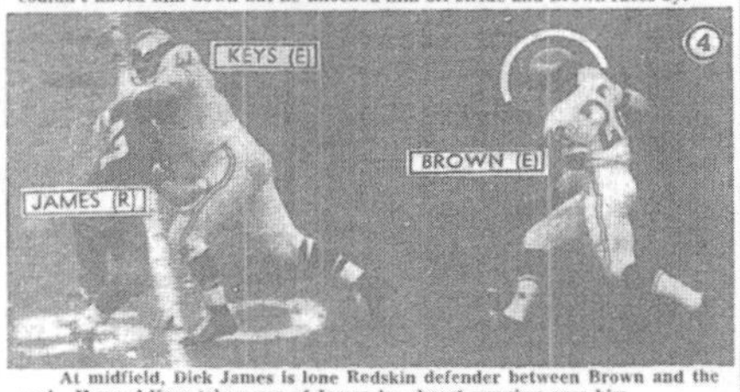
KEYS (E)
JAMES (R)
BROWN (E)
4

At midfield, Dick James is lone Redskin defender between Brown and the goal. Howard Keys takes care of James by almost running over him.

Sports Results

Professional
FOOTBALL
NFL

EAGLES 37	Washington 14
Pittsburgh 19	St. Louis 7
New York 26	Chicago 24
Dallas 45	Cleveland 21
Green Bay 41	Los Angeles 10
Detroit 21	Baltimore 14
San Francisco 35	Minnesota 12

STANDINGS
EASTERN DIVISION

	W	L	T	Pct.	Pts.	OP
x-New York	10	2	0	.833	340	239
Pittsburgh	7	5	0	.583	259	322
Cleveland	6	5	1	.545	265	230
Washington	5	5	2	.500	260	315
Dallas	5	6	1	.455	347	309
EAGLES	3	8	1	.273	230	285
St. Louis	2	9	1	.182	190	306

x-New York wins Eastern title.

WESTERN DIVISION

	W	L	T	Pct.	Pts.	OP
Green Bay	11	1	0	.917	364	110
Detroit	10	2	0	.833	278	151
Chicago	7	5	0	.583	288	273
San Francisco	6	6	0	.500	251	287
Baltimore	5	7	0	.417	217	250
Minnesota	2	9	1	.182	214	331
Los Angeles	1	10	1	.091	183	284

AFL

Buffalo 23	Dallas 14
Houston 34	Denver 17
San Diego 31	Oakland 21

Only games scheduled.

Standings

Eastern Division	W	L	T	Pct	Western Division	W	L	T	Pct
Houston	9	3	0	.750	x-Dallas	9	3	0	.750
Boston	8	3	1	.727	Denver	7	6	0	.538
Buffalo	6	6	1	.500	San Diego	4	8	0	.333
New York	5	7	0	.417	Oakland	0	12	0	.000

x-Dallas clinched Western Division title.

Continued on Page 46, Column 2

ELMORE (R)
BROWN (E)
DAVIDSON (R)
5

Magic Eye Photos by Robert L. Mooney, Inquirer Staff Photographer

Brown is in the clear at the Redskins' 36 and the chase given by Davidson and Doug Elmore is futile. This fine run started Eagles' comeback.

West Beats Judge for Title

By BILL SIMMONS

Father Judge had the All Stars but West Catholic had the team Sunday at Franklin Field

Picture on Page 46

as it spotted the Crusaders eight early points and then came roaring back to score a surprisingly easy 36-16 victory before 25,000.

The triumph, 10th in 11 games this year for Vince McAneny's Burrs, gave them their first Catholic League championship since 1951 and the right to meet Public League titlist Southern High for the City Title Saturday on the same field.

Tommy DeFelice, seeing his first action since suffering a thigh injury a month ago, looked as sound as ever passing with deadly accuracy and faking beautifully on running plays while his All-Catholic backfield mate Bobby Mahan scored four touchdowns and passed for another to lead West's attack.

The Crusaders, who placed six on the all-Catholic squad, scored with 4:10 gone in the

Continued on Page 46, Column 3

Unable to Catch Ball, McDonald Tosses for TD on 'Broken' Play

Special to The Inquirer

WASHINGTON, Dec. 2.—Irrepressible Tommy McDonald, frustrated in his favorite ploy of catching the football, turned the tables and left a lot of Redskins red-faced in embarrassment Sunday by throwing a touchdown pass on a "busted" play.

"I don't catch 'em any more," cracked McDonald, "so they're starting to let me throw 'em now. I'm like Jim Brown—my first completion for a touchdown."

Employed mostly as a decoy, McDonald caught only one pass, but his 10-yard scoring pitch to Tim Brown eased some of the sting and helped the Eagles pile up their 37-14 margin.

NEARLY INTERCEPTED

"I've thrown passes in college," related McDonald, "but this was the first for the Eagles."

"Funny thing," mused Tommy. "I nearly didn't get it off. Somebody (end Andy Stynchula) on the Redskins blitzed and I thought for a minute he was going to intercept the pitchout and run for a touchdown."

The play began as an end around and McDonald circled deep, under heavy pressure, and ran for his life. When he did get off the toss, it was deflected off Dale Hackbart, whose interception at Philadelphia killed a late Eagle rally and saved the Redskins' victory in the first meeting.

HAD TO LOB IT

"I knew I never had a chance to run it in," McDonald said. "Then I saw Hackbart coming across. I knew I had to lob it. If I threw it hard, it would have sailed right out of the end zone."

Less than seven minutes later, the Eagles had another first when Frank Budd settled under Sonny Jurgensen's long toss for a 49-yard touchdown.

"I've been waiting a long time

Continued on Page 36, Column 2

Eagles Statistics

TEAM

	Redskins	Eagles
First downs	26	21
Net yds. rushing	75	120
Net yds. passing	272	252
Passing	22-39	15-22
Passes int'cep'd by	1	2
Punts, average	2-30	3-49
Yards penalized	15	90
Fumbles lost	3	1

INDIVIDUAL LEADERS

RUSHING

EAGLES—Peaks, 7 carries for 48 net yards; Brown, 16 for 41 and 2 TD's; Jurgensen, 2 for 13.

REDSKINS—Jackson, 13 for 44; Bassler, 5, for 20; Snead, 1 for 9.

PASSING

EAGLES—Jurgensen, 14 completions in 19 attempts for 261 yards and 2 TD's; McDonald, 1 for 1 for 10 yds. and 1 TD.

REDSKINS—Snead, 16 of 29 for 211 and 2 TDs; Hall, 6 of 10 for 61.

PASS RECEIVING

EAGLES—Retzlaff, 8 catches for 135 yds.; Budd 2 for 63 and 1 TD; Brown 2 for 24 and 1 TD; McDonald 1 for 16.

REDSKINS—Mitchell, 8 for 111; Junker, 4 for 36 and 1 TD; James, 2 for 38 and 1 TD; Jackson 3 for 69.

Broken Ribs For Don?

Don Burroughs, Eagles' defensive back, will be x-rayed Monday for a possible fracture of two ribs on the right side. He suffered the injury when he was caught in a pile-up on the last play of the first half against the Redskins Sunday. Burroughs was in such pain he played only three minutes of the second half.

Tackle Jim McCusker required two stitches for a cut on his forehead. Clarence Peaks has a sprained right ankle and Timmy Brown a sprained right knee. It is expected that all three will be able to play against the Steelers next Sunday, however.

Ailing Ramblers Lose to Ducks

COMMACK, L. I., Dec. 2.—Rambler center Chuck Stuart boosted his league-leading point total with two goals Sunday night—but the second one proved to be costly.

Stuart crashed into the boards after scoring on a game-tying, first-period breakaway and was carried off on a stretcher. Without him, the Ramblers lost to the Long Island Ducks, 8-5, before 3239 fans.

Stuart was hurt moments after netting his 29th goal and his eighth in three games. He left with an injured left knee, which will be X-rayed Monday.

The Ramblers played without winger Don Graham, who hurt his knee Saturday night and was placed on the 30-day disabled list. His replacement, 20-year-old Art Chiupka, made his Rambler debut and had two assists.

Buzz Deschamps' second goal broke a 4-4 tie at 2:03 of the third period and the Ducks never

Continued on Page 36, Column 5

1962

December 3, 1962 - Eagles romp over the Washington Redskins, 37-14
Tommy McDonald throws his first career touchdown pass to Tim Brown.
Also Tim Brown scores on a 99-yard kick-off return

1963

RECORD: 2-10-2, 7TH IN NFL EAST
HEAD COACH: NICK SKORICH

SCHEDULE

REGULAR SEASON

Wk. 2	Sep 15	T	21-21	vs Pittsburgh Steelers
Wk. 3	Sep 22	L	28-24	vs St. Louis Cardinals
Wk. 4	Sep 29	L	37-14	vs New York Giants
Wk. 5	Oct 6	W	24-21	vs Dallas Cowboys
Wk. 6	Oct 13	W	37-24	at Washington Redskins
Wk. 7	Oct 20	L	37-7	at Cleveland Browns
Wk. 8	Oct 27	L	16-7	at Chicago Bears
Wk. 9	Nov 3	L	23-17	vs Cleveland Browns
Wk. 10	Nov 10	L	42-14	at New York Giants
Wk. 11	Nov 17	L	27-20	at Dallas Cowboys
Wk. 12	Nov 24	L	13-10	vs Washington Redskins
Wk. 13	Dec 1	T	20-20	at Pittsburgh Steelers
Wk. 14	Dec 7	L	38-14	at St. Louis Cardinals
Wk. 15	Dec 15	L	34-13	vs Minnesota Vikings

Timmy Brown set a new NFL record for total offense (2,436 yards; 841 rushing, 487 receiving, 11 passing, 945 kickoff returns, and 152 punt returns) in a season. With the club's outstanding shares now held by 65 stockholders, club president Frank L. McNamee said it would be put up for sale with an asking price of 4.5 million dollars. Jerry Wolman, a 36-year old builder and self-made millionaire from Washington, outbid Philadelphia businessman Jack Wolgin and became the new owner. The sale price was 5.5 million dollars. However, the Eagles flapped their wings right into last place, finishing with a dreadful 2-10-2 record. Following the season Nick Skorich was fired and replaced by Joe Kuharich.

1963 PHILADELPHIA EAGLES STATS

Passing	Comp	Att	Comp %	Yds	Y/Att	TD	Int	Rating
Sonny Jurgensen	99	184	53.8	1413	7.68	11	13	69.4
King Hill	91	186	48.9	1213	6.52	10	17	49.9
Timmy Brown	1	3	33.3	11	3.67	1	1	45.1
Ralph Guglielmi	2	7	28.6	29	4.14	0	0	44.3

Rushing	Rush	Yds	Avg	TD
Timmy Brown	192	841	4.4	6
Ted Dean	79	268	3.4	0
Clarence Peaks	64	212	3.3	1
Sonny Jurgensen	13	38	2.9	1
Paul Dudley	11	21	1.9	0
Theron Sapp	8	21	2.6	0
Ralph Guglielmi	1	20	20.0	0
Tom Woodeshick	5	18	3.6	0
King Hill	3	-1	-0.3	0

Punting	Punts	Yds	Avg	Blocked
King Hill	69	2972	43.1	0

Kicking	PAT Made	PAT Att	PAT %	FG Made	FG Att	FG %	Pts
Mike Clark	29	32	91	7	15	46.7	50

Receiving	Rec	Yds	Avg	TD
Pete Retzlaff	57	895	15.7	4
Tommy McDonald	41	731	17.8	8
Timmy Brown	36	487	13.5	4
Clarence Peaks	22	167	7.6	1
Ron Goodwin	15	215	14.3	4
Ted Dean	14	108	7.7	0
Ralph Smith	5	63	12.6	1
Paul Dudley	1	8	8.0	0
Tom Woodeshick	1	-3	-3.0	0
Theron Sapp	1	-5	-5.0	0

Interceptions	Int	Yds	Avg	TD
Don Burroughs	4	36	9.0	0
Dave Lloyd	3	30	10.0	0
Irv Cross	2	6	3.0	0
Lee Roy Caffey	1	87	87.0	1
Jimmy Carr	1	25	25.0	0
Ben Scotti	1	17	17.0	0
Maxie Baughan	1	9	9.0	0
Mike McClellan	1	0	0.0	0
Nate Ramsey	1	0	0.0	0

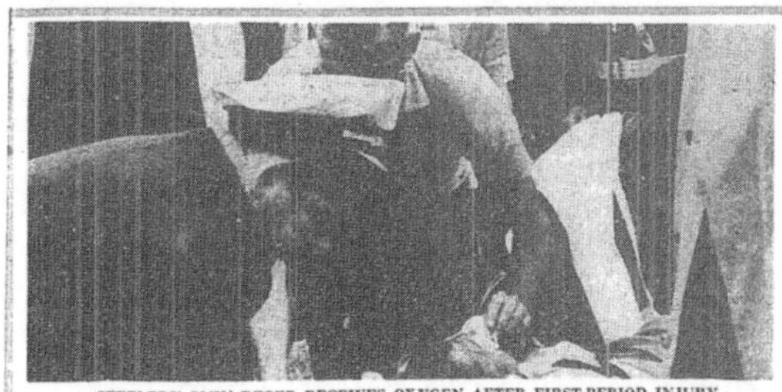

STEELERS' JOHN REGER RECEIVES OXYGEN AFTER FIRST-PERIOD INJURY.

Choking Steeler Saved From Death

DEATH was cheated Sunday on Franklin Field before 58,205 onlookers, unaware of the drama developing before them.

Only quick, skilled work by team doctors and trainers saved John Reger, Pittsburgh Steelers' linebacker, from choking to death. Reger was knocked unconscious and went into convulsions after tackling Theron Sapp of the Eagles on the last play of the first quarter.

Reger's face was blue-black from his inability to breathe after swallowing his tongue, those who rushed to his aid said.

Dr. James Nixon, the Eagles' physician, took one look at Reger writhing on the ground and rushed off for a knife with which he planned to make an on-the-spot, emergency tracheotomy if no other way could be found to give Reger life-saving air.

Meanwhile, Pittsburgh trainer Roger McGill attempted artificial respiration and then Dr. John Best, the team's physician, forced scissors between the player's teeth. When the scissors became caught in Reger's mouth, several teeth were dislodged as the instrument was withdrawn. Through the hole left by the missing teeth, it was possible to pry open Reger's mouth so that the obstruction could be removed.

* * *

IT was obvious from the moment that Reger went down that he was in serious trouble, but only a few of those present realized its nature.

As soon as the doctors saw him, they summoned a cabulance, which was driven right to his side on the playing field.

When the desperate first aid efforts partially restored Reger's breathing, treatment was continued on the field for several minutes before he was lifted on a stretcher to the cabulance and driven to nearby University Hospital.

There it was later announced that his condition was satisfactory. He was detained overnight for observation to guard against possibility of a brain injury.

HERB GOOD

The Philadelphia Inquirer

TODAY'S SPORTS

31 MONDAY, SEPTEMBER 16, 1963 h★

Also in this section . . .

Classified Advertising

Comics, Puzzles

Trailing by a point in the fourth period, the Eagles shift into a shotgun formation—and Sonny Jurgensen fires as Steelers' Lou Michaels and Ernie Stautner apply pressure. Sonny's on h is 11 as he throws the ball.

Inquirer Magic Eye Photos by Robert L. Mooney, Staff Photographer

The pass sails 50 yards through the air and falls into the waiting arms of Tommy McDonald, who grabs it in full stride and heads for the goal line. Here, he's crossing the Steelers' 35 with Glenn Glass in pursuit.

Steelers' Late PAT Fails, Eagles Tie in Opener, 21-21

By HERB GOOD

Continued from First Page

thereafter to put the Steelers on the Eagles' 36 as the game ended.

Burroughs was so incensed that he had to be restrained from following the officials to their locker room after the final whistle.

Both teams found the stalemate highly unpalatable, as each thought it should have won, and rightly so.

The Eagles, with five new men in their starting units, showed improvement over the team that finished in the cellar a year ago and delighted their fans with the way they got the jump on the Steelers and set the pace most of the way.

In addition to tossing his big bomb to McDonald, Jurgensen also threw a 13-yard TD pass to Tommy to give the Eagles a 7-0 lead in the first quarter and he tossed six yards to Ralph (Catfish) Smith for the other Eagle tally.

McDonald, who showed no signs of the charley horse that kept him out of the last exhibition game with the New York Giants, was at his sparkling finest as he grabbed seven passes in all for 179 big yards.

The Eagles outgained the Steelers in total net yardage, 353 to 315, largely due to the marksmanship of Jurgensen, who completed 16 of 26 tosses for 322 yards.

Jurgensen hit McDonald for 43 yards and Pete Retzlaff for 27 as he directed an 87-yard drive for the first TD that came at 7:58 of the first quarter.

The second TD was set up by a Jurgensen toss to Tim Brown on a play that covered 42 yards to the enemy six, following a fumble recovery by Maxie Baughan at the Steeler 41 early in the third quarter.

But it was the big bomb to McDonald that provided the game's biggest thrill, especially since it came on the surprise shotgun play coach Nick Skorich had readied for the occasion and which he feared a Pittsburgh spy might have learned at last Thursday's practice.

Obviously, the Steelers hadn't been tipped off since they were unprepared for Jurgensen taking a direct pass from center and uncorking a tremendous throw which McDonald grabbed at the Steeler 41. He raced to the goal line after eluding a diving tackle by Glenn Glass at the 23. It was the third play of an 80-yard advance.

STEELERS MOVE AHEAD

This lightning bolt came five minutes after the Steelers, who trailed, 7-6, at halftime, had gone ahead on a one-yard scoring dive by Johnson on the second play after Brady Keys had returned a punt 76 yards to the two.

Ironically, the damaging runback came on King Hill's best punt of the chilly, dreary day—a 62-yarder which skimmed off Key's fingers as he tried to catch the ball running toward

Continued on Page 36, Column 1

Records

EAGLES LOG

Sept. 15—Tied Steelers, 21-21.
Sept. 22—Cardinals.
Sept. 29—Giants.
Oct. 6—Cowboys.
Oct. 13—at Redskins.
Oct. 20—at Browns.
Oct. 27—at Bears.
Nov. 3—Browns.
Nov. 10—at Giants.
Nov. 17—at Cowboys.
Nov. 24—Redskins.
Dec. 1—at Steelers.
Dec. 8—at Cardinals.
Dec. 15—Vikings.

STEELERS LOG

Sept. 15—Tied EAGLES, 21-21.
Sept. 22—Giants.
Sept. 29—Cardinals.
Oct. 5—at Browns.
Oct. 13—at Cardinals.
Oct. 20—Redskins.
Oct. 27—Cowboys.
Nov. 3—Packers at Milwaukee.
Nov. 10—Browns.
Nov. 17—at Redskins.
Nov. 24—Bears.
Dec. 1—EAGLES.
Dec. 8—at Cowboys.
Dec. 15—at Giants.

Baseball Facts

Standings, Statistics

(September 16, 1963)

NATIONAL LEAGUE

Sunday's Results

PHILLIES, 6; Los Angeles, 1.
San Francisco, 13; Pittsburgh, 5.
Cincinnati, 3; Chicago, 1.
St. Louis, 3; Milwaukee, 2, 1st. St. Louis, 5; Milwaukee, 0, 2d.
Houston, 5; New York, 4, 1st. Houston, 5; New York, 0, 2d.

STANDING OF THE TEAMS

CLUBS	Los Angeles	St. Louis	San Francisco	Milwaukee	PHILLIES	Cincinnati	Chicago	Pittsburgh	Houston	New York	Games Won	Games Lost	Percentage	Games Behind
Los Angeles	—	9	9	8	7	10	11	11	13	13	91	59	.607	—
St. Louis	6	—	10	10	10	6	10	13	13	13	91	61	.599	1
San Francisco	9	8	—	6	9	10	8	11	10	10	81	69	.540	10
Milwaukee	10	8	9	—	10	7	4	7	13	12	80	71	.530	11½
PHILLIES	8	8	6	8	—	10	9	13	9	8	79	72	.523	12½
Cincinnati	8	7	8	9	8	—	9	11	10	10	80	73	.523	12½
Chicago	7	6	10	8	9	9	—	6	9	11	75	75	.500	16
Pittsburgh	4	5	4	11	5	7	8	—	12	14	70	79	.470	20½
Houston	5	5	8	5	6	6	9	3	—	11	58	93	.384	33½
New York	2	5	5	6	8	8	7	4	4	—	49	102	.325	42½

AMERICAN LEAGUE

Sunday's Results

Baltimore, 2; Detroit, 1.
New York, 2; Minnesota, 1.
Boston, 5; Kansas City, 3.
Cleveland, 6; Los Angeles, 3.
Chicago at Washington, postponed, rain.

STANDING OF THE TEAMS

CLUBS	New York	Chicago	Minnesota	Baltimore	Detroit	Boston	Cleveland	Los Angeles	Kansas City	Washington	Games Won	Games Lost	Percentage	Games Behind
New York	—	10	11	11	10	12	11	11	10	14	100	52	.658	—
Chicago	6	—	8	10	9	7	11	12	10	12	85	65	.567	14
Minnesota	4	10	—	9	8	9	13	9	9	14	85	67	.559	15
Baltimore	7	6	9	—	11	7	10	7	9	13	79	72	.523	20½
Detroit	8	6	7	4	—	9	8	12	13	7	74	76	.493	25
Boston	6	8	6	11	9	—	10	9	5	9	73	79	.480	27
Cleveland	6	7	4	8	10	8	—	8	8	13	72	81	.471	28½
Los Angeles	3	8	9	9	6	8	6	—	8	9	67	83	.447	32
Kansas City	4	6	9	9	3	11	6	10	—	8	68	84	.447	32
Washington	4	4	4	2	8	9	5	9	9	—	53	97	.353	46

Continued on Page 34, Column 3

Monday's Games, Pitchers & their records on Page 35.

Tittle's Passes Carry Giants to Win Over Colts

BALTIMORE, Sept. 15 (UPI).—Y. A. Tittle, the 36-year-old pass master, threw three scoring passes and ran nine yards for a go-ahead touchdown Sunday before leaving with an injury as the New York Giants scored a 37-28 victory over the Baltimore Colts.

A crowd of 60,029, largest ever to attend a National Football League game in Memorial Stadium, watched Tittle complete 16 of 23 passes for 242 yards despite a steady rain.

This was the Colts' first home opening setback in nine seasons.

Tittle was shaken up when hit hard at the goal line in running for a touchdown that gave the Giants a 30-28 lead at 7:28 of the third quarter. He did not return to the game, but during his absence the Giants added a touchdown following a pass interception by Allan Webb later in the period.

With Ralph Guglielmi at quarterback, the Giants stuck largely to a running game through the scoreless final period.

Tittle's passing rallied the Giants after a wretched 17 minutes during which they set up three Baltimore touchdowns by fumbles and fell behind, 21-3.

Tittle himself fumbled three

Continued on Page 36, Column 7

Eagles' Statistics

TEAM

	Eagles	Steelers
First downs	14	21
Net Yards rushing	58	109
Net Yards passing	295	206
Passes completed	16 of 26	18 of 34
Passes intercepted by	0	2
Punts	6-45.2	4-39.5
Yards penalized	40	15
Fumbles lost	2	2

INDIVIDUAL LEADERS

RUSHING

EAGLES—T. Brown, 7 carries for 24 net yds.; Sapp 8 for 21; Peaks 4 for 12.

STEELERS—Hoak, 15 for 55; Johnson, 13 for 40 and 1 TD; Ferguson, 3 for 7.

PASSING

EAGLES—Jurgensen, 16 completions in 26 attempts for 322 yards and 3 TDs.

STEELERS—E. Brown, 18 for 34 for 234.

RECEIVING

EAGLES—McDonald, 7 catches for 179 yards and 2 TDs; Retzlaff, 2 for 34; T. Brown, 4 for 79; R. Smith, for 6 and 1 TD.

STEELERS — Dial, 7 for 116; Carpenter, 5 for 54; Johnson, 3 for 16 and 1 TD.

It's a race between McDonald and Glass, who dives in an effort to catch Tommy on the 23.

McDonald's home free on a 75-yard TD play as he leaves Glass sprawled behind him on the 20.

Phils Win, 6-1, Shave Dodger Lead to 1 Game

By ALLEN LEWIS

Righthander Dallas Green pitched his best game of the season Sunday at Connie Mack Stadium, and it couldn't have come at a worse time for the Los Angeles Dodgers, who are fighting for their lives in another madcap National League pennant race.

Green, who has completed only three of his 12 starts this year, held the league leaders to five scattered hits and didn't give up a safety after the fifth inning as the Phillies pleased a gathering of 16,796 by winning their final home game of the season, 6-1.

That boosted the Phils' home attendance for the season to 907,141, their highest total since 1958.

The Phillies, who took advantage of three passed balls by catcher John Roseboro, treated the Dodgers' ace righthander, Don Drysdale, like just another pitcher as they scored twice in the first, twice in the sixth and once in the seventh against the hurler who beat the Phillies 13 straight times until this season.

In the eighth, Roy Sievers greeted reliefer Dick Calmus with his 17th home run to wind up the scoring.

TOMMY DAVIS HOMERS

The only run the Dodgers scored came on a home run. It was hit by Tommy Davis in the fourth inning and, like Sievers' blow, landed on the left field roof. It was Davis' 15th of the season and his second in two games.

That was the only product of the Dodger offense, however, and the Los Angeles' league lead, a comfortable seven games on Aug. 30, has now been cut to one game by the rampaging St. Louis Cardinals, who beat the Milwaukee Braves twice, 3-2, 5-0.

There may be a real connection between the fact that the Dodgers' lead has been steadily diminishing since Drysdale won his last game. Don beat San Francisco Aug. 30 for his 17th victory and hasn't won since. Sunday's loss was his 17th of the season.

Right at the outset, it didn't seem to be the Dodgers' day. Green set the visitors down on two strikeouts and a pop fly in the first and the Phillies then took the lead.

Tony Taylor singled to center, stole second on the next pitch and scored when Johnny Callison singled to right. Slugger Wes Covington surprised the Dodgers with a bunt between the mound and first base and beat it out for a hit.

Drysdale steadied to get Tony Gonzalez to bounce to shortstop into a double play, but the second pitch to Clay Dalrymple got away from Roseboro for a passed ball which allowed Callison to sprint home from third.

McMULLEN TAGGED

Cookie Rojas made a nice play to turn in a double play on John Roseboro's grounder to second after Ron Fairly singled in the second, and some more alert defensive play—and a base-running goof—stymied the Dodgers in the third.

In this frame, Willie Davis led off with a safe bunt down the first-base line and sprinted to third on Ken McMullen's single to right. Callison made a strong, low throw to the infield, although he had no chance to get the swift Davis, and shortstop Bobby Wine rushed over to cut off the ball halfway between first and second.

McMullen had rounded first and was an easy out when Wine threw the ball to Sievers. That ruined that rally. Drysdale bounced to the mound as Green held Davis at third, and Maury Wills then flied out to left.

Tommy Davis hit his homer on a no-ball two-strike pitch in the fourth, and Willie Davis singled to right in the fifth with one away. McMullen walked, but Drysdale fouled out and Wills popped up. The only other Dodg-

Continued on Page 32, Column 2

Cards Sweep Braves, Extend Win Streak to 10

ST. LOUIS, Sept. 15 (AP).—Lew Burdette and Ray Sadecki pitched St. Louis within one game of National League-leading Los Angeles Sunday as the Cardinals swept a doubleheader from Milwaukee, 3-2 and 5-0.

The two victories extended the Cardinals' winning streak to 10 games—their longest in 11 years—and gave the Cardinals 19 victories in 20 games during their drive to overhaul Los Angeles.

The Dodgers, who saw 1½ games sliced from their lead when they lost to Philadelphia Sunday, open a three-game series at St. Louis Monday night.

WHITE BELTS 27TH

Bill White's 27th home run, with a man on in the second inning, and Ken Boyer's 23d in the fourth gave the Cardinals enough to get by in the opener.

Charlie James and Tim McCarver each stroked three hits to lead a 14-hit attack in the second game against loser Dennis Lemaster and four relievers. James drove in two runs and McCarver one while Sadecki checked the Braves on five hits.

Burdette, winning his third game and second against his former mates since he joined the Cardinals in June, allowed just six hits. Hank Aaron's 42d homer with a man on in the seventh accounted for the Milwaukee runs.

BURDETTE WALKS NONE

Burdette struck out five and walked none in picking up his ninth victory against 11 defeats.

Sadecki struck out six and

Continued on Page 37, Column 5

Remaining Games

Los Angeles—At home 9, Pittsburgh 3, New York 3, Phillies 3; Away 3, St. Louis 3.

St. Louis—At home 7, Milwaukee 1, Los Angeles 3, Cincinnati 3; Away 4, Cincinnati 2, Chicago 2.

Sports Results

FOOTBALL

NFL

Sunday's Results

EAGLES	21	Pittsburgh	21
New York	37	Baltimore	28
Cleveland	37	Washington	14
Chicago	10	Green Bay	3
Minnesota	24	San Francisco	20

Saturday's Results

St. Louis	34	Dallas	7
Detroit	23	Los Angeles	2

Standings

Eastern Division

	W	L	T	P.	Pts	OP
New York	1	0	0	1.000	37	28
St. Louis	1	0	0	1.000	34	7
Cleveland	1	0	0	1.000	37	14
EAGLES	0	0	1	.000	21	21
Pittsburgh	0	0	1	.000	21	21
Washington	0	1	0	.000	14	37
Dallas	0	1	0	.000	7	34

Western Division

	W	L	T	Pct	Pts	OP
Detroit	1	0	0	1.000	23	2
Minnesota	1	0	0	1.000	24	20
Chicago	1	0	0	1.000	10	3
San Fran'co	0	1	0	.000	20	24
Baltimore	0	1	0	.000	28	37
Los Ang'les	0	1	0	.000	2	23
Green Bay	0	1	0	.000	3	10

Continued on Page 36, Column 7

1963

September 16, 1963 - Eagles tie the Steelers, 21-21
Tommy McDonald has seven catches for 179 yards and two touchdowns

1964

RECORD: 6-8, T-3RD IN NFL EAST
HEAD COACH: JOE KUHARICH

Schedule

Regular Season

Wk. 1	Sep 13	W	38-7	vs New York Giants
Wk. 2	Sep 20	L	28-24	vs San Francisco 49ers
Wk. 3	Sep 27	L	28-20	vs Cleveland Browns
Wk. 4	Oct 4	W	21-7	vs Pittsburgh Steelers
Wk. 5	Oct 11	L	35-20	at Washington Redskins
Wk. 6	Oct 18	W	23-17	at New York Giants
Wk. 7	Oct 25	W	34-10	at Pittsburgh Steelers
Wk. 8	Nov 1	L	21-10	vs Washington Redskins
Wk. 9	Nov 8	L	20-10	at Los Angeles Rams
Wk. 10	Nov 15	W	17-14	at Dallas Cowboys
Wk. 11	Nov 22	L	38-13	vs St. Louis Cardinals
Wk. 12	Nov 29	L	38-24	at Cleveland Browns
Wk. 13	Dec 6	W	24-14	vs Dallas Cowboys
Wk. 14	Dec 13	L	36-34	at St. Louis Cardinals

In the first of a series of major trades, Kuharich traded safety Jim Carr and quarterback Sonny Jurgensen to the Washington Redskins for Norm Snead in a swap of signal callers. He then traded Tommy McDonald to Dallas, Clarence Peaks to Pittsburgh, Ted Dean to Minnesota, and Lee Roy Caffey and a draft pick to Green Bay. The team that was clearly in a rebuilding mode slowly showed improvement by eventually finishing the season with a 6-8 record.

1964 Philadelphia Eagles Stats

Passing	Comp	Att	Comp %	Yds	Y/Att	TD	Int	Rating
Norm Snead	138	283	48.8	1906	6.73	14	12	69.6
Jack Concannon	12	23	52.2	199	8.65	2	1	92.5
King Hill	49	88	55.7	641	7.28	3	4	71.3
Earl Gros	0	1	0.0	0	0.00	0	0	39.6
Timmy Brown	0	2	0.0	0	0.00	0	1	0.0

Rushing	Rush	Yds	Avg	TD
Earl Gros	154	748	4.9	2
Ollie Matson	96	404	4.2	4
Timmy Brown	90	356	4.0	5
Tom Woodeshick	37	180	4.9	2
Jack Concannon	16	134	8.4	1
Norm Snead	16	59	3.7	2
Izzy Lang	12	37	3.1	0
King Hill	8	27	3.4	0
Ron Goodwin	1	-23	-23.0	0

Receiving	Rec	Yds	Avg	TD
Pete Retzlaff	51	855	16.8	8
Ray Poage	37	479	12.9	1
Earl Gros	29	234	8.1	0
Ron Goodwin	23	335	14.6	3
Ollie Matson	17	242	14.2	1
Timmy Brown	15	244	16.3	5
Red Mack	8	169	21.1	1
Izzy Lang	6	69	11.5	0
Roger Gill	4	58	14.5	0
Ralph Smith	4	35	8.8	0
Tom Woodeshick	4	12	3.0	0
Claude Crabb	1	14	14.0	0

Punting	Punts	Yds	Avg	Blocked
Sam Baker	49	2073	42.3	0
King Hill	24	968	40.3	0

Interceptions	Int	Yds	Avg	TD
Nate Ramsey	5	31	6.2	0
Irv Cross	3	109	36.3	1
Dave Lloyd	3	68	22.7	0
Joe Scarpati	3	41	13.7	1
Don Burroughs	2	5	2.5	0
Glenn Glass	1	18	18.0	0

Kicking	PAT Made	PAT Att	PAT %	FG Made	FG Att	FG %	Pts
Sam Baker	36	37	97	16	26	61.5	84

THE PHILADELPHIA INQUIRER, MONDAY MORNING, SEPTEMBER 14, 1964 a b 31

Too Many Eagles in Backfield Make It Trying Day for Tittle

Inquirer Photos by Alexander Deans, Staff Photographer

Giants' Y. A. Tittle (left) found that his "pocket" Sunday consisted all too often of Eagles instead of Giants. Floyd Peters (72), Mike Morgan (89) and Max Baughan (55) apply first-quarter rush.

Eagles' blitzing defense kept catching up with Giants' signal-caller, as linebacker Baughan applies "collar" tackle and Morgan zeroes on Yat's underpinnings.

Even the news on the sidelines wasn't good. Tittle relaxes glumly while Giants' coach Allie Sherman talks with aides upstairs as disaster unfolds.

To make day "complete," Tittle had to run 248-pound Eagle linebacker Dave Lloyd (left) out of bounds after latter had stolen Yat's pass in fourth period and returned it to Giants' nine-yard line.

September 14, 1964 - Eagles snap a six-game losing streak against the Giants by winning 38-7. QB Norm Snead makes his Eagles debut.

1964

1965

RECORD: 5-9, T-5TH IN NFL EAST
HEAD COACH: JOE KUHARICH

Schedule

Regular Season

Wk. 2	Sep 19	W	34-27	vs St. Louis Cardinals
Wk. 3	Sep 26	L	16-14	vs New York Giants
Wk. 4	Oct 3	L	35-17	vs Cleveland Browns
Wk. 5	Oct 10	W	35-24	at Dallas Cowboys
Wk. 6	Oct 17	L	35-27	at New York Giants
Wk. 7	Oct 24	L	20-14	vs Pittsburgh Steelers
Wk. 8	Oct 31	L	23-21	at Washington Redskins
Wk. 9	Nov 7	L	38-34	at Cleveland Browns
Wk. 10	Nov 14	W	21-14	vs Washington Redskins
Wk. 11	Nov 21	L	34-24	at Baltimore Colts
Wk. 12	Nov 28	W	28-24	at St. Louis Cardinals
Wk. 13	Dec 5	L	21-19	vs Dallas Cowboys
Wk. 14	Dec 12	W	47-13	at Pittsburgh Steelers
Wk. 15	Dec 19	L	35-28	vs Detroit Lions

Despite solid seasons from quarterback Norm Snead and his favorite target, tight end Pete Retzlaff (66 receptions for 1,190 and 10 touchdowns), the Eagles still had a disappointing season. The Eagles did manage to tie an NFL record with nine interceptions against Pittsburgh in 47-13 win. Unfortunately the team continued to sputter, finishing with a 5-9 record. However, the Eagles did end the season on a strong note by winning three of their last four games.

1965 Philadelphia Eagles Stats

Passing	Comp	Att	Comp %	Yds	Y/Att	TD	Int	Rating
Norm Snead	150	288	52.1	2346	8.15	15	13	78.0
King Hill	60	113	53.1	857	7.58	5	10	55.8
Earl Gros	1	2	50.0	63	31.50	1	0	135.4
Ray Poage	0	1	0.0	0	0.00	0	0	39.6
Timmy Brown	0	1	0.0	0	0.00	0	0	39.6
Jack Concannon	12	29	41.4	176	6.07	1	3	33.8

Rushing	Rush	Yds	Avg	TD
Timmy Brown	158	861	5.4	6
Earl Gros	145	479	3.3	7
Tom Woodeshick	28	145	5.2	0
Jack Concannon	9	104	11.6	0
Ollie Matson	22	103	4.7	2
Norm Snead	24	81	3.4	3
Izzy Lang	10	25	2.5	1
King Hill	7	20	2.9	2
Joe Scarpati	1	6	6.0	0

Interceptions	Int	Yds	Avg	TD
Nate Ramsey	6	74	12.3	0
Jim Nettles	3	84	28.0	1
Joe Scarpati	3	4	1.3	0
Irv Cross	3	1	0.3	0
Dave Lloyd	2	35	17.5	0
Al Nelson	2	23	11.5	0
John Meyers	2	12	6.0	0
George Tarasovic	1	40	40.0	1
Maxie Baughan	1	33	33.0	1
Don Hultz	1	6	6.0	0
Mike Morgan	1	1	1.0	0

Receiving	Rec	Yds	Avg	TD
Pete Retzlaff	66	1190	18.0	10
Timmy Brown	50	682	13.6	3
Ray Poage	31	612	19.7	5
Earl Gros	29	271	9.3	2
Ron Goodwin	18	252	14.0	1
Glenn Glass	15	201	13.4	0
Tom Woodeshick	6	86	14.3	0
Claude Crabb	2	41	20.5	0
Izzy Lang	2	30	15.0	0
Ollie Matson	2	29	14.5	1
Roger Gill	1	27	27.0	0
Fred Hill	1	21	21.0	0

Punting	Punts	Yds	Avg	Blocked
King Hill	19	813	42.8	0
Sam Baker	37	1551	41.9	0

Kicking	PAT Made	PAT Att	PAT %	FG Made	FG Att	FG %	Pts
Sam Baker	38	40	95	9	23	39.1	65
Dave Lloyd	7	7	100	1	2	50.0	10

1965

The Philadelphia Inquirer — Today's SPORTS
32 MONDAY, DECEMBER 13, 1965 h★
Also in this section: Financial News · Classified Advertising · Comics, Puzzles

Eagles Steal 9 Passes, Rip Steelers, 47-13

6 Interceptions Turned Into TDs; Nettles Grabs 3

Pittsburgh Suffers 11th Loss as Thefts Equal NFL Record

By HERB GOOD
Of The Inquirer Staff

PITTSBURGH, Dec. 12 — Using enemy passes as their most potent weapon, the Eagles rolled over the Pittsburgh Steelers on Sunday with ridiculous ease, 47-13, for their fifth victory before 22,002 in Pitt Stadium.

With rookie Jim Nettles stealing three, the Eagles intercepted nine passes to tie the National Football League record as they handed the Steelers their sixth straight loss and 11th reverse of the season.

Three of the interceptions were returned for touchdowns and three other scores stemmed from the thefts as the Eagles avenged a 20-14 setback received in a Franklin Field upset.

NETTLES SCORES

Nettles, diminutive former Wisconsin star who was pressed into service at strong-side safety when Nate Ramsey was injured early in the game, returned his second interception 86 yards for his first pro TD. Maxie Baughan, seeing most of his action at middle linebacker, raced 33 yards and George Tarasovic, a former Steeler, dashed 40 yards for scores on their interceptions.

Marv Woodson also raced 61 yards with an interception for Pittsburgh's second TD on the last play of the first half. Thus, four scoring interceptions by the two teams set a new NFL record, and the three by the Eagles tied the league mark for one team.

It was a weird, sloppy game, almost a travesty on the sport, and was played in unseasonable 64-degree weather on a somewhat soggy field outlined by sawdust at the wettest spots. Brief flurries of fisticuffs broke out three times as frustrations ignited tempers.

RETZLAFF SETS MARKS

Veteran tight end Pete Retzlaff wiped out two of Tommy McDonald's Eagle season records with five catches for 52 yards and one TD, all in the first half. He now has 65 catches, one more than McDonald made in 1961, and 1171 yards, compared with the 1146 yards McDonald contributed in 1962.

Except for this bright point, the Eagles did little to brag about offensively although running up a 34-0 lead in the first 16 minutes and scoring the most points ever made against the Steelers in this long rivalry.

Believe it or not, the Steelers had a 19-17 edge in first downs and had a total net yardage advantage of 324 to 302.

Norm Snead directed the Eagles to first-period scores on

Continued on Page 34, Column 6

RECORDS

EAGLES' LOG

Sept. 19—Defeated Cardinals, 34-27.
Sept. 26—Lost to Giants, 16-14.
Oct. 3—Lost to Browns, 35-17.
Oct. 10—Defeated Cowboys, 35-24.
Oct. 17—Lost to Giants, 35-27.
Oct. 24—Lost to Steelers, 20-14.
Oct. 31—Lost to Redskins, 23-21.
Nov. 7—Lost to Browns, 38-34.
Nov. 14—Defeated Redskins, 21-14.
Nov. 21—Lost to Colts, 34-24.
Nov. 28—Defeated Cardinals, 28-24.
Dec. 5—Lost to Cowboys, 21-19.
Dec. 12—Defeated Steelers, 47-13.
Dec. 19—Lions.

STEELERS' LOG

Sept. 19—Lost to Packers, 41-9.
Sept. 26—Lost to 49ers, 27-17.
Oct. 3—Lost to Giants, 23-13.
Oct. 9—Lost to Browns, 24-19.
Oct. 17—Lost to Cardinals, 20-7.
Oct. 24—Defeated EAGLES, 20-14.
Oct. 31—Defeated Cowboys, 22-13.
Nov. 7—Lost to Cardinals, 21-17.
Nov. 14—Lost to Cowboys, 24-17.
Nov. 21—Lost to Redskins, 31-3.
Nov. 28—Lost to Browns, 42-21.
Dec. 5—Lost to Giants, 35-10.
Dec. 12—Lost to EAGLES, 47-13.
Dec. 19—At Redskins.

Astros Fire Richards, Harris in Shakeup

Waiting eagerly for this pre-Christmas gift, Eagles' Maxie Baughan prepares to make shoestring catch of pass thrown by Steelers' sub quarterback Tommy Wade, on Steeler 33 late in the first quarter.

Inquirer Magic Eye Photos by Robert L. Mooney, Staff Photographer

In full stride after making the interception—one of nine by the Eagles—Baughan veers to his right as he nears the Steelers' 15. Ray Mansfield and Dan James race cross-field in an effort to cut him off.

Grady Hatton Promoted to Manager's Job

Tal Smith Is Named Head of Personnel; Robinson Bounced

HOUSTON, Tex., Dec. 12 (UPI).—The Houston Astros, ninth in the National League for the past three years, Sunday fired general manager Paul Richards and field manager Luman Harris in a major top-level shakeup.

The Astros' owner, Judge Roy Hofheinz, announced that former Cincinnati third baseman Grady Hatton will replace Harris as manager.

The 43-year-old Hatton moves up to the post from the managership of the Astros' Class Triple-A minor league club at Oklahoma City, which he guided to two pennants and a third-place finish in three years.

ROBINSON OUT ALSO

Also losing his job in the shakeup was Astros' farm director Eddie Robinson.

Hofheinz said Tal Smith, a key figure in laying out the fabulous Harris County domed stadium for baseball, would become a vice-president of the Astros and director of player personnel.

"Hatton and Smith will handle all decisions regarding player personnel and development throughout the Houston organization," Hofheinz said.

Hofheinz said he wished "Richards the very best in any endeavor he may undertake."

CONTRACT THROUGH 1970

Harris, who had a 65-97 record with the Astros last season, had another year to go on his contract. Hofheinz said he will be offered another position with the club.

Richards had a contract that ran through 1970.

Hatton only last Friday announced that he had an offer from the Chicago White Sox to succeed Al Lopez as manager, an offer that the White Sox denied making. The unusual nature of the Hatton announcement led to widespread speculation that he was on his way up in the Houston organization.

SOME COACHES OUT

Hatton said that he will choose his own coaches under his new job, and indicated that "some" of his present staff would not stay on. He did not say who would be fired.

Hatton joined the Houston organization less than a month

Continued on Page 35, Column 2

Hornung Gets 5 TDs As Packers Top Colts To Take Division Lead

BALTIMORE, Dec. 12 (AP)—Paul Hornung scored five touchdowns in leading the Green Bay Packers to a 42-27 victory over the crippled Baltimore Colts Sunday and moved the Packers into first place in the National Football League's Western Conference.

The Packers, winning their 10th game against three losses took a one-half game lead over the Colts and can clinch a championship playoff berth Jan. 2 against Cleveland by beating San Francisco in the final game next Sunday.

The scoring outburst by the Packers was their highest of the

See Red Smith's Column on Page 36

season and Hornung's five touchdowns were the most ever by a Packer. The Golden Boy had scored only three in the 12 previous games this season.

65-YARD PASS PLAY

As the Colts were staging their second attempt at a comeback in the last quarter, Hornung and quarterback Bart Starr pulled off a 65-yard pass and run scoring play.

In the first quarter, the same pair worked a 50-yard touchdown and Hornung ran for three more.

The Colts, with quarterback John Unitas on crutches on the sideline, and his substitute Gary Cuozzo playing the last half with an injured shoulder, had trouble with their offense until the last quarter.

They scored twice then to chop the Packer lead to 35-27. Cuozzo set up the first score with a 40-yard pass to end Raymond Berry and hit him for the second on a five-yard toss.

The Colts were blanked in the third quarter when Cuozzo was hurt and the Packers ran up a 35-13 lead with Hornung scoring twice.

The Colts muffed an opportunity to take the lead at halftime instead of trailing, 21-13.

87-YARD RETURN

They were on the Packer two and second down when Cuozzo lofted a soft pass to the flat on his right.

Linebacker Dave Robinson intercepted the ball and rambled 87 yards to the Colt 10 before being dragged down from behind. On the first play, Starr rifled a touchdown pass to end Boyd Dowler.

The sudden turn of events extinguished what had been a rally by the Colts to overcome a 14-3 Packer lead in the first quarter.

Although the Colts drew first blood on Lou Michaels' 14-yard field goal after Lenny Lyles returned an intercepted pass to the Green Bay 31, the Packers stormed for touchdowns the next two times with the ball.

They ran and passed through the Colts for 64 yards on six plays, with Hornung ramming over the last two. Hornung worked his way out in the clear the next time the Packers were in possession and Starr hit him with a pass for a 50-yard scoring play.

Michaels kicked another field goal of 45 yards and Lyles provided the offense with another chance to score by recovering a

Continued on Page 34, Column 1

Sports Results

Professional

FOOTBALL
NATIONAL LEAGUE

EAGLES	47	Pittsburgh	13
Green Bay	42	Baltimore	27
Chicago	61	San Francisco	20
Los Angeles	42	Cleveland	7
New York	27	Washington	10
Minnesota	29	Detroit	7

Saturday's Result

Dallas	27	St. Louis	13

Standings
Eastern Conference

	W	L	T	Pct.	Pts.	Op.
*Cleveland	10	3	0	.769	336	301
New York	7	6	0	.538	259	300
Dallas	6	7	0	.462	287	260
EAGLES	5	8	0	.385	335	324
St. Louis	5	8	0	.385	272	282
Washington	5	8	0	.385	222	287
Pittsburgh	2	11	0	.154	188	362

*Clinched conference title.

Western Conference

	W	L	T	Pct.	Pts.	Op.
Green Bay	10	3	0	.769	292	200
Baltimore	9	3	1	.750	369	267
Chicago	9	4	0	.692	392	251
S.Francisco	7	6	0	.538	397	378
Minnesota	6	7	0	.462	359	386
Detroit	5	7	1	.417	222	267
Los Angeles	4	9	0	.308	252	308

AMERICAN LEAGUE

San Diego	27	Houston	26
Buffalo	34	Kansas City	25
Oakland	24	New York	14
Boston	28	Denver	20

Standings
Eastern Division

	W	L	T	Pct.	Pts.	Opp.
*Buffalo	10	2	1	.833	301	212
New York	4	8	1	.333	271	291
Houston	4	9	0	.308	281	387
Boston	3	8	2	.273	202	288

Western Division

	W	L	T	Pct.	Pts.	Opp.
*San Diego	8	2	3	.800	316	213
Oakland	8	4	1	.667	284	215
Kansas City	6	5	2	.545	277	250
Denver	4	9	0	.308	288	347

* Clinched divisional title

Continued on Page 31, Column 2

Running more like a young halfback than a veteran linebacker, Maxie keeps his feet and manages to stay in bounds as he eludes Mansfield at the eight and heads for the Steeler goal line.

Crossing the five, Maxie runs into Steelers' Charlie Bradshaw, who appears to have a clean shot at the ball-carrier. But Baughan, cutting back to the inside, escapes Bradshaw's grasp.

Running hard and low, Maxie is home free at the end of his fancy-stepping dash, crossing the goal line an instant before Steelers' Mike Lind hits him. Baughan's TD gave Eagles a 27-0 lead.

Sayers' 6 TDs Equal Mark as Bears Win, 61-20

CHICAGO, Dec. 12 (AP).—Fabulous Gale Sayers scored six touchdowns Sunday, pushing his season total to 21 to set a National Football League season record, and the Chicago Bears routed the San Francisco 49ers, 61-20.

Sayers' touchdown spree established a Bear single game scoring record and also matched the one-game NFL mark.

His total of 21 bettered the league record of 20 registered last season by Baltimore's Lenny Moore and duplicated this season by Cleveland's Jimmy Brown.

BEARS AVENGE LOSS

The triumph, avenging an opening 52-24 defeat at San Francisco, kept alive the Bears' mathematical chance of sharing the Western Conference title. They now have a 9-4 mark.

The remarkable rookie from Kansas tallied this way on a rain-slick field as 46,278 fans gave him standing ovations:

First quarter — Rudy Bukich hit Sayers on a screen pass and he streaked 80 yards.

SAYERS BOLTS OVER

Second quarter—After John Arnett ran back a punt 77 yards to the 49ers' 21, Sayers bolted across on the first play. Bukich's 51-yard pass to Jimmy Jones set up Sayers' next scoring smash from the seven on a pitchout.

Third quarter — Sayers cut through tackle and raced 50

Continued on Page 35, Column *

'Guilty Conscience'

Lucky to Intercept 3, Rookie Nettles Claims

Special to The Inquirer

PITTSBURGH, Dec. 12—Nobody bothered to draft Jim Nettles when his football eligibility expired at the University of Wisconsin two years ago, so he stayed in school to pick up his degree in landscape architecture and worked at a variety of jobs.

He helped plan a John F. Kennedy Memorial Library in his home town—Muncie, Ind.—and as a membe. of the General Motors labor relations staff helped negotiate a contract with a Muncie local.

Sunday, the pint-sized defensive halfback negotiated a place for himself in the Eagles' future as he intercepted three Pittsburgh Steeler passes—a total that fell one short of a prediction he'd made before the game.

"If I get in there I think I'll pick off four," he'd said, whimsically.

Nate Ramsey's toe hurt, so Nettles got in there. He insists he stands 5-10 and weighs 175 pounds, but he must be giving his mustache credit for 15 pounds. At any rate, he covered 6-2 Clendon Thomas as persistently as a bedbug, snatching two passes intended for the rangy end.

"On the first one," said Nettles, "I sort of played him for

Continued on Page 34, Column 5

December 13, 1965 - Eagles intercepted nine passes to tie the NFL record as they roll over the Steelers 47-13

1966

RECORD: 9-5, T-2ND IN NFL EAST
HEAD COACH: JOE KUHARICH

Schedule

Regular Season

Wk. 2	Sep 11	L	16-13	at St. Louis Cardinals
Wk. 3	Sep 18	W	23-10	vs Atlanta Falcons
Wk. 4	Sep 25	W	35-17	vs New York Giants
Wk. 5	Oct 2	L	41-10	vs St. Louis Cardinals
Wk. 6	Oct 9	L	56-7	at Dallas Cowboys
Wk. 7	Oct 16	W	31-14	at Pittsburgh Steelers
Wk. 8	Oct 23	W	31-3	at New York Giants
Wk. 9	Oct 30	L	27-13	vs Washington Redskins
Wk. 10	Nov 6	W	24-23	vs Dallas Cowboys
Wk. 11	Nov 13	L	27-7	at Cleveland Browns
Wk. 12	Nov 20	W	35-34	at San Francisco 49ers
Wk. 14	Dec 4	W	27-23	vs Pittsburgh Steelers
Wk. 15	Dec 11	W	33-21	vs Cleveland Browns
Wk. 16	Dec 18	W	37-28	at Washington Redskins

Despite more trades and switching between three different quarterbacks (Norm Snead, Jack Concannon and King Hill) the Eagles actually played solid football all year, finishing with a 9-5 record for their first winning season in five years. However, the Eagles record was only good enough to land them in second place.

1966 Philadelphia Eagles Stats

Passing	Comp	Att	Comp %	Yds	Y/Att	TD	Int	Rating
Norm Snead	103	226	45.6	1275	5.64	8	11	55.1
Izzy Lang	2	3	66.7	51	17.00	0	0	109.7
King Hill	53	97	54.6	571	5.89	5	7	59.3
Earl Gros	0	1	0.0	0	0.00	0	0	39.6
Jack Concannon	21	51	41.2	262	5.14	1	4	31.7

Rushing	Rush	Yds	Avg	TD
Timmy Brown	161	548	3.4	3
Earl Gros	102	396	3.9	7
Tom Woodeshick	85	330	3.9	4
Izzy Lang	52	239	4.6	1
Jack Concannon	25	195	7.8	2
Ollie Matson	29	101	3.5	1
Norm Snead	15	32	2.1	1
Sam Baker	1	15	15.0	0
Fred Hill	1	5	5.0	0
King Hill	7	-2	-0.3	0

Punting	Punts	Yds	Avg	Blocked
Sam Baker	42	1726	41.1	0
King Hill	23	862	37.5	0

Kicking	PAT Made	PAT Att	PAT %	FG Made	FG Att	FG %	Pts
Sam Baker	38	39	97	18	25	72.0	92

Receiving	Rec	Yds	Avg	TD
Pete Retzlaff	40	653	16.3	6
Timmy Brown	33	371	11.2	3
Fred Hill	29	304	10.5	0
Earl Gros	18	214	11.9	2
Ron Goodwin	16	212	13.3	1
Ben Hawkins	14	143	10.2	0
Izzy Lang	12	107	8.9	0
Tom Woodeshick	10	118	11.8	1
Ollie Matson	6	30	5.0	1
Jack Concannon	1	7	7.0	0

Interceptions	Int	Yds	Avg	TD
Joe Scarpati	8	182	22.8	0
Jim Nettles	3	57	19.0	1
Dave Lloyd	3	46	15.3	0
Aaron Martin	1	47	47.0	0
Harold Wells	1	8	8.0	0
Mike Morgan	1	5	5.0	0
Al Nelson	1	0	0.0	0
Nate Ramsey	1	0	0.0	0
Fred Whittington	1	0	0.0	0

The Philadelphia Inquirer — 43 — MONDAY, JANUARY 9, 1967

Today's SPORTS

Also in this section: Classified Advertising, Comics, Puzzles

Colts Down Eagles in Final 14 Seconds

Subs' 12-5 Spurt Propels 76ers By Bulls, 117-108

Full-Court Press Decisive: Celtics Fall 9 Games Back

By JACK CHEVALIER
Of The Inquirer Staff

CHICAGO, Jan. 8 — A scrambling, pressing defense — executed by the 76ers' reserves while the strong men were catching their breath for the fourth quarter — carried Philadelphia to a stormy, 117-108 victory over the Chicago Bulls on Sunday night.

The unexpected surge came in the last 3:42 of the third period with Wilt Chamberlain resting his injured ankle and four other regulars out of the lineup. It changed the game, which Chicago had dominated, and sent the 76ers limping into the All-Star break with a 20-4 record.

By breaking the Bulls' spirit and silencing an International Amphitheater crowd of 7333, the 76ers opened a fat, nine-game bulge on the second-place Boston Celtics in the National Basketball Association's Eastern Division.

SUBS GET 12-5 SPURT

While the subs tied up Chicago with a sticky, full-court press, the 76ers went on a 12-5 spurt to take a 92-86 lead after three quarters. Then Chamberlain, Luke Jackson and Hal Greer returned to turn on the usual power and make the 76ers' record 7-0 against this expansion club.

With Larry Costello out for three weeks with torn knee ligaments, coach Alex Hannum started the game with a thin backcourt crew. Things got worse after only 7:33 when Villanova grad Wally Jones was ejected for fighting with Temple grad Guy Rodgers.

Rodgers also got the thumb and was sorely missed by Bulls' coach Johnny Kerr. "Nevertheless, it was the press that killed us," Kerr admitted after the game. "I'm surprised Philly didn't try it earlier."

WILT GETS REST

The proper time came with Chicago on top, 81-80, and Chamberlain—whose right achilles tendon was kicked in Friday's game against Baltimore — due for a rest. The personal foul situation strongly favored the 76ers and Hannum decided to gamble.

Dave Gambee and Chet Walker took care of the rebounds, rookies Bill Melchionni and Matt Guokas fired the points, and the Bulls made repeated mistakes in the next 3:42.

Melchionni's first hoop of the game put the 76ers on top, 84-83. He and Walker sank free throws, then Walker stole the ball at midcourt and drove for a 15-foot jumper.

Guokas, tighter than a drum during the first half, caught the

Continued on Page 44, Column 1

No 'Star' Tilt For Wilt?

CHICAGO, Jan. 8. — Wilt Chamberlain, hobbled by a swollen achilles tendon in his right ankle, said Sunday night he may not play in the NBA All-Star game on Tuesday in San Francisco.

"If this ankle doesn't feel any better tomorrow, I'll tell them I can't play," Wilt said. "I won't request it. I'll tell them."

Chamberlain, Hal Greer and Chet Walker are scheduled to represent the 76ers in the East-West game. The Knicks' Walt Bellamy, the logical replacement if Chamberlain can't play, will be in San Francisco because New York is making a West Coast swing.

Subperb

G—Goals; ST—Shots tried; F—Fouls; FT—Fouls tried; R—Rebounds; A—Assists; P—Personal fouls; PTS—Total points.

[illegible]

With only 14 seconds left in game, Colts' Tom Matte (41) crosses goal with winning touchdown after taking handoff from Johnny Unitas (19). Matte's score defeated Eagles, 20-14, in Playoff Bowl.

Guokas Plays Well

Jones, Rodgers Banished for 1st-Period Fight

Special to The Inquirer

CHICAGO, Jan. 8 — Wally Jones and Guy Rodgers, old head-to-head playground and professional basketball rivals, were ejected from Sunday night's 76ers-Chicago game after a fist fight in the first quarter.

The scuffle, in which both participants landed a couple of solid punches, occurred at 7:33 of the period after Jones tripped Rodgers, who was trying to drive toward the basket.

Chicago's Rodgers came up swinging and it took 76ers' coach Alex Hannum and the Bulls' Jim Washington, a former teammate of Jones at Villanova, to prevent Wally from making it a 10-round bout. Jones and Hannum later said that an incident earlier in the game led to the fight.

JONES CLOUTED

"Guy did something to me physically," Jones said. "He know what it is—I don't want to say."

Hannum revealed that Rodgers had clouted Jones in the mouth with an elbow during a rebound battle.

"It was a dirty, malicious play," the coach said. "Wally

Continued on Page 44, Column 7

Concannon Wanted to Run On Pivotal Interception Play

By JOHN DELL
Of the Inquirer Staff

MIAMI, Fla., Jan. 8 — "Did you get paid yet," Timmy Brown asked, holding his $500 loser's share from Sunday's Playoff Bowl game. "They're not going to give me any," Jack Concannon answered. This was in the Eagles' locker room at the Orange Bowl stadium, after the Eagles blew a whole locker-room load of $1200 winning shares.

Concannon was feeling lowest of the low, after an interception of his pass gave the Baltimore Colts a chance to get fat piggy banks, 20-14, on a touchdown 14 seconds before the end.

"I was surprised that he threw the ball," said Jerry Logan, Colts' tight safetyman, who was playing his zone, on the left side, and hoping more than expecting that the ball would be propelled within his reach on a second-and-three situation on the Eagles' 25. Logan intercepted and returned 14 to the Eagles' 35.

LOGAN CONFIDENT

"I was just happy," was the reaction of Logan, who also made an interception in the Colts' 34-24 victory over the Eagles last season, a win made possible by Bobby Boyd's interception.

"I thought John (Unitas) would take us in or we'd get

Continued on Page 44, Column 6

Inquirer Games

Tickets Now At 3 Outlets

BUY your tickets now for the 23d annual Inquirer Track Games, Saturday, Feb. 4, at Civic Center Convention Hall.

Prices are:

$5.50 $3.50
$4.50 $2.50

Tickets are now on sale at these Central City Ticket Offices:

1422 Chestnut st.

10 A. M.-5:30 P. M.

69th Street Terminal Concourse

41 Roosevelt plaza, Camden

For mail orders make check payable to Philadelphia Inquirer Charities, Inc., and mail to Central City Ticket Office, 1422 Chestnut st., Philadelphia, Pa. 19102. Include 25 cents for postage and handling.

Sports Results

Professional

FOOTBALL

NFL PLAYOFF BOWL

Baltimore 20 — EAGLES 14

BASKETBALL

NATIONAL BASKETBALL ASSN.

[illegible]

HOCKEY

NATIONAL LEAGUE

[illegible]

AMERICAN LEAGUE

[illegible]

EASTERN LEAGUE

[illegible]

School

BASKETBALL

CATHOLIC LEAGUE

[illegible]

SUBURBAN CATHOLIC LEAGUE

[illegible]

NON LEAGUE

[illegible]

Independent

BASKETBALL

SCHUYLKILL NAVY LEAGUE

[illegible]

JEWISH LEAGUE

[illegible]

Campbell's Body Still Not Found

CONISTON, England, Jan. 8 (AP).—While prayers were said for him in village churches Sunday, divers continued searching for the body of speed king Donald Campbell who died when his jet boat Bluebird crashed on Coniston Lake last Wednesday.

Bluebird's steering wheel was dredged up, but the boat's hull still lay stuck in a bed of silt 142 feet down.

Intercepted Pass Sets Up 20-14 Playoff Bowl Win

By GORDON FORBES
Of the Inquirer Staff

MIAMI, Fla., Jan. 8.—None of the plungers at Miami's gambling dens blew as much over the weekend as Jack Concannon did on one tragic play Sunday in the Orange Bowl. The Baltimore Colts latched on to an unexpected Concannon pass which they converted into a last-second touchdown and a 20-14 Playoff Bowl victory before 58,088 shirt-sleeved fans and a Nation-wide television audience.

The interception cost the Eagles a cool $28,000, the difference between $48,000, and $1200 per player for the winning team, and $20,000, and $500 per man, for the losing team.

DULL SECOND HALF

Actually, there was such a dull flavor to the second half that many of the fans were streaming for the exits when Concannon made his ill-fated pitch.

It came when the Eagles had second down at their 25 and needed only three yards for a first down with a little more than three minutes left to play.

Instead of hammering out a first down, Concannon shoved the entire stakes on his ability to hit tight end Pete Retzlaff on a sprint-out play to his right.

LOGAN INTERCEPTS

Jerry Logan, however, ranged up to grab the ball at the Eagles' 40 and joyfully dashed with it to the 35.

That left it up to Johnny Unitas, who proceeded to guide the Colts into the end zone, with Tom Matte, hero of last season's Playoff Bowl win over the Dallas Cowboys, slamming the final foot with just 14 seconds left.

It was an ironic windup for the Eagles, who had laughed at odds all season while compiling a 9-5 record.

And it was especially bitter for Concannon, who had wrested the quarterback job away from King Hill and Norm Snead with his daring, sometimes nondescript style of moving the offense.

'JUST HUNG IT UP THERE'

"I just got jammed up when I rolled out and thought I saw Retzlaff open," said a dejected Concannon in the Eagles' locker room. "I just hung it up there."

After the theft, the Eagles could have braced at the 17 when the Colts went to third-and-nine. But even so, Baltimore had Lou Michaels available for a field goal that would have erased the Eagles' 14-13 lead.

Michaels wasn't called on then because Matte ripped past Don Hultz, Gary Pettigrew and Dave Lloyd for a 10-yard gain and a first down at the seven with 1:25 to play.

INTERFERENCE PENALTY

A motion penalty pushed the Colts momentarily back to the 12 but Jim Nettles, defensing Ray Berry, was guilty of interference and Baltimore got a first down at the six.

In the final minute, it took the Colts three plays to score. Fullback Jerry Hill smashed for three; Matte went over right tackle for almost three more and then slid off linebacker Har-

Continued on Page 44, Column 3

Frank Dolson

Miami Fans Missed TV Fun

Look, there on the screen,
Is it a soap opera?
Is it a variety show?
Well, it's certainly not Super Bowl.

OKAY, so the temperature in Miami was in the 80s, the sun was shining and the voice kept saying, "It's a beautiful day for football."

And . . . let's be honest. It was a miserable day in Philadelphia, damp and dismal. Good for nothing much but sitting in front of a television screen and watching the Eagles play the Colts in the sixth annual Lesser Bowl.

FRANK DOLSON

Still, that's no reason to be jealous of those 58,088 live ones, basking in the Orange Bowl. Oh sure, they got a tan and saw a football game. But think of what they missed.

Studio audiences never see as much of a TV show as the home viewers. And, let's face it. The NFL's Lesser Bowl, pitting the team that didn't quite win the Eastern title against the team that didn't quite win the Western title, is basically a TV show. So it shouldn't be surprising that those poor, sun-bathing ticket-buyers in Miami missed practically all the fun.

* * *

COUNTING pre-game and post-game shows, they missed 25 commercials, all in living color. While the folks in the Orange Bowl yawned through all those dull, minute-long time-outs, those of us lucky enough to be home thrilled to the sight of people hawking four brands of cigarets, two makes of TV sets, two deodorants, cars, trucks, gasoline, razor blades, sun glasses, cigars, after-shave lotion, shaving cream, tires, an airline and a beer.

Best of all, was an inspired commercial for Ford pickup trucks, starring Harry Gilmer, "coach of the Detroit Lions." Gilmer played his role with striking realism, considering he was fired a couple of days ago by the owner of the Lions, William Clay Ford.

Apparently, there was a breakdown in communications between the auto branch and the football branch of the Ford family. Now that the auto branch has used Gilmer to plug cars, the football branch may get even by using the Lions to plug Edsels.

The studio audience also missed a lot of other goodies. There were isolated videotape reruns in color and slow-motion reruns in black and white. There were close-up shots of the Orange Bowl queen and her court. And there was a pre-game interview with Eagles' coach Joe Kuharich, who told home viewers: "We're hopeful that with variations of defensive maneuvers we can stymie them, at least periodically."

The Lesser Bowl, though, was much more than a TV show. In reality, it was a gigantic, three-hour-

Continued on Page 44, Column 4

The violence of pro football is well demonstrated on this play as Colts' linebacker Mike Curtis takes the legs out from under Eagles' Ron Goodwin, who has just caught a Jack Concannon pass for nine-yard gain.

Eagles' defensive back Joe Scarpati (21) hits Colt halfback Tom Matte (41) so hard he loses ball in third period of Playoff Bowl. Matte quickly recovered fumble. Colt fullback Tony Lorick (33) rushes in to aid. Colts won, 20-14.

January 9, 1967 - Eagles lose in the Playoff Bowl to the Baltimore Colts 20-14 as the Colts come back with 10 unanswered points in the second half.

1966

1967

RECORD: 6-7-1, 2ND IN NFL CAPITOL
HEAD COACH: JOE KUHARICH

Schedule

Regular Season

Wk. 3	Sep 17	W	35-24	vs Washington Redskins
Wk. 4	Sep 24	L	38-6	vs Baltimore Colts
Wk. 5	Oct 1	W	34-24	vs Pittsburgh Steelers
Wk. 6	Oct 8	W	38-7	at Atlanta Falcons
Wk. 7	Oct 15	L	28-27	vs San Francisco 49ers
Wk. 8	Oct 22	L	48-14	at St. Louis Cardinals
Wk. 9	Oct 29	W	21-14	vs Dallas Cowboys
Wk. 10	Nov 5	L	31-24	at New Orleans Saints
Wk. 11	Nov 12	L	33-17	at Los Angeles Rams
Wk. 12	Nov 19	W	48-21	vs New Orleans Saints
Wk. 13	Nov 26	L	44-7	at New York Giants
Wk. 14	Dec 3	T	35-35	at Washington Redskins
Wk. 15	Dec 10	L	38-17	at Dallas Cowboys
Wk. 16	Dec 17	W	28-24	vs Cleveland Browns

Quarterback Norm Snead and flanker Ben Hawkins set team passing (3,399 yards for 29 touchdowns) and receiving records (59 completions gaining 1,265 yards and 10 touchdowns), respectively. However, injuries to key players and a poor showing by the defense allowing 409 points led the team to a disappointing 6-7-1 record.

1967 Philadelphia Eagles Stats

Passing	Comp	Att	Comp %	Yds	Y/Att	TD	Int	Rating
Norm Snead	240	434	55.3	3399	7.83	29	24	80.0
Izzy Lang	1	1	100.0	26	26.00	0	0	118.8
King Hill	2	7	28.6	33	4.71	1	0	86.3
Benjy Dial	1	3	33.3	5	1.67	0	0	42.4

Rushing	Rush	Yds	Avg	TD
Tom Woodeshick	155	670	4.3	6
Izzy Lang	101	336	3.3	2
Timmy Brown	53	179	3.4	1
Norm Snead	9	30	3.3	2
Harry Jones	8	17	2.1	0
Gary Ballman	1	17	17.0	1
Ron Goodwin	1	1	1.0	0

Receiving	Rec	Yds	Avg	TD
Ben Hawkins	59	1265	21.4	10
Gary Ballman	36	524	14.6	6
Tom Woodeshick	34	391	11.5	4
Mike Ditka	26	274	10.5	2
Izzy Lang	26	201	7.7	3
Timmy Brown	22	202	9.2	1
Jim Kelly	21	345	16.4	4
Fred Hill	9	144	16.0	0
Ron Goodwin	6	65	10.8	0
Harry Jones	3	32	10.7	0
Harry Wilson	2	20	10.0	0

Interceptions	Int	Yds	Avg	TD
Joe Scarpati	4	99	24.8	1
Jim Nettles	4	52	13.0	0
Fred Brown	2	29	14.5	0
Ron Medved	2	23	11.5	0
Aaron Martin	2	8	4.0	0
Ike Kelley	1	18	18.0	0
Harold Wells	1	17	17.0	0
Don Hultz	1	16	16.0	1
Bob Shann	1	8	8.0	0
Floyd Peters	1	3	3.0	0
Dave Lloyd	1	1	1.0	0
Mike Morgan	1	0	0.0	0

Punting	Punts	Yds	Avg	Blocked
Sam Baker	61	2335	38.3	0

Kicking	PAT Made	PAT Att	PAT %	FG Made	FG Att	FG %	Pts
Sam Baker	45	45	100	12	19	63.2	81

The Philadelphia Inquirer
25 MONDAY, NOVEMBER 20, 1967 h
Today's SPORTS
Also in this section
Classified
Advertising
Comics, Puzzles

Snead Stars as Eagles Rout Saints, 48-21

Sandy Padwe

Tom's Policy: Get Rid of Joe

IT WAS not a good day for Tom Woodruff. It was cold in Franklin Field, the wind was blowing and it took a long while to gain the attention of the hot chocolate vendors.

SANDY PADWE

Besides that, the Eagles won, 48-21, over New Orleans. Normally that would make Tom Woodruff happy. But these are not normal times. And they won't be until Joe Kuharich is coaching some place else. Like about 12 years from now.

Tom Woodruff is the president of a rather informal society known as the "Let's Get Rid of Joe Kuharich Club."

Woodruff is the manager of an insurance agency in Abington. He's in his 30s and looks very much like Ed Snider, the former vice president of the Eagles.

"I wish I had his money," Tom Woodruff said. If he did, you know the first thing he would do. He would head straight for the Eagles office and buy up Joe Kuharich's contract.

"Listen," Woodruff said. "I like Jerry Wolman. He's a courteous man and I want to see him get out of those financial problems he's in. But if someone bought the Eagles from him, I wouldn't mind. The new owners would get rid of Kuharich.

"What did Kuharich ever do to earn a contract (15 years) like that?"

• • •

EXACTLY what is Woodruff's gripe about Kuharich? "We know it doesn't mean a thing to him to hear what the fans think," Woodruff said. "He's demonstrated that on television and through his statements in the papers.

"It's frustrating. The fans made this league what it is. I know the fans can't run the teams, but the sentiment around our section of Franklin Field and the sentiment of lots of people I've spoken to is the same as mine.

"What has he done here? He asked for four years to build a championship team. Well? What has he done to improve the defensive line? And his trades? He never gets anything in return for any of his trades.

"The man never admits individual weaknesses among his players and he has no imagination. None. If he did, he might have compensated for some of those injuries last week."

Tom Woodruff is no wild-eyed radical. He dresses conservatively. Lives in the quiet, Chestnut Hill area.

"I just love the Eagles," he said. "We have about 25 people in this club. Some work with me. I know there are a lot of people who feel this way. You hear it all over town."

Last week, the club acted officially for the first time. It sent a telegram to Maxie Baughan and Irv Cross, two players Kuharich traded to the Los Angeles Rams.

• • •

IT READ: "We're true Eagle fans, but when Mister Double Talk traded you two guys it was the biggest steal since the Louisiana Purchase. We're asking you and the rest of the Rams not just to win, but play like you've never played before and humiliate him (Kuharich) so bad that he'll want to walk home to Philadelphia just to clear his head. Our sincere wishes for the Rams to win the Western Conference."

—Tom Woodruff, president, *Get Rid of Joe Kuharich Fan Club.*

The Rams complied. But Joe took the team plane back to Philadelphia.

The club's next official act is a secret. A march around City Hall? The Eagles office? Perhaps Franklin Field at halftime of the Browns game Dec. 17?

"I'm not afraid of being called a crank," Tom Woodruff said. "There are a lot of people out there every Sunday who pay good money to see that team play. I just get mad and when I get mad I work my frustrations off by writing letters."

The man he corresponds with is Jerry Wolman. "I've never met Mr. Woodruff," Wolman said, "but I do consider him my pen pal."

It has been a long association. "Ever since the third game of the 1964 season, I've sat down after every Eagles game and written Wolman a letter," Woodruff said. "I just tell him what I think. He answers most of them, too. That's why I consider him a gentleman. How many other men in his position would take the time? On Fridays, the guys at my office have a ritual. They all come up to me and ask me if I've gotten my weekly reply from Jerry."

Wolman laughed. "If he's working his frustration off," Jerry said, "he does a good job of it."

He's got 12 more years to go, too. The post office department should be happy about that.

Inquirer Color Photo by Alexander L. Deans, Staff Photographer

Eagles' Timmy Brown runs for daylight and four-yard gain at Franklin Field before Saints' Mike Tilleman (74) moves in for tackle. Other Eagles are Jim Skaggs (70), Tom Woodeshick (37) and Lynn Hoyem (63). Saints' 81 is Doug Atkins.

60,751 See Norm Complete Four Scoring Passes

Birds Roll Up 28 In Second Period To Avenge Upset

By GORDON FORBES
Of The Inquirer Staff

For one period at least, the Eagles played like a club worth $15 million Sunday while the New Orleans Saints played like a club looking for the first decent road to the airport.

Favored by such environment quarterback Norm Snead hurled four touchdown passes in less than 20 minutes as the Eagles made off with a 48-21 romp before 60,751 chilled onlookers at Franklin Field.

REVENGE VICTORY

The lopsided victory avenged an upset dealt the Eagles in New Orleans two weeks ago. It halted an Eagles' slump which had resulted in four defeats in their last five games and gave them a 5-5 record for the season.

Snead was brilliant during the almost three periods he played. But throughout the second quarter, when the Eagles broke the game open with 24 points, and part of the third, he was close to perfect.

COMPLETES 8 IN ROW

In the second period alone, he completed eight successive passes for 145 yards and three touchdowns. And in the early minutes of the third quarter, Snead struck for a fourth score before retreating to the bench in favor of backup King Hill.

Over-all, Snead completed 19 of 27 attempts for 309 yards, including a pair of touchdown strikes to flanker Ben Hawkins and one each to running backs Tom Woodeshick and Izzy Lang.

"The game plan was to send our backs out to work on their linebackers," Snead said in the winners' dressing room. "And we noticed their backs had been playing deep in recent games.

SHORT GAME WORKS

"So we relied on our short game most of the time—and it worked."

The Eagles seized undisputed control of the game after a whacky first period dominated by cold-weather fumbles.

On the first play of that quarter, Snead completed his fourth pass and his third to tight end Jim Kelly on a drive that swept to the Saints' 11. Two plays later, Snead missed Gary Ballman in the end zone — but he didn't miss again until after halftime.

HAWKINS' GREAT CATCH

His 10-yard bullet was grabbed by a lunging Hawkins in the left corner for a touchdown, leaving defender Dave Whitsell sprawling alongside, and the Saints behind, 10-0. That completion touched off Sneads eight-in-a-row string.

A blend of Don McCall's 68-yard kickoff return, a foolish piling on penalty by bomb squad leader Ike Kelley, which cost 15 more yards, and Gary Cuozzo's 22-yard pitch to rookie split end Dan Abramowicz got the Saints back in contention at 10-7.

After that, the Saints disappeared from view.

SCARPATI INTERCEPTS

An interference call against John Douglas, defending Hawkins on a fly pattern, cost the Saints 44 yards on the next series. It put the ball on the five and Woodeshick barreled over on the next play. Sam Baker, who kicked field goals of 21 and 37 yards, converted for a 17-7 margin.

The Eagles couldn't cash in on Ernie Wheelwright's second fumble near midfield but turned

Continued on Page 26, Column 6

Flyers Nip Blues, 3-2, Then 2 Brawls Erupt As Teams Leave Ice

By JACK CHEVALIER
Of The Inquirer Staff

If they had played a fourth period Sunday night at the Spectrum, it might have been the most exciting 20 minutes in hockey history. That's because tempers were boiling, the score was close and 7102 fans were roaring after the final buzzer in the Flyers' 3-2 victory over the St. Louis Blues.

The game, actually decided by the Flyers' three-goal flurry in the first period, ended in a wild melee, with both teams conducting shoving matches on the ice around two heated fights.

Blues' defenseman Noel Picard jarred the Flyers Larry

Picture, Related Article On Page 28

Zeidel with a sucker punch and it took two linesmen and three Flyers to restrain Zeidel and push him off the ice.

POUNCES ON VAN IMPE

It was a lifeless contest until St. Louis scored twice in the third period, then pulled goalie Glenn Hall for most of the final minute.

The Blues' six-forward attack failed to produce the tying goal, so the visitors decided to have some postgame fireworks. Defenseman Gordie Kannegiessen started the brawl by pouncing on Ed Van Impe, who had scored the Flyers' winning goal.

"We were tangled up in the corner and as he pulled free, my stick hit his face," Van Impe said. "I guess he thought I hit him on purpose, so he jumped me. Pat Hannigan came over to help out and I was glad to see him."

GETS CLOUT UNDER EYE

The game had ended and some of the players were headed toward the locker rooms when they noticed Hannigan and Kannegiessen starting their main bout. They received five-minute fighting penalties, officially timed at 20:00 of the period, but they'll never be served.

Then Zeidel, who hadn't played since the first period, skated out as a peacemaker and was clouted under the left eye by Picard. Zeidel will have a shiner Monday, but he never got a solid return punch at the Blues' defenseman.

IT'LL COST 'EM $50 EACH

"They say Picard knocked out Harry Sinden (the Boston coach) with a sucker punch like that," Zeidel said later. "I must be pretty tough. I didn't go down."

Both of these combatants were

Continued on Page 28, Column 5

Answer Today?

Penn State May Go to Gator Bowl

A MEMBER of the selection committee admitted Sunday that the Gator Bowl is "very much interested" in Penn State as a participant in the Dec. 30 postseason contest in Jacksonville, Fla.

"We like to have an Eastern team because we get good press coverage and a good viewing

Related Articles, Page 29

area for television," Van Fletcher said by telephone from Jacksonville. "But we won't know anything for sure until tomorrow."

The earliest any bowl bid may be offered and accepted under NCAA regulations is 10:30 A. M. Monday.

Fletcher spiked a report that Penn State might be left at home in favor of a team it had beaten. "It's untrue that Penn State is being excluded in favor of Syracuse," Fletcher said in response to one report that had Syracuse playing the Florida-Florida State victor in the Gator Bowl.

Sports Results

Professional
FOOTBALL
NATIONAL LEAGUE
Sundays Results

EAGLES 48	New Orleans 21
Baltimore 41	Detroit 7
L. Angeles 31	Atlanta 3
Cleveland 14	Minnesota 10
New York 28	Pittsburgh 20
Chicago 30	St. Louis 3
Green Bay 13	S. Francisco 0
Washington 27	Dallas 20

Standings
Eastern Conference
Capitol Division

	W.	L.	T.	Pct.	Pts.	Opp.
Dallas	7	3	0	.700	225	183
EAGLES	5	5	0	.500	264	268
Washg'tn	4	4	2	.500	246	236
N. Orl'ns	1	9	0	.100	146	280

Century Division

	W.	L.	T.	Pct.	Pts.	Opp.
Cl'v'land	6	4	0	.600	224	202
St. Louis	5	4	1	.556	251	232
N. York	5	5	0	.500	267	304
Pittsb'gh	2	7	1	.222	196	233

Western Conference
Central Division

	W.	L.	T.	Pct.	Pts.	Opp.
Gr. Bay	7	2	1	.778	244	118
Chicago	5	5	0	.500	165	163
Detroit	3	5	2	.375	195	194
Minn's'ta	2	6	2	.250	152	213

Coastal Division

	W.	L.	T.	Pct.	Pts.	Opp.
Baltimore	8	0	2	1.000	305	128
L. Ang'l's	7	1	2	.875	286	152
San Fran.	5	5	0	.500	192	239
Atlanta	1	8	1	.111	106	218

AMERICAN LEAGUE

New York 29	Boston 24
Oakland 31	Miami 17
Denver 21	Buffalo 20
San Diego 17	Kansas City 16

Standings
Eastern Division

	W.	L.	T.	Pct.	Pts.	Opp.
New York	7	2	1	.778	269	204
Houston	5	3	1	.625	142	133
Boston	3	7	1	.300	226	277
Buffalo	3	7	1	.300	145	201
Miami	1	8	0	.111	96	279

Continued on Page 28, Column 2

Locker Room Report

Eagles' Ferocity Surprises Saint

By JOHN DELL
Of The Inquirer Staff

"I knew you fellows were mad, but I didn't think you were that mad," said Ray Rissmiller, the one-time Eagle who plays tackle for the New Orleans Saints, after the Eagles' 48-21, get-even victory Sunday at Franklin Field.

"It was a good day all around," said Jim Ringo, the durable center who was glad some of the sting of a 31-24 upset two weeks ago at New Orleans was eased on his day.

"I thought we had played our bad game against Cleveland," said Ed Khayat, a defensive tackle from the Eagles' 1960 championship team who now coaches the Saints' defensive line. Cleveland beat the Saints, 42-7, in the third game of the season and the fledgings haven't been as thoroughly humbled since. The Saints did a bit of early grave digging but their mistakes only served to make things easier for an Eagles' offense that was functioning so well that the score would have gone into the 50's if Joe Kuharich had not pulled a number of first-liners in the last quarter.

"We didn't do much different on offense than we did against them in the first game," Kuharich said of the plays that gave the Eagles a tidy 421 yards in total offense. They had made 339 yards at New Orleans.

"We added a few man-in-motion plays but 90 to 95 percent of the plays were the same as we used against them before and against Los Angeles," Kuharich said.

The man-in-motion maneuver accounted for the Eagles' easiest touchdown. On it, Norm Snead passed to Jim Kelly for the 35-yard second-quarter touchdown that made the game a runaway. It upped the lead to 24-7 and the momentum carried on until the Eagles built up a 48-7 lead.

"Timmy (Brown) was in mo-

Continued on Page 26, Column 5

Ballman Injured

Gary Ballman, Eagles split end, pulled a hamstring muscle in his right leg Sunday and will be out for possibly two weeks.

Ballman was hurt while running out for a pass in the second quarter of the Eagles 48-21 victory over the New Orleans Saints at Franklin Field. Ballman missed one game because of a similar injury earlier in the season.

Mike Ditka, tight end who tore a medial collateral ligament in his left knee in the 31-24 loss at New Orleans two weeks ago, had his cast removed after the game by Dr. James E. Nixon.

"Mike will start swimming and exercising this week and will miss at least one or two more games," Dr. Nixon said.

Concannon Tosses for 3 TDs

Bears Wallop Cards, 30-3

CHICAGO, Nov. 19 (AP). — Quarterback Jack Concannon threw three touchdown bombs, including a 93-yard strike to Dick Gordon, spiralling the Chicago Bears to a 30-3 victory Sunday over the St. Louis Cardinals in a National Football League game.

The 93-yard pass play, longest in the NFL this year, touched off a 20-point second period in which Concannon hit Bob Jones on a 51-yard scoring pass and then found Gordon again with a 67-yard touchdown pass.

The Cardinals, yielding the ball seven times on pass interceptions and twice on fumbles, scored the first time they got the ball on a 37-yard field goal by Jim Bakken but couldn't get going again.

Following Bakken's field goal, the Bears marched 70 yards with Concannon capping the drive on a six-yard run to go ahead to stay.

Early in the second quarter, St. Louis gained field position on a punt by Chuck Latourette deep into Bear territory. But Concannon, who had thrown only one touchdown pass all season, let go with a long pitch which bounced off the hands of Pat Fischer and Larry Wilson and into the hands of Gordon, who rambled the 48 yards untouched.

Midway in the period, Curt Gentry made the first of his three interceptions. After the Cardinals were hit with two penalties, Concannon threw his 51-yard touchdown pass to rookie Bob Jones, a 22-year-old hurdle champion from San Diego State.

The next time the Bears got the ball, Concannon hit Gordon with a 67-yard touchdown pass.

The victory was the third straight for the Bears who boosted their record to 5-5 while

Continued on Page 28, Column 1

4 TD Aerials Beat Cowboys

Jurgensen Passes Win for Redskins

DALLAS, Nov. 19 (UPI). — Sonny Jurgensen, working from an almost air-right pocket, picked the Dallas Cowboys' defense apart for four touchdown passes Sunday and the Washington Redskins kept their Capitol Division hopes alive with a 27-20 victory before 75,538.

Jurgensen ran his season touchdown total to 21 with 29 and 4-yard scoring tosses to Jerry Smith, a 14-yarder to A. D. Whitfield and a 5-yard pitch to Bobby Mitchell to even the Redskins' record to 4-4-2.

The Cowboys, snake-bitten with dropped touchdown passes and fumbles for most of three quarters, staged another of their patented fourth-quarter finishes that have marked this series when Craig Morton came on for limping Don Meredith and sparked the Cowboys to two touchdowns.

Morton hit Frank Clarke with a 15 yarder for one touchdown. Then, after Cowboys linebacker, Dave Edwards recovered an onside kickoff at the Washington 45, he guided them to another touchdown, which came on a 6-yard pass to Pettis Norman with Redskins hanging all over him.

The Cowboys got the ball on their own 10-yard line with 2:53 left and the crowd kept anticipating another of the final minute surges that has seen these clubs divide their last four games with each one won in the final two minutes.

But Redskins defensive back, Paul Krause abruptly blotted out that hope with a sparking interception, the Redskins' fourth of the day, at the Dallas 49-yard line with 1:40 remaining.

The Cowboys got one more chance from their own 17-yard line with 58 seconds left, but could work their way out only to the Washington 37 by game's end in the face of a terrific rush put on Morton by the Redskins' front line of Ron Snidow, Walt Barnes, Joe Rutgens and Earl Kammerer.

It was this same group that got to Meredith time and time again in the first three quarters, forced him to throw hastily or smother him for losses. He took a heavy beating and finally had to retire.

Jurgensen hit 23 of 33 passes for 265 yards and suffered only one interception, while he was not thrown for a loss a single time by the once-feared Cowboys' front line.

In contrast, Meredith hit 14 of 27 for 189 yards, Morton hit 10 of 15 for 131 yards and half-

Continued on Page 26, Column 1

1967

November 20, 1967 - Eagles enjoy their highest single-game offensive output in eight years, defeating New Orleans 48-21

1968

RECORD: 2-12, 4TH IN NFL CAPITOL
HEAD COACH: JOE KUHARICH

Schedule

Regular Season

Wk. 2	Sep 15	L	30-13	at Green Bay Packers
Wk. 3	Sep 22	L	34-25	vs New York Giants
Wk. 4	Sep 29	L	45-13	vs Dallas Cowboys
Wk. 5	Oct 6	L	17-14	at Washington Redskins
Wk. 6	Oct 13	L	34-14	at Dallas Cowboys
Wk. 7	Oct 20	L	29-16	vs Chicago Bears
Wk. 8	Oct 27	L	6-3	at Pittsburgh Steelers
Wk. 9	Nov 3	L	45-17	vs St. Louis Cardinals
Wk. 10	Nov 10	L	16-10	vs Washington Redskins
Wk. 11	Nov 17	L	7-6	at New York Giants
Wk. 12	Nov 24	L	47-13	at Cleveland Browns
Wk. 13	Nov 28	W	12-0	at Detroit Lions
Wk. 14	Dec 8	W	29-17	vs New Orleans Saints
Wk. 15	Dec 15	L	24-17	vs Minnesota Vikings

The Eagles struggled, losing their first 11 games (a team record), and then winning their last two games. By winning those two games, they ruined the probability of selecting O.J. Simpson in the draft. In the last game of the season, a 24-17 loss to Minnesota, Eagles fans where so unhappy with Coach Joe Kuharich that they turned on Santa Claus by pelting him with snowballs.

1968 Philadelphia Eagles Stats

Passing	Comp	Att	Comp %	Yds	Y/Att	TD	Int	Rating
Norm Snead	152	291	52.2	1655	5.69	11	21	51.8
Sam Baker	1	1	100.0	58	58.00	1	0	158.3
Joe Scarpati	1	2	50.0	3	1.50	0	0	56.3
John Huarte	7	15	46.7	110	7.33	1	2	54.2
King Hill	33	71	46.5	531	7.48	3	6	50.9

Rushing	Rush	Yds	Avg	TD
Tom Woodeshick	217	947	4.4	3
Izzy Lang	69	235	3.4	0
Cyril Pinder	40	117	2.9	0
Gary Ballman	1	30	30.0	0
Norm Snead	9	27	3.0	0
Harry Jones	22	24	1.1	0
Larry Conjar	8	21	2.6	0
John Huarte	2	9	4.5	0
King Hill	1	1	1.0	0

Receiving	Rec	Yds	Avg	TD
Ben Hawkins	42	707	16.8	5
Tom Woodeshick	36	328	9.1	0
Fred Hill	30	370	12.3	3
Gary Ballman	30	341	11.4	4
Izzy Lang	17	147	8.6	1
Cyril Pinder	16	166	10.4	0
Mike Ditka	13	111	8.5	2
Harry Jones	5	87	17.4	1
Chuck Hughes	3	39	13.0	0
John Mallory	1	58	58.0	1
Sam Baker	1	3	3.0	0

Punting	Punts	Yds	Avg	Blocked
Rick Duncan	5	228	45.6	0
Sam Baker	55	2248	40.9	0

Interceptions	Int	Yds	Avg	TD
Al Nelson	3	7	2.3	0
Joe Scarpati	2	22	11.0	0
Nate Ramsey	2	0	0.0	0
Harold Wells	2	0	0.0	0
Randy Beisler	1	12	12.0	0
Alvin Haymond	1	10	10.0	0
Ron Medved	1	0	0.0	0
Floyd Peters	1	0	0.0	0

Kicking	PAT Made	PAT Att	PAT %	FG Made	FG Att	FG %	Pts
Sam Baker	17	21	81	19	30	63.3	74

The Philadelphia Inquirer 33 FRIDAY, NOVEMBER 29, 1968 h★★ Today's SPORTS Comics, Puzzles Classified Advertising

76ers' Romp Ruins Lakers' 'Super' Image

Eagles' Sam Baker was set to try for field goal near the end of first half when high pass from center caused holder Joe Scarpati to start running.

Scarpati is running to the left looking for someone to throw the ball to while Baker watches and Lions' defensive back Mike Weger starts to chase the Eagle, who is now at the 48.

Inquirer Magic Eye Sequence Photos by Alexander Deans, Staff Photographer

Realizing he is trapped by several Lions, and unable to find an eligible receiver free downfield, Scarpati turns and starts to pass the ball to Baker, who was a fullback at Oregon State.

L.A. Troubles Aired by Coach After Setback

By ERNIE ACCORSI
Of The Inquirer Staff

For two weeks now, the 76ers have been doing things so excellently and so consistently, they're beginning to look a little special.

Thursday night at the Spectrum, after scrambling to stay close for two periods, they played the second half as if carrying a vendetta against Los Angeles, shooting 72.1 percent and pounding the Lakers, 122-107.

The 76ers, again inspired by Billy Cunningham, who is off to an incredible start, shot 16 for 21 in the third period, 31 for 43 for the second half, and suddenly Los Angeles was completely out of a game they had been in for 32 minutes.

NO SUPER TEAM

Only 8256 saw this attraction on Thanksgiving night and it's a shame because the 76ers punctured more holes in the Lakers' myth.

Los Angeles, you see, just isn't a super team and Laker Coach Bill van Breda Kolff isn't going to argue it.

"We don't have enough movement," van Breda Kolff said. "We're not a team of good shooters, and we're poor from the foul line."

He wasn't finished.

"We're not a good passing team," he continued, "and the main thing now is the mental approach. We're not ready to play a hungry, aggressive club.

NOT HUNGRY ENOUGH

"Our attitude is, 'Well, if we want to put it all together, we can win.' You can't do that. I don't know how many loose balls they got on us. When you're not going for them, you're not hungry. I'm just going to have to work them harder; more practice, that's all."

And if Wilt Chamberlain was supposed to be the guy who vaulted the Lakers into this imaginary "super" class, you can forget it. van Breda Kolff sounds like he'd rather have last year's club.

Jerry West missed the game because of a flu attack and the Lakers looked like they missed him much more than they missed Chamberlain during the 7-minute period van Breda Kolff benched him.

SET PICKS, WILT

"Last year," van Breda Kolff said, "if we lost Jerry we had Archie Clark and Gail Goodrich. We just don't get enough good picks now to get the good percentage shots, the ones you know you can make.

"Wilt is just going to have to move around more and set more picks."

Chamberlain didn't score his

Continued on Page 36, Column 4

Locker Room Report

Baker Gets New Experience After 14 Years in Pro Ball

By ROGER KEIM
Of The Inquirer Staff

DETROIT, Nov. 28.—Sam Baker has been kicking in the National Football League for 14 years. Thursday he received a new experience. "I never played on a field like that in the pros," said Baker after booming a field goal in each quarter at Tiger Stadium to keep the Eagles from achieving the longest one-season losing streak in NFL history.

"The key to kicking field goals on any field, wet or dry, is the holder," insisted Baker during the Eagles' somewhat restrained celebration in the locker room after a 12-0 win over the Lions. "I didn't try to kick any differently because of the conditions, but you probably react differently without thinking about it."

Tiger Stadium's turf made the average pig's quarters appear to be wall-to-wall carpeted by comparison. Baker splashed his second field goal out of an unnamed lake that kept growing as the cold, stinging rain poured throughout the game.

SLOWS THE SNAP

"I don't remember anything like this anywhere," said holder Joe Scarpati. "Normally, Sam starts his motion before I put the ball down. But today he waited to see where the ball was placed because I couldn't put my hand down to show him before the snap. It would have gotten wet.

"In practice before the game we had (center) Dave Lloyd slow the snap. I told him, 'just get the ball to me.' I figured on the field they (the Lions) wouldn't be able to charge as fast.

"Normally, I catch the ball with my holding finger over the point. Today, I just tried to catch the ball the best way possible and try to get the laces pointing forward."

Scarpati also explained the Eagles' contained clubhouse happiness. "It's great to win," he said. "But we're still 1 and 11."

SWEEPS SURPRISING

The Lions' repeated use of sweeps through the slop surprised the Eagles' defense. "After Cleveland used them last week, we were expecting them to try it," said Scarpati. "But the condition of the field and the use of a zone (defense) helped us contain their wide plays.

"Once on fourth and one (at the Eagles 30) and another time with second and two, they went wide (both sweeps lost yardage.) I never expected those plays. We used a lot of zone and tried to hide it.

"Nate (Ramsey) kept jumping around so they wouldn't see what we were doing. Fred Brown and Harold Wells did a real good job containing them."

"You can only run so much inside, then if you don't go out everybody is going to come up in the gaps," said middle linebacker Lloyd. "We really didn't do anything different. Our execution was just better. And the offense won the ball game the way they controlled the ball."

FORD SOUNDS OFF

Meanwhile, Lions' owner William Clay Ford was sounding like Detroit Coach Joe Schmidt is in jeopardy. "With all our offensive talent, we should have more points than we've shown," said Ford, whose Lions are 3-7-2, haven't won in seven weeks and were quarterbacked by rookie Greg Landry.

"I think we've become stereotyped," continued Ford. "We do too much of the same thing in the same down situations.

"I can't say I feel worse losing to the Eagles because of

Continued on Page 36, Column 7

Sandy Padwe

In the Long Run, Effort Pays Off

IT WAS cold and dark and the terrain was a bit unfamiliar. There were no police around, however, and that made things a little easier. The car had left the Villanova campus at about 3 A.M., arriving at Van Cortlandt Park in the Bronx some three hours later.

The occupants got out of the car and began fanning through the park, posting their messages in select places along the route of the National Collegiate cross-country meet.

SANDY PADWE

The messages were simple: "Make It Three." "Cats No. 1." "Villanova NCAA." There also were signs of encouragement for each member of the Villanova team. It's the type of thing you expect from college students. But usually the signs are for the football or basketball team. Not the cross-country team. And normally the sign painters are fans, not athletes.

This time, the signs were for the cross-country team and they were painted and hung by members of the freshman team, a team so strong that Villanova may just win the national title for three more years. That would make it six in a row for the Wildcats.

Villanova's record in cross country is remarkable. The trouble is not many people know about it. In this country, if a sport isn't on television and if there isn't a morning line to quote and if national prestige is not involved, people conveniently forget it.

They forget a training program that includes 120 to 140 miles of running a week; they forget an alarm clock ringing at 6:30 on a chill, winter morning; they forget that there are many athletes in many sports who never receive the recognition they should.

Perhaps this is part of the reason for the great camaraderie among distance runners. The public may not realize it, but the runners know and understand the sacrifices the other man makes in this sport.

* * *

AND maybe this is why some members of the Villanova freshman team traveled to New York at 3 A.M. Monday and hung signs along the route that the varsity would run later in the morning.

"They seem to understand more about the running at home," said Donal Walsh, one of the organizers of the sign-painting expedition. Home for Walsh is Cork, Ireland. He is the latest of Jumbo Elliott's imports and by the end of his collegiate career may be one of the best.

"At home, they don't laugh and if they see me going along the road, they'll all stop and ask me how things are; how I did in my last race. Here, people are mostly in cars and I suppose that makes a big difference."

Walsh's reason for coming to Villanova is rather simple. "In Ireland," he said, "any runner who is worth anything tries to come here. I had never seen the campus, but I had received some mail from Ian Hamilton (another Villanova runner) and I spoke with Ron Delany and Noel Carroll. They told me this was the place for me. See, in Ireland, there aren't many coaches and if you're serious about running you almost have to come to the United States.

"Well, they were right about Villanova. They make you feel at home here. From the first day, I felt that way. The varsity runners feel the same way about the freshmen as they do about each other. I guess this is the tradition of the school.

"The closeness among us is the result of this and all the time we put in practicing together. When you

Continued on Page 39, Column 6

Eagles Defeat Lions, 12-0, for 1st Win of '68

Continued from First Page

rangy rookie from Massachusetts, all the way at quarterback. He replaced regular Bill Munson, who is suffering from a sore neck and sore throwing arm.

EAGLE DEFENSE HOLDS

The Lions' No. 1 draft pick took the Lions into Eagle territory only four times during the game. Each time the Lions were rebuffed by an ambitious Eagle defense.

In the first period, the Lions reached the Eagle 36 but strong safety Nate Ramsey blew in and tossed Nick Eddy for a four-yard loss on fourth-and-one.

The Lions blew another opportunity in the second period when Tom Nowatzke fumbled and linebacker Dave Lloyd recovered at the Eagles 40-yard line.

2 INTERCEPTIONS VITAL

Two interceptions—one at the 31-yard line by linebacker Harold Wells and another at the five by Ramsey—destroyed what little hope the Lions had of winning in the final period.

Landry, the hand-picked draft selection of owner William Clay Ford, was given a three-year, no-cut contract worth $125,000. In this soggy holiday clash, he resembled George Plimpton. Landry completed seven of 15 passes for 66 yards and two of them for 30 yards came in the final three minutes.

He hit flanker Billy Gambrell with passes of 22 and 8 yards, and Gambrell's second catch, a diving reception at the nine, came with 1:33 left to play.

RAMSEY COMES THROUGH

Landry's next toss, also meant for Gambrell, was stolen by Ramsey, killing off the Lions for good and triggering a loud chorus of boos from the stands.

The Lion offense has produced only five touchdowns in the past seven games, none of which Detroit has won. Over that span, the Lions have lost five, tied two and skidded to a 3-7-2 record, worst in the Central Division.

There was a solemn note to the long-awaited victory. The Eagles presented the game ball, which quarterback Norm Snead lugged off the field, to Mrs. Anne Wolman, wife of the owner. She is still in the intensive care unit at Doctors Hospital in Washington, D. C., recovering from a massive heart attack.

WELLS IN RIGHT PLACE

The Eagles never really put the game out of reach until Baker's 35-yarder with 3:49 left in the game. Wells made it possible with his theft after Landry had given the Lions a first down at the Eagle 36 on a six-yard rollout around right end.

That came on the final play of the third period. To open the final quarter, Landry tried to hit Eddy circling out of the backfield but lofted a wobbly attempt that fell into Wells' hands at the 31.

Tom Woodeshick and Izzy Lang, who carried the ball on 16 straight running plays in the final period, couldn't hammer out a first down. But the Eagles got a big break when the Lions roughed Baker, the punter. That meant a first down at the 36.

A holding penalty might have halted the Eagles if the Lions hadn't reciprocated. A personal foul against Detroit moved the ball to the Lion 44.

Woodeshick, on five slashing

Continued on Page 38, Column 6

Baker makes the catch at about the Lions' 42, turns and starts to run as tacklers converge.

Hit at the 41, Baker manages to keep going in the sloppy footing until he reaches the 37.

Cowboys Win, Redskins' Coach Cries 'Robbery'

From Our Wire Services

DALLAS, Nov. 28. — Dallas' Doomsday Defense came to the rescue of a lethargic Cowboy offense Thursday night and defensive end Larry Cole's 5-yard scoring run with an interception provided the killing blow in a 29-20 victory over the stubborn Washington Redskins.

The triumph gave the Cowboys a 10-2 record and moved them within half a game of clinching the National Football League's Capitol Division title. Should Cleveland beat the New York Giants Sunday, the Cowboys would have a three-game lead with two to play.

GRAHAM UPSET

Coach Otto Graham charged that the officials "stole" the game from his Redskins.

Graham was referring to the 124 yards in penalties incurred by his team—several at crucial times. Dallas got 97 yards via penalties. But an interference call in the end zone set up Dallas for one touchdown. Once Graham himself was penalized 15 yards for unsportsmanlike conduct.

OTHER COMPLAINTS

"I thought the officials stole the game from us," Graham declared. "I've written to the league officials several times complaining about the officiating, but never has it been this bad. I don't mind getting beat and I can appreciate that the officials have judgment calls to make.

"But I think it's about time we got some officials who have some judgment."

PUGH HITS NINOWSKI

Cole, scoring his second touchdown of the season, had an easy walk for his 5-yard scoring sortie after big Jethro Pugh had stormed into the Redskins' Jim Ninowski at the goal line as he tried to pass.

The Cowboys' other points came on 1-yard and 9-yard runs by Craig Baynham and Don Perkins, 18- and 25-yard field goals by Mike Clark and a safety in the third quarter when defensive stalwarts George Andrie and Bob Lilly forced Ninowski to fumble out of his own end zone.

Ninowski, however, had done a very creditable job of filling in for flue-stricken Sonny Jurgensen by hitting Charley Taylor, Jim Smith and Pat Richter with touchdown passes of 29, 11 and 4 yards despite the tremendous pressure.

DAL—FG Clark 18
DAL—Baynham 1 run (Clark kick)
DAL—Perkins 9 run (Clark kick)
WASH—Taylor 29 pass from Ninowski (Gogolak kick)
DAL—Safety, Ninowski fumble out of end zone
WASH—Jo Smith 11 pass from Ninowski (Gogolak kick)
WASH—Richter 4 pass from Ninowski (kick failed)
DAL—FG Clark 25
DAL—Cole 5 interception runback (Clark kick)

STATISTICS

AFL Roundup

Chiefs Topple Oilers, Clinch Crown for Jets

From Our Wire Services

KANSAS CITY, Nov. 28. — Len Dawson got Kansas City's slow-starting offense clicking late in the first half Thursday, then picked Houston's defense apart with his pin-point passing to fire the Chiefs to a 24-10 American Football League victory over the Oilers.

The triumph kept Kansas City tied with Oakland for the Western Division lead, each with a 10-2 record. The Raiders defeated Buffalo, 13-10.

JETS GAIN TITLE

The loss eliminated the Oilers, the defending Eastern Division champions, from contention and clinched the title for the New York Jets in the East.

That means the Jets will host the AFL championship game Dec. 29.

Dawson, who has been hampered by injuries to his prime receivers as well as by his own severe thigh injury, threw scoring passes of 37 yards to Mike Garrett, and 33 and 43 yards to Frank Pitts.

10 STRAIGHT BULL'S EYES

He completed 10 passes in a row from late in the first half until the latter stages of the fourth period, including the three touchdown tosses. He had 17 completions in 23 attempts for 253 yards in all.

It was Dawson's 43-yard strike to Pitts with 7¼ minutes left that gave Kansas City a 21-10 lead.

Jan Stenerud booted a 17-yard field goal three minutes later for the final reading after Curly Culp blocked a punt and Jerry Mays recovered at the Houston 13-yard line.

Houston, trailing the Oilers 14-3 after Dawson's 33-yard scoring pass to Pitts in the second quar-

Continued on Page 36, Column 5

Tickets Available

About 800 tickets for Saturday's Army-Navy football game at Kennedy Stadium are still available and will go on sale at 9 A. M. Friday on the mezzanine floor of the Benjamin Franklin Hotel.

All tickets are priced at $8.50.

Sugar Goes To Arkansas

NEW ORLEANS, Nov. 28. (UPI).—The eighth-ranked Arkansas Razorbacks will meet unbeaten, fourth-ranked Georgia (7-0-2) in the Sugar Bowl in New Year's Day, it was announced Thursday.

Sugar Bowl president Dr. Fred Wolfe Jr. made the announcement shortly after Texas defeated Texas A & M, 35-14, to gain the host spot in the Cotton Bowl.

Sports Results

College

FOOTBALL

EAST

Hofstra 11 ...... C. W. Post 7

SOUTH

Virginia Tech 55 ...... VMI 6
Tennessee Tech 7 ...... Middle Tenn. St. 3
Tennessee A&I 48 ...... Bishop (Tex.) 12
Austin Peay 9 ...... Univ. of Tenn. 7
Presbyterian 42 ...... Newberry 7
N. Carolina A&T 21 ...... N. Carolina College 6
Texas 35 ...... Texas A&M 14
Tuskegee Inst. 23 ...... Alabama St. 21
Lenoir Rhyne 27 ...... Catawba 22
S. Carolina St. 28 ...... Johnson Smith 6
Tulsa 23 ...... Wichita St. 7
Wofford 21 ...... Furman 7

Professional

FOOTBALL

NATIONAL LEAGUE

Thursday's Results

EAGLES 12 ...... Detroit 0
Dallas 29 ...... Washington 20
(Only games scheduled.)

EASTERN CONFERENCE

Capital Division	W	L	T	Pct.	Pts.	Opp.
Dallas	10	2	0	.833	375	169
New York	7	4	0	.636	253	224
Washington	4	8	0	.333	216	331
EAGLES	1	11	0	.083	168	310
Century Division						
Cleveland	8	3	0	.727	300	215
St. Louis	6	4	1	.600	250	242
New Orleans	3	7	1	.300	188	261
Pittsburgh	2	8	1	.200	213	325

WESTERN CONFERENCE

Central Division	W	L	T	Pct.	Pts.	Opp.
Minnesota	6	5	0	.545	225	174
Green Bay	5	5	1	.500	230	157
Chicago	5	6	0	.455	183	272
Detroit	3	7	2	.300	180	229
Coastal Division						
Baltimore	10	1	0	.909	314	117
Los Angeles	9	1	1	.900	241	152
San Fran.	5	5	1	.500	242	248
Atlanta	2	9	0	.182	151	307

AMERICAN LEAGUE

Thursday's Results

Kansas City 24 ...... Houston 10

Continued on Page 36, Column 1

November 29, 1968 - After eleven straight losses, Sam Baker kicks four field goals as the Eagles defeat Detroit 12-0 for their first win of the season

1969

RECORD: 4-9-1, 4TH IN NFL CAPITOL
HEAD COACH: JERRY WILLIAMS

Schedule

Regular Season

Wk. 2	Sep 21	L	27-20	vs Cleveland Browns
Wk. 3	Sep 28	W	41-27	vs Pittsburgh Steelers
Wk. 4	Oct 5	L	38-7	vs Dallas Cowboys
Wk. 5	Oct 13	L	24-20	at Baltimore Colts
Wk. 6	Oct 19	L	49-14	at Dallas Cowboys
Wk. 7	Oct 26	W	13-10	vs New Orleans Saints
Wk. 8	Nov 2	W	23-20	at New York Giants
Wk. 9	Nov 9	T	28-28	at Washington Redskins
Wk. 10	Nov 16	L	23-17	vs Los Angeles Rams
Wk. 11	Nov 23	W	34-30	at St. Louis Cardinals
Wk. 12	Nov 30	L	26-17	at New Orleans Saints
Wk. 13	Dec 7	L	34-29	vs Washington Redskins
Wk. 14	Dec 14	L	27-3	vs Atlanta Falcons
Wk. 15	Dec 21	L	14-13	at San Francisco 49ers

Financial ruin forced owner Jerry Wolman to sell the Eagles to Leonard Tose, a millionaire trucking executive, who purchased the Eagles for a record price of 16.1 million dollars. Tose fired Kuharich immediately and replaced him with GM Pete Retzlaff, who in turn promoted assistant coach Jerry Williams to head coach. Despite the change at the top the Eagles continued to struggle, finishing in last place again with a terrible 4-9-1 record.

1969 Philadelphia Eagles Stats

Passing	Comp	Att	Comp %	Yds	Y/Att	TD	Int	Rating
Norm Snead	190	379	50.1	2768	7.30	19	23	65.7
Leroy Keyes	1	2	50.0	14	7.00	0	0	72.9
Bill Bradley	0	1	0.0	0	0.00	0	0	39.6
George Mira	25	76	32.9	240	3.16	1	5	19.6

Rushing	Rush	Yds	Avg	TD
Tom Woodeshick	186	831	4.5	4
Leroy Keyes	121	361	3.0	3
Cyril Pinder	60	309	5.2	1
Ronnie Blye	8	25	3.1	0
George Mira	3	16	5.3	0
Harold Jackson	2	10	5.0	0
Harry Wilson	4	7	1.8	0
Bill Bradley	1	5	5.0	0
Norm Snead	8	2	0.3	2
Harry Jones	1	0	0.0	0
Ben Hawkins	1	-3	-3.0	0

Receiving	Rec	Yds	Avg	TD
Harold Jackson	65	1116	17.2	9
Ben Hawkins	43	761	17.7	8
Gary Ballman	31	492	15.9	2
Leroy Keyes	29	276	9.5	0
Tom Woodeshick	22	177	8.0	0
Cyril Pinder	12	77	6.4	0
Fred Hill	6	64	10.7	1
Chuck Hughes	3	29	9.7	0
Ronnie Blye	2	-6	-3.0	0
Fred Brown	1	20	20.0	0
Kent Lawrence	1	10	10.0	0
Harry Wilson	1	6	6.0	0

Punting	Punts	Yds	Avg	Blocked
Bill Bradley	74	2942	39.8	0

Kicking	PAT Made	PAT Att	PAT %	FG Made	FG Att	FG %	Pts
Sam Baker	31	31	100	16	30	53.3	79

Interceptions	Int	Yds	Avg	TD
Joe Scarpati	4	54	13.5	1
Al Nelson	3	10	3.3	0
Nate Ramsey	2	26	13.0	1
Dave Lloyd	2	22	11.0	0
Bill Bradley	1	56	56.0	1
Wayne Colman	1	11	11.0	0
Adrian Young	1	0	0.0	0

26 a d h THE PHILADELPHIA INQUIRER, MONDAY MORNING, SEPTEMBER 29, 1969

The Norman Conquest—Snead Style

Inquirer Magic-Eye Pictures by Alexander L. Deans and William M. Brown, Staff Photographers

Gentle Ben a Better Show Than Oliver

1. With Eagles trailing 13-0 in second period, quarterback Norm Snead fired pass from pocket formed by three linemen. Steelers' Joe Greene fails in his leap to block first of 5 TD passes.

2. Wide receiver Ben Hawkins turns toward scrimmage line and leaps over defender Clarence Oliver for catch.

3. As ball settles in Hawkins' chest, his speed and momentum carry him toward goal line.

4. Hawkins falls into end zone to complete 26-yard touchdown play and ignite the rally which carried Eagles' to 41-27 victory. Eagles declined pass interference call against Steelers.

Rookie Flips Over Hawk's Move

1. It looks like Ben Hawkins is going nowhere after catching this sideline pass in front of Steelers' Coach Ch k Noll near midfield.

2. But Hawkins, without touching the ground, flips Clarence Oliver over his shoulder and keeps going.

3. Hawkins leaves Oliver, a rookie from San Diego State, on the turf and crosses the midfield stripe.

4. Headed off by linebacker Andy Russell, Hawkins changes direction and gets hemmed in by three defenders.

5. Hawkins' pivot fools the Steelers, however, and Gary Ballman rushes over to help Ben gain more yardage on third-quarter play.

6. Defensive end Lloyd Voss finally wrestles down Hawkins at Pittsburgh's 46. Play gained 15 yards.

Good Way to Get a Shiner

1. Eagles' Tim Rossovich bats arm of Steelers' Dick Shiner on third-period passing attempt and forces fumble. Tackle John Brown blocks Eagles' Mel Tom.

2. As Rossovich forces Shiner to the turf, ball bounces loose near the Steelers' 33-yard line. Tackle Mike Taylor, on all fours, spots the pigskin.

3. Taylor grabbed ball on Steelers' 29, but advanced only to the 30 before Floyd Peters nailed him. Loss of 12 yards forced Pittsburgh to punt.

September 29, 1969 - Hawkins ties a club record with four touchdowns as the Eagles defeated Pittsburgh 41-27

1969

1970's DECADE IN REVIEW

1970
The final steps of the AFL-NFL merger are put into place. Two 13-team conferences, the National and the American, now make up the National Football League.

A new phenomenon sweeps the country as the NFL and ABC-TV launch Monday Night Football. In their first MNF appearance, the Birds defeat the Giants at Franklin Field.

1971
After 13 seasons at Franklin Field, the Eagles, along with MLB's Phillies, move into then newly built Veterans Stadium (recently imploded).

Already the owner of the NFL mark for longest return of a missed field goal, Al Nelson tops that effort when he returns a missed Cowboys kick 101 yards for a TD in the Eagles' first regular season game at Veterans Stadium.

Safety Bill Bradley becomes the first Eagle ever to lead the league in interceptions in consecutive years, logging a club-record 11 in 1971 and 9 more the following season.

1972
Wide receiver Harold Jackson leads the NFL in both receptions and receiving yards (62-1,048).

1973
6'8" receiver Harold Carmichael and quarterback Roman Gabriel pace the NFL. Carmichael, who would go on to become a cornerstone of the Birds' playoff teams of the late '70s and set a club record for career games played, leads the league in receiving. Gabriel leads the NFL in nearly every passing category.

1974-77
From 1974-77 the foundation that will take the Eagles to Super Bowl XV is laid. First, Pro Bowl linebacker Bill Bergey arrives via a trade with Cincinnati. In 1976, former UCLA mentor Dick Vermeil takes over the coaching reins. One year later he acquires quarterback Ron Jaworski from the Rams and drafts running back Wilbert Montgomery, both of whom will join receiver Harold Carmichael in re-writing the Eagles' record books.

1978
The Eagles log their first winning season since 1966 and first playoff berth since 1960. They are aided by an improbable play on November 19 that becomes known as "the Miracle of the Meadowlands." Seemingly headed for defeat against the host NY Giants, cornerback Herman Edwards scoops up a fumbled handoff from Joe Pisarcik to Larry Csonka and races 26 yards for a TD – and a victory – in the final 20 seconds of play.

1979
The Eagles close the decade with an 11-5 record and win a Wild Card playoff game over Chicago before falling to Tampa Bay.

Harold Carmichael sets a then-NFL record with a reception in 106 straight games; Wilbert Montgomery sets a single-season Eagles' record with 1,512 rushing yards; and Dick Vermeil earns coach of the year honors.

The Eagles' First Game at Veterans Stadium August 1971 vs. Buffalo

The Monday Night Crew (l to R): Don Meredith, Howard Cosell and Frank Gifford

Al Nelson

Harold Carmichael

Roman Gabriel

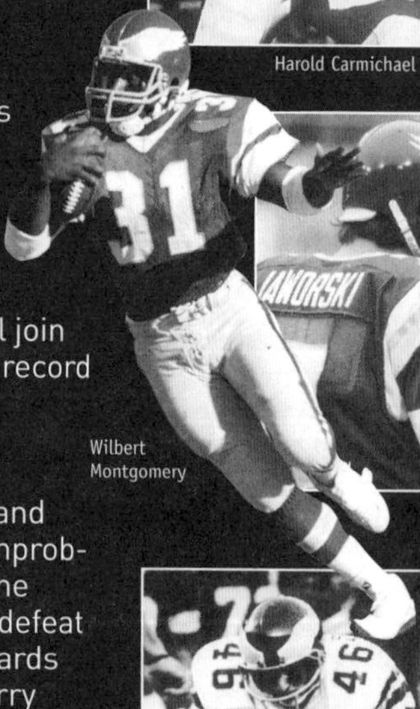
Wilbert Montgomery

Ron Jaworski and Dick Vermeil

Bill Bergey

The Miracle of the Meadowlands

No small feat: Harold Carmichael's record-setting effort earned the big receiver an even bigger trophy

1970's

70s Decade in Review

Decade Win-Loss Record:
56-84-4; (1-2 postseason record)

Home Field:
Franklin Field 1970; Veterans Stadium 1971-79

Playoff Appearances:
1978 and 1979

Championships:
None

Head Coaches:
Jerry Williams 1970-71 (3-13-1);
Ed Khayat 1971-1972 (8-15-2);
Mike McCormack 1973-75 (16-25-1);
Dick Vermeil 1976-1979 (29-31)
(1-2 postseason record)

Hall of Fame Inductees:
None

Award Winners:
Roman Gabriel, Comeback Player of the Year 1973;
Charlie Young, Rookie of the Year 1973;
Dick Vermeil, Coach of the Year 1979

All Pro:
Bill Bradley 1971-1973, Harold Jackson 1972;
Harold Carmichael 1973 and 1979;
Charlie Young 1973-1974; Bill Bergey 1974-78;
Wilbert Montgomery 1978-79;
Charlie Johnson 1979; Stan Walters 1979

Pro Bowl Selections:
Dave Lloyd 1970; Tim Rossovich 1970;
Bill Bradley 1972-74;
Harold Jackson 1970 and 1973;
Harold Carmichael 1974; Roman Gabriel 1974;
Charlie Young 1974-76;
Bill Bergey 1975 and 1977-79; Mike Boryla 1976;
Wilbert Montgomery 1979; Stan Walters 1979

First Game of the Decade:
September 20, 1970, lost to Dallas Cowboys 17-7

Last Game of the Decade:
December 16, 1979, defeated by the
Houston Oilers 26-20

Largest Margin of Victory:
December 2, 1979 vs. Detroit Lions 44-7

Largest Margin of Defeat:
November 26, 1972 vs. New York Giants 62-10

Eagle Firsts of the Decade:

First Game at Veterans Stadium
September 19, 1971, loss to the
Cincinnati Bengals 37-14

First Playoff game at the Vet
December 23, 1979, defeated the Chicago
Bears in their first postseason home game 27-17

First Overtime Game
September 27, 1976, lost to Washington
Redskins 20-17

First Monday Night Football
November 23, 1970, win over the New York
Giants 23-20 at Franklin Field

First Exhibition Game Outside the US
August 5, 1978, the New Orleans Saints defeat the
Eagles 14-7 in a preseason game held in Mexico
City

First Soccer-Style Kicker
In 1975, Horst Muhlmann became the Eagles
first Soccer-Style Kicker.

1970

RECORD: 3-10-1, 5TH IN NFC EAST
HEAD COACH: JERRY WILLIAMS

Schedule

Regular Season

Wk. 1	Sep 20	L	17-7	vs Dallas Cowboys
Wk. 2	Sep 27	L	20-16	at Chicago Bears
Wk. 3	Oct 4	L	33-21	vs Washington Redskins
Wk. 4	Oct 11	L	30-23	at New York Giants
Wk. 5	Oct 18	L	35-20	vs St. Louis Cardinals
Wk. 6	Oct 25	L	30-17	at Green Bay Packers (at Milwaukee, WI)
Wk. 7	Nov 1	L	21-17	at Dallas Cowboys
Wk. 8	Nov 8	W	24-17	vs Miami Dolphins
Wk. 9	Nov 15	T	13-13	vs Atlanta Falcons
Wk. 10	Nov 23	W	23-20	vs New York Giants
Wk. 11	Nov 29	L	23-14	at St. Louis Cardinals
Wk. 12	Dec 6	L	29-10	at Baltimore Colts
Wk. 13	Dec 13	L	24-6	at Washington Redskins
Wk. 14	Dec 20	W	30-20	vs Pittsburgh Steelers

The Eagles began the new decade on a sour note, losing their first seven games on the way to another wretched last place 3-10-1 season; it was their last season at Franklin Field. The Eagles would actually win their final game at Franklin Field 30-20 over the Pittsburgh Steelers on December 20, 1970. Also, the Eagles played in their first Monday Night Football game on November 23, 1970, when they defeated the NY Giants 23-20.

1970 Philadelphia Eagles Stats

Passing	Comp	Att	Comp %	Yds	Y/Att	TD	Int	Rating
Norm Snead	181	335	54.0	2323	6.93	15	20	66.1
Rick Arrington	37	73	50.7	328	4.49	1	3	50.5
Lee Bouggess	0	1	0.0	0	0.00	0	0	39.6
Gary Ballman	0	1	0.0	0	0.00	0	0	39.6

Rushing	Rush	Yds	Avg	TD
Cyril Pinder	166	657	4.0	2
Lee Bouggess	159	401	2.5	2
Tom Woodeshick	52	254	4.9	2
Larry Watkins	32	96	3.0	1
Harry Jones	13	44	3.4	0
Norm Snead	18	35	1.9	3
Rick Arrington	4	33	8.3	1
Bill Bradley	1	14	14.0	0
Leroy Keyes	2	7	3.5	0
Ben Hawkins	2	3	1.5	0
Harold Jackson	1	-5	-5.0	0

Receiving	Rec	Yds	Avg	TD
Lee Bouggess	50	401	8.0	2
Gary Ballman	47	601	12.8	3
Harold Jackson	41	613	15.0	5
Ben Hawkins	30	612	20.4	4
Cyril Pinder	28	249	8.9	0
Steve Zabel	8	119	14.9	1
Tom Woodeshick	6	28	4.7	0
Fred Hill	3	10	3.3	1
Larry Watkins	3	6	2.0	0
Harry Jones	1	12	12.0	0
Billy Walik	1	0	0.0	0

Punting	Punts	Yds	Avg	Blocked
Bill Bradley	61	2246	36.8	0
Mark Moseley	10	350	35.0	0

Kicking	PAT Made	PAT Att	PAT %	FG Made	FG Att	FG %	Pts
Mark Moseley	25	28	89	14	25	56.0	67

Interceptions	Int	Yds	Avg	TD
Al Nelson	2	45	22.5	0
Steve Preece	2	19	9.5	0
Adrian Young	2	19	9.5	0
Ray Jones	2	17	8.5	0
Ed Hayes	1	2	2.0	0
Nate Ramsey	1	0	0.0	0

1970

Page 19 Monday
September 21, 1970
h★

The Philadelphia Inquirer / SPORTS

Financial

Eagles Fall to Cowboys, 17-7, in Opener

FRANK DOLSON

Sacrificial Lambs Played Like Tigers

THEY CAME OUT BREATHING FIRE, riding a tide of emotion that helped them keep the Dallas Cowboys off the scoreboard for nearly the entire first half. Two rookies. Two second-year pros. Only one starter, middle linebacker Dave Lloyd, with more than five years' experience. But this green defensive unit came ready to play football.

The sacrificial lambs played like tigers Sunday, slamming down the big names in the white jerseys, play after play, until a strange sound filled Franklin Field. Cheers.

"Boy, were they fired up!" Roger Staubach said. "Our first two series we didn't do anything. Either they were fired up or we were fired down."

They were up. Up so high you could sense it in the top row of the upper deck.

The first time Calvin Hill carried the ball he was slammed down for a one-yard loss. The first time Walt Garrison carried the ball, it was belted out of his hands. The first time Staubach scrambled, the Eagles scrambled him, jolting the ball loose five yards behind the line of scrimmage.

For 28 minutes, the team that is rated odds-on to win the National East title couldn't score a point against the 1000-to-one longshots. All that preparation—the unusually long practices, the written tests, the six and seven-hour work days that made up what Lloyd called "the hardest week I've ever spent for a league game"—paid off. The Eagles lost another football game, but at least it was a respectable loss. At least the game was 57 minutes old before the first loud boos floated across the field. At least the people who paid $8 to get in got *something* in return.

Cowboys Have to Work

AT LEAST THE DALLAS COWBOYS had to work and sweat and strain for this victory.

"I feel exhausted," Calvin Hill said in that soft, pleasant voice of his after absorbing the brutal pounding the Eagles were dishing out. "I'm just drained emotionally . . . They've got a good team. Gollee, they're so much better than last year . . ."

DAVE LLOYD

Had Hill made that statement 24 hours earlier, there would have been laughter. Not now. The Eagles' defensive team made Calvin earn every one of the 117 yards he gained on this opening day. Time after time, it prevented him from breaking loose for the long gainer he wanted so badly.

Perhaps the best measure of the Eagles' tenacity was Hill's frustration, which bubbled over early in the third quarter when Mel Tom reached out from behind and hauled him down near the Dallas bench, turning a potential big play into a modest six-yarder. Calvin fired the ball at the artificial turf in disgust.

Four plays later he nearly broke another one, but the hotly pursuing Eagles held him to 11 yards. Again Hill slammed the *football*—and drew a 15-yard penalty for unsportsmanlike conduct.

"I was ticked off at myself," the Yale man said. "I was pretty psyched up. I was upset. Throwing the ball down is like banging your fist against the turf . . . I wish they'd define the rules. Sometimes you can jump (hurdle for extra yardage), sometimes you can't. Sometimes you can slam the ball down, sometimes you can't . . ."

"You mean you didn't say anything when you slammed down the ball?" a newspaperman asked.

Hill grinned. "I might have said, 'Darnit Calvin, c'mon,'" he replied. "Or maybe 'Dammit Calvin . . .'" The grin spread. "Or maybe something worse than that."

Anger, Frustration Subside

THE ANGER AND FRUSTRATION he felt on the football field had subsided. It had been a good day for Calvin Hill, despite all the Eagles did to stop him. So good that one reporter suggested that he bore a startling resemblance to Jimmy Brown.

"There's only one Jim Brown," Hill said softly. "The only resemblance is we're both black, and we both have numbers in the 30s . . ."

And then he talked about how well the Cowboys had blocked for him, and how much he had to learn about using his blockers. "If O. J. (Simpson) had the line I had, he'd gain 3000 yards," Calvin said.

Not against a defensive team that hit as hard and pursued as well as the Eagles did Sunday, he wouldn't. Not against the charged-up unit that might have held Dallas scoreless for the first half, if Tom Woodeshick hadn't fumbled on his 34 with 5½ minutes to go.

"I'm real proud of the defense," Dave Lloyd said. "If they hadn't scored that first touchdown, if they'd gone in the locker room seven points down instead of even, I don't think they'd have scored the second one . . ."

But the Cowboys had scored the first one and the second one, and they had won the football game. The 1000-to-one longshots, the pre-season laughing stocks were 0-1, as advertised.

"It's better than losing the game like we lost before," Lloyd argued. "We were determined if they beat us, it was going to be a marginal score. Not like before. Not 56-7."

So it was only 17-7. A tough 17-7. A come-from-behind 17-7. Don't sneer. This is a year when moral victories may have to do.

Sports Results

Professional
FOOTBALL
National League
Sunday Results

Dallas 17	EAGLES 7
Minnesota 27	Kansas City 10
Cincinnati 31	Oakland 21
Houston 19	Pittsburgh 7
Detroit 40	Green Bay 0
Baltimore 16	San Diego 14
S. Francisco 26	Washington 17
Atlanta 14	New Orleans 3
Boston 27	Miami 14
Denver 25	Buffalo 10

(Only games scheduled)

Saturday's Results

Chicago 24	New York 16

(Only game scheduled)

Friday's Results

Los Angeles 34	St. Louis 13

(Only game scheduled)

Continued on Page 23, Col. 1

Inquirer photo by ALEXANDER DEANS

Cowboys' Calvin Hill Sheds Eagles' Adrian Young

Hill gained four yards on this second-quarter carry, finished the game with 117 yards rushing in 25 attempts

Staubach Hits Rentzel For Key TD

Birds Lead, 7-0, Before Lapsing Into Exhibition Form

By GORDON FORBES
Of The Inquirer Staff

Unsaddled in the first half, the Dallas Cowboys were remounted by Roger Staubach and Calvin Hill and proceeded on to a 17-7 victory over the Eagles before 59,728 fans Sunday at Franklin Field.

The Eagles, rated by some as the worst team in pro football, and the Cowboys, ranked by many as the best, played far out of character.

It took a pretty 31-yard touchdown strike from Staubach to Lance Rentzel in the third period to crack an even-

Pictures, Related Article On Pages 24 and 25

up grudge match between the Eastern Division rivals. Before that, the Eagle defensive unit had laughed in the faces of Tom Landry's multiple offense.

'PRESEASON FORM'

Hill, though he did not score a single point, provided the needed ball control for the highly favored Cowboys who wore down the Eagles in the final two periods.

Offensively, the Eagles struck for an early touchdown and then reverted to their pathetic exhibition form. Dallas stole three passes from Norm Snead, the Eagles' harassed quarterback, and set up a tying touchdown by grabbing Tom Woodeshick's second-period fumble at the Eagle 34.

LINE LEAKS

The guilt on two of the interceptions thrown by Snead belonged to the offensive line which broke down and allowed the Cowboys to claw at the quarterback's passing arm.

Staubach's big scoring pass came early in the third period and followed a punt by rookie Mark Moseley that dazzled only the Eagles. It took a reverse bounce and went into the records as a 14-yard kick that carried to the Cowboy 42-yard line.

PUNISHING AND PUNISHED

Hill, a punishing runner who gained 117 yards in 25 carries, helped move the ball into Eagle territory but then was flagged down for unsportsmanlike conduct when he slammed the ball to the AstroTurf after an 11-yard run.

The penalty pushed Dallas back to its 46. But then the Eagles also sinned. A defensive holding infraction gave the Cowboys an automatic first down at the Eagle 49.

BEATS HARVEY

After Hill and Garrison moved the ball to the 31, Staubach called for Rentzel to run a "sideline takeoff" pattern. Man-to-man defense by the Eagles dictated a deep pass to Rentzel.

The receiver ran an "out" move, then accelerated for the end zone where he caught up with Staubach's perfect toss. Rookie Richard Harvey caught up with Rentzel three strides too late.

'TALKED ALL GAME'

'It was a dumb mistake on my part," said Harvey in the Eagle dressing room. "I was pressing him from the inside and he ran a six-yard out pattern. When I took a step and committed myself, it was just what he wanted.

"We talked to one another the whole game. He would say, 'Rookie, you can't cover me,' and I would tell him, 'I don't care who you are, I'll have you on your back every play.' He expressed himself as the best receiver in the league.

'DOESN'T RUN CRISP'

"My answer to him was, 'I'm just as aggressive as anybody in the league.' He (Rentzel) doesn't run real crisp moves. He gets you to make the wrong move and then he capitalizes on it."

Rentzel's catch and Mike Clark's conversion put the Cowboys in front for the first time, 14-7.

After the ensuing kickoff, Snead guided the Eagles as far as the Cowboy 45 by hit-

Continued on Page 24, Col. 5

Lions Win in Rout, Hand Packers 1st Shutout Since '58

GREEN BAY, Wis., Sept. 20 (AP)—Mel Farr scored two touchdowns and Erroll Mann kicked four field goals as the Detroit Lions crushed the Green Bay Packers, 40-0, in a National Football League opener Sunday.

It was the first time the Packers have been shut out since 1958, when the Baltimore Colts stomped them, 53-0.

The last time the Packers were blanked in Green Bay was the opening game of the 1949 season, when the Chicago Bears turned the trick, 17-0.

EX-PACKER STARS

Mann, a former Packer, opened the scoring with a 22-yard field goal in the first period. He added three-pointers from 14, 43 and 47 yards.

Farr punched across from the one-yard line to push Detroit's lead to 10-0, then added another tally on a 12-yard burst in the fourth period.

Lem Barney's 40-yard return with a pass interception and Bill Triplett's 11-yard gallop around right end finished the Lions' scoring.

STARR BOOED

Triplett's touchdown burst was set up by Greg Landry's 76-yard romp on a quarterback sneak. The Lion signal-caller finally was hauled down from behind by Al Matthews at the Green Bay 11.

Bart Starr, the veteran Green Bay quarterback who led the Packers to five NFL championships and two Super Bowl crowns, was booed by the record crowd of 56,263 at

Continued on Page 24, Col. 7

Standings, Statistics

(SEPT. 21, 1970)

Sunday's Results
NATIONAL LEAGUE

PHILLIES 7, St. Louis 4, 10 innings.
Montreal 6, Chicago 4.
Atlanta 11, Cincinnati 2.
New York 4, Pittsburgh 1, 1st.
Pittsburgh 9, New York 5, 10 innings.
Los Angeles 7, Houston 6, 14 innings
(Only games scheduled).

Saturday's Results

PHILLIES 10, St. Louis 6
Chicago 8, Montreal 4
Pittsburgh 2, New York 1
Cincinnati 7, Atlanta 4, night.
Los Angeles 6, Houston 5.
San Francisco 3, San Diego 0.

Standings
Eastern Division

	W	L	Pct.	G.B.
Pittsburgh	82	70	.539	—
Chicago	80	72	.526	2
New York	79	74	.516	3½
St. Louis	72	81	.471	10½
PHILLIES	70	83	.458	12½
Montreal	67	85	.441	15

Western Division

	W	L	Pct.	G.B.
x-Cincinnati	96	58	.623	—
Los Angeles	83	69	.546	12
San Fran.	82	70	.539	13
Atlanta	74	80	.481	22
Houston	72	80	.474	23
San Diego	59	94	.386	36½

x-Won division title.

AMERICAN LEAGUE
Sunday's Results

Minnesota 8, Chicago 1.
New York 5, Detroit 1.
Baltimore 7, Cleveland 0.
Boston 3, Washington 1.
Milwaukee 4, Kansas City 3
California 4, Oakland 2

Saturday's Results

Boston 7, Washington 3, 1st
Boston 11, Washington 3, 2d night.
New York 7, Detroit 6
Kansas City 4, Milwaukee 1
Oakland 2, California 1.
Minnesota 5, Chicago 3, night.
Cleveland 4, Baltimore 2,

Standings
Eastern Division

	W	L	Pct.	G.B.
x-Baltimore	98	54	.645	—
New York	86	67	.562	12½
Boston	80	73	.523	18½
Detroit	76	76	.500	22
Cleveland	74	79	.484	24½
Washington	70	81	.464	27½

Western Division

	W	L	Pct.	G.B.
Minnesota	92	60	.605	—
Oakland	84	69	.549	8½
California	80	72	.526	12
Kansas City	59	91	.393	32
Milwaukee	59	93	.388	33
Chicago	53	96	.356	37½

x-Won division title.

Continued on Page 20, Col. 6

Monday's Games, Pitchers, Their Records on Page 20

Gretel Spurts On 5th Leg to Beat Intrepid

From Our Wire Services

NEWPORT, R. I., Sept. 20. —Skipper Jim Hardy found the right spinnaker to complement Gretel II's speed as the Australian challenger rallied on the fifth leg to beat Intrepid by one minute, seven seconds Sunday and tie the

Picture on Page 20

1970 America's Cup yachting series at 1-1 in a race again marred by protest flags.

Hardy, off to a poor start and trailing for the first four legs, put reserve helmsman David Forbes at the wheel for the downwind fifth leg and it apparently was the right move as Gretel went in front by 50 seconds going into the last leg and kept drawing away to win by about 300 yards.

The victory in the best-of-seven series was only the seventh by a challenger in the 119-year history of America's Cup competition and the second time since 12-meter yachts took over in 1958. Both recent triumphs belonged to Sir Frank Packer, the publishing magnate whose Gretel I beat Weatherly in the second race of the 1962 series.

Intrepid sailed the 24.3-mile nautical mile course without Steve Van Dyck, its regular tactical advisor who was evacuated by helicopter to a Newport hospital for treatment of a bee sting prior to the race. Lack of wind and a mine scare that turned out to

Continued on Page 20, Col. 4

Say, Jerry . . .?

Snead Still No. 1 For a Starter

Eagles' Coach Jerry Williams answers questions from the fans telephoned to The Inquirer during the game and relayed to sports writer Chuck Newman at the scene of action. While watching or listening to next week's game at Chicago, if you have a question, dial Say Jerry at LO 3-3288 before the end of the game.

Q. Why did you start Snead over Arrington?

Chuck Armstrong
Swarthmore

A. Because Norm Snead is our No. 1 quarterback and he has not been displaced by Rick Arrington.

Q. Why didn't the Eagles play more ball control when they got the lead in the first half?

Tillman Hann
Philadelphia

A. Snead went to the air on the first down after we had the lead. I corrected him and we did try to control the ball after that.

Q. What did you say to Tom Woodeshick after he fumbled in the second period?

Chip Barrett
Wayne

A. Nothing. Physical errors that are not the result of lack of effort are not the object of my wrath.

Q. Why did you punt on fourth down and inches to go in the third period?

Cathy Kinsay
Philadelphia

A. The idea of going for it crossed my mind, but only briefly. A good punt would have given us ideal field position. If we had gone for the first down and missed, it would

Continued on Page 24, Col. 4

Pirates Split With Mets, Lead by 2

From Our Wire Services

NEW YORK, Sept. 20.—Willie Stargell's 31st homer touched off a four-run spree in the 10th inning that gave the Pittsburgh Pirates a 9-5 victory over the New York Mets

National League

for a Sunday doubleheader split and a two-game edge in the National League's three-way East Division title race.

Phillies Beat Cards, Story on Page 20

Lefthander Jerry Koosman fired a two-hitter as the Mets took the opener, 4-1, snapping a four-game losing streak.

The split sent the Pirates two games up on the second-place Chicago Cubs, who lost to Montreal, 6-4. It maintained their 3½-game margin over the third-place Mets.

Stargell opened the 10th against Met reliever Tug McGraw with a drive over the

Continued on Page 20, Col. 5

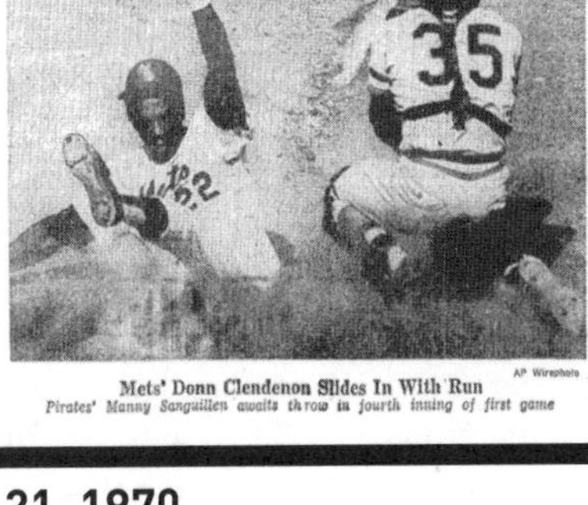

AP Wirephoto

Mets' Donn Clendenon Slides In With Run

Pirates' Manny Sanguillen awaits throw in fourth inning of first game

Sports on TV

PRO FOOTBALL
9 P. M.—New York Jets vs. Cleveland, Ch. 4.

September 21, 1970
Eagles lose home opener to the Dallas Cowboys 17-7

1971

RECORD: 6-7-1, 3RD IN NFC EAST
HEAD COACH: JERRY WILLIAMS & ED KHAYAT

SCHEDULE

REGULAR SEASON

Wk. 1	Sep 19	L	37-14	at Cincinnati Bengals
Wk. 2	Sep 26	L	42-7	vs Dallas Cowboys
Wk. 3	Oct 3	L	31-3	vs San Francisco 49ers
Wk. 4	Oct 10	L	13-0	vs Minnesota Vikings
Wk. 5	Oct 17	L	34-10	at Oakland Raiders
Wk. 6	Oct 24	W	23-7	vs New York Giants
Wk. 7	Oct 31	W	17-16	vs Denver Broncos
Wk. 8	Nov 7	T	7-7	at Washington Redskins
Wk. 9	Nov 14	L	20-7	at Dallas Cowboys
Wk. 10	Nov 21	W	37-20	at St. Louis Cardinals
Wk. 11	Nov 28	L	20-13	vs Washington Redskins
Wk. 12	Dec 5	W	23-20	at Detroit Lions
Wk. 13	Dec 12	W	19-7	vs St. Louis Cardinals
Wk. 14	Dec 19	W	41-28	at New York Giants

In their first season at Veterans Stadium, the Eagles did not start out any better than before, losing their first three games, including the first at the Vet 42-7 to the Dallas Cowboys on September 26th, when coach Jerry Williams wasfired and replaced by Ed Khayat. Under Khayat the Eagles would continue to struggle, losing their next two games. Now 0-5, the Eagles were looking for there first win both for the season and at the Vet. It finally happened on October 24, 1971,when the Eagles defeated the New York Giants 23-7. The Eagles played solid football the rest of the season, posting a 6-7-1 record, as they finished the season on a strong note by winning their last three games. Tom Dempsey made his Eagles kicking debut and earned his first win by kicking three field goals against St. Louis, with a final score of 37-20. Then, just three weeks later, the Eagles played St. Louis again and Dempsey tied a club record with four field goals, one of which was a 54-yarder---the longest in the NFL that season.

1971 PHILADELPHIA EAGLES STATS

Passing	Comp	Att	Comp %	Yds	Y/Att	TD	Int	Rating
Pete Liske	143	269	53.2	1957	7.28	11	15	67.1
Rick Arrington	55	118	46.6	576	4.88	2	5	49.3
Ronnie Bull	1	1	100.0	15	15.00	0	0	118.8
Jim Ward	1	1	100.0	4	4.00	0	0	83.3
Sonny Davis	0	1	0.0	0	0.00	0	0	39.6

Rushing	Rush	Yds	Avg	TD
Ronnie Bull	94	351	3.7	0
Lee Bouggess	97	262	2.7	2
Tom Woodeshick	66	188	2.8	0
Sonny Davis	17	163	9.6	1
Larry Watkins	35	98	2.8	1
Tony Baker	17	49	2.9	0
Tom Bailey	23	41	1.8	1
Harold Jackson	5	41	8.2	0
Pete Liske	13	29	2.2	1
Rick Arrington	5	23	4.6	0
Ben Hawkins	4	8	2.0	0
Steve Zabel	1	-5	-5.0	0

Punting	Punts	Yds	Avg	Blocked
Tom McNeill	73	3063	42.0	0
Bill Bradley	2	76	38.0	0

Kicking	PAT Made	PAT Att	PAT %	FG Made	FG Att	FG %	Pts
Tom Dempsey	13	14	93	12	17	70.6	49
Happy Feller	10	10	100	6	20	30.0	28

Receiving	Rec	Yds	Avg	TD
Harold Jackson	47	716	15.2	3
Ben Hawkins	37	650	17.6	4
Lee Bouggess	24	170	7.1	1
Harold Carmichael	20	288	14.4	0
Gary Ballman	13	238	18.3	0
Sonny Davis	11	46	4.2	0
Ronnie Bull	9	75	8.3	1
Fred Hill	7	92	13.1	0
Tom Bailey	7	55	7.9	0
Kent Kramer	6	65	10.8	1
Larry Watkins	6	40	6.7	0
Tom Woodeshick	6	36	6.0	1
Tony Baker	4	36	9.0	0
Steve Zabel	2	4	2.0	2
Jim Whalen	1	41	41.0	0

Interceptions	Int	Yds	Avg	TD
Bill Bradley	11	248	22.5	0
Leroy Keyes	6	31	5.2	0
Al Nelson	2	63	31.5	1
Tim Rossovich	1	24	24.0	0
Steve Zabel	1	14	14.0	0
Don Hultz	1	4	4.0	0

NFL Playoff Picture
(Stories on Page 36)

Cowboys vs. Vikings	Dolphins vs. Chiefs	Browns vs. Colts	Redskins vs. 49ers
(Sat., Ch. 10, 1 P.M.)	(Sat., Ch. 3, 4 P.M.)	(Sun., Ch. 3, 1 P.M.)	(Sun., Ch. 10, 4 P.M.)

Monday, Dec. 20, 1971 h★ 35 The Philadelphia Inquirer / SPORTS Television—Radio

Act Surprised, Pete

This Was the Day Scrooge Became Santa Claus

FRANK DOLSON

NEW YORK.

LEONARD TOSE ARRIVED at Yankee Stadium on Sunday wearing a red plaid sports jacket. If he had only known what was going to happen, he might have worn more fitting attire. Say, a red suit with white trim on it. Ho-ho-ho.

For the owner of the Philadelphia Eagles it was a strange, new role, but Leonard Tose played it convincingly. Maybe he was Scrooge to Jerry Williams, but on this long, cold afternoon in the Bronx he looked like Santa Claus to Pete Retzlaff and Eddie Khayat.

As the day dragged on, as the score mounted, the jolly old elf in Leonard Tose took charge. By the third quarter he was smiling, even laughing. By the fourth quarter his mind was made up. It was time to end all those nasty rumors. Time to rehire his general manager and his head coach.

"It was an easy decision to make," Tose said. "I saw no point in having these guys hang over Christmas."

Not after turning a 0-5 start into a 6-7-1 finish. Not after outclassing the New York Giants on the final day of the season.

"I thought we completely dominated the game," the Eagles' owner gushed. "I said, 'Why not (make the announcement)?' "

Complete domination. That was the key, the magic phrase that turned Scrooge into Santa. Anything short of that would have prolonged the agony.

"I would say that's a fair assessment, yes," Tose said. "I would say if this game was up for grabs I would've given it more thought. But I don't say my decision would have been different . . ."

NOR DID HE SAY HIS DECISION would have been the same.

In fact, there's some question as to exactly what Leonard Tose did say at the moment he decided to keep Retzlaff and Khayat for another two years.

"I was told about it before the announcement was made," the general manager said.

When?

"Prior to coming down here (to the locker room). Let me put it that way. He told me what he was going to say . . ."

Continued on Page 38, Column 1

★ ★ ★

"I said to myself, 'If you make a decision there's no sense vacillating.' I didn't want to be accused of killing Santa Claus." — LEN TOSE

★ ★ ★

A Gathering of Clean-Shaven, Victorious and Happy-for-the-Boss Eagles

Leroy Keyes (left) and Al Davis lead cheers after 'dunked' head coach Ed Khayat (right) was given two-year contract

Inquirer photos by GERVASE ROZANSKI

Liske Hurls For 3 TDs in Eagle Romp

By GORDON FORBES
Of The Inquirer Staff

NEW YORK. — The Eagles ended their turn-around season Sunday by humiliating the pathetic New York Giants and thrilling their demanding owner.

Minutes after the 41-28 rout was completed, Len Tose swaggered into the Eagle dressing room and announced that his interim coach, Ed Khayat, and his general manager, Pete Retzlaff, had been rehired.

Khayat and Retzlaff earned two-year contracts that reflect Tose's belief in the future of his once-shaky football team.

"Eddie's going to be our coach," Tose told a cluster of reporters after posing for pictures. "And Retzlaff is coming back, too. That's official."

Given three touchdown passes by Pete Liske and vicious gang-tackling by the defense, the Eagles wrapped up the victory as early as the third period.

Liske, who earlier hit Steve Zabel and Ben Hawkins for second-period scoring passes, hooked up with speedy Harold Jackson on a 63-yarder. That gave the Eagles a 38-14 lead and by then Tose was overjoyed.

Randy Johnson, who went all the way in place of Fran Tarkenton as the Giant quarterback, threw two meaningless touchdown passes in the final period. Johnson wound up with impressive statistics, 30 of 47 attempts for 372 yards and three TDS.

Earlier in the game when the Giants needed the big play, however, Johnson was ineffective in the face of constant pressure from the Eagle pass rush and blitzing linebackers.

Liske, on the other hand, contributed another strong

Continued on Page 38, Column 1

Flyers Fall To Plante, Leafs, 4-0

By CHUCK NEWMAN
Of The Inquirer Staff

Bernie Parent enjoyed another "homecoming" Sunday night. Smiled all the way through the Toronto Maple Leafs' 4-0 blanking of the Flyers. Never lifted a stick, never stopped a puck.

"I always like coming back," the ex-Flyer goaltender said after watching ageless Jacques Plante sleepwalk his way through a 25-shot (you should excuse the expression) shutout.

DATE VIVIDLY RECALLED

The date of Jan. 31, 1971, came back vividly to the Flyers' again last night. That was the date they sent Parent to the Leafs and failed to hold on to winger Mike Walton, who might help with a couple of goals here. If they forgot the people involved, Walton's name went up on the scoreboard after he scored a goal for the Bruins against Pittsburgh.

The Flyers also got goalie Bruce Gamble and a first-round draft choice in the deal. The draft pick turn out to be Pierre Plante, now with Richmond. Gamble got into the act last night, rescuing Doug Favell after the score was 4-0.

FANS REMEMBER

Parent, whom Plante says will be the best in the NHL very soon, likes to know he's remembered here. The sign in black letters that read, "This is 'Your' Home, Bernie," made him happy as did the one in red which said, "Hi, Bernie."

Parent has yet to play a game for Toronto here. And he has only met them once in

Continued on Page 40, Column 4

Everyone Was All Smiles After the Game, But...

GM Pete Retzlaff, left, coach Ed Khayat, right, receive Leonard Tose's congratulations

Lakers Beat 76ers for 25th; Wilt Nets 32, 33 Rebounds

Special to The Inquirer

INGLEWOOD, Calif. — The Los Angeles Lakers won a record 25th consecutive game Sunday night, repelling a determined bid by the 76ers, 154-132.

The 76ers trailed only 121-119 with 6:48 to play but then the Lakers outscored the Philadelphians, 18-1, late in the fourth quarter. Wilt Chamberlain led the way with 32 points, 33 rebounds and blocked 12 shots. It was Los Angeles' highest point total of its record-smashing season.

Bob Rule led the 76ers with 33 points while Billy Cunningham contributed 28. Gail Goodrich had 31 for the Lakers.

The 76ers started fast in hopes of accomplishing what the Lakers' last 24 opponents couldn't.

Kevin Loughery made a three-point play off the opening tipoff, and Dave Kohl followed with a short jumper for a 5-0 lead.

But the Lakers quickly caught up, and went ahead, 8-7, on a pair of free throws by Jim McMillian.

Then, the Lakers went of a

Continued on Page 40, Column 3

Sports on TV

COLLEGE FOOTBALL
9 P.M.—Liberty Bowl: Tennessee vs. Arkansas, Ch. 6.

Sports Results

Professional

FOOTBALL

Sunday's Results

EAGLES 41	N.Y. Giants 28
N.Y. Jets 35	Cincinnati 21
Cleveland 20	Washington 13
Miami 27	Green Bay 6
Los Angeles 23	Pittsburgh 14
New England 21	Baltimore 17
Atlanta 24	New Orleans 20
Minnesota 27	Chicago 10
Houston 49	San Diego 33
Kansas City 22	Buffalo 9
San Francisco 31	Detroit 27
Oakland 21	Denver 13

Saturday's Results

Dallas 31	St. Louis 12

BASKETBALL

NATIONAL BASKETBALL

Sunday's Results

Atlanta 101	Cincinnati 99
Chicago 119	Cleveland 101

Continued on Page 40, Column 1

...Retzlaff's Fate Was a Questionable Pre-Game Matter

Tose confers with rumored-on-the-way-out Pete as the Eagles warmed up

December 20, 1971 - Eagles close out the season with third consecutive win over the NY Giants 41-28

1972

RECORD: 2-11-1, 5TH IN NFC EAST
HEAD COACH: ED KHAYAT

SCHEDULE

REGULAR SEASON

Wk. 1	Sep 17	L	28-6	at Dallas Cowboys
Wk. 2	Sep 24	L	27-17	vs Cleveland Browns
Wk. 3	Oct 2	L	27-12	vs New York Giants
Wk. 4	Oct 8	L	14-0	at Washington Redskins
Wk. 5	Oct 15	L	34-3	vs Los Angeles Rams
Wk. 6	Oct 22	W	21-20	at Kansas City Chiefs
Wk. 7	Oct 29	L	21-3	at New Orleans Saints
Wk. 8	Nov 5	T	6-6	vs St. Louis Cardinals
Wk. 9	Nov 12	W	18-17	at Houston Oilers
Wk. 10	Nov 19	L	28-7	vs Dallas Cowboys
Wk. 11	Nov 26	L	62-10	at New York Giants
Wk. 12	Dec 3	L	23-7	vs Washington Redskins
Wk. 13	Dec 10	L	21-12	vs Chicago Bears
Wk. 14	Dec 17	L	24-23	at St. Louis Cardinals

Wide receiver Harold Jackson hada spectacular year, leading the NFL in both catches (62) and yards (1,048). Dempsey set another club record by scoring all the points in an 18-17 win against Houston (the Eagles second win for the season) when he kicked six field goals. However, the Eagles played terrible football all season long and finish with a wretched 2-10-1 season. Following the disastrous season, Tose accepts general manager Retzlaff's resignation and releases the entire coaching staff as part of a shake-up from the front office to the field.

1972 PHILADELPHIA EAGLES STATS

Passing	Comp	Att	Comp %	Yds	Y/Att	TD	Int	Rating
Pete Liske	71	138	51.4	973	7.05	3	7	60.4
John Reaves	108	224	48.2	1508	6.73	7	12	58.4
Rick Arrington	5	13	38.5	46	3.54	0	1	16.8

Rushing	Rush	Yds	Avg	TD
Po James	182	565	3.1	0
Tony Baker	90	322	3.6	0
Larry Watkins	67	262	3.9	1
John Reaves	18	109	6.1	1
Harold Jackson	9	76	8.4	0
Tom Bailey	7	22	3.1	0
Pete Liske	7	20	2.9	0
Tom Sullivan	13	13	1.0	0
Rick Arrington	1	2	2.0	0
Larry Crowe	1	2	2.0	0
Ben Hawkins	3	0	0.0	0

Receiving	Rec	Yds	Avg	TD
Harold Jackson	62	1048	16.9	4
Ben Hawkins	30	512	17.1	1
Harold Carmichael	20	276	13.8	2
Po James	20	156	7.8	1
Tony Baker	16	114	7.1	0
Kent Kramer	11	176	16.0	1
Gary Ballman	9	183	20.3	0
Larry Watkins	6	-2	-0.3	0
Tom Bailey	5	32	6.4	0
Tom Sullivan	4	17	4.3	0
Billy Walik	1	15	15.0	1

Punting	Punts	Yds	Avg	Blocked
Tom McNeill	7	290	41.4	0
Bill Bradley	56	2250	40.2	0

Kicking	PAT Made	PAT Att	PAT %	FG Made	FG Att	FG %	Pts
Tom Dempsey	11	12	92	20	35	57.1	71

Interceptions	Int	Yds	Avg	TD
Bill Bradley	9	73	8.1	0
Nate Ramsey	3	14	4.7	0
Ron Porter	2	10	5.0	0
Leroy Keyes	2	0	0.0	0
John Bunting	1	45	45.0	0
Chuck Allen	1	15	15.0	0
Dick Absher	1	7	7.0	0

Houston a Panacea to Ailing Philadelphians

HOUSTON.

AH, FINALLY A CITY with pro teams we can handle.

Saturday night the Houston Rockets.

Sunday afternoon the Houston Oilers.

Tomorrow the world . . .

Derek Sanderson was right. Think positive. Any time your pro football team can get outscored, two touchdowns to none, and win — well, things can't be THAT bad.

Although, in all honesty, they almost were.

The Eagles came within a few inches — a foot perhaps? — of losing to a team they seemed capable of clobbering. And yet with 16 seconds to go, there was Skip Butler flexing his right leg, getting ready to kick the 43-yard field goal that would win it for the Oilers.

Skip Butler, of all people.

For Tom Dempsey, who had booted six field goals in seven tries, it would have been an awful way to lose. After all, Butler was the guy who took Dempsey's job in New Orleans last year.

"He took it with a 12-yard field goal and three kickoffs out of bounds," Tom said in a voice that still contained a hint of bitterness.

And now Butler was on the verge of stealing the glory on Dempsey's most productive day.

FRANK DOLSON

A kicker lives for the moment when it's just him and one second (to go)," Tom said. 'If he doesn't live for that he shouldn't be out there . . . That's when it's fun to kick, unless you miss."

The snap was good. The snap was good. The hold was perfect. The kick was in the air . . .

For the better part of three hours the fans in the half-filled Astrodome had done more booing than rooting. Now they were on their feet, ready to holler themselves hoarse.

Dempsey stood in front of the Eagles' bench, hoping the ball would curve to the left of that yellow upright, thinking not about the six field goals he had kicked, but the one he hadn't kicked.

"I was watching the official," Tom said.

And he was listening to the people in the end zone seats, waiting for their reaction . . .

"The fans started yelling. I thought, 'Oh ——.' "

But the ball curved. The yell died. The Eagles won. Now Tom Dempsey could think about the six field goals he had kicked, and forget about the 22-yarder he had pulled to the left of the same yellow upright.

Wipe Away the Tears

And Skip Butler could do nothing but stand in front of his locker, press a towel to his face and wipe away the tears.

Like Dempsey, he lived for the moment when a football game hung in the balance, when a place-kick could make the difference.

And, like Dempsey and Jim Bakken last week in Philadelphia, he failed.

"It missed by a foot," Butler said in a voice choked by emotion. "A foot . . . ."

But it missed. That's all that mattered. "It should have been down the gut," he kept saying. "That's what a kicker gets paid for. When you miss one, especially one like that . . . ."

The voice trailed away. He was sobbing again. Finally, with a visible effort, he controlled himself.

"You want to help the team so damn much. Seems like when you need it most you can't come through. . . . That's what the game's all about. It's a game of inches. A game of pressure. . . ." He seemed startled by his own words. "No," he said, "I don't think it was the pressure. I just hit the ball bad. I got a good snap, a good hold and I just came across it a little bit."

So little that for a few, excruciating moments nobody on the sidelines could possibly tell.

A Save for Pastorini

So little that Dan Pastorini, the young, hard-throwing Oiler quarterback, thought Skip Butler had taken him off the hook.

"I thought he made it," Pastorini said, and he tore a strip of tape off his ankle, crushed it into a ball and threw it against his locker.

He wasn't angry at Butler's miss. He was angry at his own stupidity. If Dan Pastorini had known what down it was in the final minute of the first half, when he drove the Oilers deep into Eagles' territory, it would have been a different ball game.

It was third-and-seven on the Eagles' 17 when Pastorini dumped a screen pass to Fred Willis, who could have settled for a first down, but tried to go for six points instead. Retreating a yard or so as he looked for running room, Willis was thrown just inside the 11. Now it was fourth-and-one. Pastorini thought it was first-and-10.

Had he known it was fourth down, he would have called Houston's last time out of the first half and given Butler a chance to kick an 18-yard field goal. Instead he threw a pass that Bill Bradley intercepted in the end zone.

"We had sent in word from the bench," Oiler coach Bill Peterson said. "If it's fourth down, take a time out. . . . But Dan thought he made first down. Hell, anybody can make mistakes. Fred had run around. It was one of those things . . . ."

"It was a screw-up on my part," Pastorini said, holding a hand to the side of his head, the anger still flashing in his eyes.

"Mental mistakes . . . ." He was talking to himself. "How do you expect to make a quarterback with mistakes like that?" He looked up, seemingly aware of his audience for the first time. "That game was my fault," the kid said. "Nobody else's."

Okay, they were both willing to accept full blame for the defeat — the quarterback who didn't know what down it was in the last minute of the first half, the place-kicker who missed by a foot in the last minute of the game.

And the Eagles were just as willing to accept Sunday afternoon's one-point victory over the Oilers as the 76ers were to take Saturday night's two-pointer over the Rockets.

Helluva town, Houston.

The Philadelphia Inquirer / SPORTS Dial (a) Score LO 3-2842
For Late Results
Monday, Nov. 13, 1972 13

Dempsey's Boots Beat Oilers, 18-17

Eagles Win on 6 Field Goals

Longest of Tom Dempsey's six field goals was this 52-yarder for Eagles in first period UPI Telephoto

By GORDON FORBES
Of The Inquirer Staff

HOUSTON—The Eagle offense fainted seven times at the sight of the end zone Sunday.

Fortunately, Tom Dempsey took the notoriously in-and-out unit off a giant hook with a flurry of six field goals. The Eagles needed every one to pull out an 18-17 victory over the incredibly inept Houston Oilers inside the glittering Astrodome.

As sometimes happens in one of these pro football capers, the ending was packed with drama. Skip Butler, the newest in a succession of Oiler placekickers, barely missed a 43-yard try with 16 seconds left to play.

"It didn't miss by a helmet," said Super Bill Bradley. "It missed by (the width of) a football. I thought it was going to hit the bar."

When Butler's kick curled to the left of the upright, the Eagles were assured of their second one-point victory of the season against six losses and a tie.

The Oilers, roundly jeered by a half-filled Astrodome including many millionaire Texans trying to stay awake in their super-suites, dropped to 1-8, the worst record of any team in pro football.

"I was plain nervous when Butler lined up," admitted Bob Creech, the young Eagle linebacker. "I thought it missed by about three feet. I was just happy to see it go by."

With any kind of offensive thrust in the scoring zones, the Eagles should have been coasting in the final period.

As it was, Dempsey's sixth field goal, a 22-yarder in the first minute of the final period, provided an uneasy cushion of 18-10.

Quarterback Dan Pastorini, the adopted scapegoat of Oiler fans, somehow brought his team back to within a point with an unorthodox 64-yard thrust midway through the fourth quarter. It was unusual because the drive included only one tough pass, a 14-yard play-action toss to right end Alvin Reed. It was called on, of all downs, fourth-and-one.

A fail-safe flat pass to Paul Robinson gained five more yards and Pastorini scrambled for six to the Eagle 30.

Robinson then got two vicious blocks from guards Tom Regner and Ron Saul, located a power alley up the right side, and exploded for a 30-yard touchdown. Butler's kick with 5:39 left cut the Eagle lead to a single point, 18-17.

The offense then put the Eagles in a big hole. Pete Liske ran Ben Hawkins on a deep reverse that lost 15 yards back to the 15. That series ended with Bradley getting off a towering punt that fluttered away from returner Ken Houston and was finally downed at the Oiler 11 with 3:27 to go.

"It was left up to us, just like at Kansas City," grinned Richard Harris, the big end. "We decided we couldn't give it (a field goal) up.

"I was thinking all we had to do was try to contain Pastorini from running. Put on a big rush. Hope the backs could cover the receivers.

"OUR PURPOSE then was to keep them out of field goal range. They got inside but we just kept up the pressure. It was a lucky shot for us."

Fullback Fred Willis, who rushed for 119 yards, rammed for two tough yards and a first down at the 22 to get the drive started. Pastorini

Continued on Page 18, Column 1

★ ★ ★

Tom's Feat One Short

Tom Dempsey of the Eagles was one short of the National Football League record when he kicked six field goals in the Eagles' 18-17 victory over the Oilers Sunday at Houston.

Jim Bakken of the 1967 St. Louis Cardinals kicked seven against the Pittsburgh Steelers.

Here's rundown of Dempsey's connections:

Distance	Score
First Quarter	
33 yards	3-0
52 yards	6-0
Second Quarter	
22 yards	9-3
12 yards	12-3
38 yards	15-3
Fourth Quarter	
20 yards	18-10

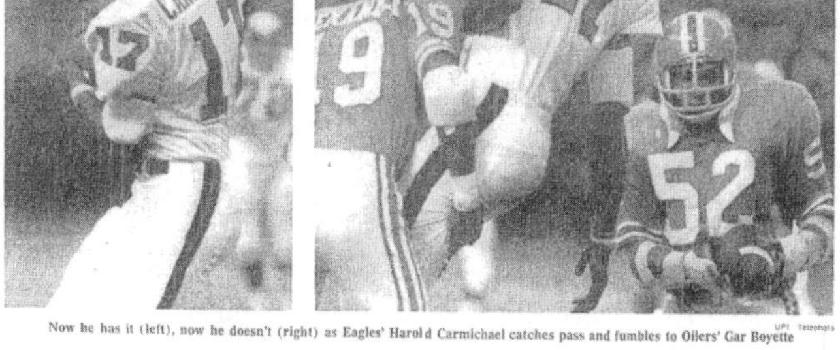

Now he has it (left), now he doesn't (right) as Eagles' Harold Carmichael catches pass and fumbles to Oilers' Gar Boyette UPI Telephoto

Giant Coach Accuses 'Skins Of Trying to Run Up Score

WASHINGTON (AP) — With 24 seconds remaining and Washington leading New York, 20-13, Redskin Coach George Allen called a timeout to stop the clock, much to the dismay of Giant Coach Alex Webster.

On the next play, running back Larry Brown plowed four yards for a touchdown.

Webster said afterward, "Why did he call the time out? You guys know what he's like, don't you."

IN REPLY Allen said, "Somebody said Larry needed only one yard to go over 1,000 yards for the season," said Allen. "My only thought was to give Larry an opportunity to crack the mark.

"And you have to remember, the score was only 20-13 at the time, so another touchdown wouldn't have hurt. You know, anything can happen at the end of a game."

Brown, the NFL's leading ground-gainer, carried the ball 30 times for 106 yards, the sixth time this season he has rushed for 100 or more yards. He was shy of the 1,000-yard mark by five.

Related Story, Photo on Page 16

Allen also denied giving Webster the cold shoulder.

"Before a game, I'm so tight that I don't say anything to anyone," he said. "And afterward, I would have liked to shake hands with Red (Webster's nickname) but I was concerned with more fights breaking out. I didn't want Sam to break his hand."

ALLEN SAID he thought there were two points in the game where the Redskins assured themselves of victory.

The Giants ran the second-half kickoff back to the Redskins 13, but six plays later had to settle for a field goal.

The second turning point was in the Redskins series of downs after the field goal.

On a second-and-19 on Washington's 13-yard line, quarterback Bill Kilmer's pass hit Giant linebacker Jim Files on the hands and bounced out but Redskin receiver Roy Jefferson made a one-hand catch for a 14-yard gain. The Skins went on to score.

Sports on TV

PRO FOOTBALL.
9 P. M.—Cleveland vs. San Diego, Ch. 6.

COLLEGE FOOTBALL.
Midnight — Temple - Rhode Island highlights, Ch. 29.

NFL RESULTS

Sunday's Results

EAGLES 18, Houston 17
Dallas 33, St. Louis 24
Pittsburgh 16, Kansas City 7
Washington 27, N. Y. Giants 13
N. Y. Jets 41, Buffalo 3
Oakland 20, Cincinnati 14
Miami 52, New England 0
Atlanta 36, New Orleans 20
Green Bay 23, Chicago 17
Minnesota 16, Detroit 14
San Francisco 24, Baltimore 21
Denver 16, Los Angeles 10

NATIONAL CONFERENCE						
East Division						
Washington	8	1	0	.889	227	124
Dallas	7	2	0	.778	217	149
N.Y. Giants	5	4	0	.556	215	[illegible]
EAGLES	2	6	1	.278	86	[illegible]
St. Louis	2	6	1	.278	122	[illegible]
Central Division						
Green Bay	6	3	0	.667	179	[illegible]
Minnesota	5	4	0	.556	[illegible]	[illegible]
Detroit	5	4	0	.556	[illegible]	[illegible]
Chicago	3	5	1	.375	[illegible]	145
West Division						
Los Angeles	5	3	1	.611	[illegible]	[illegible]
Atlanta	5	4	0	.556	[illegible]	[illegible]
S. Francisco	4	4	1	.500	[illegible]	[illegible]
New Orleans	1	7	1	.167	[illegible]	[illegible]
AMERICAN CONFERENCE						
East Division						
Miami	9	0	0	1.000	[illegible]	[illegible]
N.Y. Jets	6	3	0	.667	[illegible]	[illegible]
N. England	3	6	0	.333	[illegible]	[illegible]
Buffalo	[illegible]	[illegible]	[illegible]	[illegible]	[illegible]	[illegible]
Baltimore	2	7	0	.222	[illegible]	[illegible]
Central Division						
Pittsburgh	7	2	0	.778	[illegible]	[illegible]
Cleveland	[illegible]	[illegible]	[illegible]	[illegible]	[illegible]	[illegible]
Cincinnati	5	4	0	.556	[illegible]	[illegible]
Houston	1	8	0	.111	104	[illegible]
West Division						
Oakland	5	3	1	.611	[illegible]	[illegible]
Kansas City	5	4	0	.556	[illegible]	[illegible]
Denver	3	6	0	.333	181	[illegible]
San Diego	[illegible]	[illegible]	[illegible]	[illegible]	152	[illegible]

Flyers Score 8 Goals in Last 2 Periods To Wallop Seals, 8-3, Take Lead in West

By CHUCK NEWMAN
Of The Inquirer Staff

Former City Representative Abe Rosen would have taped it. It wasn't even in style in his days in office. "We're No. 1. We're No. 1."

The chant, that has been heard in Pittsburgh, Dallas, Baltimore, Boston and points east, west, north and south of the city, came to Philadelphia at 9:02 P. M. "We're No. 1, We're No. 1."

It rang out from 15,974 assembled at the Spectrum at 9:02 P. M. Sunday night. "We're No. 1, We're No. 1." The Flyers had made it possible by burying the California Golden Seals, 8-3, on eight goals in the last two periods as the scoreboard showed the New York Rangers on their way to a win over Los Angeles.

And an usher at the happening summed it up the best. "Even if it's only for one day," he said, "the fans have waited a long while."

IT HASN'T been since the 1967-68 hockey and basketball seasons here that a city sports team has been in first place this deep into the season. The Flyers are there. In first place in the West Division of the National Hockey League.

They made it in convincing fashion. Unlike their predecessors they went out and ate up a 1-0 deficit after one period with an offensive barrage that had Seals' goalie Marv Edwards making a couple of trips to the bench for a breather.

THE FLYERS got even 1-1 on Bobby Clarke's goal at 2:15. At 4:23 of the second period they were down again, 2-1. Visions of the stinker they played here in a 4-1 loss to the last-place Seals on Oct. 21 came back.

But, according to Coach Fred Shero and the players, this is no longer a defensive hockey team. Defenseman Brent Hughes tied the game and the Flyers were off to four straight goals and first place.

Shero has heard the chant before. In Buffalo when his teams were 20 points ahead of the pack in the American Hockey League. "It feels good even then. It gives you a lift," Shero said, almost showing some elation.

"I'd like to be there at the end," he rationalized. "But

Continued on Page 14, Column 3

Inside Our Pages

1972

November 13, 1972 - Tom Dempsey sets club record by kicking six field goals to defeat the Houston Oilers 18-17.

1973

RECORD: 5-8-1, 3RD IN NFC EAST
HEAD COACH: MIKE McCORMACK

Schedule

Regular Season

Wk. 1	Sep 16	L	34-23	vs St. Louis Cardinals
Wk. 2	Sep 23	T	23-23	at New York Giants
Wk. 3	Sep 30	L	28-7	vs Washington Redskins
Wk. 4	Oct 7	L	27-26	at Buffalo Bills
Wk. 5	Oct 14	W	27-24	at St. Louis Cardinals
Wk. 6	Oct 21	L	28-21	at Minnesota Vikings
Wk. 7	Oct 28	W	30-16	vs Dallas Cowboys
Wk. 8	Nov 4	W	24-23	vs New England Patriots
Wk. 9	Nov 11	L	44-27	vs Atlanta Falcons
Wk. 10	Nov 18	L	31-10	at Dallas Cowboys
Wk. 11	Nov 25	W	20-16	vs New York Giants
Wk. 12	Dec 2	L	38-28	at San Francisco 49ers
Wk. 13	Dec 9	W	24-23	vs New York Jets
Wk. 14	Dec 16	L	38-20	at Washington Redskins

Under new head coach Mike McCormick and new quarterback Roman Gabriel, the Eagles had an exciting offensive season but could only muster a 5-8-1 record. In his first year as a full-time receiver, Harold Carmichael became the second consecutive Eagle to lead the NFL in receptions with 67. Meanwhile quarterback Roman Gabriel became the NFL Comeback Player of the Year, after passing for 3,219 yards and 23 touchdowns.

1973 Philadelphia Eagles Stats

Passing	Comp	Att	Comp %	Yds	Y/Att	TD	Int	Rating
Roman Gabriel	270	460	58.7	3219	7.00	23	12	86.0
John Reaves	5	19	26.3	17	0.89	0	1	17.7

Rushing	Rush	Yds	Avg	TD
Tom Sullivan	217	968	4.5	4
Norm Bulaich	106	436	4.1	1
Po James	36	178	4.9	1
Tom Bailey	20	91	4.6	0
Harold Carmichael	3	42	14.0	0
Lee Bouggess	15	34	2.3	1
Charlie Young	4	24	6.0	1
Roman Gabriel	12	10	0.8	1
Greg Oliver	1	6	6.0	0
John Reaves	2	2	1.0	0
Bill Bradley	1	0	0.0	0\

Receiving	Rec	Yds	Avg	TD
Harold Carmichael	67	1116	16.7	9
Charlie Young	55	854	15.5	6
Tom Sullivan	50	322	6.4	1
Norm Bulaich	42	403	9.6	3
Don Zimmerman	22	220	10.0	3
Po James	17	94	5.5	0
Tom Bailey	10	80	8.0	1
Ben Hawkins	6	114	19.0	0
Lee Bouggess	4	18	4.5	0
Greg Oliver	1	9	9.0	0
Stan Davis	1	6	6.0	0

Punting	Punts	Yds	Avg	Blocked
Tom McNeill	46	1881	40.9	0
Bill Bradley	18	735	40.8	0

Kicking	PAT Made	PAT Att	PAT %	FG Made	FG Att	FG %	Pts
Tom Dempsey	34	34	100	24	40	60.0	106

Interceptions	Int	Yds	Avg	TD
Randy Logan	5	38	7.6	0
Bill Bradley	4	21	5.3	0
John Outlaw	2	48	24.0	1
Steve Zabel	2	13	6.5	0
John Sodaski	1	0	0.0	0
Dennis Wirgowski	1	0	0.0	0

Monday, Dec. 17, 1973 The Philadelphia Inquirer / SPORTS Dial a Score LO 3-2842 For Late Results Section C

Associated Press

O. J. Simpson gets hero's ride from mates after breaking NFL rushing mark

2,003

O. J. Runs to Records as Bills Bury Jets

By SKIP MYSLENSKI
Inquirer Staff Writer

NEW YORK. — He had endured a hectic week, so now, as the Buffalo Bills chartered jet flew toward New York, O. J. Simpson was able to more appreciate the moments alone.

But as he relaxed, Johnny Ray, the team's irrepressible linebacker coach, moved down the aisle, noted his fashionable three-piece gray suit and chortled. "Hey, Juice," Ray kidded, "you look so good someone would think you're on your way to close some business deal."

Simpson looked up and smiled wanly. "That," he answered, "all depends."

At 1:25 Sunday afternoon in a snowy Shea Stadium, all doubts were removed. Joe Ferguson, Buffalo's rookie quarterback, knelt in the huddle and called "I-5 right," once again for O. J. Simpson to run the ball. At the snap, he turned and handed it to Simpson, then watched as this splendid runner followed fullback Jim Braxton over left tackle for six yards.

As they lay on the ground together, Braxton looked over. "That a big enough hole for ya?" he asked.

"Yea, man," Simpson said back. "Not bad. Not bad at all."

With that simple run the momentous countdown ended. O.J. Simpson upped his season total to 1,869 yards and eclipsed Jim Brown's old mark by six.

Before the game ended in a Bills' 34-14 victory, others too would fall. Simpson himself would go on to carry 34 times for a season-total of 332, breaking the old mark by 27; he would run for 200 yards, his season total then ending at a prodigious 2,003; and the Bills as a team gained 314 yards rushing, surpassing the

(See O.J. on 2-C)

JIM BROWN, 1963

Opponent	Atts.	Yds.	Avg.
Washington	15	162	10.8
Dallas	20	232	11.6
Los Angeles	22	95	4.3
Pittsburgh	21	175	8.3
New York Giants	23	123	5.3
Philadelphia	25	144	5.8
New York Giants	9	40	4.4
Philadelphia	28	223	8.0
Pittsburgh	19	99	5.2
St. Louis	22	154	7.0
Dallas	17	51	3.0
St. Louis	29	179	6.2
Detroit	13	61	4.7
Washington	28	125	4.5
TOTALS	291	1,863	6.4

O. J. SIMPSON, 1973

Opponent	Atts.	Yds.	Avg.
New England	29	250	8.6
San Diego	22	103	4.7
New York Jets	24	123	5.1
Philadelphia	27	171	6.3
Baltimore	22	166	7.5
Miami	14	55	3.9
Kansas City	39	157	4.0
New Orleans	20	79	3.9
Cincinnati	20	99	4.9
Miami	20	120	6.0
Baltimore	15	124	8.3
Atlanta	24	137	5.7
New England	22	219	10.0
New York Jets	34	200	5.9
TOTALS	332	2,003	6.0

Redskins Defeat Eagles, Gain Playoffs

FRANK DOLSON

Eagles Still Believe After Final Defeat

WAHINGTON.—Sure, it would have been nice to end the season with a victory. Especially a victory over a team fighting to make the playoffs. And most especially a victory over a team coached by George Allen.

But Mike McCormack's first season as Eagles' head coach had ended with a defeat, and now, as the writers entered the locker room, he was walking from locker to locker, player to player. He patted Kermit Alexander on the back, shook hands with Bill Bradley, embraced Jerry Sisemore, playfully mussed Mark Nordquist's hair, thanked them all for what they had done. And what they had tried to do.

MIKE McCORMACK
. . . looks to next year

Maybe to his old boss—the guy down the hall in the winners' locker room on this dismal day—losing was like death. But not this defeat. Not to this man.

Mike McCormack's Eagles had started something this season—something that didn't end in the snow and mud and disappointment of Sunday's game.

I think we have an outstanding young football team," the losing coach said after he had patted the last back, grasped the last hand, mussed the last lock of hair.

Sure, this was a painful defeat. But it wasn't the end of the world, merely the end of the first season—even if the winning coach was named George Allen.

"We had a lot of guys on this team who wanted to win the game so bad it hurt," said super rookie Charley Young, and he began ticking off names. McCormack . . . Alexander . . . Boyd Dowler . . . Roman Gabriel . . . Marlin McKeever, all the Eagles who had been with Allen in past years. "You could see it in their faces."

Maybe so. But now that it was over, you could see something else in most of those faces. And it wasn't despair. Nor humiliation.

George Allen had won the game he simply had to win against a team crippled on defense. Nothing extraordinary about that.

"He's a great coach," Gabriel said. "No doubt about it. His record proves that. We had a lot of emotion going today because we had the opportunity of knocking them out of the

(See DOLSON on 4-C)

Charley Young is hot as his touchdown catch, against Redskins' Ken Houston, gives Eagles 10-0 lead . . .

Playoff Picture

The lineup for National Football League playoff games (all times Eastern Standard):

NATIONAL CONFERENCE

FIRST ROUND

Dec. 22—Washington (10-4) at Minnesota (12-2), 1 P.M., CBS-TV (Ch. 10).

Dec. 23—Los Angeles (12-2) at Dallas (10-4), 4 P.M., CBS-TV (Ch. 10).

CHAMPIONSHIP GAME

Dec. 30—At Dallas or Los Angeles, time to be announced, CBS-TV (Ch. 10).

AMERICAN CONFERENCE

FIRST ROUND

Dec. 22—Pittsburgh (10-4) at Oakland (9-4-1), 4 P.M., NBC-TV (Ch. 3).

Dec. 23—Cincinnati (10-4) at Miami (12-2), 1 P. M., NBC-TV (Ch. 3).

CHAMPIONSHIP GAME

Dec. 30—Site priority: Miami, Oakland, Cincinnati, time to be announced; NBC-TV (Ch. 3).

SUPER BOWL

Jan. 13—National champion vs. American champion at Rice Stadium, Houston, 3:30 P.M., CBS-TV (Ch. 10).

Philadelphia Inquirer / RICHARD M. TITLEY

. . . but Young is cold and forlorn on snow-kissed bench late in game

Brown Stars in 38-20 Win

By GORDON FORBES
Inquirer Staff Writer

WASHINGTON — Confronted by natural and man-made obstacles, Larry Brown cut loose for four touchdowns Sunday to propel the desperate Washington Redskins into the playoffs for the third straight season.

Neither a swirling snowstorm that made footing treacherous at RFK Stadium nor an off-beat 4-4 defense could halt Brown throughout the Redskins' 38-20 triumph over the outmanned Eagles.

Brown scored twice as the Redskins erupted for 24 points in an intimidating show of offensive firepower in the second period.

"We couldn't stop them," said Coach Mike McCormack, conceding the obvious. "Larry came alive today. I think he scored four times without being touched."

George Allen, a fanatic for perfection on the Redskin specialty teams, had the pleasure of seeing McCormack's units break down repeatedly. In the second period alone, a roughing-the-punter penalty and a high snap generously helped the Redskins to their second and third touchdowns.

The Eagles managed to end the Redskins flurry, getting a 15-yard field goal from Tom Dempsey just before halftime to trail, 24-13.

Then Brown fled 64 yards with a screen pass from Billy Kilmer to finish the Eagles late in the third period.

"He was my coverage on the screen," said linebacker Dean Halverson. "I got cut down by Charley Taylor. Hell, I was down all the time. The ice and mud would just cake up on your cleats."

Halverson slipped and fell trying to defend Brown while the Eagles were trying to protect a 10-0 lead. The result was an easy 14-yard touchdown pass to Brown that triggered the Redskin surge.

After the Redskins had gone ahead, 31-13, on the screen pass to Brown, the Eagle options narrowed to Roman Gabriel throwing deep.

Harold Carmichael outleaped 5-9 cornerback Pat Fischer for one of Gabe's tosses, shook off Brig Owens with a vicoius stiff-arm and legged it to the one-yard line for a 73-yard play.

Tom Sullivan, who fell 32 yards short in his quest for 1,000 yards rushing, scored from the one for the final Eagle touchdown.

Gabriel wound up unloading 39 passes into the tough Redskin defense, completing 22 for 302 yards. He managed to reach Carmichael twice more

(See EAGLES on 5-C)

Flyers Whip Islanders, 4-0

By CHUCK NEWMAN
Inquirer Staff Writer

Denis Potvin, the New York Islander's $100,000-plus draft choice, missed the bus. That's not why the laughing stock of the National Hockey League is so bad. It's really because their general manager, Bill Torrey, missed the boat when it came to choosing a profession.

"Torrey's Turkeys' lost another one last night, 4-0, to the Flyers at the Spectrum. And they bored the 13,181 paying customers who had braved the snowstorm.

The Islanders were saved from falling to the position they are so accustomed to, last in the East Division, by another Vancouver nosedive.

But stay tuned; they're only one point away and charging.

Potvin, who lives a five-minute drive in his $17,000 Mercedes from the Nassau County Coliseum where the Islanders allegedly play, couldn't make the distance. The Islanders' bus left for Philadelphia at 10:06. But Coach Al Arbour, who deserves a better fate, waited. The bus was scheduled to leave at 10 o'clock.

"I knew I wouldn't make it and would be suspended and fined anyway so I just forgot about it," Potvin told a New York reporter.

He'll face something," Arbour, who proably can't do much about Potvin, said after the game. "We'll sit down and talk to the boy."

The worse they can do to Potvin is make him rejoin this crew, which Torrey is molding into the same type of failure he fashioned at California.

The victory kept the Flyers one point ahead of Chicago in the West Division of the NHL.

(See FLYERS on 6-C)

Sports on the Air

TELEVISION
College Football
1 P. M.—Liberty Bowl, North Carolina, Kansas, Ch. 1.

RADIO
Thoroughbred Racing
1:15 P.M., Race of the Day from ... Park, WCAM-1310, WTMR-800.

December 17, 1973
After a 10-0 lead the Eagles lose to Washington 38-20.

1973

1974

RECORD: 7-7, 4TH IN NFC EAST
HEAD COACH: MIKE McCORMACK

SCHEDULE

REGULAR SEASON

Wk. 1	Sep 15	L	7-3	at St. Louis Cardinals
Wk. 2	Sep 23	W	13-10	vs Dallas Cowboys
Wk. 3	Sep 29	W	30-10	vs Baltimore Colts
Wk. 4	Oct 6	W	13-7	at San Diego Chargers
Wk. 5	Oct 13	W	35-7	vs New York Giants
Wk. 6	Oct 20	L	31-24	at Dallas Cowboys
Wk. 7	Oct 27	L	14-10	at New Orleans Saints
Wk. 8	Nov 3	L	27-0	at Pittsburgh Steelers
Wk. 9	Nov 10	L	27-20	vs Washington Redskins
Wk. 10	Nov 17	L	13-3	vs St. Louis Cardinals
Wk. 11	Nov 24	L	26-7	at Washington Redskins
Wk. 12	Dec 1	W	36-14	vs Green Bay Packers
Wk. 13	Dec 8	W	20-7	at New York Giants
Wk. 14	Dec 15	W	28-17	vs Detroit Lions

The Eagles made a trade with Cincinnati to acquire linebacker Bill Bergey. Bergey bolstered the defense and wons Pro Bowl honors along with Charlie Young, who becomes the third consecutive Eagle to lead the league in pass receptions with 63. Newly acquired linebacker Bill Bergey led an improved defense as the Eagles get off to a solid start, winning four of their first five games. However, a six-game losing streak would doom the Eagles playoff hopes, as they needed to win their final three games just to finish with a 7-7 record.

1974 PHILADELPHIA EAGLES STATS

Passing	Comp	Att	Comp %	Yds	Y/Att	TD	Int	Rating
Mike Boryla	60	102	58.8	580	5.69	5	3	78.9
Roman Gabriel	193	338	57.1	1867	5.52	9	12	66.8
Harold Carmichael	0	1	0.0	0	0.00	0	0	39.6
John Reaves	5	20	25.0	84	4.20	0	2	5.0

Rushing	Rush	Yds	Avg	TD
Tom Sullivan	244	760	3.1	11
Po James	67	276	4.1	2
Norm Bulaich	50	152	3.0	0
Roman Gabriel	14	76	5.4	0
Charlie Young	6	38	6.3	0
Tom Bailey	10	32	3.2	0
Mike Boryla	6	25	4.2	0
Greg Oliver	7	19	2.7	0
John Reaves	1	8	8.0	0
Randy Jackson	7	3	0.4	2
Merritt Kersey	1	2	2.0	0
Harold Carmichael	2	-6	-3.0	0

Punting	Punts	Yds	Avg	Blocked
Merritt Kersey	82	2959	36.1	0
Bill Bradley	2	67	33.5	0

Kicking	PAT Made	PAT Att	PAT %	FG Made	FG Att	FG %	Pts
Tom Dempsey	26	30	87	10	16	62.5	56

Receiving	Rec	Yds	Avg	TD
Charlie Young	63	696	11.0	3
Harold Carmichael	56	649	11.6	8
Tom Sullivan	39	312	8.0	1
Po James	33	230	7.0	0
Don Zimmerman	30	368	12.3	2
Norm Bulaich	28	204	7.3	0
Randy Jackson	17	0	0.0	0
Tom Bailey	6	27	4.5	0
Charlie Smith	1	28	28.0	0

Interceptions	Int	Yds	Avg	TD
Bill Bergey	5	57	11.4	0
John Bunting	2	23	11.5	0
John Outlaw	2	22	11.0	0
Bill Bradley	2	19	9.5	0
Steve Zabel	2	12	6.0	0
Randy Logan	2	2	1.0	0
Joe Lavender	1	37	37.0	1
Jerry Patton	1	4	4.0	0
Dean Halverson	1	0	0.0	0

Sportscene 3
Scoreboard 6
Calendar 6
Horse Racing 7
High Schools 8

The Philadelphia Inquirer
sports

section C

Monday, Dec. 2, 1974

In Packer Weather, Boryla Makes Impressive Debut

BILL LYON

For four nights Mike Boryla had a squirrel scurrying around inside his stomach.

For four nights Mike Boryla counted blitzing linebackers in his sleep and listened to the wild pounding of his own heart, dreaming of the ecstasy of a touchdown pass, the agony of an interception.

Because last Wednesday Mike McCormack decided to rest Roman Gabriel's battered body and start Mike Boryla, whose regular-season experience his rookie season had consisted of 59 seconds of one game.

"Mike just told me I'd start and he was going to keep it quiet so the Packers wouldn't be able to prepare for me, set up blitzes and stunts to pressure me," Mike Boryla said.

So that gave Mike Boryla four nights to wait. And worry. And stew in his own bubbling juices. And feel that damned squirrel running around loose in his gut.

"Sure, I got the shakes and the nerves," Mike Boryla admitted. "But I think I would rather know in advance that I was starting instead of the last minute.

"A lot of people on the team talked to me. They all had advice for me," he smiled.

"I just told myself this is what you were waiting for. Now it's your chance. I've always felt I could play up here. If I didn't feel that way, I wouldn't belong in the pros. I've always had confidence. But you don't always have to be talking about it just to prove it."

So Mike Boryla, low key, quiet, a rookie in experience only, went out and completed 16 of 32 passes, two of them for scores, engineered two impressive touchdown drives of 80 and 41 yards, and the Eagles took out six weeks worth of frustration on fumbling, butter-fingered Green Bay, 36-14.

It was an impressive debut for the QB from Stanford, because the game was played in the kind of weather the Packers invented.

The sky was black and glowering. The Vet echoed with thunderclaps. Sheets of rain splattered down. And the wind was whirlpool treacherous, blowing in cold, buffeting currents with downdrafts that grabbed spirals and drove them into the artificial turf.

Yet Mike Boryla threw with accuracy and variety. Lobs to skyscraping Harold Carmichael. Darts to Charles Young. Flares to Norm Bulaich. Sideline zingers to Don Zimmerman.

(See LYON on 4-C)

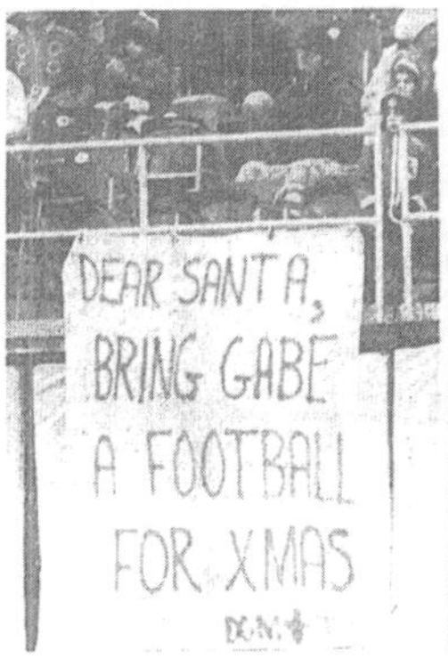

Philadelphia Inquirer / ALEXANDER DEANS

If Mike Boryla keeps it up, will Christmas be the next time Roman Gabriel (right) gets the ball?

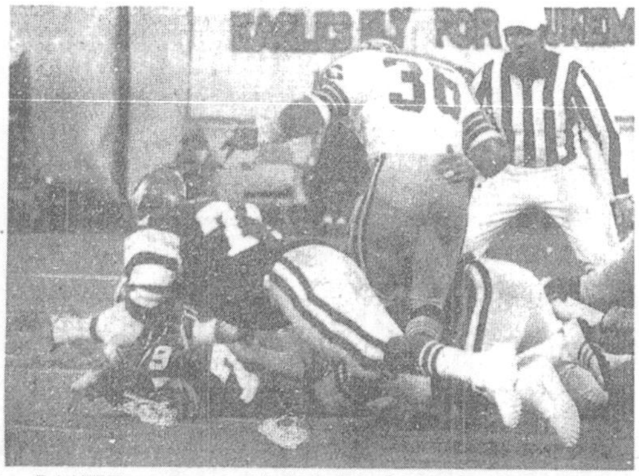

Eagles' Will Wynn pounces on one of five fumbles Packers lost, this by MacArthur Lane (36) . . .

. . . picks it up and takes off 87 yards for a touchdown with a phalanx of blockers to protect him . . .

Philadelphia Inquirer / ALEXANDER DEANS

. . . so it's no wonder he has a Wynning smile

Eagles End Slump, Rack Pack, 36-14

By GORDON FORBES
Inquirer Staff Writer

Mike Boryla made his quarterback debut in the pro football bigs Sunday and it would be nice to say that he corrected everything that was wrong with the Eagle offense when it belonged to Roman Gabriel.

It would also be untrue.

Sure, Boryla played with poise against natural and human obstacles, but what accelerated the Eagles in their totally enjoyable 36-14 win over the bungling Green Bay Packers was an awesome defense.

"That was the best defensive effort we've had all around," said middle linebacker Bill Bergey. "The guys in front of me were just knocking people over. And the defensive secondary played well.

"After six straight losses," Bergey added, fingering a long, thin cigar, "maybe we had to go back to basic things. We gave the game ball to Mike McCormack, but I thought 30 or 40 people could have gotten game balls."

McCormack handled the ball flawlessly. The Packers should have been so fortunate. They fumbled eight times against the aroused Eagle defense, losing the ball five times. Out of these five turnovers, the Eagles gleefully produced 29 points to the delight of the 42,030 fans in attendance. The miserable weather accounted for 24,022 no-shows.

Boryla, who got the call from McCormack over an unhappy John Reaves, had to battle swirling winds and a tough Packer defense that had limited its last three opponents to 10 points. Bergey's hitters removed much of the pressure by turning the ball over to the offense three times in Packer territory and supplying a touchdown outright on Will Wynn's spectacular 87-yard run with MacArthur Lane's fumble.

The rookie took the Eagles 60 yards late in the second period for their fourth straight touchdown and a 29-0 lead over the dazed Packers.

Green Bay got it together offensively in the second half, closing to within 29-14 on quarterback John Hadl's three-yard rollout pass to MacArthur Lane. And on the

(See EAGLES on 4-C)

Associated Press

Now find the other 24,558 who watched the Browns-49ers game

A No-Show Sunday

From Inquirer Wire Services

Things were rough all over Sunday.

An ice storm forced cancellation of the 10-race program at Penn National Race Course in Grantville, Pa.

The World Hockey Association game between the Cleveland Crusaders and the Michigan Stags at Richfield, O., was snowed out.

So was the National Hockey League game between the Toronto Maple Leafs and the Detroit Red Wings. It seems the Maple Leafs made it to Olympic Stadium in Detroit just fine, but all except one Red Wing were stranded at their homes.

And although no National Football League games were called off, maybe a few should've been.

An NFL record for no-shows was set in Chicago where 36,951 decided not to attend a Bears-New York Giants game played in freezing rain and snow. Some 18,602 did show up.

But the record didn't last out the day. Two hours later in Atlanta, where it was 33 degrees with 15-MPH winds, 18,648 ticket holders showed and 40,202 didn't.

In other sellouts, there were 29,365 no-shows in Cleveland (24,559 showed); 24,022 at Veterans Stadium, where 42,030 watched the Eagles; 9,155 no-shows in Pittsburgh (41,195 braved freezing rain); approximately 4,000 in Buffalo (79,540 showed) and 3,900 in Oakland, where 54,020 attended in good weather.

Elsewhere, attendance was 44,402 at Minnesota, 41,863 in snowy St. Louis and 44,888 at Shea Stadium where the New York Jets beat San Diego, 27-14, in showers and blustery winds.

K.C.'s Not-So-Good Scouts Lambasted by Flyers, 10-0

By CHUCK NEWMAN
Inquirer Staff Writer

Tom Capaccio and Mike Fore were the starting linesmen in Sunday night's so-called hockey game between the Flyers and the Kansas City Scouts.

Don't look for them in the National Hockey League roster of officials. They usually work Junior A games in South Jersey and toil as stickboys at the Flyers' games at the Spectrum.

Ironically, Capaccio and Fore were not out of place when fouled-up weather forced the use of stand-ins until referee Andy Van Hellemond could manage the three-hour car drive from Washington.

In a game that should erase all thoughts of further expansion, the Flyers scored five times in the first period and four more times in the second en route to a 10-0 annihilation of the Scouts.

The win pushed the Flyers back atop Division One of the NHL, two points ahead of idle Atlanta.

"It was a tough game to coach," Flyers' Coach Fred Shero explained. "You have to stop the players from going goofy."

Shero used four lines in an effort to hold the score down and held a seminar with his team after the first and second periods, concentrating on the mistakes his team was making.

"I told them after the second period that we could go out there and score five more goals and give up two

(See FLYERS on 6-C)

Jabbar Scores 35, Bucks Zap 76ers

Special to The Inquirer

RACINE, Wis.—Kareem Abdul-Jabbar scored 20 of his 35 points in the third period and the revived Milwaukee Hawks beat the 76ers, 117-112, before 1,632 Sunday night.

The loss was the 76ers' fourth in succession and the victory was the Bucks' sixth in seven games. They lost 13 of their first 14 while Jabbar was sidelined with a broken hand.

Jabbar spent the last 15 minutes of the first half on the bench after picking up his third personal foul but the Bucks led at intermission, 58-56, on a field goal by Gary Brokaw, the only basket in the half by the rookie from Notre Dame.

In the third period, Jabbar dominated the boards and began scoring regularly. He was a one-man show for the Bucks, although the 76ers twice forged four-point leads, 79-75 and 83-79.

But Jabbar paced a Buck rally and Brokaw scored his second field goal on a fast break to put the Bucks ahead to stay, 88-87, as the third period ended.

The Bucks gradually increased their lead in the final period as the losers ran into foul trouble. With 4½ minutes to play, Jabbar made a perfect pass to Mickey Davis underneath for a goal and a 107-98 Milwaukee advantage.

The 76ers then rallied as Doug Collins and Allan Bristow led the way. Bristow's second three-point play of the spurt cut the Milwaukee edge to 109-108 before Jim Price, fouled by Steve Mix with 2:01

(See 76ERS on 6-C)

NFL Playoff Picture

Standings and remaining games for teams in contention for National Football League playoff berths (six division champions and the second-place team with the best record in each conference qualify):

	W	L	T	Dec. 8	Dec. 15
NATIONAL CONFERENCE					
Eastern Division					
y-St. Louis	9	3	0	at N. Orleans	N. Y. Giants
Washington	8	4	0	at L. Ang. (M)	Chicago
Dallas	7	5	0	Cleveland (S)	at Oakland (S)
Central Division					
x-Minnesota	8	4	0	Atlanta (S)	at Kan. City (S)
Detroit	6	6	0	at Cincinnati	at Eagles
Western Division					
x-L. Angeles	9	3	0	Washing. (M)	Buffalo
AMERICAN CONFERENCE					
Eastern Division					
Buffalo	9	3	0	at N. Y. Jets	at Los Angeles
Miami*	8	3	0	at Baltimore	New England
N. England	7	5	0	Pittsburgh	at Miami
Central Division					
Pittsburgh	8	3	1	at N. England	Cincinnati (S)
Cincinnati*	7	4	1	Detroit	at Pitts. (S)
Western Division					
x-Oakland	10	2	0	at Kan. City	Dallas (S)
Denver	6	5	1	Houston	at San Diego

*Cincinnati plays at Miami tonight
x-clinched division title y-clinched playoff berth
S-scheduled preceding Saturday; M-following Monday

December 2, 1974 - In his Eagles debut QB Mike Boryla defeats the Green Bay Packers 36-14

1975

RECORD: 4-10, 5TH IN NFC EAST
HEAD COACH: MIKE McCORMACK

Schedule

Regular Season

Wk. 1	Sep 21	L	23-14	vs New York Giants
Wk. 2	Sep 28	L	15-13	at Chicago Bears
Wk. 3	Oct 5	W	26-10	vs Washington Redskins
Wk. 4	Oct 12	L	24-16	at Miami Dolphins
Wk. 5	Oct 19	L	31-20	at St. Louis Cardinals
Wk. 6	Oct 26	L	20-17	vs Dallas Cowboys
Wk. 7	Nov 3	L	42-3	vs Los Angeles Rams
Wk. 8	Nov 9	L	24-23	vs St. Louis Cardinals
Wk. 9	Nov 16	W	13-10	at New York Giants
Wk. 10	Nov 23	L	27-17	at Dallas Cowboys
Wk. 11	Nov 30	W	27-17	vs San Francisco 49ers
Wk. 12	Dec 7	L	31-0	vs Cincinnati Bengals
Wk. 13	Dec 14	L	25-10	at Denver Broncos
Wk. 14	Dec 21	W	26-3	at Washington Redskins

The Eagles suffered a season of setbacks, finishing in last place with a terrible 4-10 record. Following the season coach Mike McCormick was fired and replaced by fiery UCLA coach Dick Vermeil.

1975 Philadelphia Eagles Stats

Passing	Comp	Att	Comp %	Yds	Y/Att	TD	Int	Rating
Roman Gabriel	151	292	51.7	1644	5.63	13	11	67.8
Mike Boryla	87	166	52.4	996	6.00	6	12	52.7

Rushing	Rush	Yds	Avg	TD
Tom Sullivan	173	632	3.7	0
James McAlister	103	335	3.3	1
Art Malone	101	325	3.2	0
Po James	43	196	4.6	1
Charlie Smith	9	85	9.4	0
Roman Gabriel	13	70	5.4	1
Mike Boryla	8	33	4.1	0
John Tarver	7	20	2.9	0
Charlie Young	2	1	0.5	0
Spike Jones	1	-1	-1.0	0

Receiving	Rec	Yds	Avg	TD
Charlie Young	49	659	13.4	3
Harold Carmichael	49	639	13.0	7
Charlie Smith	37	515	13.9	6
Po James	32	267	8.3	1
Tom Sullivan	28	276	9.9	0
Art Malone	20	120	6.0	0
James McAlister	17	134	7.9	2
John Tarver	5	14	2.8	0
Keith Krepfle	1	16	16.0	0

Punting	Punts	Yds	Avg	Blocked
Spike Jones	68	2742	40.3	0
Merritt Kersey	15	489	32.6	0

Kicking	PAT Made	PAT Att	PAT %	FG Made	FG Att	FG %	Pts
Horst Muhlmann	21	24	88	20	29	69.0	81

Interceptions	Int	Yds	Avg	TD
John Outlaw	5	23	4.6	0
Frank LeMaster	4	133	33.3	1
Artimus Parker	4	15	3.8	0
Joe Lavender	3	59	19.7	1
Bill Bergey	3	48	16.0	0
John Bunting	1	6	6.0	0
Randy Logan	1	4	4.0	0

The Scene 3
High Schools 5
Classified Ads 7
Comics 16
Feature Page 17

The Philadelphia Inquirer
sports
section D
Tuesday, Nov. 4, 1975

A Helpless McCormack

By FRANK DOLSON

It was quite a switch for Howard. Two nights before he had been in New York City doing Saturday Night Live. Last night he was in Philadelphia doing Monday Night Dead . . .

Game-time approached and you could feel the excitement mounting. So what if the Eagles were 1-and-5? The nation was watching, the stadium was packed.

Half a minute before the opening kickoff and a roar thundered across Veterans Stadium, imploring the home team to win one for Mike McCormack or Roone Arledge or Leonard Tose's friend, Gene Mauch, who was sitting in the owner's box . . . or somebody. Anybody . . .

The people were ready. The Eagles weren't. What a shame for the 64,601 in the Vet and the 40 million non-paying spectators who missed Archie Bunker to see this.

And especially what a shame for Mike McCormack . . .

"I like Mike McCormack," Bill Bergey had said 24 hours before the dreadful mismatch. "I think he's a good coach. I think he prepares us well. He's got a knack of keeping things going when things are dark and dismal."

But last night, with all those people watching, with Howard Cosell talking, with all those friends of the owner sitting in the executive box, things got so dark, so dismal that the fired-up crowd started leaving in the third quarter. One disgruntled group in the end zone went so far as to hold up a sign they had brought along in the event of just such a shellacking. "Bring Back Joe," it said, apparently referring to former Eagles Coach Joe Kuharich.

Poor Mike McCormack. He stood there near midfield, his arms folded across his huge chest, watching the game get out of control, listening to the cheers turn to jeers.

Bill Bergey isn't the only person who likes Mike McCormack. To know the man is to like him . . . and, at a time like this, to feel sorry for him. When a game disintegrates there is nothing a coach can do — except maybe wish it hadn't disintegrated with the nation watching.

"I couldn't think of anything to stem the tide," McCormack said. "I'd have taken messages from Heaven, from the pressbox, from anyplace if anybody knew how to stop it."

Outwardly, he was still calm, still in control of his emotions. But there was one clue to the agony he must have felt inside. In his left hand, he held a red-colored lead pencil, and as he stood there, leaning against the wooden platform in his office, he gripped the pencil tighter and tighter until, finally, it snapped in two.

Before the ordeal was over, the pencil was in tiny fragments, the lead was jammed through the rubber eraser. Here was a man going through hell—and yet, no matter how unpleasant the questions, never once acting anything but a man.

"I don't know any other profession that affects you so much personally," he had said before the game. "You get in a losing streak, you don't want to go out of the house, to see anyone . . ."

It happened to Nick Skorich. It happened to Kuharich. It happened to Jerry Williams, and to Eddie Khayat, and now it was happening to Mike McCormack.

"In professional sports," he knew, "people pay to see a winner."

(See DOLSON on 2-D)

Philadelphia Inquirer / RICHARD M. TITLEY

Mike McCormack: "I'd have taken messages from Heaven"

'In seven years, we haven't made any progress at all.'
—Leonard Tose

Rams Humiliate Eagles

Sixth Defeat (42-3) Worst Since 1972

Philadelphia Inquirer / RICHARD M. TITLEY

On the bench, Tom Sullivan (right) rages against a hopeless situation . . .

By GORDON FORBES
Inquirer Staff Writer

The Eagles suffered another of those humiliating defeats last night that have so often marked their pathetic past. This time it was a 42-3 drubbing at the hands of the awesome Los Angeles Rams before a jeering sellout crowd of 64,601 fans and a national television audience of 40 million.

The last time the Eagles were wiped out that badly was three years ago in a 62-10 wipeout by the New York Giants. That was the season that owner Len Tose chose to fire Eddie Khayat and replace him with Mike McCormack. And out of the Monday Night Massacre came the obvious question: Is Tose in the mood to replace McCormack?

The owner wasn't saying. But McCormack, wearing his customary grim face after watching his team taken apart, admitted this was the worst defeat in his three-year head coaching career.

"It's going to be short and sweet this time gentlemen," he told reporters afterwards. "We had our butts kicked by a very good football team. They did everything they wanted to and we couldn't seem to do anything against them."

The Eagles, now 1-6 and badly slipping, fell behind, 21-3 at halftime as quarterback James Harris whipped both cornerbacks on deep touchdown passes to fleet Harold Jackson, the former Eagle gamebreaker. On the first of Harris' throws, a 54-yard bomb, Jackson ran past defender John Outlaw. On the second, he beat Cliff Brooks for a 30-yard score.

The Rams turned it into a rout in the third quarter, scoring twice more. Harris hurled a 42-yard touchdown strike to backup receiver Jack Snow and later Fred Dryer, the flanky defensive end, rubbed it in by grabbing a fumble by Roman Gabriel and racing 20 yards for another score.

"They weren't as good as we made them out to be," Outlaw said in the silent Eagle dressing room. "We knew they were going to put the ball in the air. We just didn't do the job.

"He (Jackson) just ran a short out and then a fly. I just didn't come out of my turn quick enough. He just outran me. With Snow, we were in zone coverage and he just split the seam on us," Outlaw said as he stared off into space. "You just want to go somewhere and bury yourself. There's not a whole lot you can say."

Dryer's touchdown opened a 35-3 lead for the Rams (6-1) and McCormack gave Gabriel a 10th series before turning the sputtering offensive over to Mike Boryla with 6:36 left in the third period.

Boryla produced a touchdown all right—for the Rams. On the second play of the final period, the young quarterback tried to go short but linebacker Isiah Robertson intercepted and sprinted 76 yards down the left sideline to wrap up the scoring.

"It wasn't any fun," Dryer said

(See EAGLES on 2-D)

Leonard Tose: A Bitter Man

By BILL LYON

Leonard Tose went on the Mutual Radio Network at halftime last night and did what Howard Cosell is always braying about. He told it like it is.

"In seven years," said the Eagles' owner, "We haven't made any progress at all in my opinion."

"We're 1-and-5 and we're headed for 1-and-6 and that doesn't make me happy. We've slipped a lot."

Tose did not amplify on that. Not during the game. But afterwards.

Two weeks ago he was asked if he thought his coach, Mike McCormack, was doing a good job. He refused comment, and that of course triggered all sorts of speculation that McCormack, in his third year of a three-year contract, faced the ultimatum that confronts all coaches—win or else.

The Eagles, facing a grim schedule, would have to sweep the second half of their season to emerge with a winning record. In the wake of last night's humiliation, you can make your own odds on that possibility.

"Well, I'll tell ya," said Fred Dryer. "I emphathesize with these guys (the Eagles).

"I've been through that before, Man, I could stand here and talk to you 'til next week about my days with the Giants."

Dryer, a defensive end traded from New York to the Rams, rumbled 20 yards with a Roman Gabriel fumble to score one of six LA TDs against the Eagles. And the Eagles, he said, reacted predictably.

"Some of 'em quit and some of 'em didn't," he said. "I'm not gonna name names. I imagine the films will show that. It happens when you get behind. Believe me, I know. They got half a season left. They can either say, screw it, or they can try to correct whatever is wrong. I'll tell you, they got some damn good players."

So does the fault lie with the coaches?

"Who the hell knows?" replied Dryer. "From what I can tell McCormack is a good coach. Look at Atlanta. They fire a coach and the next day they beat New Orleans. Now figure that.

"I think the Eagles can turn themselves around. I hope they do. Really. Otherwise, it's a long damn season.

"I think if they got some points on us early they'd have really stuck it to us."

But the sticking was done instead by the Roadrunner, Harold Jackson. Ex-Eagle. Two TD catches.

"The first one is called 85 X-go, if you really care," Jackson said with a grin. "John Outlaw was setting on me, hanging for the short stuff. So on the sideline I said, hey, let me run a fly right by him.

"The second one, (Clifford) Brooks was expecting me to go inside. So I

(See LYON on 2-D)

Philadelphia Inquirer / RICHARD M. TITLEY

. . . while on the field, the hopelessness is the reality of a Roman Gabriel fumble, following Larry Brooks' sack

November 4, 1975 - Eagles get clobbered by the LA Rams 42-3, worst loss since 1972.

1976

RECORD: 4-10, 4TH IN NFC EAST
HEAD COACH: DICK VERMEIL

Schedule

Regular Season

Wk. 1	Sep 12	L	27-7	at Dallas Cowboys
Wk. 2	Sep 19	W	20-7	vs New York Giants
Wk. 3	Sep 27	L	20-17	vs Washington Redskins (OT)
Wk. 4	Oct 3	W	14-13	at Atlanta Falcons
Wk. 5	Oct 10	L	33-14	at St. Louis Cardinals
Wk. 6	Oct 17	L	28-13	at Green Bay Packers
Wk. 7	Oct 24	L	31-12	vs Minnesota Vikings
Wk. 8	Oct 31	W	10-0	at New York Giants
Wk. 9	Nov 7	L	17-14	vs St. Louis Cardinals
Wk. 10	Nov 14	L	24-3	at Cleveland Browns
Wk. 11	Nov 21	L	26-7	vs Oakland Raiders
Wk. 12	Nov 28	L	24-0	at Washington Redskins
Wk. 13	Dec 5	L	26-7	vs Dallas Cowboys
Wk. 14	Dec 12	W	27-10	vs Seattle Seahawks

After 10 straight non-winning seasons, the Eagles new coach Dick Vermeil was a change of direction. Vermeil, a workaholic perfectionist, came into camp and worked the Eagles hard. Many players rejected the hard-driving Vermeil, as the Eagles did not play any better posting another 4-10 record. However, they did win their home opener 20-7 against the NY Giants.

1976 Philadelphia Eagles Stats

Passing	Comp	Att	Comp %	Yds	Y/Att	TD	Int	Rating
Mike Boryla	123	246	50.0	1247	5.07	9	14	53.4
Spike Jones	1	1	100.0	-4	-4.00	0	0	79.2
Roman Gabriel	46	92	50.0	476	5.17	2	2	63.5
Harold Carmichael	0	2	0.0	0	0.00	0	0	39.6
John Walton	12	28	42.9	125	4.46	0	2	26.6

Rushing	Rush	Yds	Avg	TD
Mike Hogan	123	561	4.6	0
Tom Sullivan	99	399	4.0	2
Dave Hampton	71	267	3.8	1
James McAlister	68	265	3.9	0
Herb Lusk	61	254	4.2	0
Mike Boryla	29	166	5.7	2
Bill Olds	36	120	3.3	1
Charlie Smith	9	25	2.8	1
Art Malone	2	14	7.0	1
Charlie Young	1	6	6.0	0
Roman Gabriel	4	2	0.5	0
John Walton	2	1	0.5	0

Receiving	Rec	Yds	Avg	TD
Harold Carmichael	42	503	12.0	5
Charlie Young	30	374	12.5	0
Charlie Smith	27	412	15.3	4
Mike Hogan	15	89	5.9	0
Tom Sullivan	14	116	8.3	1
Herb Lusk	13	119	9.2	0
James McAlister	12	72	6.0	0
Dave Hampton	12	57	4.8	0
Bill Olds	9	29	3.2	0
Keith Krepfle	6	80	13.3	1
Art Malone	1	-3	-3.0	0
Frank LeMaster	1	-4	-4.0	0

Punting	Punts	Yds	Avg	Blocked
Spike Jones	94	3445	36.6	0

Kicking	PAT Made	PAT Att	PAT %	FG Made	FG Att	FG %	Pts
Horst Muhlmann	18	19	95	11	16	68.8	51

Interceptions	Int	Yds	Avg	TD
Bill Bradley	2	63	31.5	0
Bill Bergey	2	48	24.0	0
John Outlaw	2	19	9.5	0
Randy Logan	1	38	38.0	0
Tom Ehlers	1	27	27.0	0
Al Clark	1	0	0.0	0

Scoreboard 2
The Scene 3
Horse racing 6
High schools 7

The Philadelphia Inquirer
sports

Section
C

Monday, Nov. 1, 1976

By FRANK DOLSON

Sports Editor

Tale of Jolly Lean Giants

EAST RUTHERFORD, N.J. — Come to think of it, this has been a heckuva sports year for New York. The Yankees made it to the World Series. The Knicks won three games before losing. The Islanders got off to a flying start in the National Hockey League. And, perhaps best of all from the standpoint of rebuilding the city's sports image, the Giants left town.

Their record might be the worst this side of Tampa Bay. Their execution might be abysmal. Their personnel might be questionable. Their offense might be invisible. But nobody can criticize their timing.

What better season to escape to the other side of the river. What more perfect year to flee across state lines. The move was sheer genius. As the New York Giants, descendants of a proud heritage, this club would be a disgrace. But as the East Rutherford Giants (Midgets?) they're — well, they're the best damned football team East Rutherfordians have ever had.

A great sports town, East Rutherford. Maybe the greatest of all time. Imagine selling 76,000 tickets — at $9 and $11.50 a crack — to see a 0-and-7 team that hasn't scored a point in five quarters extend their winless streak to eight and their scoreless streak to nine.

Listing flagship

Across the way, on the other side of the Hudson, the natives must be laughing themselves silly. Not only is it now possible for them to totally disown this team, but yesterday — thanks to the foresight of the local CBS television station — it was impossible to watch the Giants play in New York. Given a choice between carrying the sold-out East Rutherford-Philadelphia game or Dallas-Washington, the station chose the latter. It may have been CBS' sharpest move since the cancellation of "Ball Four."

"When you're talking about the Giants you're talking about the flagship of the NFL," East Rutherford's new head coach, John McVay told a New York writer the other day. Either McVay has a good sense of humor or the NFL has a bad flagship.

The Giants were so impotent yesterday that even the most loyal East Rutherfordians were tempted to act like hardened New Yorkers. Their boos floated across these reclaimed marshlands; their frustrations over the inability of Craig Morton to put points on those fancy, electronic scoreboards drove them to chant: "We want Snead ... We want Snead." (In fairness to the East Rutherford sports fans, however, those may have been Eagles' rooters screaming for McVay to use Snead.)

Poor McVay. A short, chunky, personable man who inherited this mess from Bill Arnsparger days before, he handled the postgame inquisition with patience and grace.

"We moved the ball a little bit," he said in the tone of voice of a coach grateful for small favors, "but we dropped a touchdown pass in the end zone and we missed a field goal. You're not supposed to do things like that in a professional football game."

First and no goal

Nor are you supposed to get a first down on the other team's 3, try three running plays and wind up with a fourth down on the 6. But the Giants did in the fourth quarter — with a major assist from the Eagles' defensive unit, and no small help from themselves. On the first play Marsh White slipped and lost 3. Second-and-goal on the 6. In came another play from the sidelines, designed for a goal-line defense. But the Eagles weren't in a goal-line defense, and Morton called time.

A conference, then a handoff to — surprise! — Larry Csonka, only his seventh carry of the day. He struggled to the 5. Then a quick pitch to Doug Kotar, and a loss as Manny Sistrunk hauled him down from behind. And finally, a pass that bounced harmlessly in the end zone, far over the head of wide-receiver Ray Rhodes, who obviously didn't run the pattern Morton expected him to run. BOO-O-O.

"We were down in there (close)," McVay said. "It was my decision, let's go in for a score. Then an onside kick, then ..."

That was quite a finish John McVay had worked out in his mind, but it bore no resemblance to what the Giants came up with on the field.

"Holding hurt us," the coach was saying. "And our inability to get outside. And we dropped some balls."

They did what losing football teams have been doing for years in much more exotic places than East Rutherford, N.J. And McVay said what his predecessor had been saying for weeks: "We've got good personnel ... football players."

"Well," Csonka would say later in that big, plush locker room, "we'd

(See DOLSON on 5-C)

Eagles win with basics

Associated Press

His footing unsecure, tight end Bob Tucker of the Giants goes down at the hands of the Eagles' John Bunting in the last period

Defeat Giants by 10-0

By Gordon Forbes
Inquirer Staff Writer

After seven weeks of frustration in the defensive trenches, the Eagles finally discovered an offensive line they could handle and a quarterback they could knock down.

They needed both edges to achieve a 10-0 victory over the winless, struggling New York Giants yesterday at the Meadowlands Complex on a day when the Eagle offense didn't dazzle anybody either.

"We just went back to basics," said Bill Dunstan, who went all the way inside at both tackle spots as the Eagles put together their first shutout in 105 games, or since late in 1968. "We stressed coming off the football and it finally is coming around now. We just began rolling off the ball ... starting with step one and reading our keys second."

"We knew beginning on Wednesday that we weren't going to be doing that much blitzing," said Blenda Gay, the strongside end. "That's because they flared their backs a lot. Most teams give solid protection and the backs can help defense the ends."

Gay grinned. "You know," he said, "it's much easier to hit a still target than a moving target."

The still target was poor Craig Morton, the beleaguered Giant quarterback, who was sacked six times by the furious Eagle rush and booed continually by angry fans who pleaded for a relief appearance by Norm Snead.

The boos began as early as the second period when Morton was on the field for three running plays and then off. On the next two series, quarterback Mike Boryla guided the Eagles to a 10-point lead that stood up only because they were playing the Giants.

It would have stood up in their first game when the Giants scored a single touchdown. And it was enough yesterday because the Giants, playing their first game under new coach John McVay, never developed any offensive rhythm or consistency.

"I've seen three Giant games on film," said linebacker John Bunting, "and our defensive front four has just played unbelievable against the Giants. It makes it so much easier on the linebackers. They play that way and you know Bill Bergy will make all-pro. Hell, even Frank LeMaster and me might be all-pro, too."

Boryla gave the Eagles a 7-0 lead

(See EAGLES on 5-C)

Wind-helped kick levels Vikings

Associated Press

CHICAGO — Bob Parsons plays for the Chicago Bears who play in the Windy City and knows something about shifting winds.

Parsons outdueled Neil Clabo in a kicking game that went a long way in providing the Chicago Bears with a 14-13 victory yesterday as they handed the Minnesota Vikings their first loss of the season.

A pair of squibbed punts by Clabo into a 17-m.p.h. wind quickly were turned into touchdowns by the Bears and Parsons recalled that he had shanked three punts at Minnesota earlier in the season when the Vikings edged the Bears, 20-19.

"I felt sorry for Clabo," said Parsons. "I know how he feels. I work on kicking into the wind every day. I was able to get my punts high into the wind which enabled our guys to cover well."

Clabo admitted the wind was a factor but said, "All kickers have bad days," and Minnesota Coach Bud Grant added, "Kicking definitely was a factor. Our's was as bad as it has been since I can remember."

Bear Coach Jack Pardee said the wind was against the Vikings on their last possession and was a factor in keeping them from getting into range for a game-winning field goal.

Walter Payton's 39-yard touchdown run in the first quarter and a couple of breaks which led to another touchdown in the fourth period helped the Bears even their record at 4-4.

Minnesota is now 6-1-1.

With the Bears leading, 7-6, after Fred Cox had booted a pair of 24-yard field goals for the Vikings, Nate Wright was called for pass interference which gave the Bears the ball on the Viking 3-yard line. Johnny Musso then fumbled and recovered the ball in the end zone for what proved to be the winning touchdown

Minnesota came right back with a touchdown on an 80 yard drive which was helped by a pass interference call before Fran Tarkenton, who earlier broke the last of Johnny Unitas' passing records, rolled out 2 yards to score.

Tarkenton completed 24 of 46 passes for 272 yards and a career total of 40,421,, surpassing Unitas' total of 40,239.

It marked the Bears' first victory over the Vikings since 1972 after eight regular-season losses.

Tarkenton, who a year ago sur-

(See BEARS on 4-C)

Bakken's OT kick wins for Cards

Associated Press

ST. LOUIS — "We just blew them out," guard Bob Young said. "They stunted some in the first half, but they never beat us one on one."

The 270-pound Young was describing the 39-yard St. Louis Cardinals march in overtime, overcoming the vaunted defense of the San Francisco 49ers in a 23-20 National Football League game yesterday.

The Cards, after recovering a fumble at the 49er 43-yard line, called on Jim Otis for five straight carries in their parade to within the shadow of the San Francisco goalpost.

Then, after Otis was halted at the 4 on third down, veteran Jim Bakken coolly kicked a 21-yard field goal for the triumph with 6 minutes 42 seconds gone in the extra period.

"We have nothing to be ashamed about in losing," said San Francisco Coach Monte Clark, who watched his team begin with a costly mistake and lose in the same fashion.

"Aside from a couple mistakes, I thought we outplayed them, but they (Cardinals) are a championship-type team," Clark added.

"Our effort was great," Clark said. "It's just too bad that as great as

(See CARDINALS on 4-C)

Flyers blast LoPresti to wallop Stars, 9-1

Gary Ronberg
Inquirer Staff Writer

Down there on the frosty Spectrum ice, his head encased in white plastic and the rest of him wrapped in pads that would never be more vital to his survival, Pete LoPresti was all alone last night. Into his pads, against his stick, clanging off the glass and the bright red posts on either side of him, and feeling like hot coals when it wound up in his glove, more rubber was poured at LoPresti than into tire factory molds.

And many times — too many times — it billowed in the net behind him as the Flyers thrashed the Minnesota North Stars, 9-1, and pulled into a first-place tie with the New York Islanders, pending the outcome of tonight's Islanders-Canucks match in Vancouver.

"It's hard to explain," said LoPresti, son of Sam LoPresti, a former National Hockey League goaltender who after he gets word of last night may wish his son had chosen other endeavors.

"You just try to keep going. You give it your best, so that at least you can walk out of the building with your head up. Everybody has bad games now and then. But with a goaltender, it goes up there on the board where everybody can see it."

The thing is, LoPresti was probably the best North Star on the ice. Indeed, if he gave up a bad goal, it was only one — Reggie Leach's short-side strike on a first-period power play.

"If you saw a bad goal against him tonight, I didn't," said Minnesota Coach Ted Harris. "None of what happened tonight was his fault. I wouldn't have been him (LoPresti) tonight for a million bucks."

Perhaps it was the game at Long Island Saturday night that aroused these Flyers. Or maybe it was that they decided to cease playing down to

(See FLYERS on 2-C)

Philadelphia Inquirer / RICHARD M. TITLEY

Flyer Paul Holmgren upsets North Star Tom Reid last night at the Spectrum

Syracuse coach: No honest day's work by officials

By Chuck Newman
Inquirer Staff Writer

College roundup

Syracuse Coach Frank Maloney will violate football decorum at his weekly football press conference today. Not only will he question the judgment of the officials who worked his game at Pittsburgh Saturday, but he will question their INTEGRITY.

"I'm going to ask for an investigation of the whole thing," he said after viewing films of two downs on which Syracuse short yardage specialist Jim Sessler failed — according to head linesman Cliff Fair — to make inches for a first down at the Panther 10-yard line, with second-ranked Pitt nursing a 7-point lead. Pitt won, 23-13.

Maloney drew a 15-yard penalty after Syracuse was stopped with 3 minutes 23 seconds left to play for questioning the placement of the ball. "It was obvious in the films that his (Sessler's) shoulders were inside the 10-yard line," he said yesterday. "He made it even if he was carrying the ball between his legs."

There are extenuating circumstances to the controversy. The official who made the call on the placement of the ball is a member of the Tri-State officials, who mainly handle Pitt, Penn State and West Virginia games. He was one of four Tri-State officials in the crew Two others were assigned from the ECAC, of which Syracuse is a member.

Maloney left the field thinking he had been bilked. He vent his ire on two officials, neither of whom had anything to do with the marking of the ball. "I couldn't find Fair," he said.

"They are a great football team," he said of the Panthers. "Maybe, if we had scored, they would have come back to win. But we had a chance at one of the major college upsets of the year if not many years."

You could understand his thinking had his team been given the first down. Quarterback Bill Hurley was doing a surgical number (365 yards in offense) on Pitt's vaunted defense and there seemed no way they could have stopped him from getting 10 yards in four more downs.

"People say you're supposed to keep quiet," Maloney steamed. "I get attacked when I make bad calls, so why can't I attack them. I have no control over the officials who work the game. We coaches don't have as much power as you think. It's ridiculous. Everybody knows those Tri-State officials better not offend anybody if they want to keep working the games of those three schools.

"I'm not going to milquetoast this thing. Question not only the judg-

(See COLLEGES on 7-C)

1976

November 1, 1976 - Eagles first shutout since 1968, when they defeated the NY Giants 10-0.

1977

RECORD: 5-9, 4TH IN NFC EAST
HEAD COACH: DICK VERMEIL

Schedule

Regular Season

Wk. 1	Sep 18	W	13-3	vs Tampa Bay Buccaneers
Wk. 2	Sep 25	L	20-0	at Los Angeles Rams
Wk. 3	Oct 2	L	17-13	at Detroit Lions
Wk. 4	Oct 9	W	28-10	at New York Giants
Wk. 5	Oct 16	L	21-17	vs St. Louis Cardinals
Wk. 6	Oct 23	L	16-10	vs Dallas Cowboys
Wk. 7	Oct 30	L	23-17	at Washington Redskins
Wk. 8	Nov 6	W	28-7	vs New Orleans Saints
Wk. 9	Nov 13	L	17-14	vs Washington Redskins
Wk. 10	Nov 20	L	21-16	at St. Louis Cardinals
Wk. 11	Nov 27	L	14-6	at New England Patriots
Wk. 12	Dec 4	L	24-14	at Dallas Cowboys
Wk. 13	Dec 11	W	17-14	vs New York Giants
Wk. 14	Dec 18	W	27-0	vs New York Jets

QB Ron Jaworski was obtained from the Los Angeles Rams in exchange for the rights to tight end Charlie Young. Bill Bergey, keying the newly installed 3-4 defense of coordinator Marion Campbell, won All-Pro and All-Conference honors and was selected to play in his third Pro Bowl. The Eagles would end the lackluster season on a strong note by taking their last two games in convincing fashion to finish with a 5-9 record. The Birds did show improvement on the field, but earned only one more victory than the previous season.

1977 Philadelphia Eagles Stats

Passing	Comp	Att	Comp %	Yds	Y/Att	TD	Int	Rating
Ron Jaworski	166	346	48.0	2183	6.31	18	21	60.4
Roman Gabriel	1	3	33.3	15	5.00	0	0	50.7

Rushing	Rush	Yds	Avg	TD
Mike Hogan	155	546	3.5	0
Keith Krepfle	27	530	19.6	3
Tom Sullivan	125	363	2.9	0
James Betterson	62	233	3.8	1
Herb Lusk	52	229	4.4	2
Wilbert Montgomery	45	183	4.1	2
Ron Jaworski	40	127	3.2	5
Frank LeMaster	1	30	30.0	0
Charlie Smith	2	13	6.5	0
Cleveland Franklin	1	0	0.0	0
Wally Henry	1	-2	-2.0	0

Receiving	Rec	Yds	Avg	TD
Harold Carmichael	46	665	14.5	7
Charlie Smith	33	464	14.1	4
Tom Sullivan	26	223	8.6	2
Mike Hogan	19	118	6.2	1
Herb Lusk	5	102	20.4	1
James Betterson	4	41	10.3	0
Wilbert Montgomery	3	18	6.0	0
Wally Henry	2	16	8.0	0
Vince Papale	1	15	15.0	0
Richard Osborne	1	6	6.0	0

Punting	Punts	Yds	Avg	Blocked
Spike Jones	93	3463	37.2	0

Interceptions	Int	Yds	Avg	TD
Deac Sanders	6	122	20.3	0
Herman Edwards	6	9	1.5	0
Randy Logan	5	124	24.8	0
John Outlaw	2	41	20.5	0
Bill Bergey	2	4	2.0	0

Kicking	PAT Made	PAT Att	PAT %	FG Made	FG Att	FG %	Pts
Horst Muhlmann	17	19	89	3	8	37.5	26
Nick Mike-Maye	7	7	100	3	3	100.0	16
Ove Johannson	1	3	33	1	4	25.0	4

1977

Sports/People 2
NFL roundup 4
Horse racing 6
Colleges 7
Schools 7

The Philadelphia Inquirer
sports

section
C

Monday, December 19, 1977

Another titanic battle, another big Flyers loss

By Gary Ronberg
Inquirer Staff Writer

After a buildup of 10 weeks, it was equal to what the most rabid Montreal or Flyers fan might have expected. One of grand emotion, of gut-wrenching skating, an absolute blur of red and white shirts up and down the frosty ice of the Spectrum. And when it was over, after a final, desperate chance by the Flyers had been destroyed by a referee's whistle with only 2 minutes 6 seconds to play, the Montreal Canadiens again had defeated the Flyers, this time by 2-0 last night.

Obviously it was not an explosive struggle, replete with heart-stopping opportunities and sprawling saves; but to observe the effort put forth by these rivals was worth double the admission price of the Spectrum's most expensive ticket. All one had to do was drop by the dressing cubicle of Joe Watson, that veteran defenseman who has been through so many games he has stopped counting, and the entire evening was put into perspective.

"Wasn't that," Watson sighed, "a titanic struggle? It seemed like one out there, but you watched it."

Yes, Joe, it was.

For the Flyers, riding the crest of an 11-game undefeated streak, leading the National Hockey League with 46 points, and already flirting with the same Stanley Cup spirit that had infused them several years ago, this was the night to put an end to the Canadiens' jinx once and for all. It was a night, THE NIGHT, to puncture that 0-11-1 Flyers' record against Montreal dating to Feb. 15, 1976.

For these Canadiens were not only hurting, they were sick. The finest player in the world today, Guy Lafleur, was back in Montreal with tonsillitis and the flu. So was an all-star defenseman, Guy LaPointe, with a bad knee and the flu. So were Yvan Cournoyer and Pierre LaRouche, both with knee injuries.

And coming into the Spectrum,
(See FLYERS on 3-C)

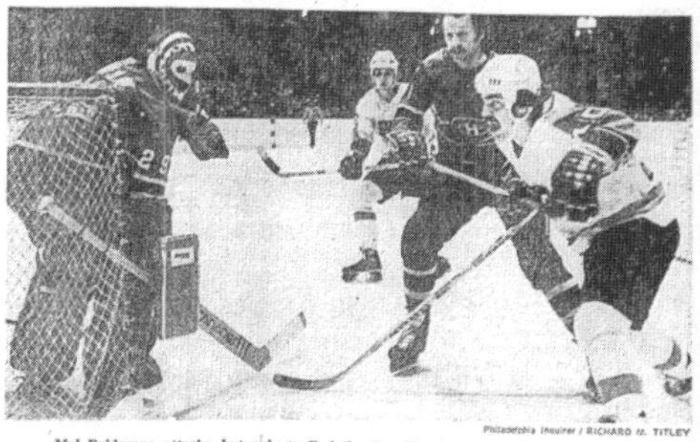

Philadelphia Inquirer / RICHARD M. TITLEY
Mel Bridgman attacks, but only to find the Canadiens' Dan Dryden waiting — again

By FRANK DOLSON

Sports Editor

Nothing game? Not for Eagles

There was so much water on the artificial turf yesterday they should have renamed the place Veterans Lake.

There were so many empty seats in the upper deck you'd have thought Temple was playing.

It was raining so hard you kept expecting to see the Phillies take the field for a playoff game against the Dodgers.

The weather was so downright miserable Chub Feeney should have been forced to spend the entire two and a half hours sitting in an uncovered box seat without an umbrella.

"The halftime show," quipped a member of the Eagles' official family, "is being produced by Aquarama. For the highlight, Johnny Weissmuller is going to dive off the 30-second clock."

Yes, friends, it was THAT bad yesterday at the Vet, where the Eagles and the Jets played one of those nothing games that dot the NFL schedule this time of the year. It was a day when you might expect a 3-10 team and a 4-9 team to go through the motions ... but only the 3-10 team did.

They played for keeps

The Eagles played this nothing game with the Jets as if it really mattered to them that they finish Dick Vermeil's second season 5-9 instead of 4-10. Neither the weather nor the strange-looking collection of starters the Jets threw out into the rain nor those 43,000-plus empty seats could kill their lust for battle.

If you didn't know better you'd have sworn a playoff berth was on the line in those closing minutes. Why else would Vince Papale come leaping off the bench in ecstasy as Bill Bergey intercepted a soggy, misdirected Richard Toss pass? Why else would Bergey display all that emotion as the clock ran down on yet another losing season, balling his battered hands into fists and thrusting them high over his head as the faithful chanted his name?

The Eagles, with all their losing tradition, have won meaningless, season-ending games before; in fact, they've now closed out four straight seasons with victories. But the way they acted yesterday you'd have thought they were challenging the Cowboys for first place, not the Giants for last. Grown men don't embrace at the end of nothing games, so obviously to the Eagles — to Bergey and Keith Krepfle and Randy Logan and all the others wrapped in last-minute bear hugs — this game, this 27-0 victory, meant something.

Praise from Vermeil

"I get a kick out of playoff teams saying they can't get up for nothing games," Vermeil said. "I wonder how some of those teams would play in the Eagles' situation, when half of the season is nothing games."

Would they go through the motions on a day like this? Or would they play the way this team played, would they care the way Bill Bergey and John Bunting cared?

"With about four minutes to go John Bunting threw a little fit out there," Bergey said. "He wanted that shutout."

The members of the defensive unit had been talking shutout all week — big talk when you consider that Eagles teams had won only two shutouts in two decades, and hadn't blanked anybody before the home fans since 1955, when home was Connie Mack Stadium.

"We kept saying and yelling and screaming for a shutout all week in practice," Bergey said. And so, with 4 minutes left and the Jets on their first drive of the day, Bunting ex-
(See DOLSON on 5-C)

Eagles swamp Jets, 27-0

Philadelphia Inquirer / EDWARD J. FREEMAN
The Eagles' Wilbert Montgomery (31), with Mike Hogan (35) and Wade Key (72) leading the way, makes a third-quarter gain

End year with five victories

By Gordon Forbes
Inquirer Staff Writer

It was the kind of miserable weather in which the winners invariably pull away to an early lead, grind out the yards with a running attack and try to destroy the senses of the other team's quarterback.

In gusting winds and swirling rain yesterday at the Vet, the Eagles did all three to humiliate the New York Jets, 27-0 and set quarterback Richard Todd's education back at least another season. It was all over after the first 12 minutes for the Jets, who fell behind, 17-0, and then fell victim to a solid if not spectacular Eagle ground game and a wild pass rush off Marion Campbell's 3-4 defense.

"I think under those conditions, we had it put away when it was 17-0," said Eagle quarterback Ron Jaworski. "It's really difficult to throw the ball when you get behind as they did. We kept the pressure on Todd and that ball, it must have weighed four pounds."

The lopsided win enabled the Eagles to finish 5-9, an improvement over last year's 4-10 record that was much more significant than the statistics if you believe Coach Dick Vermeil. The Jets, who lost nine of their last 10 games, fell to 3-11, but managed to escape the AFC East cellar by a single point in head-to-head competition with the lowly Buffalo Bills.

"There isn't any comparison between the two squads," Vermeil said. "This squad is totally committed to working together and getting better. Nobody is grumbling to go anywhere else and nobody is mad at this coach and that coach. We have the foundation. It'll just take time."

It was an afternoon in which the Eagles kept approaching and passing old records and the Jets put on display their team of the '80s by starting eight backup players. The Eagle pass rush, led by third-down specialist Lem Burnham, got to Todd seven times, bringing the season sack total to 47 to match a club record. Split end Harold Carmichael routinely caught two passes, the first extending his consecutive-game streak to 80 games, tieing another club mark, and the second giving him 300 catches in his accelerating seven-year career.

Only 19,241 Eagle fanatics turned out (prompting record 43,013 no-
(See EAGLES on 5-C)

The playoffs: Who's in, who's not

Associated Press

In a dramatic final day of the regular-season that included one critical game that went into overtime and another in which the winner came back from an 18-point deficit, the National Football League yesterday filled its lineup for next weekend's playoffs.

With the dust — and snow — now cleared, the first round of the playoffs shapes up like this:

In the NFC, the Eastern Division champion Dallas Cowboys (12-2) will face the wild-card entry Chicago Bears (9-5) at Dallas and the Western Division champion Los Angeles Rams (10-4) will play the Central Division champion Minnesota Vikings (9-5) at Los Angeles, both next Monday.

In the AFC, the Eastern Division champion Baltimore Colts (10-4) will meet the wild-card Oakland Raiders (11-3) at Baltimore and the Western Division champion Denver Broncos (12-2) will play the Central Division champion Pittsburgh Steelers (9-5) at Denver, both on Saturday.

The Bears, Colts, and Steelers wrapped up the last four playoff berths yesterday, with the Bears and Colts doing it in particularly dramatic fashion.

Chicago, which had to defeat the New York Giants to wrest the NFC wild-card spot from the Washington Redskins, succeeded by a 12-9 margin in overtime on a snow-covered field at East Rutherford, N.J., winning on Bob Thomas' 28-yard field goal with 9 seconds left in the sudden-death overtime.

The Colts got their playoff spot — and bumped out the Miami Dolphins — by coming back to a 30-24 victory over the New England Patriots after New England had taken a 21-3 lead early in the third quarter. Quarterback Bert Jones threw three touchdown passes in the Baltimore rally.

Pittsburgh, which needed a Cincinnati Bengals defeat to have a shot at the AFC Central title, got that when the Houston Oilers upset the Bengals, 21-16, and then took advantage of the break by edging the San Diego Chargers, 10-9, to clinch its berth.

More joy in Tampa Bay

By Skip Myslenski
Inquirer Staff Writer

TAMPA, Fla. — When, eight days ago, it was about to happen for the very first time, Lee Roy Selmon looked long and lovingly at the scoreboard in the New Orleans Superdome. The clock was stopped for the 2-minute warning, and the numbers showed that his team, the Tampa Bay Buccaneers, was leading the Saints, 33-14, and at last he was certain. "They shouldn't be able to score that many points," he thought. Then he smiled softly and a single word popped into his mind: "Wow!"

At the same time linebacker Richard Wood looked at the people suddenly surrounding the Buc bench and said to no one in particular, "I can't wait to get into the dressing room so I can cry. A grown man ought not to cry out here in front of these people."

"It was a totally different feeling," Lee Roy Selmon recalled. "It was great. It's one of the best I've ever had. It's hard to describe. To see a little success after so long, well" — and here his voice trailed off before he continued — "right
(See BUCS on 8-C)

Associated Press
Walter Payton managed only 47 yards

Bears make it; Payton doesn't

"Oh, my life is worth more than 6 seconds. It couldn't pass in front of me in 6 seconds. But, if I'd missed, I saw an exit sign over to the left. I fugure the Giants would've been happy, they'd have let me run through 'em, and I could've got away.

"I'd probably have forwarded my mail to Asia."

—Chicago placekicker Bob Thomas

By Bill Livingston
Inquirer Staff Writer

EAST RUTHERFORD, N.J. — Actually, it all happened with 9 seconds left in overtime, but let us not accuse Bob Thomas of being overly dramatic.

The 28-yard field goal he nailed through flying sleet and snow, after skittering up to the football over treacherous patches of ice with 9 seconds to play, gave the Chicago Bears a 12-9 victory over the New York Giants and their first NFL playoff berth in 14 years.

So, although Bear running back Walter Payton was able to slalom his way to only 47 yards in 15 carries, a full 151 short of O.J. Simpson's surreal one-season record, the game neeed no hype.

It needed little more than the actual, numbing sequences of opportunity and futility that sent the Bears pratfalling around the field for 74 minutes and 51 seconds in their frantic pursuit of the National Conference wild-card playoff spot.

It needed little more than Thomas' final frantic kick, which redeemed the third-year kicker from Notre Dame for two earlier missed field goals of 23 and 35 yards (the second
(See BEARS on 4-C)

December 19, 1977 - Wilbert Montgomery makes his first NFL start and the Eagles achieve their only shutout for the season by defeating the NY Jets 27-0

1978

RECORD: 9-7, 2ND IN NFC EAST
HEAD COACH: DICK VERMEIL

Schedule

Regular Season

Wk. 1	Sep 3	L	16-14	vs Los Angeles Rams
Wk. 2	Sep 10	L	35-30	at Washington Redskins
Wk. 3	Sep 17	W	24-17	at New Orleans Saints
Wk. 4	Sep 24	W	17-3	vs Miami Dolphins
Wk. 5	Oct 1	W	17-14	at Baltimore Colts
Wk. 6	Oct 8	L	24-14	at New England Patriots
Wk. 7	Oct 15	W	17-10	vs Washington Redskins
Wk. 8	Oct 22	L	14-7	at Dallas Cowboys
Wk. 9	Oct 29	L	16-10	vs St. Louis Cardinals
Wk. 10	Nov 5	W	10-3	vs Green Bay Packers
Wk. 11	Nov 12	W	17-9	vs New York Jets
Wk. 12	Nov 19	W	19-17	at New York Giants
Wk. 13	Nov 26	W	14-10	at St. Louis Cardinals
Wk. 14	Dec 3	L	28-27	at Minnesota Vikings
Wk. 15	Dec 10	L	31-13	vs Dallas Cowboys
Wk. 16	Dec 17	W	20-3	vs New York Giants

Post Season

Wild Card Playoffs

	Dec 24	L	14-13	at Atlanta Falcons

The Eagles continued to show improved as they post a 9-7 record, their first winning season since 1966, and making the playoffs for the first time since 1960. Wilbert Montgomery, in his first starting season, rushes for 1,220 yards to become the first Eagle since Steve Van Buren to surpass 1,000 in a season. In a game against the Giants dubbed the "Miracle of the Meadowlands," the Giants were trying to run out the clock and with the Eagles were seemingly headed towards defeat. Somehow Eagle Herman Edwards started the "Miracle" when he scooped up a fumbled handoff from Joe Pisarcik to Larry Csonka and races 26 years for a TD in the final 20 seconds of play before a stunned Giants Stadium. The win propels the Eagles into the playoffs for the first time since 1960. In the NFC Wild Card playoff game in Atlanta, the Eagles lost on what was to be 34-yard game winning field goal when Eagles Kicker Mike Michel missed the attempt with only 1:34 left to play.

1978 Philadelphia Eagles Stats

Passing	Comp	Att	Comp %	Yds	Y/Att	TD	Int	Rating
Ron Jaworski	206	398	51.8	2487	6.25	16	16	67.9
Rick Engles	1	1	100.0	-2	-2.00	0	0	79.2
John Walton	0	1	0.0	0	0.00	0	0	39.6
John Sciarra	0	1	0.0	0	0.00	0	0	39.6

Rushing	Rush	Yds	Avg	TD
Wilbert Montgomery	259	1220	4.7	9
Mike Hogan	145	607	4.2	4
Billy Campfield	61	247	4.0	0
Cleveland Franklin	60	167	2.8	0
Ron Jaworski	30	79	2.6	0
James Betterson	11	32	2.9	0
Frank LeMaster	2	29	14.5	0
Harold Carmichael	1	21	21.0	0
Ken Payne	1	17	17.0	0
Rick Engles	1	16	16.0	0
John Sciarra	8	11	1.4	2
Louie Giammona	4	6	1.5	0
Larry Barnes	1	4	4.0	1
John Walton	2	0	0.0	0
Mike Michel	1	0	0.0	0

Punting	Punts	Yds	Avg	Blocked
Rick Engles	33	1307	39.6	0
Mike Michel	58	2078	35.8	0

Kicking	PAT Made	PAT Att	PAT %	FG Made	FG Att	FG %	Pts
Nick Mike-Mayer	21	22	95	8	17	47.1	45
Mike Michel	9	12	75	0	0	0.0	9

Receiving	Rec	Yds	Avg	TD
Harold Carmichael	55	1072	19.5	8
Wilbert Montgomery	34	195	5.7	1
Mike Hogan	31	164	5.3	1
Keith Krepfle	26	374	14.4	3
Billy Campfield	15	101	6.7	0
Ken Payne	13	238	18.3	1
Richard Osborne	13	145	11.2	0
Charlie Smith	11	142	12.9	2
Cleveland Franklin	7	46	6.6	0
James Betterson	2	8	4.0	0

Interceptions	Int	Yds	Avg	TD
Herman Edwards	7	59	8.4	0
Deac Sanders	5	43	8.6	1
Bill Bergey	4	70	17.5	0
Frank LeMaster	3	22	7.3	1
Bob Howard	3	15	5.0	0
Randy Logan	2	15	7.5	0
John Sciarra	1	21	21.0	0
Dennis Harrison	1	12	12.0	0
John Bunting	1	9	9.0	0
Drew Mahalic	1	5	5.0	0

1978

The Philadelphia Inquirer
Sports Extra

section D

Monday, Dec. 25, 1978

Eagles fail to follow through and the Falcons win by 14-13

Philadelphia Inquirer / AKIRA SUWA

Amidst the jubilation of Atlanta players and fans sits dejected Eagles kicker Mike Michel as teammate John Sciarra (21) walks off after a missed field goal

Missed FG ends season

By Gordon Forbes
Inquirer Staff Writer

ATLANTA — The Eagles lost their first NFL playoff in 18 years yesterday — in a cold drizzle, to the amazing Atlanta Falcons, and by a 14-13 score. They will be forced to remember it as a game they tried to win without a field-goal kicker.

With 13 seconds left and the crowd at Atlanta-Fulton County Stadium in an uproar after the Falcons had scored twice in 3 minutes 17 seconds to take a 14-13 lead, Mike Michel lined up to try a 34-yard, game-winning field goal. He missed.

But don't blame Michel. He is the Eagle punter who was pressed into double-duty as a placekicker six weeks ago when Nick Mike-Mayer broke two ribs.

"Mike is a punter who was sort of transposed to kicker," said linebacker Frank LeMaster in the silent Eagle dressing room. "He did all he could. I think he did an adequate job. I'd be more upset if it was his job and it came down to that. I know Mike feels terrible. It came down to (the point where) he could have been the villain or the hero and he missed being the hero by three or four inches."

Michel also missed a conversion after the first Eagle touchdown. So when the Falcons, who have won four games in the final 10 seconds and six in the final two minutes, exploded for two touchdowns in the last five minutes yesterday, they had the winning margin.

There were some glaring breakdowns in the coverage by the Eagle secondary which allowed Falcon quarterback Steve Bartkowski to hurl a 20-yard scoring pass to tight end Jim Mitchell with 4:56 left and a 37-yarder to split end Wallace Francis with 1:39 to play. Rookie Tim Mazzetti, the former Penn kicker

(See EAGLES on 5-D)

Michel took his darkest moment like a man

By FRANK DOLSON

Sports editor

ATLANTA — Sports can be so cruel. So damnably, relentlessly cruel. So often the big game — the entire season — comes down to a matter of seconds, or a matter of inches. After more than 160 baseball games, after 17 football games, one play becomes all or nothing, one man becomes hero or goat.

Two months ago, Garry Maddox, who can practically catch fly balls in his sleep, failed to catch one in Dodger Stadium and wound up facing the toughest inquisition of his life. To his credit, he handled it like the man he is.

Yesterday it was Mike Michel's turn . . . and he, too, handled it like a man.

With the final seconds ticking off on the Atlanta Stadium clock, Michel went through both the giddiest high and the most shattering low of his career. Bang-bang, just like that.

One moment he was leaving his feet, his arm raised, his hopes soaring to the cloudy skies. This punter-turned-emergency-place-kicker had never kicked a field goal in a regular season or postseason National Football League game, but for a giddy instant he thought, his teammates thought, we all thought that he had kicked the Atlanta Falcons into oblivion and the Eagles into the next round of the playoffs.

"I hit it good," the slender, dark-haired, bearded young man would say later.

The ball seemed headed for three-point territory just inside the right post. For a right-footed kicker, that should have meant success. Usually, Michel's kicks hook to the left. But his first point-after-touchdown try didn't. And neither did this field-goal attempt. Instead of a hook, Michel got the tiniest slice. Not much. Just enough to send those fans who hadn't quit on the Falcons when they were down, 13-0, into a wild celebration.

Just enough to turn what had started out as a jump for joy by Mike Michel into a backward somersault of despair. The football sailed to the right of the upright . . . and in that moment Mike Michel's ecstasy turned into agony.

"I thought it would come back," he said. "They usually do. They usually have a slight hook on them. This one didn't come back at all."

And so this finest Eagle season in more than a decade was suddenly, shatteringly over. Thousands of Atlanta fans poured onto the field, delaying the final 13 seconds of the game for fully five minutes. While the fans cavorted, Michel remained on the wet ground for what seemed like a very long time, then got up and slowly edged through the mob.

God, how a moment like this can tear a man apart. He had come so close to being the storybook hero, so close to making his first official NFL field goal one of the most memorable in the history of the franchise. If only that kick had hooked when it was supposed to hook; if only Mike Michel had followed all the way through with that right leg.

"I just didn't come back enough. I didn't swing through it well enough."

A crowd gathered in front of his locker; as luck would have it, Michel's stall was the one nearest the main entrance to the visiting locker room. Then another crowd. And another. Michel made no effort to hide, or to run or to plead for privacy. Handling those waves of questioners at a time like this had to be as difficult as . . . well, as kicking a 34-

(See DOLSON on 4-D)

'Dual' catch saves Falcons, leaves bitter taste for Birds

By Allen Lewis
Inquirer Staff Writer

ATLANTA — To Atlanta Falcons quarterback Steve Bartkowski, it was the key play of the game. To Falcons flanker Wallace Francis, it was the play that set up Atlanta's first touchdown. To Eagles defensive back John Sanders, it was an official's decision that will live in infamy.

THE play occurred when the Eagles seemingly had this National Football League playoff game sewed up. They were riding the crest of a 13-0 lead and stopping the Falcons' offense with consistency.

There was less than 8 minutes left, and it was second down and 10 yards to go for the Falcons with the ball on their 26 when Bartkowski faded back and fired a bomb down the middle.

Free safety Sanders leaped at the Eagles' 26-yard line and was joined by Wallace a split second after the Philadelphia player seemingly had the ball. They went down in a heap. An official ran over and signaled Atlanta first down — a 49-yard gain.

Sanders couldn't believe it. "He never had the ball," Sanders said emphatically after Atlanta's thrilling 14-13 victory. "I caught the ball before he ever got to me. I rolled over with the ball and I had it until I saw the official signal first down. Then is the first time I gave it up. And besides, he pushed me before the ball got there.

"He said he caught it?" Sanders asked incredulously. "He knew he didn't."

As for the official, Sanders said, "He must have been intimidated by the crowd."

Francis, of course, had a different view of the controversial play.

"He may have caught it first, I don't know," the six-year veteran said. "But I know I came down with it. I'd have to look at the films to see who caught it first. I know I didn't push him."

As controversial as that catch was, there was no problem involved with either Atlanta scoring pass. Four plays after the dual-possession pass, Atlanta got on the scoreboard as Bartkowski threw a 20-yard strike to tight end Jim Mitchell, who caught the ball a step from the goal line and went in untouched.

When the Falcons gained possession again, they drove 49 yards in six plays, and the scoring toss was a 37-yarder to a wide-open Francis, who made a fall-down grab and landed on his back just over the goal line.

"We used three wide receivers on that play," Francis said. "I took the place of the tight end in the slot. I ran a post pattern. If it was zone, I was supposed to hook up in the middle. If it was man, I was supposed to keep going, and that's what I did. Steve (Bartkowski) read the coverage real well and I was open.

"I didn't know how open I was and I didn't know I was at the goal. I just concentrated on catching the ball. It was the same play as the other one (dual catch play).

"My greatest day? I don't know. My greatest day hasn't happened yet. It was my best since I caught seven against the Giants.

"On the touchdown, I caught him playing me square, and I gave him a step to the inside and he went for it.

"I had told Steve I was open on the pattern a few plays before the touchdown."

He was so open, Eagles Coach Dick Vermeil said, "Someone was responsible, that's definite."

United Press International

Celebrating his TD reception is Atlanta's Wallace Francis

Pastorini leads Oilers over Miami

By Dan Sewell
Associated Press

MIAMI — Dan Pastorini, wearing a specially designed flak jacket able to withstand the pounding of onrushing defensive linemen, had his best passing game in three seasons, leading the Houston Oilers to a 17-9 victory over the Miami Dolphins in an NFL wild-card playoff game yesterday.

Pastorini completed 20 of 29 passes for 306 yards, including a 13-yard touchdown pass to Tim Wilson, despite knee and rib injuries.

The Oilers quarterback took a pain-killing shot and wore a brace to ward off the effects of a wrenched knee, and wore the flak jacket given to him by a man in Houston.

The jacket's effectiveness was demonstrated to him by the man, who wore the jacket while a friend pounded him — without effect — with a baseball bat.

"I said, 'I want one of those,'" Pastorini recalled.

"The flak jacket spreads the shock

(See OILERS on 6-D)

December 25, 1978 - Eagles lose their first NFL playoff game in 18 years to the Atlanta Falcons 14-13, when Mike Michel with 13 seconds left in the game missed a 34-yard game winning field goal.

1979

RECORD: 11-5, 2ND IN NFC EAST
HEAD COACH: DICK VERMEIL

SCHEDULE

REGULAR SEASON

Wk. 1	Sep 2	W	23-17	vs New York Giants
Wk. 2	Sep 10	L	14-10	vs Atlanta Falcons
Wk. 3	Sep 16	W	26-14	at New Orleans Saints
Wk. 4	Sep 23	W	17-13	at New York Giants
Wk. 5	Sep 30	W	17-14	vs Pittsburgh Steelers
Wk. 6	Oct 7	W	28-17	vs Washington Redskins
Wk. 7	Oct 14	W	24-20	at St. Louis Cardinals
Wk. 8	Oct 21	L	17-7	at Washington Redskins
Wk. 9	Oct 28	L	37-13	at Cincinnati Bengals
Wk. 10	Nov 4	L	24-19	vs Cleveland Browns
Wk. 11	Nov 12	W	31-21	at Dallas Cowboys
Wk. 12	Nov 18	W	16-13	vs St. Louis Cardinals
Wk. 13	Nov 25	W	21-10	at Green Bay Packers
Wk. 14	Dec 2	W	44-7	vs Detroit Lions
Wk. 15	Dec 8	L	24-17	vs Dallas Cowboys
Wk. 16	Dec 16	W	26-20	at Houston Oilers

POST SEASON

Wild Card Playoffs				
	Dec 23	W	27-17	vs Chicago Bears
Divisional Playoffs				
	Dec 29	L	24-17	at Tampa Bay Buccaneers

The Eagles came soaring out of the gate, winning six of their first seven games. Then a midseason three-game slide threatened their season. The Eagles would end their slide with a 31-21 win over the Cowboys in Dallas that got them right in thick of the race for first place. Unfortunately the Eagles could never shake off the Cowboys, and with a record of 10-4 entered a showdown in the Vet with the NFC East on the line. The Eagles would fall 24-17 as the Cowboys held on to win the division via tiebreaker, as the Eagles settled for a Wild Card with an 11-5 record. In the playoffs the Eagles beat the Chicago Bears 27-17 in the first playoff game in Philadelphia in 19 years. However, a week later their season ended with a disappointing 24-17 loss to the Buccaneers in Tampa. Wilbert Montgomery set a club record with 1,512 rushing yards, and Harold Carmichael set an NFL record on November 4, 1979, by catching a pass in his 106th consecutive game. Rookie barefoot kicker Tony Franklin booted the second longest field goal in NFL history---59 yards---in a 31-21 win at Dallas. Dick Vermeil was voted NFL Coach of the Year.

1979 PHILADELPHIA EAGLES STATS

Passing	Comp	Att	Comp %	Yds	Y/Att	TD	Int	Rating
Ron Jaworski	190	374	50.8	2669	7.14	18	12	76.8
John Walton	19	36	52.8	213	5.92	3	1	86.9

Rushing	Rush	Yds	Avg	TD
Wilbert Montgomery	338	1512	4.5	9
Leroy Harris	107	504	4.7	2
Billy Campfield	30	165	5.5	3
Ron Jaworski	43	119	2.8	2
Larry Barnes	25	74	3.0	1
Louie Giammona	5	38	2.5	0
Frank LeMaster	1	15	15.0	0
Harold Carmichael	1	0	0.0	0
Earl Carr	1	-1	-1.0	0
John Walton	6	-5	-0.8	0

Receiving	Rec	Yds	Avg	TD
Harold Carmichael	52	872	16.8	11
Keith Krepfle	41	760	18.5	3
Wilbert Montgomery	41	494	12.0	5
Charlie Smith	24	399	16.6	1
Leroy Harris	22	107	4.9	0
Billy Campfield	16	115	7.2	0
Scott Fitzkee	8	105	13.1	1
John Spagnola	2	24	12.0	0
Larry Barnes	1	6	6.0	0
Earl Carr	1	2	2.0	0
Jerrold McRae	1	-2	-2.0	0

Punting	Punts	Yds	Avg	Blocked
Max Runager	74	2927	39.6	0
Tony Franklin	1	32	32.0	0

Kicking	PAT Made	PAT Att	PAT %	FG Made	FG Att	FG %	Pts
Tony Franklin	36	39	92	23	31	74.2	105

Interceptions	Int	Yds	Avg	TD
Brenard Wilson	4	70	17.5	0
Randy Logan	3	57	19.0	0
Bob Howard	3	34	11.3	0
Herman Edwards	3	6	2.0	0
John Sciarra	2	47	23.5	0
Al Chesley	2	39	19.5	0
John Bunting	2	13	6.5	0
Reggie Wilkes	2	0	0.0	0
Bill Bergey	1	0	0.0	0

The NBA 2
Scoreboard 4
Colleges 9
Horse racing 10
High schools 12

The Philadelphia Inquirer
sports
Section D
Sunday, December 30, 1979

Bucs end Eagles' season, 24-17

Philadelphia Inquirer / VICKI VALERIO

Ricky Bell, whom the Eagles had a difficult time figuring out yesterday, appears to be casting a spell on linebacker Reggie Wilkes

Bell, Williams engineer upset

By Gordon Forbes
Inquirer Staff Writer

TAMPA, Fla. — Doug Williams and the young, ambitious Tampa Bay Buccaneers came out running yesterday, and the Eagles came out retreating, all the way out of the National Football Conference playoffs.

The Bucs lined up in a double-tight-end formation, pulled both guards, led into the power alley with their fullback and pitched the ball back to magnificent Ricky Bell. They ran all the way to a 24-17 victory over the helpless Eagles before 71,402, mostly fanatical Bucs' lovers.

The Eagles were overpowered in the trenches, especially the left side of their wilting defense — end Claude Humphrey, outside linebacker John Bunting and cornerback Bobby Howard. Bell, who set an NFL playoff record with 38 carries and rushed for 142 yards, kept beating the Eagles defenders to the corner, at least those who were still standing.

"If you're asking me where to put the blame," Humphrey said afterward in the subdued losers' dressing room, "I don't know where to put it. I do know this. They've got a better football team. That's where to put some of the blame."

As lopsided as the game statistics were in favor of the tough-hitting Bucs, 318 total yards to 227, 186 rushing yards to 48, 70 offensive plays to 58, the Eagles miraculously still had a chance to pull it out in the final, dramatic 2 minutes.

For maybe the first time in the game, Humphrey got penetration and slammed Bell down for a seven-yard loss on third-and-one, forcing the Bucs to punt. With 2 minutes, 11 seconds left, quarterback Ron Jaworski led his battered offense back onto the field for one last shot.

"I was confident," said Jaworski, who hooked up with Harold Carmichael on a late 37-yard touchdown pass that brought the Eagles within 24-17 with 3:36 left. "But I was also realistic, too. I realized you're limited in what you can do. You get down to no timeouts and you can't be going for five or six yards. And it's a risky thing when you throw downfield."

While cornerback Jeris White was dropping two game-ending interceptions, Jaworski kept firing. The Polish Rifle completed a low, 16-yarder to Carmichael, an 18-yard crossover on fourth down (which was nullified by a penalty) and a 25-yarder to Charlie Smith at the Bucs 45 with a little more than a minute left.

It was the kind of drive of which miracles are made. But it ended 17 tense seconds later after three incompletions and a dropped third-down pass by Billy Campfield.

On fourth-and-10 from the 45, Jaworski backpedaled, searched for Carmichael along the right sideline and threw. The ball flew out of bounds as Carmichael broke inside.

"It was good coverage," said Jaworski, who was pressured into a dreadful 15-for-38 afternoon in bright, balmy Florida weather. "I just tried to lead him away from the defense. They had him covered, and by the time he came off the ball, I had already let it go."

The Eagles already had let go of their chance for another eagerly awaited rematch with Dallas, assuming that the Cowboys get past the Los Angeles Rams in today's other NFC divisional playoff. The Eagles' greatest contribution to the Bucs' highly emotional upset was an inability to handle Tampa Bay's running game.

"They were like cutting it back," said Howard, who may have played his final game as an Eagle. "They started out and they executed real well. Their execution really helped them. They had us (the Eagles defense) down real well. They played super today. You could tell from the start. It was like they were caged and they were letting them out."

Incredibly, the no-offense Bucs (11-

(See EAGLES on 6-D)

Eagles' title hopes were drowned in a sea of orange

By FRANK DOLSON

Sports editor

TAMPA, Fla. — The stadium was a sea of orange, and from the very start of yesterday's playoff game the Philadelphia Eagles were battling desperately to stay afloat. At the end, the wonder of it wasn't that the Tampa Bay Bucs, a 4-year-old professional football team, won the game, 24-17, but that the Eagles were that close.

Seldom has an underdog football team so thoroughly dominated a game of this importance . . . and yet each time the visitors were on the verge of sinking out of sight, somebody threw them a life raft and the Eagles clutched it, prolonging the agony. Had they somehow pulled out yesterday's game — and Stan Walters, among others, thought "we were going to get overtime; I really did" — it would have been a terrible miscarriage of justice. Even the most partisan of Eagles fans would have been forced to admit that.

In retrospect, it might be fair to say the Eagles really lost this game — and with it the chance to go to the NFC championship game — three weeks ago at Veterans Stadium, when the Dallas Cowboys beat them out of the Eastern Division championship and the home-field playoff advantage that went with it. Had that sea of orange been an ocean of green, perhaps the Eagles would have been inspired to play the kind of game that the Bucs played yesterday.

"I realize now," Walters said after the Eagles had finally gone down for the last time, "the importance of playing at home. If I had to make one objective statement, it would be that if we ever get another shot to win a game for the division (title), we've got to take full advantage of it and get the home field and the week's rest and everything else that goes with it."

Don't underestimate the importance of that home field, the impact of a roaring crowd. Above all, don't underestimate the importance of getting a week off before plunging into the playoffs.

"Their execution showed two weeks of practice," Dick Vermeil said. "We've been practicing since Wednesday."

It was not an excuse, merely a simple statement of the facts. But not even those facts should have added up to so great a superiority on the playing field as the Bucs displayed. "It's just impossible to gain a mental edge in a playoff game," Vermeil had said, "because there's no such thing as a team not being ready to play." Maybe not, but the Bucs were more ready to play than the Eagles. That much was clear.

The team that wasn't supposed to have much of an offense, the team that had scored a not-so-grand total of 10 points in its last three games, merely took the opening kickoff and rammed the ball down the Eagles' throats. For 18 plays the Bucs controlled the football. For close to 9½ minutes they ran Ricky Bell again and again and again. Sweep right. Sweep right. A draw, then another sweep, this time to the left.

And it was "draft choices right" and "draft choices left." The Eagles, no great shakes against the run all year as Vermeil was quick to point out, simply were incapable on this day of stopping Tampa Bay's basic plays.

"The Eagles are not good enough to win unless we play super," Vermeil

(See DOLSON on 6-D)

Philadelphia Inquirer / VICKI VALERIO

Jimmy Giles rejoices after scoring the touchdown that put Tampa Bay ahead, 24-10, on a nine-yard pass from Doug Williams

Flyers edge the rallying Rockies, 3-2

By Al Morganti
Inquirer Staff Writer

DENVER — Just another night on the road with the usual stuff: a record-breaking crowd jacked up beyond belief; an opposing team jacked up even higher, and the usual uneven officiating.

Despite it all, just as they seemingly have done for an eternity, the Flyers rumbled out of McNichols Arena with a gasping, 3-2 win over the Colorado Rockies, thus extending their unbeaten streak to 33 games and raising their lead over Buffalo, which lost to Montreal, to seven points with two games in hand.

The Flyers looked as if they finally were going to win one with a little room to spare when they went into the final period leading, 3-0, but two frantic Colorado goals within less than two minutes of the final period — one very controversial — made the Flyers sweat their usual bullets through the closing seconds.

With 9 minutes, 22 seconds remaining, Rene Robert scored the first Rockies goal, ending Phil Myre's shutout bid and throwing the record-crowd of 16,452 into ecstacy.

Like the night before in Winnipeg, where a record-breaking crowd went out to see the Flyers, the Colorado crowd was primed to see the Flyers' streak come to a halt.

"This whole team, this whole place was ready for us," Bob Dailey said. "We knew this was going to be a tough place to play when we got here."

It got very tough in that last period when, with 7:57 left, Mike McEwen scored a disputed goal that ignited a final Colorado charge.

The goal began as a simple icing call when linesman Bob Luther put

(See FLYERS on 3-D)

Up from the dump: How sweet it is for Bucs

By BILL LYON

TAMPA, Fla. — You say you don't believe in miracles?

Try this one: In its four-year history, a football team tha has played 61 games and managed to lose 43 of them is one step from the Super Bowl.

"Yeah, it kinda blows your mind, doesn't it?" said Steve Wilson, standing there with a grin cutting a wide swath through his bush of a beard.

Wilson is an original Buccaneer, which, until now, was a dubious distinction at best. Kind of like being the driver of the getaway car for The Gang That Couldn't Shoot Straight. Or the navigator aboard the Titanic.

Wilson is the center for Tampa Bay, the only one they've ever had, so he stood there amid the locker room frenzy yesterday and sucked in deep gulps of air, almost as if he were trying to cleanse the purgatory of the last four seasons.

One of the attendants came by to take his helmet so the dents could be hammered out, and on the back of the attendant's shirt was the Tampa Bay slogan:

"Five Year Plan — From Worst To First."

The Bucs certainly fulfilled the first part of that plan. For a long time they were the worst team in pro football. Second worst was far behind.

"What was it like?" Wilson repeated the question. "Well, it was depressing. Like living in a garbage dump, I guess. You know how a bad smell won't go away no matter what you do? That's what it was like. We'd work and work and work, but nothing good would ever seem to happen.

"Then you'd start doubting yourself, wondering if you were good enough to play up here. That's a terrible thing, doubting yourself. It's slow death."

Well, the Bucs moved out of the low-rent district yesterday. They vacated the garbage dump and moved uptown to a fancy address. And now, despite a record of 18 wins and 43 defeats, the Bucs are close to taking up residence in the penthouse of the NFL.

They achieved that by blowing out

(See LYON on 7-D)

Oilers stifle Chargers in 17-14 upset

Associated Press

SAN DIEGO — Safety Vernon Perry, leading an aroused Houston defense that took up the slack for missing offensive stars, intercepted four passes by Dan Fouts and blocked a field-goal attempt, and the Oilers, riding Gifford Nielsen's clutch touchdown pass to Mike Renfro, beat San Diego, 17-14, yesterday in the American Football Conference playoffs.

Nielsen, making only his second career start in the NFL, teamed with Renfro on a 47-yard scoring play with 2 minutes, 5 seconds left to play in the third quarter for the touchdown that vaulted Houston into the AFC championship game Jan. 6, against the winner of today's contest between Miami and the defending Super Bowl champion Pittsburgh Steelers.

"Ain't no such thing as a one- or two-man team," said Perry, whose play helped compensate for the absence of NFL rushing champion Earl Campbell and quarterback Dan Pastorini.

"We knew when we signed him as a free agent out of Canada that the kid was a player," Houston coach Bum Phillips said of Perry, who came out of Jackson State, failed to make it as a Chicago Bears draft choice and wound up with the Canadian Football League's Montreal Alouettes.

"If the Canadian League never does anything else for the NFL," Phillips said, "they did something for us."

In fact, the last big game Perry had was in the Canadian Grey Cup. In that game he had two interceptions and a blocked punt.

"He was a college teammate of (Houston linebacker) Robert Bra-

(See OILERS on 5-D)

December 30, 1979 - Tampa Bay rolls over the Eagles 24-17 in the NFC Divisional Playoff game.

1980's DECADE IN REVIEW

Wilbert Montgomery sets his sights... On the end zone

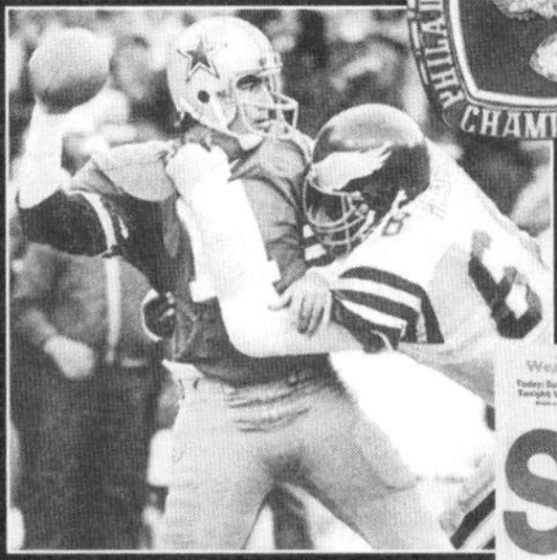

Dennis Harrison greets QB Danny White

Bill Bergey tackles Jim Plunkett in Super bowl XV

1980
'he Eagles open the 1980s just as they had the '60s: with an Eastern Division itle and a shot at the NFL crown. In the NFC Championship Game at Veterans Stadium, coach Dick Vermeil's club uses a 194-yard rushing effort by Wilbert Montgomery to top their arch rivals, the Dallas Cowboys, 20-7, and earn a berth in Super Bowl XV against the Oakland Raiders. Although the Raiders prevail, the loss does not obscure a bright season in which quarterback Ron Jaworski earns NFL and NFC player of the year honors.

1982
'he season, marked by a nine-week work stoppage (one of two players' strikes that interrupt the decade), is followed by Dick Vermeil's decision to step down as coach. Defensive coordinator Marion Campbell will succeed Vermeil.

1983
Mike Quick posts a league-leading, club-record 1,409 receiving yards and goes on to be named to five straight Pro Bowls.

1984
Paul McFadden, a barefoot, rookie kicker, sets a club single-season scoring record with 116 points.

1985
After owner Leonard Tose nearly moves the Eagles to Phoenix in December of '84, he sells the club to Norman Braman and Ed Leibowitz, Miami automobile dealers and Philadelphia-area natives, for a reported $65 million. Within two years, Braman becomes sole owner of the club.

'he Eagles draft QB Randall Cunningham. In time, the versatile Cunningham - a major threat as a passer, rusher, and sometimes punter - would be labeled by Sports Illustrated as "the ultimate weapon."

n August, the rival United States Football League folds after three seasons and former Memphis Showboats defensive end Reggie White joins the Eagles. White will go on to become perhaps the greatest lineman in the history of the game while setting club and league records for most quarterback sacks in a career.

Quarterback Ron Jaworski and wide receiver Mike Quick end an overtime game vs. Atlanta and tie an NFL record when they team up on a 99-yard TD pass play.

Ron Jaworski

Mike Quick

1986
n January, shortly after the Bears win Super Bowl XX, Buddy Ryan, the architect of Chicago's famed "46 defense," becomes the Eagles head coach. 'he outspoken Ryan instills a swagger in the Eagles, who go on to reach the playoffs three straight times beginning in 1988.

Buddy Ryan

1988
'he Eagles' divisional playoff game at Chicago, known as "the Fog Bowl," becomes one of the most memorable games in NFL history. While the game begins under bright, sunny skies, a thick fog rolls in over Soldier Field during the 2nd quarter. The fog blankets the field for the remainder of the contest, making visibility difficult for those on the field and in the stands, as well as for those viewing the broadcast on national TV.

1st Half of the "The Fog Bowl"

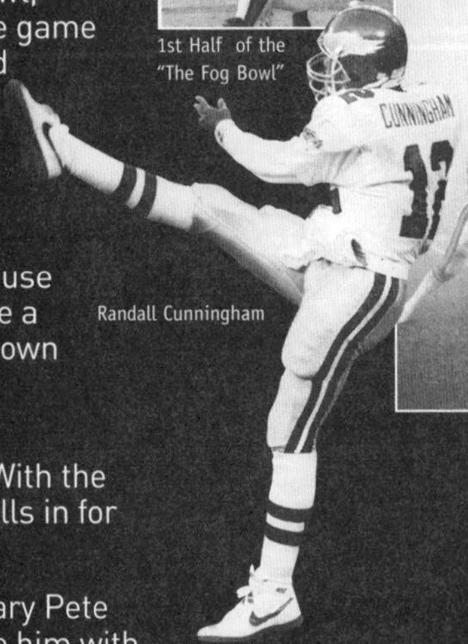

Randall Cunningham

2nd Half of the "The Fog Bowl

1989
Ryan's Eagles reach the playoffs again with three key wins. First they use a team-record 447 passing yards by Randall Cunningham to overcome a 20-point deficit at Washington. Then a 27-0 win at Dallas becomes known as "the Bounty Bowl" when the Cowboys allege that Ryan has placed "bounties" on their kicker and quarterback.

A late-season win over the Giants becomes remembered for a punt. With the game tied 17-17 and the Eagles at their own goal line, Cunningham fills in for the injured John Teltschik and launches a club-record 91-yard boot.

'he end of the decade also marks the end of an era when the legendary Pete Rozelle, NFL Commissioner since 1960, retires. Team owners replace him with Paul Tagliabue, the NFL's accomplished legal counsel.

1980's

80s Decade in Review

Decade Win-Loss Record:
76-74-2; (2-4 postseason record)

Home Field:
Veterans Stadium 1980-89

Playoff Appearances:
1980, 1981, 1988, and 1989

Championships:
Division Champions 1980 (NFC East)
NFL/NFC Champion Game 1980
Super Bowl Appearance XV (1980)

Head Coaches:
Dick Vermeil 1980-83 (25-16) (2-2 postseason record);
Marion Campbell 1983-85 (17-29-1);
Fred Bruney 1985 (1-0);
Buddy Ryan 1986-89 (33-29-1) (0-2 postseason record)

Hall of Fame Inductees:
None

Award Winners:
Ron Jaworski MVP 1980;
Randall Cunningham MVP 1988;
Reggie White Defensive MVP 1987;
Keith Jackson Rookie of the Year 1988;
Paul McFadden NFC Rookie of the Year 1984

All Pro:
Harold Carmichael 1980;
Charlie Johnson 1980-81;
Randy Logan 1980;
Jerry Robinson 1980-81 and 1983;
Mike Quick 1983, 1985 and 1987;
Wes Hopkins 1984-85;
Reggie White 1986-89;
Randall Cunningham 1988:
Keith Jackson 1988-89;
Jerome Brown 1989

Pro Bowl Selections:
Wilbert Montgomery 1980; Stan Walters 1980;
Wally Henry 1980; Harold Carmichael 1980-81;
Ron Jaworski 1981; Charlie Johnson 1980-81;
Randy Logan 1980-81; Frank LeMaster 1982;
Jerry Robinson 1982; Jerry Sisemore 1980 & 82;
Roynell Young 1982; Dennis Harrison 1983;
Mike Quick 1984-88; Wes Hopkins 1986;
Reggie White 1987-89;
Randall Cunningham 1989-89;
Keith Jackson 1989

First Game of the Decade:
September 7, 1980 defeated
the Denver Broncos 27-6

Last Game of the Decade:
December 24, 1989 defeated
the Phoenix Cardinals 31-14

Largest Margin of Victory:
November 18, 1981 vs. the
St. Louis Cardinals 52-10

Largest Margin of Defeat:
October 16, 1983 vs. the Dallas Cowboys 37-7

Eagle Firsts of the Decade:
First Quarterback to lead team in Rushing,
Randall Cunningham did it from 1987-1990

1980

RECORD: 12-4,1ST IN NFC EAST
HEAD COACH: DICK VERMEIL

Schedule

Regular Season

Wk. 1	Sep 7	W	27-6	vs Denver Broncos
Wk. 2	Sep 14	W	42-7	at Minnesota Vikings
Wk. 3	Sep 22	W	35-3	vs New York Giants
Wk. 4	Sep 28	L	24-14	at St. Louis Cardinals
Wk. 5	Oct 5	W	24-14	vs Washington Redskins
Wk. 6	Oct 12	W	31-16	at New York Giants
Wk. 7	Oct 19	W	17-10	vs Dallas Cowboys
Wk. 8	Oct 26	W	17-14	vs Chicago Bears
Wk. 9	Nov 2	W	27-20	at Seattle Seahawks
Wk. 10	Nov 9	W	34-21	at New Orleans Saints
Wk. 11	Nov 16	W	24-0	at Washington Redskins
Wk. 12	Nov 23	W	10-7	vs Oakland Raiders
Wk. 13	Nov 30	L	22-21	at San Diego Chargers
Wk. 14	Dec 7	L	20-17	vs Atlanta Falcons
Wk. 15	Dec 14	W	17-3	vs St. Louis Cardinals
Wk. 16	Dec 21	L	35-27	at Dallas Cowboys

Post Season

Divisional Playoffs				
	Jan 3	W	31-16	vs Minnesota Vikings
Conference Championship				
	Jan 11	W	20-7	vs Dallas Cowboys
Superbowl				
	Jan 25	L	27-10	vs Oakland Raiders (at New Orleans, LA)

The Eagles led by QB Ron Jaworski threw for 3,527 yards and 27 touchdowns. He was named NFL player of the year by the Maxwell Football Club and NFC player of the year by UPI. As the Eagles won 11 of their first 12 games and went on to a 12-4 capturing the NFC East Championship. Harold Carmichael's then-record NFL receiving streak is snapped at 127 games when he fails to catch a pass in the regular season finale at Dallas after sustaining a back injury in the first half. In the divisional playoffs, the Eagles trounced on the Vikings 31-16, then in the NFC Championship game against the Cowboys. The Eagles defeated them 20-7, as the Cowboys wore their blue uniforms on a frigid day in Philadelphia before a loud sellout crowd at the Vet and a berth in Super Bowl XV. In their first Super Bowl, the Eagles were matched up against the Oakland Raiders in New Orleans. The Eagles would go into the game, as the heavy favorite because the Raiders were just a wild card team. The Oakland Raiders prevailed in the game 27-10.

1980 Philadelphia Eagles Stats

Passing	Comp	Att	Comp %	Yds	Y/Att	TD	Int	Rating
Ron Jaworski	257	451	57.0	3529	7.82	27	12	91.0
Louie Giammona	3	3	100.0	55	18.33	1	0	158.3
Joe Pisarcik	15	22	68.2	187	8.50	0	0	94.3
Wilbert Montgomery	0	1	0.0	0	0.00	0	0	39.6

Rushing	Rush	Yds	Avg	TD
Wilbert Montgomery	193	778	4.0	8
Louie Giammona	97	361	3.7	4
Leroy Harris	104	341	3.3	3
Perry Harrington	32	166	5.2	1
Billy Campfield	44	120	2.7	1
Ron Jaworski	27	95	3.5	1
Mike Hogan	12	44	3.7	1
Charlie Smith	5	33	6.6	0
Frank LeMaster	2	21	10.5	0
Scott Fitzkee	1	15	15.0	0
John Sciarra	3	11	3.7	0
Zachary Dixon	2	8	4.0	0
Jim Culbreath	1	3	3.0	0
Keith Krepfle	1	2	2.0	0
Joe Pisarcik	3	-3	-1.0	0

Punting	Punts	Yds	Avg	Blocked
Max Runager	75	2947	39.3	0

Kicking	PAT Made	PAT Att	PAT %	FG Made	FG Att	FG %	Pts
Tony Franklin	48	48	100	16	31	51.6	96

Receiving	Rec	Yds	Avg	TD
Wilbert Montgomery	50	407	8.1	2
Harold Carmichael	48	815	17.0	9
Charlie Smith	47	825	17.6	3
Keith Krepfle	30	450	15.0	4
Billy Campfield	26	275	10.6	2
John Spagnola	18	193	10.7	3
Louie Giammona	17	178	10.5	1
Leroy Harris	15	207	13.8	1
Rodney Parker	9	148	16.4	1
Scott Fitzkee	6	169	28.2	2
Wally Henry	4	68	17.0	0
Perry Harrington	3	24	8.0	0
Lewis Gilbert	1	7	7.0	0
Zachary Dixon	1	5	5.0	0

Interceptions	Int	Yds	Avg	TD
Brenard Wilson	6	79	13.2	0
Roynell Young	4	27	6.8	0
Herman Edwards	3	12	4.0	0
Charles Johnson	3	9	3.0	0
Jerry Robinson	2	13	6.5	0
Richard Blackmore	2	0	0.0	0
Randy Logan	1	16	16.0	0
Bill Bergey	1	7	7.0	0
Frank LeMaster	1	7	7.0	0
Carl Hairston	1	0	0.0	0
Reggie Wilkes	1	0	0.0	0

Sports Extra: Four pages of the Eagles

SPORTS FINAL

The Philadelphia Inquirer

Vol. 304, No. 12 © 1981, The Philadelphia Inquirer Monday, January 12, 1981 20 CENTS

Eagles Head for the Super Bowl

The Big Act

Philadelphia Inquirer / VICKI VALERIO

Cowboy Tony Dorsett lies despondent after dropping a pass as Herm Edwards (46) and Bill Bergey congratulate each other

Cowboys fall; on to Raiders

The Philadelphia Eagles yesterday won their first trip to the Super Bowl with a 20-7 thrashing of their nemesis, the Dallas Cowboys, at Veterans Stadium.

A sellout crowd of 70,696 endured a combination of cold and brisk winds that made the temperature feel as though it was 15 degrees below zero. Most sat bundled like Eskimos, but several inspired fans paraded through the stands bare-chested.

The victory gave the Eagles the National Football Conference championship and a berth in Super Bowl XV against the American Football Conference champion Oakland Raiders, who beat the San Diego Chargers 34-27. The Jan. 25 game in the New Orleans Superdome will be the first time the Eagles have played for the National Football League championship since 1960, when they defeated the Green Bay Packers 17-13.

The victory touched off the second jubilant celebration at the South Philadelphia stadium in three months — since that day in October when the Philadelphia Phillies won the World series, setting off a mad celebration that gripped the city for days.

There was much cause for reminiscence yesterday. Just as in October, the Philadelphia police encircled the field with mounted officers and police dogs to contain the crowd as the final moments ticked away.

Like the Phillies

Just as in October, a cordon of helmeted officers escorted the coach — this time Dick Vermeil, the architect of the Eagles' rise from mediocrity — to the jubilant locker room.

And as the victorious Eagles filed off the field, CBS television announcer Brent Musburger proclaimed Philadelphia, just as in October, the "city of champions."

Indeed, the Eagles' ticket to the Super Bowl completes a remarkable sports year for the city. In 1980, all four of the city's major sport teams — the Sixers, the Phillies, the Flyers and the Eagles — have made it to the final round of championship play. The Flyers and Sixers were unsuccessful in their bids for the top, but then on came the Phillies.

There was little dancing in the streets after the latest triumph, but that was more a reflection on the frigid temperatures than the mood of the fans in the city.

Many of those who attended the game refused to leave, prancing through the stands chanting and cheering long after the players had left the field. Then they piled into cars and headed home through congested streets with horns honking wildly.

Those who headed north toward Center City were greeted at Broad Street and Snyder Avenue by several hundred celebrants.

Additional police were also summoned to Frankford and Cottman Avenues in the Northeast to control a crowd estimated at more than 150.

Game coverage, Page 1-B.

Softer line from Iran on money

Bill could be a compromise

From Inquirer Wire Services

The Iranian Parliament went into closed session today to discuss what was believed to be a bill concerning compromises with the United States on financial terms of negotiations for the release of the 52 American hostages.

Iran has dropped its demand that the U.S. deposit $24 billion in Algerian banks before the release of the hostages, a top Iranian negotiator was quoted as saying yesterday.

In the first indication from Iran that it would waive the deposit demand, negotiator Ahmad Azizi told the Iranian newspaper Enghelab Islami: "The Iranian government has accepted Algerian proposals asking the United States for international guarantees instead of placing a deposit with the Algerian bank."

U.S. officials in Washington said they had not been notified by Iran that their demand had been dropped and could not independently confirm Azizi's statement.

However, sources close to the Algerian delegation in Tehran, which is serving as intermediary in the hostage talks, said yesterday that the Algerians believe a breakthrough is near.

And Iranian government spokesman and Executive Affairs Minister Benzad Nabavi, a key figure in the negotiations Azizi, presented a bill in the parliament early today "concerning the financial and legal problems" between the two countries.

There was no immediate indication of the bill's contents, but it was believed to be a compromise resulting from intensive negotiating over the last few days.

Negotiator Azizi would not specify the kind of guarantees his government would accept, but they presumably would be connected with Iranian claims on assets frozen in the United States and claims on the wealth of the late shah, Mohammed Reza Pahlavi.

He was quoted as saying that Iran would formally respond to the Algerian suggestion today or tomorrow.

On Saturday, Azizi told another Tehran newspaper, Kayhan, that Iran "in all likelihood" would accept the Algerian draft and that he thought the initiative would also be acceptable to the United States.

Last week, an American official who asked not to be identified said that Iran was prepared to revise its demand for the Algerian bank deposit, but Azizi's comments yesterday were the first indication from Iran that the deposit condition was negotiable.

American negotiators extended their stay in the Algerian capital yesterday to reply to additional Iranian questions about the latest American proposal. American officials said Deputy Secretary of State Warren M.

(See IRAN on 2-A)

Jaworski: Vermeil's pregame pessimism was a ploy

By Gordon Forbes
Inquirer Staff Writer

Ron Jaworski, giggling after a scattershot championship game, says the Dallas Cowboys were conned by Dick Vermeil.

"Everything was a setup," Jaworski said in the congested winners' dressing room. "They were set up. Dick made them think we were disorganized and scrambling. That we didn't have a chance to win. He told us, 'Let everybody think you're unsettled and worried.' But in our private meetings, he said we were going to kick. . .

"Hey, we're America's new team. You believe that, buddy, and I've got some costume jewelry back here."

Jaworski, who struggled through a 9-for-29 game in bitter, 16-degree weather, accompanied by tricky January winds, said Vermeil set up the Cowboys by using the media.

"The way the Eagles were all week in Tampa, we were very low-key publicly," Jaworski said. "You've got to give credit to Dick. He made it seem as if we didn't have a chance to win. But in meetings, we set 'em up a little bit. He set up the Cowboys through the press. He did nothing but blow up that Dallas balloon.

"I just don't think the Cowboys were flying around. I don't think they had the intensity they had in the last game in Dallas. Maybe they came in here too cocky, a little bit too confident."

Jaworski said that Vermeil told the Eagles they could win the National Football Conference title without playing a great game. "He just felt if

(See VICTORY on 8-A)

Begin ally quits; collapse imminent

By William Claiborne
Washington Post Service

JERUSALEM — Israeli Finance Minister Yigael Hurvitz made good on his threat to resign yesterday, thereby virtually assuring the collapse of the government of Prime Minister Menachem Begin.

Yigael Hurvitz
Israeli finance minister

After nearly eight hours of uninterrupted debate in which Begin fruitlessly sought to reach a compromise in a ministerial impasse over Israel's deteriorating economy, Begin announced through a spokesman that the cabinet would meet again today to discuss the "political implications" of Hurvitz's resignation.

But because Hurvitz will take with him the three votes of the parliamentary Rafi faction, thus further diminishing Begin's already paper-thin Likud coalition majority, the only practical option that appeared available to the prime minister was to submit a motion to dissolve the Knesset (parliament) and schedule national elections.

The cabinet ministers appeared unanimous on the inevitability of the collapse of the government, with Justice Minister Moshe Nissim saying, "I think this can be assumed," and Health Minister Eliezer Shostak declaring, "Of course the government will (fall). One has to go to early elections, and I think this will be the opinion of the prime minister."

The opposition Labor Party said yesterday that it would give the government until Wednesday to dissolve

(See BEGIN on 2-A)

AS MAYOR of Philadelphia, James H.J. Tate was not known for long talks with the press. But now years out of office, Tate talks freely. People, Page 1-C.

Weather & Index

MOSTLY SUNNY today. High 15 to 20. Partly cloudy and not so cold tonight. Low 10 to 15. Mostly cloudy tomorrow with a chance of snow flurries. Full weather report, Page 17-D.

Action Line	2-C	Horoscope	16-D
The Arts	6-C	Obituaries	18-D
Business	4-D	People	1-C
Classified	5-D	Puzzles	17-D
Comics	16-D	Sports	1-B
Editorials	6-A	TV/Radio	14-D

An anti-busing folk hero

By Jane P. Shoemaker
Inquirer Staff Writer

ALEXANDRIA, La. — The judge's office is overflowing with mementos of past conquests — photographs of the fallen deer, of the record fishing catch, of the ducks hunted with a passion.

Richard E. Lee takes his competition seriously, against fish or game — or any man who interferes with the way he runs his court.

It was in a Rapides Parish courtroom here that Lee gave his blessing to a hastily arranged custody agreement that, in effect, allowed three white teenage girls to avoid being bused away from all-white Buckeye High School under a federal desegregation plan.

And it was a block away in the granite and marble federal courthouse that U.S. District Judge Nauman Scott, who wrote the desegregation plan, ruled that Lee was out of line to interfere with desegregation. Scott ordered the three girls out of Buckeye High and into a school with a racially mixed enrollment.

Lee ordered them back to Buckeye. Scott ordered them out. Lee ordered them back. Scott ordered them out.

Lee *took* them back. Scott ordered them out, filed contempt citations against parents, guardians, school officials and Lee, and threatened everyone with fines of $500 to $1,000 a day if the girls returned to Buckeye High. They did not, and will not be going to any school pending a courtroom confrontation between Scott and Lee Thursday.

Is this the end of the battle, with the federal government proving it

(See JUDGE on 4-A)

A bitter federal prison strike wears on

By David Zucchino
Inquirer Staff Writer

MARION, Ill. — The first day of refusal, Sept. 15, began with a passive retreat. The men of Marion Prison declined, silently and almost to a man, to answer the morning work call.

For Marion, a secluded warehouse for the nation's most resourceful and independent felons, a work stoppage was hardly a remarkable event. Two other strikes had come and gone earlier in 1980, each aborted with a whimper as the prison ladled out minor concessions.

But now, as the strike enters its 18th week, the men who run Marion find themselves struggling to keep the lid on what has become the longest strike in federal prison history. It is now no ordinary strike — and fittingly, for Marion is no ordinary prison.

For years, career convicts have come to know and fear Marion. From the day it opened in 1962 as the federal government's maximum-security prison, it was "the lab," "behavior mod," the new Alcatraz, the toughest turn of the screw in the federal prison system.

Marion is a catch basin for the men who, in the judgment of prison officials, cannot be "controlled" in any

(See PRISON on 4-A)

1980

January 12, 1981 - After 20 years the Eagles make it to the Super Bowl, however lose to Oakland Raiders 27-10

1981

RECORD: 10-6, 2ND IN NFC EAST
HEAD COACH: DICK VERMEIL

SCHEDULE

REGULAR SEASON

Wk. 1	Sep 6	W	24-10	at New York Giants
Wk. 2	Sep 13	W	13-3	vs New England Patriots
Wk. 3	Sep 17	W	20-14	at Buffalo Bills
Wk. 4	Sep 27	W	36-13	vs Washington Redskins
Wk. 5	Oct 5	W	16-13	vs Atlanta Falcons
Wk. 6	Oct 11	W	31-14	at New Orleans Saints
Wk. 7	Oct 18	L	35-23	at Minnesota Vikings
Wk. 8	Oct 25	W	20-10	vs Tampa Bay Buccaneers
Wk. 9	Nov 1	L	17-14	vs Dallas Cowboys
Wk. 10	Nov 8	W	52-10	at St. Louis Cardinals
Wk. 11	Nov 15	W	38-13	vs Baltimore Colts
Wk. 12	Nov 22	L	20-10	vs New York Giants
Wk. 13	Nov 30	L	13-10	at Miami Dolphins
Wk. 14	Dec 6	L	15-13	at Washington Redskins
Wk. 15	Dec 13	L	21-10	at Dallas Cowboys
Wk. 16	Dec 20	W	38-0	vs St. Louis Cardinals

POST SEASON

Wild Card Playoffs				
	Dec 27	L	27-21	vs New York Giants

With running back Wilbert Montgomery's return from injury to rush for 1,402 yards, the Eagles got off to a high flying start by winning their first 6 games. The Eagles would continue to play solid football and sat atop the NFC East at 9-2. However, a four-game losing streak would drop them out of first. The Eagles won their final game to finish with a 10-6 record, and appear in the playoffs for the fourth consecutive year, but were upset at home in the NFC Wild Card Game by the NY Giants, 27-21 at the Vet. The Birds' defense ranked first in the NFL in fewest yards allowed (4,447) and fewest points allowed (221). On offense, Harold Carmichael enjoyed the third 1,000-yard receiving year of his career and Wilbert Montgomery rushed for 1,402 yards.

1981 PHILADELPHIA EAGLES STATS

Passing	Comp	Att	Comp %	Yds	Y/Att	TD	Int	Rating
Ron Jaworski	250	461	54.2	3095	6.71	23	20	73.8
Joe Pisarcik	8	15	53.3	154	10.27	2	2	89.3

Rushing	Rush	Yds	Avg	TD
Wilbert Montgomery	286	1402	4.9	8
Hubie Oliver	75	329	4.4	1
Perry Harrington	34	140	4.1	2
Calvin Murray	23	134	5.8	0
Ron Jaworski	22	128	5.8	0
Booker Russell	38	123	3.2	4
Billy Campfield	31	115	3.7	1
Louie Giammona	35	98	2.8	1
Steve Atkins	1	21	21.0	0
Frank LeMaster	1	7	7.0	0
Ron Smith	1	7	7.0	0
Charlie Smith	2	5	2.5	0
Joe Pisarcik	7	1	0.1	0
Harold Carmichael	1	1	1.0	0
John Sciarra	1	0	0.0	0
Wally Henry	1	-2	-2.0	0

Punting	Punts	Yds	Avg	Blocked
Max Runager	63	2567	40.7	0
Tony Franklin	1	13	13.0	0

Kicking	PAT Made	PAT Att	PAT %	FG Made	FG Att	FG %	Pts
Tony Franklin	41	43	95	20	31	64.5	101

Receiving	Rec	Yds	Avg	TD
Harold Carmichael	61	1028	16.9	6
Wilbert Montgomery	49	521	10.6	2
Charlie Smith	38	564	14.8	4
Billy Campfield	36	326	9.1	3
Keith Krepfle	20	210	10.5	5
Hubie Oliver	10	37	3.7	0
Wally Henry	9	145	16.1	2
Perry Harrington	9	27	3.0	0
Rodney Parker	8	168	21.0	2
John Spagnola	6	83	13.8	0
Louie Giammona	6	54	9.0	1
Ron Smith	4	84	21.0	0
Calvin Murray	1	7	7.0	0
Booker Russell	1	-5	-5.0	0

Interceptions	Int	Yds	Avg	TD
Brenard Wilson	5	73	14.6	0
Roynell Young	4	35	8.8	0
Herman Edwards	3	1	0.3	0
Al Chesley	2	66	33.0	0
Richard Blackmore	2	43	21.5	0
Frank LeMaster	2	28	14.0	0
Reggie Wilkes	2	18	9.0	0
Randy Logan	2	-1	-0.5	0
Jerry Robinson	1	3	3.0	0
Charles Johnson	1	0	0.0	0
Ray Phillips	1	0	0.0	0
John Sciarra	1	0	0.0	0

The Philadelphia Inquirer
Sports Extra
section C
Monday, December 28, 1981

Eagles dig hole, Giants bury 'em

Philadelphia Inquirer / VICKI VALERIO

Dick Vermeil makes sure that Eagles assistant coach John Becker (left) wigwags correct signal to Ron Jaworski; sub QB Joe Pisarcik (center) also flashes sign

Carpenter heroic in 27-21 win

By Gordon Forbes
Inquirer Staff Writer

The strategy that was supposed to send the Eagles winging toward Super Bowl XVI was simple enough.

On defense, to gang-tackle the Giants' Rob Carpenter and force young Scott Brunner to throw before his receivers made their break. On offense, to control the ball with a unique, three-back I-formation and just enough passes to keep the tough New York defense honest.

It all sounded nice enough, but on a dreary afternoon at Veterans Stadium yesterday, the Giants kicked the aging Eagles and Dick Vermeil's game plans around in a stunning 27-21 upset before 71,611 gloomy fans. The unexpected victory sends the wild-card Giants to San Francisco for a divisional playoff against the 49ers on Sunday.

How bad were the Eagles?

The Giants (10-7), jumping on two disastrous kick fumbles by Wally Henry, rushed out to a 20-0 first-period lead before Ron Jaworski got to throw a pass. The Eagles (10-7) never recovered from that nightmarish start, although they finally found their poise to close within a touchdown of victory with 2 minutes, 51 seconds left.

Carpenter gains 161

That left it up to the defense to gang up on Carpenter, who carried 33 times for 161 yards — more than any other runner had gained against the Eagles this season. He did it with classic inside cutbacks from a one-back set. Philadelphia's 3-4 defense, with its reputation for jamming up the run, suddenly seemed old and never got the ball back for Jaworski's offense.

"It was a shock that they did that much in so short a time," said defensive end Carl Hairston in a dressing room where the mood was a perfect match for the weather. "I'm hurting. I was looking forward to winning this game. This one was tougher to take than the Super Bowl because we didn't play well. This was almost like a championship game for us."

Linebacker Frank LeMaster stood in disbelief in front of his locker stall. "This loss is the most disappointing and frustrating I've ever had," he said, "mainly because my expectations were higher. We've got too much talent here. The higher your expectations are, the more frustration there is. I wish I had the answers."

Reece recovers

The Eagles began their fumbling and bumbling exit from the NFC playoffs on the first Giants series. Continuing a streak of dreadful special-teams play, Henry fumbled Jennings' punt with the Giants' Pro Bowl linebacker, rookie Lawrence Taylor, in his face. Beasley Reece recovered for the Giants at the 25-yard line.

Brunner, who completed only nine passes but burned the Eagles for three touchdowns, took the Giants into the end zone in six plays. After Carpenter moved it to the four on five power runs, tackle Gordon King was called for a false start, leaving the Giants with third-and-goal at the nine.

Brunner overcame. The Giants flowed their receivers inside and sent Leon Bright, a speed runner,

(See EAGLES on 5-C)

Their 'science' left in rubble, erring Eagles reveal courage

By FRANK DOLSON

Sports editor

They talk about the "science" of pro football. The Dick Vermeils of the world work deep into the night studying films, looking for a clue here, an edge there before coming up with that precious thing known as a "game plan."

And then the game begins and almost quicker than you can say "Wait 'til next year," the plan is shot to pieces.

That's the crazy thing about football. All those hours running a projector, all that precise, scientific planning, all those brilliant X's and O's aren't worth a hoot when a team keeps giving away the football, when a fumbled punt and a fumbled kickoff add up to two gift touchdowns in the very first period.

As the Eagles discovered yesterday, a game plan is reduced to rubble when your offensive unit has been on the field for a total of four plays (for a net gain of one yard) in the first quarter and the score is 20-0 against you.

Suddenly, shockingly, sickeningly, the game they found themselves in bore absolutely no resemblance to the tight, tough, defensive game they had made such elaborate plans to play.

In this season of devastating mistakes, that was the final irony. Not even the hardest-working, best-prepared coaching staff in all of football could have foreseen the rash of blunders that shot down the '81 Philadelphia Eagles.

There were those holding penalties by the kickoff-return team that kept the Eagles stuck in terrible field position the first time they played Dallas. There was the fumbled snap on what was supposed to be the game-winning field-goal try at Washington. And the fumbled punt that cost the

(See DOLSON on 4-C)

Philadelphia Inquirer / JOHN PAUL FILO

Wally Henry tries to get ball after fumbling kickoff

Associated Press

Buffalo wide receiver Frank Lewis wins the race to the end zone for a first-quarter touchdown

Bills roll up early lead, then hold off Jets, 31-27

By Chuck Newman
Inquirer Staff Writer

NEW YORK — Jim Haslett, who has, on occasion, publicly pronounced his hatred for the New York Jets and the house they play in, was praying at the end.

"Lord, please give us one more break," thought Haslett, a linebacker for the Buffalo Bills, who were staggering at the end of yesterday's AFC wild-card game at Shea Stadium.

While Haslett was praying, teammate Joe Cribbs had his eyes closed. "I couldn't bear to watch the last 2 minutes," the Bills' 1,060-yard runner said. "I kept thinking about last year."

Last year, the Bills lost a playoff game to the Chargers in the final minutes, when Ron Smith (now an Eagle) scored on a pass play that will live in infamy in Haslett's mind.

The victim of Smith's reception was safety Bill Simpson, who yesterday answered Haslett's prayers, intercepting a Richard Todd pass at the Buffalo one-yard line with 2 seconds left to play to rescue a 31-27 victory. The win sent the Bills (11-6) to Cincinnati, for a second-round NFL playoff game on Sunday, and the frustrated Jets (10-6-1) went to an early vacation, to ponder what might have been.

Simpson's second interception of the game killed a frantic Jets drive that began at the New York 20-yard line with 2:36 to play. The Jets devoured 69 yards before the Bills were able to cut short what would have been one of the great comebacks in NFL history.

That the game would have come down to the final seconds had seemed highly unlikely.

Buffalo built a 24-0 lead in just over 24 minutes of play, fueled by the fastest touchdown in an NFL playoff since 1974. Cornerback Charles Romes picked up a fumble on the

(See BILLS on 6-C)

NFL playoffs

CONFERENCE SEMIFINALS

Saturday

Tampa Bay Buccaneers (9-7) at Dallas Cowboys (12-4), 1 p.m.

San Diego Chargers (10-6) at Miami Dolphins (11-4-1), 5 p.m.

Sunday

Buffalo Bills (11-6) at Cincinnati Bengals (12-4), 1 p.m.

New York Giants (10-7) at San Francisco 49ers (13-3), 5 p.m.

CONFERENCE CHAMPIONSHIPS

Jan. 10

Sites and times to be determined.

SUPER BOWL XVI

Jan. 24

Pontiac, Mich., 4 p.m.

Sixers, unable to overcome their Phoenix jinx, tumble to 99-96 loss

By George Shirk
Inquirer Staff Writer

PHOENIX, Ariz. — The 76ers always save their worst for Phoenix. It's a tradition.

Last night, after four days of rest, the Sixers gave their worst shooting performance of the season and lost to the Suns, 99-96.

On paper, the loss appeared unlikely. The Suns were playing their third game in three days and, by all rights, should have been two steps slower and three times more ragged. But it didn't turn out that way at all. So, in front of a capacity crowd of 14,660 — the Suns' first sellout of the season — with Truck Robinson collecting 25 points and 15 rebounds, Phoenix beat the Sixers. Again.

The loss was Philadelphia's fifth straight here since March 1978. To make matters worse, it dropped the Sixers, now 20-6, a half-game behind Boston in the NBA's Atlantic Division.

Phoenix, which jumped its record to 16-12, had lost to Golden State on Saturday evening in Oakland and had lost to Los Angeles at home on Friday. Yet it was the Sixers, who were playing without injured Bobby Jones, who were a step slow and off balance.

"It was hard to tell which team was the one that had played three games in three nights," coach Billy Cunningham said with a wry laugh after the game. "We just didn't get anything generated on a consistent basis, either defensively or offensively. I thought we had several opportunities to win the game, but we either committed a foul, didn't get a rebound, missed foul shots, etc. I can name about 20 [opportunities]."

The Sixers shot a pitiful 40.2 percent from the field. It was not only their poorest effort this season but worse than any last season.

Julius Erving, who led the club with 20 points, was 7 for 17. Darryl Dawkins, who fouled out of the game in the fourth quarter and who scored nine points, all in the first half, shot 2 for 7. Mo Cheeks, who had nine points and six assists, was three for 11, Lionel Hollins 6 for 15 and Caldwell Jones 3 for 8.

In addition, the Sixers were pounded on the boards, losing the rebounding battle, 56-40.

Given those circumstances, it was remarkable that they were even in the game when time began running out on them in the fourth quarter. But they were indeed in it, thanks to 22 Phoenix turnovers, right up until the last seconds.

They were down by 99-96 and had the ball and a timeout with 14 seconds to go. They also had Andrew Toney, who, with 41 seconds left, had hit a three-point field goal to bring them that close.

All eyes, therefore, were on Toney, who is the best three-point man on the club, as the Sixers put the ball in bounds.

Cunningham had designed a play that would have gotten the ball first to C. Jones, who would have the option of passing to Erving, Cheeks, Toney or Steve Mix for a three-point try. The play went awry.

"We were looking for a three-point shot, obviously," Cunningham said. "We were going to have five people

(See SIXERS on 7-C)

December 28, 1981 - Eagles lose in the NFC Wild Card game 27-21 to the NY Giants

1981

1982

RECORD: 3-6, 13TH IN NFC
HEAD COACH: DICK VERMEIL

SCHEDULE

REGULAR SEASON

Wk. 1	Sep 12	L	37-34	vs Washington Redskins (OT)
Wk. 2	Sep 19	W	24-21	at Cleveland Browns
Wk. 10	Nov 21	L	18-14	vs Cincinnati Bengals
Wk. 11	Nov 28	L	13-9	at Washington Redskins
Wk. 12	Dec 5	L	23-20	vs St. Louis Cardinals
Wk. 13	Dec 11	L	23-7	at New York Giants
Wk. 14	Dec 19	W	35-14	vs Houston Oilers
Wk. 15	Dec 26	W	24-20	at Dallas Cowboys
Wk. 16	Jan 2	L	26-24	vs New York Giants

An NFL players' strike took place after two games and stopped play for eight weeks. When play resumed on November 21, 1982, the long layoff hurt the Eagles. After splitting the first two games of the season, the Birds came back from the strike to lose four in a row and miss the playoff for the first time since 1977. A 24-20 Eagles victory at Dallas on December 26, 1982, is the last victory in the Philadelphia career of head coach Dick Vermeil, who resigned sighting burnout shortly following the season after compiling a 56-51-0 overall record.

1982 PHILADELPHIA EAGLES STATS

Passing	Comp	Att	Comp %	Yds	Y/Att	TD	Int	Rating
Ron Jaworski	167	286	58.4	2076	7.26	12	12	77.5
Joe Pisarcik	1	1	100.0	24	24.00	0	0	118.8
Louie Giammona	0	1	0.0	0	0.00	0	1	0.0

Rushing	Rush	Yds	Avg	TD
Wilbert Montgomery	114	515	4.5	7
Perry Harrington	56	231	4.1	1
Leroy Harris	17	39	2.3	2
Louie Giammona	11	29	2.6	1
Ron Jaworski	10	9	0.9	0
Melvin Hoover	1	5	5.0	0
Billy Campfield	1	2	2.0	0
Frank LeMaster	1	-1	-1.0	0

Receiving	Rec	Yds	Avg	TD
Harold Carmichael	35	540	15.4	4
Ron Smith	34	475	14.0	1
John Spagnola	26	313	12.0	2
Wilbert Montgomery	20	258	12.9	2
Billy Campfield	14	141	10.1	1
Perry Harrington	13	74	5.7	0
Mike Quick	10	156	15.6	1
Louie Giammona	8	67	8.4	0
Vyto Kab	4	35	8.8	1
Leroy Harris	3	17	5.7	0
Lawrence Sampleton	1	24	24.0	0

Punting	Punts	Yds	Avg	Blocked
Max Runager	44	1784	40.5	0

Kicking	PAT Made	PAT Att	PAT %	FG Made	FG Att	FG %	Pts
Tony Franklin	23	25	92	6	9	66.7	41

Interceptions	Int	Yds	Avg	TD
Herman Edwards	5	3	0.6	0
Roynell Young	4	0	0.0	0
Jerry Robinson	3	19	6.3	0
Richard Blackmore	1	20	20.0	1
John Bunting	1	0	0.0	0
Brenard Wilson	1	0	0.0	0

The Philadelphia Inquirer

Sports Extra

section C

Monday, September 20, 1982

Carmichael, Eagles seem to have 'picks' down pat

Gordon Forbes: Inside report

CLEVELAND — It is one of the lickest tricks in pro football, one hat defensive coaches scream about nd offensive coaches swear they never use.

Coach Dick Vermeil said that the Eagles put together those two superb ouchdown drives yesterday to stun he Cleveland Browns without beneit of a single "pick" play. But Harold Carmichael, his dead-honest receiver, who set up the winning score by beating a s-l-o-w safety named Judson Flint, wasn't so sure.

"Well, yeah, you could say that I was using the pick," Carmichael said, with a sheepish grin, following the 24-21 thriller at Cleveland Stadium. "I could pick on it or get open on it. I'm trying to get open, but if the guy holds me up and if I can see him in 'man' [man-to-man coverage], I can set a pick. I pick the other guy."

Vermeil said that there weren't any picks on either of the critical drives — ones that showcased Ron Jaworski's poise and ability to read a nickel defense and the vastly improved Eagles receiving corps. But he had also pleaded innocent after the Eagles won a 1979 National Football Conference wild-card game over the Chicago Bears in which Carmichael threw a pick to spring Billy Campfield for a 63-yard touchdown.

Pick plays usually work inside the 20-yard line. With the defense almost always in man-to-man coverage, one receiver runs a simple crossing pattern, forcing a defender into traffic and into a pick. And what receiver on the Eagles is better suited to pick off linebacker Tom Cousineau, who is still learning about National Football League pass coverages, than Carmichael?

The Eagles probably used the pick on both of Campfield's catches yesterday — an all-or-nothing 12-yarder on fourth-and-10 for a first down at the Cleveland 16 and an 11-yarder on third-and-five for a go-ahead touchdown. Both times, Carmichael went inside on motion out of the shotgun while Campfield, on a delay route, slipped outside.

"The first one was just like the Bears," said Campfield, who has developed into a solid shotgun receiver. "I came off him [Carmichael], and Ron saw me. I don't think it was really a pick. I was just one-on-one [against Cousineau].

"The second one, I was hoping to get one-on-one again with the linebacker, but they zoned it up. I slowed it up and got open."

The Eagles drove 68 of the toughest yards they'll ever earn to spring Campfield into the end zone. It wasn't so much the Browns' nickel that made them tough as it was the way the Eagles stuck themselves in two third-and-10 holes and one fourth-and-10 hole.

With starting left cornerback Ron Bolton out, the Browns were forced to play five small backs against Carmichael and the other Eagles leapers. Their only speed back was Hanford Dixon, a young, talented corner whom the Eagles avoided. Out of

(See FORBES on 6-C)

Associated Press

Leroy Harris barrels over Eddie Johnson for the Eagles' game-winning TD with 22 seconds left

Eagles' offense strikes in time

By Jeré Longman
Inquirer Staff Writer

CLEVELAND — These were the Cardiac Kids all right, but they were in different jerseys now, wearing Eagles green instead of Cleveland brown.

This time it wasn't Brian Sipe doing his Harry Blackstone routine in the autumn moments, as he had seven times in 1980. Yesterday that bit of magic belonged to Ron Jaworski.

After Ozzie Newsome picked Roynell Young's pocket for a 34-yard touchdown with 57 seconds remaining, Jaworski drove the Eagles right back, composing a 65-yard drive with three crisp passes.

With the clock wound down to its final half-minute, he pitched left to his butterball fullback, Leroy Harris, who rolled in from the two to give the Eagles a 24-21 win over the Browns (1-1) before a stunned audience of 78,830 at Cleveland Stadium.

It's becoming clear that to make it through the Eagles' season — if there is any more of a season — the average fan will need a respirator and a handful of nitroglycerin tablets. The fourth quarter produced 35 of the 45 points.

For the second time in eight days, the offense surged ahead just when most people were ready to call it Miller Time. Last week, Harold Carmichael's supine catch gave the Eagles a 34-31 lead with 1 minute, 4 seconds left.

Then the defense failed, and Mark Moseley won it for Washington with two field goals. This time, the defense avoided a last-second mugging, and Herman Edwards, picked on relentlessly by the Redskins, intercepted Sipe at the Cleveland 41 about the time CBS cut away to a final beer commercial.

It was a curious game for the Eagles, whose offense clanked and groaned like the Broad Street Sub-

(See EAGLES on 5-C)

Pro football

Dallas 24, St. Louis 7
Detroit 19, L. A. Rams 14
Pittsburgh 26, Cincinnati 20, ovt.
L. A. Raiders 38, Atlanta 14
New York Jets 31, New England 7
New Orleans 10, Chicago 0
Kansas City 19, San Diego 12
Denver 24, San Francisco 21
Houston 23, Seattle 21
Washington 23, Tampa Bay 13
Miami 24, Baltimore 20

Detailed coverage Pages 4-C and 5-C

Associated Press

Harold Carmichael beats Judson Flint, sets up winning score

If this was the end, it sure was a beauty

By BILL LYON

CLEVELAND — The first three quarters here in Baghdad-by-the-Sewer had been as inconclusive as mud-wrestling.

The harder the Eagles and Browns tried, the more they spun their wheels. They had tugged and shoved and taffy-pulled with each other, and they had moved the ball briskly, but only between the 20-yard lines. Each time either nudged close to a score, a wheel would come off and the offense would spray the ball into Lake Erie. Where, of course, it would promptly stick.

So Cleveland led, 7-3, going into the fourth period. And then, with no warning whatsoever, the game exploded into the star-spangled, rockets-bursting, cymbals-crashing crescendo that has made professional football *the* sport of our civilization.

It was a graphic reminder of just what spectaculars the mercenaries of Sunday are capable of generating, and at the same time, it was a cruel, mocking tease, for it is quite possible that the season will end tonight. No more fixes for NFL junkies unless labor and management end their stalemate.

So after producing only 10 points in the first, sputtering 47 minutes, 17 seconds, the Eagles and Browns crammed 35 points into the final

(See LYON on 6-C)

Phils fall to Bucs, 8-1, find backs against wall

By Jayson Stark
Inquirer Staff Writer

In the context of great Philadelphia disasters, this one isn't even in the top 10.

Great disasters need goats and villains, and moments to remember for three decades. This one has been lifeless — a collapse without a central tragic event.

No Chico Ruiz. No Manny Mota. No John Milner grand slams. Just a sudden pulling of the plug. One minute, there was a pennant race. The next minute, there was nothing there.

Seven days ago, the Phillies were in first place. Now, after yesterday's 8-1 horror-show loss to the Pirates, they are 4½ games behind the Cardinals and in need of some quick CPR.

They have 14 games to play. The magic number for elimination is 10.

They have won two of their last eight games. The Cardinals have won seven straight, including five this weekend over the clinically dead Mets.

The St. Louis staff has allowed a total of eight runs in its last seven games. The Phillies have scored two runs or fewer in nine of their last 17.

The Phillies' starting eight hit .172 on this 2-4 homestand. The Cardinals won yesterday with Keith Hernandez and Lonnie Smith taking days off.

The Phillies' plight is as grim as all that data makes it sound — and maybe grimmer. They move on to St. Louis tonight for the first of two make-or-break games, and the match-

(See PHILLIES on 8-C)

Philadelphia Inquirer / GERALD S. WILLIAMS

Willie Stargell: 'My final season has been like a gourmet meal'

A day for Stargell

Phils honor a star-studded career

By Gary Ronberg
Inquirer Staff Writer

To millions of fans of the Grand Old Game, the memory of Wilver Dornel Stargell probably will be that of a mountain of a man in Pittsburgh's gold and black, rotating his bat in anticipation of the next pitch and launching another white blur toward the upper deck in right.

In fact, so commanding did Stargell's presence as a slugger become that the memory of his taking batting practice might well be followed by an exclamation point.

"Oh, could Willie do a number in BP," said the Phillies' pitching coach, Claude Osteen. "He'd windmill that bat and mash the balls flat on one side. Just hit 'em up into no-man's land."

Few athletes, if any, have seen dusk fall on their careers in quite the way that Stargell has in this last month of his 20th and final year as a Pirate. The memory that will linger most in the minds of the 37,352 who witnessed his final appearance in Veterans Stadium yesterday afternoon may well be that of a burly man with a white towel around his neck. For as Willie Stargell, 42, has demonstrated on several occasions already this month, grown men *do* cry.

"How many other ballplayers have been given a 'day' in just about every ballpark in the National League?"

(See STARGELL on 12-C)

Kenyan breezes to world half-marathon record in Phila. Distance Run

By Ron Reid
Inquirer Staff Writer

In a performance as stunning as it ppeared effortless, Michael Musyoki of Kenya won the Philadelphia Distance Run yesterday, covering the 13.1-mile course in the world-record time of 1 hour, 1 minute, 35 seconds.

He was chased to the wire by George Malley, a former Penn State runner who has returned to competition after 16 months of injury problems. His revived health evident, Malley was timed in 1:01:42, an American record.

Stan Mavis, a former world record-holder at this half-marathon distance, finished third in 1:04:06.

In all, the first 12 runners each took less than 65 minutes to complete the finest race in the five-year history of the event. But the victory went to Musyoki, the most durable talent in the field and perhaps the most graceful.

Taking the lead at the halfway point — shortly before the race would lose Rod Dixon, its two-time defending champion, to a severe leg cramp — Musyoki glided with the elegance of an impala.

Knocking off mile after mile with fluid ease, the man who holds the world records for 10 and 15 kilometers ran at a pace of 4 minutes, 42 seconds a mile, even though he was never seriously challenged after going to the front.

When the race ended at JFK Plaza, Musyoki appeared about as winded as a man waiting for a bus. While one competitor finished the race on a stretcher and others consigned their breakfasts to the pavement en route, Musyoki was a study in tranquility.

That could be credited in part to a cool, crisp, sunlit morning that was ideal for a distance run. But for the world record, Musyoki could thank race director Bill Jackson, who added a catalyst named Gabriel Kamau to field of 6,100.

Kamau, another Kenyan, entered the race — which was sponsored by the Philadelphia YMCA, Nike and The Inquirer — as the designated "rabbit," one of those runners who sets a fast early pace for the record-breaking benefit of others.

Kamau set a blistering pace. He led the pack through the first four miles in 18:25 — 1 minute, 7 seconds faster than the same distance had been run here last year — and he covered the first 10 kilometers (6.2 miles) in just over 29 minutes before yielding the lead to Musyoki.

By the seven-mile mark, it was a two-man race, with some in the field trailing Musyoki and Malley by as much as four miles.

Malley, a liquor-store employee, almost had elected to have surgery last summer for a chronic heel-tendon problem.

"I backed out at the last minute," he said, "and then I had this miraculous healing. Now I've had 19 solid weeks of training. I'm glad I held off."

Pointing to his American record on the electronic timer, he added, "And I'm happier about this."

Several times, Malley closed to within 40 yards of Musyoki, only to fall back, but he, like Musyoki, broke the course record of 1:02:12 set by Dixon a year ago.

This time, Dixon set a new stan-

(See RUN on 8-C)

1982

September 20, 1982 - Jaworski is successful with his second consecutive 300-yard game as the Eagles defeat the Cleveland Browns 24-21

1983

RECORD: 5-11, 4TH IN NFC EAST
HEAD COACH: MARION CAMPBELL

Schedule

Regular Season

Wk. 1	Sep 3	W	22-17	at San Francisco 49ers
Wk. 2	Sep 11	L	23-13	vs Washington Redskins
Wk. 3	Sep 18	W	13-10	at Denver Broncos
Wk. 4	Sep 25	L	14-11	vs St. Louis Cardinals
Wk. 5	Oct 2	W	28-24	at Atlanta Falcons
Wk. 6	Oct 9	W	17-13	at New York Giants
Wk. 7	Oct 16	L	37-7	at Dallas Cowboys
Wk. 8	Oct 23	L	7-6	vs Chicago Bears
Wk. 9	Oct 30	L	22-21	vs Baltimore Colts
Wk. 10	Nov 6	L	27-20	vs Dallas Cowboys
Wk. 11	Nov 13	L	17-14	at Chicago Bears
Wk. 12	Nov 20	L	23-0	vs New York Giants
Wk. 13	Nov 27	L	28-24	at Washington Redskins
Wk. 14	Dec 4	W	13-9	vs Los Angeles Rams
Wk. 15	Dec 11	L	20-17	vs New Orleans Saints (OT)
Wk. 16	Dec 18	L	31-7	at St. Louis Cardinals

Marion Campbell replaced Dick Vermeil as head coach after six seasons as the defensive coordinator. Owner and president Leonard Tose announced in January that his daughter, Susan Fletcher, the Eagles vice president and legal counsel, would eventually succeed him as primary owner of the Eagles. The Eagles got off to a solid start, winning four of their first six games. However, they came crashing down to earth quickly during a crippling seven game losing streak. The Eagles went on to finish in last place with a 5-11 record. The Birds' offense was highlighted by first-team all-pro and AFC-NFC Pro Bowl selection Mike Quick, who led the league and set club records with 1,409 yards receiving on 69 catches.

1983 Philadelphia Eagles Stats

Passing	Comp	Att	Comp %	Yds	Y/Att	TD	Int	Rating
Ron Jaworski	235	446	52.7	3315	7.43	20	18	75.1
Harold Carmichael	1	1	100.0	45	45.00	1	0	158.3
Joe Pisarcik	16	34	47.1	172	5.06	1	0	72.2
Dan Pastorini	0	5	0.0	0	0.00	0	0	39.6

Rushing	Rush	Yds	Avg	TD
Hubie Oliver	121	434	3.6	1
Michael Williams	103	385	3.7	0
Michael Haddix	91	220	2.4	2
Wilbert Montgomery	29	139	4.8	0
Ron Jaworski	25	129	5.2	1
Perry Harrington	23	98	4.3	1
Major Everettt	5	7	1.4	0
Max Runager	1	6	6.0	0
Dan Pastorini	1	0	0.0	0
Joe Pisarcik	3	-1	-0.3	0

Punting	Punts	Yds	Avg	Blocked
Max Runager	59	2459	41.7	0
Tom Skledany	27	1062	39.3	0

Kicking	PAT Made	PAT Att	PAT %	FG Made	FG Att	FG %	Pts
Tony Franklin	24	27	89	15	26	57.7	69

Receiving	Rec	Yds	Avg	TD
Mike Quick	69	1409	20.4	13
Hubie Oliver	49	421	8.6	2
Harold Carmichael	38	515	13.6	3
Michael Haddix	23	254	11.0	0
Vyto Kab	18	195	10.8	1
Michael Williams	17	142	8.4	0
Melvin Hoover	10	221	22.1	0
Wilbert Montgomery	9	53	5.9	0
Tony Woodruff	6	70	11.7	2
Al Dixon	4	54	13.5	0
Glen Young	3	125	41.7	1
Lawrence Sampleton	2	28	14.0	0
Major Everettt	2	18	9.0	0
Perry Harrington	1	19	19.0	0
Ron Smith	1	8	8.0	0

Interceptions	Int	Yds	Avg	TD
Anthony Griggs	3	61	20.3	0
Ray Ellis	1	18	18.0	0
Herman Edwards	1	0	0.0	0
Elbert Foules	1	0	0.0	0
Randy Logan	1	0	0.0	0
Roynell Young	1	0	0.0	0

The Philadelphia Inquirer

Sports Extra

section D

Monday, December 19, 1983

Eagles fall on their faces one last time

By FRANK DOLSON

Sports editor

The Eagles go slip-slidin' away

ST. LOUIS — Somewhere, that old, ex-Eagle, Tom Brookshier, was probably sitting in an easy chair in front of a warm fire yesterday, his feet propped up, looking at a television screen and laughing.

Red-jerseyed Cardinals were romping up and down the snow-slicked field while red-faced Eagles were slipping and sliding on a day when the wind-chill factor was minus-10 degrees. And to think, the big shots at CBS-TV thought they were *punishing* Brookshier by taking him off the game, a suspension for comments made on the air during last week's Eagles-Saints game.

It was a day unfit for man, beast or television announcer, and the game was perfectly suited to the day — a virtually meaningless exercise in which grown men took pratfalls in the snow and 21,902 spectators thumbed their frozen noses at double pneumonia.

It was so miserable out there that Cardinals' veteran Dan Dierdorf, retiring at the end of this, his 13th pro season, accepted a plaque before the game, stepped to the microphone and said, "I don't want anybody to think I'm going to talk long enough to delay the start of this football game. I'm as cold as you are."

Unfortunately for the Eagles, Dierdorf quit talking at that point and let the game begin.

It was horrendous, a game only a Cardinals fanatic could love. The playing surface looked more like a hockey rink than a football field, and the Eagles, getting into the spirit of things, looked like the New Jersey Devils.

The only thing the visitors were to win on this frostbitten afternoon was the opening toss. They elected to receive. Had they known then what they know now, they would have elected to leave.

While the Eagles' running backs spun their wheels and went nowhere, collectively gaining a net 14 yards, the Cardinals' Ottis Anderson personally ran for 156.

"They had good traction ... a lot better traction than we had," Eagles coach Marion Campbell said when it was over, indicating that the Cardinals wore shoes better suited to the playing suface.

Maybe so. But watching this game between a Cardinals team that had won six of its last nine and an Eagles team that had lost eight of its last nine, you got the feeling they could have been playing in Miami Beach and it wouldn't have made much difference in the final result.

The Eagles were so helpless that they didn't gain anything until their eighth play from scrimmage — a Ron Jaworski-to-Hubie Oliver pass that picked up three yards on a second-and-12 play. Their first seven offensive plays netted minus-14 yards.

Their running game was so bad that they went 12½ minutes before

(See DOLSON on 6-D)

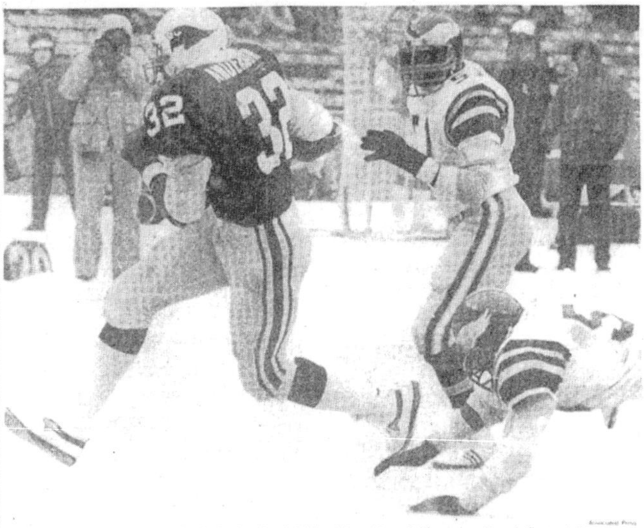

Associated Press

Ottis Anderson (32) darts past Eagles linebackers Reggie Wilkes (51) and Jerry Robinson for a 12-yard, first-period touchdown

Cardinals cruise, 31-7, in the snow

By Jere Longman
Inquirer Staff Writer

ST. LOUIS — The other sho[e] dropped on the Eagles yesterday.

Make that the wrong shoe.

In a season in which everythin[g] imaginable has gone askew, the Ea[gles] reached a new low in yester[day's] finale, a 31-7 loss to St. Louis — they wore the wrong shoes.

That's right.

The Cardinals appeared relativel[y] immune to the blowing snow and 1[0] degree temperature at Busch Stadi[um], but the Eagles went skatin[g] across the frozen turf like Eric He[iden].

St. Louis, it seems, wore a brand o[f] shoe called Acton, which was origi[nally] designed for rainy weather an[d] is often used in the Canadian Foot[ball] League. Its most attractive fea[ture] is longer rubber cleats than th[e] standard turf shoe.

The Eagles, meanwhile, went sli[p] sliding around in their normal tur[f] shoes, missing tackles, falling o[n] pass patterns and generally bein[g] unable to generate any traction.

"I almost fell down just coming ou[t] of the huddle," center Guy Morri[ss] said.

Partly because the Eagles couldn['t] stay on their feet, they slipped t[o] their 11th loss in 16 games. Yeste[r]day's inglorious conclusion marke[d] their worst season since Dick Ve[r]meil was hired as coach in 1976 an[d] posted a 4-10 record. The last time th[e] Eagles lost 11 games was 1972, whe[n] they finished 2-11-1.

"It was just a poor performance o[n] our part," said coach Marion Cam[p]bell, that master of understatemen[t]. "We didn't get anything going offe[n]sively or defensively."

Some examples:

• The Eagles managed a grand t[o]tal of 14 yards rushing on 12 carrie[s]. If Max Runager hadn't skated for [...] yards on a fake punt, that total woul[d] have been 8 yards on 11 carries. [...] was the most pitiful rushing perfo[r]mance by the Eagles since the[y] plowed up 10 yards against the G[i]ants on Nov. 20.

• Ron Jaworski completed 21 of [...] passes for 298 yards, but he als[o] threw four interceptions, matchin[g] his career high. The pickoffs wer[e] costly, setting up three St. Lou[is] touchdowns and a field goal.

• Jaworski, hounded all day by [a] fierce pass rush, also was sacked [...] times. 4½ sacks went to defensiv[e] end Curtis Greer and three mor[e] went to defensive end Bubba Bake[r].

The only reason the Eagles score[d] was St. Louis' insistence on passin[g] even with a 31-0 lead in the fourt[h] quarter. With 28 seconds remainin[g] quarterback Neil Lomax lost the ba[ll] while trying to scramble, an[d] Jaworski salvaged the day with a 2[...] yard touchdown pass to Mike Quic[k] at the final gun.

With his four catches, Quick set a[n] Eagles season record of 69 rece[p]tions. His touchdown also tied Tom[my] McDonald's club mark of 13 in [a] season. There was another record o[f] sorts. Harold Carmichael, with fiv[e] catches, tied Fred Biletnikoff fo[r] fifth place on the all-time NFL lis[t] with 589 career receptions.

But yesterday's frosty denouemen[t] will not be remembered for record[s]

(See EAGLES on 6-D)

Wild finishes complete playoff field

From Inquirer Wire Services

The battle for the last playoff berths in the National Football Conference went down to the final seconds yesterday when field goals eliminated two of the five teams vying for the three spots available on the final Sunday of the National Football League regular season.

Mike Lansford's 42-yard field goal with 2 seconds left gave the visiting Los Angeles Rams a 26-24 victory, earned them a postseason date and dashed the playoff hopes of the New Orleans Saints, who were bidding also for the first winning season in the franchise's 17-year history.

Minutes later in Chicago, Bob Thomas kicked a 22-yard field goal with 10 seconds remaining to give the Bears a 23-21 victory over Green Bay and eliminate the Packers from playoff consideration.

In the American Football Conference, the Seattle Seahawks decided their own destiny by defeating the New England Patriots, 24-6, to survive a four-team run at the remaining AFC postseason berth, a wild-card spot.

The ouster of the Saints paved the way to the playoffs for the Rams and San Francisco 49ers, who meet Dallas tonight (9 o'clock, TV-Channel 6) in the final game of the regular season.

If the 49ers defeat Dallas, they will be NFC West Division champions and the Rams will be the Cowboys'

(See PLAYOFFS on 4-D)

United Press International

Lansford cheers as his field goal gives the Rams a playoff spot

Pro football

REGULAR-SEASON FINALES

Atlanta 31, Buffalo 14
Baltimore 20, Houston 10
Chicago 23, Green Bay 21
Cleveland 30, Pittsburgh 10
Detroit 23, Tampa Bay 20
Kansas City 48, Denver 17
L.A. Raiders 30, San Diego 14
L.A. Rams 26, New Orleans 24
Seattle 24, New England 6

PLAYOFF QUALIFIERS

NFC division champions — Washington (14-2), Detroit (9-7) and San Francisco (9-6) or L.A. Rams (9-7).

NFC wild cards — Dallas (12-3) and San Francisco or L.A. Rams.

AFC division champions — Miami (12-4), Pittsburgh (10-6) and L.A. Raiders (12-4).

AFC wild cards — Denver (9-7) and Seattle (9-7).

PLAYOFF SCHEDULE

First round — AFC: Denver at Seattle, Saturday, 4 p.m. NFC: San Francisco or L.A. Rams at Dallas, Dec. 26, 2:30 p.m.

Conference semifinals — Dec. 31 and Jan. 1.

Conference championships — Jan. 8.

Super Bowl XVIII — Jan. 22 at Tampa, Fla., 4:30 p.m.

Detailed coverage of the NFL begins on Page 4-D.

Giant Steps

Second of five excerpts from the autobiography of Kareem Abdul-Jabbar.

Learning to walk tall in Harlem

By Kareem Abdul-Jabbar
and Peter Knobler

On the New York streets where I was growing up, if you didn't know how to fight you were in big trouble, and I just didn't have the instinct. I didn't have that many fights; I just lost all of them.

When I was born in 1947, my parents — Cora and Ferdinand Lewis "Al" Alcindor — were living in Harlem. Back then, Harlem was by no means paradise, but it wasn't the war zone it is today. When I was growing up, everyone around us had a job; to be on welfare was an embarrassment. My mother would take me to play in Central Park with no fear. People would leave their front doors open. Stealing was not tolerated. Anybody who got caught snatching a purse got handled by the people in the community. Some of the worst offenders would get thrown off the roof. People didn't play around.

We moved to the Dyckman Street projects in the Inwood section of Manhattan in 1950. By then, I already knew what to expect from my parents.

It was important to them to be respectable; they were definitely not going to have a thug for a son. Their primary focus, as far as I was concerned, was my education. In fact, it was almost all we talked about.

There wasn't a lot of emotion on display in the Alcindor household. My father was stern and powerful. I knew he loved me, but he didn't often go out of his way to let me hear about it. A large man — 6 feet, 3 inches tall, 200 pounds — he carried himself as if his mere bulk and the silence he maintained were a life statement.

But there was clearly a muse on the loose inside him as well. He enrolled in the Juilliard School of Music right after I was born and gradu-

(See GIANT STEPS on 7-D)

Philadelphia Daily News

Abdul-Jabbar says he was no prodigy at basketball

Tribune Company Syndicate Inc.

A young Lew Alcindor; education was a priority

Flyers and Red Wings battle to another 3-3 tie

By Angelo Cataldi
Inquirer Staff Writer

Bobby Clarke sat frozen in the Flyers' net, a look of disbelief on his face. The clock above him indicated that time had elapsed, that the Flyers had won. The red light behind him suggested otherwise.

And so, ultimately, did the scoreboard and the standings, as the Flyers watched a win dissolve into a 3-3 tie with the Detroit Red Wings last night before 16,049 disbelieving fans at the Spectrum.

The tying goal, by Detroit's Steve Yzerman, beat Flyers goalie Pelle Lindbergh and the clock by the narrowest of margins — a couple of inches and 1 haunting second — and closed out a weekend home-and-home series in which the teams produced back-to-back 3-3 ties.

"It's disappointing," said dejected and angry Flyers coach Bob McCammon. "I think we beat ourselves when we missed all of those scoring chances before that. That was just a tough game."

The game also was more than a little controversial. McCammon attacked on several fronts after the contest, and the officiating was again the primary target of his venom.

First, he wondered about the two apparent Flyers goals — especially the last one — that referee Bryan Lewis nullified. Second, he questioned the events of those final seconds. Finally, he openly criticized the lack of calls during an inconse[quential] 5-minute overtime.

"If the period wasn't over," he sa[id] of the tying goal, which was official[ly] recorded at 19 minutes, 59 seconds, "why didn't we have a face-off afte[r] that? I don't understand. He [Lewis] was so excited rooting for Detroit, [I] guess he forgot.

"There were at least three penal[ties] in that overtime, and he didn'[t] call any of them. When a penalty's a penalty, they've got to call them. I[f] they keep it up like this, they'r[e] going to hurt the game."

The final goal was an exercise in futility that exceeded even the Fly[ers'] norm in this frustrating season. The Wings pulled their goalie, Eddi[e] Mio, with 49 seconds remaining, and then pressed the Flyers relentlessly. On several occasions the puck bounced precariously close to the goal, but it wasn't until the final seconds were ticking off that the real danger arose.

With about three ticks left, the puck snaked into the crease, and Lindbergh dived for it. Just before he reached it, it bounded off Ron Duguay's stick and out to Yzerman, who snapped it through a knot of bodies and into the net. Long after the play, Clarke remained in the net, as the crowd grew silent.

"One second, 5 seconds, 20 seconds, it doesn't matter," reasoned Lindbergh. "I'm disappointed, of course.

(See FLYERS on 11-D)

December 19, 1983
Eagles are humiliated by St. Louis 31-7

1984

RECORD: 6-9-1, 5TH IN NFC EAST
HEAD COACH: MARION CAMPBELL

Schedule

Regular Season

Wk. 1	Sep 2	L	28-27	at New York Giants
Wk. 2	Sep 9	W	19-17	vs Minnesota Vikings
Wk. 3	Sep 16	L	23-17	at Dallas Cowboys
Wk. 4	Sep 23	L	21-9	vs San Francisco 49ers
Wk. 5	Sep 30	L	20-0	at Washington Redskins
Wk. 6	Oct 7	W	27-17	at Buffalo Bills
Wk. 7	Oct 14	W	16-7	vs Indianapolis Colts
Wk. 8	Oct 21	W	24-10	vs New York Giants
Wk. 9	Oct 28	L	34-14	vs St. Louis Cardinals
Wk. 10	Nov 4	T	23-23	at Detroit Lions (OT)
Wk. 11	Nov 11	L	24-23	at Miami Dolphins
Wk. 12	Nov 18	W	16-10	vs Washington Redskins
Wk. 13	Nov 25	L	17-16	at St. Louis Cardinals
Wk. 14	Dec 2	L	26-10	vs Dallas Cowboys
Wk. 15	Dec 9	W	27-17	vs New England Patriots
Wk. 16	Dec 16	L	26-10	at Atlanta Falcons

After a 1-4 start, the Eagles posted a 5-5-1 record in their final 11 games. Philadelphia's swarming defense set a then-club record of 60 quarterback sacks and was the catalyst for the team's improved play. Wilbert Montgomery established the Eagles' career rushing record for yards (6,538) and attempts (1,465), surpassing Steve Van Buren from 1944-1951. Kicker Paul McFadden established an Eagles' season scoring record with 116 points (top among rookies), surpassing Bobby Walston's 30-year mark of 114, and was named NFC Rookie of the Year. Quarterback Ron Jaworski suffered a broken leg at St. Louis in week 13, snapping his streak of 116 consecutive starts. Mike Quick was selected to the AFC-NFC Pro Bowl for the second straight year. By the end of the season there were widespread rumors of the team's owner Leonard Tose's financial problems.

1984 Philadelphia Eagles Stats

Passing	Comp	Att	Comp %	Yds	Y/Att	TD	Int	Rating
Ron Jaworski	234	427	54.8	2754	6.45	16	14	73.5
Joe Pisarcik	96	176	54.5	1036	5.89	3	3	70.6
Dean May	1	1	100.0	33	33.00	0	0	118.8
Wilbert Montgomery	0	2	0.0	0	0.00	0	0	39.6

Rushing	Rush	Yds	Avg	TD
Wilbert Montgomery	201	789	3.9	2
Hubie Oliver	72	263	3.7	0
Michael Haddix	48	130	2.7	1
Michael Williams	33	83	2.5	0
Andre Hardy	14	41	2.9	0
Joe Pisarcik	7	19	2.7	2
Ron Jaworski	5	18	3.6	1
Mike Quick	1	-5	-5.0	0

Receiving	Rec	Yds	Avg	TD
John Spagnola	65	701	10.8	1
Mike Quick	61	1052	17.2	9
Wilbert Montgomery	60	501	8.4	0
Michael Haddix	33	231	7.0	0
Hubie Oliver	32	142	4.4	0
Tony Woodruff	30	484	16.1	3
Kenny Jackson	26	398	15.3	1
Vyto Kab	9	102	11.3	3
Michael Williams	7	47	6.7	0
Melvin Hoover	6	143	23.8	2
Andre Hardy	2	22	11.0	0
Gregg Garrity	2	22	11.0	0

Punting	Punts	Yds	Avg	Blocked
Mike Horan	92	3880	42.2	0

Interceptions	Int	Yds	Avg	TD
Ray Ellis	7	119	17.0	0
Wes Hopkins	5	107	21.4	0
Elbert Foules	4	27	6.8	0
Herman Edwards	2	0	0.0	0
Brenard Wilson	1	28	28.0	0
Reggie Wilkes	1	6	6.0	0

Kicking	PAT Made	PAT Att	PAT %	FG Made	FG Att	FG %	Pts
Paul McFadden	26	27	96	30	37	81.1	116

The Philadelphia Inquirer

Sports Extra

section F

Monday, November 26, 1984

Last-minute kick sinks Eagles

WILEY PRICE, Associated Press

Jaworski, in the grasp of David Galloway (right) and Curtis Greer (bottom), on the play in which he was injured

O'Donoghue connects as Cards win, 17-16

By Jere Longman
Inquirer Staff Writer

ST. LOUIS — The Eagles saw the light at the end of the tunnel yesterday. As usual, it was a fatal vision.

It has happened with frustrating regularity over the last two seasons. Always, the Eagles are close. Seldom are they close enough.

Last season, the Eagles lost six games by a total of 15 points. This year, they have tied Detroit and lost three one-point games, the latest coming in yesterday's 17-16 heartbreaker won by St. Louis.

As Neil O'Donoghue's 44-yard field goal drifted over the crossbar with 8 seconds left, the Eagles drifted to 5-7-1. They will have to finish the season with virtually no playoff hopes and without Ron Jaworski, who broke the fibula in his left leg three plays into the game.

Safety Ray Ellis has called the Eagles the best "almost" team in the National Football League. However, the standings measure only wins and losses.

"We've been so close, yet so far from victory," Ellis said. "We're almost there, but that's not good enough. The only thing that counts is the final score. I'd rather be the best winning team in football than the best losing team. But so far, we've been on the short end of the stick."

The Eagles had plenty of chances to win yesterday. Again, they found a way to lose. Three mistakes nailed the coffin shut.

• Early in the second quarter, with the Eagles trailing 7-3, Joe Pisarcik, in replacement of Jaworski, launched a perfect rainbow down the left sideline to Melvin Hoover.

Safety Bennie Perrin and cornerback Lionel Washington ran into a pick by Mike Quick, freeing Hoover for what should have been a 50-yard touchdown pass. Instead, the ball bounced harmlessly off Hoover's right shoulder inside the 5.

"No comment," Hoover said.

Said Pisarcik, "I got hit, so I didn't see the play, but I heard he should have caught it."

• With 4:18 left in the game and the Eagles trailing 14-13, Paul McFadden lined up for a chip shot. This one was a 26-yard field goal attempt, a glorified extra point.

McFadden would kick three field goals before the game ended — from 31, 43 and 32 yards. He would set an Eagles season record with 26 field goals. But this chip shot, this 26-yarder, he would hook to the left.

"I have no excuses," McFadden said. "I just pulled the ball. The snap was fine, the hold was fine, the pro-

(See EAGLES on 7-F)

Pro football

Cincinnati 35, Atlanta 14
Washington 41, Buffalo 14
Cleveland 27, Houston 10
New York Giants 28, Kansas City 27
Los Angeles Rams 34, Tampa Bay 33
Pittsburgh 52, San Diego 24
Chicago 34, Minnesota 3
L.A. Raiders 21, Indianapolis 7
San Francisco 35, New Orleans 3
Seattle 27, Denver 24

Coverage of the rest of the NFL begins on Page 4-F

His streak, and his season, ends

By FRANK DOLSON

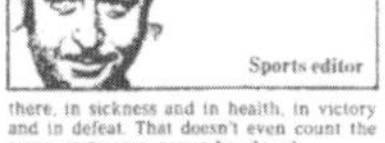

Sports editor

ST. LOUIS — The human body was not designed to play pro football. Not on those schoolyard-hard, plastic, green carpets that cover too many big-league playing fields in this age of multipurpose stadiums. Not when high-speed collisions with 250- and 260-pounders are all in a day's work.

Somehow, Ron Jaworski had survived in this world of super-hard knocks. From the day he made his debut as quarterback for the Philadelphia Eagles — Sept. 18, 1977 — through yesterday at Busch Stadium, Jaworski never missed a starting call. For 116 straight times — the most consecutive starts ever by an NFL quarterback — he went out there, in sickness and in health, in victory and in defeat. That doesn't even count the seven postseason games he played.

Sure, there have been much longer iron-man streaks in professional sports. Heck, Lou Gehrig made it through 2,130 consecutive games for the Yankees. But Gehrig was a baseball player, not a quarterback. He had to face only 90 m.p.h. fastballs, not King Kong-sized defensive ends and blitzing linebackers.

One of the remarkable aspects of Jaworski's streak — surely one of the most noteworthy in all of professional sports — is that hardly anybody paid any attention to it. Maybe folks were too busy chanting, "We want Joe," when the Eagles' offense sputtered. More likely, they simply took it for granted that No. 7 would be out there, shrugging off the blitzes

(See DOLSON on 6-F)

Off the bench, Pisarcik almost pulls out a win

By Jere Longman
Inquirer Staff Writer

ST. LOUIS — When Ron Jaworski's left leg was placed in a cast yesterday, Joe Pisarcik was suddenly cast as the Eagles' No. 1 quarterback.

The Eagles lost the game, 17-16, but Pisarcik never lost his poise. He threw 39 passes and completed 24 for 226 yards, including a 16-yard touchdown pass to Mike Quick.

"Joe did an outstanding job," Jaworski said. "He does a good job of preparing every week. He doesn't get a chance to play that often, but he's prepared to play every time. I've got so much respect for him."

With Pisarcik at quarterback, the Eagles controlled the ball for 35 of the game's 60 minutes. In fact, they controlled everything but the final score.

Pisarcik was sacked four times, but he remained relaxed in the pocket, throwing to Tony Woodruff and John Spagnola over the middle, hitting Quick on curls and corner patterns and discreetly dumping off to the running backs.

If Melvin Hoover had not dropped a potential 50-yard touchdown pass in the first half, Pisarcik — not St. Louis kicker Neil O'Donoghue — probably would have been the hero of this game.

"It's my job to come in and play the best I can and help the team to win," Pisarcik said. "This is my 11th year. I think it's expected of me to come in

(See PISARCIK on 6-F)

Joe Pisarcik
After McFadden's missed FG

Jamaican native wins Philadelphia marathon

By Mike Bruton
Inquirer Staff Writer

Ringo Adamson attacked The Hill while those all around him respected it, and that was the key to his winning the Philadelphia Independence Marathon yesterday.

Adamson, a native of Jamaica who lives in Glassboro, N.J., separated himself from a cluster of front-runners just past the 12-mile mark on a torturous incline in Chestnut Hill and held off second-place finisher Geoff Mearns to finish first in 2 hours, 16 minutes, 39 seconds.

Mearns, who came back to challenge Adamson from the 17th through the 21st mile, faltered about 2 miles from the finish line and came in at 2:17:29. Philadelphia's Mike Patterson, the pre-race favorite, was fifth at 2:20:56.

Barbara Filutze, a 38-year-old mother of three from Erie, Pa., was the women's champion with a time of 2:42:30.

The starter's gun started 3,740 runners, roughly 10 percent of them women, on their trek from Temple University's Ambler campus to the finish line at Fifth and Chestnut Streets in downtown Philadelphia.

It was a perfect day for a marathon. The air was still and crisp, with the temperature climbing into the 50s before the race was over. The Hill was the only adverse element along the picturesque 26-mile, 385-yard course.

Adamson, 24, conquered the mile-long slope that rises 285 feet, even as that slope was intimidating other competitors.

"Everyone gets scared of running those things," said Adamson, who finished 51st in this year's Olympic marathon under the Jamaican flag. "I'm really good at running them. I really break people like that."

Adamson, the assistant manager of an athletic footwear store at Deptford Mall, had a mile split of 6:08 on The Hill.

Mearns, a 23-year-old first-year law student at the University of Virginia, fell back about 50 yards, leaving him just ahead of Terry Colton of England, Patterson and Frank Melo of Newark, N.J., on the slope.

"The hill seems to divide the race very quickly," said Mearns, who finished second here in 1982 and fifth last year. "My theory is that you can't win a race like that — on a hill. You

(See MARATHON on 12-F)

The Philadelphia Inquirer / BRYAN GRIGSBY

Ringo Adamson signals his victory as he reaches the finish line at Fifth and Chestnut

Analysis

Flyers soaring at quarter pole

By Al Morganti
Inquirer Staff Writer

Again and again, you hear complaints that the National Hockey League's regular season is meaningless.

Yet when you consider that before Thanksgiving — before the season was a quarter over — coaches had been fired in Vancouver and Minnesota, it becomes clear that the regular season must mean something.

It is especially meaningful in Philadelphia, where the Flyers are trying to use an almost completely restructured team to get back in the hunt for the Stanley Cup.

Although it can be argued that the early season has little bearing on what will happen in April, the young Flyers, rookie coach Mike Keenan and new general manager Bob Clarke need measuring sticks such as the quarter pole (20 games), which they reached with a 4-4 tie in Hartford Saturday night.

With that tie, the Flyers not only extended their unbeaten streak to

(See FLYERS on 9-F)

•

The Flyers have some surprising statistics after 20 games. Page 4-F.

1984

November 26, 1984 - Eagles QB Ron Jaworski snaps his streak of 116 consecutive starts when he breaks his leg in a loss to St. Louis 17-16

1985

RECORD: 7-9, 4TH IN NFC EAST
HEAD COACH: MARION CAMPBELL & FRED BRUNEY

SCHEDULE

REGULAR SEASON

Wk. 1	Sep 8	L	21-0	at New York Giants
Wk. 2	Sep 15	L	17-6	vs Los Angeles Rams
Wk. 3	Sep 22	W	19-6	at Washington Redskins
Wk. 4	Sep 29	L	16-10	vs New York Giants (OT)
Wk. 5	Oct 6	L	23-21	at New Orleans Saints
Wk. 6	Oct 13	W	30-7	vs St. Louis Cardinals
Wk. 7	Oct 20	W	16-14	vs Dallas Cowboys
Wk. 8	Oct 27	W	21-17	vs Buffalo Bills
Wk. 9	Nov 3	L	24-13	at San Francisco 49ers
Wk. 10	Nov 10	W	23-17	vs Atlanta Falcons (OT)
Wk. 11	Nov 17	W	24-14	at St. Louis Cardinals
Wk. 12	Nov 24	L	34-17	at Dallas Cowboys
Wk. 13	Dec 1	L	28-23	vs Minnesota Vikings
Wk. 14	Dec 8	L	17-12	vs Washington Redskins
Wk. 15	Dec 15	L	20-14	at San Diego Chargers
Wk. 16	Dec 22	W	37-35	at Minnesota Vikings

On March 12,1985, Leonard Tose, the Eagles owner since 1969, announced an agreement to sell the team to Norman Braman and Ed Leibowitz for a reported $65 million. Braman officially became the Eagles' new owner on April 29 1985. That same day, Braman elevated Harry Gamble, general manager since February 4, to vice president-general manager overseeing day-to-day operations of the club. All-time Eagles rushing leader Wilbert Montgomery did not report to camp and was traded to Detroit for linebacker Garry Cobb in the preseason. Reggie White signed a free-agent contract and ended the season as the NFC Defensive Rookie of the Year. The Eagles would struggle out of the gate again, losing four of their first five games. The Eagles would recover by winning five of their next six games to get into playoff contention.
However, a four-game losing streak would end all postseason hopes, and Coach Marion Campbell was fired on December 16. In the final game of the season interim coach Fred Bruney led the Eagles to a win over the Vikings in Minnesota as the Eagles finish with a 7-9 record. Following the season the Eagles named Buddy Ryan, who was the defensive coordinator for the Chicago Bears, as their new Coach. Mike Quick, who caught 71 passes to break his own club season record, and Wes Hopkins represent Philadelphia in the AFC-NFC Pro Bowl.

1985 PHILADELPHIA EAGLES STATS

Passing	Comp	Att	Comp %	Yds	Y/Att	TD	Int	Rating
Ron Jaworski	255	484	52.7	3450	7.13	17	20	70.2
Herman Hunter	1	2	50.0	38	19.00	1	0	135.4
Randall Cunningham	34	81	42.0	548	6.77	1	8	29.8

Rushing	Rush	Yds	Avg	TD
Earnest Jackson	282	1028	3.6	5
Michael Haddix	67	213	3.2	0
Randall Cunningham	29	205	7.1	0
Herman Hunter	27	121	4.5	1
Ron Jaworski	17	35	2.1	2
Major Everettt	4	13	3.3	0
Hubie Oliver	1	3	3.0	0

Interceptions	Int	Yds	Avg	TD
Wes Hopkins	6	36	6.0	1
Ray Ellis	4	32	8.0	0
Herman Edwards	3	8	2.7	1
Evan Cooper	2	13	6.5	0
Rich Kraynak	1	26	26.0	0
Mike Reichenbach	1	10	10.0	0
Roynell Young	1	0	0.0	0
Reggie Wilkes	0	2	0.0	0

Receiving	Rec	Yds	Avg	TD
Mike Quick	73	1247	17.1	11
John Spagnola	64	772	12.1	5
Michael Haddix	43	330	7.7	0
Kenny Jackson	40	692	17.3	1
Herman Hunter	28	405	14.5	1
Ron Johnson	11	186	16.9	0
Earnest Jackson	10	126	12.6	1
Gregg Garrity	7	142	20.3	0
Dave Little	7	82	11.7	0
Major Everettt	4	25	6.3	0
Keith Baker	2	25	12.5	0
Hubie Oliver	1	4	4.0	0

Punting	Punts	Yds	Avg	Blocked
Mike Horan	91	3777	41.5	0

Kicking	PAT Made	PAT Att	PAT %	FG Made	FG Att	FG %	Pts
Paul McFadden	29	29	100	25	30	83.3	104

The Philadelphia Inquirer

Sports Extra

section D

Monday, November 11, 1985

Eagles work overtime for 23-17 win

The Philadelphia Inquirer / CLEM MURRAY

Pelle Lindbergh with his mask, ready for action

A 'Little Swede' with a big heart and a love of life

By Al Morganti
Inquirer Staff Writer

The Stanley Cup seems like a trinket now, the Vezina Trophy nothing more than worthless metal, and sports in general so much trivia.

All that matters now is that Pelle Lindbergh, 26, is brain-dead, connected to a life-support system in a New Jersey hospital.

His beating heart might seem to be caught up in a futile effort, but for those who know Pelle Lindbergh, there can be no doubt that he would give every last push to carry on with life.

An appreciation

It doesn't seem possible that it's over so quickly.

It doesn't seem possible that Lindbergh won't be at practice this morning as usual, dressing in his locker with the little Swedish flag on top, calling people over to look at his latest trinket and then skating onto the ice with his teammates.

It doesn't seem possible that Pelle Lindbergh is likely to soon be only a memory. Of course, his number 31 is likely to hang from the Spectrum's rafters, and his name will remain on the Vezina Trophy that he won as the NHL's best goalie last season.

But to those who know him, Lindbergh is so much more than a goalie. He is a very special person whose love of life made his transition from playing in Sweden to playing in North America as smooth as if he'd grown up in Philadelphia.

Think back to what he means, and the montage is a strange collection of on-the-ice and off-the-ice happenings. On the hockey side, there are the great saves, so many that they run into each other, and the white fiberglass mask that became both his trademark and, literally, his game face.

Away from the rink, there is the memory of Lindbergh at the Flyers' Christmas party, holding hands and skating with his fiancee, Kerstin Pietzsch; the bizarre picture of the Little Swede wearing the floppy cowboy hat at last season's all-star game in Calgary, and the sight of him driving away from practice in his red Porsche.

His love of cars was just another extension of his love of life — a fast, fun life. He wasn't a hard liver, not in the traditional sense. In fact, he hardly drank, and he was far too worried about his health to run around at all hours.

But he did love speed, and he had expensive toys. In addition to his Porsche 930 Turbo, he had a speedboat in Sweden and a collection of miniature toy cars at his home in Marlton.

Ultimately, he found tragedy in his love of driving.

"We warned him about driving too fast," said Flyers general manager Bob Clarke. "I guess I shouldn't say that, I don't know that he drove fast. But with that car and all, we were all worried about him.

"I guess, when you're that young, and that strong, and feel that much on top of the world, I guess you feel invincible. Hey,

(See APPRECIATION on 8-D

The Philadelphia Inquirer / JOHN PAUL FILO

Mike Quick is halted by the Falcons' Wendell Cason after making a first-half pass reception

99-yard pass tops Falcons

By Angelo Cataldi
Inquirer Staff Writer

The Eagles played another game of Russian roulette yesterday at Veterans Stadium and dodged another bullet.

This time, it was the usually lethal left foot of Atlanta kicker Mick Luckhurst that misfired. This time, it was the normally deadly feet of Mike Quick that didn't.

The scoreboard showed a 23-17 overtime victory for the Eagles over the Falcons, but the difference between success and failure in this curious game was more accurately measured in yards than in points.

Luckhurst's potential game-winning field-goal attempt missed the left upright by no more than a couple of tantalizing yards, and safety Scott Case's bid for an interception on the final play of the game fell one straining stride short.

Case's ill-advised gamble permitted Quick to collect a blur of a pass by quarterback Ron Jaworski at about the 20-yard line and then chug 80 free, happy yards to the end zone for a 99-yard touchdown and a victory that squared the Eagles' record at 5-5.

Temporarily obscured in the explosion of cheers by the 63,694 fans after Quick's jaunt was the fact that the Eagles had given away a 17-point fourth-quarter lead — and almost their season — against one of the NFL's sorriest teams.

"We dodged another bullet," nose tackle Kenny Clarke said through a relieved smile. "That's what you've got to do. There are 16 games in a season, and every one's an adventure."

If the end truly justifies the means, then the Eagles probably will rerun the film of that final play until it unravels on the reel. This was survival football at its sweetest — and its most precarious.

There were 13 minutes, 20 seconds remaining in overtime when — on second down from his 1-foot-line — Jaworski dropped back into the end zone and delivered the ball on a timing pattern to Quick, who had slipped between cornerback Bobby Butler and Case up the seam of a zone defense.

When Quick turned to look upfield after collecting the ball, he already knew what he would see there. Nothing.

"I knew there was no stopping me unless I tripped and fell," he said. "I knew I had them."

"The safety went for it," Jaworski said. "Maybe he thought I was too old to throw it like that anymore."

And so it was that the Eagles posted the first overtime victory in their history and once again rescued their hopes of making the playoffs.

(See EAGLES on 4-D)

Eagles forced to go the distance by yet another 'patsy' opponent

By FRANK DOLSON

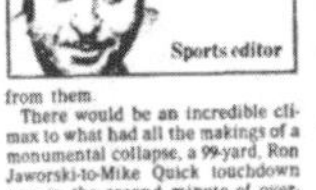

Sports editor

The good news for the fainthearted among Eagles rooters is that their heroes have no more "patsies" to play, no more "sure victories" on their National Football League schedule.

Two weeks ago, hosting a Buffalo team that had won only one game, the Eagles didn't start playing until they were 17 points down in the final quarter, and they barely managed to pull out a 21-17 victory.

Yesterday, against an Atlanta team that had won only one game, the Eagles stopped playing in the fourth quarter, blew a 17-point lead, and came within a few feet of having the game, and their season, slip away from them.

There would be an incredible climax to what had all the makings of a monumental collapse, a 99-yard, Ron Jaworski-to-Mike Quick touchdown pass in the second minute of overtime. But as spectacular as that goal-

(See DOLSON on 5-D)

NFL results

Dallas	13	Washington	7
Cincinnati	27	Cleveland	10
Chicago	24	Detroit	3
Green Bay	27	Minnesota	17
Buffalo	20	Houston	0
New England	34	Indianapolis	15
New York Giants	24	Los Angeles Rams	19
Pittsburgh	36	Kansas City	28
Tampa Bay	16	St. Louis	0
Seattle	27	New Orleans	3
San Diego	40	L. A. Raiders	34
Miami	21	New York Jets	17

Detailed NFL coverage begins on Page 5-D

Earnest Jackson
Rushed for 74 yards

The Philadelphia Inquirer / VICKI VALERIO

The Sixers observing a moment of silence for goalie Pelle Lindbergh before last night's game

Determined Malone scores 35 to lift Sixers to 105-97 win over Bucks

By Mike Bruton
Inquirer Staff Writer

The Sixers won last night, in large part because Moses Malone wanted to win.

But there were other reasons why the 76ers, a team that seemed to be bent on self-destruction Friday night in a humiliating loss to San Antonio, defeated the Milwaukee Bucks, 105-97, before a crowd of 10,090 in the Spectrum.

One of them was Milwaukee forward Terry Cummings' failure to score in double figures for the first time since he entered the league in 1982-83.

Because of Charles Barkley's defense, with help off the bench from Terry Catledge, Cummings played like a man who had wandered into the building.

Cummings' six-point effort snapped a 239-game streak of double-digit scoring. He had been second in that category to the Lakers' Kareem Abdul-Jabbar, who has 624 straight games with 10 or more points.

Another reason was Julius Erving's ability to neutralize Milwaukee point forward Paul Pressey.

There was a stirring of emotion in the Sixers' locker room before the game. Obviously, they were upset about Friday's 107-95 loss to San Antonio, but they also had Flyers goalie Pelle Lindbergh on their minds.

Lindbergh had been listed as brain-dead after suffering multiple injuries in an automobile crash at 5:41 a.m. yesterday in Somerdale, N.J.

"It wasn't a good day for all of Philadelphia, including myself," said Erving, who had 20 points, 12 rebounds, 3 assists and 3 steals. "We were very, very quiet before we went out. Our hearts go out to the Flyers because it's a genuine sports tragedy."

Against the Bucks, the Sixers were at their predatory best, protecting the lane and scoring 17 points off 16 steals.

The Sixers' defense fueled the offense, and they ran the fastbreak the way coach Matt Guokas had hoped they would in every game.

It all started with Malone, who set a relentless pace from the start of the game.

The Sixers center had 25 points and 12 rebounds at halftime and finished with 35 points and 14 boards.

Malone, who used Milwaukee centers Alton Lister, Paul Mokeski and Randy Breuer like props in a personal highlight film, had 15 points in

(See SIXERS on 3-D)

November 11, 1985 - Eagles win their first overtime win in team history against Atlanta 23-17. Jaworski hits Quick with a 99-yard TD reception, tying the longest TD in NFL history.

1986

RECORD: 5-10-1, 4TH IN NFC EAST
HEAD COACH: BUDDY RYAN

Schedule

Regular Season

Wk. 1	Sep 7	L	41-14	at Washington Redskins
Wk. 2	Sep 14	L	13-10	at Chicago Bears (OT)
Wk. 3	Sep 21	L	33-7	vs Denver Broncos
Wk. 4	Sep 28	W	34-20	vs Los Angeles Rams
Wk. 5	Oct 5	W	16-0	at Atlanta Falcons
Wk. 6	Oct 12	L	35-3	at New York Giants
Wk. 7	Oct 19	L	17-14	vs Dallas Cowboys
Wk. 8	Oct 26	W	23-7	vs San Diego Chargers
Wk. 9	Nov 2	L	13-10	at St. Louis Cardinals
Wk. 10	Nov 9	L	17-14	vs New York Giants
Wk. 11	Nov 16	L	13-11	vs Detroit Lions
Wk. 12	Nov 23	L	24-20	at Seattle Seahawks
Wk. 13	Nov 30	W	33-27	at Los Angeles Raiders (OT)
Wk. 14	Dec 7	T	10-10	vs St. Louis Cardinals (OT)
Wk. 15	Dec 14	W	23-21	at Dallas Cowboys
Wk. 16	Dec 21	L	21-14	vs Washington Redskins

Buddy Ryan, defensive coordinator of the Chicago Bears' Super Bowl XX Champions, was named the seventeenth head coach in Eagles history on January 29, 1986. On July 16, Norman Braham became the sole owner of the team, purchasing the remaining 35 percent from his brother-in-law Ed Leibowitz. Harry Gamble was promoted to president-chief operating officer. Ryan made sweeping changes in the Eagles roster, keeping young players and releasing several veterans. The youthful Birds struggle to a 5-10-1 record against the toughest schedule in the league. One highlight of the season was the play of second-year quarterback Randall Cunningham, who became a double threat with his throwing arm and his scrambling abilities; Cunningham took the starting job away from Ron Jaworski. The Birds placed two players on the AFC-NFC Pro Bowl roster: wide receiver Mike Quick and defensive end Reggie White. White tied a Pro Bowl record with four sacks and was named MVP of the game.

1986 Philadelphia Eagles Stats

Passing	Comp	Att	Comp %	Yds	Y/Att	TD	Int	Rating
Randall Cunningham	111	209	53.1	1391	6.66	8	7	72.9
Ron Jaworski	128	245	52.2	1405	5.73	8	6	70.2
Keith Byars	1	2	50.0	55	27.50	1	0	135.4
Matt Cavanaugh	28	58	48.3	397	6.84	2	4	53.6

Rushing	Rush	Yds	Avg	TD
Keith Byars	177	577	3.3	1
Randall Cunningham	66	540	8.2	5
Anthony Toney	69	285	4.1	1
Michael Haddix	79	276	3.5	0
Junior Tautalatasi	51	163	3.2	0
Charles Crawford	28	88	3.1	1
Ron Jaworski	13	33	2.5	0
Matt Cavanaugh	9	26	2.9	0
Mike Waters	5	8	1.6	0
Kenny Jackson	1	6	6.0	0
John Teltschik	1	0	0.0	0

Interceptions	Int	Yds	Avg	TD
Andre Waters	6	39	6.5	0
Roynell Young	6	9	1.5	0
Alonzo Johnson	3	6	2.0	0
Terry Hoage	1	18	18.0	0
Elbert Foules	1	14	14.0	0
Jody Schulz	1	11	11.0	0
Seth Joyner	1	4	4.0	0
Garry Cobb	1	3	3.0	0
Evan Cooper	0	3	0.0	20

Receiving	Rec	Yds	Avg	TD
Mike Quick	60	939	15.7	9
Junior Tautalatasi	41	325	7.9	2
John Spagnola	39	397	10.2	1
Kenny Jackson	30	506	16.9	6
Michael Haddix	26	150	5.8	0
Dave Little	14	132	9.4	0
Anthony Toney	13	177	13.6	0
Gregg Garrity	12	227	18.9	0
Ron Johnson	11	207	18.8	1
Keith Byars	11	44	4.0	0
Phil Smith	6	94	15.7	0
Mike Waters	2	27	13.5	0
Byron Darby	2	16	8.0	0
Bobby Duckworth	1	7	7.0	0

Punting	Punts	Yds	Avg	Blocked
John Teltschik	108	4493	41.6	0
Randall Cunningham	2	54	27.0	0

Kicking	PAT Made	PAT Att	PAT %	FG Made	FG Att	FG %	Pts
Paul McFadden	26	27	96	20	31	64.5	86

1986

The Philadelphia Inquirer

Sports Extra

section D

Monday, October 6, 1986

Eagles make Falcons shutout victims

The Philadelphia Inquirer / JOHN PAUL FILO

Von Hayes signs autographs for fans before the game at the Vet.

Phils cap season by beating Expos

By Peter Pascarelli
Inquirer Staff Writer

The Final Day passed with some personal goals unrealized, but the big picture remained rosy for the Phillies.

The Phils ended the 1986 season with a yawn-filled 2-1 win in 10 innings yesterday over the Montreal Expos. That left the Phils with an 86-75 record, the first time all season they were 11 games over .500.

A crowd of 25,293 left the Phils with a season home attendance of 1,933,335.

"I think we're all very satisfied with the way things went," said manager John Felske, who earlier yesterday received a contract extension through 1988.

"At no time could anyone question the players' effort," he said, "even when we didn't play well. And I think it will be exciting to look at ways to make us better over the winter, because a lot of our people are just going to get better."

If there was any disappointment yesterday, it was the failure of Von Hayes and Mike Schmidt to meet personal goals.

Hayes fell 2 RBIs short of 100, his big chance coming in the sixth inning, when he popped up with the bases loaded.

"I wanted the 100 RBIs, no doubt about it," said Hayes, who finished his magnificent season with a .305 average, 19 homers, 98 RBIs, 107 runs scored (tied for the league lead) and 46 doubles (a league high).

"But you have to give that Expos pitcher [Bob] Sebra credit. He had four pitches, and he would throw you off-speed stuff when behind in the count.

"I feel good about the season. Before opening day, I set my goal as driving in between 80 and 100 runs, and next year I'm going to raise my sights. . . . And the biggest thing was that we finished [11] games over .500. I think that makes it a successful year and an indication that we're a good team that is going to get better."

Meanwhile, Schmidt, who did not start yesterday, popped up in his only at-bat. He fell 2 RBIs short of equaling his career high of 121, finishing the year with a .290 average and with league-leading totals in homers (37) and RBIs (119). Those are numbers that likely are good enough for him to win his third Most Valuable Player award.

"I feel I have a good shot at MVP," Schmidt said. "I just came into today with nothing left. I just couldn't grind it out anymore, so it didn't make sense to play. I'm also unhappy with the way I hit the last week or so of the season, when I wanted to put up some more numbers. . . . But the year ends with the definite feeling that this team is very close to being right up there. I don't think the Mets are any better than the Phillies right now, but over 162 games they obviously were."

A big part of the Phils' strong second half and their optimism for next year was Bruce Ruffin, who yesterday pitched nine innings without a decision in his final start, allowing one run and eight hits.

"Winning nine games in a little over half of a season is pretty satisfying," Ruffin said. "If I can come out of spring training strong . . . I think winning 20 games could be a realistic goal for me."

Ruffin was nicked for a second-

(See PHILLIES on 3-D)

Bad start, promising ending

By Peter Pascarelli
Inquirer Staff Writer

Months ago such a news conference had seemed impossible. But yesterday in a final-day affirmation of the Phillies' 1986 success, club president Bill Giles announced the following developments:

- As expected, manager John Felske has had his contract extended through the 1988 season, and all five of the Phils' coaches — Lee Elia, Jim Davenport, Del Unser, Claude Osteen and Mike Ryan — have been rehired for next season.
- While Giles acknowledged that the Phils' catching was "not what it should be," he said he believed the club must improve that position from within rather than try to deal for an established catcher.
- The Phillies would like an established starting pitcher and a left-handed reliever and will seek them through trades and possibly the free-agent market. But Giles added, "I don't anticipate making a lot of deals because at least this year I don't think we have a lot we can afford to trade."

In that vein, Giles later added, "We have four players in Schmidt, Hayes, Samuel and Wilson who we will not

(See SEASON on 3-D)

The Philadelphia Inquirer / GREG LANIER

Mike Quick hauls in a pass from Ron Jaworski over Atlanta's Scott Case in the third quarter.

TD catch by Quick sets tone

By Angelo Cataldi
Inquirer Staff Writer

ATLANTA — As Mike Quick twist ed his body away from the defende and stretched his left arm to its ful lest extension, only his fingertip were able to touch the fading foot ball on its flight through the end zone.

But then an amazing thing hap pened yesterday at Atlanta-Fulton County Stadium. The ball stuck. I didn't bounce away, it didn't slithe off and it didn't flop to the ground i a cloud of dust and distress.

This time, neither the chance for a miraculous play nor the opportunity for a magnificent victory would slip through the fingers of an Eagle team that had a score to settle with the Atlanta Falcons — and settled i with this remarkable score: 16-0.

The victory was the second in a row for the Eagles after three losses and it was their first shutout since a 38-0 win against St. Louis on Dec. 20 1981. Atlanta, which had the top rated offense in the NFL before the game — but certainly not after it — lost its first contest of the season.

Yet this was a game to be measured not by statistics so much as by snip pets of action that suggested a star tling change in fortune — and i perspective — for an Eagles fran chise that has languished through four consecutive losing seasons.

It was a contest to be remembered for linebacker Garry Cobb's four stampeding sacks, halfback Junior Tautalatasi's daring 56-yard dance through the Atlanta secondary, quar terback Ron Jaworski's precise spi rals and — above all — Quick's magi cal catch.

The game was scoreless late in the second quarter, and the Eagles were 8 tantalizing yards from the Atlanta goal line when Jaworski uncorked an arching toss toward Quick, who had cut to the middle of the field and then hooked back toward the righ sideline.

There was no conceivable way for Quick to control the ball on his fin gertips, pull it into his body and then land on the ground without jarring it loose. But Quick snatched it with his left hand, tucked it into his mid section and then landed with a roll that shielded the ball from his im pact with the clumpy turf.

"I knew I had a chance to get my hand on the ball," Quick said, "and once I got it there, it stuck. It just stuck. I think that was one of the best catches I've ever made."

"When Mike makes a catch like that, all I can do is shake my head," said fellow wide receiver Ron John

(See EAGLES on 4-D)

On Atlanta's sideline, Campbell couldn't hide his frustrations

By FRANK DOLSON

Sports editor

ATLANTA — He came out onto the field at the last possible minute, presumably to avoid any emotional pregame hellos, and when it was over, after his old team, the Eagles, had shocked his present team, the Falcons, 16-0, and a parade of winners had come over to shake his hand and wish him luck, Marion Campbell was the first man to dash out of the Atlanta locker room.

But it wasn't necessary to talk to him yesterday to sense how much he wanted to win this game, how badly he wanted to beat Buddy Ryan, Ron Jaworski and the rest of the guys in green.

Normally, the man who was head coach of the Philadelphia Eagles through two full seasons and 15 games of a third isn't the demonstrative type.

"Marion, as you all know, likes to do all his talking and performing on the field," said Atlanta linebacker Reggie Wilkes, another longtime wearer of the green. "He doesn't try to get involved in the pregame hype or the postgame hype. He deserves a lot of credit and a lot of respect. He's a class act, whatever adjective you want to use. He's a good man."

And yesterday, on a rare October

(See DOLSON on 4-D)

Pro football

Washington	14	New Orleans	6
Chicago	23	Minnesota	0
New England	34	Miami	7
New York Giants	13	St. Louis	6
Cleveland	27	Pittsburgh	24
Detroit	24	Houston	13
Cincinnati	34	Green Bay	28
L.A. Raiders	24	Kansas City	17
Denver	29	Dallas	14
San Francisco	35	Indianapolis	14
New York Jets	14	Buffalo	13
L.A. Rams	26	Tampa Bay	20

Roy Hinson
A 7-footer in a 6-9 body

Hinson has the right stuff to avoid disappearing in Barkley's shadow

By Mike Bruton
Inquirer Staff Writer

LANCASTER — When you play alongside Charles Barkley, anonymity can become a formidable opponent.

You might as well have the word *FORWARD* stitched across the back of your jersey.

If, perchance, fans are curious, they can look you up in the game program to discover that your first name is "Other."

Bobby Jones, now retired, had no problem with that situation. He preferred keeping a low profile.

Jones' likely replacement, a pleasant man, also is not one to grapple for recognition. But it may take more than playing opposite Barkley to keep him from being noticed.

Roy Hinson is listed as being 6 feet, 9 inches tall, but he is all arms and legs, and he looks — and plays — more like a 7-footer.

When he spreads his arms in the lane, he casts an imposing shadow on any point guard looking to get the ball inside. Getting a pass by him must be like trying to throw the ball by a windmill.

The 25-year-old Trenton native is the type of player who makes opposing shooters hesitate before pulling the trigger, wondering, "Where is Hinson?" for they know they could end up with the word *Spalding* imprinted on their foreheads.

Hinson runs well, soars fluidly, scores when called on and rebounds. He is sinewy and as strong as

(See SIXERS on 8-D)

Sails are hoisted Down Under to spar for the Auld Mug

By Al Morganti
Inquirer Staff Writer

FREMANTLE, Australia — The walls of the Auld Mug Tavern on High Street are lined with pictures of J-boats, sloops and sleek 12-meter yachts that have raced for past America's Cups, but crew members aren't allowed to arm-wrestle in the pub anymore.

They still have some lively arguments about what kind of keel is going to work best in the slop and chop of the Indian Ocean, whether the vicious wind called The Doctor will blow anybody overboard, and if New Zealand really has a shot with its fiberglass boats.

The crew members can argue all they want, but arm-wrestling is taboo.

The end of that tradition, which used to settle many an argument, was sounded with a loud *snap* during the 12-meter world championships here in February. It was during those races that a winch-grinder from New Zealand broke the arm of one of his counterparts from Australia.

Some people are wondering if the tradition would have been ended if the Aussie had broken the New Zealander's arm. But that's a moot point — this is the Australians' show.

The Aussies rule the waves. So, until they lose, it's Aussie rules.

Technically, this will be the 26th defense of the America's Cup. But down here, the Americans' 132-year hold on the Cup seems to have been erased from memory, and the competition, which began yesterday, is being billed as "Australia's First Defence."

This isn't Newport, and the Americans — especially the New York Yacht Club — are given no special treatment. All right, so maybe the Aussies are looking at the Yanks as their biggest threat, but there are no guarantees that an American boat will even reach the finals.

In all probability, one of the six American teams will match up with an Australian defender in the best-of-seven America's Cup races, which are scheduled to begin Jan. 31.

But until then, the Americans have just five entries among 13 from six countries that will attempt to earn the right to challenge for the Cup. The Australians will run a simultaneous series to choose a defender.

Within the Auld Mug Tavern, there is some disagreement about which American team could come out on top. The opinion is split between America II, which is the entry of the venerable New York Yacht Club, and Stars & Stripes '87, which has Dennis Conner, now sailing for the San Diego Yacht Club, at the helm.

Conner, who won the Auld Mug as

(See CUP on 10-D)

Index

Australia's Pat Cash defeated Brad Gilbert in four sets to give his country an insurmountable lead over the United States in the Davis Cup semifinals. Sports in brief, Page 8-D.

Penn State's offense has been more imaginative than last year's. Page 7-D.

October 6, 1986 - Eagles defeat Atlanta 16-0 for their first shutout since 1981

1987

RECORD: 7-8, 4TH IN NFC EAST
HEAD COACH: BUDDY RYAN

SCHEDULE

REGULAR SEASON

Wk. 1	Sep 13	L	34-24	at Washington Redskins
Wk. 2	Sep 20	W	27-17	vs New Orleans Saints
Wk. 4	Oct 4	L	35-3	vs Chicago Bears
Wk. 5	Oct 11	L	41-22	at Dallas Cowboys
Wk. 6	Oct 18	L	16-10	at Green Bay Packers (OT)
Wk. 7	Oct 25	W	37-20	vs Dallas Cowboys
Wk. 8	Nov 1	W	28-23	at St. Louis Cardinals
Wk. 9	Nov 8	W	31-27	vs Washington Redskins
Wk. 10	Nov 15	L	20-17	vs New York Giants
Wk. 11	Nov 22	L	31-19	vs St. Louis Cardinals
Wk. 12	Nov 29	W	34-31	at New England Patriots (OT)
Wk. 13	Dec 6	L	23-20	at New York Giants (OT)
Wk. 14	Dec 13	L	28-10	vs Miami Dolphins
Wk. 15	Dec 20	W	38-27	at New York Jets
Wk. 16	Dec 27	W	17-7	vs Buffalo Bills

In March, quarterback Ron Jaworski was put on waivers after the club decided not to guarantee his contract. The Eagles split their first two games before a NFL players' strike led to the use of replacement players. The Eagles replacement team was not even competitive, losing all three games, to put the Eagles into a 1-4 hole. Making matters worse, the Cowboys regulars who crossed the picket line rolled up to score in a 41-22 humiliation in Dallas. The Eagles would get revenge in a 37-20 win when the regulars returned at the Vet. The Eagles would go on to finish with a 7-8 record, as the regulars went 7-5. Offensively, wide receiver Mike Quick earned his fifth consecutive trip to the AFC-NFC Pro Bowl while quarterback Randall Cunningham (Pro Bowl first alternate) emerged as a rising talent. Cunningham threw 23 touchdown passes and became the first quarterback to lead his team in rushing (505 yards) since the Bears' Bobby Douglass did so in 1972. Defensive end Reggie White, who was named the NFL's defensive player of the year, led the defense. White's 21 sacks set an NFC record and fell one shy of the NFL mark.

1987 PHILADELPHIA EAGLES STATS

Passing	Comp	Att	Comp %	Yds	Y/Att	TD	Int	Rating
Randall Cunningham	223	406	54.9	2786	6.86	23	12	83.0
Scott Tinsley	48	86	55.8	637	7.41	3	4	71.7
Marty Horn	5	11	45.5	68	6.18	0	0	65.7
Guido Merkens	7	14	50.0	70	5.00	0	0	64.6
Anthony Toney	0	1	0.0	0	0.00	0	0	39.6
Cris Carter	0	1	0.0	0	0.00	0	0	39.6
Otis Grant	0	1	0.0	0	0.00	0	0	39.6

Rushing	Rush	Yds	Avg	TD
Randall Cunningham	76	505	6.6	3
Anthony Toney	127	473	3.7	5
Keith Byars	116	426	3.7	3
Michael Haddix	59	165	2.8	0
Reggie Brown	39	136	3.5	0
Jacque Robinson	24	114	4.8	0
Junior Tautalatasi	26	69	2.7	0
Alvin Ross	14	54	3.9	1
John Teltschik	3	32	10.7	0
Kenny Jackson	6	27	4.5	0
Otis Grant	1	20	20.0	0
Bobby Morse	6	14	2.3	0
Scott Tinsley	4	2	0.5	0
Topper Clemons	3	0	0.0	0
Marty Horn	1	0	0.0	0
Matt Cavanaugh	1	-2	-2.0	0
Guido Merkens	3	-8	-2.7	0

Interceptions	Int	Yds	Avg	TD
Elbert Foules	4	6	1.5	0
Andre Waters	3	63	21.0	0
Seth Joyner	2	42	21.0	0
Michael Kullman	2	25	12.5	0
Jerome Brown	2	7	3.5	0
Terry Hoage	2	3	1.5	0
Evan Cooper	2	0	0.0	0
Roynell Young	1	30	30.0	0
Byron Evans	1	12	12.0	0
Cedrick Brown	1	9	9.0	0
Troy West	1	0	0.0	0

Receiving	Rec	Yds	Avg	TD
Mike Quick	46	790	17.2	11
Anthony Toney	39	341	8.7	1
John Spagnola	36	350	9.7	2
Junior Tautalatasi	25	176	7.0	0
Kenny Jackson	21	471	22.4	3
Keith Byars	21	177	8.4	1
Otis Grant	16	280	17.5	0
Gregg Garrity	12	242	20.2	2
Mike Siano	9	137	15.2	1
Eric Bailey	8	69	8.6	0
Reggie Brown	8	53	6.6	0
Jimmie Giles	7	95	13.6	1
Michael Haddix	7	58	8.3	0
Kevin Bowman	6	127	21.2	1
Cris Carter	5	84	16.8	2
Jay Repko	5	46	9.2	0
Alvin Ross	5	41	8.2	0
Jacque Robinson	2	9	4.5	0
Topper Clemons	1	13	13.0	1
Dave Little	1	8	8.0	0
Bobby Morse	1	8	8.0	0
Randall Cunningham	1	-3	-3.0	0
Reggie Singletary	1	-11	-11.0	0

Punting	Punts	Yds	Avg	Blocked
Mark Royals	5	209	41.8	0
John Teltschik	82	3131	38.2	0
Dave Jacobs	10	369	36.9	0
Guido Merkens	2	61	30.5	0

Kicking	PAT Made	PAT Att	PAT %	FG Made	FG Att	FG %	Pts
Paul McFadden	36	36	100	16	26	61.5	84
Dave Jacobs	2	4	50	3	5	60.0	11

1987

The Philadelphia Inquirer
Sports Extra
section C
Monday, October 5, 1987

Ersatz Eagles lay an embarrassing egg

The Philadelphia Inquirer / CLEM MURRAY

Guido Merkens fumbles after being hit by Jim Althoff for one of Chicago's 11 sacks. Merkens, who was sacked 10 times, recovered.

Replacement Bears romp to 35-3 victory

By Bill Ordine
Inquirer Staff Writer

When Eagles owner Norman Braman promised "good" and "competitive" football in the NFL's replacement games, most folks knew enough to snicker at the "good" part but conceded that there probably would be a measure of competitiveness between equally ragged and ill-prepared teams.

Yesterday, however, it was evident that there are degrees of ragged and ill-prepared. Beyond bad, there is worse. Beyond worse, there is worst. And beyond worst, there are the replacement Philadelphia Eagles.

In the slapstick farce that unfolded in the empty cavern of Veterans Stadium yesterday, the only thing missing was Guido Merkens, the backup quarterback and sometime punter, getting hit in the face by a custard pie as the inept Eagles fill-ins were mauled by the fill-in Bears, 35-3.

The last time anyone saw a bunch of guys take as many pratfalls as the Eagles did yesterday, Mack Sennett was coaching the Keystone Kops.

In a game featuring two teams that had practiced for all of 10 days, it wasn't surprising to see a punt blocked, a high snap out of shotgun formation produce a loss of 32 yards and the ball, and an improvised run out of punt formation lose 9 yards. What was surprising is that all of that happened to just one team — the Eagles.

And there was more:

• The Eagles gave up 11 sacks for 70 yards. Merkens took 10 of those sacks.

• Yellow flags were falling like — well, like Guido Merkens — as Philadelphia was penalized 11 times.

• The Eagles fumbled five times, losing the ball on two of those occasions, and averaged 2.2 yards per

(See EAGLES on 4-C)

Strike Sunday: A day for losers

By FRANK DOLSON

Sports editor

You've heard it said time and time again: Nobody wins in a strike. That may be true, but seldom have we seen as many losers as turned up yesterday at Veterans Stadium.

It wasn't just the strikebreaking team disguised as the Philadelphia Eagles who lost, and lost big, to a strikebreaking team disguised as the Chicago Bears. That alone would have been no big deal.

It wasn't just Buddy Ryan, coach of the green-and-white-shirted, red-faced squad that came out on the short end of a 35-3 score (not that surprising when you consider he spent much of the week making fun of his players), who lost, and lost big.

It wasn't just the National Football League, which decided it was more important to play these games with makeshift teams and count them in the standings than to consider the best interests of the fans and the integrity of the sport, that lost, and lost big.

Sadly, the biggest loser on this day may have been the City of Philadelphia, its image battered and beaten every bit as badly as Buddy Ryan's bogus and bewildered Birds.

Surely, the lasting image of this miserable excuse for a football game will be that televised one of a fan walking out of the Vet — and smack dab into a sucker punch thrown by one of the union types who massed outside the stadium.

It was a day on which Norman Braman, the owner of the Eagles,

(See DOLSON on 5-C)

Pro football

				Attendance
Chicago	35	EAGLES	3	4,074
Tampa Bay	31	DETROIT	27	4,919
LOS ANGELES RAIDERS	35	Kansas City	17	7,500
Indianapolis	47	BUFFALO	6	9,860
Dallas	38	NEW YORK JETS	24	12,370
Green Bay	23	MINNESOTA	16	13,911
Cleveland	20	NEW ENGLAND	10	14,830
Pittsburgh	28	ATLANTA	12	16,667
San Diego	10	CINCINNATI	9	18,074
SEATTLE	24	Miami	20	19,448
WASHINGTON	28	St. Louis	21	27,728
NEW ORLEANS	37	Los Angeles Rams	10	29,745
Houston	40	DENVER	10	38,494

Home team in CAPITALS.

Report: Union ready to end strike

From Inquirer Wire Services

Player representatives from the 28 NFL teams are scheduled to meet tonight in Chicago amid growing speculation that the NFL Players Association soon will ask striking players to return to work.

Quoting unnamed union sources, yesterday's Daily Breeze in Torrance, Calif., reported that the NFLPA would announce today or tomorrow that it was dropping its demands for free agency and would ask players to return to their teams.

The sources told the paper that the union's decision to drop free agency as an issue in the 13-day strike was prompted by the massive defection of players who crossed picket lines on Friday and the threat of entire teams crossing this week. Eighty-six players have crossed the picket lines so far.

"Teams in as many as seven cities have told the union they will come across en masse this week unless free agency is dropped and bargaining resumes," one of the sources said.

Members of the Cleveland Browns, San Francisco 49ers and Los Angeles Raiders all have mentioned the possibility of having their teams cross picket lines after this weekend's games.

NFLPA executive director Gene Upshaw said that the meeting would be an attempt to get the stalled negotiations started again.

"We have to do something to get the parties to negotiate," he said. "Gene Upshaw has never represented his view, but represented the players. If the players change their mind, it's Gene Upshaw's job to change his mind.

"The player reps will determine tomorrow what we do. The majority will rule. . . . We have to do what's good for all of us."

Doug Allen, the union's assistant director, said that the fact that a meeting was being called did not mean that the union was going to concede anything.

"There is no plan to throw in the towel, no plan to go back to work without a contract," Allen said. "It's going to take good-faith negotiations

(See STRIKE on 7-C)

Afleet tops Lost Code in Derby

By Don Clippinger
Inquirer Staff Writer

Afleet, seemingly beaten in Philadelphia Park's stretch, found another gear yesterday and roared back to defeat Lost Code by 2¼ lengths in the $300,000 Pennsylvania Derby.

Afleet, ridden by Gary Stahlbaum, had matched strides with Arlington Classic winner Lost Code almost from the start. But Afleet fell back on the Bucks County track's final turn and handed Lost Code a 2½-length lead in midstretch.

The Pennsylvania Derby appeared to be over as the two front-runners headed toward the wire. But Afleet kicked in and surged again, blasting past Lost Code with 100 yards left to run and drawing away to the wire.

Although the early fractions were relatively slow, Afleet completed the Pennsylvania Derby's 1⅛ miles in a stakes record 1 minute, 48 1/5 sec-

(See DERBY on 10-C)

Index

The Cards' Ozzie Smith doesn't have much size, and he doesn't have *any* home runs. The question is, should that make any difference?

United Press International

The case for Ozzie as MVP

By Jayson Stark
Inquirer Staff Writer

ST. LOUIS — He stands 5-foot-11. And he weighs 160 pounds. And if you stood him up next to Andre Dawson, he would look practically like Emmanuel Lewis.

Well, Ozzie Smith knows that people who are built like the star of *Webster* haven't won a whole lot of MVP awards. He also knows that people who go two years without hitting a home run haven't won a whole lot of MVP awards. He also knows that people who are famous mostly for their defensive acrobatics haven't won a whole lot of MVP awards.

But there's a funny thing going on. An increasing number of people think that the most valuable player in the National League this year just might be none other than Osborne Earl Smith, diminutive and homerless and glove-oriented as he might be.

His manager, Whitey Herzog, is now branding the Wizard "a very bona fide candidate." In fact, the manager is boosting Smith's candidacy these days more than the candidacy of Jack Clark — the man who was the clear-cut MVP of the first four months but only the Amelia Earhart of the last two.

And remember, the manager made a big case for Smith as the MVP in 1982, when he was just a .248-hitting leatherworker. Herzog's premise in those days was that Ozzie Smith stopped 100 runs a year with that Gold Glove of his, and heck, that was the same as knocking in 100, right?

Now here we are five years later, and he still stops as many runs as ever. But in case you hadn't noticed, Ozzie Smith doesn't just play defense anymore.

He possesses the eighth-highest batting average (.303) in the National League. And is second

(See OZZIE SMITH on 4-C)

Tigers edge Jays, rejoice over title

By Angelo Cataldi
Inquirer Staff Writer

DETROIT — While the Detroit Tigers charged onto the field in a stampede of arm-waving hysteria late yesterday afternoon, the Toronto Blue Jays stood transfixed in their dugout, unable to remove their gaze from the celebration.

After seven memorable games in 11 tense days, the emotions finally drained from both teams in that one final tableau — whoops and high fives and hugs among the winners, tears and trauma and introspection among the losers.

Every season provides a similiar scene at the end of a long, taut pennant race, but yesterday's 1-0 victory by the Tigers offered an especially vivid illustration of what it feels like to succeed, and also to fail.

"This is the best moment, the biggest moment, of my career in baseball," said Detroit manager Sparky Anderson, whose team overcame a 3½-game deficit in the final eight days of the season to win the American League East championship. "I said all year that I was proudest of this team because they gave me everything I asked, everything they had."

"You can't undo what happened," Toronto manager Jimy Williams said

(See TIGERS on 3-C)

Phillies lose, 4-2, to end season on a dismal note

By Peter Pascarelli
Inquirer Staff Writer

PITTSBURGH — During the Phillies' disheartening finish, Lee Elia resisted the temptation to emphatically enforce his will upon an often listless ball club.

But before the Phils' sorry 1987 season ended with them tied for fourth place after yesterday's 4-2 loss to the Pittsburgh Pirates, Elia made it clear that the team's lackluster season-ending play did not go unnoticed. He also said that what the Phils will need in a big way in 1988 is something called character.

"The most important thing I'd like to see is this club develop a sense of character, a sense of team," Elia said. "I've seen it at times, but I've also seen it disappear at times too.

"We simply have to get away from the singular approach to everything that has been too prevalent around here. I don't think our club has an understanding of what you call constructive criticism. Everything is taken too personally.

"It's nice to know you're good, but

(See PHILLIES on 3-C)

October 5, 1987 - Eagles replacement players are embarrassed by Chicago Bears 35-3

1988

RECORD: 10-6, 1ST IN NFC EAST
HEAD COACH: BUDDY RYAN

Schedule

Regular Season

Wk. 1	Sep 4	W	41-14	at Tampa Bay Buccaneers
Wk. 2	Sep 11	L	28-24	vs Cincinnati Bengals
Wk. 3	Sep 18	L	17-10	at Washington Redskins
Wk. 4	Sep 25	L	23-21	at Minnesota Vikings
Wk. 5	Oct 2	W	32-23	vs Houston Oilers
Wk. 6	Oct 10	W	24-13	vs New York Giants
Wk. 7	Oct 16	L	19-3	at Cleveland Browns
Wk. 8	Oct 23	W	24-23	vs Dallas Cowboys
Wk. 9	Oct 30	L	27-24	vs Atlanta Falcons
Wk. 10	Nov 6	W	30-24	vs Los Angeles Rams
Wk. 11	Nov 13	W	27-26	at Pittsburgh Steelers
Wk. 12	Nov 20	W	23-17	at New York Giants (OT)
Wk. 13	Nov 27	W	31-21	vs Phoenix Cardinals
Wk. 14	Dec 4	L	20-19	vs Washington Redskins
Wk. 15	Dec 10	W	23-17	at Phoenix Cardinals
Wk. 16	Dec 18	W	23-7	at Dallas Cowboys

Post Season

Divisional Playoffs				
	Dec 31	L	20-12	at Chicago Bears

Under third-year head coach Buddy Ryan; the Eagles would get off to a slow start losing 3 straight after winning their season opener. The Eagles would continue to play mediocre football until the middle of the season when they sat at 4-5. However, the Eagles would catch fire winning 6 of their final 7 games to capture the NFC East with a 10-6 record. Driving the Eagles Division Title run is QB Randall Cunningham who passes 3,808 yards and adds 624 yards with his legs. However, in the Divisional Playoffs the Eagles traveled to Chicago for an NFC Divisional Playoff game against the Bears and a place in NFL history. The game, which begins in sunny, 29-degree weather, would later be dubbed "The Fog Bowl," after a thick fog rolls off Lake Michigan late in the 2nd quarter. Due to the fog, visibility on the playing field was extremely difficult and the Bears prevail, 20-12.

1988 Philadelphia Eagles Stats

Passing	Comp	Att	Comp %	Yds	Y/Att	TD	Int	Rating
Randall Cunningham	301	560	53.8	3808	6.80	24	16	77.6
Matt Cavanaugh	7	16	43.8	101	6.31	1	1	59.6
John Teltschik	1	3	33.3	18	6.00	0	0	54.9
Keith Byars	0	2	0.0	0	0.00	0	0	39.6

Rushing	Rush	Yds	Avg	TD
Randall Cunningham	93	624	6.7	6
Keith Byars	152	517	3.4	6
Anthony Toney	139	502	3.6	4
Michael Haddix	57	185	3.2	0
Terry Hoage	1	38	38.0	1
John Teltschik	2	36	18.0	0
Junior Tautalatasi	14	28	2.0	0
Walter Abercrombie	5	14	2.8	0
Cris Carter	1	1	1.0	0

Interceptions	Int	Yds	Avg	TD
Terry Hoage	8	116	14.5	0
Eric Allen	5	76	15.2	0
Wes Hopkins	5	21	4.2	0
Seth Joyner	4	96	24.0	0
William Frizzell	3	19	6.3	0
Andre Waters	3	19	6.3	0
Roynell Young	2	5	2.5	0
Eric Everett	1	0	0.0	0
Jerome Brown	1	-5	-5.0	0
Todd Bell	0	24	0.0	0

Receiving	Rec	Yds	Avg	TD
Keith Jackson	81	869	10.7	6
Keith Byars	72	705	9.8	4
Cris Carter	39	761	19.5	6
Anthony Toney	34	256	7.5	1
Mike Quick	22	508	23.1	4
Ron Johnson	19	417	21.9	2
Gregg Garrity	17	208	12.2	1
Michael Haddix	12	82	6.8	0
Jimmie Giles	6	57	9.5	1
Junior Tautalatasi	5	48	9.6	0
Mark Konecny	1	18	18.0	0
Walter Abercrombie	1	-2	-2.0	0

Punting	Punts	Yds	Avg	Blocked
Randall Cunningham	3	167	55.7	0
John Teltschik	98	3958	40.4	0

Kicking	PAT Made	PAT Att	PAT %	FG Made	FG Att	FG %	Pts
Luis Zendajas	30	31	97	19	24	79.2	87
Dean Dorsey	9	9	100	4	7	57.1	21
Dale Dawson	3	3	100	0	1	0.0	3

The Philadelphia Inquirer
SUNDAY
January 1, 1989
SPORTS
SECTION E

Eagles mauled by their mistakes

The Philadelphia Inquirer / JERRY LODRIGUSS

Luis Zendejas (right) watches as the third of his four field goals sails toward the goal posts through the fog that descended on Soldier Field in the second quarter.

Bears to play for NFC title

By Bill Ordine
Inquirer Staff Writer

CHICAGO — Through a surreal fog, a Soldier Field crowd serenaded Buddy Ryan with a mocking rendition of "Auld Lang Syne" as the game clock ticked off the final seconds of the Eagles' season yesterday.

Ryan, whose defense had paced the Bears' Super Bowl drive three years ago, fell short of making a triumphant postseason return to Chicago, his Eagles stumbling, 20-12, in an NFC divisional playoff game.

It was a game destined to be remembered as the "Fog Bowl," if not by some similar appellation. An incredibly dense mist crept over the south end of the stadium late in the second quarter and engulfed the field for the rest of the afternoon.

While the Bears and Eagles both groped in the gray soup, the Eagles were in a mental fog. Penalties, dropped passes and missed defensive assignments were the chief culprits in their elimination from the playoffs.

"The only thing we felt could beat us today was ourselves, and that's what happened," middle linebacker Mike Reichenbach said.

On offense, the Eagles moved inside the Chicago 20-yard line nine times without scoring a touchdown. Two TDs were called back by penalties, and tight end Keith Jackson dropped a potential scoring pass with no one around him.

As for the defense, a blown assignment in the secondary allowed the Bears to jump ahead by 7-0 in the first period, and it was a lead that Chicago would not relinquish. The touchdown came on a 64-yard pass from quarterback Mike Tomczak to a wide-open receiver Dennis McKinnon 3 minutes, 2 seconds into the game.

"We missed all kinds of opportunities, and you have to credit the Bears' defense for that," Ryan said. "They kept us out of the end zone.

"We had a couple of touchdowns called back early on because of penalties, and it just seemed like, every time we went down there, nothing was happening for us.

"All year, it's been happening for us, but we couldn't make it happen today. So you have to credit the Bears for making the plays to keep us out of the end zone."

Through their stretch drive to the NFC East championship, the Eagles

(See EAGLES on 8-E)

Birds earned their loss, but with an assist by NFL

By FRANK DOLSON

Sports editor

CHICAGO — In 30-some years of covering sports, I thought I'd seen just about everything. Yesterday, sitting in a 50-yard-line seat at Soldier Field, I saw practically nothing.

Don't feel sorry for me, though. Think, instead, of the fans who paid to see a football game and spent the entire second half in a fog. Literally. Visiting teams dream about taking the home crowd "out of the game," but this was ridiculous.

"They ran a play on the other side, and I can't see what's going on over there," Buddy Ryan would say when it was over. "The guy sounds like he's going for 1,000 yards, and he only makes 2. You don't know what the hell's going on."

You know the fog's pretty thick when even the Eagles' head coach admits he's in it.

Barely 30 minutes after word spread that the game had ended, the fog lifted. As this is being written, it is possible to watch the Soldier Field ground crew pulling sections of tarpaulin over the field. Why, you wonder, didn't the NFL, in its infinite wisdom, in its quest for fair play, in its deep concern for its paying patrons, hold up the game until some visibility was restored?

Funny you should ask. Eagles owner Norman Braman and president/general manager Harry Gamble were asking the same thing, even though Ryan insisted he was perfectly content that the game went on.

"That's baseball, where you delay for rain and all that," he said. "This is football. . . ."

It was good of him to tell us. For the last hour or so, it was hard to tell what it was we weren't seeing.

The fog had appeared without warning, billowing in from the south with a little less two minutes to go in the first half and Eagles trailing, 17-6. It happened so fast and looked so thick that it might have been smoke from a nearby fire. A two-alarmer, at least. But no, it was a freak of nature, a cruel twist of fate that provided a

(See DOLSON on 10-E)

When all went blank, Bears led

By BILL LYON

CHICAGO — They had won a game they hadn't really seen, against the coach who once designed their carnivorous defense. They had won the right to crow, but it was the right to advance in the Super Bowl tournament that meant more to them.

So the Bears, who have never been accused of good table manners, were subdued yesterday when celebrating their fog-shrouded triumph over the Eagles in the NFC playoffs. As near as anyone could tell, the score was 20-12.

The day before, Buddy Ryan had ordered the team bus to circle Soldier Field, horn honking in a sophomoric show of defiance. And now the blowsy, blustery Bears, never candidates for Miss Manners role models, surely were primed to taunt their former coach with something like: "Yo, Buddy, honk this!"

But no such vindictiveness was forthcoming.

No window-smashing, furniture-breaking carousal this time. No, they were quite content to take their win and creep gratefully away. On little cat feet. Just like, ahem, fog.

The Bears had the good fortune to be in the lead when a fog bank off Lake Michigan suddenly cloaked Soldier Field and reduced visibility to invisibility. It was like trying to watch — and play — a game through gauze. And while it is true that both teams had to play, sort of, in the same squinting haze, the team on the front end of the score suddenly had a big edge when the world went blank.

The Bears seemed to know this. And they seemed, too, to realize that if Randall Cunningham could actually have seen whom he was throwing

(See LYON on 10-E)

The Philadelphia Inquirer / JERRY LODRIGUSS

Anthony Toney, being halted by Chicago's Mike Singletary on a carry in the second period, suffered through an afternoon he will not remember fondly. Story on Page 11-E.

What you saw was all you got

By Ron Reid
Inquirer Staff Writer

CHICAGO — The Eagles and Bears reportedly contested an exceedingly important playoff game yesterday at Soldier Field, but as to the key plays and star performers, most fans hadn't the foggiest.

What the fans did see, in the Bears' 20-12 victory that wrote a gloomy finish to the Eagles' season, was a pea-soup fog that drifted in off Lake Michigan with about two minutes left in the first half.

Eerily, within a matter of minutes, the fog quickly reduced visibility to about 10 yards and produced the most bizarre NFL contest in memory.

Through most of the second half, disgruntled fans who couldn't see what was happening on the field were kept informed by the public-address announcer, doing play-by-

(See FOG on 10-E)

Poulin ends drought as Flyers top Sabres

By Al Morganti
Inquirer Staff Writer

BUFFALO — It wasn't so very long ago that Dave Poulin was the Flyers' No. 1 offensive center, the guy who pulled the trigger for wingers Tim Kerr and Brian Propp.

But times have changed, and the Flyers captain has been assigned to a defensive role, which is why last night's performance must have been so sweet.

Poulin emerged from his role as a checking center to score a dramatic, picture-perfect backhanded goal with less than five minutes to play at the Buffalo Auditorium, where the Flyers defeated the Sabres, 3-2.

Poulin, who had only four goals during the first half of the season, broke into the Sabres' zone as part of a three-on-two break with linemates Scott Mellanby and Derrick Smith. Mellanby fed Poulin a pass from the right-wing boards, and Poulin placed a perfect backhanded shot over the blocker of goalie Daren Puppa with 4 minutes, 44 seconds to play.

Flyers goalie Ron Hextall made a couple of big saves during a Buffalo

(See FLYERS on 5-E)

Index

While the L.A. Lakers charted their downhill course, the Houston Rockets took off for a stay — albeit a brief one — atop the Midwest Division. Bob Ford, Page 3-E.

Here's how baseball can do America's hockey fans a big favor. Al Morganti, Page 4-E.

NHL, NBA	2-E	Ben Callaway	16-E
Flyers notes	5-E	Horse racing	16-E

Associated Press

The Bengals' Ickey Woods takes an aerial route to the goal line.

Woods and Cincinnati roll past Seattle, 21-13

By Dave Caldwell
Inquirer Staff Writer

CINCINNATI — He is a self-styled trend-setter who wears his hair in a pony tail and is the creator of the post-touchdown dance that he immodestly named the "Ickey Shuffle."

After himself, of course.

Cincinnati Bengals fullback Ickey Woods is only a rookie, but he already has made it quite clear he wants to be known as a man who likes to zig when others zag — on the field and off. And in yesterday's *other* NFL playoff game, Woods almost ran out of his wardrobe to boost Cincinnati to a dramatic 21-13 victory over Seattle.

As Woods, a 233-pound rookie from Nevada-Las Vegas, rumbled for a game-high 126 yards on 23 carries, a split in the seat of his white game pants widened. But Woods, like any trouper, never considered a costume change in mid-act.

"Hey," said Cincinnati tackle Anthony Munoz, "he was into the game, and he didn't want to change his pants. When he's running like that, you let him do whatever he wants."

Woods truly made an appropriate fashion statement, because Cincinnati (13-4) had to hang on by the seat of its pants for the victory over the rambling, gambling Seahawks (9-8), who registered two touchdowns in the fourth quarter to turn an apparent blowout into a white-knuckle finish.

"It's frustrating; the finality of it all is just a situation that's so hard to

(See BENGALS on 13-E)

Previews of today's playoff games — Vikings vs. 49ers and Oilers vs. Bills — are on Page 12-E.

January 1, 1989 - Eagles lose the NFC Divisional Playoff game to Chicago 20-12 in the infamous "Fog Bowl"

1989

RECORD: 11-5, 2ND IN NFC EAST
HEAD COACH: BUDDY RYAN

Schedule

Regular Season

Wk. 1	Sep 10	W	31-7	vs Seattle Seahawks
Wk. 2	Sep 17	W	42-37	at Washington Redskins
Wk. 3	Sep 24	L	38-28	vs San Francisco 49ers
Wk. 4	Oct 2	L	27-13	at Chicago Bears
Wk. 5	Oct 8	W	21-19	vs New York Giants
Wk. 6	Oct 15	W	17-5	at Phoenix Cardinals
Wk. 7	Oct 22	W	10-7	vs Los Angeles Raiders
Wk. 8	Oct 29	W	28-24	at Denver Broncos
Wk. 9	Nov 5	L	20-17	at San Diego Chargers
Wk. 10	Nov 12	L	10-3	vs Washington Redskins
Wk. 11	Nov 19	W	10-9	vs Minnesota Vikings
Wk. 12	Nov 23	W	27-0	at Dallas Cowboys
Wk. 13	Dec 3	W	24-17	at New York Giants
Wk. 14	Dec 10	W	20-10	vs Dallas Cowboys
Wk. 15	Dec 18	L	30-20	at New Orleans Saints
Wk. 16	Dec 24	W	31-14	vs Phoenix Cardinals

Post Season

Wild Card Playoffs				
	Dec 31	L	21-7	vs Los Angeles Rams

The Eagles used an aggressive, ball-hungry defense -- which led the NFL in takeaways (56) and interceptions (30), and set a team record with 62 QB sacks -- to improve their regular season record to 11-5. However, they would have to settle for the Wild Card despite beating the first place New York Giants twice. In the first post-season game at the Vet since 1981, the Los Angeles Rams shocked the Eagles by winning 21-7 on a rainy afternoon in Philadelphia and won the NFC Wild Card game.

1989 Philadelphia Eagles Stats

Passing	Comp	Att	Comp %	Yds	Y/Att	TD	Int	Rating
Randall Cunningham	290	532	54.5	3400	6.39	21	15	75.5
Roger Ruzek	1	1	100.0	22	22.00	1	0	158.3
Matt Cavanaugh	3	5	60.0	33	6.60	1	1	79.6

Rushing	Rush	Yds	Avg	TD
Randall Cunningham	104	621	6.0	4
Anthony Toney	172	582	3.4	3
Keith Byars	133	452	3.4	5
Mark Higgs	49	184	3.8	0
Heath Sherman	40	177	4.4	2
Robert Drummond	32	127	4.0	0
Mike Reichenbach	1	30	30.0	0
John Teltschik	1	23	23.0	0
Cris Carter	2	16	8.0	0
Ron Johnson	1	3	3.0	0
Matt Cavanaugh	2	-3	-1.5	0
Carlos Carson	1	-9	-9.0	0

Interceptions	Int	Yds	Avg	TD
Eric Allen	8	38	4.8	0
Eric Everett	4	64	16.0	1
William Frizzell	4	58	14.5	0
Izel Jenkins	4	58	14.5	0
Byron Evans	3	23	7.7	0
Al Harris	2	18	9.0	0
Clyde Simmons	1	60	60.0	1
Mike Golic	1	23	23.0	0
Andre Waters	1	20	20.0	0
Todd Bell	1	13	13.0	0
Seth Joyner	1	0	0.0	0

Receiving	Rec	Yds	Avg	TD
Keith Byars	68	721	10.6	0
Keith Jackson	63	648	10.3	3
Cris Carter	45	605	13.4	11
Ron Johnson	20	295	14.8	1
Anthony Toney	19	124	6.5	0
Robert Drummond	17	180	10.6	1
Jimmie Giles	16	225	14.1	2
Mike Quick	13	228	17.5	2
Gregg Garrity	13	209	16.1	2
Heath Sherman	8	85	10.6	0
Henry Williams	4	32	8.0	0
Mark Higgs	3	9	3.0	0
Anthony Edwards	2	74	37.0	0
Dave Little	2	8	4.0	1
Carlos Carson	1	12	12.0	0

Punting	Punts	Yds	Avg	Blocked
Randall Cunningham	6	319	53.2	0
John Teltschik	57	2246	39.4	0
Rick Tuten	7	256	36.6	0
Max Runager	17	568	33.4	0

Kicking	PAT Made	PAT Att	PAT %	FG Made	FG Att	FG %	Pts
Luis Zendajas	23	23	100	9	15	60.0	50
Roger Ruzek	14	14	100	8	11	72.7	38
Steve DeLine	3	3	100	3	7	42.9	12

The Philadelphia Inquirer

MONDAY
January 1, 1990

SPORTS EXTRA

SECTION D

Playoffs arrive, Eagles depart

Henry Ellard jumps for joy after his 39-yard TD catch in the first quarter. Eric Everett (42) was unable to prevent the TD after teammate Izel Jenkins' ill-fated leap.

L.A. rides fast start to victory

By Bill Ordine
Inquirer Staff Writer

The Eagles expected to take a Great Step Forward this season, but yesterday they were stopped cold in their tracks.

For the second year in a row, Buddy Ryan's team lost its opening playoff game, and the Eagles probably played worse in yesterday's NFC wild-card game than they did in their loss to the Chicago Bears in the divisional playoffs a year ago.

"I think we need to mature as a team," linebacker Seth Joyner said. "With the way we ended up last year and the way we ended up this year, it's the same. You'd think we'd learn something, but we didn't. We played terribly in a playoff game again."

The Eagles were short on offensive weapons going into the game, and the few they did have were defused by a smothering Los Angeles Rams defense. Stung by a pair of early touchdowns, the Eagles never recovered, and they exited from the playoffs, 21-7, at soggy Veterans Stadium.

"I wanted us to take that one step forward, but today wasn't the day to do it," Ryan said, repeating his often stated hope for the Eagles for this season. "We didn't make it happen, but we need to do that. I don't know how many times the Rams have been to the playoffs and didn't get past the first round."

Quarterback Randall Cunningham did not complete a pass for more than 2 yards until the Eagles trailed by 14-0. He finished with 24 completions in 40 attempts for 238 yards and no touchdowns, and he threw one interception. At halftime, he had thrown for only 78 yards and run for 9. The Eagles had only three first downs and had turned the ball over twice.

The Philadelphia game plan was to run, with Cunningham calling one of a couple of predetermined plays at the line of scrimmage. But two Rams touchdowns in the first 7 minutes, 20 seconds derailed that scheme. Then, when Cunningham went looking for his short-range receivers, he found a cordon of pass defenders in tight zone coverage.

"They [prepared] for what our offense does," Cunningham said. "They took [tight end] Keith Jackson away early. They took our wideouts away and our short passing game, as far as our tight end and halfbacks were concerned. I have to tip my hat to their defensive coordinator [Fritz Shurmur].

"A lot of times, I'd roll around the corner, and when I do that, normally I can get a fullback or a tight end coming across. But they did a great job."

Once Mike Quick was shelved for the season after the sixth game by knee surgery, the Eagles lacked any-

(See EAGLES on 4-D)

Inside

- The Rams took a novel approach on defense. — Page 4-D.
- Greg Bell's big run. — Page 4-D.
- Highlights and lowlights. — Page 5-D.
- A stunned secondary. — Page 6-D.

By FRANK DOLSON

Sports editor

Eagles talked, Rams listened

One team talked a good game.

The other team played it.

You might think that sort of pregame hype wouldn't matter in the pros. Think again. Football players are kids at heart. They spike footballs. They gesture. They strut. They taunt.

And when the other side talks too much, they listen. And remember. And use it to fuel their fire.

The Eagles did a lot of talking this past week. It's their style under Buddy Ryan. Be aggressive. Intimidate the opposition.

"Once the game starts, we got to go to war and take care of business," Jerome Brown had said, "because that's the way Buddy wants us to play."

It's their trademark, their strength. But talking about it isn't enough. You have to do it, too.

The Los Angeles Rams had heard it all. They weren't intimidated; they were motivated.

"We loved that," Jim Everett, their

(See DOLSON on 5-D)

Randall Cunningham and Keith Jackson after the defeat.

A dreary day, a dreary effort

By BILL LYON

And so, once again, the Eagles perish in pea soup.

Last season, in Chicago, young and inexperienced and still new to this bewildering thing called the NFL playoffs, they expired in impenetrable fog, far from home, on tough, alien turf.

This time, with the comforts and reassurances of home, a year older and supposedly a year wiser, allegedly better equipped to cope with playoff pressure, they came out and played in a fog, literally and figuratively.

In dark, dank gloom, pelted by a cold, relentless rain, their parka-clad followers sat in sullen silence, waiting for a reason to come to life.

None came.

The Eagles' fate then fell, as it usually does, at the feet of their quarterback.

The feet, on this day, were salt and pepper. Randall Cunningham was shod schizophrenically — white low-cut cleat on his right foot, black high-top on his left, as if he couldn't make up his mind. That footwear turned out to be symbolic of the way he — and the other Eagles — performed.

Bewildered by a Rams defense that he later conceded the Eagles were unprepared for, Cunningham sputtered through another fitful, indecisive afternoon. It should be pointed out that he was severely restricted by his own team, too. The Eagles' offense is sorely limited and offers precious few options.

The result was a 21-7 loss to the Rams, who at last escaped that surfer-boys-who-can't-win-beyond-the-beach rap. And the Eagles thus concluded, abruptly and unsatisfactorily, a season that will be perceived as a disappointment even though it was a winning one.

And Buddy Ryan, who built and promotes his reputation on defensive schematics, was outcoached in his area of expertise. The Rams' game plan, especially on defense, was obviously superior. A bitter footnote is that the Eagles lost to a team

(See LYON on 5-D)

Anderson's 50-yard FG lifts Steelers past Oilers

By Mike Bruton
Inquirer Staff Writer

HOUSTON — The stadium the Houston Oilers proudly call "The House of Pain" became a pleasure palace yesterday for the Pittsburgh Steelers.

Just 3 minutes, 26 seconds into overtime, Gary Anderson kicked a 50-yard field goal to give the Steelers a 26-23 victory over the Oilers in the AFC wild-card game.

Only moments after the kick — Anderson's longest attempt of the season — split the uprights, the Steelers erupted in celebration as the Oilers, widely expected to win this game, disappeared into the bowels of the Astrodome.

Anderson's performance, which also included field goals of 25, 30 and 48 yards, punctuated a gritty Pittsburgh showing against the self-proclaimed bad boys of the AFC.

In fact, the play that put the Steelers in position for Anderson's final kick was of the kind that Houston coach Jerry Glanville loves to see his players make.

Pittsburgh cornerback Rod Woodson, aided by nose tackle Gerald Williams, put a savage hit on running back Lorenzo White, forcing a fumble on Houston's only offensive play in overtime.

Woodson recovered his own trophy at the Houston 46-yard line and, five plays later, Anderson kicked the ball that spoiled extraordinary performances by Oilers quarterback Warren Moon and wide receiver Ernest Givins.

"It wasn't real pretty," said Steelers quarterback Bubby Brister. "It's not San Francisco. It's Pittsburgh Steeler football. It's knock-down, drag-out. It's blood and guts. We're playing hard, dirty football."

It was almost a replay of Houston's

(See AFC on 6-D)

Index

NBA, NHL	2-D
Sixers	2-D
Baseball	8-D
Sports in brief	8-D
Horse racing	10-D

Gary Anderson is all smiles after his winning kick in overtime.

Orange Bowl: Emotion runs deep

By Jere Longman
Inquirer Staff Writer

MIAMI — Before he died of cancer in September, Sal Aunese, Colorado's suffering, inspiring quarterback, wrote a message to his teammates.

The note was read posthumously. In part, it said: "Do not be saddened that you no longer see me in the flesh, because I assure you I will always be with you in spirit. Strive only for victory each time we play . . . go get 'em, and bring home the Orange Bowl."

Thus inspired, the top-ranked Buffaloes roamed to a perfect 11-0 season. A victory over Notre Dame tonight (Channel 3, 8 o'clock) in the Orange Bowl would give Colorado its first national championship.

"Sal is the main ingredient for getting this team close together," said all-America guard Joe Garten. "We told him we'd bring home the Orange Bowl. We didn't tell him we'd get this far and fall flat on our face."

A victory for the fourth-ranked Irish (11-1) would give Notre Dame claim to its second consecutive national title. Coach Lou Holtz's team will have played nine bowl teams after tonight. It has lost only once in the last 24 games. However, the wire service polls, not tonight's game, will ultimately decide Notre Dame's fate.

Holtz may have thrown some gasoline onto Colorado's emotional fire last week when remarks he made to his team at practice were picked up by a Denver television station and

(See ORANGE BOWL on 8-D)

Flyers and Canucks skate to 2-2 tie

By Joe Juliano
Inquirer Staff Writer

VANCOUVER — For its final game of the 1980s, the National Hockey League sent the Flyers to Canada's Pacific Coast for a New Year's Eve contest that was in progress while their fans toasted and welcomed the new year.

While it wasn't enough to rank on anyone's list of greatest games of the decade, the Flyers and the Canucks engaged in a crisp-checking affair that ended in a 2-2 tie before 15,778 would-be revelers at the Pacific Coliseum.

Pete Peeters, one of the NHL's best goalies during a portion of the '80s but reduced to part-time status now, played a good game in goal for the Flyers in his first action since Nov. 25. He turned aside 23 of 25 Vancouver shots but remained without a win this season.

Playing without defenseman Jay Wells, who was shaken up by a shot from Tom Laidlaw in the second period of Saturday night's 6-3 win over Los Angeles, the Flyers held leads of 1-0 and 2-1 in this game.

Keith Acton scored with less than three minutes gone in the game, but Vancouver's Brian Bradley tied it midway through the opening period. The Flyers' Doug Sulliman made it 2-1 early in the second, but ex-Flyer Rich Sutter scored with just 1 minute, 25 seconds left in the period to tie the game at 2-2.

The Flyers kept the heat on Canucks goalie Kirk McLean late in the

(See FLYERS on 3-D)

January 1, 1990 - First home playoff game at the Vet since 1981, the Eagles get defeated by the LA Rams 21-7 in the NFC Wild Card game

1989

1990's Decade in Review

1990
The decade opens with a closing ... of the Buddy Ryan era. Ryan's teams, though powerful, drop their playoff opener for the third straight year and at season's end owner Norman Braman hands over the coaching duties to offensive coordinator Rich Kotite.

QB Randall Cunningham leads the NFC in touchdown passes with 30 and the Eagles in rushing yards with 942.

1991
The Eagles lose Randall Cunningham to a season-ending knee injury on opening day but ride the league's best defense to a 10-6 finish. The defense becomes only the fifth unit in history to lead the league across the board. The defense also sends Reggie White, Jerome Brown, Clyde Simmons, Seth Joyner and Eric Allen to the Pro Bowl.

1992
Newly acquired running back Herschel Walker helps the Birds return to post-season play and win a playoff game at New Orleans, but the season is overshadowed by the death of Pro Bowl DT Jerome Brown in a June auto accident. Players honor their fallen teammate with special patches on their jerseys and the club retires his #99.

Off the field, a court ruling paves the way for NFL players to enjoy a more liberal form of free agency.

1993
Cornerback Eric Allen ties an NFL record and becomes only the third player in NFL history to return four interceptions for TDs in a single season.

1994
Boston native and Hollywood-based movie producer Jeffrey Lurie purchases the club from Norman Braman for nearly $200 million.

RB Herschel Walker becomes the first player in NFL history to log a 90-plus yard run, reception, and kickoff return for a score in a single season.

1995
In February, Jeffrey Lurie makes Ray Rhodes, defensive coordinator of the Super Bowl champion 49ers, the 19th head coach in Eagles history and the third African-American head coach in the modern NFL era. Running back Ricky Watters, the NFL's most prominent free agent acquisition that spring, also arrives from the 49ers.

The Birds crush Detroit in a Wild Card playoff game when they surge to a 51-7 lead and coast to a 58-37 win in the highest-scoring NFL playoff game ever.

Lurie is named NFL owner of the year by The Sporting News and Rhodes wins coach of the year honors.

Lurie and his wife, Christina, see to it that the Eagles will be a dynamic force in the community by launching Eagles Youth Partnership. The club's charitable wing, EYP focuses on enriching the health and education of at-risk youth.

1996
Powered by the NFC's #1 ranked offense, the Birds reach the playoffs for a second straight year. RB Ricky Watters leads the league in total yards from scrimmage and WR Irving Fryar sets a team record with 88 receptions. Eagles LB James Willis picks off a pass in the end zone at Dallas and laterals to CB Troy Vincent, who finishes off an NFL record 104-yard interception return.

1997
Ricky Watters becomes the first back in Eagles history to rush for over 1,000 yards in three straight seasons.

1999
Lurie replaces head coach Ray Rhodes with Packers QB's coach Andy Reid who, during his tenure in Green Bay, helped Brett Favre earn league MVP honors three straight times.

Reid uses the second overall pick in the draft to select Syracuse QB Donovan

Randall Cunningham

Herschel Walker

The Eagles' 1991 "Gang Green" defense

Eric Allen

Clyde Simmons, Eric Allen, Jerome Brown, Seth Joyner and Reggie White

Jerome Brown

THE CITY OF PHILADELPHIA
WELCOMES JEFFREY LURIE

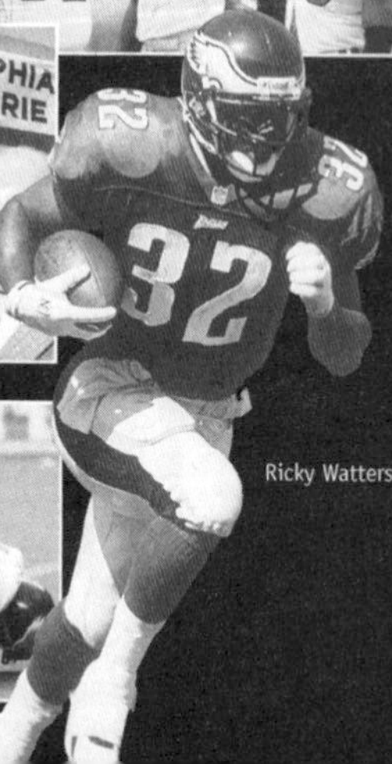
Ricky Watters

The Eagles crush Detroit in a 1995 Wild Card playoff game

1990's

DECADE WIN-LOSS RECORD:
80-79-1 (2-4 postseason record)

HOME FIELD:
Veterans Stadium 1990-1999

PLAYOFF APPEARANCES:
1990, 1992, 1995 and 1996

CHAMPIONSHIPS:
None

HEAD COACHES:
Buddy Ryan 1990 (10-6) (0-1 postseason record);
Rich Kotite 1991-94 (36-28) (1-1 postseason record);
Ray Rhodes 1995-98 (29-34-1) (1-2 postseason record);
Andy Reid 1999 (5-11)

HALL OF FAME INDUCTEES:
None

AWARD WINNERS:
Randall Cunningham, MVP 1990, Offensive MVP 1990,
C omeback Player of the Year 1992;
Reggie White, Defensive MVP 1991;
Eric Allen, NFC Defensive MVP 1993;
Jim McMahon, Comeback Player of the Year 1991;
Ray Rhodes, Coach of the Year 1995

ALL PRO:
Jerome Brown 1990-91;
Randall Cunningham 1990 and 1992;
Byron Evans 1990 and 1992;
Keith Jackson 1990; Reggie White 1990-92;
Eric Allen 1991 and 1992; Seth Joyner 1991-93,
Clyde Simmons 1991-92; Vai Sikahema 1992;
William Fuller 1995; Andy Harmon 1995;
William Thomas 1995

PRO BOWL SELECTIONS:
Jerome Brown 1991-92;
Randall Cunningham 1990-01;
Keith Jackson 1990-91; Reggie White 1990-92;
Eric Allen 1990, 1992-95;
Seth Joyner 1992 and 1994;
Clyde Simmons 1992-93; Fred Barnett 1993;
William Fuller 1995-97; William Thomas 1996-97;
Ricky Watters 1996-97; Irving Fryar 1997-98;

FIRST GAME OF THE DECADE:
September 9, 1990 loss to the
New York Giants 27-20

LAST GAME OF THE DECADE:
December 19, 1999 win over the
New England Patriots 24-9

LARGEST MARGIN OF VICTORY:
October 2, 1994 vs. the San Francisco 49ers 40-8

LARGEST MARGIN OF DEFEAT:
September 6, 1998 vs. the Seattle Seahawks 38-0

EAGLE FIRSTS OF THE DECADE:

NEW UNIFORM AND LOGO
In 1996, changed to Midnight Green with a fiercer screaming Eagle head

FIRST NFL STADIUM WITH A COURTROOM AND JUDGE:
Judge Seamus P. McCaffrey presided during games

FIRST NFL PLAYER TO SCORE ON 90-YARD RECEIVING, RUSHING, AND RETURNING PLAYS IN ONE SEASON:
In 1994 Herschel Walker achieved this feat.

1990

RECORD: 10-6, 2ND IN NFC EAST
HEAD COACH: BUDDY RYAN

Schedule

Regular Season

Wk. 1	Sep 9	L	27-20	at New York Giants
Wk. 2	Sep 16	L	23-21	vs Phoenix Cardinals
Wk. 3	Sep 23	W	27-21	at Los Angeles Rams
Wk. 4	Sep 30	L	24-23	vs Indianapolis Colts
Wk. 6	Oct 15	W	32-24	vs Minnesota Vikings
Wk. 7	Oct 21	L	13-7	at Washington Redskins
Wk. 8	Oct 28	W	21-20	at Dallas Cowboys
Wk. 9	Nov 4	W	48-20	vs New England Patriots
Wk. 10	Nov 12	W	28-14	vs Washington Redskins
Wk. 11	Nov 18	W	24-23	at Atlanta Falcons
Wk. 12	Nov 25	W	31-13	vs New York Giants
Wk. 13	Dec 2	L	30-23	at Buffalo Bills
Wk. 14	Dec 9	L	23-20	at Miami Dolphins (OT)
Wk. 15	Dec 16	W	31-0	vs Green Bay Packers
Wk. 16	Dec 23	W	17-3	vs Dallas Cowboys
Wk. 17	Dec 29	W	23-21	at Phoenix Cardinals

Post Season

Wild Card Playoffs				
	Jan 5	L	20-6	vs Washington Redskins

In February, Buddy Ryan hired Rich Kotite as offensive coordinator to improve the Eagles' sluggish attack. At season's end, the offense led the NFL in rushing (2,556) and time of possession (33:19) and the NFC in scoring (396) and touchdown passes (34). On the other side of the ball, the defense led the NFL in stopping the run (1, 169), thereby making the Birds the first team to lead the league in both rushing categories since Chicago did so in 1985. A 10-6 record put Philadelphia in the playoffs once again, but the Eagles suffered their third opening round defeat in as many seasons. The 20-6 Wild Card Game loss to Washington signaled an end to the five-year Ryan era. On January 8, 1991, owner Norman Braman announced that Ryan would not be offered a new contract. On the same day, he elevated Kotite to the head coaching position, noting that it was time for the Eagles "to reach the next plateau." Under Kotite, quarterback Randall Cunningham flourished with an NFC-leading 30 touchdown passes, 942 rushing yards, and a selection to the Pro Bowl, while rookie wide receivers Calvin Williams and Fred Barnett combined to make 17 touchdown receptions. Tight end Keith Jackson, defensive end Reggie White, and defensive tackle Jerome Brown also earned Pro Bowl berths, but running back Keith Byars, who tied a team record with 81 receptions and also threw four touchdown passes, was overlooked.

1990 Philadelphia Eagles Stats

Passing	Comp	Att	Comp %	Yds	Y/Att	TD	Int	Rating
Randall Cunningham	271	465	58.3	3466	7.45	30	13	91.6
Keith Byars	4	4	100.0	53	13.25	1	0	158.3
Jim McMahon	6	9	66.7	63	7.00	0	0	86.8
Jeff Feagles	0	1	0.0	0	0.00	0	0	39.6

Rushing	Rush	Yds	Avg	TD
Randall Cunningham	118	942	8.0	5
Heath Sherman	164	685	4.2	1
Anthony Toney	132	452	3.4	1
Thomas Sanders	56	208	3.7	1
Keith Byars	37	141	3.8	0
Roger Vick	16	58	3.6	1
Robert Drummond	8	33	4.1	1
Calvin Williams	2	20	10.0	0
Fred Barnett	2	13	6.5	0
Jeff Feagles	2	3	1.5	0
Jim McMahon	3	1	0.3	0

Interceptions	Int	Yds	Avg	TD
Wes Hopkins	5	45	9.0	0
William Frizzell	3	91	30.3	1
Eric Allen	3	37	12.3	1
Ben Smith	3	1	0.3	0
Byron Evans	1	64	64.0	1
Reggie White	1	33	33.0	0
Mike Golic	1	12	12.0	0
Seth Joyner	1	9	9.0	0
Terry Hoage	1	0	0.0	0

Receiving	Rec	Yds	Avg	TD
Keith Byars	81	819	10.1	3
Keith Jackson	50	670	13.4	6
Calvin Williams	37	602	16.3	9
Fred Barnett	36	721	20.0	8
Heath Sherman	23	167	7.3	3
Mickey Shuler	18	190	10.6	0
Anthony Toney	17	133	7.8	3
Mike Quick	9	135	15.0	1
Robert Drummond	5	39	7.8	0
Thomas Sanders	2	20	10.0	0
Kenny Jackson	1	43	43.0	0
Marvin Hargrove	1	34	34.0	1
Harper Le Bel	1	9	9.0	0

Punting	Punts	Yds	Avg	Blocked
Jeff Feagles	72	3026	42.0	2

Kicking	PAT Made	PAT Att	PAT %	FG Made	FG Att	FG %	Pts
Roger Ruzek	45	48	94	21	29	72.4	108

Lease a Loser

City's Dream Deal Isn't: **Page 3**

Tails & Heads

Why Style Hangs On: **Page 37**

MONDAY
DECEMBER 17, 1990

PHILADELPHIA DAILY
NEWS
THE PEOPLE PAPER

LATE SPORTS
35¢
50 CENTS OUTSIDE METROPOLITAN PHILADELPHIA
FOR HOME DELIVERY PHONE 665-1234

Playoff Power

GEORGE REYNOLDS/ DAILY NEWS

Eagles Randall Cunningham (left) and Anthony Toney rejoice during a 31-0 win that clinched a wild-card spot; seven pages in **Sports**

**December 17, 1990 - First home shutout since 1981,
Eagles 31-0 over Green Bay and clinch Wild Card spot**

1990

1991

RECORD: 10-6, 3RD IN NFC EAST
HEAD COACH: RICH KOTITE

SCHEDULE

REGULAR SEASON

Wk. 1	Sep 1	W	20-3	at Green Bay Packers
Wk. 2	Sep 8	L	26-10	vs Phoenix Cardinals
Wk. 3	Sep 15	W	24-0	at Dallas Cowboys
Wk. 4	Sep 22	W	23-14	vs Pittsburgh Steelers
Wk. 5	Sep 30	L	23-0	at Washington Redskins
Wk. 6	Oct 6	L	14-13	at Tampa Bay Buccaneers
Wk. 7	Oct 13	L	13-6	vs New Orleans Saints
Wk. 9	Oct 27	L	23-7	vs San Francisco 49ers
Wk. 10	Nov 4	W	30-7	vs New York Giants
Wk. 11	Nov 10	W	32-30	at Cleveland Browns
Wk. 12	Nov 17	W	17-10	vs Cincinnati Bengals
Wk. 13	Nov 24	W	34-14	at Phoenix Cardinals
Wk. 14	Dec 2	W	13-6	at Houston Oilers
Wk. 15	Dec 8	W	19-14	at New York Giants
Wk. 16	Dec 15	L	25-13	vs Dallas Cowboys
Wk. 17	Dec 22	W	24-22	vs Washington Redskins

On January 8th, team owner Norman Braman opted not to renew the contract of Buddy Ryan, the Eagles' head coach since 1986. On the same day, Braman promoted then-offensive coordinator Rich Kotite, making him the 18th head coach in club history. They opened with a 3-1 mark, their best start since 1981, despite having lost QB Randall Cunningham for the year due to a knee injury suffered at Green Bay on opening day. After coming on to lead the Eagles to their solid start, backup QB Jim McMahon was also injured in game 5. With McMahon sidelined, the Birds suffered through a four game skid. By midseason, Philadelphia had used five quarterbacks in eight games and seen its record sink to 3-5. The Eagles regrouped, however, and surged into contention for a playoff spot with a six-game winning streak (the club's longest since the start of '81) that upped their record to 9-5. But a loss at home to Dallas in game 15 ended Philadelphia's playoff hopes. They ended the season with a record of 10-6, and joined the 49ers as the only NFL clubs to post 10-or-more wins in each of the last four seasons. The defense finished the season ranked #1 in the NFL in terms of fewest yards allowed overall, vs. the run, and vs. the pass. As such, the Birds became only the fifth club in NFL history and the first since 1975 to accomplish this rare triple.

1991 PHILADELPHIA EAGLES STATS

Passing	Comp	Att	Comp %	Yds	Y/Att	TD	Int	Rating
Jim McMahon	187	311	60.1	2239	7.20	12	11	80.3
Jeff Kemp	57	114	50.0	546	4.79	5	5	60.1
Randall Cunningham	1	4	25.0	19	4.75	0	0	46.9
Brad Goebel	30	56	53.6	267	4.77	0	6	27.0
Pat Ryan	10	26	38.5	98	3.77	0	4	10.3
Keith Byars	0	2	0.0	0	0.00	0	1	0.0

Rushing	Rush	Yds	Avg	TD
James Joseph	135	440	3.3	3
Keith Byars	94	383	4.1	1
Heath Sherman	106	279	2.6	0
Thomas Sanders	54	122	2.3	1
Jeff Kemp	16	73	4.6	0
Jim McMahon	22	55	2.5	1
Robert Drummond	12	27	2.3	2
Brad Goebel	1	2	2.0	0
Fred Barnett	1	0	0.0	0
Jeff Feagles	3	-1	-0.3	0
Pat Ryan	1	-2	-2.0	0

Interceptions	Int	Yds	Avg	TD
Wes Hopkins	5	26	5.2	0
Eric Allen	5	20	4.0	0
Seth Joyner	3	41	13.7	0
Rich Miano	3	30	10.0	0
Otis Smith	2	74	37.0	1
Byron Evans	2	46	23.0	0
Ben Smith	2	6	3.0	0
John Booty	1	24	24.0	0
Mike Golic	1	13	13.0	0
Andre Waters	1	0	0.0	0
Reggie White	1	0	0.0	0

Receiving	Rec	Yds	Avg	TD
Fred Barnett	62	948	15.3	4
Keith Byars	62	564	9.1	3
Keith Jackson	48	569	11.9	5
Calvin Williams	33	326	9.9	3
Roy Green	29	364	12.6	0
Heath Sherman	14	59	4.2	0
James Joseph	10	64	6.4	0
Thomas Sanders	8	62	7.8	0
Mickey Shuler	6	91	15.2	0
Maurice Johnson	6	70	11.7	2
Kenny Jackson	4	29	7.3	0
Rod Harris	2	28	14.0	0
Jim McMahon	1	-5	-5.0	0

Punting	Punts	Yds	Avg	Blocked
Jeff Feagles	87	3640	41.8	1

Kicking	PAT Made	PAT Att	PAT %	FG Made	FG Att	FG %	Pts
Roger Ruzek	27	29	93	28	33	84.8	111

1991

MONDAY, SEPTEMBER 16, 1991

FOR LATE SPORTS, SCORES: PAGE 99

PHILADELPHIA DAILY NEWS

Sports

Grand day for Bream, Braves

See page 82

SACKS MANIACS

BIRDS DROP AIKMAN 11 TIMES IN 24-0 WIN OVER DALLAS

MICHAEL MERCANTI / DAILY NEWS

Jerome Brown is congratulated by Seth Joyner (left) and Reggie White after fourth-quarter sack

SEE PAGE 98

NFL WEEK 3

Detroit 17	**Pittsburgh 20**	**Chicago 20**	**Washington 34**	**Green Bay 15**	**Minnesota 17**
Miami 13	New England 6	NY. Giants 17	Phoenix 0	Tampa Bay 13	SanFrancisco 14
Cleveland 14	**Denver 16**	**Atlanta 13**	**Buffalo 23**	**LA Raiders 16**	**New Orleans 24**
Cincinnati 13	Seattle 10	San Diego 10	NY Jets 20	Indianapolis 0	LA Rams 7

September 16, 1991 - Eagles manhandle the Cowboys 24-0, had a team-record 11 sacks in single game

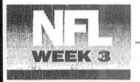

1992

RECORD: 11-5, 2ND IN NFC EAST
HEAD COACH: RICH KOTITE

Schedule

Regular Season

Wk. 1	Sep 6	W	15-13	vs New Orleans Saints
Wk. 2	Sep 13	W	31-14	at Phoenix Cardinals
Wk. 3	Sep 20	W	30-0	vs Denver Broncos
Wk. 5	Oct 5	W	31-7	vs Dallas Cowboys
Wk. 6	Oct 11	L	24-17	at Kansas City Chiefs
Wk. 7	Oct 18	L	16-12	at Washington Redskins
Wk. 8	Oct 25	W	7-3	vs Phoenix Cardinals
Wk. 9	Nov 1	L	20-10	at Dallas Cowboys
Wk. 10	Nov 8	W	31-10	vs Los Angeles Raiders
Wk. 11	Nov 15	L	27-24	at Green Bay Packers (at Milwaukee, WI)
Wk. 12	Nov 22	W	47-34	at New York Giants
Wk. 13	Nov 29	L	20-14	at San Francisco 49ers
Wk. 14	Dec 6	W	28-17	vs Minnesota Vikings
Wk. 15	Dec 13	W	20-17	at Seattle Seahawks (OT)
Wk. 16	Dec 20	W	17-13	vs Washington Redskins
Wk. 17	Dec 27	W	20-10	vs New York Giants

Post Season

Wild Card Playoffs	Jan 3	W	36-20	at New Orleans Saints
Divisional Playoffs	Jan 10	L	34-10	at Dallas Cowboys

Tragedy struck at the heart of the Eagles before the season even started, when linebacker Jerome Brown was killed in an automobile accident a month before the start of training camp. The Eagles dedicated the season to Brown by wearing a patch in his honor and retired his number 99. With the return of Randall Cunningham the Eagles got off to a solid 4-0 start. After struggling through the middle of the season the Eagles closed with four straight wins to make the playoffs with a solid 11-5 record. The team returned to the playoffs after a one-year absence and earned a Wild Card victory over the Saints in New Orleans 36-20. The win over the Saints was the team's first postseason victory since 1981 and its first road playoff conquest since 1949. Unfortunately, a week later their season would end in a 34-10 loss to the Cowboys in Dallas at the Divisional Playoffs. Following the season the Eagles, who had already lost tight end Keith Jackson to free agency, lost defensive end Reggie White.

1992 Philadelphia Eagles Stats

Passing	Comp	Att	Comp %	Yds	Y/Att	TD	Int	Rating
Randall Cunningham	233	384	60.7	2775	7.23	19	11	87.3
Jim McMahon	22	43	51.2	279	6.49	1	2	60.1
Herschel Walker	0	1	0.0	0	0.00	0	0	39.6
Keith Byars	0	1	0.0	0	0.00	0	0	39.6

Rushing	Rush	Yds	Avg	TD
Herschel Walker	267	1070	4.0	8
Heath Sherman	112	583	5.2	5
Randall Cunningham	7	549	6.3	5
Keith Byars	41	176	4.3	1
Jim McMahon	6	23	3.8	0
Vai Sikahema	2	2	1.0	0
Fred Barnett	1	-15	-15.0	0

Interceptions	Int	Yds	Avg	TD
Seth Joyner	4	88	22.0	2
Byron Evans	4	76	19.0	0
Eric Allen	4	49	12.3	0
John Booty	3	22	7.3	0
Wes Hopkins	3	6	2.0	0
William Thomas	2	4	2.0	0
Rich Miano	1	39	39.0	0
Andre Waters	1	23	23.0	0
Mark McMillian	1	0	0.0	0
Otis Smith	1	0	0.0	0

Receiving	Rec	Yds	Avg	TD
Fred Barnett	67	1083	16.2	6
Keith Byars	56	502	9.0	2
Calvin Williams	42	598	14.2	7
Herschel Walker	38	278	7.3	2
Heath Sherman	18	219	12.2	1
Vai Sikahema	13	142	10.9	0
Roy Green	8	105	13.1	0
Pat Beach	8	75	9.4	2
Floyd Dixon	3	36	12.0	0
Maurice Johnson	2	16	8.0	0

Punting	Punts	Yds	Avg	Blocked
Jeff Feagles	82	3459	42.2	0

Kicking	PAT Made	PAT Att	PAT %	FG Made	FG Att	FG %	Pts
Roger Ruzek	40	44	91	16	25	64.0	88

MONDAY PHILADELPHIA DAILY NEWS SEPTEMBER 21, 1992

Sports

Morandini makes history with solo tripleplay, but Phils lose again anyway
Page 102

NFL WEEK 3

Eagles 30	Denver 0
Washington 13	Detroit 10
Dallas 31	Phoenix 20
Pittsburgh 23	San Diego 6
Miami 26	LA Rams 10
Cleveland 28	Raiders 16
Minnesota 26	Tampa Bay 20
New Orleans 10	Atlanta 7
San Francisco 31	NY Jets 14
Houston 23	Kansas City 20 (ot)
Buffalo 38	Indianapolis 0
Seattle 10	New England 6
Green Bay 24	Cincinnati 23

NOT YOUR DAY, ELWAY

Birds crush Broncos to go to 3-0: Page 118

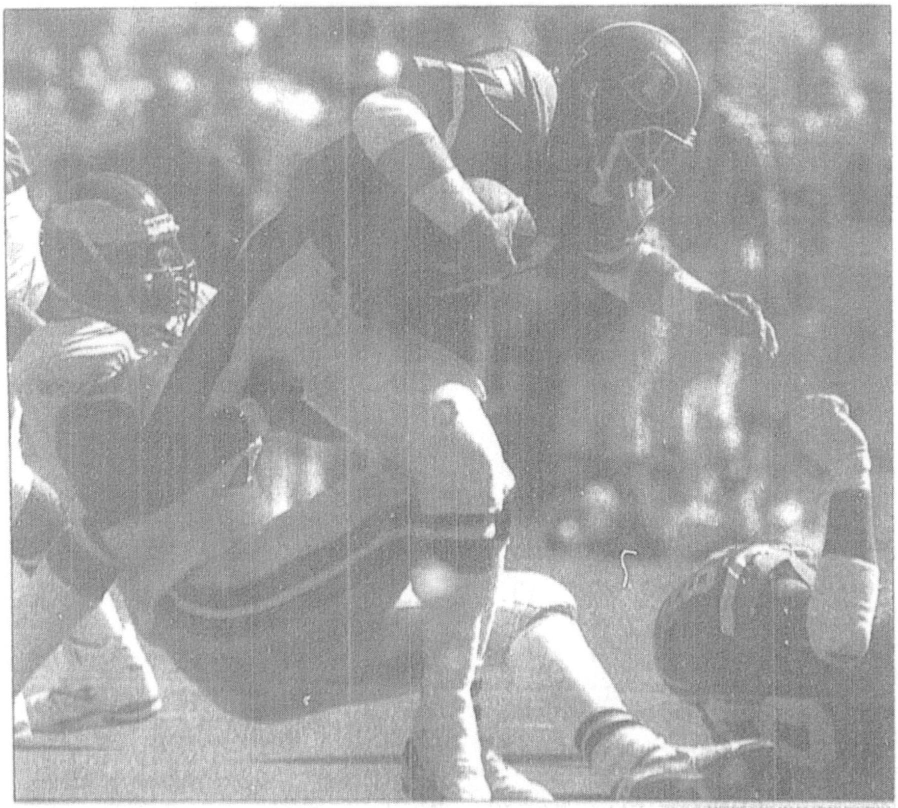

ANDREA MIHALIK / DAILY NEWS

Clyde Simmons drops John Elway in third quarter, one of the Eagles' four sacks

1992

September 21, 1992 - Eagles soar over Denver 30-0
Calvin Williams and Fred Barnett gain 100 yards each, first time since 1983

1993

RECORD: 8-8, 3RD IN NFC EAST
HEAD COACH: RICH KOTITE

Schedule

Regular Season

Wk. 1	Sep 5	W	23-17	vs Phoenix Cardinals
Wk. 2	Sep 12	W	20-17	at Green Bay Packers
Wk. 3	Sep 19	W	34-31	vs Washington Redskins
Wk. 5	Oct 3	W	35-30	at New York Jets
Wk. 6	Oct 10	L	17-6	vs Chicago Bears
Wk. 7	Oct 17	L	21-10	at New York Giants
Wk. 9	Oct 31	L	23-10	vs Dallas Cowboys
Wk. 10	Nov 7	L	16-3	at Phoenix Cardinals
Wk. 11	Nov 14	L	19-14	vs Miami Dolphins
Wk. 12	Nov 21	L	7-3	vs New York Giants
Wk. 13	Nov 28	W	17-14	at Washington Redskins
Wk. 14	Dec 6	L	23-17	at Dallas Cowboys
Wk. 15	Dec 12	L	10-7	vs Buffalo Bills
Wk. 16	Dec 19	W	20-10	at Indianapolis Colts
Wk. 17	Dec 26	W	37-26	vs New Orleans Saints
Wk. 18 (OT)	Jan 3	W	37-34	at San Francisco 49ers

After a flying start in which the Birds jumped out to a 4-0 record on the strength of three consecutive dramatic come-from-behind wins, season-ending injuries to quarterback Randall Cunningham, Pro Bowl wide receiver Fred Barnett and others were followed by a six-game losing streak. Despite suffering their worst skid since 1983, the resilient Eagles bounced back behind the fine play of back-up QB Bubbly Brisker to win four of their final six contests---a stretch that kept them in the playoff hunt until the final week of the season. The Eagles' injury-riddled, roller-coaster ride of the 1993 campaign produced an 8-8 record.

1993 Philadelphia Eagles Stats

Passing	Comp	Att	Comp %	Yds	Y/Att	TD	Int	Rating
Randall Cunningham	76	110	69.1	850	7.73	5	5	88.1
Bubby Brister	181	309	58.6	1905	6.17	14	5	84.9
Ken O'Brien	71	137	51.8	708	5.17	4	3	67.4

Rushing	Rush	Yds	Avg	TD
Herschel Walker	174	746	4.3	1
Heath Sherman	115	406	3.5	2
Vaughn Hebron	84	297	3.5	3
James Joseph	39	140	3.6	0
Randall Cunningham	18	110	6.1	1
Bubby Brister	20	39	2.0	7
Ken O'Brien	5	17	3.4	0
Jeff Feagles	2	6	3.0	0

Interceptions	Int	Yds	Avg	TD
Eric Allen	6	201	33.5	4
Rich Miano	4	26	6.5	0
William Thomas	2	39	19.5	0
Mark McMillian	2	25	12.5	0
Britt Hager	1	19	19.0	0
Byron Evans	1	8	8.0	0
Seth Joyner	1	6	6.0	0
Wes Hopkins	1	0	0.0	0
Clyde Simmons	1	0	0.0	0
Otis Smith	1	0	0.0	0

Receiving	Rec	Yds	Avg	TD
Herschel Walker	75	610	8.1	3
Calvin Williams	60	725	12.1	10
Mark Bavaro	43	481	11.2	6
Victor Bailey	41	545	13.3	1
James Joseph	29	291	10.0	1
Fred Barnett	17	170	10.0	0
Mike Young	14	186	13.3	2
James Lofton	13	167	12.8	0
Heath Sherman	12	78	6.5	0
Vaughn Hebron	11	82	7.5	0
Maurice Johnson	10	81	8.1	0
Jeff Sydner	2	42	21.0	0
Reggie Lawrence	1	5	5.0	0

Punting	Punts	Yds	Avg	Blocked
Jeff Feagles	83	3323	40.0	0

Kicking	PAT Made	PAT Att	PAT %	FG Made	FG Att	FG %	Pts
Matt Bahr	18	19	95	8	13	61.5	42
Roger Ruzek	13	16	81	8	10	80.0	37

MONDAY | PHILADELPHIA DAILY NEWS | SEPTEMBER 13, 1993

Sports

Pete Sampras makes U.S. Open his 2nd Slam of year
Page 88

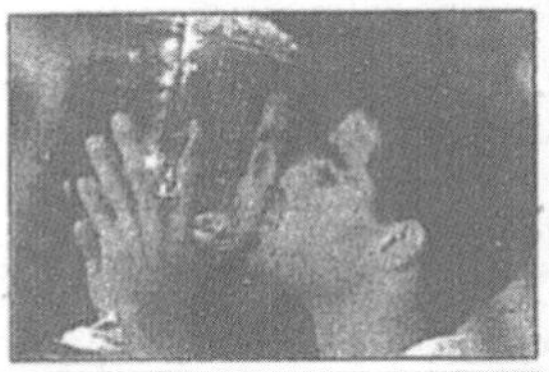

MAKING AMENS

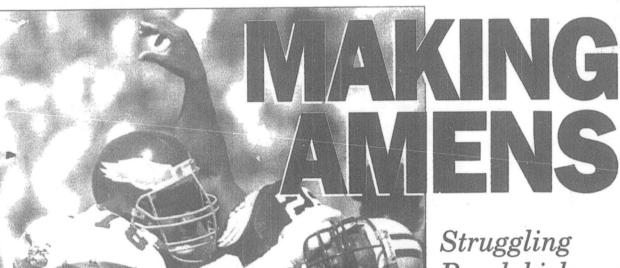

Struggling Ruzek kicks game-winner as Eagles stun Packers, spoil White's impressive performance

Pages 99-94

Eagles tackle Antone Davis gets in the face of former teammate Reggie White.

GEORGE REYNOLDS / DAILY NEWS

PHILLIES LOSE; LEAD DOWN TO 5
PAGES 93-91

MAGIC NUMBER

15

	W	L	Pct.	GB
Phillies	87	56	.608	
Montreal	82	61	.573	5

GRANNY HAMNER DEAD AT 66
PAGE 90

September 13, 1993 - Reggie White's first game back as a Packer, but Eagles win 20-17

1994

RECORD: 7-9, 4TH IN NFC EAST
HEAD COACH: RICH KOTITE

Schedule

Regular Season

Wk. 1	Sep 4	L	28-23	at New York Giants
Wk. 2	Sep 12	W	30-22	vs Chicago Bears
Wk. 3	Sep 18	W	13-7	vs Green Bay Packers
Wk. 5	Oct 2	W	40-8	at San Francisco 49ers
Wk. 6	Oct 9	W	21-17	vs Washington Redskins
Wk. 7	Oct 16	L	24-13	at Dallas Cowboys
Wk. 8	Oct 24	W	21-6	vs Houston Oilers
Wk. 9	Oct 30	W	31-29	at Washington Redskins
Wk. 10	Nov 6	W	17-7	vs Arizona Cardinals
Wk. 11	Nov 13	L	26-7	vs Cleveland Browns
Wk. 12	Nov 20	L	12-6	at Arizona Cardinals
Wk. 13	Nov 27	L	28-21	at Atlanta Falcons
Wk. 14	Dec 4	L	31-19	vs Dallas Cowboys
Wk. 15	Dec 11	L	14-3	at Pittsburgh Steelers
Wk. 16	Dec 18	L	16-13	vs New York Giants
Wk. 17	Dec 24	L	33-30	at Cincinnati Bengals

A new chapter in Philadelphia Eagle history began on April 6th as Norman Braman, the Birds' owner since 1985, reached an agreement in principle to sell the franchise to Boston native and Hollywood-based movie producer Jeffrey Lurie. The Eagles would lose their season opener but would win 7 of their next 8 to sit right in thick of the playoff hunt with a 7-2 record. However the team would suddenly start to struggle losing their final 7 games to finish with a disappointing 7-9 record. Two days after the season finale, Rich Kotite's 4-year reign as head coach of the Birds ended when he was relieved of his duties. Despite the dismal ending, several Eagles provided memorable performances throughout the year. RB Herschel Walker etched his name into the NFL record books, as he became the first player in the 75-year history of the league to record a 90-plus yard run, reception, and kickoff return in a single season. Rookie RB Charlie Garner became only the 7th back in NFL history to eclipse the 100-yard rushing mark in his first two contests.

1994 Philadelphia Eagles Stats

Passing	Comp	Att	Comp %	Yds	Y/Att	TD	Int	Rating
Randall Cunningham	265	490	54.1	3229	6.59	16	13	74.4
Bubby Brister	51	76	67.1	507	6.67	2	1	89.1

Rushing	Rush	Yds	Avg	TD
Herschel Walker	113	528	4.7	5
Charlie Garner	109	399	3.7	3
Vaughn Hebron	82	325	4.0	2
Randall Cunningham	65	288	4.4	3
James Joseph	60	203	3.4	1
Bubby Brister	1	7	7.0	0
Calvin Williams	1	7	7.0	0

Punting	Punts	Yds	Avg	Blocked
Randall Cunningham	1	80	80.0	0
Bryan Barker	66	2696	40.8	0
Mitch Berger	25	951	38.0	0

Kicking	PAT Made	PAT Att	PAT %	FG Made	FG Att	FG %	Pts
Eddie Murray	33	33	100	21	25	84.0	96

Receiving	Rec	Yds	Avg	TD
Fred Barnett	78	1127	14.4	5
Calvin Williams	58	813	14.0	3
Herschel Walker	50	500	10.0	2
James Joseph	43	344	8.0	2
Maurice Johnson	21	204	9.7	2
Victor Bailey	20	311	15.6	1
Vaughn Hebron	18	137	7.6	0
Mark Bavaro	17	215	12.6	3
Charlie Garner	8	74	9.3	0
David Alexander	2	1	0.5	0
Jeff Sydner	1	10	10.0	0

Interceptions	Int	Yds	Avg	TD
Greg Jackson	6	86	14.3	1
Michael Zordich	4	39	9.8	1
Eric Allen	3	61	20.3	0
Bill Romanowski	2	8	4.0	0
Mark McMillian	2	2	1.0	0

William Thomas, Byron Evans, Britt Hager, and Andy Harmon all had one interception.

MONDAY THE PHILADELPHIA DAILY NEWS OCTOBER 10, 1994

Sports

Thomas, Cardinals meet, but nothing is imminent
Page 100

ALEJANDRO A. ALVAREZ/ DAILY NEWS
Randall Cunningham flips past Andre Collins on 20-yard TD run

BACK *to* EARTH

Birds follow giddy romp over 49ers with close win vs. Redskins, 21-17

Pages 115-107

Cowboys humble Buddy, await Eagles
Page 106

October 10, 1994 - Charlie Garner is the Eagles first rookie to gain over 100-yards in back-to-back games as Eagles defeated Washington 21-17

1995

RECORD: 10-6, 2ND IN NFC EAST
HEAD COACH: RAY RHODES

Schedule

Regular Season

Wk. 1	Sep 3	L	21-6	vs Tampa Bay Buccaneers
Wk. 2	Sep 10	W	31-19	at Arizona Cardinals
Wk. 3	Sep 17	L	27-21	vs San Diego Chargers
Wk. 4	Sep 24	L	48-17	at Oakland Raiders
Wk. 5	Oct 1	W	15-10	at New Orleans Saints
Wk. 6	Oct 8	W	37-34	vs Washington Redskins (OT)
Wk. 7	Oct 15	W	17-14	at New York Giants
Wk. 9	Oct 29	W	20-9	vs St. Louis Rams
Wk. 10	Nov 6	L	34-12	at Dallas Cowboys
Wk. 11	Nov 12	W	31-13	vs Denver Broncos
Wk. 12	Nov 19	W	28-19	vs New York Giants
Wk. 13	Nov 26	W	14-7	at Washington Redskins
Wk. 14	Dec 3	L	26-14	at Seattle Seahawks
Wk. 15	Dec 10	W	20-17	vs Dallas Cowboys
Wk. 16	Dec 17	W	21-20	vs Arizona Cardinals
Wk. 17	Dec 24	L	20-14	at Chicago Bears

Post Season

Wild Card Playoffs				
	Dec 30	W	58-37	vs Detroit Lions
Divisional Playoffs				
	Jan 7	L	30-11	at Dallas Cowboys

Under new coach Ray Rhodes the Eagles play sluggish football, losing three of their first four games, prompting Rhodes to bench quarterback Randall Cunningham. Under Cunningham's replacement Rodney Peete, the Birds rode the legs of running backs Ricky Watters and Charlie Garner to win nine of their final 12 games. Philadelphia's defense also chipped in with 48 sacks (second best in the league). The result was a 10-6 record and a spot in the playoffs as the NFC's top Wild Card team. In the Wild Card Game at the Vet the Eagles quickly soared in front to a 51-7 lead, and coasted the rest the way to a 58-37 slaughtering of the Detroit Lions at the Vet. However, a week later it was the Eagles who were slaughtered 30-11 by the Cowboys in Dallas. At season's end, Watters, defensive end William Fuller (an NFC-high 13 sacks), and linebacker William Thomas (whose seven interceptions were the most by an NFL linebacker since 1983) represented the Eagles in the Pro Bowl. Defensive tackle Andy Harmon and a pair of rookies, cornerback Bobby Taylor and punter Tom Hutton, also received numerous honors. Eleven months and a playoff victory later, first year head coach Ray Rhodes received numerous NFL Coach of the Year honors.

1995 Philadelphia Eagles Stats

Passing	Comp	Att	Comp %	Yds	Y/Att	TD	Int	Rating
Rodney Peete	215	375	57.3	2326	6.20	8	14	67.3
Randall Cunningham	69	121	57.0	605	5.00	3	5	61.5

Rushing	Rush	Yds	Avg	TD
Ricky Watters	337	1273	3.8	11
Charlie Garner	108	588	5.4	6
Rodney Peete	33	147	4.5	1
Randall Cunningham	21	98	4.7	0
Kevin Turner	2	9	4.5	0
Derrick Witherspoon	2	7	3.5	0
Fred McCrary	3	1	0.3	1
Tom Hutton	1	0	0.0	0
James Saxon	1	0	0.0	0
Calvin Williams	1	-2	-2.0	0

Interceptions	Int	Yds	Avg	TD
William Thomas	7	104	14.9	1
Mark McMillian	3	27	9.0	0
Bobby Taylor	2	52	26.0	0
Bill Romanowski	2	5	2.5	0
Kurt Gouveia	1	20	20.0	0
Greg Jackson	1	18	18.0	0
Michael Zordich	1	10	10.0	0
Derrick Frazier	1	3	3.0	0
Barry Wilburn	1	0	0.0	0

Receiving	Rec	Yds	Avg	TD
Calvin Williams	63	768	12.2	2
Ricky Watters	62	434	7.0	1
Fred Barnett	48	585	12.2	5
Rob Carpenter	29	318	11.0	0
Ed West	20	190	9.5	1
Kelvin Martin	17	206	12.1	0
Charlie Garner	10	61	6.1	0
Fred McCrary	9	60	6.7	0
Art Monk	6	114	19.0	0
Jimmie Johnson	6	37	6.2	0
Reggie Johnson	5	68	13.6	2
Chris T. Jones	5	61	12.2	0
Kevin Turner	4	29	7.3	0

Punting	Punts	Yds	Avg	Blocked
Tom Hutton	85	3682	43.3	1

Kicking	PAT Made	PAT Att	PAT %	FG Made	FG Att	FG %	Pts
Gary Anderson	33	32	103	30	22	136.4	123

1995

The Philadelphia Inquirer

Sunday **Sports**

Coping with comparisons
Penn State's Wally Richardson follows a very tough act. **C12.**

Section C

Sunday, December 31, 1995

Philadelphia Online:

Eagles win in a big, big way

Eagles show remarkable resiliency

Bill Lyon

How can you not hand over your heart to this team of liquor-store clerks and truck drivers and other refugees from the real world who splattered the best offense in the NFL yesterday?

Really now, if you had heard only the score before kickoff, 58-37, wouldn't you have assumed that Detroit was the one with the 58?

Ray Rhodes has a way of rousing his team, but even he couldn't believe he'd end up with a laugher.

This had the look of a Super Bowl. Detroit generously played the part of the AFC team.

So the Eagles learned exactly how much the home field is worth in the playoffs.

And this is what happens to roofed teams that are forced to come outdoors and play in December and beyond.

The Eagles obliterated the Lions in yesterday's NFC wild-card playoff game at the Vet, exposing them as just another domed fraud. There were a lot of reasons for the machine-gunning, but none more compelling than this: The Eagles were much the tougher team mentally.

Harder and hardier and heartier.

The Lions didn't even get a real taste of the Northeast in winter, but they shriveled up and died a hothouse plant's death anyway. The first turnover and they were looking for the exits. Since 1990, when the Lions have played teams with

See **HEART** on C8

The Philadelphia Inquirer / RON CORTES

The Eagles' Charlie Garner straight-arms Detroit cornerback Ryan McNeil in a bid to get outside. Garner piled up 78 yards on 12 carries.

Crush Lions in Round 1 of playoffs

By Frank Fitzpatrick
INQUIRER STAFF WRITER

Lions	37
Eagles	58

Veterans Stadium shook like the Market Street El in full throttle. The Eagles' lead resembled a Sixers first-period deficit. And Rodney Peete, his index finger jabbing the sky in jubilant vindication, nearly outran his 18th and final first-half pass to the Lions' end zone.

Peete's remarkable 43-yard touchdown heave to Rob Carpenter, on the last play of a nearly perfect hometown half, left the Lions stunned and still. It sent the Eagles dancing to the locker room with a 38-7 lead. And it typified Philadelphia's wondrous fortune on an afternoon that would fill NFL record books and embarrass Lomas Brown for eternity.

With a revived Peete throwing for 270 yards and three touchdowns, with a realigned defense intercepting six passes, and with 66,099 fans howling in green-tinged joy, the Eagles disassembled Detroit, 58-37, yesterday in a first-round NFC playoff game.

"All week, all we heard about was how great Detroit was, how potent their offense was," coach Ray Rhodes said. "I think everybody overlooked this football team."

The lopsided victory, featuring the most points by two teams in NFL postseason history and the second-most ever for the Eagles, emphatically ended the Lions' seven-game winning streak and their season.

"We never thought that just because we had been playing good football, the Eagles were going to roll over and die," said Lions coach Wayne Fontes, his job security in jeopardy again. "They beat us in every way possible."

The win was the Eagles' first at home in the postseason since Jan. 11, 1981, when they defeated Dallas

See **EAGLES** on C8

Detroit's Brown readily eats words

He'd predicted the wild-card game would be over quickly. He didn't know how right — and how wrong — he would be.

By Phil Sheridan
INQUIRER STAFF WRITER

Here it is, the recipe for Words a la Lomas:

Saute lightly, adding a pinch of humility, and serve with a smile.

"Yes, I'm eating it today," said Lomas Brown, the veteran offensive tackle who surprised friends and teammates last week by guaranteeing a Detroit Lions victory over the Eagles.

Last week, Brown told reporters he expected the NFC wild-card playoff to be over early. He couldn't have known how right and how wrong he would be: it was the Eagles who took a 38-7 lead by halftime.

"They were the better team today," Brown said. "I have no problem admitting that. What I said was out of pure confidence. It was a reflection of how I felt about the guys in this locker room, about the type of team I thought we had.

"I have to take my hat off to Coach (Ray) Rhodes and to the Philadelphia Eagles. They beat us, handily beat us. The way we played, we could have played against a high school team today and not beaten them. You can't be the team to turn the ball over seven times and expect to win a playoff game."

When the record-breaking 58-37 loss was over, Brown spoke on the field with several Eagles, including Rhodes. After a brief talk with reporters at midfield, Brown jogged toward the tunnel to the Lions' locker room. Dozens of Eagles fans were waiting in the stands above the tunnel, chanting "Lomas ... Lomas" and bowing toward the man who sprayed kerosene on the Eagles' competitive fire.

"I told Coach Rhodes I would give him a call Tuesday," Brown said. "I would rather keep our conversation between him and me. Me and Coach Rhodes go way back. When he was in San Francisco, he coached some Pro Bowl squads. And I've met him a

See **LIONS** on C7

The Philadelphia Inquirer / RON CORTES

The Eagles' William Thomas (right) and Kurt Gouveia celebrate after Thomas scored in the fourth quarter on a 30-yard interception return.

Barnett and Garner serve special treats

The receiver dished up a surprise package with his best performance of the season. The running back provided the initial spice.

By Ron Reid
INQUIRER STAFF WRITER

Starting their playoff season yesterday with an amazing 58-37 victory over Detroit, the Eagles confronted their fans like a banquet table — offering too many good things to savor, many of them unexpected.

Chief among the latter was the play of Fred Barnett, the Eagles' six-year veteran wide receiver who could hardly have chosen a better time to turn in his finest, most surprising performance of the year.

The familiar treat was Charlie Garner, the explosive running back who scored the game's first touchdown on a scintillating 15-yard run. He racked up 78 yards on 12 carries, as the game's leading ground-gainer, and set up a field goal with a 30-yard run.

"We do have some guys who can help ignite our football team," said Eagles coach Ray Rhodes. "Charlie Garner is definitely one of them."

Garner didn't hang around to discuss his contributions with the media.

Arkansas Fred, as he used to be known, caught eight passes for 109 yards and a touchdown in what was a throwback to his earlier seasons with the team, when he routinely turned in the brilliant catch to scorch cornerbacks throughout the NFL.

Barnett's TD reception came in

See **BARNETT** on C7

NFL Playoffs

Wild-card round.

Yesterday

- **Eagles 58, Detroit 37**
- **Buffalo 37, Miami 22**

Today

- **Atlanta at Green Bay**, 12:30 p.m., Ch. 29.
- **Indianapolis at San Diego**, 4 p.m., Ch. 10.

Inside Sports

Villanova rallies after trailing Delaware. **C10.**

Dolphin loss Shula finale?

The Bills ousted the Dolphins from the playoffs, 38-22, yesterday and the humiliating defeat may wind up ending Don Shula's long tenure in Miami. **C7.**

Osborne's halo is slipping

A year ago, Nebraska head coach Tom Osborne was hailed as the nice guy with the model football program who finally won a national title. Now, his program and image are tarnished. **C2.**

Barber new Hershey coach

Bill Barber was named head coach of the AHL Hershey Bears. Meanwhile, the Flyers go for their second win in a row today, against Vancouver. **C2.**

College Basketball

Villanova 71, Delaware 58	Missouri 95, Hawaii 89
SMU 79, Penn 67	Cincinnati 103, McNeese St. 89
Oklahoma St. 49, Temple 41	Texas 74, North Carolina 72
UCLA 92, San Francisco 58	Clemson 67, Campbell 43
Georgetown 123, St. Leo 66	Virginia 76, Liberty 48
Drexel 68, Montana St. 62	Georgia 86, Jacksonville 59
Connecticut 102, Hartford 63	Louisville 96, Towson St. 72
Illinois 85, No. Carolina St. 76	**Coverage: C10-11.**

December 31, 1995 - Eagles set postseason scoring record with a huge win over the Lions 58-37 in the NFC Wild Card game

1996

RECORD: 10-6, 2ND IN NFC EAST
HEAD COACH: RAY RHODES

Schedule

Regular Season

Wk. 1	Sep 1	W	17-14	at Washington Redskins
Wk. 2	Sep 9	L	39-13	at Green Bay Packers
Wk. 3	Sep 15	W	24-17	vs Detroit Lions
Wk. 4	Sep 22	W	33-18	at Atlanta Falcons
Wk. 5	Sep 30	L	23-19	vs Dallas Cowboys
Wk. 7	Oct 13	W	19-10	at New York Giants
Wk. 8	Oct 20	W	35-28	vs Miami Dolphins
Wk. 9	Oct 27	W	20-9	vs Carolina Panthers
Wk. 10	Nov 3	W	31-21	at Dallas Cowboys
Wk. 11	Nov 10	L	24-17	vs Buffalo Bills
Wk. 12	Nov 17	L	26-21	vs Washington Redskins
Wk. 13	Nov 24	L	36-30	at Arizona Cardinals
Wk. 14	Dec 1	W	24-0	vs New York Giants
Wk. 15	Dec 5	L	37-10	at Indianapolis Colts
Wk. 16	Dec 14	W	21-20	at New York Jets
Wk. 17	Dec 22	W	29-19	vs Arizona Cardinals

Post Season

Wild Card Playoffs				
	Dec 29	L	14-0	at San Francisco 49ers

The Eagles got off to a quick start, winning three of their first four games, before a Monday Night showdown with the Dallas Cowboys at the Vet. The Eagles lost the game 23-19 and lost quarterback Rodney Peete for the season due to a freak knee injury. Since the Eagles released Randall Cunningham prior to the season, they were forced to turn to Ty Detmer. Detmer played well, leading the Eagles to a four-game winning streak, as running back Ricky Watters stepped up and supplied the offense with a career best 1,411-yard season. The Eagles went on to finish with a 10-6 record and earned a Wild Card spot. However their season would be ended quickly as their offense got stuck in the mud in a 14-0 loss to the 49ers in San Francisco. The 1996 season marked the second consecutive year in which the Eagles compiled a 10-6 regular season record and earned a Wild Card playoff berth. As such, Ray Rhodes became the first coach to lead the Eagles into the playoffs in each of his first two seasons at the helm.

1996 Philadelphia Eagles Stats

Passing	Comp	Att	Comp %	Yds	Y/Att	TD	Int	Rating
Ty Detmer	238	401	59.4	2911	7.26	15	13	80.8
Rodney Peete	80	134	59.7	992	7.40	3	5	74.6
Mark Rypien	10	13	76.9	76	5.85	1	0	116.2

Rushing	Rush	Yds	Avg	TD
Ricky Watters	353	1411	4.0	13
Charlie Garner	66	346	5.2	1
Ty Detmer	31	59	1.9	1
Kevin Turner	18	39	2.2	0
Rodney Peete	21	31	1.5	1
Irving Fryar	1	-4	-4.0	0

Interceptions	Int	Yds	Avg	TD
Michael Zordich	4	54	13.5	0
Troy Vincent	3	144	48.0	1
William Thomas	3	47	15.7	0
Brian Dawkins	3	41	13.7	0
Bobby Taylor	3	-1	-0.3	0
James Willis	1	14	14.0	0
James Fuller	1	4	4.0	0
Ray Farmer	1	0	0.0	0

Receiving	Rec	Yds	Avg	TD
Irving Fryar	88	1195	13.6	11
Chris T. Jones	70	859	12.3	5
Ricky Watters	51	444	8.7	0
Kevin Turner	43	409	9.5	1
Mark Seay	19	260	13.7	0
Jason Dunn	15	332	22.1	2
Charlie Garner	14	92	6.6	0
Freddie Solomon	8	125	15.6	0
Ed West	8	91	11.4	0
Jimmie Johnson	7	127	18.1	0
Mark Ingram	2	33	16.5	0
Calvin Williams	2	8	4.0	0
Guy McIntyre	1	4	4.0	0

Punting	Punts	Yds	Avg	Blocked
Tom Hutton	73	3107	42.6	1

Kicking	PAT Made	PAT Att	PAT %	FG Made	FG Att	FG %	Pts
Gary Anderson	40	40	100	25	29	86.2	115

MONDAY PHILADELPHIA DAILY NEWS DECEMBER 23, 1996

Sports

Flyers scored upon, but tie hawks: *Page 68*

500 for Hull: *Page 69*

RETURN TICKET

Eagles squash Cards, enter playoffs vs. 49ers in homecoming for Rhodes and Watters

Pages 83-78

GEORGE REYNOLDS / DAILY NEWS

Eagles defensive end Mike Mamula sacks Arizona quarterback Kent Graham on second play of game, forcing fumble that he picked up and returned for a 4-yard touchdown.

YONG KIM / DAILY NEWS

GRAND PRIZE GO FOR IT!

Super Bowl or Pro Bowl? Take your shot at a special trip in our Pick-a-Bowl Blitz contest. Details: Pages 75, 69

December 23, 1996
Gary Anderson boots five field goals to defeat the Cardinals 29-19

1996

1997

RECORD: 6-9-1, 3RD IN NFC EAST
HEAD COACH: RAY RHODES

Schedule

Regular Season

Wk. 1	Aug 31	L	31-17	at New York Giants
Wk. 2	Sep 7	W	10-9	vs Green Bay Packers
Wk. 3	Sep 15	L	21-20	at Dallas Cowboys
Wk. 5	Sep 28	L	28-19	at Minnesota Vikings
Wk. 6	Oct 5	W	24-10	vs Washington Redskins
Wk. 7	Oct 12	L	38-21	at Jacksonville Jaguars
Wk. 8	Oct 19	W	13-10	vs Arizona Cardinals (OT)
Wk. 9	Oct 26	W	13-12	vs Dallas Cowboys
Wk. 10	Nov 2	L	31-21	at Arizona Cardinals
Wk. 11	Nov 10	L	24-12	vs San Francisco 49ers
Wk. 12	Nov 16	T	10-10	at Baltimore Ravens (OT)
Wk. 13	Nov 23	W	23-20	vs Pittsburgh Steelers
Wk. 14	Nov 30	W	44-42	vs Cincinnati Bengals
Wk. 15	Dec 7	L	31-21	vs New York Giants
Wk. 16	Dec 14	L	20-17	at Atlanta Falcons
Wk. 17	Dec 21	L	35-32	at Washington Redskins

With a record of 1-1 the Eagles were poised to beat the Cowboys in a Monday Night showdown in Dallas as they set up for field goal slightly longer then a PAT in the final seconds. However, the snap was mishandled and the Eagles lost 21-20 in one of the most embarrassing moments in team history. The Eagles recovered, and sat at 4-4 through the first 8 games. However, quarterback struggles began to catch up with Eagles, as Rodney Peete, Ty Detmer, and Bobby Hoying all struggled. The Eagles dropped their final three games and finished with a disappointing 6-9-1 record.

1997 Philadelphia Eagles Stats

Passing	Comp	Att	Comp %	Yds	Y/Att	TD	Int	Rating
Bobby Hoying	128	225	56.9	1573	6.99	11	6	83.8
Rodney Peete	68	118	57.6	869	7.36	4	4	78.0
Ty Detmer	134	244	54.9	1567	6.42	7	6	73.9

Rushing	Rush	Yds	Avg	TD
Ricky Watters	285	1110	3.9	7
Charlie Garner	116	547	4.7	3
Kevin Turner	18	96	5.3	0
Bobby Hoying	16	78	4.9	0
Ty Detmer	14	46	3.3	1
Rodney Peete	8	37	4.6	0
Duce Staley	7	29	4.1	0
Tom Hutton	1	0	0.0	0

Interceptions	Int	Yds	Avg	TD
Brian Dawkins	3	76	25.3	1
Troy Vincent	3	14	4.7	0
Charles Dimry	2	25	12.5	0
William Thomas	2	11	5.5	0
Rhett Hall	1	39	39.0	0
Michael Zordich	1	21	21.0	0
Matt Stevens	1	0	0.0	0
James Willis	1	0	0.0	0

Receiving	Rec	Yds	Avg	TD
Irving Fryar	86	1316	15.3	6
Kevin Turner	48	443	9.2	3
Ricky Watters	48	440	9.2	0
Michael Timpson	42	484	11.5	2
Freddie Solomon	29	455	15.7	3
Charlie Garner	24	225	9.4	0
Jimmie Johnson	14	177	12.6	1
Mark Seay	13	187	14.4	1
Chad Lewis	12	94	7.8	4
Jason Dunn	7	93	13.3	2
Chris T. Jones	5	73	14.6	0
Duce Staley	2	22	11.0	0

Punting	Punts	Yds	Avg	Blocked
Tom Hutton	87	3660	42.1	1

Kicking	PAT Made	PAT Att	PAT %	FG Made	FG Att	FG %	Pts
Chris Boniol	33	33	100	22	31	71.0	99

PHILADELPHIA DAILY NEWS

THE PEOPLE PAPER

MONDAY, DECEMBER 1, 1997 60¢ LATE SPORTS

'HOME ALONE 3'
Win tickets: Page 43
Keepsake photo:
Pull out Page 40

ALIVE & KICKING

Eagles still in the playoff chase – and the fans are loving it

Sports and Page 3

Quarterback Bobby Hoying leaves the field after yesterday's 44-42 victory over the Bengals

GEORGE REYNOLDS / DAILY NEWS

12 DAYS OF CHRISTMAS WIN A SUPER BOWL TRIP Page 64

December 1, 1997 - Eagles QB Bobby Hoying throws for four touchdowns as the Eagles edge the Bengals 44-42

1997

1998

RECORD: 3-13, 5TH IN NFC EAST
HEAD COACH: RAY RHODES

Schedule

Regular Season

Wk. 1	Sep 6	L	38-0	vs Seattle Seahawks
Wk. 2	Sep 13	L	17-12	at Atlanta Falcons
Wk. 3	Sep 20	L	17-3	at Arizona Cardinals
Wk. 4	Sep 27	L	24-21	vs Kansas City Chiefs
Wk. 5	Oct 4	L	41-16	at Denver Broncos
Wk. 6	Oct 11	W	17-12	vs Washington Redskins
Wk. 7	Oct 18	L	13-10	at San Diego Chargers
Wk. 9	Nov 2	L	34-0	vs Dallas Cowboys
Wk. 10	Nov 8	W	10-9	vs Detroit Lions
Wk. 11	Nov 15	L	28-3	at Washington Redskins
Wk. 12	Nov 22	L	20-0	at New York Giants
Wk. 13	Nov 29	L	24-16	at Green Bay Packers
Wk. 14	Dec 3	W	17-14	vs St. Louis Rams
Wk. 15	Dec 13	L	20-17	vs Arizona Cardinals (OT)
Wk. 16	Dec 20	L	13-9	at Dallas Cowboys
Wk. 17	Dec 27	L	20-10	vs New York Giants

With the loss of Ricky Watters to free agency, Deuce Staley stepped in at runningback and supplied a solid season with 1,065 rushing yards. However, since all three Eagles quarterbacks struggled, the team went into a season long nose-dive that saw them finish with a woeful 3-13 record. Nobody demonstrated these struggles more then Bobby Hoying, who was sacked 35 times, and intercepted nine times, all without throwing a single touchdown pass. Following the season the Eagles made a change in direction that started by replacing head coach Ray Rhodes with Andy Reid.

1998 Philadelphia Eagles Stats

Passing	Comp	Att	Comp %	Yds	Y/Att	TD	Int	Rating
Koy Detmer	97	181	53.6	1011	5.59	5	5	67.7
Rodney Peete	71	129	55.0	758	5.88	2	4	64.7
Bobby Hoying	114	224	50.9	961	4.29	0	9	45.6

Rushing	Rush	Yds	Avg	TD
Duce Staley	258	1065	4.1	5
Charlie Garner	96	381	4.0	4
Kevin Turner	20	94	4.7	0
Bobby Hoying	22	84	3.8	0
Corey Walker	12	55	4.6	0
Irving Fryar	3	46	15.3	0
Rodney Peete	5	30	6.0	1
Koy Detmer	7	20	2.9	0
Dietrich Jells	2	9	4.5	0
Karl Hankton	1	-4	-4.0	0
Jason Dunn	1	-5	-5.0	0

Receiving	Rec	Yds	Avg	TD
Duce Staley	57	432	7.6	1
Irving Fryar	48	556	11.6	2
Jeff Graham	47	600	12.8	2
Kevin Turner	34	232	6.8	0
Freddie Solomon	21	193	9.2	1
Charlie Garner	19	110	5.8	0
Russell Copeland	18	221	12.3	0
Jason Dunn	18	132	7.3	0
Chris Fontenot	8	90	11.3	0
Kaseem Sinceno	3	42	14.0	1
Dietrich Jells	2	53	26.5	0
Corey Walker	2	35	17.5	0
Jimmie Johnson	2	14	7.0	0
Andrew Jordan	2	9	4.5	0
Bubba Miller	1	11	11.0	0

Punting	Punts	Yds	Avg	Blocked
Tom Hutton	104	4339	41.7	0

Interceptions	Int	Yds	Avg	TD
Brian Dawkins	2	39	19.5	0
Troy Vincent	2	29	14.5	0
Michael Zordich	2	18	9.0	0
Mike Caldwell	1	33	33.0	0
William Thomas	1	21	21.0	0
Tim McTyer	1	18	18.0	0

Kicking	PAT Made	PAT Att	PAT %	FG Made	FG Att	FG %	Pts
Chris Boniol	15	17	88	14	21	66.7	57

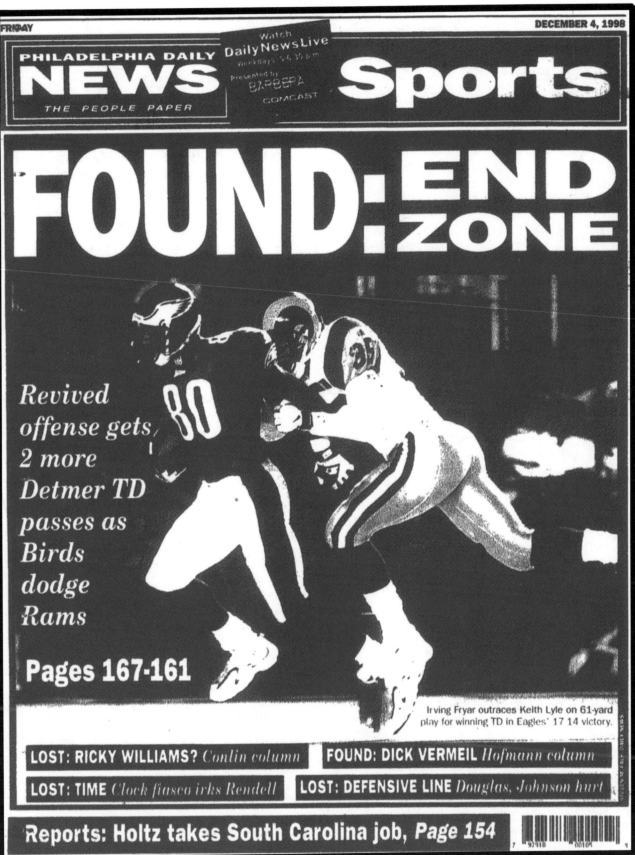

FRIDAY DECEMBER 4, 1998

PHILADELPHIA DAILY
NEWS
THE PEOPLE PAPER

Watch
DailyNewsLive
Presented by
BARBERA
COMCAST

Sports

FOUND: END ZONE

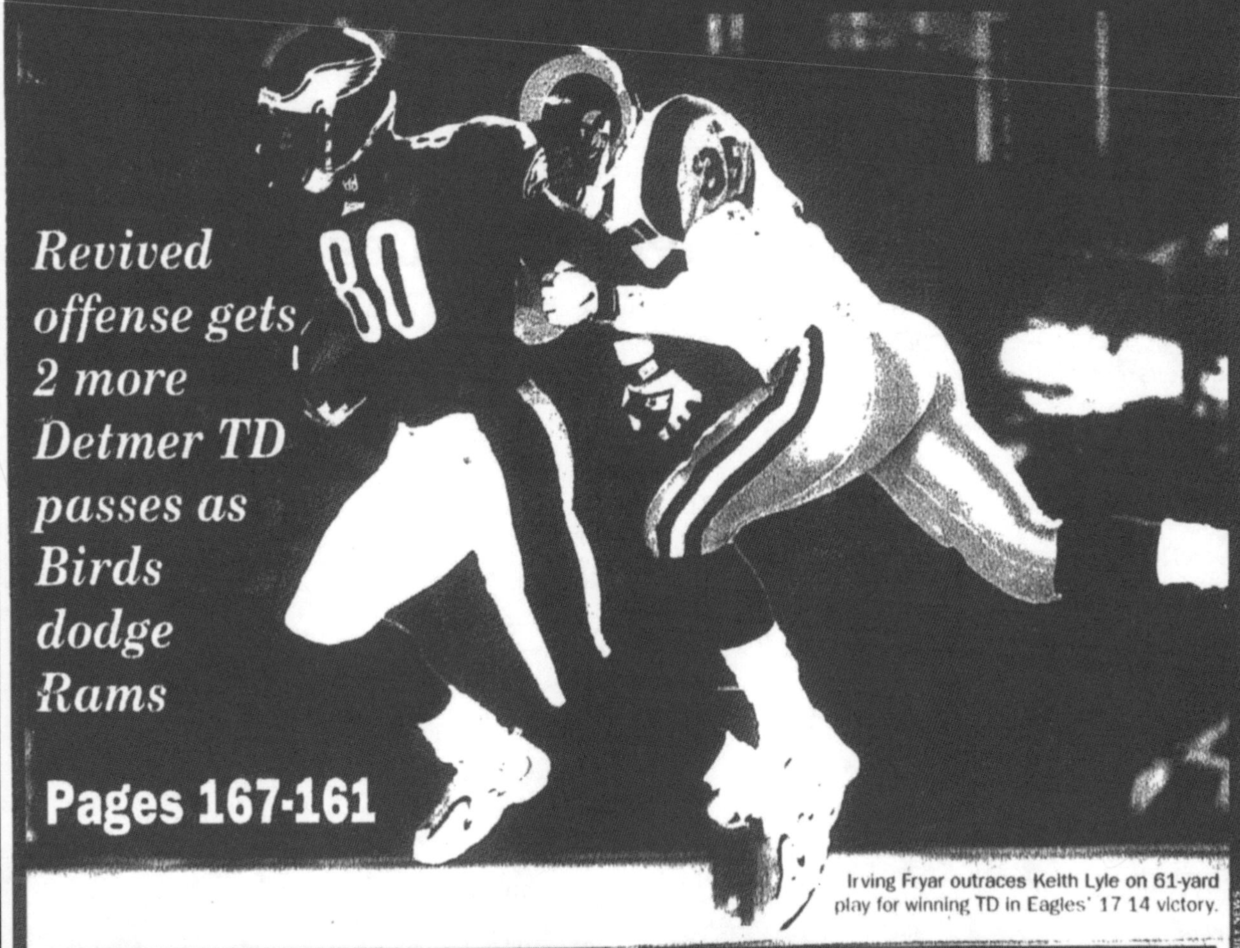

Revived offense gets 2 more Detmer TD passes as Birds dodge Rams

Pages 167-161

Irving Fryar outraces Keith Lyle on 61-yard play for winning TD in Eagles' 17 14 victory.

LOST: RICKY WILLIAMS? *Conlin column*

FOUND: DICK VERMEIL *Hofmann column*

LOST: TIME *Clock fiasco irks Rendell*

LOST: DEFENSIVE LINE *Douglas, Johnson hurt*

Reports: Holtz takes South Carolina job, *Page 154*

1998

December 4, 1998 - Eagles barely win this game 17-14 over the Rams

1999

RECORD: 5-11, 5TH IN NFC EAST
HEAD COACH: ANDY REID

Schedule

Regular Season

Wk. 1	Sep 12	L	25-24	vs Arizona Cardinals
Wk. 2	Sep 19	L	19-5	vs Tampa Bay Buccaneers
Wk. 3	Sep 27	L	26-0	at Buffalo Bills
Wk. 4	Oct 3	L	16-15	at New York Giants
Wk. 5	Oct 10	W	13-10	vs Dallas Cowboys
Wk. 6	Oct 17	W	20-16	at Chicago Bears
Wk. 7	Oct 24	L	16-13	at Miami Dolphins
Wk. 8	Oct 31	L	23-17	vs New York Giants (OT)
Wk. 9	Nov 7	L	33-7	at Carolina Panthers
Wk. 10	Nov 14	W	35-28	vs Washington Redskins
Wk. 11	Nov 21	L	44-17	vs Indianapolis Colts
Wk. 12	Nov 28	L	20-17	at Washington Redskins (OT)
Wk. 13	Dec 5	L	21-17	at Arizona Cardinals
Wk. 14	Dec 12	L	20-10	at Dallas Cowboys
Wk. 15	Dec 19	W	24-9	vs New England Patriots
Wk. 17	Jan 2	W	38-31	vs St. Louis Rams

To improve their quarterback situation the Eagles drafted Donovan McNabb with the second overall pick in the draft. However, McNabb started the season on the bench as the Eagles struggled, losing their first four games. McNabb got his chance in the second half of the season and shined as the Eagles finished on a strong note, winning their last two games to finish with a 5-11 record.

1999 Philadelphia Eagles Stats

Passing	Comp	Att	Comp %	Yds	Y/Att	TD	Int	Rating
Doug Pederson	119	227	52.4	1276	5.62	7	9	62.9
Donovan McNabb	106	216	49.1	948	4.39	8	7	60.1
Koy Detmer	10	29	34.5	181	6.24	3	2	62.6
Torrance Small	0	2	0.0	0	0.00	0	0	39.6

Rushing	Rush	Yds	Avg	TD
Duce Staley	325	1273	3.9	4
Donovan McNabb	47	313	6.7	0
Eric Bieniemy	12	75	6.3	1
Doug Pederson	20	33	1.7	0
James Bostic	5	19	3.8	0
Edwin Watson	4	17	4.3	0
Kevin Turner	6	15	2.5	0
Cecil Martin	3	3	1.0	0
Koy Detmer	2	-2	-1.0	0

Interceptions	Int	Yds	Avg	TD
Troy Vincent	7	91	13.0	0
Al Harris	4	151	37.8	1
Brian Dawkins	4	127	31.8	1
Bobby Taylor	4	59	14.8	1
Jeremiah Trotter	2	30	15.0	0
Mike Mamula	1	41	41.0	1
James Darling	1	33	33.0	0
Rashard Cook	1	29	29.0	0
Damon Moore	1	28	28.0	0
Brandon Whiting	1	22	22.0	1
Mike Caldwell	1	12	12.0	0
Tim Hauck	1	2	2.0	0

Receiving	Rec	Yds	Avg	TD
Torrance Small	49	655	13.4	4
Duce Staley	41	294	7.2	2
Charles Johnson	34	414	12.2	1
Luther Broughton	26	295	11.3	4
Na Brown	18	188	10.4	1
Jed Weaver	11	91	8.3	0
Cecil Martin	11	22	2.0	0
Dietrich Jells	10	180	18.0	2
Kevin Turner	9	46	5.1	0
Dameane Douglas	8	79	9.9	1
Chad Lewis	7	76	10.9	3
James Bostic	5	8	1.6	0
Eric Bieniemy	2	28	14.0	0
Brian Finneran	2	21	10.5	0
Troy Smith	1	14	14.0	0
Donovan McNabb	1	-6	-6.0	0

Punting	Punts	Yds	Avg	Blocked
Sean Landeta	107	4524	42.3	1

Kicking	PAT Made	PAT Att	PAT %	FG Made	FG Att	FG %	Pts
Norm Johnson	25	25	100	18	25	72.0	79
David Akers	2	2	100	3	6	50.0	11

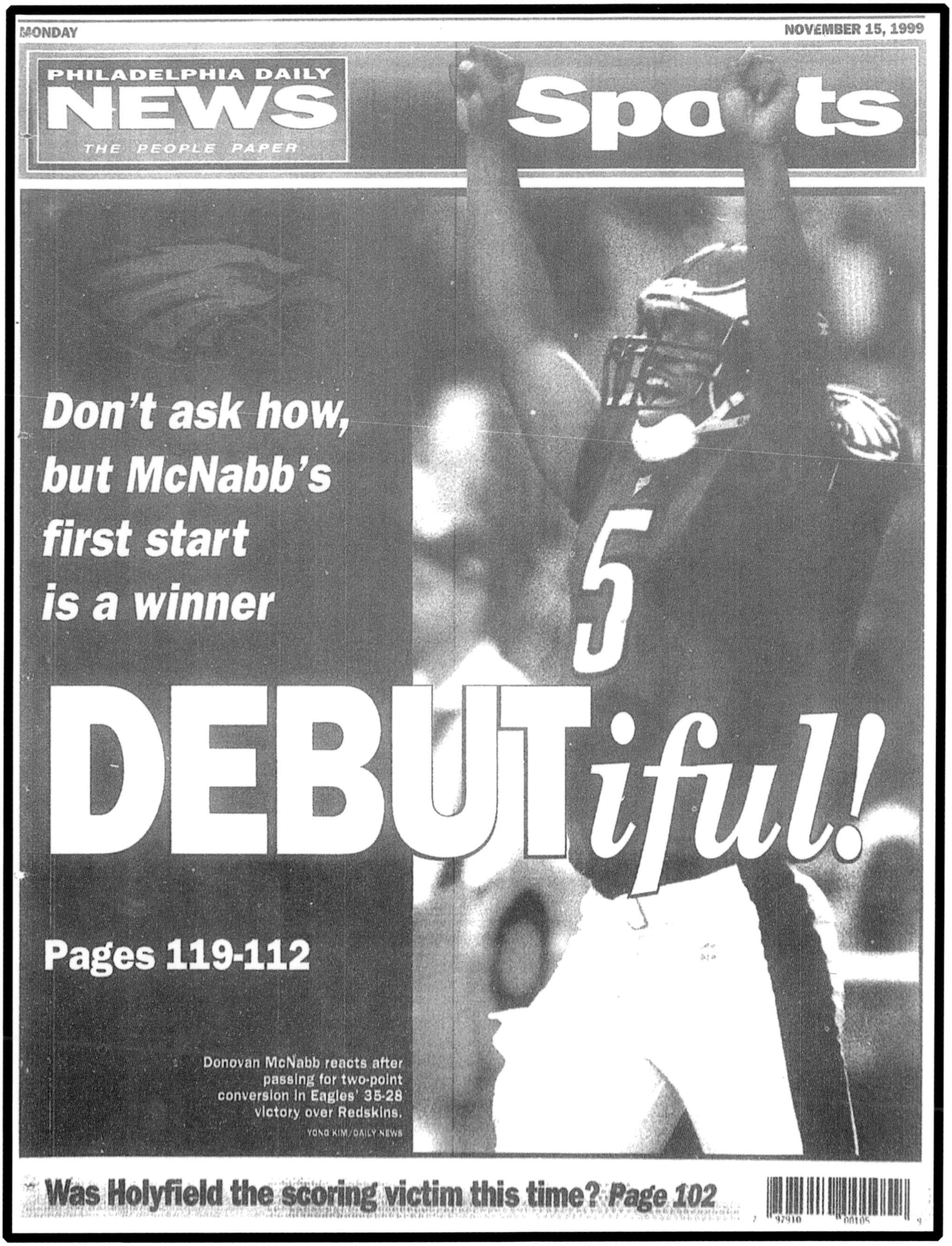

MONDAY NOVEMBER 15, 1999

PHILADELPHIA DAILY NEWS
THE PEOPLE PAPER

Sports

Don't ask how, but McNabb's first start is a winner

DEBUT*iful!*

Pages 119-112

Donovan McNabb reacts after passing for two-point conversion in Eagles' 35-28 victory over Redskins.

YONG KIM/DAILY NEWS

Was Holyfield the scoring victim this time? *Page 102*

November 15, 1999 - Rookie QB Donovan McNabb makes his first start for the Eagles as the Eagles defeat the Redskins 35-28

2000's

City Council President Anna Verna, NovaCare President Ed Miersch, Mayor John Street, Eagles Owner/President Jeffrey Lurie and his wife, Christina, at groundbreaking ceremonies for the NovaCare Complex.

Quarterback Donovan McNabb leads the Eagles in passing and rushing in just his second NFL season

DE Hugh Douglas's sack of Sean King sets up the Eagles' first TD in their 20-3 Wild Card Playoff Game victory over Tampa Bay on December 31, 2000

2000

The Eagles and NovaCare broke ground on the NovaCare Complex on February 14. Located on the grounds of the former Philadelphia Naval Hospital, the NovaCare Complex stands as the crown jewel in one of the most integrated and progressive corporate partnership deals in sports history. The 108,000-square foot facility houses the Eagles' corporate headquarters and practice facility as well as the NovaCare Center for Rehabilitation Excellence.

Over the latter half of the season, second-year quarterback Donovan McNabb came of age... and the Eagles took flight. McNabb helped the Eagles clinch a spot in the playoffs when he fired 4 TD passes at Cleveland.

On November 16, Lurie and representatives of the Phillies joined Mayor Street in announcing a deal that will result in the construction of 2 state-of-the-art stadiums in South Philadelphia.

On New Year's Eve, a national TV audience saw the Eagles dominate Tampa Bay in a 21-3, playoff game victory at Veterans Stadium. Andy Reid, whose efforts earned him numerous Coach of the Year honors, watched McNabb throw for two scores and run for another. Hugh Douglas, Philadelphia's Pro Bowl defensive end, set the tone early on when his sack of Shaun King caused a fumble and set up the Eagles' first TD.

2001

The winter/spring of 2001 literally marked the beginning of a new era in Eagles history. In March, the Eagles opened their $37 million NovaCare Complex - a state-of-the-art corporate headquarters and training facility – to rave reviews.

On June 7, years of visionary thinking and painstaking effort on the part of Eagles Chairman & CEO Jeffrey Lurie and team President Joe Banner turned a dream into reality as ground is broken for the Eagles' new stadium.

Led by head coach Andy Reid, a stellar defensive unit that sent four players to the Pro Bowl, and by quarterback Donovan McNabb, the Eagles marched to an 11-5 record, their first NFC East Division crown since 1988. Dramatic playoff victories over the visiting Buccaneers and on the road at Chicago vaulted the Eagles into the NFC Championship Game for the first time since 1980.

2002

In the Eagles' 31st and final season at Veterans Stadium, the club set a team record for points scored (415) and Andy Reid earned consensus NFL coach of the year honors after guiding the club to the top record in the NFC.

Donovan McNabb, who was sidelined by a broken ankle, returned for the postseason and directed a win over Atlanta in the Divisional playoff. But the Eagles fell short, 27-10, in the NFC title game to visiting Tampa Bay.

After being injured in the 1st quarter of game 10, McNabb still managed to fire 4 TD passes and engineered a win. A week later in a Monday Night win at San Francisco, backup QB Koy Detmer shined before suffering a dislocated elbow. The injury opened the door for third string passer A.J. Feeley, who went on to start the final five games, winning his first four.

The Eagles' stingy defense finished in the top five in numerous categories and sent four players to the Pro Bowl, including CBs Troy Vincent and Bobby Taylor and FS Brian Dawkins. The offensive line also featured multiple Pro Bowl selections for the first time since 1980 as Tra Thomas, Jon Runyan and Jermane Mayberry were honored. Kicker David Akers earned a Pro Bowl berth with a team record 133 points.

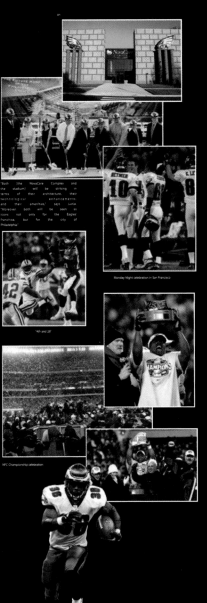

"Both [the NovaCare Complex and the stadium] will be striking in terms of their architecture, their technological enhancements, and their amenities," says Lurie. "Moreover, both will be seen as icons not only for the Eagles' franchise, but for the city of Philadelphia."

2003

The Eagles began the 2003 season by christening their new, state-of-the-art home, Lincoln Financial Field, with a breathtaking laser and fireworks show and a nationally televised matchup against the defending Super Bowl champion Buccanneers. In the months to come, the Birds would ultimately author a fireworks show of their own. Powered by a high-scoring offense and a suffocating defense, this Eagles season - like the two campaigns that came before - would end with Philadelphia on the brink of the Super Bowl.

Along the way, it was a huge, nine-game win streak that thrust the Eagles into contention for NFC superiority. The catalyst for the streak, however, was Brian Westbrook, who returned a punt 84 yards for a touchdown in the final minutes of a week six contest against the host NY Giants, lifting the team to an improbable victory.

Monday Night celebration in San Francisco

"4th and 26"

In the postseason, Donovan McNabb and Freddie Mitchell teamed up for an equally improbable 4th-and-26 completion that set up David Akers' game-tying field goal in the closing seconds of regulation play vs. Green Bay. Minutes later, Akers' overtime FG propelled the Eagles to a third consecutive berth in the NFC title game.

2004

One of the most eventful off-seasons in team history helped propel the Eagles to their first NFC Championship and their first Super Bowl appearance in 24 years. Although they would subsequently fall just tantalizingly short in the thrilling contest that was Super Bowl XXIX, the 24-21 loss to the New England Patriots in Jacksonville could not dull what was a glorious season marked by team success and great individual achievement. The milestones were plentiful as the Eagles captured their fourth consecutive NFC East division title and racked up a franchise-best 13 regular season wins. Along the way, head coach Andy Reid became the all-time winningest coach in franchise history surpassing the legendary Greasy Neale.

NFC Championship celebration

An unparalleled, aggressive approach to the off-season began on the first day of free agency when the Eagles inked all-pro DE Jevon Kearse. Shortly thereafter Philadelphia bolstered its offense with a highly-publicized trade involving Baltimore and San Francisco that sent all-pro WR Terrell Owens to the Eagles.

Philadelphia stormed out to a 7-0 record before stumbling at Pittsburgh. The Eagles, however, bounced back to clinch the NFC East title with five games remaining and locked up home field advantage in the NFC by compiling a 13-1 mark with two games still to play. In the playoffs, Philadelphia topped Minnesota to move on to a fourth straight NFC title game. This time, their third consecutive year hosting the big game, would be the charm. The Eagles subsequently downed Atlanta, 27 - 10 to advance to the Super Bowl. There, Eagles fans - a fervent bunch long known for their unparalleled passion and dedication - would turn Jacksonville into an unforgettable rolling sea of midnight green and silver.

2005

Reggie White's #92 was officially retired in an emotional halftime ceremony of a Monday night contest vs. Seattle on December 5. The ceremony included Reggie's wife, Sara, and their two children, as well as more than 20 of his former teammates and coaches.

The 2006 Eagles showed great character and toughness in claiming their fifth NFC Ea
Division Championship in six years, as they reeled off five consecutive wins at the end of th
regular season to finish 10-6. Their season began with a 4-1 start which perched them atc
the NFC Eas

The hot start was capped off by an emotional 38-24 victory at home vs. Terrell Owens and th
Dallas Cowboys on October 8th, in which Pro Bowl cornerback Lito Sheppard made two cruci
interceptions, the second of which he returned 102 yards for a touchdown in th
waning second

After losing five of their next six games and the services of Donovan McNabb to injury, 3
year-old Jeff Garcia was handed the reins of the quarterback position and rallied the Eagle
to five straight wins and a division title, including three straight wins on the road vs. NFC Eas
foes. They took the division lead for good on Christmas Day at Dallas in a decisive 23-7 victor

Brian Westbrook became the focal point of the Eagles offense, as he posted four 100-yar
rushing performances in the final eight games of the year, on his way to his first 1,000-yar
rushing season. Westbrook also amassed 1,916 yards from scrimmag
third most in team histor

The Eagles celebrated a 23-20 Wild Card game victory the following week against the Giants with a walk-off 38-yard field goal b
David Akers. A week later, however, the Eagles came out on the losing end of a 27-24 battle at New Orlean

200

In the team's 75th anniversary season, the Eagles could not overcome a 1-3 start as they finished 8-8 and out of the playof
for the just the 2nd time this decade

The Eagles welcomed back starting quarterback Donovan McNabb, who underwent a grueling rehabilitation after sufferin
a season-ending knee injury in November, 2006. He completed 61.5% of his passes (2nd best percentage of his career) fo
3,324 yards and an 89.9 QB rating. Although he missed two games due to ankle and thumb injuries, McNabb regained hi
mobility and confidence as the season progressed

As McNabb recaptured his touch, his multi-talented backfield mate, RB Brian Westbrook, set two single-season tear
records for total yards from scrimmage (2,104) and receptions (90). He became the first Eagle to lead the league in tota
yards from scrimmage since 1996 (Ricky Watters) and the first NFL player from a non-Division I-A school to do so since 197
(Philadelphia's Wilbert Montgomery). Westbrook also logged career highs in rushing yards (1,333), receiving yards (771
touches (368), and offensive touchdowns (12

WR Kevin Curtis posted career highs in catches (77), yards (1,110), and total touchdowns (8) in his first season i
Philadelphia after signing a lucrative free agent contract. For the first time in franchise history, the Eagles featured thre
players (Westbrook, Curtis, WR Reggie Brown) with over 60 catches and 700 yards each

With all those numbers, though, the Eagles failed to score 21 points in 10 of their games
including five of their first six. After that 1-3 start, the team managed to fight their wa
back to a 5-5 record as they headed into Gillette Stadium to face the 10-0 New Englan
Patriots. A valiant effort by back-up QB A.J. Feeley and the Eagles fell just three point
short in a 31-28 loss and the team subsequently dropped their next two tightly-contested
games (28- 24 to Seattle and 16-13 to the Giants) to fall to 5-8 and virtually out of playof
contention

Philadelphia ended the season on a high note, winning their final three games, including
victories at Dallas and New Orleans. Westbrook and RG Shawn Andrews both earned Pro
Bowl honors, while DE Trent Cole was selected as a first alternate after leading the team
with 12.5 sacks. Cole (103 stops) and DT Mike Patterson (114) became the first pair o
Eagles defensive lineman to notch 100 tackles in the same season since 1991

2000's

2000s DECADE IN REVIEW

2000-2007 Win-Loss Record:
83-45 (8-6* postseason record)

Home Field:
Veterans Stadium 2000-02;
Lincoln Financial Field 2002-Present

Playoff Appearances:
2000, 2001, 2002, 2003, 2004 and 2006

Championships:
Divisional Champions: 2001, 2002, 2003, 2004 and 2006

NFL/NFC Championship Games:
2001, 2002, 2003, and 2004

Super Bowl Appearance: XXXIV (2004)

Head Coaches:
Andy Reid 2000-2007 (83-45) (8-6 postseason record)

Hall of Fame Inductees:
None

Award Winners:
Donovan McNabb, NFC MVP 2000 and 2004;
Andy Reid, NFL Coach of the Year 2000 and 2002

All Pro:
Hugh Douglas 2000 and 2002; Jeremiah Trotter 2000;
David Akers 2001-02, 2004; Brian Dawkins 2001-04, 2006;
Corey Simon 2001; Jermane Mayberry 2002;
Bobby Taylor 2002; Tra Thomas 2002;
Troy Vincent 2002-03; Michael Lewis 2004;
Terrell Owens 2004; Ike Reese 2004,
Lito Sheppard 2004; Tra Thomas 2004;
Shawn Andrews 2006; Brian Westbrook 2008

Pro Bowl Selections:
Hugh Douglas 2001-03; Chad Lewis 2001-03;
Donovan McNabb 2001-05;
Jeremiah Trotter 2001-02, 2005-06;
Troy Vincent 2000-04; David Akers 2002-03, 2005;
Brian Dawkins 2000, 2002-03, 2005-07;
William Thomas 2002-03, 2005;
Jermane Mayberry 2003; Jon Runyan 2003;
Bobby Taylor 2003; Corey Simon 2004;
Terrell Owens 2005; Ike Reese 2005;
Lito Sheppard 2005, 2007; Michael Lewis 2005;
Brian Westbrook 2005, 2008, Mike Bartrum 2006;
Shawn Andrews 2007-08; Trent Cole 2008

First Game of the Decade:
September 3, 2000 defeated the Dallas Cowboys 41-14

Last Game of the Decade:
December 2009, not played yet

Largest Margin of Victory:
September 18, 2005 vs. San Francisco 49ers, 42-3

Largest Margin of Defeat:
December 5, 2005 vs. Seattle Seahawks, 42-0

Eagle Firsts of the Decade:

First Game at Lincoln Financial Field
September 8, 2003, lost to Tampa Bay Buccaneers 17-0

First Win at the Linc
October 5, 2002 vs. Washington Redskins 27- 25

First Playoff Game at the Linc
January 11, 2004, win over the Green Bay Packers 20-17

First Game Cancelled
August 13, 2001 vs. Baltimore Ravens in a preseason game due to poor field conditions at Veterans Stadium

First NFL Player to Intercept a Pass, Recover a Fumble, Record a Sack, and Catch a Touchdown Pass All in One Game.
September 29, 2002, was achieved by Brian Dawkins against the Houston Texans

First Super Bowl Appearance of the Decade
February 6, 2005, loss to New England Patriots 24-21

2000

RECORD: 11-5, 2ND IN NFC EAST
HEAD COACH: ANDY REID

Schedule

Regular Season

Wk. 1	Sep 3	W	41-14	at Dallas Cowboys
Wk. 2	Sep 10	L	33-18	vs New York Giants
Wk. 3	Sep 17	L	6-3	at Green Bay Packers
Wk. 4	Sep 24	W	21-7	at New Orleans Saints
Wk. 5	Oct 1	W	38-10	vs Atlanta Falcons
Wk. 6	Oct 8	L	17-14	vs Washington Redskins
Wk. 7	Oct 15	W	33-14	at Arizona Cardinals
Wk. 8	Oct 22	W	13-9	vs Chicago Bears
Wk. 9	Oct 29	L	24-7	at New York Giants
Wk. 10	Nov 5	W	16-13	vs Dallas Cowboys (OT)
Wk. 11	Nov 12	W	26-23	at Pittsburgh Steelers (OT)
Wk. 12	Nov 19	W	34-9	vs Arizona Cardinals
Wk. 13	Nov 26	W	23-20	at Washington Redskins
Wk. 14	Dec 3	L	15-13	vs Tennessee Titans
Wk. 15	Dec 10	W	35-24	at Cleveland Browns
Wk. 17	Dec 24	W	16-7	vs Cincinnati Bengals

Post Season

Wild Card Playoffs	Dec 31	W	21-3	vs Tampa Bay Buccaneers
Divisional Playoffs	Jan 7	L	20-10	at New York Giants

In his first season as starter Donovan McNabb established himself as a rising star by passing for 3,365 yards and rushing for an additional 629 yards. Behind McNabb the Eagles played solid football all season, sometimes winning games in heart-stopping fashion while compiling an 11-5 record. However, two costly losses to the New York Giants cost the Eagles the division title. Settling for the Wild Card, the Eagles hosted the Tampa Bay Buccaneers in the Vet in the first round of the playoffs. In his first playoff game Donovan McNabb simply took over as the Eagles dominated the Bucs all day on the way to a 21-3 win. However, a week later the Eagles would be stymied by the Giants again, 20-10 in the Meadowlands.

2000 Philadelphia Eagles Stats

Passing	Comp	Att	Comp %	Yds	Y/Att	TD	Int	Rating
Donovan McNabb	330	569	58.0	3365	5.91	21	13	77.8
Brian Mitchell	1	4	25.0	21	5.25	0	0	49.0
Koy Detmer	0	1	0.0	0	0.00	0	1	0.0
Torrance Small	0	1	0.0	0	0.00	0	1	0.0

Rushing	Rush	Yds	Avg	TD
Donovan McNabb	86	629	7.3	6
Duce Staley	79	344	4.4	1
Darnell Autry	112	334	3.0	3
Stanley Pritchett	58	225	3.9	1
Brian Mitchell	25	187	7.5	2
Cecil Martin	13	77	5.9	0
Chris Warren	15	42	2.8	0
Charles Johnson	5	18	3.6	0
Koy Detmer	1	8	8.0	0
David Akers	1	2	2.0	0
Amp Lee	1	2	2.0	0
Torrance Small	1	1	1.0	0

Interceptions	Int	Yds	Avg	TD
Troy Vincent	5	34	6.8	0
Brian Dawkins	4	62	15.5	0
Bobby Taylor	3	64	21.3	0
Damon Moore	2	24	12.0	0
Carlos Emmons	2	8	4.0	0
Jeremiah Trotter	1	27	27.0	1
Mike Caldwell	1	26	26.0	1
Hugh Douglas	1	9	9.0	0
Al Harris	0	1	0.0	0

Receiving	Rec	Yds	Avg	TD
Chad Lewis	69	735	10.7	3
Charles Johnson	56	642	11.5	7
Torrance Small	40	569	14.2	3
Cecil Martin	31	219	7.1	0
Duce Staley	25	201	8.0	0
Stanley Pritchett	25	193	7.7	0
Darnell Autry	24	275	11.5	1
Brian Mitchell	13	89	6.8	1
Luther Broughton	12	104	8.7	0
Todd Pinkston	10	181	18.1	0
Jeff Thomason	10	46	4.6	5
Na Brown	9	80	8.9	1
Donovan McNabb	2	5	2.5	0
Amp Lee	1	20	20.0	0
Dameane Douglas	1	9	9.0	0
Bubba Miller	1	9	9.0	0
Alex Van Dyke	1	8	8.0	0
Chris Warren	1	1	1.0	0

Punting	Punts	Yds	Avg	Blocked
Sean Landeta	86	3635	42.3	0

Kicking	PAT Made	PAT Att	PAT %	FG Made	FG Att	FG %	Pts
David Akers	34	36	94	29	33	87.9	121

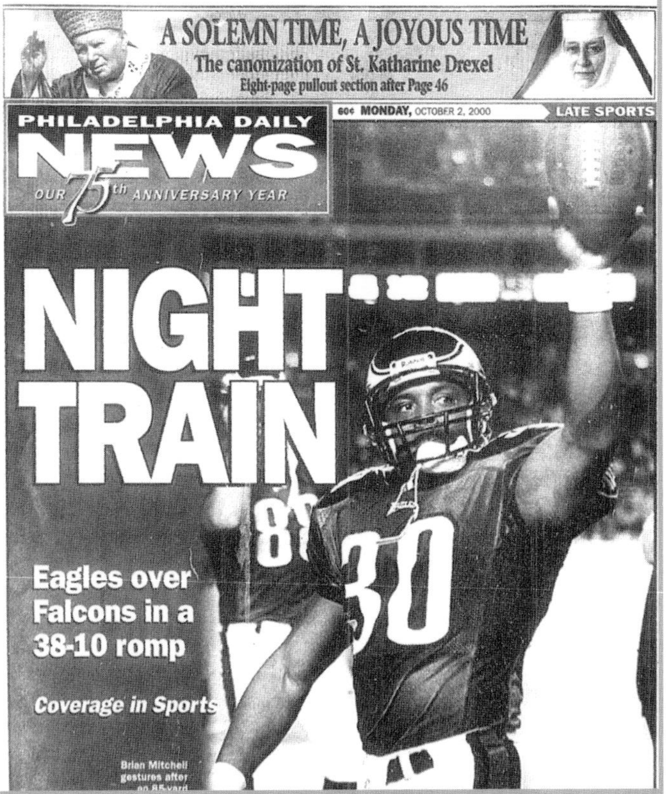

A SOLEMN TIME, A JOYOUS TIME
The canonization of St. Katharine Drexel
Eight-page pullout section after Page 46

PHILADELPHIA DAILY NEWS
OUR 75th ANNIVERSARY YEAR

60¢ MONDAY, OCTOBER 2, 2000 LATE SPORTS

NIGHT TRAIN

Eagles over Falcons in a 38-10 romp

Coverage in Sports

Brian Mitchell gestures after an 85-yard

October 2, 2000
Eagles over Falcons in a 38-10 romp

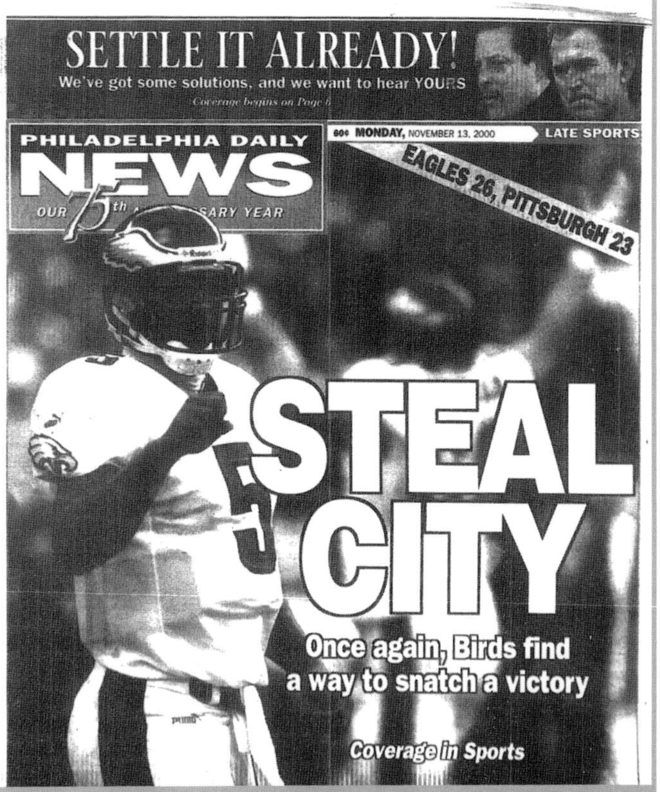

SETTLE IT ALREADY!
We've got some solutions, and we want to hear YOURS
Coverage begins on Page 6

PHILADELPHIA DAILY NEWS
OUR 75th ANNIVERSARY YEAR

60¢ MONDAY, NOVEMBER 13, 2000 LATE SPORTS

EAGLES 26, PITTSBURGH 23

STEAL CITY

Once again, Birds find a way to snatch a victory

Coverage in Sports

November 13, 2000
Eagles steal one from the Steelers 26- 23

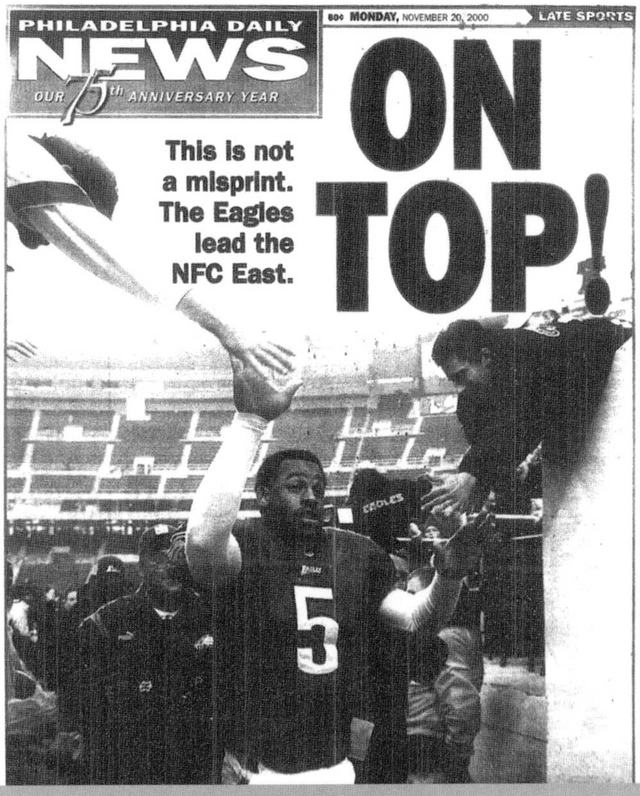

PHILADELPHIA DAILY NEWS
OUR 75th ANNIVERSARY YEAR

60¢ MONDAY, NOVEMBER 20, 2000 LATE SPORTS

ON TOP!

This is not a misprint. The Eagles lead the NFC East.

November 20, 2000
Eagles fly over Cardinals 34-9

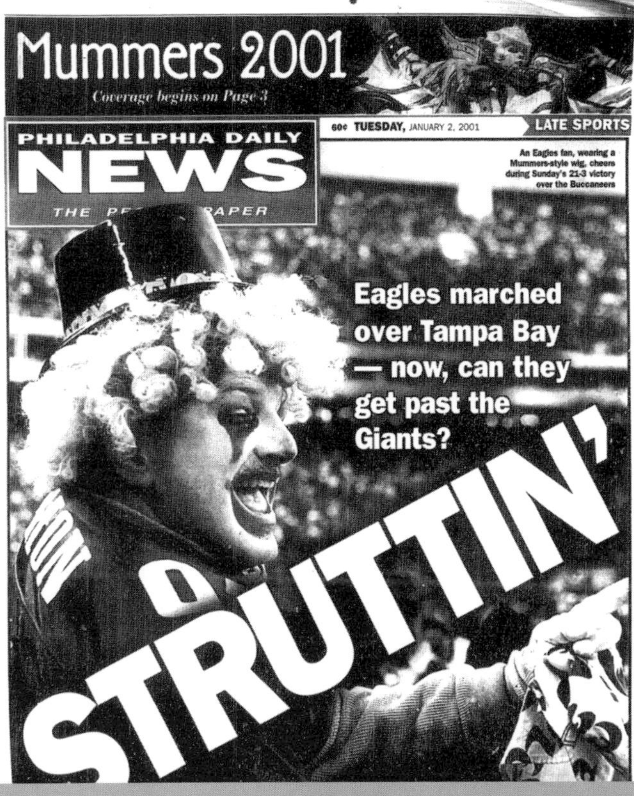

Mummers 2001
Coverage begins on Page 3

PHILADELPHIA DAILY NEWS
THE PEOPLE PAPER

60¢ TUESDAY, JANUARY 2, 2001 LATE SPORTS

An Eagles fan, wearing a Mummers-style wig, cheers during Sunday's 21-3 victory over the Buccaneers

Eagles marched over Tampa Bay — now, can they get past the Giants?

STRUTTIN'

January 2, 2001
Eagles strut over Buc's 21-3

2000

2001

RECORD: 11-5, 1ST IN NFC EAST
HEAD COACH: ANDY REID

Schedule

Regular Season

Wk. 1	Sep 9	L	20-17	vs St. Louis Rams (OT)
Wk. 2	Sep 23	W	27-3	at Seattle Seahawks
Wk. 3	Sep 30	W	40-18	vs Dallas Cowboys
Wk. 4	Oct 7	L	21-20	vs Arizona Cardinals
Wk. 6	Oct 22	W	10-9	at New York Giants
Wk. 7	Oct 28	L	20-10	vs Oakland Raiders
Wk. 8	Nov 4	W	21-7	vs Arizona Cardinals
Wk. 9	Nov 11	W	48-17	vs Minnesota Vikings
Wk. 10	Nov 18	W	36-3	at Dallas Cowboys
Wk. 11	Nov 25	L	13-3	vs Washington Redskins
Wk. 12	Nov 29	W	23-10	at Kansas City Chiefs
Wk. 13	Dec 9	W	24-14	vs San Diego Chargers
Wk. 14	Dec 16	W	20-6	at Washington Redskins
Wk. 15	Dec 22	L	13-3	at San Francisco 49ers
Wk. 16	Dec 30	W	24-21	vs New York Giants
Wk. 17	Jan 6	W	17-13	at Tampa Bay Buccaneers

Post Season

Wild Card Playoffs				
	Jan 12	W	31-9	vs Tampa Bay Buccaneers
Divisional Playoffs				
	Jan 19	W	33-19	at Chicago Bears
Conference Championship				
	Jan 27	L	29-24	at St. Louis Rams

The Eagles captured their first NFC Eastern Division Championship since 1988 and their first appointment in the NFC title game since 1980. Adversity hit this club early and often. The first preseason game was cancelled due to problems with the Veterans Stadium Nexturf. Starting C Bubba Miller was lost to a season ending foot injury. And they dropped their season opener in overtime to the Rams before true adversity devastated the entire world on September 11th when terrorist attacks struck the World Trade Center and the Pentagon. As a result, a week's worth of NFL games were postponed. The Eagles were 2-2 before beating the Giants, 10-9, on Monday Night Football for the first time since 1996 (a span of nine games). The Eagles won 8 of their last 10 games, including a dramatic 24-21 win over the Giants on December 30 to clinch the NFC East title. In the playoffs, the Eagles defeated the Bucs again, 31-9, and in the Divisional playoffs, Donovan McNabb made his homecoming to Chicago a sweet one, winning 33-19 at Soldier Field.

2001 Philadelphia Eagles Stats

Passing	Comp	Att	Comp %	Yds	Y/Att	TD	Int	Rating
Donovan McNabb	285	493	57.8	3233	6.56	25	12	84.3
A. J. Feeley	10	14	71.4	143	10.21	2	1	114.0
Freddie Mitchell	0	1	0.0	0	0.00	0	0	39.6
Koy Detmer	5	14	35.7	51	3.64	0	1	17.3

Rushing	Rush	Yds	Avg	TD
Duce Staley	166	604	3.6	2
Correll Buckhalter	129	586	4.5	2
Donovan McNabb	82	482	5.9	2
James Thrash	6	57	9.5	0
Cecil Martin	9	27	3.0	0
Brian Mitchell	7	9	1.3	0
Koy Detmer	8	6	0.8	0
Rod Smart	2	6	3.0	0
Todd Pinkston	1	5	5.0	0
Freddie Mitchell	2	-4	-2.0	0

Interceptions	Int	Yds	Avg	TD
Troy Vincent	3	0	0.0	0
Jeremiah Trotter	2	64	32.0	1
Al Harris	2	22	11.0	0
Brian Dawkins	2	15	7.5	0
Damon Moore	2	2	1.0	0
William Hampton	1	33	33.0	1
Rashard Cook	1	11	11.0	0
Bobby Taylor	1	5	5.0	0\

Receiving	Rec	Yds	Avg	TD
James Thrash	63	833	13.2	8
Duce Staley	63	626	9.9	2
Todd Pinkston	42	586	14.0	4
Chad Lewis	41	422	10.3	6
Cecil Martin	24	124	5.2	2
Freddie Mitchell	21	283	13.5	1
Correll Buckhalter	13	130	10.0	0
Na Brown	7	95	13.6	0
Brian Mitchell	6	122	20.3	0
Dameane Douglas	5	77	15.4	2
Tony Stewart	5	52	10.4	1
Jeff Thomason	5	33	6.6	0
Gari Scott	2	26	13.0	0
Jamie Reader	2	14	7.0	0
Mike Bartrum	1	4	4.0	1

Punting	Punts	Yds	Avg	Blocked
Sean Landeta	97	4221	43.5	0

Kicking	PAT Made	PAT Att	PAT %	FG Made	FG Att	FG %	Pts
David Akers	37	38	97	26	31	83.9	115

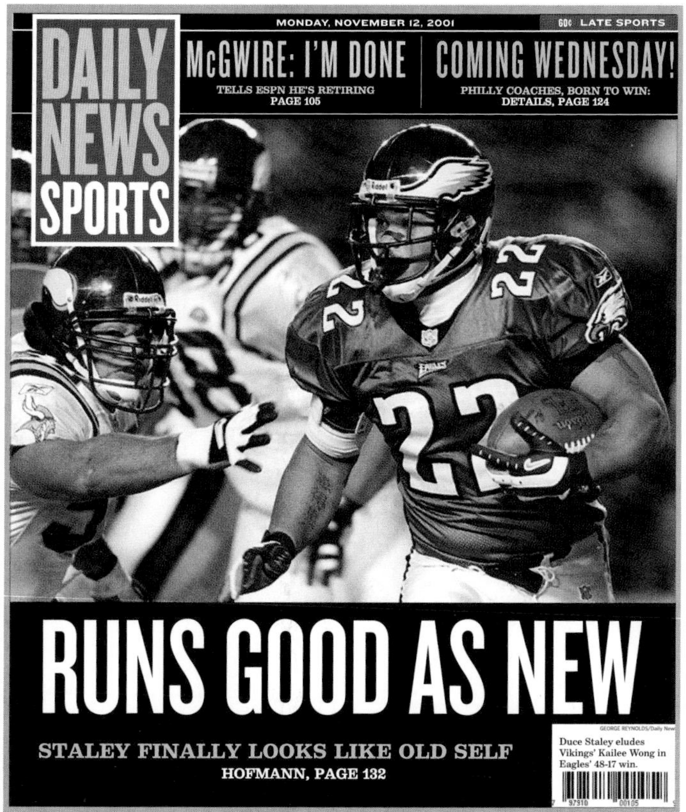
MONDAY, NOVEMBER 12, 2001 60¢ LATE SPORTS

DAILY NEWS SPORTS

McGWIRE: I'M DONE
TELLS ESPN HE'S RETIRING
PAGE 105

COMING WEDNESDAY!
PHILLY COACHES, BORN TO WIN:
DETAILS, PAGE 124

RUNS GOOD AS NEW

STALEY FINALLY LOOKS LIKE OLD SELF
HOFMANN, PAGE 132

GEORGE REYNOLDS/Daily News
Duce Staley eludes Vikings' Kailee Wong in Eagles' 48-17 win.

November 12, 2001
Eagles run all over Vikings 48-17

MONDAY, DECEMBER 17, 2001 LATE SPORTS 60¢

PHILADELPHIA DAILY NEWS
THE PEOPLE

THIS TIME, EAGLES DOMINATE WASHINGTON

SWEET REVENGE!

BIRD WATCH: PAGES 130-120

Brian Mitchell gets a hug from Donovan McNabb after the game.
GEORGE REYNOLDS/Daily News

December 17, 2001
Eagles dominate Redskins 20-6

MONDAY, DECEMBER 31, 2001 HOME EDITION 60¢

PHILADELPHIA DAILY NEWS
THE PEOPLE PAPER

CLINCH!

EAGLES SURVIVE LAST-SECOND SCARE, BEAT GIANTS, WIN NFC EAST CROWN

BIRD WATCH: PAGES 110-100

Corey Simon lets out a yell after the too-close-for-comfort ending to yesterday's 24-21 victory.
YONG KIM/Daily News

December 31, 2001
Eagles win NFC East defeating Giants 24-21

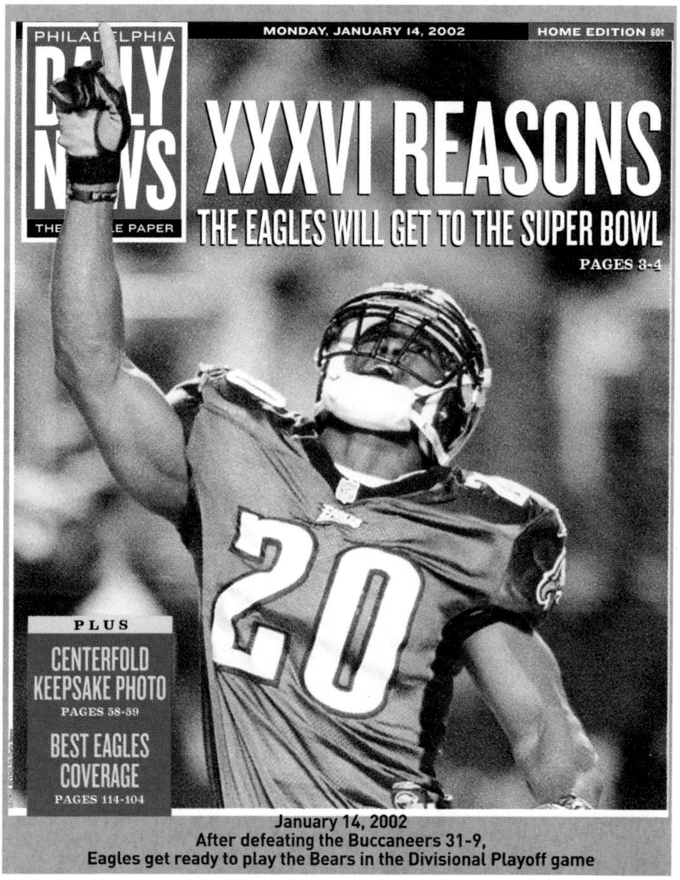
MONDAY, JANUARY 14, 2002 HOME EDITION 60¢

PHILADELPHIA DAILY NEWS
THE PEOPLE PAPER

XXXVI REASONS
THE EAGLES WILL GET TO THE SUPER BOWL
PAGES 3-4

PLUS
CENTERFOLD KEEPSAKE PHOTO
PAGES 58-59
BEST EAGLES COVERAGE
PAGES 114-104

January 14, 2002
After defeating the Buccaneers 31-9,
Eagles get ready to play the Bears in the Divisional Playoff game

2001

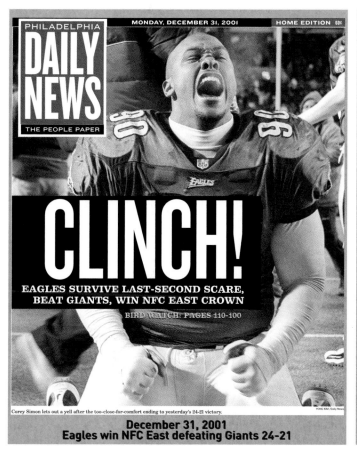

2002

RECORD: 12-4, 1ST IN NFC EAST
HEAD COACH: ANDY REID

Schedule

Regular Season

Wk. 1	Sep 8	L	27-24	at Tennessee Titans
Wk. 2	Sep 16	W	37-7	at Washington Redskins
Wk. 3	Sep 22	W	44-13	vs Dallas Cowboys
Wk. 4	Sep 29	W	35-17	vs Houston Texans
Wk. 5	Oct 6	L	28-25	at Jacksonville Jaguars
Wk. 7	Oct 20	W	20-10	vs Tampa Bay Buccaneers
Wk. 8	Oct 28	W	17-3	vs New York Giants
Wk. 9	Nov 3	W	19-13	at Chicago Bears
Wk. 10	Nov 10	L	35-13	vs Indianapolis Colts
Wk. 11	Nov 17	W	38-14	vs Arizona Cardinals
Wk. 12	Nov 24	W	38-17	at San Francisco 49ers
Wk. 13	Dec 1	W	10-3	vs St. Louis Rams
Wk. 14	Dec 8	W	27-20	at Seattle Seahawks
Wk. 15	Dec 15	W	34-21	vs Washington Redskins
Wk. 16	Dec 21	W	27-3	at Dallas Cowboys
Wk. 17	Dec 28	L	10-7	at New York Giants (OT)

Post Season

Divisional Playoffs

	Jan 11	W	20-6	vs Atlanta Falcons

Conference Championship

	Jan 19	L	27-10	vs Tampa Bay Buccaneers

In the 31st and final season at Veterans Stadium, the Eagles set a team record for points scored (415) and sent a league-high 10 players to the Pro Bowl. However, they fell in the NFC Championship game for the second consecutive season. Andy Reid, the consensus coach of the year, proved the Eagles were not a one-man show, winning five of six games without Donovan McNabb (broken ankle). McNabb returned for the playoffs and directed a win in the Divisional playoff after 3rd QB A.J. Feeley started the final five games, winning his first four. Although the Eagles lost their season finale to the Giants, they were still able to clinch home field after the Jets trounced the Packers in the same stadium one day later.

2002 Philadelphia Eagles Stats

Passing	Comp	Att	Comp %	Yds	Y/Att	TD	Int	Rating
Donovan McNabb	211	361	58.4	2289	6.34	17	6	86.0
A. J. Feeley	86	154	55.8	1011	6.56	6	5	75.4
Brian Mitchell	1	1	100.0	57	57.00	1	0	158.3
Brian Westbrook	1	1	100.0	25	25.00	1	0	158.3
Koy Detmer	19	28	67.9	224	8.00	2	0	115.8
Dorsey Levens	0	2	0.0	0	0.00	0	0	39.6
Freddie Mitchell	0	1	0.0	0	0.00	0	0	39.6

Rushing	Rush	Yds	Avg	TD
Duce Staley	269	1029	3.8	5
Donovan McNabb	63	460	7.3	6
Dorsey Levens	75	411	5.5	1
Brian Westbrook	46	193	4.2	0
James Thrash	18	126	7.0	2
David Akers	1	10	10.0	0
A. J. Feeley	12	6	0.5	0
Koy Detmer	2	4	2.0	1
Sean Landeta	1	0	0.0	0
Cecil Martin	1	-4	-4.0	0
Todd Pinkston	1	-15	-15.0	0

Punting	Punts	Yds	Avg	Blocked
Sean Landeta	52	2229	42.9	0
Lee Johnson	14	523	37.4	0
Jason Baker	13	445	34.2	0

Kicking	PAT Made	PAT Att	PAT %	FG Made	FG Att	FG %	Pts
David Akers	43	43	100	30	34	88.2	133

Receiving	Rec	Yds	Avg	TD
Todd Pinkston	60	798	13.3	7
James Thrash	52	635	12.2	6
Duce Staley	51	541	10.6	3
Antonio Freeman	46	600	13.0	4
Chad Lewis	42	398	9.5	3
Dorsey Levens	19	124	6.5	1
Cecil Martin	15	126	8.4	0
Freddie Mitchell	12	105	8.8	0
Jeff Thomason	10	128	12.8	2
Brian Westbrook	9	86	9.6	0
Brian Dawkins	1	57	57.0	1
Mike Bartrum	1	8	8.0	0

Interceptions	Int	Yds	Avg	TD
Bobby Taylor	5	43	8.6	1
Shawn Barber	2	81	40.5	1
Sheldon Brown	2	41	20.5	0
Brian Dawkins	2	27	13.5	0
Troy Vincent	2	1	0.5	0
Al Harris	1	0	0.0	0
Michael Lewis	1	0	0.0	0

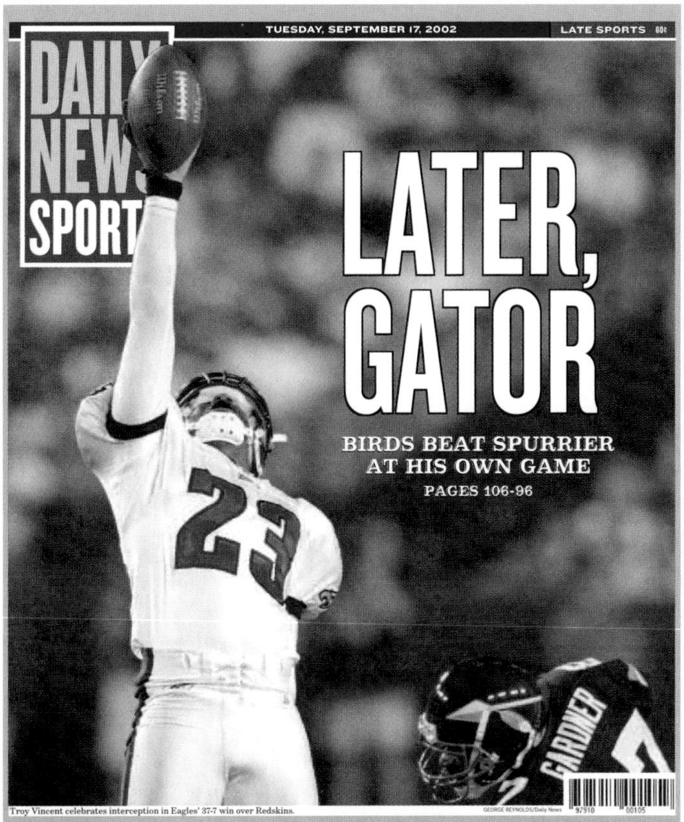
TUESDAY, SEPTEMBER 17, 2002 LATE SPORTS 60¢

DAILY NEWS SPORTS

LATER, GATOR

BIRDS BEAT SPURRIER AT HIS OWN GAME

PAGES 106-96

Troy Vincent celebrates interception in Eagles' 37-7 win over Redskins.

GEORGE REYNOLDS/Daily News

September 17, 2002
Eagles skin the Redskins 37-7

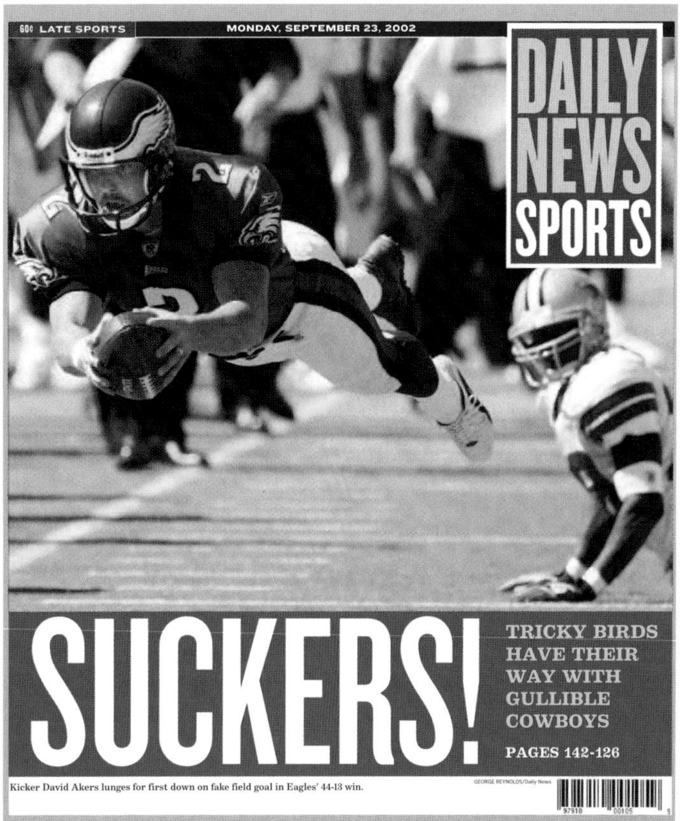
60¢ LATE SPORTS MONDAY, SEPTEMBER 23, 2002

DAILY NEWS SPORTS

SUCKERS!

TRICKY BIRDS HAVE THEIR WAY WITH GULLIBLE COWBOYS

PAGES 142-126

Kicker David Akers lunges for first down on fake field goal in Eagles' 44-13 win.

GEORGE REYNOLDS/Daily News

September 23, 2002
Eagles trick the Cowboys and win 44-13

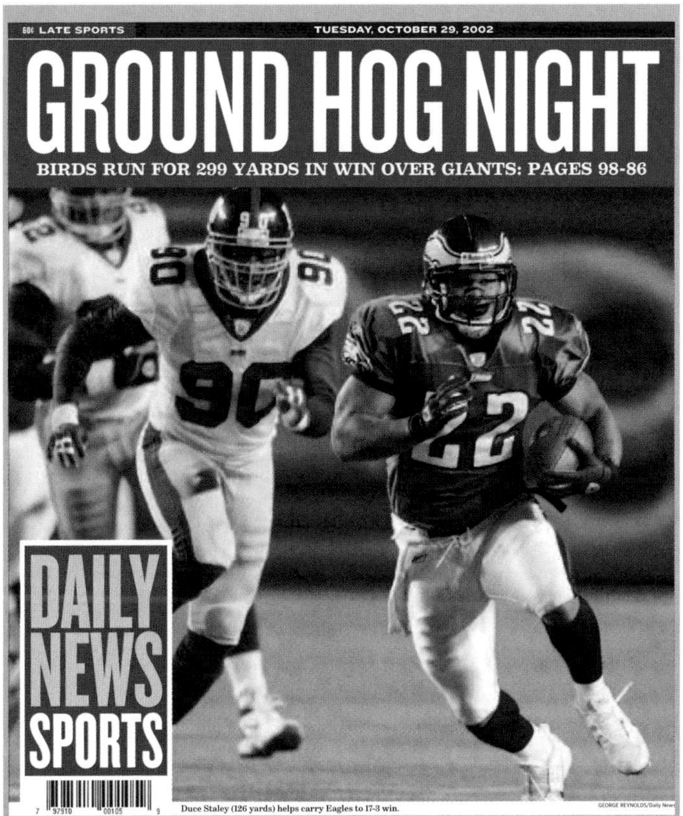
60¢ LATE SPORTS TUESDAY, OCTOBER 29, 2002

GROUND HOG NIGHT

BIRDS RUN FOR 299 YARDS IN WIN OVER GIANTS: PAGES 98-86

DAILY NEWS SPORTS

Duce Staley (126 yards) helps carry Eagles to 17-3 win.

GEORGE REYNOLDS/Daily News

October 29, 2002
Eagle run all over the Giants 17-3

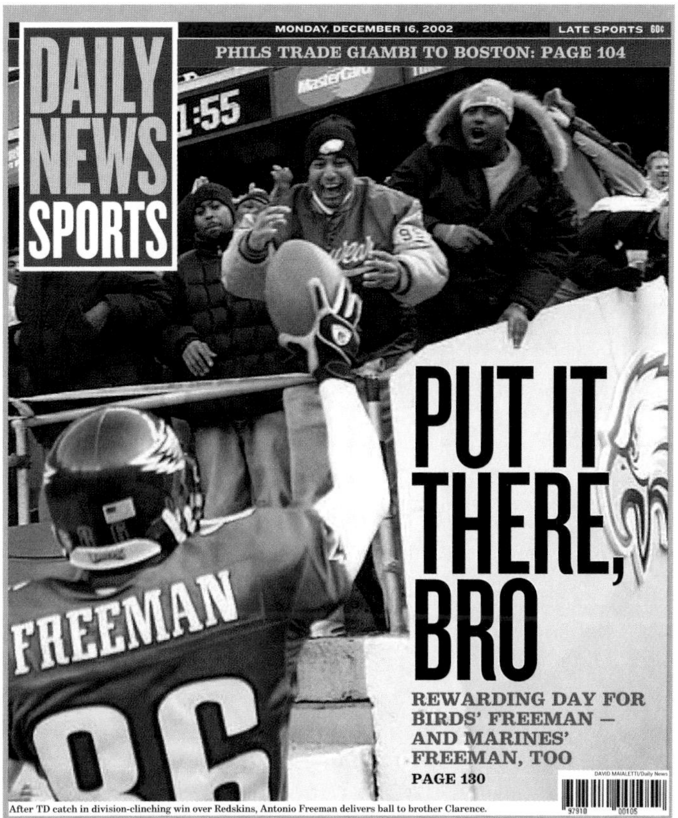
MONDAY, DECEMBER 16, 2002 LATE SPORTS 60¢

DAILY NEWS SPORTS

PHILS TRADE GIAMBI TO BOSTON: PAGE 104

PUT IT THERE, BRO

REWARDING DAY FOR BIRDS' FREEMAN — AND MARINES' FREEMAN, TOO

PAGE 130

After TD catch in division-clinching win over Redskins, Antonio Freeman delivers ball to brother Clarence.

DAVID MAIALETTI/Daily News

December 16, 2002
Eagles defeated the Redskins 34-21

2002

2003

RECORD: 12-4, 1ST IN NFC EAST
HEAD COACH: ANDY REID

Schedule

Regular Season

Wk. 1	Sep 8	L	17-0	vs Tampa Bay Buccaneers
Wk. 2	Sep 14	L	31-10	vs New England Patriots
Wk. 4	Sep 28	W	23-13	at Buffalo Bills
Wk. 5	Oct 5	W	27-25	vs Washington Redskins
Wk. 6	Oct 12	L	23-21	at Dallas Cowboys
Wk. 7	Oct 19	W	14-10	at New York Jets
Wk. 8	Oct 26	W	24-17	vs New York Jets
Wk. 9	Nov 2	W	23-16	at Atlanta Falcons
Wk. 10	Nov 10	W	17-14	at Green Bay Packers
Wk. 11	Nov 16	W	28-10	vs New York Giants
Wk. 12	Nov 23	W	33-20	vs New Orleans Saints
Wk. 13	Nov 30	W	25-16	at Carolina Panthers
Wk. 14	Dec 7	W	36-10	vs Dallas Cowboys
Wk. 15	Dec 15	W	34-27	at Miami Dolphins
Wk. 16	Dec 21	L	31-28	vs San Francisco 49ers (OT)
Wk. 17	Dec 27	W	31-7	at Washington Redskins

Post Season

Divisional Playoffs				
	Jan 11	W	20-17	vs Green Bay Packers (OT)
Conference Championship				
	Jan 18	L	14-3	vs Carolina Panthers

Lincoln Financial Field officially became the Eagles new nest with a season opening Monday Night contest vs. Tampa Bay. But the Eagles not only lost their first two contests, they were left without the services of Pro Bowl defensive backs Brian Dawkins and Bobby Taylor for a large chunk of the regular season (foot injuries). After a 2-3 start, the Eagles rattled off nine straight wins, tying a team record previously set in 1960. That win streak was propelled by an improbable win at NYG on October 19. Trailing the Giants 10-7 with 1:34 remaining, no timeouts and a sputtering offense, Westbrook fielded a bouncing punt and raced 84 yards for the dramatic, game-winning score. During that win streak, the Eagles toughed out a crucial win at Green Bay with a last-minute, game-winning drive directed by Donovan McNabb and ended up earning home-field advantage in the playoffs for the 2nd straight season. The Eagles captured their third consecutive NFC East division title and third straight trip to the NFC title game. However McNabb suffering from a rib injury sustained against Green bay wasn't able to finish the Championship game and was sidelined in the 4th quarter as the Eagles loss to Carolina 14-3.

2003 Philadelphia Eagles Stats

Passing	Comp	Att	Comp %	Yds	Y/Att	TD	Int	Rating
Donovan McNabb	275	478	57.5	3216	6.73	16	11	79.6
Freddie Mitchell	1	1	100.0	25	25.00	1	0	158.3
Koy Detmer	3	5	60.0	32	6.40	0	0	78.8

Rushing	Rush	Yds	Avg	TD
Brian Westbrook	117	613	5.2	7
Correll Buckhalter	126	542	4.3	8
Duce Staley	96	463	4.8	5
Donovan McNabb	71	355	5.0	3
James Thrash	5	52	10.4	0
Jon Ritchie	1	1	1.0	0
Todd Pinkston	1	-11	-11.0	0

Interceptions	Int	Yds	Avg	TD
Michael Lewis	3	31	10.3	0
Troy Vincent	3	28	9.3	0
Lito Sheppard	1	34	34.0	0
Nate Wayne	1	33	33.0	0
Ndukwe Kalu	1	15	15.0	1
Sheldon Brown	1	10	10.0	0
Roderick Hood	1	5	5.0	0
Bobby Taylor	1	2	2.0	0
Brian Dawkins	1	0	0.0	0

Receiving	Rec	Yds	Avg	TD
James Thrash	49	558	11.4	1
Brian Westbrook	37	332	9.0	4
Todd Pinkston	36	575	16.0	2
Duce Staley	36	382	10.6	2
Freddie Mitchell	35	498	14.2	2
L. J. Smith	27	321	11.9	1
Chad Lewis	23	293	12.7	1
Jon Ritchie	17	86	5.1	3
Correll Buckhalter	10	133	13.3	1
Greg Lewis	6	95	15.8	0
Reno Mahe	1	5	5.0	0
Billy McMullen	1	2	2.0	0
Donovan McNabb	1	-7	-7.0	0

Punting	Punts	Yds	Avg	Blocked
Dirk Johnson	79	3207	40.6	1

Kicking	PAT Made	PAT Att	PAT %	FG Made	FG Att	FG %	Pts
David Akers	42	42	100	24	29	82.8	114

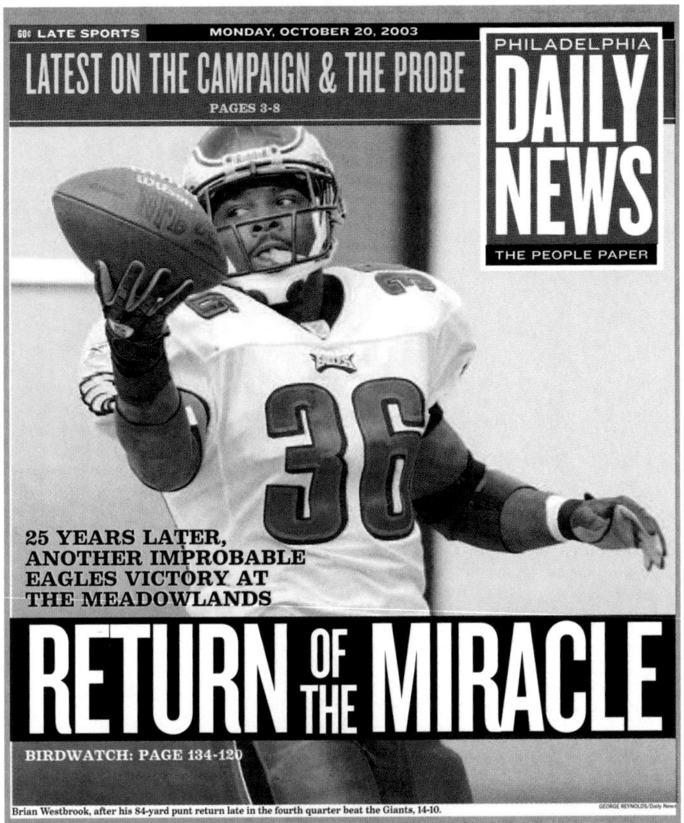
60¢ LATE SPORTS MONDAY, OCTOBER 20, 2003

LATEST ON THE CAMPAIGN & THE PROBE

PAGES 3-8

PHILADELPHIA DAILY NEWS THE PEOPLE PAPER

25 YEARS LATER, ANOTHER IMPROBABLE EAGLES VICTORY AT THE MEADOWLANDS

RETURN OF THE MIRACLE

BIRDWATCH: PAGE 134-120

Brian Westbrook, after his 84-yard punt return late in the fourth quarter beat the Giants, 14-10. GEORGE REYNOLDS/Daily News

October 20, 2003
Eagles defeated Jets 14-10

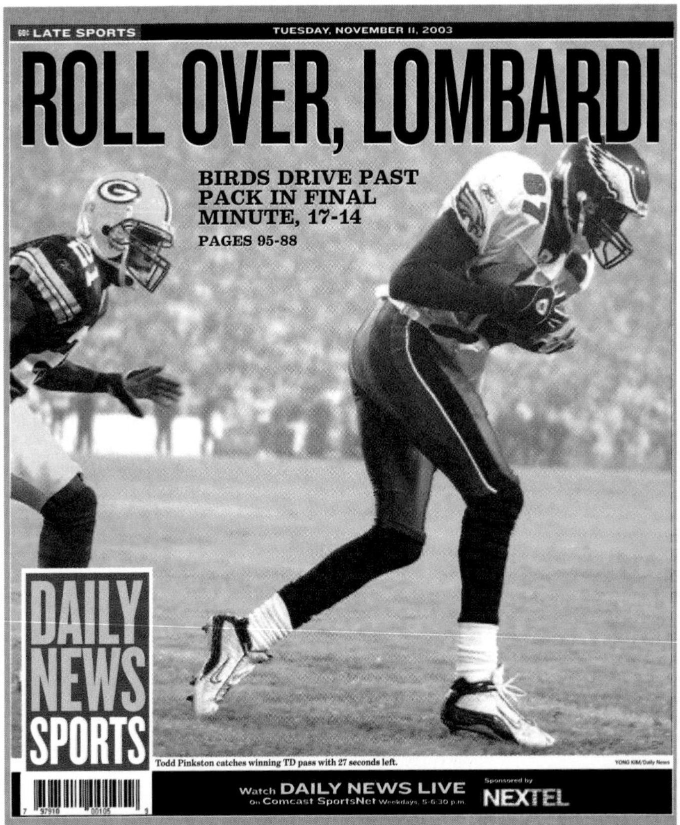
60¢ LATE SPORTS TUESDAY, NOVEMBER 11, 2003

ROLL OVER, LOMBARDI

BIRDS DRIVE PAST PACK IN FINAL MINUTE, 17-14

PAGES 95-88

DAILY NEWS SPORTS

Todd Pinkston catches winning TD pass with 27 seconds left. YONG KIM/Daily News

Watch DAILY NEWS LIVE On Comcast SportsNet Weekdays, 5-6:30 p.m. Sponsored by NEXTEL

November 11, 2003
Eagles last drive defeats Packers 17-14

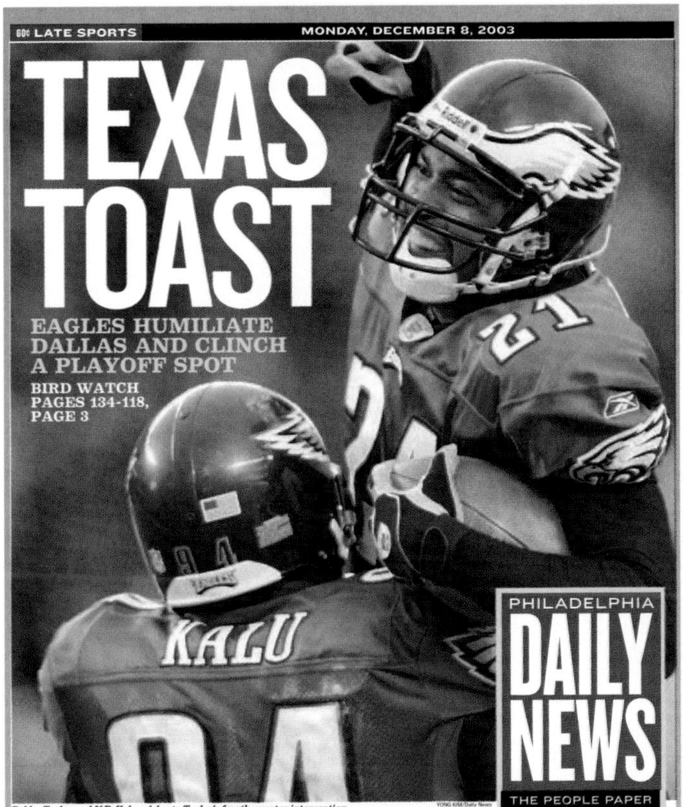
60¢ LATE SPORTS MONDAY, DECEMBER 8, 2003

TEXAS TOAST

EAGLES HUMILIATE DALLAS AND CLINCH A PLAYOFF SPOT

BIRD WATCH PAGES 134-118, PAGE 3

PHILADELPHIA DAILY NEWS THE PEOPLE PAPER

Bobby Taylor and N.D. Kalu celebrate Taylor's fourth-quarter interception. YONG KIM/Daily News

December 8, 2003
Eagles Humiliate Cowboys 36-10

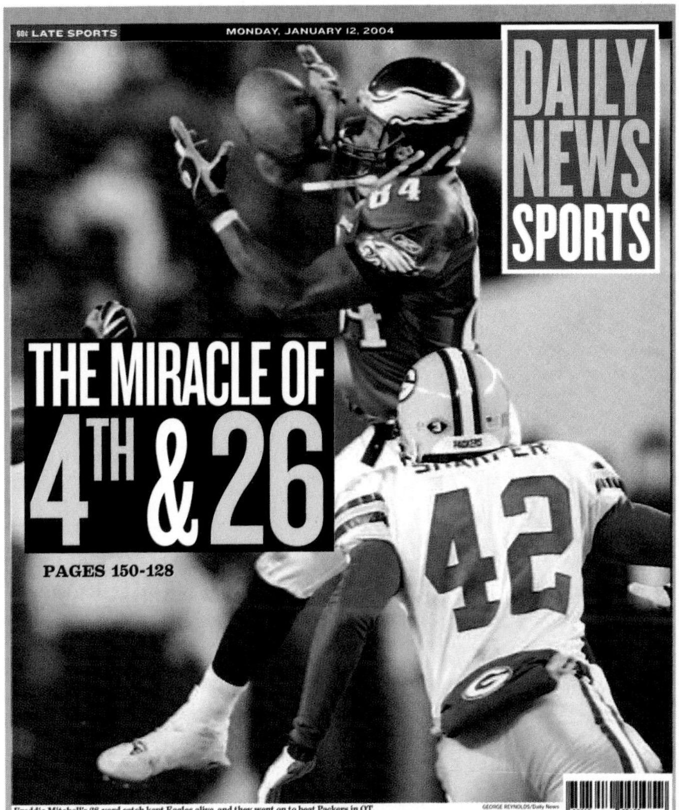
60¢ LATE SPORTS MONDAY, JANUARY 12, 2004

DAILY NEWS SPORTS

THE MIRACLE OF 4TH & 26

PAGES 150-128

Freddie Mitchell's 28-yard catch kept Eagles alive, and they went on to beat Packers in OT. GEORGE REYNOLDS/Daily News

January 12, 2004
Eagles "go for it" and defeat the Packers 20-17

2003

2004

RECORD: 13-3, 1ST IN NFC EAST
HEAD COACH: ANDY REID

SCHEDULE

REGULAR SEASON

Wk. 1	Sep 12	W	31-17	vs New York Giants
Wk. 2	Sep 20	W	27-16	vs Minnesota Vikings
Wk. 3	Sep 26	W	30-13	at Detroit Lions
Wk. 4	Oct 3	W	19-9	at Chicago Bears
Wk. 6	Oct 17	W	30-8	vs Carolina Panthers
Wk. 7	Oct 24	W	34-31	at Cleveland Browns (OT)
Wk. 8	Oct 31	W	15-10	vs Baltimore Ravens
Wk. 9	Nov 7	L	27-3	at Pittsburgh Steelers
Wk. 10	Nov 15	W	49-21	at Dallas Cowboys
Wk. 11	Nov 21	W	28-6	vs Washington Redskins
Wk. 12	Nov 28	W	27-6	at New York Giants
Wk. 13	Dec 5	W	47-17	vs Green Bay Packers
Wk. 14	Dec 12	W	17-14	at Washington Redskins
Wk. 15	Dec 19	W	12-7	vs Dallas Cowboys
Wk. 16	Dec 27	L	20-7	at St. Louis Rams
Wk. 17	Jan 2	L	38-10	vs Cincinnati Bengals

POST SEASON

Divisional Playoffs				
	Jan 16	W	27-14	vs Minnesota Vikings
Conference Championship				
	Jan 23	W	27-10	vs Atlanta Falcons
Superbowl				
	Feb 6	L	24-21	vs New England Patriots (at Jacksonville)

One of the most eventful off-seasons in team history, the Eagles signed Jevon Kearse and Terrell Owens both helped the Eagles to their first NFC Championship and subsequent Super Bowl appearance in 24 years. The Eagles captured their 4th consecutive NFC East division title and won a franchise record 13 regular season games, while Andy Reid became the all-time winningest coach in franchise history surpassing Greasy Neale. QB Donovan McNabb became the first player in NFL history to finish a season with 30+ TD passes and fewer than 10 INTs and his 24 consecutive completions over a span of two games set an NFL record previously held by Joe Montana (22) in 1987. Eagles kicker David Akers set an NFL record with 17 FGs of 40-yards or more. The Eagles stormed out to a 7-0 record and after a win at NYG on November 28, clinched the NFC East title with 5 games remaining. They went on to clinch home field advantage in the NFC after compiling a 13-1record. In the playoffs, the Eagles topped Minnesota 27-14 in the Divisional playoff and defeated Atlanta 27-10 in the NFC Championship game. In Super Bowl XXXIV, the Eagles lost a hard-fought battle to the Patriots, 24-21, played in Jacksonville, Florida.

2004 PHILADELPHIA EAGLES STATS

Passing	Comp	Att	Comp %	Yds	Y/Att	TD	Int	Rating
Donovan McNabb	300	469	64.0	3875	8.26	31	8	104.7
Jeff Blake	18	37	48.6	126	3.41	1	1	54.6
Koy Detmer	18	40	45.0	207	5.18	0	2	40.3
Mike Bartrum	0	1	0.0	0	0.00	0	0	39.6

Rushing	Rush	Yds	Avg	TD
Brian Westbrook	177	812	4.6	3
Dorsey Levens	94	410	4.4	4
Donovan McNabb	41	220	5.4	3
Reno Mahe	23	91	4.0	0
Eric McCoo	9	54	6.0	0
Thomas Tapeh	12	42	3.5	0
Greg Lewis	4	16	4.0	0
Jeff Blake	3	6	2.0	0
Terrell Owens	3	-5	-1.7	0
Koy Detmer	10	-7	-0.7	0

Interceptions	Int	Yds	Avg	TD
Lito Sheppard	5	172	34.4	2
Brian Dawkins	4	40	10.0	0
Sheldon Brown	2	33	16.5	0
Ike Reese	2	22	11.0	0
Roderick Hood	1	20	20.0	0
Dhani Jones	1	0	0.0	0
Michael Lewis	1	0	0.0	0
Quintin Mikell	1	0	0.0	0

Receiving	Rec	Yds	Avg	TD
Terrell Owens	77	1200	15.6	14
Brian Westbrook	73	703	9.6	6
Todd Pinkston	36	676	18.8	1
L. J. Smith	34	377	11.1	5
Chad Lewis	29	267	9.2	3
Freddie Mitchell	22	377	17.1	2
Greg Lewis	17	183	10.8	0
Reno Mahe	14	123	8.8	0
Dorsey Levens	9	92	10.2	0
Josh Parry	9	75	8.3	0
Mike Bartrum	5	45	9.0	1
Jon Ritchie	4	36	9.0	0
Billy McMullen	3	24	8.0	0
Eric McCoo	2	15	7.5	0
Thomas Tapeh	2	15	7.5	0

Punting	Punts	Yds	Avg	Blocked
Dirk Johnson	72	3032	42.1	0
David Akers	1	36	36.0	0

Kicking	PAT Made	PAT Att	PAT %	FG Made	FG Att	FG %	Pts
David Akers	41	42	98	27	32	84.4	122

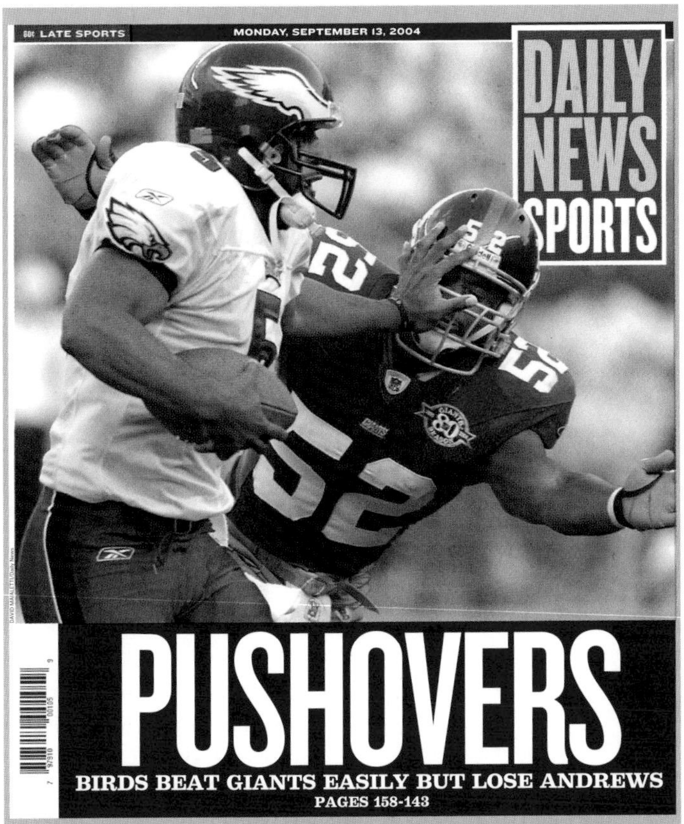
60¢ LATE SPORTS
MONDAY, SEPTEMBER 13, 2004
DAILY NEWS SPORTS
PUSHOVERS
BIRDS BEAT GIANTS EASILY BUT LOSE ANDREWS
PAGES 158-143

September 13, 2004
Eagles beat Giants easily 31-17

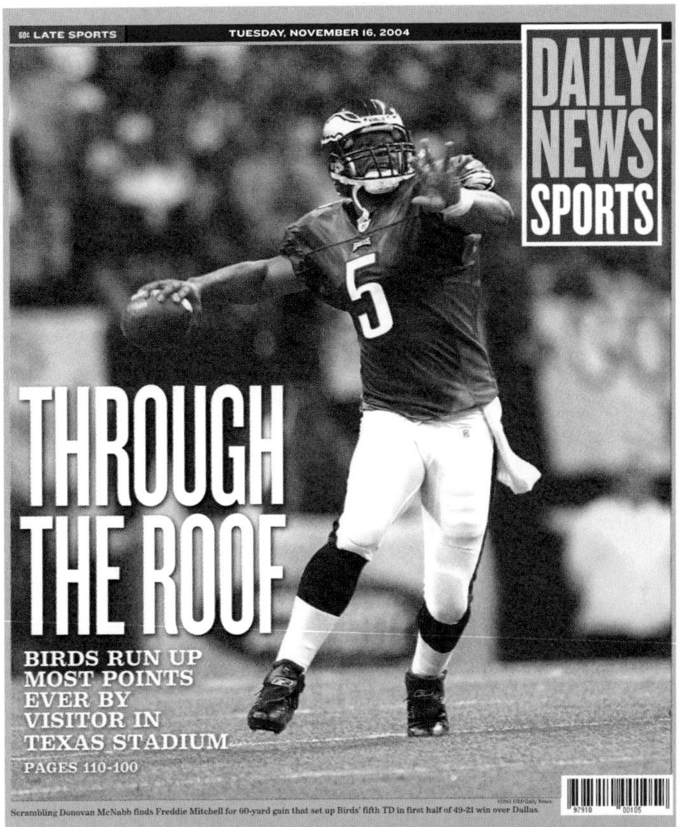
60¢ LATE SPORTS
TUESDAY, NOVEMBER 16, 2004
DAILY NEWS SPORTS
THROUGH THE ROOF
BIRDS RUN UP MOST POINTS EVER BY VISITOR IN TEXAS STADIUM
PAGES 110-100
Scrambling Donovan McNabb finds Freddie Mitchell for 60-yard gain that set up Birds' fifth TD in first half of 49-21 win over Dallas.

November 16, 2004
Eagles destroy the Cowboys 49-21

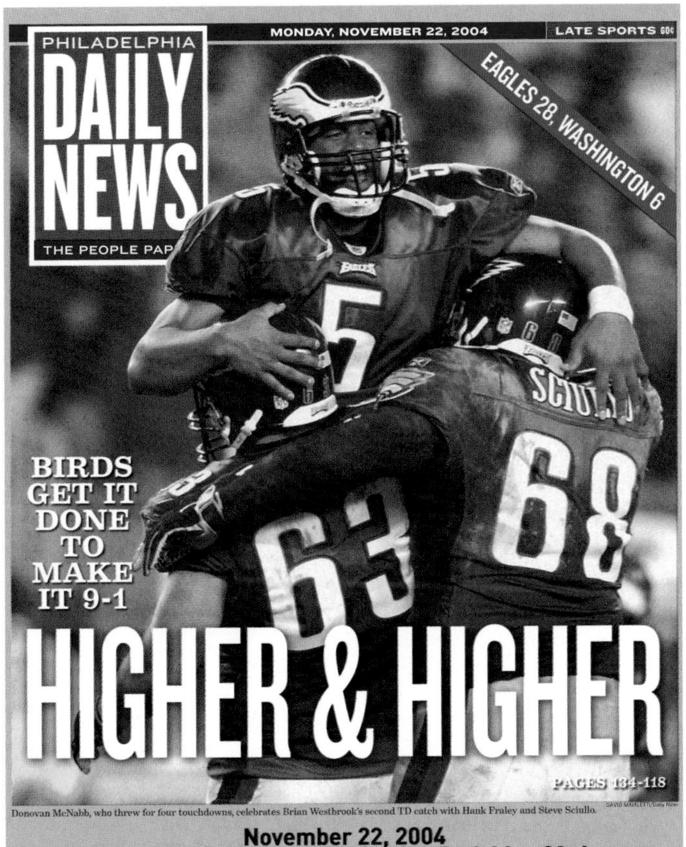
PHILADELPHIA DAILY NEWS
THE PEOPLE PAPER
MONDAY, NOVEMBER 22, 2004
LATE SPORTS 60¢
EAGLES 28, WASHINGTON 6
BIRDS GET IT DONE TO MAKE IT 9-1
HIGHER & HIGHER
PAGES 134-118
Donovan McNabb, who threw for four touchdowns, celebrates Brian Westbrook's second TD catch with Hank Fraley and Steve Sciullo.

November 22, 2004
Eagles record 9th win defeating Redskins 28-6

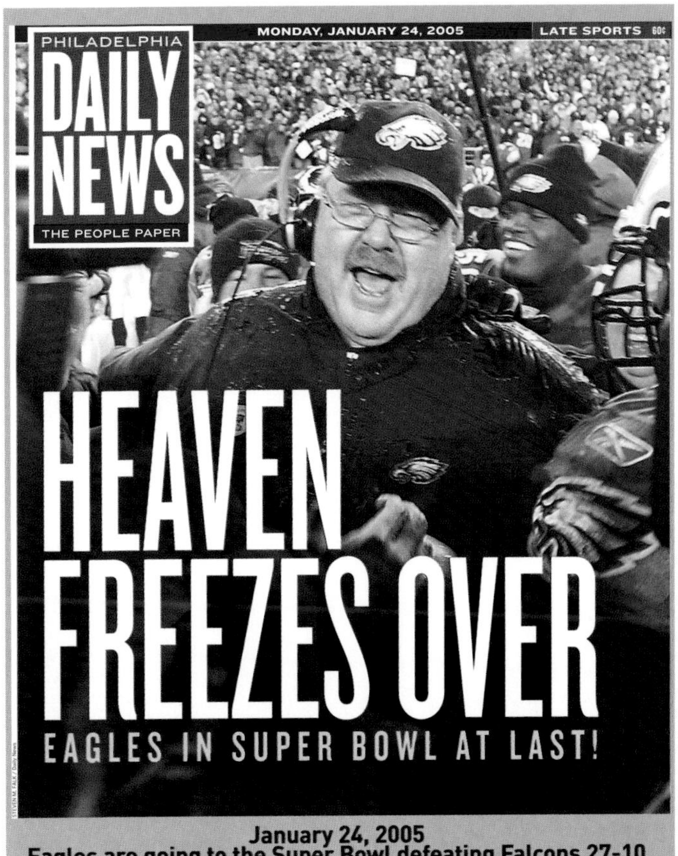
PHILADELPHIA DAILY NEWS
THE PEOPLE PAPER
MONDAY, JANUARY 24, 2005
LATE SPORTS 60¢
HEAVEN FREEZES OVER
EAGLES IN SUPER BOWL AT LAST!

January 24, 2005
Eagles are going to the Super Bowl defeating Falcons 27-10

2004

2005

RECORD: 6-10, 4TH IN NFC EAST
HEAD COACH: ANDY REID

Schedule

Regular Season

Wk. 1	Sep 12	L	14-10	at Atlanta Falcons
Wk. 2	Sep 18	W	42-3	vs San Francisco 49ers
Wk. 3	Sep 25	W	23-20	vs Oakland Raiders
Wk. 4	Oct 2	W	37-31	at Kansas City Chiefs
Wk. 5	Oct 9	L	33-10	at Dallas Cowboys
Wk. 7	Oct 23	W	20-17	vs San Diego Chargers
Wk. 8	Oct 30	L	49-21	at Denver Broncos
Wk. 9	Nov 6	L	17-10	at Washington Redskins
Wk. 10	Nov 14	L	21-20	vs Dallas Cowboys
Wk. 11	Nov 20	L	27-17	at New York Giants
Wk. 12	Nov 27	W	19-14	vs Green Bay Packers
Wk. 13	Dec 5	L	42-0	vs Seattle Seahawks
Wk. 14	Dec 11	L	26-23	vs New York Giants (OT)
Wk. 15	Dec 18	W	17-16	at St. Louis Rams
Wk. 16	Dec 24	L	27-21	at Arizona Cardinals
Wk. 17	Jan 1	L	31-20	vs Washington Redskins

Coming off their loss in Super Bowl XXXIX, the Eagles looked like they would return to the "Bowl." However the 2005 season was a difficult one for Head Coach Andy Reid, as he was unprepared to deal with wide receiver Terrell Owens's flamboyant persona, which led Reid to permanently deactivate him midway through the season. A couple of weeks later, quarterback Donovan McNabb suffered a season ending injury, leaving the Eagles without the services of both of their star players. The team was stymied by various player injuries throughout the season. The Eagles starting the 2005 season with a loss to the Atlanta Falcons on Monday Night Football, then they won the next three games and the season looked promising. They split the next two games and then the Eagles lost eight of their last ten games and finished 6-10. This was the first time since 1999, when Andy Reid took over the team that the Eagles didn't make the playoffs. One key moment of the Eagles season was the official retirement of Reggie White's #92 jersey in an emotional halftime ceremony on Monday Night Football (against Seattle December 5).

2005 Philadelphia Eagles Stats

Passing	Comp	Att	Comp %	Yds	Y/Att	TD	Int	Rating
Donovan McNabb	211	357	59.1	2507	7.02	16	9	85.0
Mike McMahon	94	207	45.4	1158	5.59	5	8	55.2
Koy Detmer	32	56	57.1	238	4.25	0	3	45.1

Rushing	Rush	Yds	Avg	TD
Brian Westbrook	156	617	4.0	3
Ryan Moats	55	278	5.1	3
Lamar Gordon	54	182	3.4	1
Mike McMahon	34	118	3.5	3
Reno Mahe	20	87	4.4	0
Bruce Perry	16	74	4.6	0
Donovan McNabb	25	55	2.2	1
Greg Lewis	2	13	6.5	0
Reggie Brown	1	5	5.0	0
Terrell Owens	1	2	2.0	0
Koy Detmer	1	1	1.0	0

Punting	Punts	Yds	Avg	Blocked
Sean Landeta	34	1483	43.6	0
Dirk Johnson	39	1615	41.4	0
Nick Murphy	7	275	39.3	0
Reggie Hodges	19	699	36.8	0

Kicking	PAT Made	PAT Att	PAT %	FG Made	FG Att	FG %	Pts
David Akers	23	23	100	16	22	72.7	71
Todd France	5	5	100	6	7	85.7	23
Jose Cortez	3	3	100	0	0	0.0	3
Mark Simoneau	1	2	50	0	0	0.0	1

Receiving	Rec	Yds	Avg	TD
L. J. Smith	61	682	11.2	3
Brian Westbrook	61	616	10.1	4
Greg Lewis	48	561	11.7	1
Terrell Owens	47	763	16.2	6
Reggie Brown	43	571	13.3	4
Billy McMullen	18	268	14.9	1
Josh Parry	13	89	6.8	0
Reno Mahe	12	68	5.7	0
Lamar Gordon	11	79	7.2	0
Stephen Spach	7	42	6.0	0
Darnerien McCants	5	87	17.4	0
Chad Lewis	5	64	12.8	0
Ryan Moats	4	7	1.8	0
Mike Bartrum	2	6	3.0	2

Interceptions	Int	Yds	Avg	TD
Sheldon Brown	4	67	16.8	1
Lito Sheppard	3	72	24.0	0
Brian Dawkins	3	24	8.0	0
Roderick Hood	3	17	5.7	0
Michael Lewis	2	13	6.5	0
Jeremiah Trotter	1	2	2.0	0
Dhani Jones	1	0	0.0	0

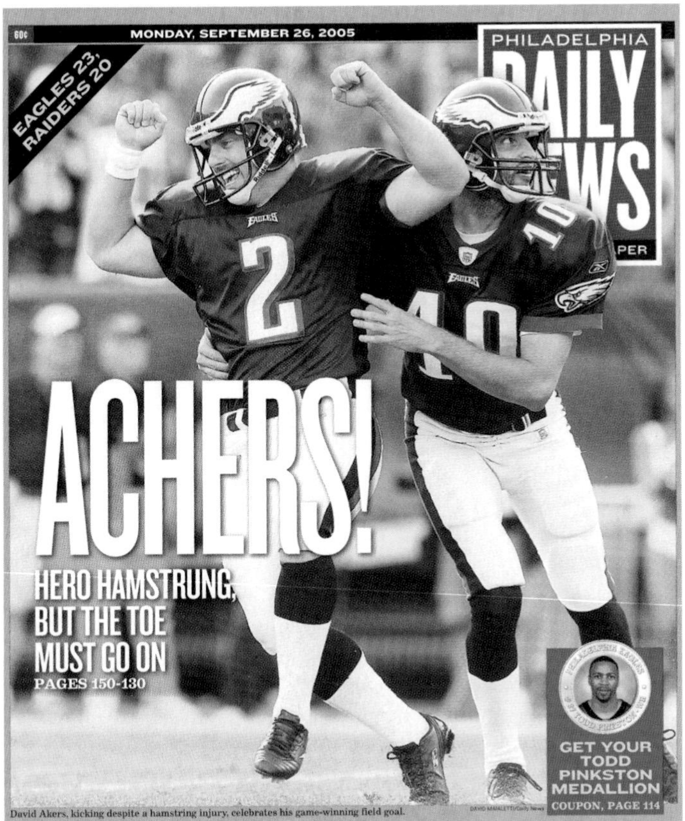
60¢ MONDAY, SEPTEMBER 26, 2005
PHILADELPHIA DAILY NEWS
EAGLES 23, RAIDERS 20
ACHERS!
HERO HAMSTRUNG, BUT THE TOE MUST GO ON
PAGES 150-130
GET YOUR TODD PINKSTON MEDALLION
COUPON, PAGE 114
David Akers, kicking despite a hamstring injury, celebrates his game-winning field goal.

September 26, 2005
Eagles kick the Raiders 23-20

60¢ MONDAY, OCTOBER 3, 2005
PHILADELPHIA DAILY NEWS
BREAST CANCER AWARENESS MONTH
THE PEOPLE PAPER
EAGLES 37, CHIEFS 31
NEW PUZZLE
WE'VE GOT SUDOKU!
READ ALL ABOUT IT: PAGE 33
DO IT: PAGE 41
SLAPPED 'EM SILLY
BAD START, BUT BIRDS PREVAIL: PAGES 119-97
PHILLIES
ALL OVER BUT THE CRITICISM
PAGES 126-122
Sheldon Brown (right) and Mike Patterson celebrate Brown's interception for a touchdown.

October 3, 2005
Eagles defeated the Chiefs 37-31

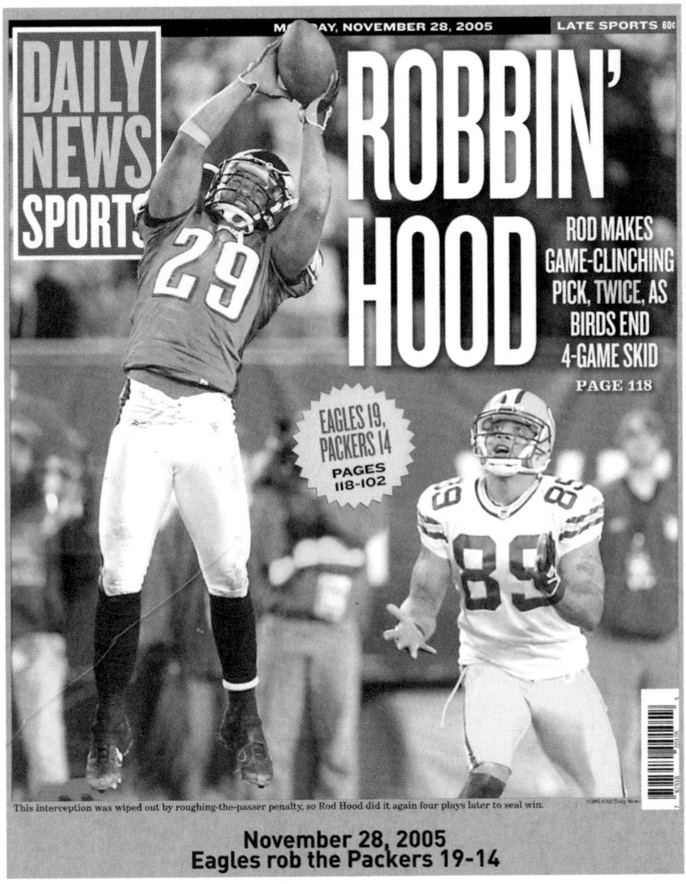
MONDAY, NOVEMBER 28, 2005 LATE SPORTS 60¢
DAILY NEWS SPORTS
ROBBIN' HOOD
ROD MAKES GAME-CLINCHING PICK, TWICE, AS BIRDS END 4-GAME SKID
PAGE 118
EAGLES 19, PACKERS 14
PAGES 118-102
This interception was wiped out by roughing-the-passer penalty, so Rod Hood did it again four plays later to seal win.

November 28, 2005
Eagles rob the Packers 19-14

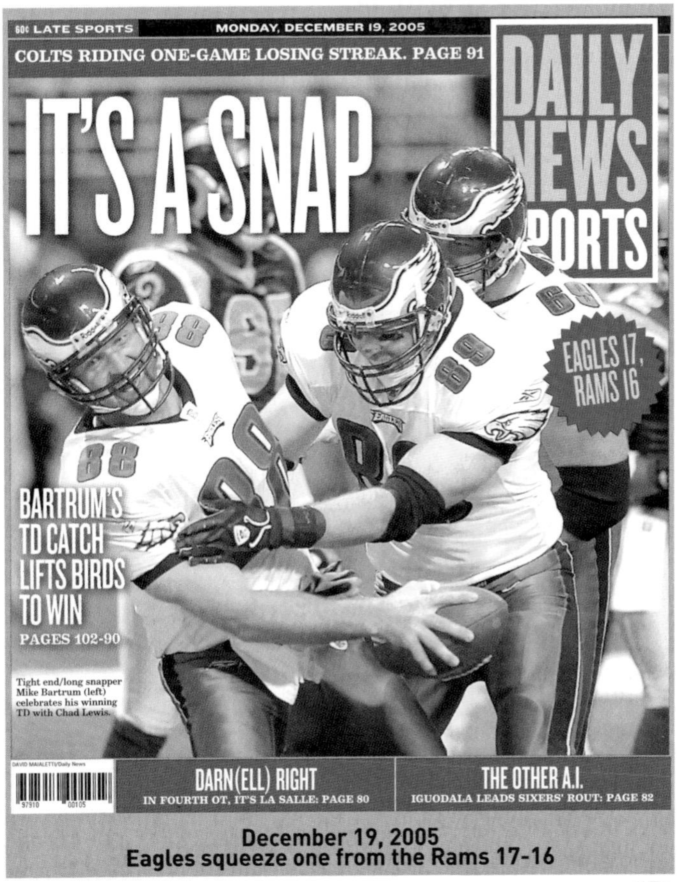
60¢ LATE SPORTS MONDAY, DECEMBER 19, 2005
COLTS RIDING ONE-GAME LOSING STREAK. PAGE 91
DAILY NEWS SPORTS
IT'S A SNAP
EAGLES 17, RAMS 16
BARTRUM'S TD CATCH LIFTS BIRDS TO WIN
PAGES 102-90
Tight end/long snapper Mike Bartrum (left) celebrates his winning TD with Chad Lewis.
DARN(ELL) RIGHT
IN FOURTH OT, IT'S LA SALLE: PAGE 80
THE OTHER A.I.
IGUODALA LEADS SIXERS' ROUT: PAGE 82

December 19, 2005
Eagles squeeze one from the Rams 17-16

2005

2006

RECORD: 10-6, 1ST IN NFC EAST
HEAD COACH: ANDY REID

Schedule

Regular Season

Wk. 1	Sep 10	W	24-10	at Houston Texans
Wk. 2	Sep 17	L	30-24	vs New York Giants (OT)
Wk. 3	Sep 24	W	38-17	at San Francisco 49ers
Wk. 4	Oct 1	W	31-9	vs Green Bay Packers
Wk. 5	Oct 8	W	38-24	vs Dallas Cowboys
Wk. 6	Oct 15	L	27-24	at New Orleans Saints
Wk. 7	Oct 22	L	23-21	at Tampa Bay Buccaneers
Wk. 8	Oct 29	L	13-6	vs Jacksonville Jaguars
Wk. 10	Nov 12	W	27-3	vs Washington Redskins
Wk. 11	Nov 19	L	31-13	vs Tennessee Titans
Wk. 12	Nov 26	L	45-21	at Indianapolis Colts
Wk. 13	Dec 4	W	27-24	vs Carolina Panthers
Wk. 14	Dec 10	W	21-19	at Washington Redskins
Wk. 15	Dec 17	W	36-22	at New York Giants
Wk. 16	Dec 25	W	23-7	at Dallas Cowboys
Wk. 17	Dec 31	W	24-17	vs Atlanta Falcons

Post Season

Wild Card Playoffs				
	Jan 7	W	23-20	vs New York Giants
Divisional Playoffs				
	Jan 13	L	27-24	at New Orleans Saints

The Eagles enjoyed a roller coaster campaign under Head Coach Andy Reid in 2006. The season appeared to be lost by October with another season-ending injury to star quarterback Donovan McNabb. The team turned a 4 and 1 start into a mid-season breakdown, which left the team 5-5. After an embarrassing defeat at the hands of the Indianapolis Colts, the Eagles were on the verge of elimination from the playoffs. Reid's game plan changed when backup quarterback Jeff Garcia rallied the 5-6 Eagles to inspiring victories over NFC rivals: the Carolina Panthers, the Washington Redskins, the New York Giants, and the hated Dallas Cowboys. The Eagles, at 10-6, won the NFC East division title, as well as winning the NFC Wild Card game against the New York Giants as David Akers kicked a 38-yard field goal. However the Eagles failed to defeat the New Orleans Saints in the NFC Divisional Round.

2006 Philadelphia Eagles Stats

Passing	Comp	Att	Comp %	Yds	Y/Att	TD	Int	Rating
Jeff Garcia	116	188	61.7	1309	6.96	10	2	95.8
Donovan McNabb	180	316	57.0	2647	8.38	18	6	95.5
A. J. Feeley	26	38	68.4	342	9.00	3	0	122.9
David Akers	1	1	100.0	11	11.00	0	0	112.5
Hank Baskett	0	1	0.0	0	0.00	0	1	0.0

Rushing	Rush	Yds	Avg	TD
Brian Westbrook	240	1217	5.1	7
Correll Buckhalter	83	345	4.2	2
Donovan McNabb	32	212	6.6	3
Jeff Garcia	25	87	3.5	0
Ryan Moats	22	69	3.1	0
Reggie Brown	3	24	8.0	1
Reno Mahe	4	18	4.5	0
Thomas Tapeh	5	9	1.8	0
A. J. Feeley	1	3	3.0	0
Dirk Johnson	1	0	0.0	0

Interceptions	Int	Yds	Avg	TD
Lito Sheppard	6	157	26.2	1
Brian Dawkins	4	38	9.5	0
Michael Lewis	2	105	52.5	1
Sheldon Brown	1	70	70.0	1
Trent Cole	1	19	19.0	1
Jeremiah Trotter	1	17	17.0	0
Omar Gaither	1	16	16.0	0
Sean Considine	1	12	12.0	0
Darwin Walker	1	6	6.0	0
LaJuan Ramsey	1	-12	-12.0	0

Receiving	Rec	Yds	Avg	TD
Brian Westbrook	77	699	9.1	4
L. J. Smith	50	611	12.2	5
Reggie Brown	46	816	17.7	8
Donte' Stallworth	38	725	19.1	5
Greg Lewis	4	348	14.5	2
Correll Buckhalter	24	256	10.7	1
Hank Baskett	22	464	21.1	2
Thomas Tapeh	16	85	5.3	1
Matt Schobel	14	214	15.3	2
Jason Avant	7	68	9.7	1
Reno Mahe	5	23	4.6	0

Punting	Punts	Yds	Avg	Blocked
Dirk Johnson	78	3326	42.6	0

Kicking	PAT Made	PAT Att	PAT %	FG Made	FG Att	FG %	Pts
David Akers	48	48	100	18	23	78.3	102

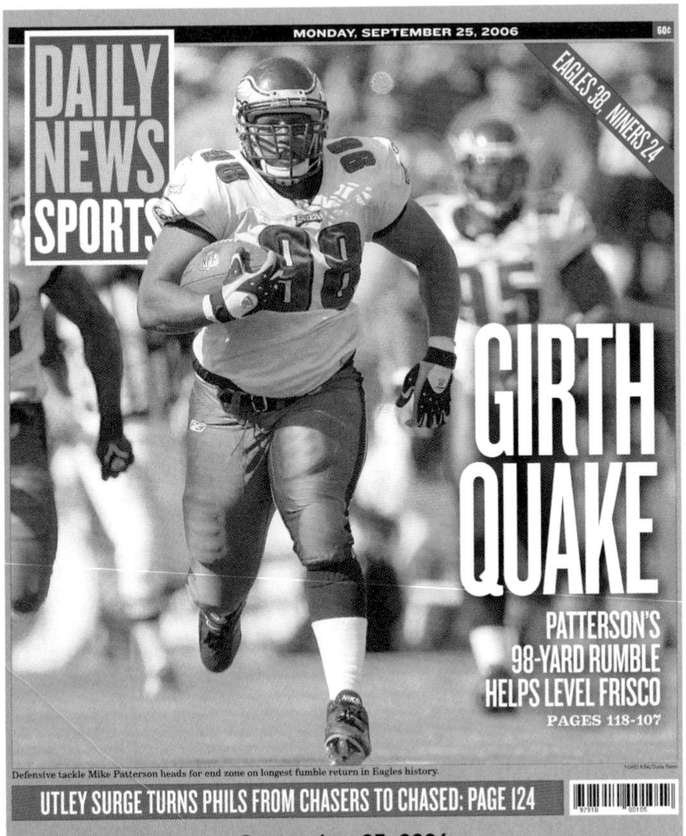
MONDAY, SEPTEMBER 25, 2006 60¢

DAILY NEWS SPORTS

EAGLES 38, NINERS 24

GIRTH QUAKE

PATTERSON'S 98-YARD RUMBLE HELPS LEVEL FRISCO

PAGES 118-107

Defensive tackle Mike Patterson heads for end zone on longest fumble return in Eagles history.

UTLEY SURGE TURNS PHILS FROM CHASERS TO CHASED: PAGE 124

September 25, 2006
Eagles rumble over the Niners 38-24

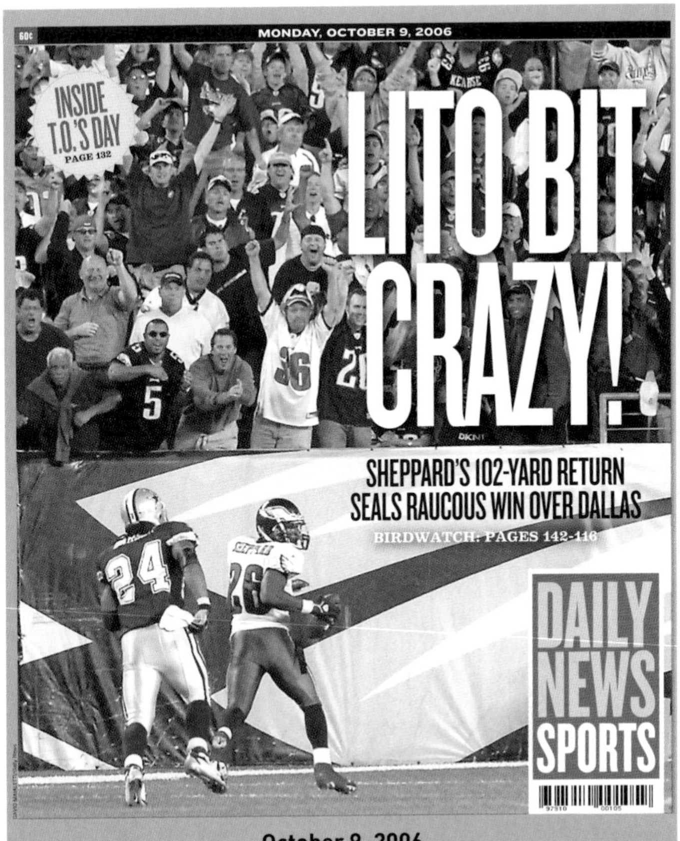
60¢ MONDAY, OCTOBER 9, 2006

INSIDE T.O.'S DAY PAGE 132

LITO BIT CRAZY!

SHEPPARD'S 102-YARD RETURN SEALS RAUCOUS WIN OVER DALLAS

BIRDWATCH: PAGES 142-116

DAILY NEWS SPORTS

October 9, 2006
Eagles destroy Cowboys 38-24

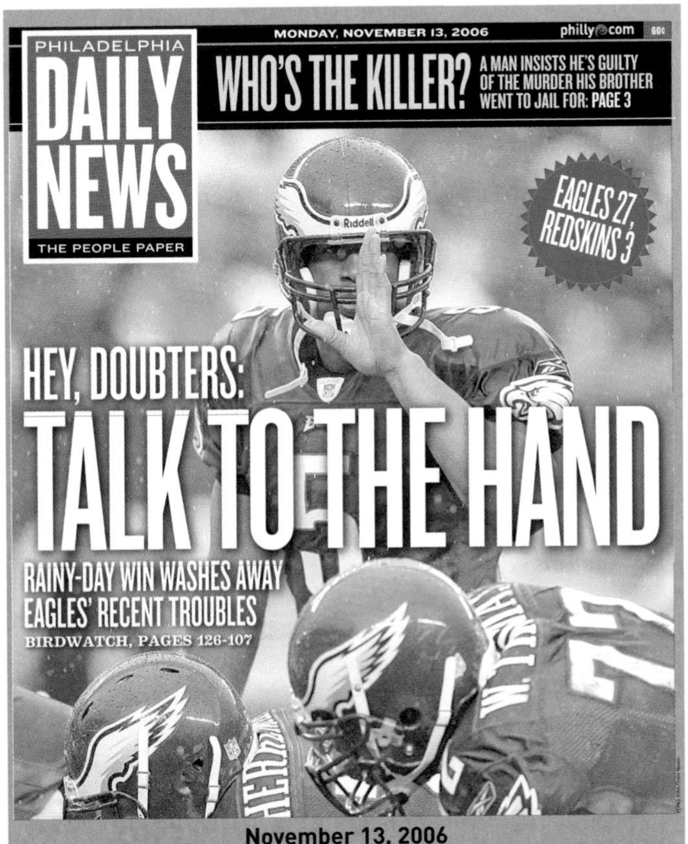
MONDAY, NOVEMBER 13, 2006 philly.com 60¢

PHILADELPHIA DAILY NEWS THE PEOPLE PAPER

WHO'S THE KILLER? A MAN INSISTS HE'S GUILTY OF THE MURDER HIS BROTHER WENT TO JAIL FOR: PAGE 3

EAGLES 27, REDSKINS 3

HEY, DOUBTERS: TALK TO THE HAND

RAINY-DAY WIN WASHES AWAY EAGLES' RECENT TROUBLES

BIRDWATCH, PAGES 126-107

November 13, 2006
Eagles have a holiday romp defeating Cowboys 23-7

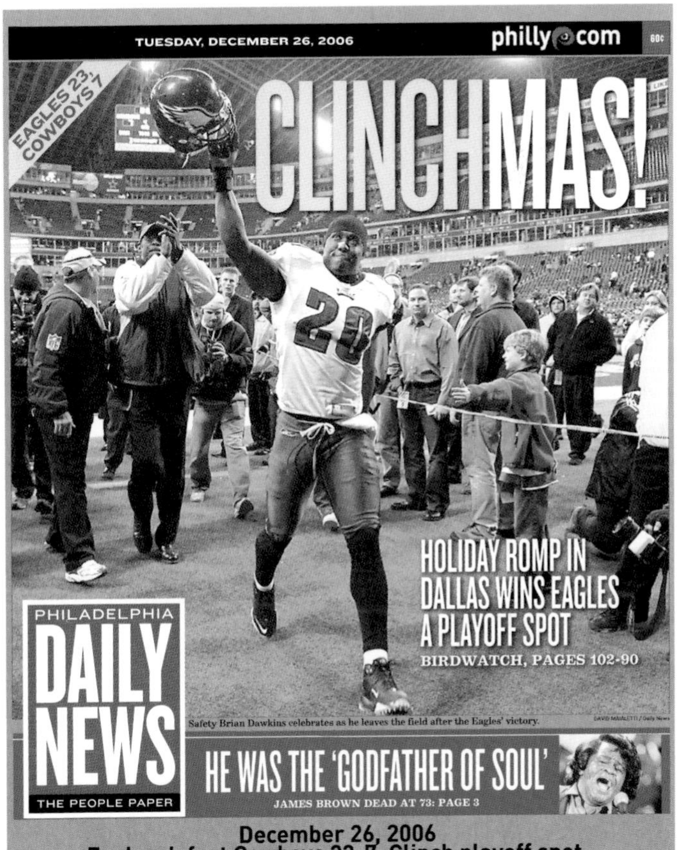
TUESDAY, DECEMBER 26, 2006 philly.com 60¢

EAGLES 23, COWBOYS 7

CLINCHMAS!

HOLIDAY ROMP IN DALLAS WINS EAGLES A PLAYOFF SPOT

BIRDWATCH, PAGES 102-90

Safety Brian Dawkins celebrates as he leaves the field after the Eagles' victory.

PHILADELPHIA DAILY NEWS THE PEOPLE PAPER

HE WAS THE 'GODFATHER OF SOUL'

JAMES BROWN DEAD AT 73: PAGE 3

December 26, 2006
Eagles defeat Cowboys 23-7, Clinch playoff spot.

2007

RECORD: 8-8, 4TH IN NFC EAST
HEAD COACH: ANDY REID

Schedule

Regular Season

Wk 1	Sep 9	L	16-13	at Green Bay Packers
Wk 2	Sep 17	L	20-12	vs Washington Redskins
Wk 3	Sep 23	W	56-21	vs Detroit Lions
Wk 4	Sep 30	L	16-3	at New York Giants
Wk 6	Oct 14	W	16-9	at New York Jets
Wk 7	Oct 21	L	19-16	vs Chicago Bears
Wk 8	Oct 28	W	23-16	at Minnesota Vikings
Wk 9	Nov 4	L	38-17	vs Dallas Cowboys
Wk 10	Nov 11	W	33-25	at Washington Redskins
Wk 11	Nov 18	W	17-7	vs Miami Dolphins
Wk 12	Nov 25	L	31-28	at New England Patriots
Wk 13	Dec 2	L	28-24	vs Seattle Seahawks
Wk 14	Dec 9	L	16-13	vs New York Giants
Wk 15	Dec 16	W	10-6	at Dallas Cowboys
Wk 16	Dec 23	W	38-23	at New Orleans Saints
Wk 17	Dec 30	W	17-9	vs Buffalo Bills

The Eagles commenced their 75th anniversary season with new starters at five different positions, including an entirely new group of linebackers. After a dismal 1-3 start, they managed to finish the season 8-8. This was only the second time this decade that the Eagles did not reach the playoffs. The team struggled offensively, being held to under 21 points in 10 of their 16 games.

There are still many highlights of the season. Quarterback Donovan McNabb completed 61.5% (2nd best percentage of his career) of his passes for 3,324 yards and had a QB rating of 89.9%. Running back Brian Westbrook was able to set single-season team records for total yards from scrimmage (2,104) and receptions (90). He became the first Eagle to lead the league in total yards from scrimmage since 1996 (Ricky Watters) and the first NFL player from a non-Division I-A school to do so since 1979 (Philadelphia's Wilbert Montgomery). Westbrook also logged career highs in rushing yards (1,333), receiving yards (771), touches (368), and offensive touchdowns (12). Wide receiver Kevin Curtis posted career highs in catches (77), yards (1,110), and total touchdowns (8) in his first season in Philadelphia. For the first time in franchise history, the Eagles featured three players (Westbrook, Curtis, and WR Reggie Brown) with over 60 catches and 700 yards each. RB Brian Westbrook and RG Shawn Andrews both earned Pro Bowl honors, while DE Trent Cole was selected as a first alternate after leading the team with 12.5 sacks. DE Trent Cole (103) and DT Mike Patterson (114) became the first pair of Eagles defensive linemen, since 1991, to record 100 tackles in the same season.

2007 Philadelphia Eagles Stats

Passing	Comp	Att	Comp %	Yds	Y/Att	TD	Int	Rating
Donovan McNabb	291	473	61.5	3324	7.0	19	7	89.9
A.J. Feeley	59	103	57.3	681	6.6	5	8	61.2
Greg Lewis	0	1	0.0	0	0.0	0	0	39.6

Rushing	Rush	Yds	Avg	TD
Brian Westbrook	278	1333	4.8	7
Correll Buckhalter	62	313	5.0	4
Donovan McNabb	50	236	4.7	0
Reggie Brown	5	36	7.2	0
A.J. Feeley	7	23	3.3	0
Thomas Tapeh	5	18	3.6	0
Tony Hunt	10	16	1.6	1
Jason Avont	1	1	1.0	0
Kevin Kolb	3	-2	-0.7	0

Interceptions	Int	Yds	Avg	TD
Sheldon Brown	3	3	1.0	0
Lito Sheppard	2	25	12.5	0
Omar Gaither	1	49	49.0	0
Quintin Mikell	1	20	20.0	0
Stewart Bradley	1	13	13.0	0
Brian Dawkins	1	1	1.0	0
Sean Considine	1	0	0.0	0
William James	1	0	0.0	0

Receiving	Rec	Yds	Avg	TD
Brian Westbrook	90	771	8.6	5
Kevin Curtis	77	1110	14.4	6
Reggie Brown	61	780	12.8	4
Jason Avant	23	267	11.6	2
L.J. Smith	22	236	10.7	1
Brent Celek	16	178	11.1	1
Hank Baskett	16	142	8.9	1
Greg Lewis	13	265	20.4	3
Correll Buckhalter	12	87	7.3	0
Matt Schobel	11	108	9.8	1
Tomas Tapeh	8	50	6.3	0
Reno Mahe	1	11	11.0	0

Punting	Punts	Yds	Avg	Blocked
Sav Rocca	73	3066	42.0	0

Kicking	PAT Made	PAT Att	PAT %	FG Made	FG Att	FG %	Pts
David Akers	36	36	100.0	24	32	75.0	108

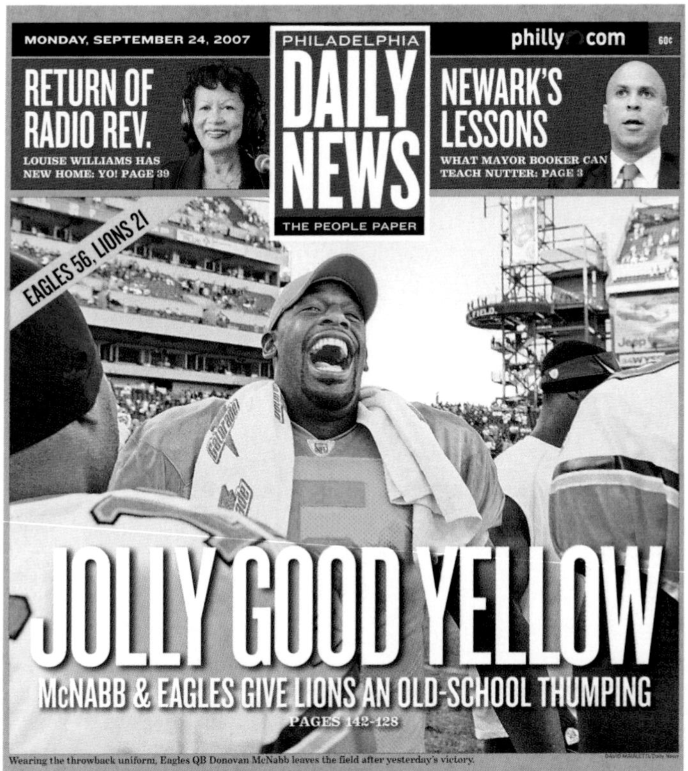
MONDAY, SEPTEMBER 24, 2007
PHILADELPHIA DAILY NEWS
THE PEOPLE PAPER
philly.com 60¢

RETURN OF RADIO REV.
LOUISE WILLIAMS HAS NEW HOME: YO! PAGE 39

NEWARK'S LESSONS
WHAT MAYOR BOOKER CAN TEACH NUTTER: PAGE 3

EAGLES 56, LIONS 21

JOLLY GOOD YELLOW
McNABB & EAGLES GIVE LIONS AN OLD-SCHOOL THUMPING
PAGES 142-128

Wearing the throwback uniform, Eagles QB Donovan McNabb leaves the field after yesterday's victory.

September 24, 2007
Eagles give Lions an old-school thumping 56-21

60¢ philly.com
MONDAY, OCTOBER 15, 2007
PHILADELPHIA DAILY NEWS
THE PEOPLE PAPER

EAGLES 16, JETS 9

GOOD BYE
THROWBACK JETS NO MATCH FOR REID'S WELL-RESTED EAGLES
BIRDWATCH, PAGES 142-130

NEW PLACE IN PHILLY FOR WOUNDED VETS
BYKOFSKY, PAGE 3

RAPPER T.I. BUSTED ON GUN CHARGES
PAGE 7

Kevin Curtis heads for a touchdown on a 75-yard pass in the first quarter.

October 15, 2007
Eagles defeat Jets 16-9

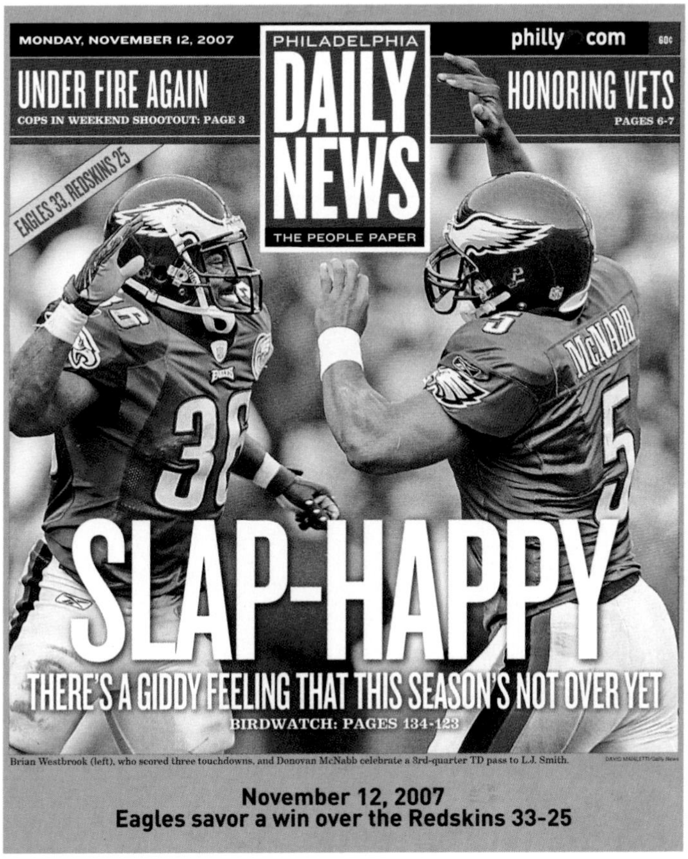
MONDAY, NOVEMBER 12, 2007
PHILADELPHIA DAILY NEWS
THE PEOPLE PAPER
philly.com 60¢

UNDER FIRE AGAIN
COPS IN WEEKEND SHOOTOUT: PAGE 3

HONORING VETS
PAGES 6-7

EAGLES 33, REDSKINS 25

SLAP-HAPPY
THERE'S A GIDDY FEELING THAT THIS SEASON'S NOT OVER YET
BIRDWATCH: PAGES 134-123

Brian Westbrook (left), who scored three touchdowns, and Donovan McNabb celebrate a 3rd-quarter TD pass to L.J. Smith.

November 12, 2007
Eagles savor a win over the Redskins 33-25

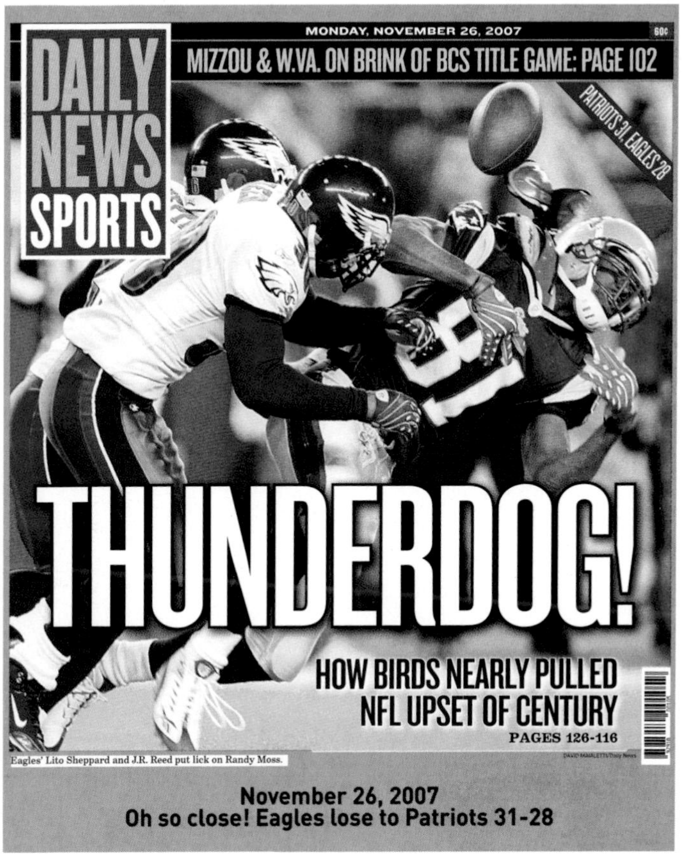
MONDAY, NOVEMBER 26, 2007 60¢
DAILY NEWS SPORTS
MIZZOU & W.VA. ON BRINK OF BCS TITLE GAME: PAGE 102

PATRIOTS 31, EAGLES 28

THUNDERDOG!
HOW BIRDS NEARLY PULLED NFL UPSET OF CENTURY
PAGES 126-116

Eagles' Lito Sheppard and J.R. Reed put lick on Randy Moss.

November 26, 2007
Oh so close! Eagles lose to Patriots 31-28

LOOKING BACK 75 YEARS

September 23, 2007 was the official "Throwback Jersey Game" marked the Eagles' 75th Season by the players wearing the original blue and yellow uniform colors from the Eagles' inaugural season in 1933 and the game field was painted in blue and yellow with an image of a throwback helmet as the centerpiece. The Eagles defeated the Detroit Lions 56-21.

Clockwise, from top right: (1) #25 Tommy McDonald & Swoop,(2) #60 Chuck Bednarik, (3) #21 Eric Allen, #99 Dee Brown, #96 Clyde Simmons and #59 Seth Joyner , (4) #83 Vince Papale, (5) #99 Dee Brown, son of the late Jerome Brown. (Center) #17 Harold Carmichael

THIS EAGLES' 75TH ANNIVERSARY TEAM WAS SELECTED BY MORE THAN 600,000 EAGLES FANS WHO VOTED FOR THEIR FAVORITE EAGLES PLAYER BY POSITION ON PHILADELPHIAEAGLES.COM.

Front Row: (Left to Right): K David Akers (1999-Present), QB Donovan McNabb (1999-Present), P Sean landeta (1999-2002, 2005), Head Coach Andy Reid (1999-Present), WR Harold Carmichael (1971-1983), FS Brian Dawkins (1996-Present), CB Eric Allen (1988-1994)

Middle Row: KR Timmy Brown (1960-1967), CB Troy Vincent (1996-2003), WR Tommy McDonald (1957-1963), PR Brian Westbrook (2002-Present), FB Keith Byars (1986-1992), OLB Seth Joyner (1986-1993)

Back Row: MLB and C Chuck Bednarik (1949-1962), RT Jon Runyan (2000-Present), LG Wade Key (1970-1980), LT William Thomas (1998-Present), RG Shawn Andrews (2004-Present), Special Teams Vince Papale (1976-1978), DT Clyde Simmons (1986-1993)

Not Pictured: RB Steve Van Buren (1944-1951), SS Andre Waters (1984-1993), TE Pete Pihos (1947-1955), OLB Alex Wojciechowicz (1946-1950), DT Charlie Johnson (1977-1981), DE Reggie White (1985-1992), DT Jerome Brown (1987-1991)

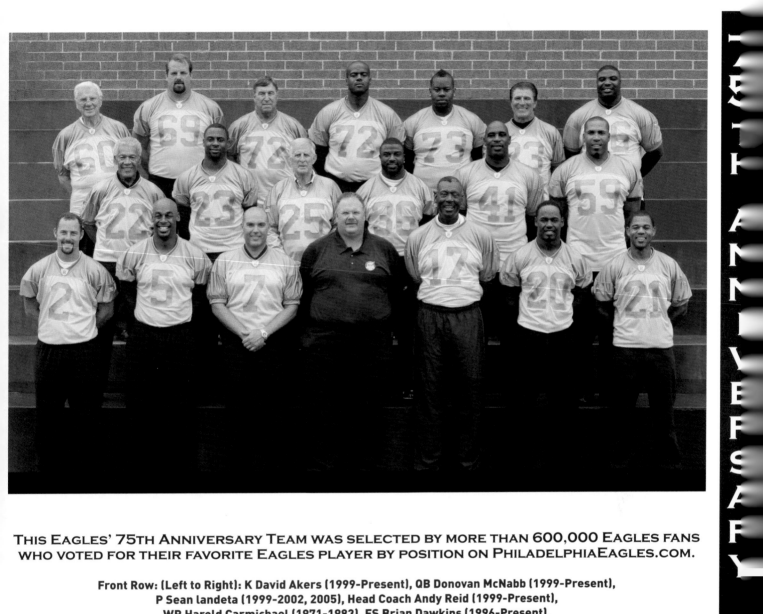

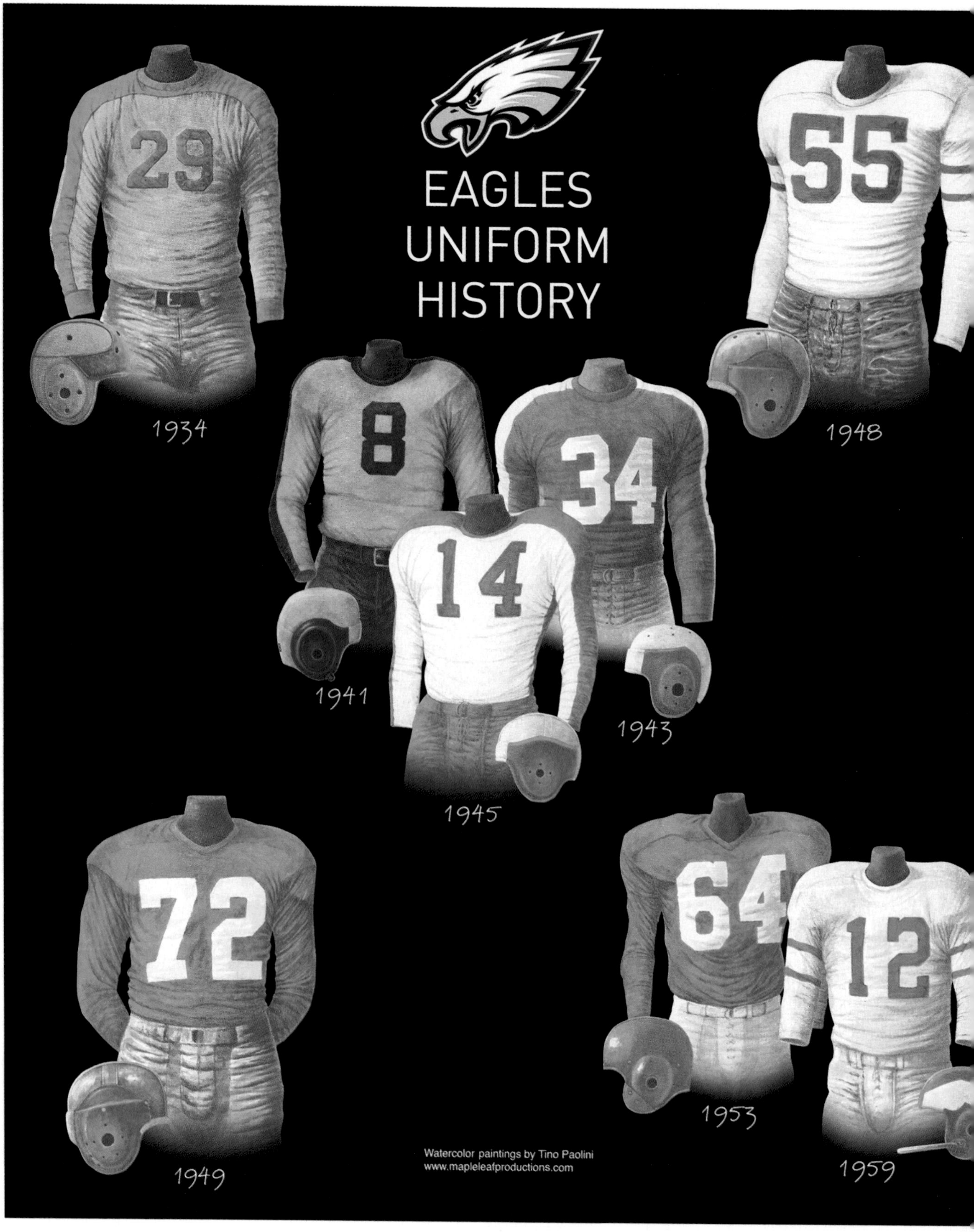
EAGLES
UNIFORM
HISTORY
29
1934
8
1941
34
1943
14
1945
55
1948
72
1949
64
1953
12
1959
Watercolor paintings by Tino Paolini
www.mapleleafproductions.com

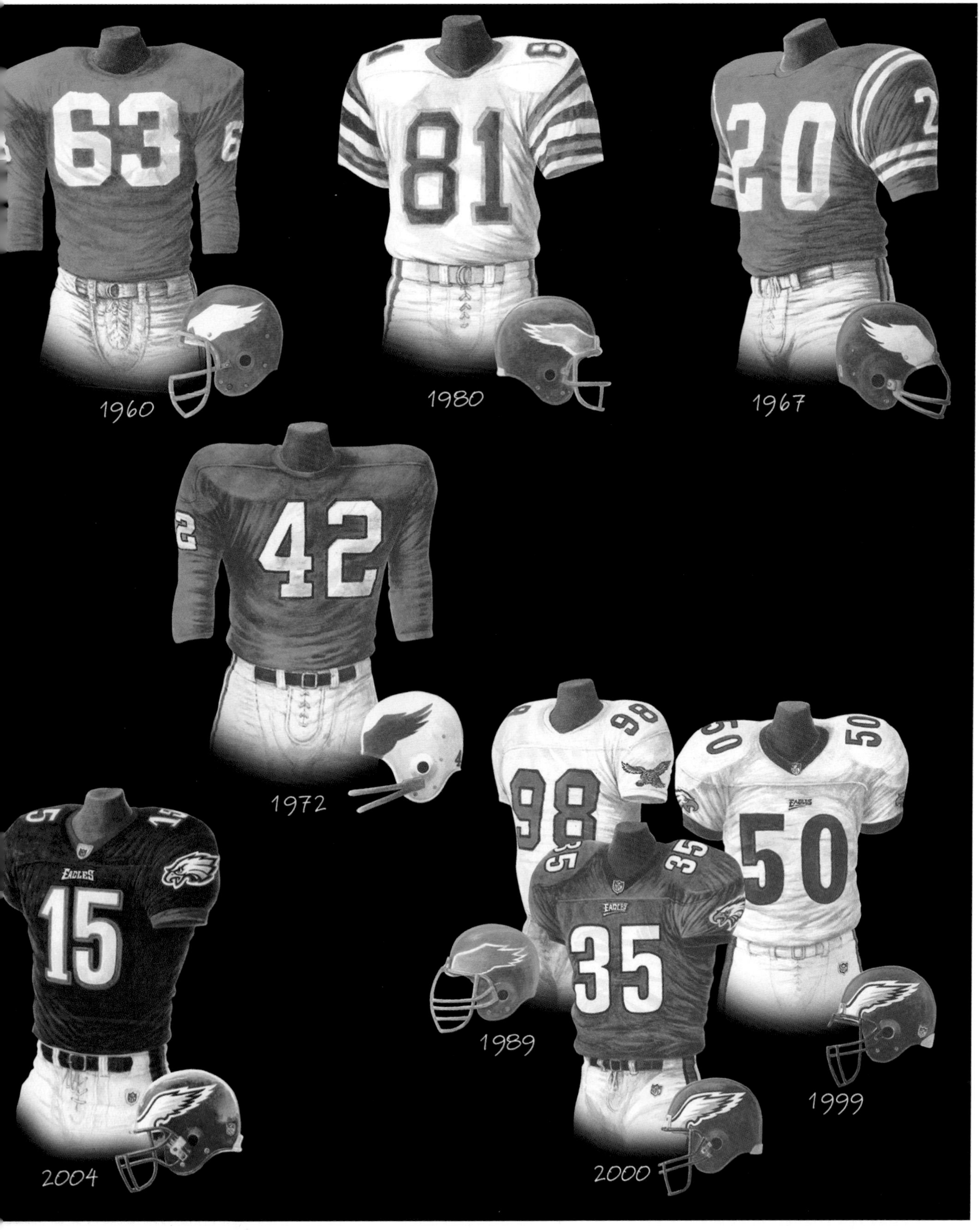
1960
1980
1967
1972
2004
1989
2000
1999

29
1934

1934

This yellow jersey that you see is the first jersey the team wore. Notice the blue stripes that runs from one sleeve cuff all the way up the arm, across the shoulders, and down the next arm. The numbers are small and placed high on the chest. Note also the helmet. It is very different than what we are used to seeing!

8
34
14
1941
1943
1945

1941

This jersey isn't quite as flashy as the 1934 jersey we see on this poster. The colors have changed to black and gray, and not only on the jersey, but the helmet as well.

1945

This white jersey is a nice change from the dark colored 1941 jersey. Notice how the helmet has also changed color to match the uniform.

55
1948

1948

This white jersey has green lettering on the front, while the stripes along the shoulders and arms are removed. Note the two green horizontal stripes on the arms. The helmet has changed slightly, adding a color where there was once white.

1949

The team decides to stick with the basics as they remove all the stripes, and keep the same helmet as the previous season.

1953

This green jersey hasn't changed much since 1949, with exception to the numbering. Note the helmet: it is now all green, and matches the jersey.

1959

This white jersey has adopted the green horizontal stripes on the arms once again, only this time adding white matching pants. Note the change of the helmet. They have added white eagles wings, as well as a safety bar.

1960

This green jersey has replaced the white stripes with white player numbers. Note also the change of the mask on the helmet. The logo of eagles' wings is also on the sides.

1967

This green jersey adds once again the white stripes, however changing them slightly, adding them to the arms as well as around the shoulders. The player numbers, however, are still on the arms. The helmet changes slightly, changing the mask.

1972

This jersey has abandoned the stripes, and added a black outline to the player numbers. Notice the helmet has changed the mask, and has changed to a white helmet, making the eagles wings green.

1980

This white jersey, as you can see, has added more stripes than ever, with five green stripes and two gray stripes. The player numbers have been moved to the shoulder, and if you look closely, you'll see that the collar of the jersey is also green. Note also the mask on the helmet is changed. The helmet is green, and the logo has changed, outlining the wings with white, and coloring it in with gray.

98
50
35
1989
1999
2000

1989

This white jersey, as you can see, now has short sleeves, with no stripes. The numbers are left on the shoulder, and have been outlined with black. If you look closely, a new eagle's logo has been added to the arm of jersey. Note the mask on the helmet has changed.

2000

If you look closely at this jersey, you will note a smaller patch the NFL shield on the jersey's neckline. Most NFL uniforms added the NFL logo patch to the neck and upper left thigh of the pants beginning in 1991 - an exception being in 1994 when teams occasionally wore "throwback" uniforms celebrating the NFL's 75th anniversary.

Note the change of the mask on the helmet. This jersey is still green, although the color has changed throughout the years. The most recent change of color happened after the 1995 season. When asked about the color change, owner Jeffrey Lurie stated that "our fans want us to look less like the Jets."

2004

This Eagles black jersey was first introduced in 2003 when the Eagles played the Giants in Week 11. It is virtually opposite in color scheme to their green home jerseys and was an immediate hit with fans.

This jersey is what is referred to nowadays as a "3rd jersey". A 3rd jersey is a concept that became commonplace in baseball and hockey in the 1990's, and in the 2000's in the NFL. Most 3rd jerseys are worn occasionally at home as well as on the road, giving a team a third option as to what uniform to wear.

15
2004

#15 Steve Van Buren, 1944-51 (RB)
1944-50 All Pro Selection

#40 Tom Brookshier, 1953, 1956-61 (CB)
1959-60 All Pro Selection;
1960-61 Pro Bowl

#44 Pete Retzlaff, 1956-66 (TE)
1958, 1964-66 All Pro Selection;
1959, 1961, 1964-66 Pro Bowl;
1965 NFL MVP

 # 60 Chuck Bednarik, 1949-62 (C)/LB
1950-57, 1960-61 All Pro Selection;
1951-55, 1957-58, 1961 Pro Bowl
1954 Pro Bowl MVP

#70 Al Wistert, 1943-51 (T)
1944-51 All Pro Selection;
1951 Pro Bowl

#92 Reggie White, 1985-92 (DE)
1986-92 All Pro Selection;
1987-93 Pro Bowl;
1987 Pro Bowl MVP;
1987, 1991 NFL Defensive MVP;
1987, 1991 NFC Defensive MVP

#99 Jerome Brown, 1987-91 (DT)
1989-91 All Pro Selection;
1991-92 Pro Bowl
1992 Ed Block Courage Award

#1
Happy Feller (K) 1971
Nick Mike-Mayer (K) 1977-78
Tony Franklin (K) 1979-83
Gary Anderson (K) 1995-9

#2
Joe Pitconis (E) 1934
Mike Michel (P/K) 1978
Mike Horan (P) 1984-85
Dean Dorsey (K) 1988
Steve DeLine (K) 1989
David Akers (K) 1999-07*

#3
Roger Kirkman (B) 1934-35
Jack Concannon (QB) 1964-66
Mark Moseley (K) 1970
Eddie Murray (K) 1994

#4
Benjy Dial (QB) 1967
Max Runager (P) 1979-83, 1989
David Jacobs (K) 1987r
Dale Dawson (K) 1988
Bryan Barker (P) 1955-98
Kevin Kolb (QB) 2007*

#5
Joe Kresky (G) 1934-35
Roman Gabriel (QB) 1973
Tom Skladany (P) 1983
Dean May (QB) 1984
Mark Royals (P) 1987r
Jeff Feagles (P) 1990-93
Donovan McNabb (QB) 1999-07*

#6
Jim MacMurdo (T) 1934-36
Gary Adams (DB) 1969
John Reaves (QB) 1972
Spike Jones (P) 1975-77
Dan Pastorini (QB) 1982-83
Matt Cavanaugh (QB) 1986-89
Bubby Brister (QB) 1993-94
Lee Johnson (P) 2002
Sav Rocca (P) 2007*

#7
Roy Zimmerman (QB) 1943-46
John Huarte (QB) 1968
Jim Ward (QB) 1971
John Reaves (QB) 1972-74
Ron Jaworski (QB) 1977-86
Roger Ruzek (K) 1989-93
Ken O'Brien (QB) 1993
Bobby Hoying (QB) 1996-98
Sean Landeta (P) 1999-02
Jason Baker (P) 2002
Jeff Garica (QB) 2006

#8
Charles Hajek (C) 1934
Davey O'Brien (QB) 1939-40
Al Coleman (DB) 1972
Paul McFadden (K) 1984-87
Luis Zendejas (K) 1988-89
Brad Goebel (QB) 1991
Preston Jones (QB) 1993
Dirk Johnson (P) 2003-06

#9
James Zyntell (G) 1934
Sonny Jurgensen (QB) 1957-63
Jim Nettles (DB) 1965-68
Billy Walik (WR) 1970-72
Joe Pisarcik (QB) 1980-84
Don McPherson (QB) 1988-90
Jim McMahon (QB) 1990-92
Rodney Peete (QB) 1995-98
Norm Johnson (K) 1999

#10
George Kavel (B) 1934
Marv Ellstrom (B) 1934
Isadore Weinstock (B) 1935
Don Jackson (B) 1936
Maurice Harper (C) 1937-40
Tommy Thompson (QB) 1941-42
Al Sherman (B) 1943-47
Frank Tripucka (QB) 1949
Adrian Burk (QB) 1951-56
Al Dorow (QB) 1957
King Hill (QB) 1961-68
George Mira (QB) 1969
Mike Boryla (QB) 1974-76
Ove Johansson (K) 1977
John Walton (QB) 1978-79
John Teltschik (P) 1986-90
Pat Ryan (QB) 1991
Koy Detmer (QB) 1997-06

#11
Lee Woodruff (B) 1933
Joe Knapper (B) 1934
Ed Manske (E) 1936
John Ferko (G) 1937
Bernie Lee (B) 1938

PLAYERS BY THE NUMBERS

Francis Murray (B) 1939-40
Lou Ghecas (B) 1941
Richard Erdlitz (B) 1942
Tommy Thompson (QB) 1945-50
John Rauch (QB) 1951
Bobby Thomanson (QB) 1952-57
Norm Van Brocklin (QB) 1958-60
Rick Arrington (QB) 1970-73
John Walton (QB) 1976-77
Jeff Christensen (QB) 1984-85
Kyle Mackey (QB) 1986
Scott Tinsley (QB) 1987r
Casey Weldon (QB) 1992
Matt Bahr (K) 1993
Jay Fiedler (QB) 1994-95
Mark Rypien (QB) 1996
Ron Powlus (QB) 2000
Tim Hasselbeck (QB) 2002
Jeff Blake (QB) 2004
Jeremy Bloom (WR/KR) 2006

#12
John Roberts (B) 1933-34
Ed Matesic (B) 1934-35
Art Buss (T) 1936-37
Herschel Ramsey (E) 1938-40
Kent Lawrence (WR) 1969
Tom McNeill (P) 1973
Bill Troup (QB) 1975
Bob Holly (QB) 1984
Randall Cunningham (QB) 1985-95

#13
George Kenneally (E) 1933-35
Dave Smukler (B) 1936-39
Leonard Barnum (B) 1940-42
Chuck Hughes (WR) 1967-69
Rick Engles (P) 1978

#14
Swede Hanson (B) 1933-36
Rudy Gollomb (G) 1936
Elwood Dow (B) 1938-40
Bob Gambold (B) 1953
Pete Liske (QB) 1971-72
Marty Horn (QB) 1987r
Rick Tuten (P) 1969
Jeff Wilkins (K) 1994
Ty Detmer (QB) 1996-97
Doug Pederson (QB) 1999
A.J. Feeley (QB) 2001-03, 2006-07*

#15
Laf Russell (B) 1933
Dick Lackman (B) 1933
Osborne Willson (G) 1934-35
Stumy Thomason (B) 1936
William Hughes (C) 1937
Clem Woltman (T) 1938-40
Lou Tomasetti (B) 1940-41
Ted Laux (B) 1942-43
Steve Van Buren (RB) 1944-51
RETIRED

#16
Harry O'Boyle (B) 1933
Sylvester Davis (B) 1933
James Zyntell (G) 1935
John Kusko (B) 1937-38
Elmer Kolberg (B) 1940
Norm Snead (QB) 1964-70
Vern Davis (DB) 1971
Horst Muklmann (K) 1975-77
Rob Hertel (QB) 1980
Jeff Kemp (QB) 1991
Gari Scott (WR) 2000

#17
Joe Carter (E) 1935-40
James Russell (T) 1937
Ebert Van Buren (B) 1951
Fred Erike (B) 1952
Jerry Reichow (E) 1960
Ralph Guglielmi (QB) 1963
Taft Reed (B) 1967
Harold Carmichael (WR) 1971-83
Mitch Berger (P) 1994
Freddie Solomon (WR) 1995
Lonny Callicchio (K) 1997

#18
Nick Prisco (B) 1933
Porter Lainhart (B) 1933
Albert Weiner (B) 1934
Joe Pilconis (E) 1936-37
Herbert Roton (E) 1937
Rankin Britt (E) 1939
Ray Hamilton (E) 1940
Ben Hawkins (WR) 1966-73
Roman Gabriel (QB) 1974-77
Dave Archer (QB) 1991-92
Chris Bonial (K) 1997-98
Donte Stallworth (WR) 2006

#19
Roger Kirkman (B) 1933
Jim Leonard (B) 1934-37
Herman Bassman (B) 1936
Tom Burnette (B) 1938
John Ferko (G) 1938
George Somers (T) 1939-40
Harold Pegg (C) 1940
Dan Berry (B) 1967
Tom Dempsey (K) 1971-74
Guido Merkens (QB) 1987r
Tony Smith (WR) 1999
Sean Morey (WR) 2001

#20
John Lipski (C) 1933-34
Howard Bailey (T) 1935
Clyde Williams (T) 1935
Pete Stevens (C) 1936
Henry Reese (C/LB) 1937-39
Jim MacMurdo (T) 1937
Elmer Hackney (B) 1940-41
Don Stevens (B) 1952, 1954
Ed Bawel (B) 1955-56
Jim Harris (B) 1957
Frank Budd (E) 1962
Leroy Keyes (DB) 1969-72
John Outlaw (DB) 1973-78
Leroy Harris (FB) 1979-82
Andre Waters (S/LB) 1984-93
Vaughn Herbron (RB) 1994-95
Brian Dawkins (S/LB) 1996-07*

#21
James Zyntell (G) 1933
Paul Cuba (T) 1934-35
John Kusko (B) 1936
Herschel Stockton (G) 1937-38
Allison White (T) 1939
Chuck Cherundolo (C) 1940
William Boedeker (B) 1950
Al Pollard (B) 1951-53
Jim Carr (S) 1959-63
Joe Scarpati (S) 1964-69, 1971
Ray Jones (DB) 1970
Jackie Allen (DB) 1972
Wes Chesson (WR) 1973-73
Al Clark (CB) 1976
John Sciarra (DB) 1978-83
Evan Cooper (DB) 1984-87
Eric Allen (CB) 1988-94
Bobby Taylor (CB) 1995-03
Matt Ware (CB) 2004-07???
Dustin Fox (DB) 2006
Will Peterson (DT) 2006
William James (CB) 2007*

#22
Henry Obst (G) 1933
Edward Storm (B) 1934-35
James Russell (T) 1936
Elmer Kolberg (B) 1939
Don Jones (B) 1940
Ralph Goldston (B) 1952, 1954-55
Lee Riley (DB) 1956, 1958-59
Tim Brown (RB) 1960-67
Cyril Pinder (RB) 1968-70
Larry Marshall (KR) 1974-77
Brenard Wilson (S) 1979-86
Robert Lavette (RB) 1987
Jacque Robinson (FB) 1987r
Mark Higgs (RB) 1989
Vai Sikahema (KR) 1992-93
Marvin Goodwin (S) 1994
James Saxon (FB) 1995
James Fuller (S) 1996
Duce Staley (RB) 1997-03
Eric McCoo (RB) 2004
Joselio Hanson (DB) 2006-07*

#23
Paul Cuba (T) 1933
Vince Zizak (T) 1934-37
Phil Poth (G) 1934
Harry Shaub (G) 1935
Bill Wilson (E) 1938
Zed Coston (C) 1939
Raymond George (T) 1940
William Roffler (B) 1954
Ken Keller (B) 1956-57
Carl Taseff (DB) 1961
Mike McClellan (B) 1962-63
Claude Crabb (DB) 1964-65
Willie Brown (WR) 1966
Harry Jones (RB) 1967-72
Roger Williams (DB) 1973
Clifford Brooks (DB) 1975-76
Bob Howard (CB) 1978-79
Cedrick Brown (CB) 1987
Willie Turral (RB) 1987r
Health Sherman (RB) 1989-93
Derrick Frazier (CB) 1994-95
Troy Vincent (CB) 1996-03
Ryan Moats (DB) 2005-07*

#24
Joe Carpe (T) 1933
Howard Auer (T) 1933
Dick Lackman (B) 1933-35
Joe Knapper (B) 1934
Herman Bassman (B) 1936
Joe Pilconis (E) 1937
Allen Keen (B) 1937-38
Bill Schneller (B) 1940
Dom Moselle (B) 1954
George Taliaferro (B) 1955
Don Schaefer (B) 1956
Nate Ramsey (DB) 1963-72
Artimus Parker (DB) 1974-76
Henry Monroe (CB) 1979
Zac Henderson (S) 1980
Ray Ellis (S) 1981-85
Rusell Gary (DB) 1986

PLAYERS BY THE NUMBERS

Allen Reid (RB) 1987
Reggie Brown (RB) 1987r
Alan Dial (DB) 1989
Corey Barlow (CB) 1992-94
Tim McTyer (CB) 1997-98
Darnell Autry (RB) 2000
Rod Smart (RB) 2001
Blaine Bishop (S) 2002
Sheldon Brown (CB) 2002-07*

#25
Osborne Willson (G) 1933
Leonard Gudd (E) 1934
Henry Reese (C/LB) 1935-36
Emmett Kriel (G) 1939
Russ Thompson (T) 1940
Hugh McCullough (B) 1943
Toy Ledbetter (B) 1950, 1953-55
Pete Retzlaff (TE) 1956
Tommy McDonald (WR) 1957-63
Bill Mack (WR) 1964
Bob Shann (B) 1965, 1967
Larry Conjar (FB) 1968
Tommy Sullivan (RB) 1972-77
Bill Bryant (CB) 1978
Zach Dixon (RB) 1980
Dennis DeVaughn (DB) 1982-83
Anthony Toney (FB) 1986-90
Tom Gerhart (DB) 1992
Charlie Garner (RB) 1994
Greg Tremble (DB) 1995
Deral Boykin (S) 1996
Willie Clay (CB) 1997
Allen Rossum (KR) 1998-99
Je'rod Cherry (S) 2000
Monty Montgomery (CB) 2001
Dorsey Levens (RB) 2002, 2004
Dustin Fox (CB) 2006

#26
Joe Kresky (G) 1933
Dan Barnhardt (B) 1934
Javk Norby (B) 1934
Forrest McPherson (T) 1935-36
Winford Baze (B) 1937
Herschel Giddens (T) 1938
Lester McDonald (E) 1940
Dave DiFilippo (G) 1941
Clarence Peaks (FB) 1957-63
Al Nelson (DB) 1965-73
Art Malone (RB) 1975-76
John Sanders (DB) 1977-79
Michael Haddix (FB) 1983-88
Ben Smith (DB) 1990-93
Al Jackson (CB) 1994
Jerome Henderson (CB) 1995
Darnell Autry (RB) 1998
Lito Sheppard (CB) 2002-07*

#27
Milton Leathers (G) 1933
Robert Gonya (T) 1933-34
Jack Dempsey (T) 1934, 1937
Burle Robinson (E) 1935
George Rado (E) 1937-38
Milton Trost (T) 1940
Sam Bartholomew (B) 1941
Bob Davis (B) 1942
John Butler (B) 1943, 1945
Ted Laux (B) 1944
Pete Kmetovic (B) 1946
Tom Johnson (B) 1948
Clyde Scott (B) 1949-52
Neil Ferris (B) 1952
Hal Giancanelli (B) 1953-56
Billy Wells (B) 1948
Gene Johnson (B) 1959-60
Irv Cross (DB) 1961-65
Trent Johnson (WR) 1966
Po James (RB) 1972-74
Richard Blackmore (CB) 1979-82
Topper Clemons (RB) 1987r
Siran Stacy (RB) 1992
Eric Zomalt (S) 1994-96
James Bostic (RB) 1998-99
Julian Jones (S) 2001
Quintin Mikell (DB) 2003-07*

#28
Richard Thorton (B) 1933
Myers Clark (B) 1934
Guy Turnbow (T) 1934
Max Padlow (E) 1935
Harry Kloppenberg (T) 1936
Stumpy Thomason (B) 1936
Joe Pilconis (E) 1937
Ray Keeling (T) 1938-39
Bob Jackson (B) 1960
Don Jonas (B) 1962
Paul Dudley (B) 1963
Jim Gray (B) 1967
Bill Bradley (S) 1969-76
Lou Rash (CB) 1984
Greg Harding (DB) 1987r
Don Griffen (CB) 1996
Mel Gray (KR) 1997
Clarence Love (CB) 1998
Amp Lee (RM) 2000
Correll Buckhalter (RB) 2001-2007*

#29
Ray Smith (C) 1933
Richard Fenci (E) 1933
Stephen Banas (B) 1935
Glenn Campbell (E) 1935
Stumpy Thomason (B) 1935
Herman Bassman (B) 1936
Joe Pivarnick (G) 1936
Clares Knox (T) 1937
William Hughes (C) 1938-40
John Nocera (LB) 1959-62
Israel Lang (FB) 1964-68
Harold Jackson (WR) 1969-72
Mark Burke (DB) 1976
Al Latimer (CB) 1979
Jo Jo Heath (DB) 1981
Elbert Foules (CB) 1983-87
Mark McMillian (CB) 1992-95
Adam Wlker (FB) 1996
Corey Walker (RB) 1998
Darrel Crutchfield (CB) 2001
Roderick Hood (CB) 2003-2006
Tony Hunt (RB) 2007*

#30
Art Koeninger (C) 1933
Barnes Milon (G) 1934
Harry Benson (G) 1935
Bob Masters (B) 1937-38
Don Looney (E) 1940
Mort Landsberg (B) 1941
Bosh Pritchard (B) 1942, 1946-51
John Binotto (B) 1942
Richard Erdlitz (B) 1945
Milton Smith (E) 1945
Theron Sapp (B) 1959-63
Alvin Haymond (DB) 1968
Jim Raye (DB) 1969
Joe Lavender (CB) 1973-75
Ron Lou (C) 1975
Cleveland Franklin (RB) 1977-78
Mike Hogan (FB) 1980
Don Calhoun (RB) 1982
Chris Johnson (DB) 1987r
Otis Smith (CB) 1991-94
Charlie Garner (RB) 1995-98
Brian Mitchell (KR) 2000-02
J.R. Reed (S) 2004-5, 2007*

#31
Joe Carter (E) 1933-34
Tom Graham (G) 1935
Irv Kupcinet (B) 1935
William Brian (T) 1935-36
Emmett Mortell (B) 1937-39
Jerry Ginney (G) 1940
Phil Ragazzo (T) 1940
Jim Macioszcyk (B) 1944, 1947
Dan Sandifer (DB) 1950-51
Elbert Van Buren (B) 1952-53
Ron Goodwin (E) 1963
Tom Bailey (B) 1971-74
Wilbert Montgomery (RB) 1977-84
Troy West (S) 1987r
Tyrone Jones (DB) 1989
Brian O'Neal (FB) 1994
Derrick Witherspoon (RB) 1995-97
Al Harris (CB) 1998-02
Daryon Brutley (CB) 2003
Dexter Wynn (CB) 2004-06

#32
Everitt Rowan (E) 1933
Fred Felber (E) 1933
Glenn Frey (B) 1936-37
Hugh Wolfe (B) 1940
Irving Hall (B) 1942
Charlie Gauer (E) 1943-44
Toimi Jarvi (B) 1944
John Rogalla (B) 1945
Jack Myers (B) 1948-50
Neil Worden (RB) 1954, 1957
Joe Pagliei (B) 1959
Roger Gill (B) 1964-65
Rick Duncan (P) 1968
Jack Smith (QB) 1971
Charles Ford (DB) 1974
Herb Lusk (RB) 1976-78
Earl Carr (RB) 1979
Jim Culbreath (FB) 1980
Booker Russell (FB) 1981
Michael Williams (RB) 1983-84
Michael Ulmer (QB) 1987r
Walter Abercomie (RB) 1988
James Joseph (RB) 1991-94
Ricky Watters (RB) 1995-97
Jason Bostic (RB) 1999-2000
Michael Lewis (S) 2000-06

#33
Guy Turnbow (T) 1933
Ray Spillers (T) 1937
Taldon Manton (B) 1940
Jack Banta (B) 1941, 1944-45
Bob Masters (B) 1942
Steve Sader (B) 1943
Russ Craft (B) 1946-53
Roy Barni (B) 1954-55
Willie Berzinski (B) 1956
Billy Ray Barnes (RB) 1957-61
Merrill Douglas (B) 1962
Ollie Matson (RB) 1964-66
Ron Blye (RB) 1969
Steve Preece (DB) 1970-72
Randy Jackson (RB) 1974

PLAYERS BY THE NUMBERS

Po James (RB) 1975
Louie Giammona (RB) 1978-82
William Frizzell (S) 1986-90, 1992-93
Mike Waters (FB) 1986
Kevin Bouie (Rb) 1996
Tim Watson (S) 1997
Aaron Hayden (RB) 1998
Eric Bieniemy (RB) 1999
Thomas Hamner (RB) 2000
Terrence Carroll (S) 2001
Clinton Hart (S) 2003-04

#34
Roy Lechthaler (G) 1933
Laurence Steinbach (T) 1933
Mike Sebastian (B) 1935
Jay Arnold (B) 1937-40
Lee Roy Caffey (LB) 1963
Earl Gros (FB) 1964-66
Larry Watkins (B) 1970-72
Dave Hampton (RB) 1976
James Betterson (RB) 1977-78
Hubie Oliver (FB) 1981-85
Terry Hoage (S) 1986-90
Herschel Walker (RB) 1992-94
Kevin Turner (FB) 1995-99
Jamie Reader (FB) 2001
Reno Mahe (RB) 2003-06

#35
Charles Leyendecker (T) 1933
Dick Smith (C) 1933
Forrest McPherson (T) 1937
Drew Ellis (T) 1938-40
Dick Bassi (G) 1940
Pete Pihos (E) 1947-55
Ted Dean (RB) 1960-63
Ray Poage (E) 1964-65
Adrian Young (LB) 1968-72
Mike Hogan (FB) 1976-78
Perry Harrington (RB) 1980-83
Mike Kullman (S) 1987r
Mark Konecny (RB) 1988
Kevin Bouie (RB) 1995
Deauntee Brown (CB) 1997
Anthony Marshall (S) 1998
Edwin Watson (RB) 1999
Chis Warren (RB) 2000
Bruce Perry (RB) 2005-06
Nick Graham (CB) 2007*

#36
Ed Manske (E) 1935
Carl Kane (B) 1936
Herbert Roton (E) 1937
Joe Bukant (B) 1938-40
Terry Fox (B) 19411945
John Stackpool (B) 1942
Dean Steward (B) 1943
Joe Muha (B) 1946-50
Jerry Cowhig (B) 1951
John Brewer (B) 1952-53
Dick Bielski (B) 1955-59
Tom McNeill (P) 1971-72
Norm Bulaich (RB) 1973-74
Herman Hunter (RB) 1985
Bobby Morse (RB) 1987
Robert Drummond (RB) 1989-91
Mike Zordich (S) 1994-98
Stanley Pritchett (FB) 2000
Brian Westbrook (RB) 2002-2007*

#37
Irv Kupcinet (B) 1935
Robert Rowe (B) 1935
Winford Baze (B) 1937
John Cole (B) 19381940
Bree Cuppoletti (G) 1939
Fred Gloden (B) 1941
Ernie Steele (B) 1942-48
Tom Woodeshick (RB) 1963-71
Merritt Kersey (P) 1974-75
Tommy Campbell (DB) 1976
Billy Campfield (RB) 1978-82
Taivale Tautalatasi (RB) 1986-88
Sammy Lilly (DB) 1989-90
Sean Woodson (S) 1998
Sean Considine (DB) 2005-07*

#38
Bill Fiedler (G) 1938
Jake Schuehle (B) 1939
John Huzvar (B) 1952
Rob Goode (B) 1955
Sam Baker (K) 1964-69
Tony Baker (B) 1971-72
George Amundson (RB) 1975
Bill Olds (RB) 1976
Larry Barnes (FB) 1978-79
Steve Atkins (FB) 1981
Mickey Fitzgerald (FB) 1981
Jairo Penaranda (RB) 1985
Russell Gary (DB) 1986
Rich Miano (DB) 1991-94
Dexter McNabb (FB) 1995
Charles Dimry (DB) 1997
Ceil Martin (FB) 1999-02
Thomas Tapeh (FB) 2004, 2006-07*

#39
Harry Benson (G) 1935
Bob Pylman (T) 1938-39
Foster Watkins (B) 1940
Bill Mackrides (B) 1947-51
Pete Emelianchik (E) 1967
Kermitt Alexander (DB) 1972-73
Bill Olds (RB) 1976
Bob Torrey (FB) 1980
Major everett (FB) 1983-85
Victor Bellamy (CB) 1987r
Tony Brooks (RB) 1992-93
Corey Walker (RB) 1997
Michael Reed (FB) 1998

#40
Charles Newton (B) 1939-40
Wesley McAfee (B) 1941
Sonny Karnofsky (B) 1945
Elliott Ormsbe (B) 1946
Leslie Palmer (B) 1948
Frank Reagan (B) 1949-51
Don Johnson (B) 1953-55
Tom Brookshier (CB) 1956-61
RETIRED

#41
Ted Schmidt (C) 1938-40
Foster Watkins (B) 1941
Gil Steinke (B) 1945-48
Busit Warren (B) 1945
Frank Ziegler (B) 1949-53
Jerry Norton (DB) 1954-58
Bob Freeman (DB) 1960-61
Howard Cassady (B) 1962
Harry Wilson (B) 1967-70
Richard Harvey (DB) 1970
Randy Logan (S) 1973-83
Earnest Jackson (RB) 1985-86
Keith Byars (RB) 1987-92
Alvin Ross (FB) 1987r
Fred McCrary (FB) 1995
Johnny Thomas (CB) 1996
William Hampton (CB) 2001

#42
Carl Jorgensen (T) 1935
George Mulligan (E) 1936
Swede Hanson (B) 1936-37
Raymond George (T) 1940
Raymond Hamilton (E) 1940
Bob Hudson (B) 1954-55, 1957-58
Bob Harrison (LB) 1962-63
Aaron Martin (DB) 1966-67
Dennis Morgan (KR) 1975
Steve Wagner (S) 1980
Calvin Murray (HB) 1981-82
Keith Byars (RB) 1986
Angelo James (CB) 1987r
Eric Everett (CB) 1988-89
John Booty (DB) 1991-92
Mike Reid (S) 1993-94
David Whitmore (S) 1995
Dialleo Burks (WR) 1996
Rashard Cook (S) 1999-02

#43
Jack Hinkle (HB) 1941, 1943-47
William Jefferson (B) 1942
James Lankas (B) 1942
Jim Palmer (B) 1948-56
Robert Smith (B) 1956
Walt Kowalczyk (B) 1958-59
Ralph Heck (LB) 1963-65
Al Davis (B) 1971-72
James McAllister (RB) 1975-76
Roynell Young (CB) 1980-88
Roger Vick (RB) 1990
Erik McMillan (S) 1993
Randy Kinder (CB) 1997
Damon Moore (S) 1999-01

#44
Franklin Emmons (B) 1940
Albert Johnson (B) 1942
Ben Kish (B) 1943-49
Norm Willey (DE) 1950-51
Bob Stringer (B) 1952-53
Harry Dowda (B) 1954-55
Pete Retzlaff (TE) 1957-66
RETIRED

#45
Leo Raskowski (T) 1935
Thomas Bushby (B) 1935
Art Buss (T) 1937
Dick Riffle (B) 1938-40
Noble Doss (B) 1947-48
Joe Sutton (B) 1950-52
Tom Brookshier (CB) 1953
Rocky Ryan (E) 1956-58
Paige Cothren (B) 1959
Don Burroughs (DB) 1960-64
Ron Medved (DB) 1966-70
Pat Gibbs (DB) 1972
Marion Reeves (DB) 1974
Von Mansfield (DB) 1982
Charles Crawford (RB) 1986-87
Jeff Griffin (CB) 1987r
Thomas Sanders (RB) 1990-91
Vaughn Hebron (RB) 1993
Barry Wilburn (S) 1995-96
Matt Stevens (S) 1997-98
Tim Hauck (S) 1999-01

#46
Don Miller (B) 1954

PLAYERS BY THE NUMBERS

Ted Wegert (B) 1955-56
Brad Myers (B) 1958
Glen Amerson (B) 1961
Lee Bouggess (RB) 1970-73
Herm Edwards (CB) 1977-85
Chris Gerhard (S) 1987r
Izel Jenkins (CB) 1988-92
Markus Thomas (RB) 1993
Fredric Ford (CB) 1997
Quintin Mikell (S) 2003-04
Jon Dorenbos (LS) 2006-07*

#47
Nick Basca (B) 1941
John Mallory (B) 1968
Ed Hayes (DB) 1970
Ron Bull (RB) 1971
Larry Crowe (RB) 1972
Charlie Williams (CB) 1978
Andre Hardy (RB) 1984
Greg Jackson (S) 1994-95
Charles Emanuel (S) 1997

#48
Eberle Schultz (G) 1940
Ben Scotti (CB) 1962-63
Jay Johnson (LB) 1969
Greg Oliver (RB) 1973-74
Martin Mitchell (DB) 1977
Wes Hopkins (S) 1983-93
Steve Hendrickson (LB) 1995
Andre President (TE) 1997
Jon Ritchie (FB) 2003-2004

#49
Dan DeStantis (B) 1941
Robert Thurbon (B) 1943
Mel Bleeker (B) 1944-46
Pat McHugh (B) 1947-51
Jerry Williams (B) 1953-54
Glenn Glass (B) 1964-65
Wayne Colman (LB) 1968-69
Jim Thrower (DB) 1970-72
John Tarver (RB) 1975
Eric Johnson (DB) 1977-78
Tom Caterbone (CB) 1987r
Todd Bell (LB) 1989
Luther Broughton (TE) 1997
Andrew Jordan (TE) 1998

#50
Alabama Pitts (B) 1935
Don Jackson (B) 1936
Robert Bjorklund (C) 1941
Ken Hayden (C) 1942
Alabama Wukits (C) 1943
Baptiste Manzini (C) 1944-45
Bob Kelley (C) 1955-56
Darrel Aschbacher (G) 1959
Dave Recher (C) 1966-68
Ron Porter (LB) 1969-72
Guy Morriss (C) 1974-83
Garry Cobb (LB) 1985-87
Dave Rimington (C) 1988-89
Ephesians Bartley (LB) 1992
James Willis (LB) 1995-98
Alonzo Ephraim (C) 2003
Mark Simoneau (LB) 2004
Torrance Daniels (LB) 2006
Matt McCoy (LB) 2005-07*

#51
Lyle Graham (C) 1941
Al Milling (G) 1942
Robert Wear (C) 1942
Enio Conti (G) 1944-45
Ray Graves (C) 1946
Boyd Williams (C) 1947
Frank Szymanski (C) 1948
Chuck Weber Weber (LB) 1959-61
Jim Schrader (C) 1962-64
Dave Recher (C) 1965
Dwight Kelley (LB) 1966-72
Dick Cunningham (LB) 1973
Ron Lou (C) 1975
Reggie Wilkes (LB) 1978-85
Chuck Gorecki (LB) 1987r
Ricky Shaw (LB) 1989-90
William Thomas (LB) 1991-99
Carlos Emmons (LB) 2000-03
Takeo Spikes (LB) 2007*

#52
Ray Graves (C) 1942-43
Vic Lindskag (C) 1944-51
Wayne Robinson (LB) 1952-56
Dave Lloyd (LB) 1963-70
Kevin Reilly (LB) 1973-74
Ray Phillips (LB) 1978-81
Rich Kraynak (LB) 1983-86
Matt Battaglia (LB) 1987r
Todd Bell (LB) 1988
Jessie Small (LB) 1989-91
Louis Cooper (LB) 1993
Vaughan Johnson (LB) 1994
Sylvester Wright (LB) 1995-96
DeShawn Fogle (LB) 1997
Jon Haskins (LB) 1998
Barry Gardner (LB) 1999-02
Jason Short (LB) 2004-06
Pago Togafau (LB) 2007*

#53
Walt Masters (B) 1936
Alex Wojciechowicz (C) 1946-50
Ken Farragut (C) 1951-54
Bob Pellegrini (LB) 1956, 1958-61
John Simerson (C) 1957
Bob Butler (G) 1962
Harold Wells (LB) 1965-68
Fred Whittingham (LB) 1971
Dick Absher (LB) 1972
Dennis Franks (C) 1976-78
Jody Schulz (LB) 0983-84
Adwayne Jiles (LB) 1985-89
Fred Smalls (LB) 1987r
Maurice Henry (LB) 1990
John Roper (LB) 1993
Bill Romanowski (LB) 1994-95
N.D. Kalu (DE) 1997
Hugh Douglas (DE) 1998-02,2004
Mark Simoneau (LB) 2003
Dedrick Roper (LB) 2005-06

#54
Gerry Huth (G) 1959
Bill Lapham (C) 1960
Jim Ringo (C) 1964-67
Gene Ceppetelli (C) 1968-69
Calvin Hunt (C) 1970
Chuck Allen (LB) 1972
Tom Roussel (LB) 1973
Jim Opperman (LB) 1975
Drew Mahalic (LB) 1976-78
Zach Valentine (LB) 1982-83
Jon Kimmel (LB) 1985
Alonozo Johnson (LB) 1986-87
Kelly Kirchbaum (LB) 1987r
Britt Hager (LB) 1989-94
Kurt Gouveia (LB) 1995
Terry Crews (LB) 1996
DeShawn Fogle (LB) 1997
Jeff Herrod (LB) 1997
Jeremiah Trotter (LB) 1998-01, 2004-06
Nate Waynes (LB) 2003

#55
Frank Bausch (C) 1941
Basillio Marchi (C) 1942
Maxie Baughan (LB) 1960-65
Fred Brown (LB) 1967-68
Jerry Strum (C) 1972
Frank LeMaster (LB) 1974-83
Ray Farmer (LB) 1996-98
Quinton Carver (LB) 2001
Tyreo Harrison (LB) 2003
Dhani Jones (LB) 2004-06
Stewart Bradley (LB) 2007*

#56
Bill Hewitt (E) 1936-39
Fred Whittingham (LB) 1966
Bill Hobbs (LB) 1969-71
Bill Overmeyer (LB) 1972
Dean Halverson (LB) 1973-76
Jerry Robinson (LB) 1979-84
Byron Evans (LB) 1987-94
David Brown (LB) 1987r
Joe Kelly (LB) 1996
Darrin Smith (LB) 1997
Mike Caldwell (LB) 1998-01
Shawn Barber (LB) 2002, 2006
Derrick Burgess (DE) 2003-04

#57
Ernie Calloway (DT) 1969
James Reed (LB) 1977
Mike Osborn (LB) 1978
Mike Curcio (LB) 1981-82
Bill Cowher (LB) 1983-84
Tom Polley (LB) 1985
Scott Kowalkowski (LB) 1991-93
Marc Woodard (LB) 1994-96
James Darling (LB) 1997-00
Keith Adams (LB) 2002-04
Chris Gocong (LB/DE) 2007*

#58
Dave Cahill (LB/DT) 1966
Mel Tom (DE) 1967-70
Bob Creech (LB) 1971-72
Steve Colavito (LB) 1975
Terry Tautolo (LB) 1976-79
Anthony Griggs (LB) 1982-85
Byron Lee (LB) 1986-87
Ty Allert (LB) 1987-89
Derrick Oden (LB) 1993-95
Whit Marshall (LB) 1996
Ike Reese (LB) 1998-04
Trent Cole (DE) 2005-07*

#59
Joseph Wendlick (B) 1940
Mike Evans (C) 1968-73
Tom Ehlers (LB) 1975-77
Al Chesley (LB) 1979-82
Joel Williams (LB) 1983-85
Seth Joyner (LB) 1986-93
Carlos Bradley (LB) 1987r
Mike Mamula (DE) 1995-00
Derrick Burgess (DE) 2001-02
Tyreo Harrison (LB) 2002
Justin Ena (LB) 2003
Mike Labinjo (LB) 2004
Nick Cole (OL) 2006-07*

PLAYERS BY THE NUMBERS

#60
Bob Suffridge (G) 1941
Alvin Thacker (G) 1942
Ed Michaels (G) 1943-46
Don Weedon (G) 1947
Chuck Bednarik (C/LB) 1949-62
RETIRED

#61
Tony Cemore (G) 1941
Joseph Frank (T) 1943
Gordon Paschka (G) 1943
Duke Maronic (G) 1944-50
John Michels (G) 1953
Tom Louderback (LB) 1958-59
Howard Keys (T/C) 1960-64
Arunas Vasys (LB) 1966-68
Tony Guillory (LB) 1969
Bill Dunstan (DT) 1973-76
Mark Slater (C) 1979-83
Ben Tamburello (C/G) 1987-90
Matt Long (C) 1987r
Eric Floyd (G) 1992-93
Theo Adams (G) 1995
Steve Everitt (C) 1997-99
Giradie Mercer (DT) 2000

#62
Elwood Gerber (G) 1941-42
Mike Mandarino (G) 1944-45
Augie Lio (G) 1946
Don Talcott (T) 1947
Bill Horrell (G) 1952
Knox Ramsey (G) 1952
John Wittenborn (G) 1960-62
Jerry Mazzanti (E) 1963
Mike Dirks (G) 1968-71
Guy Morriss (C) 1973
Bill Lueck (G) 1975
Johnny Jackson (DE) 1977
Pete Perot (G) 1979-84
Nick Haden (G) 1986
Dennis McKnight (G) 1991
Brian Baldinger (G) 1992-93
Guy McIntyre (G) 1995-96
Ian Beckles (G) 1997-98
Dwight Johnson (DE) 2000
Scott Peters (OL) 2002
Max Jean-Gilles (G) 2006-07*

#63
Ralph Fritz (G) 1941
Rupert Pate (G) 1942
Bruno Banducci (G) 1944-45
Albert Baisi (G) 1947
Leo Skladany (E) 1949
Norm Willey (DE) 1952
Ken Huxhold (G) 1954-58
Tom Catlin (LB) 1959
Mike Woulfe (LB) 1962
Lynn Hoyem (G) 1964-67
Tom Luken (G) 1972-78
Ron Baker (G) 1980-88
Daryle Smith (T) 1991-92
Joe Panos (G) 1994
Raleigh McKenzie (C) 1995-96
David Diaz-Infante (G) 1999
Hank Fraley (C) 2000-04

#64
Robert McDonough (G) 1946
Mario Giannelli (G) 1948-51
George Savirsky (T) 1949
Menil Mavraides (G) 1954
Russ Carroccio (G) 1955
Abe Gibron (G) 1956-57
Bob Gaona (T) 1957
Galen Laack (G) 1958
John Simerson (C) 1958
Roy Hord (G) 1962
Ed Blaine (G) 1963-66
Dean Wink (DT) 1967-68
Randy Beisler (DE) 1968
Norm Davis (G) 1970
Joe Jones (DE) 1974-75
Ernie Janet (T) 1975
Ed George (T) 1976-78
Garry Puetz (T) 1979
Dean Miraldi (t) 1982-84
Mike Perrino (T) 1987r
Joe Rudolph (G) 1995
Sean Love (G) 1997
Stefan Rodgers (G) 2006-07*

#65
Cliff Patton (G) 1946-50
Dan Rogas (G) 1952
Jess Richardson (DT) 1953
Tom Dimmick (T) 1956
Menil Mavraides (G) 1957
Hal Bradley (G) 1958
Gerry Huth (G) 1960
Jim Beaver (G) 1962
John Mellekas (DT) 1963
Bill Stetz (G) 1967
Henry Allison (G) 1971-72
Roy Kirksey (G) 1974
Roosevelt Manning (DT) 1975
Charlie Johnson (DT) 1977-81
Mark Dennard (C) 1984-85
Bob Landsee (G/C) 1986-87
Gary Bolden (DT) 1987r
Ron Solt (G) 1988-91
Ron Hallstrom (G) 1993
Moe Elewonibi (T) 1995
Bubba Miller (C/G) 1996-01
Jamel Green (DE) 2004

#66
John Wyhonic (G) 1946-47
Baptiste Manzini (C) 1948
Ed Sharkey (T) 1954-55
Frank D'Agostino (G) 1956
Ed Meadows (E) 1958
Joe Robb (DE) 1959-60
Will Renfro (E) 1961
Bill Byrne (G) 1963
Bruce Van Dyke (G) 1973
Gordon Wright (G) 1967
Don Chuy (G) 1969
Bill Cody (LB) 1972
Roy Kirksey (G) 1973
Bill Bergey (LB) 1974-80
Ken Reeves (T) 1985-89
John Hudson (G) 1991-95
Mike Zandofsky (G) 1997
Jerry Crafts (G) 1997
Jeff Dellenbach (G/C) 1999
Bobbie Williams (G) 2000, 2003
Trey Darelik (G/T) 2004
Kimo von Oelhoffen (DT) 2007*

#67
Enio Conti (G) 1941-43
John sanders (G) 1945
John Magee (G) 1948-55
Proverb Jacobs (T) 1958
Stan Campbell (G) 1959-61
Pete Case (G) 1962-64
Erwin Will (DT) 1965
Vern Winfield (G) 1972-73
Herb Dobbins (T) 1974
Jeff Bleamer (T) 1975-76
Lem Burnham (DE) 1977-80
Gerry Feehery (C/G) 1983-87
Steve Gabbard (T) 1989
Ryan Schau (G/T) 1999-01
Jamaal Jackson (C/G) 2005-07*

#68
Ray Romero (G) 1951
Maurice Nipp (G) 1952-53
Dick Murley (T) 1956
Bill Koman (LB) 1957-58
Bill Striegel (G) 1959
Bobby Richards (DE) 1962-65
Mark Nordquist (G) 1968-74
Blenda Gay (DE) 1975-76
Dennis Harrison (DE) 1978-84
Reggie Singletary (DT/G) 1987-90
Pete Walters (G) 1987r
Tom McHale (G/T) 1993-94
Frank Cornish (C) 1995
Morris Unutoa (C) 1996-98
Steve Sciullo (G) 2004
Pat McCoy (T) 2006-07*

#69
Dave DiFilippo (G) 1941
Joe Tyrell (G) 1952
Carl Gersbach (LB) 1970
Rich Glover (DT) 1975
Woody Peoples (G) 1978-80
Dwaine Morris (DT) 1985
Jeff Tupper (DE) 1986
Jim Angelo (G) 1987r
Bruce Collie (G) 1990-91
Burt Grossman (DE) 1994
Harry Boatswain (G/T) 19951997
George Hegamin (G/T) 1998
Jon Runyan (T) 2000-07*

#70
Joseph Frank (T) 1941
Leo Brennan (T) 1942
Al Wistert (T) 1943-51
RETIRED
Don Owens (T) 1958-60
Jim Skaggs (G) 1963-72

#71
Cecil Sturgeon (T) 1941
Frank Hrabetin (T) 1942
Eberle Schultz (G) 1943
Edmund Eiden (B) 1944
George Fritts (T) 1945
Otis Douglas (T) 1946-49
Tom Higgins (T) 1954-55
Jim Ricca (T) 1955-56
Don King (T) 1956
John Wilcox (T) 1960
Joe Lewis (T) 1962
Dick Hart (G) 1967-71
William Wynn (DE) 1973-76
Ken Clarke (DT) 1978-87
Cecil Gray (G/DT) 1990-91
Mike Chalenski (DL) 1993-95
Jermane Mayberry (G/T) 1996-04
Scott Young (G) 2005-07*

#72
Hodges West (T) 1941
Leon Cook (T) 1942
Stephen Levanities (T) 1942
Ted Doyle (T) 1943
Bob Friedman (G) 1944

PLAYERS BY THE NUMBERS

Marshall Shires (T) 1945
Thomas Campion (T) 1947
Roger Harding (C) 1947
Dick Steere (T) 1951
George Mrkonic (T) 1953
Jess Richardson (DT) 1954-61
Frank Fuller (T) 1963
Flyod Peters (DT) 1964-69
Wade Key (G/T) 1970-80
Jim Fritzsche (T/G) 1983
Dave Pacella (G/C) 1984
Kevin Allen (T) 1985
David Alexander (C) 1987-94
Jeff Wenzel (T) 1987r
Joe Panos (G) 1995-97
William "Tra" Thomas (T) 1998-07*

#73
Ed Kasky (T) 1942
Rocco Canale (G) 1943-45
Henry Gude (G) 1946
Alfred Bauman (T) 1947
Fred Hartman (T) 1948
Roscoe Hansen (T) 1951
Lum Snyder (T) 1952-55
Sid Youngelman (T) 1956-88
Ed Khayat (DT) 1958-61,1964-5
Jim Norton (T) 1968
Richard Stevens (T) 1970-74
Pete Lazetich (DT) 1976-77
Steve Kenney (G) 1980-85
Paul Ryczek (C) 1987r
Ron Heller (T) 1988-92
Lester Holmes (G) 1993-96
Jerry Crafts (T/G) 1997
Steve Martin (DT) 1998
Oliver Ross (T) 1999
Jim Pyne (C/G) 2001
Shawn Andrews (G) 2004-07*

#74
Walter Barnes (G) 1948-51
Frank Wydo (T) 1957
Len Szafaryn (T) 1958
Gerry Delucca (T) 1958
Riley Gunnels (T) 1960-64
Donnie Green (T) 1977
Frank Molden (T) 1968
Steve Smith (T) 1972-74
John Niland (G) 1975-76
Leonard Mitchell (T) 1984-86
Mike Pitts (DL) 1987-92
Tim Mooney (DE) 1987r
Gerald Nichols (DT) 1993
Bernard Williams (T) 1994
Ed Jasper (DT) 1997-98
Doug Brzezinski (G) 1999-02
Winston Justice (OT) 2006-07*

#75
Bill Halverson (T) 1942
Bob Suffridge (G) 1945
George Savitsky (T) 1948-49
Walt Stickel (T) 1950-51
Frank Wydo (T) 1952-56
Tom Saidock (T) 1957
Jim McCusker (T) 1959-62
John Meyers (T) 1964-67
Tuufuli Upersa (G) 1971
Houston Antwine (DT) 1972
Dennis Wirgowski (DE) 1973
Willie Cullars (DE) 1974
Stan Walters (T) 1975-83
Jim Gilmore (T) 1986
Scott Leggett (G) 1987r
Louis Cheek (T) 1990
Daryle Smith (T) 1990
Rob Selby (G) 1991-94
Troy Drake (T) 1995-97
John Michels (T) 1999
Juqua Thomas (DE) 2005-07*

#76
Lester McDonal (E) 1940
John Eibner (T) 1941-42
Bucko Kilroy (T) 1943-55
Len Szafaryn (T) 1957
Volney Peters (T) 1958
J.D. Smith (T) 1959-63
Bob Brown (T) 1964-68
Joe Carollo (T) 1969-70
Jerry Sisemore (T) 1973-84
Adam Schreiber (C/G) 1986-88
Broderick Thompson (T) 1993-94
Barret Brooks (T) 1995-98
John Welbourn (G/T) 1999-03
Alonzo Ephraim (C/G) 2004

#77
Phil Ragazzo (T) 1941
Bennie Kaplan (G) 1942
Tex Williams (G) 1942
Carl Fagioli (G) 1944
John Eibner (T) 1946
Jim Kekeris (T) 1947
Gus Cifelli (T) 1954
Jim Weatherall (T) 1955-57
Don Oakes (T) 1961-62
John Kapele (T) 1962
Ray Mansfield (C) 1963
Ray Rissmiller (T) 1966
Ernie Calloway (DT) 1970-72
Gerry Philbin (DE) 1973
Jerry Patton (DT) 1974
Don Ratliff (DE) 1975
Dennis Nelson (T) 1976-77
Rufus Mayes (T) 1979
Tom Jelesky (T) 1985
Michael Black (T/G) 1986
Donald Evans (DE) 1988
Antone Davis (T) 1991
Keith Millard (D/T) 1993
Howard Smothers (G) 1995
Richard Cooper (T) 1996-98
Lonnie Palelei (T/G) 1999
Artis Hicks (T) 2002-04
LaJuan Ramsey (DT) 2006-07*

#78
Mike Jarmoluk (T) 1949-55
Marion Campbell (DT) 1956-61
John Baker (DE) 1962
Dave Graham (T) 1963-69
Steve Smith (T) 1971
Wayne Mass (T) 1972
Jim Cagle (DT) 1974
Carl Hairston (DE) 1976-83
Matt Darwin (C) 1986-90
Mike Nease (C/T) 1987r
Antone Davis (T) 1991-95
Hollis Thomas (DT) 1996-04
Victor Abiamiri (DE) 2007*

#79
Vic Sears (T) 1941-43, 1945-53
Buck Lansford (T) 1955-57
Lum Snyder (T) 1958
Gene Gossage (E) 1960-62
Lane Howell (T) 1965-69
Mitch Sutton (DT) 1974-75
Manny Sistrunk (DT) 1976-79
Frank Giddens (T) 1981-82
Rusty Russell (T) 1984
Joe Conwell (T) 1986-87
Mike Schad (G) 1989-93
Mike Finn (T) 1994
Greg Jackson (DE) 1995-00
Jeremy Siechta (DT) 2002
Ian Allen (T) 2004
Todd Herremans (G/T) 2005-07*

#80
Granville Harrison (E) 1941
Kirk Hershey (E) 1941
Leonard Supulski (E) 1942
Fred Meyer (E) 1943
Bert Kuczynski (E) 1946
Neill Armstrong (E) 1947-51
Bill Stribling (E) 1955-57
Gene Mitcham (E) 1958
Ken MacAfee (E) 1959
John Tracey (DE) 1961
Ken Gregory (E) 1962
Gary Henson (E) 1963
Randy Beisler (DE) 1966-68
Don Brumm (DE) 1970-71
Clark Hoss (TE) 1972
Don Zimmerman (WR) 1973-76
Art Thomas (DE) 1977
Lither Blue (WR) 1980
Alvin Hooks (WR) 1981
Byron Williams (WR) 1983
Joe Hayes (WR) 1964
Keith Baker (WR) 1985
Bobby Duckworth (WR) 1986
Cris Carter (WR) 1987-89
Rod Harrison (WR) 1990-91
Marvin Hargrove (WR) 1990
Reggie Lawrence (WR) 1993
James Lofton (WR) 1993
Reggie Johnson (TE) 1995
Irving Fryar (WR) 1996-98
Torrance Small (WR) 1999-00
James Thrash (WR) 2001-03
Billy McMullen (WR) 2003-05
Kevin Curtis (WR)*

#81
Dick Humbert (E) 1941, 1945-49
Robert Priestly (E) 1942
Ray Reutt (E) 1943
Walt Nowak (E) 1944
John Yovicsin (E) 1944
Don McDonald (E) 1944-46
John O'Quinn (E) 1961
Ed Bawel (B) 1952
Willie Irvin (B) 1953
Eddie Bell (DB) 1955-58
Ron Goodwin (E) 1963-68
Jim Whalen (TE) 1971
Larry Estes (DE) 1972
Stan Davis (B) 1973
Oren Middlebrook (WR) 1978
Scott Fitzkee (WR) 1979-80
Ron Smith (WR) 1981-83
Kenny Jackson (WR) 1984-85
Otis Grant (WR) 1987r
Shawn Beals (WR) 1988
Henry Williams (WR) 1989
Mike Bellamy (WR) 1990
Roy Green (WR) 1991-92
Paul Richardson (WR) 1933
Robert Carpenter (WR) 1995
Mark Seay (WR) 1996-97
Jeff Graham (WR) 1998

Players by the Numbers

Charles Johnson (WR) 1999-00
Tony Stewart (TE) 2001
Billy McMullen (WR) 2003
Terrell Owens (WR) 2004-2005
Jason Avant (WR) 2006-07*

#82
Robert Krieger (E) 1941
William Combs (E) 1942
Bill Hewitt (E) 1943
Milton Smith (E) 1945
Rudy Smeja (E) 1946
Danny DiRenzo (P) 1948
Joe Restic (E) 1952
Tom Scott (DE) 1953-58
George Tarasovic (DE) 1963-65
Tim Rossovich (LB) 1968-71
Bob Picard (WR) 1973-76
Ken Payne (WR) 1978
Jerrold McRae (WR) 1979
Mike Quick (WR) 1982-90
Mickey Shuler (TE) 1991
Victor Bailey (WR) 1993-94
Chris Jones (WR) 1995-97
Karl Hankton (WR) 1998
Dameane Douglas (WR) 1999-02
L.J. Smith (TE) 2003-07*

#83
Jack Ferrante (E) 1941
Jack Smith (E) 1942
John Smith (T) 1945
Bobby Walston (E/K) 1951-62
Bill Qinlan (DE) 1963
Don Hultz (DT) 1964-73
Vince Papale (WR) 1976-78
Rodney Parker (WR) 1980-81
Tony Woodruff (WR) 1982-84
Phil Smith (WR) 1986
Jimmie Giles (TE) 1987-89
Kevin Bowman (WR) 1987r
Kenny Jackson (WR) 1990-91
Pat Beach (TE) 1992
Michael Young (WR) 1993
Ed West (TE) 1995-96
Michael Timpson (WR) 1997
Dietrich Jells (WR) 1998-99
Troy Smith (WR) 1999
Jeff Thomason (TE) 2000-02
Greg Lewis (WR) 2003-07*

#84
Larry Cabrelli (E) 1941-47
Leslie Palmer (B) 1948
Hank Burnine (E) 1956-57
Leo Sugar (DE) 1961
Mike Clark (K/E) 1963
Don Thompson (E) 1964
Jim Kelly (E) 1965-67
Richard Harris (DE) 1971-73
Keith Krepfle (TE) 1975-81
Vyto Kab (TE) 1982-85
Kenny Jackson (WR) 1986-88
Mike McCloskey (TE) 1987
Anthony Edwatds (WR) 1989-90
Floyd Dixon (Wr) 1992
Mark Bavaro (TE) 1993-94
Kelvin Martin (WR) 1995
Freddie Soloman (WR) 1996-98
Jamie Asher (TE) 1999
Luther Broughton (TE) 2000
Freddie Mitchell (WR) 2001-04
Hank Baskett (WR) 2006-07*

#85
John Shonk (E) 1941
Tony Bova (E) 1943
Bob Friedlund (E) 1944
Charlie Gauer (E) 1945
Jay MacDowell (E) 1946
Billy Hix (E) 1950
Bob Schnelker (E) 1953
Ralph Smith (E) 1962-64
Gary Ballman (TE) 1967-72
Marlin McKeever (LB) 1973
Charlrs Smith (WR) 1974-81
Mel Hoover (WR) 1982-84
Ron Johnson (WR) 1985-89
Jesse Bendross (Wr) 1987r
Mickey Shuler (TE) 1990
Jeff Sydner (WR) 1992-94
Art Monk (WR) 1995
Mark Ingram (WR) 1996
Antwuan Wyatt (WR) 1997
Chris Fontenot (TE) 1998
Na Brown (WR) 1999-01
Freedie Milons (WR) 2002
Sean Morey (WR) 2003
Jeff Thomason (TE) 2004

#86
Harold Presott (E) 1947-49
Bob McChesney (E) 1950
Bud Grant (E) 1951-52
Norm Willey (DE) 1953-57
Ed Cooke (E) 1958
Dick Stafford (E) 1962-63
Fred Hill (E) 1965-71
Charles Young (TE) 1973-76
Richard Osborne (TE) 1977-78
Ken Dunek (TE) 1980
Lewis Gilbert (TE) 1980
Steve Folsom (TE) 1981
Al Dixon (TE) 1983
Gregg Garrity (WR) 1984-89
Mike Siano (WR) 1987r
Fred Barnett (WR) 1990-95
Dialleo Burks (WR) 1996
Justin Armour (WR) 1997
Luther Broughton (TE) 1997
Russell Copeland (WR) 1998
Alex Van Dyke (WR) 1999-00
Brian Finneran (WR) 1999
Gari Scott (WR) 2000
Antonio Freeman (WR) 2002
Kori Dickerson (TE) 2003
Reggie Brown (WR) 2005-07*

#87
Jack Ferrante (E) 1944-50
Andy Nacelli (E) 1958
Art Powell (WR) 1959
Dick Lucas (E) 1960-63
Bill Cronin (E) 1965
Dave Lince (E) 1966-67
Fred Brown (LB) 1969
Kent Kramer (TE) 1971-74
Claude Humphrey (DE) 1979-81
Lawrence Sampleton (TE) 1982-84
John Goode (TE) 1985
Eric Bailey (TE) 1987r
Ron Fazio (TE) 1987r
Carlos Carson (WR) 1989
Harper LeBel (TE) 1990
Maurice Johnson (TE) 1991-94
Frank Wainwright (TE) 1995
Jason Dunn (TE) 1996-98
Jed Weaver (TE) 1999
Todd Pinkston (WR) 2000-2004
Brent Celek (TE) 2007*

#88
John Durko (E) 1944
Herschel Ramsey (E) 1945
Jay MacDowell (E) 1947-51
John Zilly (E) 1952
Bob Hudson (B) 1953
Jerry Wilson (E) 1959-60
Gary Pettigrew (DT) 1966-74
Richard Osborne (TE) 1976
Bill Larson (TE) 1978
John Spagnola (TE) 1979-87
Keith Jackson (TE) 1988-91
Jimmie Johnson (TE) 1995-98
Kevin McKenzie (WR) 1998
Luther Broughton (TE) 1999
Mike Bartrum (TE) 2000-06

#89
Henry Piro (E) 1941
Fred Meyer (E) 1942
Tom Miller (E) 1943-44
Ben Agajanian (G) 1945
Robert Krieger (E) 1946
John Green (E) 1947-51
Bob Oristaglio (E) 1952
Don Luft (E) 1954
John Bredice (E) 1956
Mike Morgan (LB) 1964-67
Mike Ditka (E) 1968
Steve Zabel (LB) 1970-74
Wally Henry (WR) 1977-82
Glen Young (WR) 1983
Dave Little (TE) 1985-89
Jay Repko (TE) 1987r
Calvin Williams (WR) 1990-96
Dialleo Burks (WR) 1996
Chad Lewis (TE) 1997-04
Kaseem Sinceno (TE) 1998
Ron Leshinski (TE) 1999
Ed Smith (TE) 1999
Justin Swift (TE) 1999
Matt Schobel (TE) 2006-07*

#90
Aaron Brown (LB) 1985
Mike Golic (DT) 1987-92
Randall Mitchell (NT) 1987r
William Perry (DT) 1993-94
Ronnie Dixon (DT) 1995-96
Jon Harris (DE) 1997-98
Ben Williams (DT) 1999
Corey Simon (DT) 2000-04
Darren Howard (DE) 2006-07*

#91
Tim Golden (LB) 1985
Reggie White (DE) 1985
Ray Conlin (DT) 1987r
George Cumby (LB) 1987r
Scott Curtis (LB) 1988
Greg Mark (DE) 1990
Andy Harmon (DT) 1991-97
Steve Martin (DT) 1999
Uhuru Hamiter (DE) 2000-01
Sam Rayburn (DT) 2003-06

#92
Smiley Creswell (DE) 1985
Reggie White (DE) 1985-92
RETIRED

#93
Tom Strauthers (DE) 1983-86
John Dumbauld (DE) 1987-88
Ray Phillips (DE) 1987r
Dave Bailey (DE) 1990
Greg Townsend (DE) 1994

Dan Stubbs (DE) 1995
Darion Conner (DE) 1996-97
Pernell Davis (DT) 1999-00
Levon Kirkland (LB) 2002
Jevon Kearse (DE) 2004-07*

#94
Byron Darby (DE/TE) 1983-86
Dan McMillen (DE) 1987r
Steve Kaufusi (DE) 1989-90
Leonard Renfro (DT) 1993-94
Kevin Johnson (DT) 1995-96
Bill Johnson (DT) 1998-99
Kelly Gregg (DT) 1990-00
N.D. Kalu (DE) 2001-03
Montae Reagor (DT) 2007*

#95
John Bunting (LB) 1972-82
Jody Schulz (LB) 1985-87
Doug Bartlett (DT) 1988
Al Harris (LB) 1989-90
Mike Flores (DT) 1991-93
William Fuller (DE) 1994-96
Richard Dent (DE) 1997
Henry Slay (DT) 1998
Tyrone Williams (DE) 1999-00
Justin Ena (LB) 2002
Jerome McDougle (DE) 2003-07*

#96
John Sodaski (LB) 1972-73
Clyde Simmons (DE) 1986-93
Harvey Armstrong (DT) 1982-84
Marvin Ayers (DE) 1987r
Mike Flores (DT) 1994
Mark Gunn (DL) 1995-96
Keith Rucker (DT) 1996
Al Wallace (DE/LB) 1997-99
Paul Grasmanis (DT) 2000-04
Omar Gaither (LB) 2006-07*

#97
Thomas Brown (DE) 1980
Reggie Singletary (DT/G) 1986
John Klingel (DE) 1987-88
Jim Auer (DE) 1987r
Dick Chapura (DT/G) 1990
Leon Seals (DT/G) 1992
Tim Harris (DE) 1993
Rhett Hall (DT/G) 1995-98
Mark Wheeler (DT/G) 1999
Darwin Walker (DT/G) 2001-06
Brodrick Bunkley (DT) 2006-07*

#98
Mike Ditka (E) 1967
Greg Brown (DE) 1981-86
Elois Grooms (DE) 1987r
Tommy Jeter (DT) 1992-95
Michael Samson (DT) 1996
Jimmie Jones (DL) 1997
Brandon Whiting (DL) 1998-03
Mike Patterson (DT) 2005-07*

#99
Mel Tom (DE) 1971-73
Leonard Mitchell (DL) 1981-83
Joe Drake (DT) 1985
Skip Hamilton (DT) 1987r
Greg Liter (DE) 1987r
Jerome Brown (DT) 1987-91
RETIRED

*** - players on the 2007**

EAGLES RADIO BROADCASTERS

YEAR	STATION	PLAY-BY-PLAY	COLOR ANALYST
1939	WCAU	Taylor Grant	Bob Hall, Harry McTique
1940-41	WCAU	Byrum Saam	Bob Hall
1942-44	WCAU	Byrum Saam	Chuck Thompson
1945	WCAU	Byrum Saam	Claude Haring
1946-49	WIBG	Byrum Saam	Claude Haring
1950	WPEN	Franny Murray	Del Parks, Jules Rind
1951	WCAU	Bill Sears	-
1952-54	WCAU	Byrum Saam	Claude Haring
1955	WCAU	Byrum Saam	Claude Haring, Bill Bransome
1956	WCAU	Bill Campbell	Bill Bransome
1957	WCAU	Bill Campbell	Bill Bransome Ed Romance
1958-59	WCAU	Bill Campbell	Bill Bransome
1960	WCAU	Bill Campbell	Ed Harvey Russ Hall
1961	WCAU	Bill Campbell	Ed Harvey Russ Hall Jack Buck Tommy Roberts
1962	WCAU	Bill Campbell	Bobby Thomason Tom Brookshier
1963	WCAU	Bill Campbell	Tom Brookshier
1964	WCAU	Bill Campbell	Byrum Saam Tom Brookshier
1965	WCAU	Andy Musser	Charlie Gauer Stan Hockman
1966-67	WCAU	Andy Musser	Charlie Gauer Ed Harvey
1968	WCAU	Andy Musser	Charlie Gauer
1969	WIP	Charlie Swift	Clarence Peaks Thatcher Longstreth
1970	WIP	Charlie Swift	Al Pollard Clarence Peaks Thatcher Longstreth
1971-76	WIP	Charlie Swift	Al Pollard
1977	WIP	Charlie Swift	Merrill Reese Herb Adderley
1978-81	WIP	Merrill Reese	Jim Barniak
1982	WIP	Merrill Reese	Jim Barniak Bill Bergey
1983	WIP	Merrill Reese	Bill Bergey
1984-91	WIP	Merrill Reese	Stan Walters
1992-97	WYSP	Merrill Reese	Stan Walters
1998-2007	WYSP	Merrill Reese	Mike Quick

TRAINING CAMP LOCATIONS

1933	ATLANTIC CITY, NJ
1934	ATLANTIC CITY, NJ
1935	CHESTNUT HILL ACADEMY, PHILADELPHIA
1936	TEMPLE UNIVERSITY, (HILLCREST HOTEL, FLOURTOWN, PA)
1937	TEMPLE UNIVERSITY, (OAK LANE COUNTRY DAY SCHOOL)
1938	WEST CHESTER STATE TEACHERS COLLEGE, WEST CHESTER, PA
1939	ST. JOSEPH'S COLLEGE, PHILADELPHIA
1940	WEST CHESTER STATE TEACHERS COLLEGE, WEST CHESTER, PA
1941	TWO RIVERS, WISCONSIN
1942	TWO RIVERS, WISCONSIN
1943	ST. JOSEPH'S COLLEGE, PHILADELPHIA, PA
1944	WEST CHESTER STATE TEACHERS COLLEGE, WEST CHESTER, PA
1945	WEST CHESTER STATE TEACHERS COLLEGE, WEST CHESTER, PA
1946	SARANAC LAKE, NEW YORK
1947	SARANAC LAKE, NEW YORK
1948-50	GRAND RAPIDS, MINNESOTA
1951-67	HERSHEY, PA (1964 2 WEEKS AT CHERRY HILL INN, NJ)
1968-72	ALBRIGHT COLLEGE, READING, PA
1973-79	WIDENER COLLEGE, CHESTER, PA
1980-95	WEST CHESTER UNIVERSITY, WEST CHESTER, PA
1996-PRESENT	LEHIGH UNIVERSITY, BETHLEHEM, PA

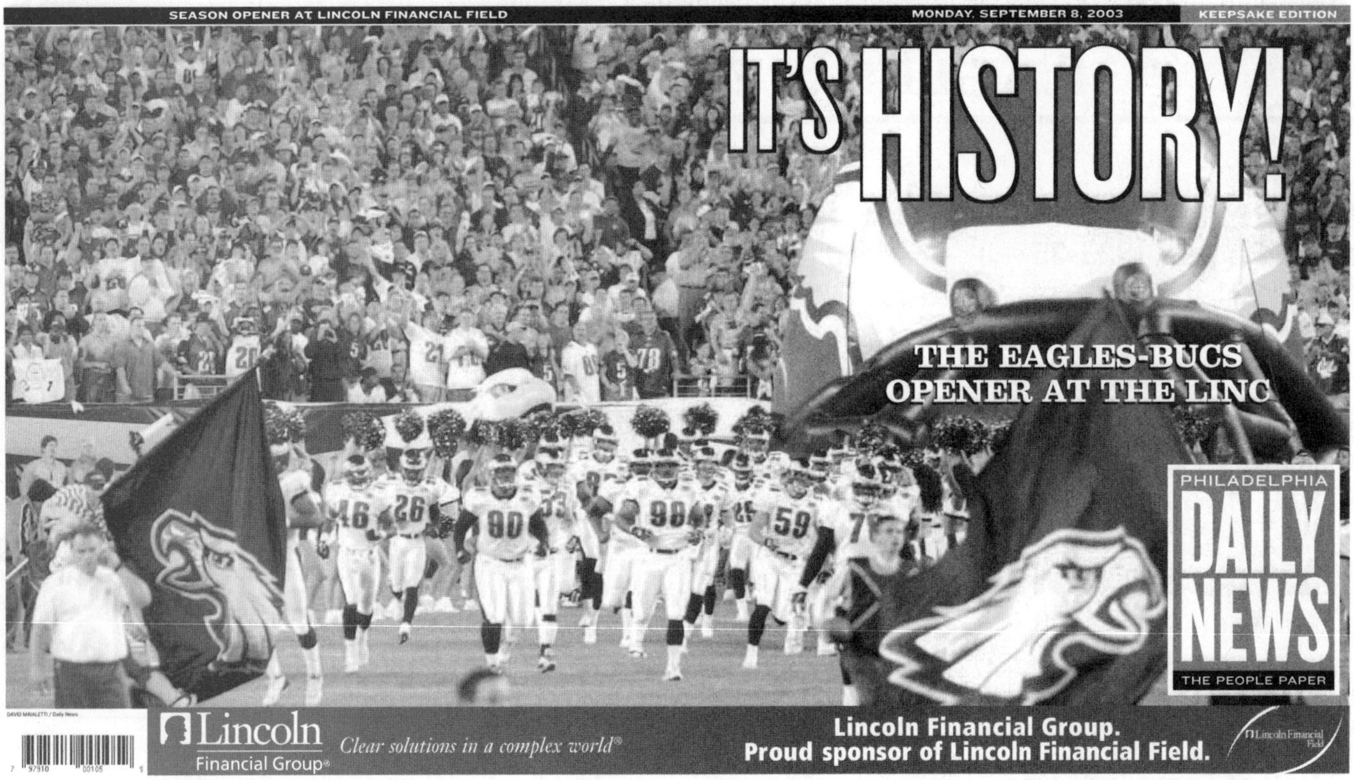
SEASON OPENER AT LINCOLN FINANCIAL FIELD
MONDAY, SEPTEMBER 8, 2003
KEEPSAKE EDITION
IT'S HISTORY!
THE EAGLES-BUCS OPENER AT THE LINC
PHILADELPHIA DAILY NEWS
THE PEOPLE PAPER
Lincoln Financial Group
Clear solutions in a complex world
Lincoln Financial Group.
Proud sponsor of Lincoln Financial Field.

HOME FIELD RECORDS (1933 - 2007)

STADIUM		RECORD	PLAYOFFS
BAKER BOWL	(1933-35)	3-11-1	0-0
TEMPLE STADIUM	(1934-35)	1-1-0	0-0
POINT STADIUM	(JOHNSTOWN, PA - 1936)	0-1-0	0-0
LAIDLEY FIELD	(CHARLESTON, WV - 1938)	1-0-0	0-0
WAR MEMORIAL STADIUM	(CHARLESTON, WV - 1942)	0-1-0	0-0
FORBES FIELD	(PITTSBURGH, PA - 1943)	2-0-0	0-0
MUNICIPAL STADIUM	(1936-39, 1941,1947, 1950, 1954)	5-14-2	0-0
SHIBE PARK/CONNIE MACK STADIUM	(1940-57)	57-35-6	1-0
FRANKLIN FIELD	(1958-70)	41-45-2	1-0
VETERANS STADIUM	(1971-2002)	144-111-2	7-4
LINCOLN FINANCIAL FIELD	(2003-2007)	28-17	4-1
TOTALS		282-236-13*	13-5

NOTE: * TOTAL INCLUDES PLAYOFF RESULTS

EAGLES ALL-TIME RECORD

Regular Season Total	Postseason Total	Overall Total
479-524-25	17-17	496-541-25

Note: The Eagles and Steelers were combined in 1943 and played under the name Steagles.
Their 5-4-1 record from that season is included in this total.

Eagles Head Coaches

Lud Wray
Coached Eagles: 1933-35
Record: 9-21-1

Bert Bell
Coached Eagles: 1936-1940
Record: 10-44-2
1963 Hall of Fame Inductee

Earle "Greasy" Neale
Coached Eagles: 1941-50
Record: 66-44-5
Post Season Record: 3-1
1948 NFL Coach of the Year
1969 Hall of Fame Inductee

Bo McMillin
Coached Eagles: 1951
Record: 2-0

Wayne Millner
Coached Eagles: 1951
Record: 2-8

Jim Trimble
Coached Eagles: 1952-55
Record: 25-20-3

Hugh Devore
Coached Eagles: 1956-57
Record: 7-16-1

Buck Shaw
Coached Eagles: 1958-60
Record: 20-16-1
Post Season Record: 1-0
1960 NFL Coach of the Year

Nick Skorich
Coached Eagles: 1961-63
Record: 15-24-3

Joe Kuharich
Coached Eagles: 1964-68
Record: 28-41-1

Jerry Williams
Coached Eagles: 1969-71
Record: 7-22-2

Ed Khayat
Coached Eagles: 1971-72
Record: 8-15-2

Mike McCormack
Coached Eagles: 1973-75
Record: 16-25-1

Dick Vermeil
Coached Eagles: 1976-82
Record: 57-51-0
Post Season Record: 3-4
1979 NFL Coach of the Year;
1978, 1979 NFC Coach of the Year

Marion Campbell
Coached Eagles: 1983-85
Record: 17-29-1

Fred Bruney
Coached Eagles: 1985
Record: 1-0

Buddy Ryan
Coached Eagles: 1986-90
Record: 43-38-1
Post Season Record: 0-3

Rich Kotite
Coached Eagles: 1991-94
Record: 37-29
Post Season Record: 1-1

Ray Rhodes
Coached Eagles: 1995-98
Record: 30-36-1
Post Season Record: 1-2
1995 NFL Coach of the Year
1995 NFC Coach of the Year

Andy Reid
Coached Eagles: 1999- 2007*
Record: 96-62-0*
Post Season Record: 8-6*
2000,2002 NFL Coach of the Year

* As of the end of the 2007 season

EAGLES OWNERS

1933 TO 1935, BERT BELL AND LUD WRAY

In 1933,with three other former college teammates (including Lud Wray, first head coach), Burt Bell became co-owner of the Eagles for $2,500.

Lud Wray was a professional American football player, coach, and co-founder, with college teammate Bert Bell, of the Philadelphia Eagles of the National Football League. He was the first coach of the Boston Braves (now Washington Redskins) in 1932 and of the Eagles, 1933-1935. His coaching record with the Eagles was 9-21-1.

1935 TO 1940, BERT BELL

Taking the approach of making the overall league stronger, Bell was credited with establishing the NFL draft in 1935. He served as Eagles head coach from 1936 to 1940. By 1937, the Eagles had lost $90,000 and were put up for public auction. Bell became sole owner with a winning bid of $4,500, but after continuing financial struggles, he became co-owner of the Pittsburgh Steelers with his friend Art Rooney in a bizarre transaction in which Rooney sold the Steelers to Philadelphia businessman Alexis Thompson, who then traded franchises with Bell. By 1943, a wartime manpower shortage led the Steelers and Eagles to temporarily merge into the "Pennsylvania Steagles" (officially known as "Phil-Pitt"). The following year, the Steelers merged with the Chicago Cardinals.
In 1937, Bell founded the Maxwell Football Club, which awards the Maxwell Award to the top college football player and the Bert Bell Award to the top professional.

1940 TO 1949, LEX THOMPSON

In 1940, Lex Thompson reportly purchased the franchise for $165,000. He became the first Eagles owner to win a championship. Hired head coach Greasy Neale who at the time was an assistant football coach at his alma mater Yale. Right before selling the team, the Eagles selected Chuck Bednarik as their number one draft selection. Thompson sold the team on January 15, 1949 for $250,000 to a group of investors known as the "100 Brothers."

1949 TO 1962, JAMES P. CLARK

James P. Clark was a successful businessman who organized a group of 100 Philadelphia businessman to invest $3,000 each to purchase the eagles team from Lex Thompson for the sum of $250,000. That season the Eagles won their second straight NFL champioship title. This was one first of two titles the Eagles would win under the "100 Brothers" ownership before selling the team to Jerry Wolman in 1963.

1963 TO 1969, JERRY WOLMAN

Jerry Wolman bought the Eagles franchise in 1963 for a sale price of $5.5 million . He was the youngest owner in the NFL at age 36. While living in the Washington, DC area he saw that the Redskins had a marching band for their football club. So he wanted this for he Eagles. He put together a 220-member marching band called the Philadelphia Eagles Sound of Brass. Wolman hired Joe Kuharich and after his first winning season was rewarded with a 15-year new contract as the team's coach and general manager.

He was also one of the founding owners, briefly in 1967, of the Philadelphia Flyers of the National Hockey League. Over the next two years, his $100-million financial empire crumbled into bankruptcy, and he was forced to give up his interests in both teams. In 1967, he sold his Flyers interest to his co-owners, with Ed Snider assuming control. In 1969, the team was placed on the auction block where he was forced to sell the Eagles to Leonard Tose for a reported $16.1 million, then a record price for a professional sports team.

EAGLES OWNERS

1969 TO 1985, LEONARD TOSE

In 1969 Tose bought the Philadelphia Eagles from Jerry Wolman for $16 million, then a record for a professional sports franchise. Tose's first official act was to fire Coach Joe Kuharich. He followed this by naming former Eagles receiving great Pete Retzlaff as General Manager and Jerry Williams as coach.

In 1976 he, along with General Manager Jimmy Murray, lured Dick Vermeil from UCLA to coach the hapless Eagles, who had one winning season from 1962-75. Vermeil's 1980 team lost to Oakland in the Super Bowl. In January 1983, Tose announced that his daughter, Susan Fletcher, the Eagles' vice president and legal counsel, would eventually succeed him as primary owner of the Eagles.

In 1985 Tose was forced to sell the Eagles to Norman Braman and Ed Leibowitz, highly successful automobile dealers from Florida, for a reported $65 million to pay off his more than $25 million in gambling debts at Atlantic City casinos.

1985 TO 1994, NORMAN BRAMAN

Norman Braman was an American football team owner. He was the owner of the Philadelphia Eagles. Norman and his brother-in-law, Ed Leibowitz, officially became the owners of the Eagles on April 29, 1985. Norman owned 65 percent of the team while Ed owned 35 percent until July 16, 1986 Norman bought the rest of the team from Ed. Braman will be remembered as the person who hired coach Buddy Ryan. But also fired him after the Eagles lost in the first round of the playoffs for the third consecutive year. Replacing him with offensive coorrdinator Rich Kotite. During his tenure as owner of the Eagles, the team twice won eleven games in a single season and went to the playoffs four times.

Braman was a very successful automoblie dealer in Florida and as the Eagles owner brought an aggressive marketing style to the organization. He was able to raise the Eagles fan base by some 15,000 fans and increased ticket prices three times during his first five years as owner. With new TV deals and expansion teams paid large amounts of money, Braman decided it was time to get out. He sold the Eagles franchise to Jeffrey Lurie.

1994 TO PRESENT, JEFFREY LURIE

Jeffrey Lurie is a former Hollywood producer turned NFL team owner. Lurie bought the Philadelphia Eagles on May 6, 1994 from then owner Norman Braman. Lurie paid $195 million for the team. The club is now estimated to be worth $1 billion, as valuated in 2006 by Forbes.

In 1999, Lurie hired Green Bay packers assistant coach Andy Reid as his new head coach. Reid drafted Donovan McNabb in the first round. Since becoming owner of the Eagles, Lurie has been named NFL "Owner of the Year by The Sporting News in 1995 and by Pro Football Insider in 2000. He is also responsible for helping push through the deal to build a new $512 million, 68,500-seat football stadium, now called Lincoln Financial Field. Lurie currently is a member of eight different NFL committees, making him one of the most active owners.

EAGLES IN THE HALL OF FAME

CHUCK BEDNARIK — **CENTER-LINEBACKER**
PLAYED WITH THE EAGLES 1949-62 — **CLASS OF 1967**

Charles Philip Bednarik. . .Two-time Pennsylvania All-America. . . Eagles' bonus draft choice, 1949. . .NFL's last "iron man" star. . . Rugged, durable, bulldozing blocker, bone-jarring tackler. . . Missed only three games in 14 years. . .Nine times All-NFL. . . Played in eight Pro Bowls, MVP in 1954 game. . .Named NFL's all-time center, 1969. . .Played 58 minutes, made game-saving tackle, 1960 NFL title game. . .Born May 1, 1925, in Bethlehem, Pennsylvania.

BERT BELL — **OWNER- HEAD COACH**
YEARS WITH EAGLES 1933-40 — **CLASS OF 1963**

De Benneville Bell. . Weathered heavy financial losses as Eagles owner, 1933-1940, Steelers co-owner, 1941-1946. . . Built NFL image to unprecedented heights as commissioner, 1946-1959. . . Generalled NFL's war with AAFC. . .Set up far-sighted television policies. . . Established strong anti-gambling controls. . . Recognized NFL Players Association. . . Born February 25, 1895, in Philadelphia, Pennsylvania. . . Died October 11, 1959, at age of 64.

BOB BROWN — **OFFENSIVE TACKLE**
PLAYED WITH THE EAGLES 1964-68 — **CLASS OF 2004**

Robert Stanford Brown. . .First-round draft pick (2nd overall), 1964 draft. . .Aggressive blocker who utilized great size and strength. . .Battled knee injury for much of career. . .Named first-team All-NFL seven times. . .Earned NFL/NFC offensive lineman of the year three times. . .Elected to six Pro Bowls – three with Eagles, two with Rams, and one with Raiders. . . Named to the NFL's All-Decade team of the 1960s. . .Born December 8, 1941, in Cleveland, Ohio.

MIKE DITKA — **TIGHT END**
PLAYED WITH THE EAGLES 1967-68 — **CLASS OF 1988**

Michael Keller Ditka. . .Consensus All-America, 1960. . . Bears' No. 1 pick, 1961. . .First tight end elected to Hall. . . Fast, rugged, outstanding blocker, great competitor. . .Big-play star of Bears' 1963 title team. . . Scored final touchdown in Cowboys' Super Bowl VI win. . .Rookie of the Year, 1961. . . All-NFL four years, in five straight Pro Bowls. . .Career record: 427 receptions, 5,812 yards, 43 TDs. . . Born October 18, 1939, in Carnegie, Pennsylvania.

SID GILLMAN — **COACH**
YEARS WITH EAGLES 1979-80 — **CLASS OF 1983**

Sidney Gillman. . .Innovative coach, dynamic administrator. . . Recognized as leading authority on passing theories, tactics . . .18-year pro record: 123-104-7. . .First to win divisional titles in both NFL, AFL. . . Won 1963 league, five division crowns in AFL's first six years. . .Major factor in developing AFL's image, impetus, respect. . .AFC Coach of the Year, 1974 . . .Played in first College All-Star game, 1934. . .Born October 26, 1911, in Minneapolis, Minnesota. . .Died January 3, 2003, at age of 91.

EAGLES HALL OF FAME

EAGLES IN THE HALL OF FAME

BILL HEWITT
PLAYED WITH THE EAGLES 1937-39
END
CLASS OF 1971

William Ernest Hewitt. . .First to be named All-NFL with two teams - 1933, 1934, 1936 Bears, 1937 Eagles. . .Famous for super-quick defensive charge. . .Fast, elusive, innovative on offense. . .Invented many trick plays to fool opposition. . . Middle man on forward-lateral that gave Bears 1933 NFL title. . .Played without helmet until rules change forced use . . .Born October 8, 1909, in Bay City, Michigan. . .Died January 14, 1947, at age of 37.

SONNY JURGENSEN
PLAYED WITH THE EAGLES 1957-63
QUARTERBACK
CLASS OF 1983

Christian Adolph Jurgensen, III. . .Exceptional passer, superb team leader, intelligent, determined, competitive, poised against pass rush. . .Career 82.625 passing rating... Won three NFL individual passing titles. . .Surpassed 3,000 yards in five seasons, 300 yards in 25 games, 400 yards in five games. . .Career totals: 2,433 completions, 32,224 yards, 255 touchdowns. . .Excelled in spite of numerous injuries. . . Born August 23, 1934, in Wilmington, North Carolina.

MARV LEVY
YEARS WITH EAGLES 1969
COACH
CLASS OF 2001

Marvin Daniel Levy. . .Led Bills to unprecedented four straight Super Bowls. . .Had 154-120-0 overall record. . .His coaching victories ranked 10th in NFL history at time of retirement. . . Quickly improved Chiefs from 4-12 to 9-7. . . Guided Buffalo to eight playoff appearances in 11 seasons. . .NFL Coach of the Year, 1988. . .AFC Coach of the Year, 1988, 1993, 1995. . .Born August 3, 1925, in Chicago, Illinois.

JAMES LOFTON
PLAYED WITH THE EAGLES 1993
WIDE RECEIVER
CLASS OF 2003

James David Lofton. . .Selected by Green Bay in 1st round (6th player overall) of 1978 NFL Draft. . .A deep-threat receiver, possessed both speed and great hands. . .recorded more than 50 receptions in a season nine times. . .First NFL player to score a touchdown in 1970s, 1980s, and 1990s. . .In 16 seasons, he caught 764 passes for 14,004 yards - an NFL record at the time of his retirement. . .Named All-Pro four times, All-NFC three times, selected to play in eight Pro Bowls. . .Born July 5, 1956, at Fort Ord, California.

OLLIE MATSON
PLAYED WITH THE EAGLES 1964-66
HALFBACK
CLASS OF 1972

llie Genoa Matson. . .San Francisco defensive All-America. . .U.S. Olympic medal winner in track, 1952. . .No. 1 draft pick, 1952. . .All-NFL four years, 1954-1957. . .Traded to Rams for nine players, 1959. . .Career ledger: 12,884 combined net yards, 5,173 yards rushing, 222 receptions, 438 points, nine TDs on punt, kickoff returns. . . Elected to six Pro Bowl games. . .MVP in 1956 Pro Bowl. . .Born May 1, 1930, in Trinity, Texas.

EAGLES IN THE HALL OF FAME

TOMMY MCDONALD — **WIDE RECEIVER**
PLAYED WITH THE EAGLES 1957-63 — **CLASS OF 1998**

Thomas Franklin McDonald. . .Eagles' third-round draft pick, 1957. . . Career statistics: 495 receptions, 8,410 yards, 84 touchdowns. . . Selected to six Pro Bowls. . .Scored 56 touchdowns in 63 games, 1958-1962. . .Career ratio of touchdowns to receptions 1 to 5.9. . .Led NFL in reception yardage and touchdowns, 1961. . .Ranked sixth all-time in receptions, fourth in yards receiving and second in touchdown catches at time of retirement. . . Born July 26, 1934, in Roy, New Mexico.

EARLE (GREASY) NEALE — **COACH**
YEARS WITH EAGLES 1941-50 — **CLASS OF 1969**

Alfred Earle Neale. . .Extensive college coaching career preceded entry into NFL in 1941. . .Quickly built second-division Eagles into a contender. . . Produced three straight Eastern Division crowns and NFL championships in 1948 and 1949. . . Both NFL titles came by shutout scores. . .Using an assumed name, played end with the pre-NFL Canton Bulldogs. . .Born November 5, 1891, in Parkersburg, West Virginia. . . Died November 2, 1973, at age of 81.

PETE PIHOS — **END**
PLAYED WITH THE EAGLES 1947-55 — **CLASS OF 1970**

Peter Louis Pihos. . .Indiana All-America, 1943. . .Fifth-round draft pick in 1945 even though he couldn't play until 1947 . . .60-minute star on Eagles title teams, 1948-1949. . . Caught winning TD pass in 1949 NFL championship. . .All-NFL six times in nine seasons, once at defensive end, 1952. . .Played in six Pro Bowls. . . Three-time NFL receiving champ, 1953-1955. . . Career record: 373 catches for 5,619 yards, 378 points. . . Born October 22, 1923, in Orlando, Florida.

JIM RINGO — **CENTER**
PLAYED WITH THE EAGLES 1964-67 — **CLASS OF 1981**

James Stephen Ringo. . .No. 7 draft choice, 1953. . . All-Pro status preceded Packers dynasty years. . . All-NFL seven times . . .Played in 10 Pro Bowls, three NFL championship games. . . Small for offensive lineman, but quick, determined, intelligent, superb team leader. . . Excellent down-field blocker, pass protector. . . Ignored numerous injuries to start in then-record 182 straight games, 1954-1967. . . Born November 21, 1931, in Orange, New Jersey.

NORM VAN BROCKLIN — **QUARTERBACK**
PLAYED WITH THE EAGLES 1958-60 — **CLASS OF 1971**

Norman Mack Van Brocklin. . .Oregon All-America, 1948. . . Rams' No. 4 draftee, 1949. Led NFL in passing three years, punting twice. . .Career mark: 1,553 completions for 23,611 yards, 173 TDs. . . 73-yard pass gave Rams 1951 title. . . Passed for 554 yards one game, 1951. . . Generalled Eagles to 1960 NFL crown. . .NFL's Most Valuable Player, 1960. . . Selected to nine Pro Bowl games. . .Born March 15, 1926, in Eagle Butte, South Dakota. . .Died May 2, 1983, at age of 57.

EAGLES IN THE HALL OF FAME

ALEX WOJCIECHOWICZ
PLAYED WITH THE EAGLES 1946-50

LINEBACKER
CLASS OF 1968

Alexander Francis Wojciechowicz. . .Two-time Fordham All-America, center of famed "Seven Blocks of Granite" line. . . Lions' No. 1 draft pick, 1938. . .Played four games first week as pro. . .Authentic "iron man" for 8 1/2 years with Lions. . . Joined Eagles as defensive specialist strictly. . . Known for exceptionally wide center stance. . . Outstanding pass defender with 19 lifetime interceptions. . .Born August 12, 1915, in South River, New Jersey. . .Died July 13, 1992, at age of 76.

REGGIE WHITE
PLAYED WITH THE EAGLES 1985-92

DEFENSIVE END
CLASS OF 2006

Reginald Howard White. . .Selected fourth overall in 1984 NFL Supplemental Draft... Recorded more sacks (124) than games played (121) in eight seasons with Eagles. Became Packers' all-time sack leader with 68.5. . .Recorded 12 seasons with 10-plus sacks. . . NFL Defensive Player of the Year in 1987, 1991, 1998. . . Elected to 13 straight Pro Bowls. . .Named All-Pro 13 of 15 seasons including 10 as first-team selection. . .Born December 19, 1961 in Chattanooga, Tennessee. . .Died December 26, 2004 at age of 43.

STEVE VAN BUREN
PLAYED WITH THE EAGLES 1944-51

HALFBACK
CLASS OF 1965

Stephen W. Van Buren. . .No. 1 draft pick, 1944. . .All-NFL six straight years. . . Provided Eagles a battering-ram punch. . . Won NFL rushing title four times. . .1944 punt return, 1945 kickoff return champ. . . Scored only TD in 7-0 title win, 1948 . . . Rushed for then-record 196 yards in 1949 finale. . .Career mark: 5860 yards rushing, 464 points scored. . .Surpassed 1,000 yards in rushing twice. . .Born December 28, 1920, in La Ceiba, Honduras.

Eagles Honor Roll

In 1987, the Eagles Honor Roll was established to honor outstanding members of the organization. Included in the inagural induction ceremony were 11members of the Hall of Fame that played with the Eagles.

#60 Chuck Bednarik, C-LB, 1949-62, Inducted 1987

Bert Bell, founder-owner, 1933-40, Inducted 1987

#17 Harold Carmichael, WR, 1971-83, Inducted 1987

#56 Bill Hewitt, TE-DE, 1936-39 and 1943, Inducted 1987

#9 Sonny Jurgensen, QB, 1957-63, Inducted 1987

#31 Wilbert Montgomery, RB, 1977-84, Inducted 1987

"Greasy" Neale, Head Coach, 1941-50, Inducted 1987

#35 Pete Pihos, TE-DE, 1947-55, Inducted 1987

#33 Ollie Matson, RB, 1964-66, Inducted 1987

#54 Jim Ringo, C, 1964-67, Inducted 1987

#11 Norm Van Brocklin, QB, 1958-60, Inducted 1987

#15 Steve Van Buren, RB-S, 1944-51, Inducted 1987

#53 Alex Wojciechowicz, C-DT, 1946-50, Inducted 1987

#66 Bill Bergey, LB, 1974-80, Inducted 1988

#25 Tommy McDonald, WR, 1957-63, Inducted 1988

#40 Tom Brookshier, CB, 1954-61, inducted 1989

#44 Pete Retzlaff, TE, 1956-66, inducted 1989

#22 Timmy Brown, RB,1960-67, inducted 1990

#76 Jerry Sisemore, OT, 1973-84, inducted 1991

#75 Stan Walters, OT, 1975-83, Inducted 1991

#7 Ron Jaworski, QB, 1977-86, Inducted 1992

#28 Bill Bradley, S-P, 1969-76, Inducted 1993

Dick Vermeil, Head Coach, 1976-82, Inducted 1994

Jim Gallagher team executive, 1949-95, Inducted 1995

#82 Mike Quick, WR, 1982-90, Inducted 1995

#99 Jerome Brown, DT, 1987-91, Inducted 1996

Otho Davis, head trainer, 1973-95, Inducted 1999

1948 & 1949 NFL Championship Teams Inducted 1999

MONDAY NIGHT FOOTBALL GAMES

On November 23, 1970 the Eagles debuted on "Monday Night Football" on ABC versus the New York Giants in a home game played at Franklin Field which was bitter cold. The Eagles had a horrible record of 1-7-1. Eagles owner Leonard Tose threw a pregame party to celebrate the event. Impatient Howard Cosell was looking for a drink and asked that the bar be opened earlier. Well after throwing back a few vodka martinis, Howard Cosell kept on drinking trying to stay warm throughtout the broadcast. Until he finally could not finish the broadcast after halftime. The Eagles came from behind to defeat the Giants 23-20.

Another noteable game played on Monday Night was on November 12, 1990, when the Washington Redskins came into the Vet in now the infamous "Body Bag Game" in which Eagles head Coach Buddy Ryan promised a beaten so severe, that the Redskins would have to be "hauled off in body bags." Eagles won 28 –14.

On January 3, 1994 the Eagles were playing the San Francisco 49ers. The Eagles missed a game-winning field goal as the overtime period expired, which would have left the game a tie. However, a penalty against the 49ers allowed a re-kick, and the Eagles were granted one untimed down. On the second attempt, the field goal was good and the dead Eagles won
37-34 in overtime.

November 10, 1997 the Eagles on national television against the 49ers received additional attention when a fan fired off a flare gun in Veterans Stadium leading to the introduction of a courtroom which was located on the lower level of the stadium. The Eagles lost that game 24-12.

September 9, 2003, was a rematch of the previous season's NFC Champs Tampa Bay Buccaneers and it was also the first regular season game played at Lincoln Financial Field. In a much hyped rematch game the Eagles were defeated again 17-0.

November 15, 2004, The Eagles were playing the Dallas Cowboys. ABC ran a controversial "Desperate Housewives" commercial prior to the game featuring Eagle Terrell Owens and Nicolette Sheridan. Owens caught three touchdowns as the Eagles crushed the Cowboys 49-21.

"Monday Night Football" has been good to the Eagles over the years. They have a winning record of (24-21).

MONDAY NIGHT FOOTBALL GAMES

The Philadelphia Inquirer / SPORTS

Snead Runs, Passes Eagles to 23-20 Win

Frank Dolson: Harkness Picture Earns X Rating

Giants Bow As Norm Scores Pair

Eagles' Locker Room: Long Underwear, Victory Glow Keep Williams Warm

State Rejects Bid; Dartmouth Spurns Paterno

Police in N. Y. Seize $50,000 Bet on Game

Say Jerry!

Bradley Still Punts; 2d Injury Feared

Eagles' Back Picks Up Five Tough Yards Against Giants

November 23, 1970:
New York Giants 20, Philadelphia Eagles 23

Tose: Eagles Playing Without Character... Hochman: 55

Philadelphia Daily News Sports

Reaves Learns Hard —Snead Knows Well

McKinney — Johnson and Johnson and Johnson and Johnson: Page 58

Motorcyclist Lolich Makes Tigers Easier Riders

Fryman: He Faces Biggest Game Tonight With a Pretzel: Page 59

No Hits: Stoneman Stops Mets Easier Than Phillies: Page 61

October 2, 1972:
New York Giants 27, Philadelphia Eagles 12

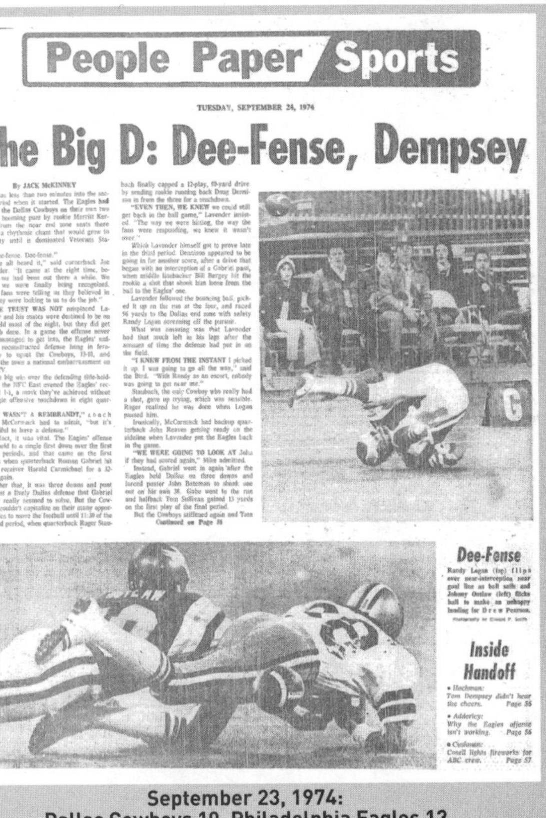

People Paper Sports

TUESDAY, SEPTEMBER 24, 1974

The Big D: Dee-Fense, Dempsey

Dee-Fense

Inside Handoff

September 23, 1974:
Dallas Cowboys 10, Philadelphia Eagles 13

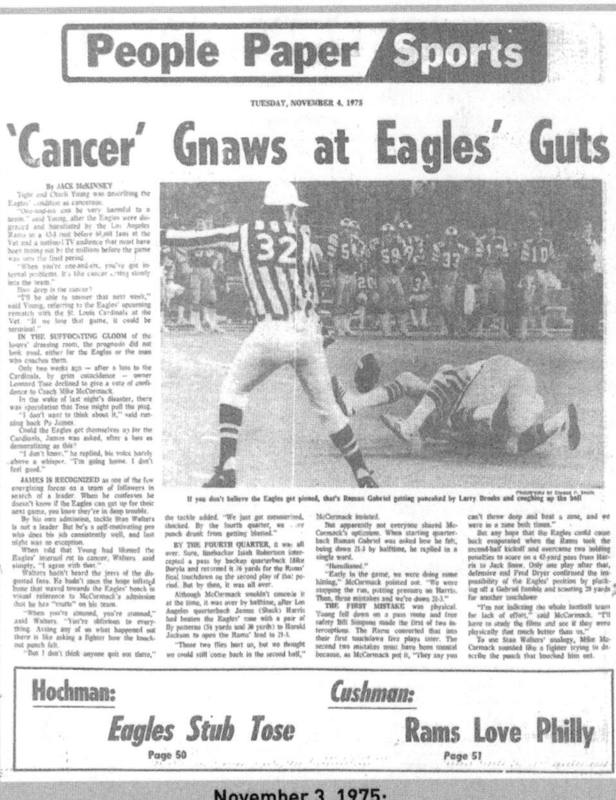

People Paper Sports

TUESDAY, NOVEMBER 4, 1975

'Cancer' Gnaws at Eagles' Guts

Hochman: Eagles Stub Tose — Page 50

Cushman: Rams Love Philly — Page 51

November 3, 1975:
Los Angeles Rams 42, Philadelphia Eagles 3

Monday Night Football Games

People Paper Sports

TUESDAY, SEPTEMBER 28, 1976

A Game Eagles Couldn't Win

This One Hurt

By PHIL JASNER

This was a game the Eagles could not win.

This is the kind of night it was for the Eagles, as Jake Scott flies over the prone James McAlister who dropped TD pass in second period.

Continued on Page 62

Cushman: Ali Inside 12 Page 58

Hochman: Ali in the 6th Page 59

Phillies' JVs Win Page 63

Alston Calls it Quits Page 57

September 27, 1976:
Washington Redskins 20, Philadelphia Eagles 17, OT

Eagles Ride Herd

Cowboys Sag As Birds End 13-Year Jinx

PHILADELPHIA DAILY NEWS SPORTS

Tuesday, November 13, 1979

By GARY SMITH

Eagles' owner Leonard Tose (right) hugs Coach Dick Vermeil during wild locker-room scene

Continued on Page 66

More on Eagles

- Win Puts Smile on Wilbert: Cushman on Page 71
- Franklin Gives Dallas Hot Foot: Smith on Page 70
- Beaten Cowboys Are Pointing Fingers: Page 66
- A Wild Day for Birds' Fans: Hochman on Page 64

November 12, 1979:
Philadelphia Eagles 31, Dallas Cowboys 21

Eagles Go Down the Tube

Falcons Win, 14-10, on National Television

By GARY SMITH

PHILADELPHIA DAILY NEWS SPORTS

Tuesday, September 11, 1979

Harold Carmichael lies on AstroTurf after missing a pass while Ray Easterling (32) and Rolland Lawrence celebrate

Continued on Page 70

Today

- Meyers Finds NBA Tough: Cushman, Page 71
- Carmichael's Big Night: Smith, Page 70
- Brenard Wilson Worries: Greenberg, Page 69
- Falcons' Runner a Surprise: Jasner, Page 67
- Battle of the Birds: Pictures, Page 66
- Highlights, Lowlights for ABC: Quinn, Page 64

Tomorrow

September 10, 1979:
Atlanta Falcons 14, Philadelphia Eagles 10

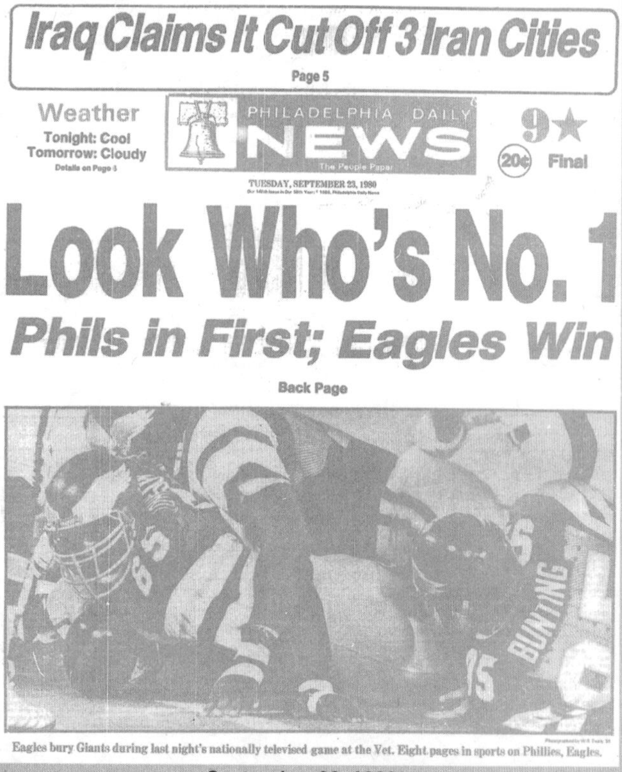

Iraq Claims It Cut Off 3 Iran Cities

Page 5

Weather
Tonight: Cool
Tomorrow: Cloudy

PHILADELPHIA DAILY NEWS
The People Paper

9★ 20¢ Final

TUESDAY, SEPTEMBER 23, 1980

Look Who's No. 1

Phils in First; Eagles Win

Back Page

Eagles bury Giants during last night's nationally televised game at the Vet. Eight pages in sports on Phillies, Eagles.

September 22, 1980:
New York Giants 3, Philadelphia Eagles 35

Monday Night Football Games

Eagles Sinking Fast

By BUD SHAW

PHILADELPHIA DAILY NEWS SPORTS
Tuesday, December 1, 1981 Mike Rathet, Sports Editor

MIAMI — This was supposed to be a nationally televised revival, a night of fire and brimstone that would send shivers down the spine of Texas. The Cowboys' lease on first place in the NFC East was believed to be short-termed, lasting only as long as it took the Eagles to digest their turkey dinners.

The Birds were supposed to restore order to a season that was perfect in its conception but lately has been looking a little haggard. This was the beginning of the Eagles' stretch run, a three-week sprint that was supposed to end with the Birds and Cowboys in an elbow-to-elbow struggle for the tape.

It just may be that the theory was based on a false hypothesis. The Eagles' 6-0 start is only a memory now. It has been replaced by the stark reality that they're just 3-4 over the last seven weeks, which means all is not good in Dick Vermeil's neighborhood. Can you say wild card?

IF THE EAGLES care to look in the mirror today, they'll find their Bo Derek season is looking more and more like Phyllis Diller. The latest wrinkle was last night's ridiculous 13-10 loss to the Dolphins, a game that left Ron Jaworski speechless and Dick Vermeil shrugging his shoulders. It seemed that nobody wanted to say the obvious. This does not look like a team ready for a showdown with Dallas in two weeks.

Instead, it's a team with a sagging offense that has scored just 20 points in its last two games. It's a team that was shut out by the Giants in the second half last week and managed just one field goal in the final 30 minutes last evening.

The Eagles are now 9-4, one game behind the Cowboys, who were probably giggling in their living rooms last night. This was, it seems, a game that only the people of Texas could love.

The Eagles lost because they blew a 10-3 lead with just under six minutes left in the game. They lost because cornerback Roynell Young slipped and fell, allowing Dolphins wide receiver Duriel Harris to catch a 17-yard TD pass from Don Strock. And because Ron Jaworski threw an interception that led to a 27-yard field goal by Uwe von Schamann with 1:04 left in the game.

But the real reason why the Eagles now find themselves at the bottom of a steep uphill climb was an offense that managed just three first downs in the second half. And while Dick Vermeil may have been able to pass off his Alfred E. Neumann imitation down here last evening, it doesn't change the fact that there's plenty to worry about.

"THE ONLY THING I can say is that it was one helluva football game," Vermeil said after shrugging his shoulders to open last night's postgame press conference. "The breaks at the end went their way.

"What went wrong with our offense was the Miami defense. It was the same with us. The Eagles' defense stopped their offense. That's all.

"Last week, we played poorly against a good defense. This time, we played as hard as we could. Miami is just a good defensive team."

All of which should come as news to Don Shula, who has bags under his eyes as proof that the Dolphins' defense should not be confused with

Continued on Page 76

Photographed by E.W. Fandom

Mortal Blow This is it, the 27-yard field goal off the foot of Miami's Uwe von Schamann that killed the Eagles last night in the Orange Bowl. It came with 1:01 left to play, about three minutes after Lyle Blackwood's interception of a Ron Jaworski pass. But the really big news is that the Eagles have now lost four of their last seven games and are firmly entrenched in second place behind Dallas in the NFC East.

Do Cavs Want Chuck Daly? Phil Jasner on Page 62

ABC Angers No. 1 Clemson Gene Quinn on Page 64

November 30, 1981:
Philadelphia Eagles 10 , Miami Dolphins 13

Birds Snap Falcon Hex

PHILADELPHIA DAILY NEWS SPORTS
Tuesday, October 6, 1981 Mike Rathet, Sports Editor

Photographed by E.W. Fandom

Defensive end Greg Brown holds ball high for all to see after recovering third period fumble for the Eagles, who held off Atlanta

By BUD SHAW

It took a little more than three hours to complete the exorcism, and when the spirit finally left their bodies a couple of minutes after midnight the Eagles were weak-kneed and exhausted.

The Eagles had swallowed three consecutive losses to the Atlanta Falcons before last night, each one casting another shadow on a series that was haunting an entire city. This wasn't just another Monday night with Howard and Frank. It was a nationally televised seance.

In the end, the Eagles clutched a 16-13 win with their fingertips. It left them with a 5-0 record, and nobody else in the league has the same credentials. It also gave them room to bless themselves at the top of the NFC East, but that was just an aside to the bigger melodrama being played out on the field.

For 12 seconds last night, the Eagles' past flashed before their eyes. One minute they were leading the Falcons, 13-0. The next it was 13-10. It all looked too familiar, the same scary story line of the last three games with the Falcons.

Atlanta kicker Mick Luckhurst had kicked a 35-yard field goal with 4:17 left in the third quarter to make it 13-3, and 70,000 people were holding their breath.

WHAT HAPPENED next was the stuff of nightmares. Wally Henry fumbled the kickoff, the ball bouncing into the arms of Falcons' cornerback Kenny Johnson, who sprinted 20 yards to the end zone. The lead was cut to three and there still was a whole quarter left for fate to smile on the Falcons again.

"Nobody can relate to how you feel in that situation," Henry would say later. "I felt about as low as an ant's ass. I'm probably happier than anyone on this team that things turned out the way they did."

"Something like that really ticks you off," said nose guard Charlie Johnson. "Don't get me wrong. I'm not blaming anybody. Fumbles are a part of the game.

"But something like that burns you up. Here you are, holding them down and holding them down and then they have it (a touchdown). They get a cheap score and they're back in the game. All it does is make you go back out there wanting to kick their behinds even more."

The Eagles went back out there and arm-wrestled the Falcons to a draw. There was very little butt-kicking, the game being decided by the bare foot of 5-9 placekicker Tony Franklin, who chose this night to continue a personal exorcism of sorts.

Franklin kicked two first-half field goals of 36 and 34 yards, helping the Eagles take advantage of interceptions by Al Chesley and Reggie Wilkes early in the first quarter.

RON JAWORSKI threw a 35-yard TD pass to Charlie Smith with 1:31 left in the half to make

Continued on Page 70

Chicago Green's Kind of Town?

By BILL CONLIN

The dual job reportedly would pay Green at least $1 million for five years, plus fringe benefits that might include a liberal profit-sharing plan. Green will earn about $150,000 as Phillies manager this season.

It is a bombshell that has far wider implications for the Phillies' future than the mere departure of a field manager to a position that two years ago would have been beyond Green's wildest dreams.

Continued on Page 63

October 5, 1981:
Atlanta Falcons 13, Philadelphia Eagles 16

2,000 Fire Deaths: The Reasons Why

20-Year Survey Finds Clues in the Ashes: Special Report Begins on Page 4

TUESDAY
OCTOBER 11, 1988

PHILADELPHIA DAILY NEWS
THE PEOPLE PAPER

LATE SPORTS
35¢
50 CENTS OUTSIDE METROPOLITAN PHILADELPHIA
FOR HOME DELIVERY PHONE 665-1234

Giant-Killers

7 Pages in Sports on a Monday Night To Savor

GEORGE REYNOLDS/DAILY NEWS

Eagle Reggie White (left) pressures Giants' quarterback Phil Simms en route to Philadelphia's nationally televised 24-13 victory last night at the Vet

U.S. Reported Offering Deal to Marcos: Page 3

October 10, 1988:
New York Giants 13, Philadelphia Eagles 24

PHILADELPHIA DAILY NEWS / TUESDAY, OCTOBER 3, 1989

Night Cap: Page 72

SPORTS

It's Foggy Again

MICHAEL MERCANTI/DAILY NEWS

Bears defensive end Richard Dent registers one of four sacks against Eagles quarterback Randall Cunningham

Chicago Victory Clouds Eagles' Bright Hopes

By Tim Kawakami
Daily News Sports Writer

CHICAGO — No blanket of fog found its way onto Soldier Field this time. No referee's piercing vision left the Eagles lost in the clouds.

They did not walk off the field boiling with the belief that they had played a better game than their conquerors, or that they had proven they could not be stopped.

No, last night, these bubbly, bouncy, cocky Eagles just quietly walked off the field, kept to themselves and tried to forget their 27-13 manhandling by the Chicago Bears, the team that drowned their playoff dreams last season in the infamous Fog Bowl.

In that game, the Eagles galloped up and down the field all day, but did not have the good fortune or the ability to put the football into the end zone. Then they were doomed by the arrival of the cloud that settled over the stadium for the entire second half.

They waited nine months for revenge, the chance to let the world know the greatness to which they feel they are destined. They will have to wait some more.

In front of a national television audience and a bellowing Bears sellout crowd, the Eagles laid an e... and suddenly that startling 2-0 s... has been transformed into the dull buzz of 2-2 going into Sunday's game against the unbeaten New York Giants at Veterans Stadium.

"It hurts," said Eagles wide receiver Mike Quick, who definitely was not speaking about the sore knee that kept him out of most of the second half. "It *hurts*. This is a big loss."

"That," added coach Buddy Ryan, who now is 0-4 against archrival and former boss Mike Ditka, "was a very disappointing loss, probably more disappointing than the 'bowl we had in the playoffs."

And assuredly — from the opening kickoff through the hail of french fries that pelted Ryan from the stands as he bolted off the field at the end — more unsettling.

The Bears took no prisoners, did not need the assistance of any weather front fortune and left no avenue open for logical excuses on the Eagles' part.

The Bears simply played a lot better, which is a pretty simple explanation for a pretty simple game, the Eagles' 13th loss in 13 tries in Chicago.

The Eagles were beaten in all of the areas in which they have been beaten for a couple of years now, and the game showed once again that, no, this is not yet a perfect football team.

"I don't think they surprised us," said offensive tackle Ron Heller. "I think they flat-out steamrolled us. They lined up and overpowered us."

The Bears, who presumably did not much appreciate the Eagles' nine-

See BEARS Page 88

INSIDE ON THE EAGLES

Rich Hofmann: Page 87
Stan Hochman: Page 85
Fans Target Buddy: Page 84
Ditka Fires Back: Page 83
Costly Penalty: Page 83
Mike Tomczak: Page 83
Notebook: Page 82
Statistics: Page 82
TV Tuesday: Page 81

October 2, 1989:
Philadelphia Eagles 13, Chicago Bears 27

MONDAY NIGHT FOOTBALL

MONDAY NIGHT FOOTBALL GAMES

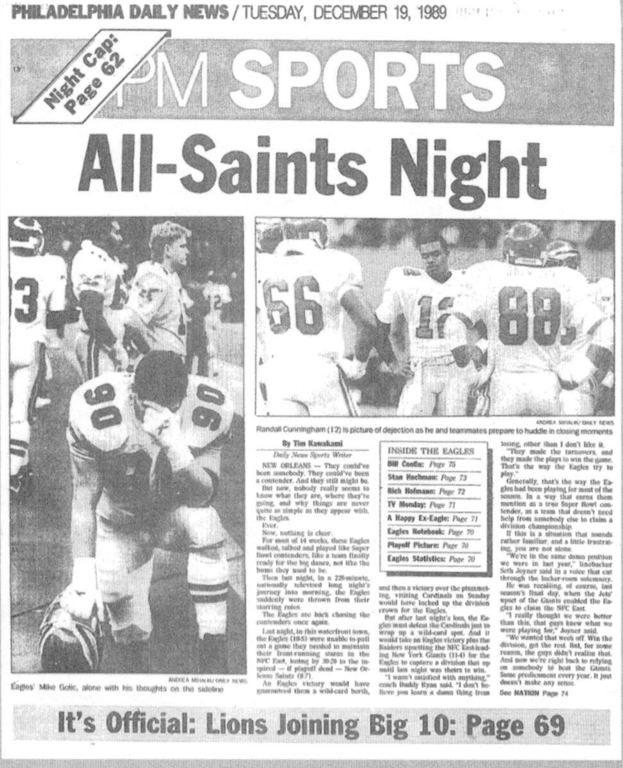

PHILADELPHIA DAILY NEWS / TUESDAY, DECEMBER 19, 1989

Night Cap: Page 62

PM SPORTS

All-Saints Night

Eagles' Mike Golic, alone with his thoughts on the sideline

ANDREA MIHALIK/DAILY NEWS

Randall Cunningham (12) is picture of dejection as he and teammates prepare to huddle in closing moments

By Tim Kawakami

Daily News Sports Writer

NEW ORLEANS — They could've been somebody. They could've been a contender. And they still might be.

But now, nobody really seems to know what they are, where they're going, and why things are never quite as simple as they appear with the Eagles.

Ever.

Now, nothing is clear.

For most of 14 weeks, these Eagles walked, talked and played like Super Bowl contenders, like a team finally ready for the big dance, not like the bums they used to be.

Then last night, in a 228-minute, nationally televised long night's journey into morning, the Eagles suddenly were thrown from their starring roles.

The Eagles are back chasing the contenders once again.

Last night, in this waterfront town, the Eagles (10-5) were unable to pull out a game they needed to maintain their front-running status in the NFC East, losing by 30-20 to the inspired — if playoff dead — New Orleans Saints (8-7).

An Eagles victory would have guaranteed them a wild-card berth, and then a victory over the plummeting, visiting Cardinals on Sunday would have locked up the division crown for the Eagles.

But after last night's loss, the Eagles must defeat the Cardinals just to wrap up a wild-card spot. And it would take an Eagles victory plus the Raiders upsetting the NFC East-leading New York Giants (11-4) for the Eagles to capture a division that up until last night was theirs to win.

"I wasn't satisfied with anything," coach Buddy Ryan said. "I don't believe you learn a damn thing from losing, other than I don't like it.

"They made the turnovers, and they made the plays to win the game. That's the way the Eagles try to play."

Generally, that's the way the Eagles had been playing for most of the season. In a way that earns them mention as a true Super Bowl contender, as a team that doesn't need help from somebody else to claim a division championship.

If this is a situation that sounds rather familiar, and a little frustrating, you are not alone.

"We're in the same damn position we were in last year," linebacker Seth Joyner said in a voice that cut through the locker-room solemnity.

He was recalling, of course, last season's final day, when the Jets' upset of the Giants enabled the Eagles to claim the NFC East.

"I really thought we were better than this, that guys knew what we were playing for," Joyner said.

"We wanted that week off. Win the division, get the rest. But, for some reason, the guys didn't realize that. And now we're right back to relying on somebody to beat the Giants. Same predicament every year. It just doesn't make any sense."

See NATION Page 74

INSIDE THE EAGLES

- Bill Conlin: Page 75
- Stan Hochman: Page 73
- Rich Hofmann: Page 72
- TV Monday: Page 71
- A Happy Ex-Eagle: Page 71
- Eagles Notebook: Page 70
- Playoff Picture: Page 70
- Eagles Statistics: Page 70

It's Official: Lions Joining Big 10: Page 69

December 18, 1989:
Philadelphia Eagles 20, New Orleans Saints 30

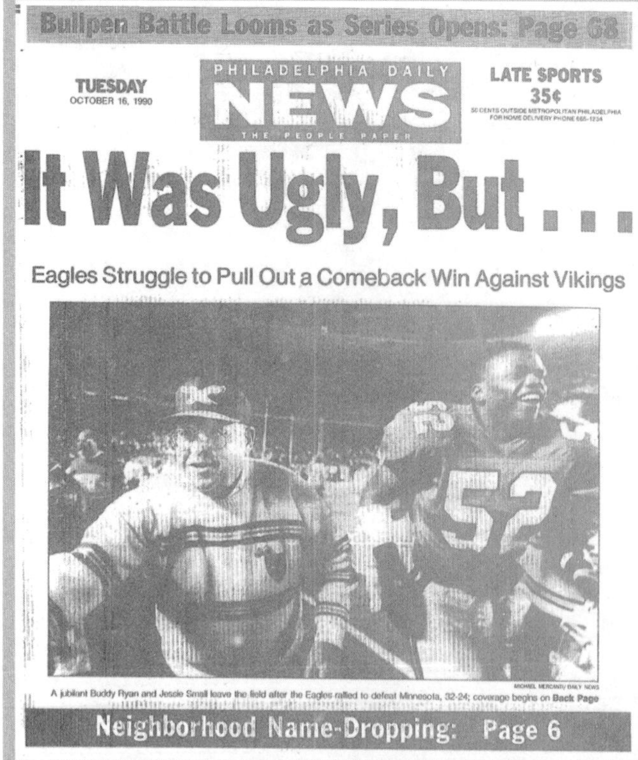

Bullpen Battle Looms as Series Opens: Page 68

TUESDAY
OCTOBER 16, 1990

PHILADELPHIA DAILY NEWS
THE PEOPLE PAPER

LATE SPORTS
35¢
50 CENTS OUTSIDE METROPOLITAN PHILADELPHIA
FOR HOME DELIVERY PHONE 665-1234

It Was Ugly, But . . .

Eagles Struggle to Pull Out a Comeback Win Against Vikings

MICHAEL MERCANTI/DAILY NEWS

A jubilant Buddy Ryan and Jessie Small leave the field after the Eagles rallied to defeat Minnesota, 32-24; coverage begins on Back Page

Neighborhood Name-Dropping: Page 6

October 15, 1990:
Minnesota Vikings 24, Philadelphia Eagles 32

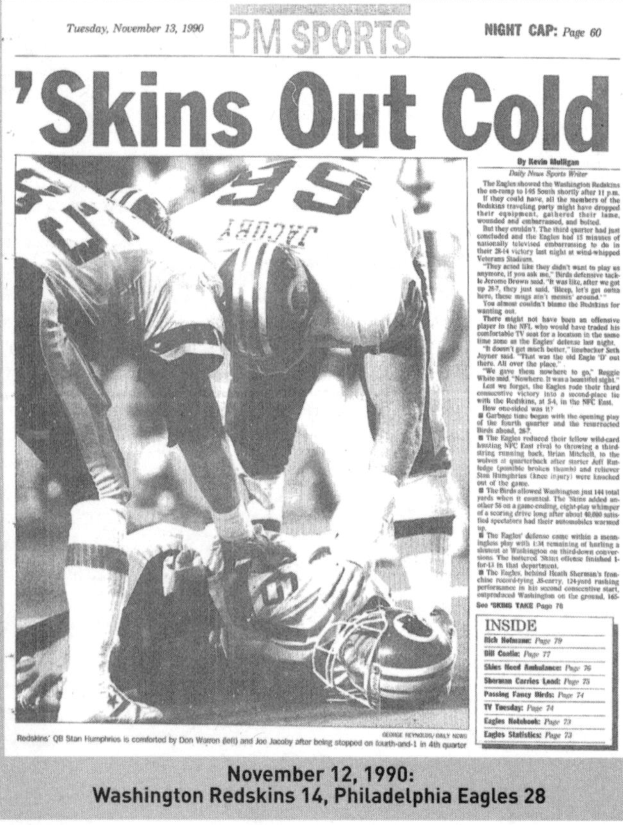

Tuesday, November 13, 1990

PM SPORTS

NIGHT CAP: *Page 60*

'Skins Out Cold

By Kevin Mulligan

Daily News Sports Writer

The Eagles showed the Washington Redskins the on-ramp to I-95 South shortly after 11 p.m.

If they could have, all the members of the Redskins traveling party might have dropped their equipment, gathered their lame, wounded and embarrassed, and bolted.

But they couldn't. The third quarter had just concluded and the Eagles had 15 minutes of nationally televised embarrassing to do in their 28-14 victory last night at wind-whipped Veterans Stadium.

"They acted like they didn't want to play us anymore, if you ask me," Birds defensive tackle Jerome Brown said. "It was like, after we got up 28-7, they just said, 'Bleep, let's get outta here, these mugs ain't messin' around.'"

You almost couldn't blame the Redskins for wanting out.

There might not have been an offensive player in the NFL who would have traded his comfortable TV seat for a location in the same time zone as the Eagles' defense last night.

"It doesn't get much better," linebacker Seth Joyner said. "That was the old Eagle 'D' out there. All over the place."

"We gave them nowhere to go," Reggie White said. "Nowhere. It was a beautiful sight."

Lest we forget, the Eagles rode their third consecutive victory into a second-place tie with the Redskins, at 5-4, in the NFC East.

How one-sided was it?

- Garbage time began with the opening play of the fourth quarter and the resurrected Birds ahead, 28-7.
- The Eagles reduced their fellow wild-card hunting NFC East rival to throwing a third-string running back, Brian Mitchell, to the wolves at quarterback after starter Jeff Rutledge (possible broken thumb) and reliever Stan Humphries (knee injury) were knocked out of the game.
- The Birds allowed Washington just 144 total yards when it counted. The 'Skins added another 56 on a game-ending, eight-play whimper of a scoring drive long after about 40,000 satisfied spectators had their automobiles warmed up.
- The Eagles' defense came within a meaningless play with 1:34 remaining of hurling a shutout at Washington on third-down conversions. The battered 'Skins offense finished 1-for-13 in that department.
- The Eagles, behind Heath Sherman's franchise record-tying 35-carry, 124-yard rushing performance in his second consecutive start, outproduced Washington on the ground, 165-

See 'SKINS TAKE Page 76

INSIDE

- Rich Hofmann: Page 79
- Bill Conlin: Page 77
- Skins Need Ambulance: Page 76
- Sherman Carries Load: Page 75
- Passing Fancy Birds: Page 74
- TV Tuesday: Page 74
- Eagles Notebook: Page 73
- Eagles Statistics: Page 73

GEORGE REYNOLDS/DAILY NEWS

Redskins' QB Stan Humphries is comforted by Don Warren (left) and Joe Jacoby after being stopped on fourth-and-1 in 4th quarter

November 12, 1990:
Washington Redskins 14, Philadelphia Eagles 28

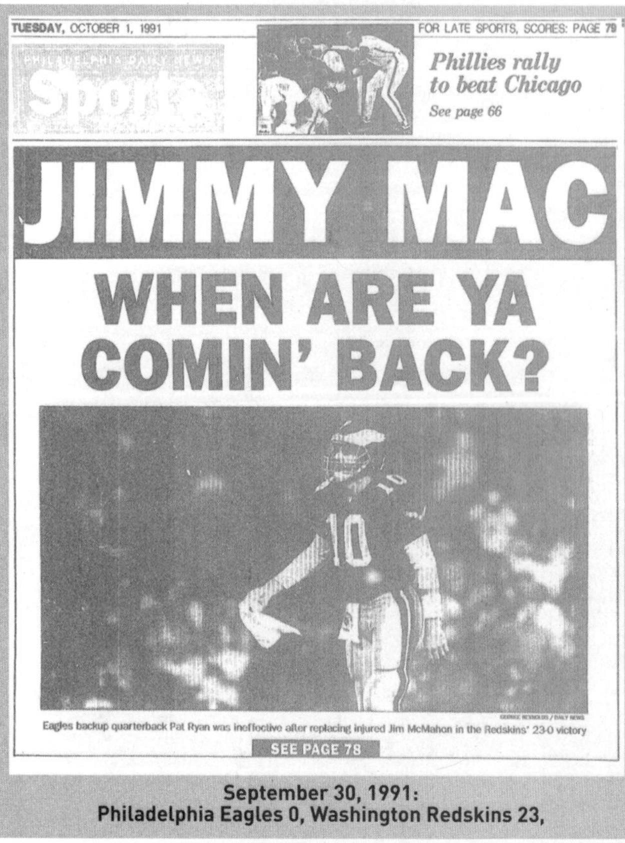

TUESDAY, OCTOBER 1, 1991

FOR LATE SPORTS, SCORES: PAGE 79

PHILADELPHIA DAILY NEWS Sports

Phillies rally to beat Chicago

See page 66

JIMMY MAC

WHEN ARE YA COMIN' BACK?

GEORGE REYNOLDS/DAILY NEWS

Eagles backup quarterback Pat Ryan was ineffective after replacing injured Jim McMahon in the Redskins' 23-0 victory

SEE PAGE 78

September 30, 1991:
Philadelphia Eagles 0, Washington Redskins 23,

Monday Night Football Games

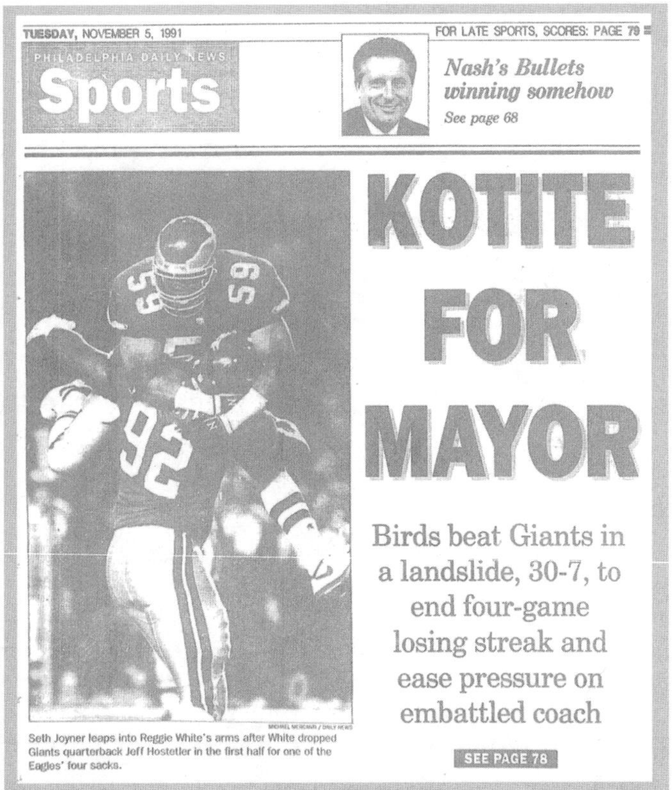

TUESDAY, NOVEMBER 5, 1991 FOR LATE SPORTS, SCORES: PAGE 79

PHILADELPHIA DAILY NEWS **Sports**

Nash's Bullets winning somehow
See page 68

KOTITE FOR MAYOR

Birds beat Giants in a landslide, 30-7, to end four-game losing streak and ease pressure on embattled coach

Seth Joyner leaps into Reggie White's arms after White dropped Giants quarterback Jeff Hostetler in the first half for one of the Eagles' four sacks.

SEE PAGE 78

November 4, 1991:
New York Giants 7, Philadelphia Eagles 30

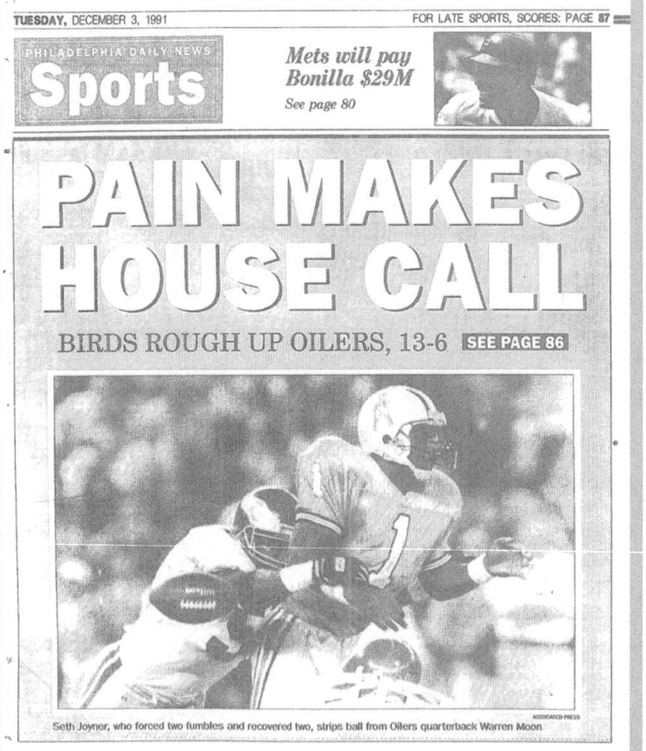

TUESDAY, DECEMBER 3, 1991 FOR LATE SPORTS, SCORES: PAGE 87

PHILADELPHIA DAILY NEWS **Sports**

Mets will pay Bonilla $29M
See page 80

PAIN MAKES HOUSE CALL

BIRDS ROUGH UP OILERS, 13-6 SEE PAGE 86

Seth Joyner, who forced two fumbles and recovered two, strips ball from Oilers quarterback Warren Moon

December 2, 1991:
Philadelphia Eagles 13, Houston Oilers 6

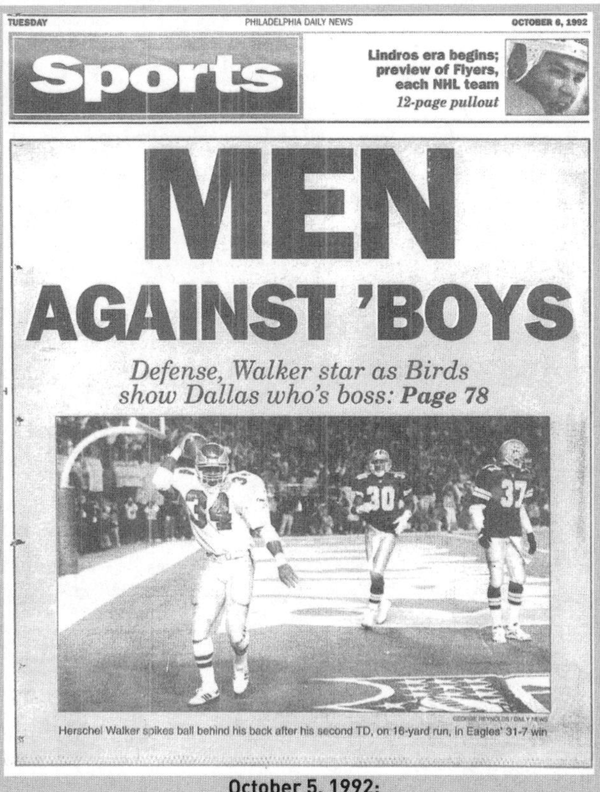

TUESDAY PHILADELPHIA DAILY NEWS OCTOBER 6, 1992

Sports

Lindros era begins; preview of Flyers, each NHL team
12-page pullout

MEN AGAINST 'BOYS

*Defense, Walker star as Birds show Dallas who's boss: **Page 78***

Herschel Walker spikes ball behind his back after his second TD, on 16-yard run, in Eagles' 31-7 win

October 5, 1992:
Dallas Cowboys 7, Philadelphia Eagles 31

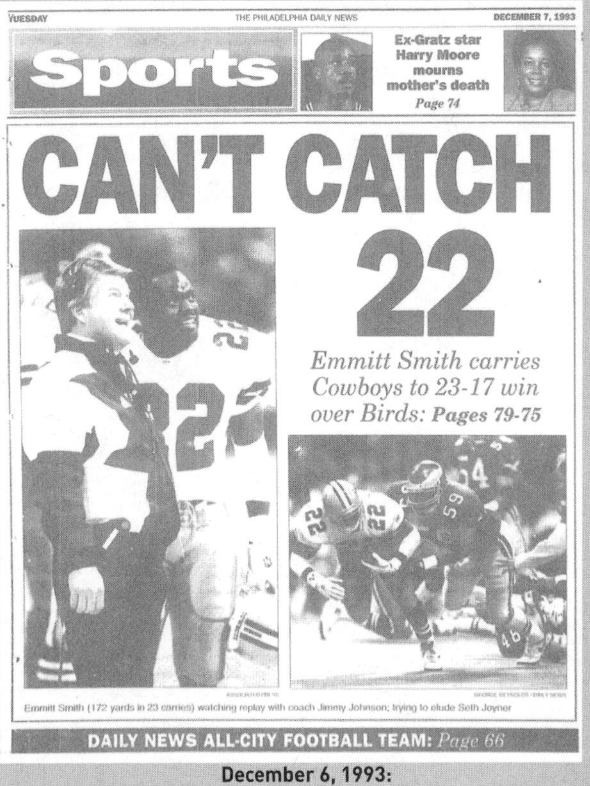

TUESDAY THE PHILADELPHIA DAILY NEWS DECEMBER 7, 1993

Sports

Ex-Gratz star Harry Moore mourns mother's death
Page 74

CAN'T CATCH 22

*Emmitt Smith carries Cowboys to 23-17 win over Birds: **Pages 79-75***

Emmitt Smith (172 yards in 23 carries) watching replay with coach Jimmy Johnson; trying to elude Seth Joyner

DAILY NEWS ALL-CITY FOOTBALL TEAM: *Page 66*

December 6, 1993:
Philadelphia Eagles 17, Dallas Cowboys 23

Monday Night Football Games

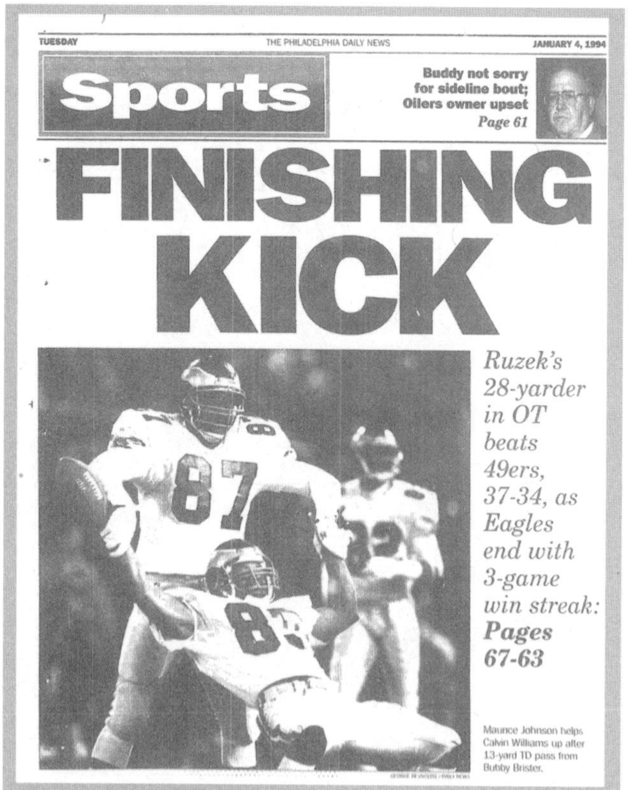

TUESDAY THE PHILADELPHIA DAILY NEWS JANUARY 4, 1994

Sports

Buddy not sorry for sideline bout; Oilers owner upset *Page 61*

FINISHING KICK

Ruzek's 28-yarder in OT beats 49ers, 37-34, as Eagles end with 3-game win streak: ***Pages 67-63***

Maurice Johnson helps Calvin Williams up after 13-yard TD pass from Bubby Brister.

January 3, 1994:
San Francisco 49ers 34, Philadelphia Eagles 37, OT

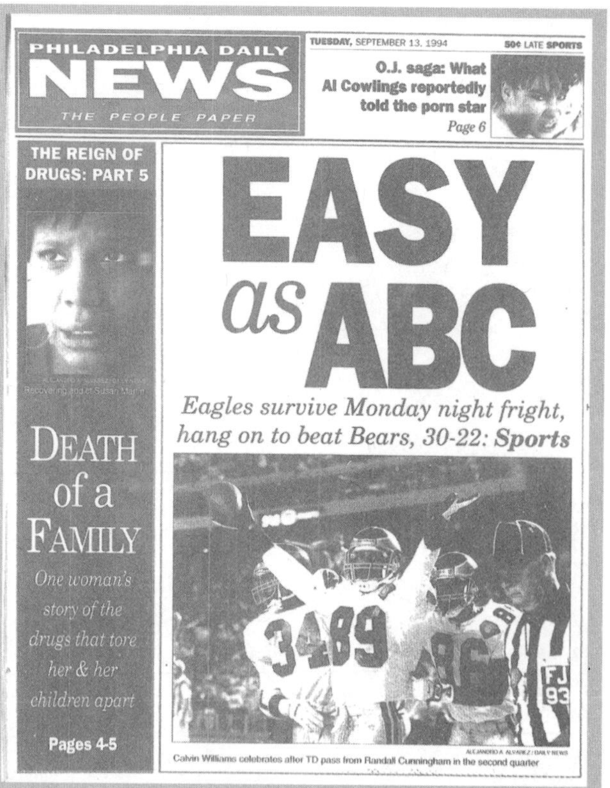

PHILADELPHIA DAILY NEWS
THE PEOPLE PAPER

TUESDAY, SEPTEMBER 13, 1994 50¢ LATE SPORTS

O.J. saga: What Al Cowlings reportedly told the porn star *Page 6*

THE REIGN OF DRUGS: PART 5

Recovering addict Susan Martin

DEATH of a FAMILY

One woman's story of the drugs that tore her & her children apart

Pages 4-5

EASY as ABC

Eagles survive Monday night fright, hang on to beat Bears, 30-22: ***Sports***

Calvin Williams celebrates after TD pass from Randall Cunningham in the second quarter

September 12, 1994:
Chicago Bears 22, Philadelphia Eagles 30

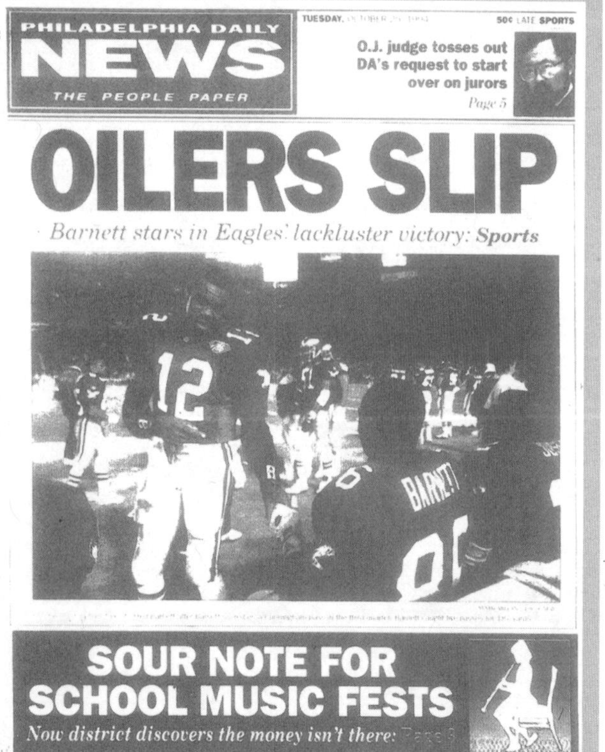

PHILADELPHIA DAILY NEWS
THE PEOPLE PAPER

TUESDAY, OCTOBER 25, 1994 50¢ LATE SPORTS

O.J. judge tosses out DA's request to start over on jurors *Page 5*

OILERS SLIP

Barnett stars in Eagles' lackluster victory: ***Sports***

SOUR NOTE FOR SCHOOL MUSIC FESTS

Now district discovers the money isn't there: Page 3

October 24, 1994:
Houston Oilers 6, Philadelphia Eagles 21

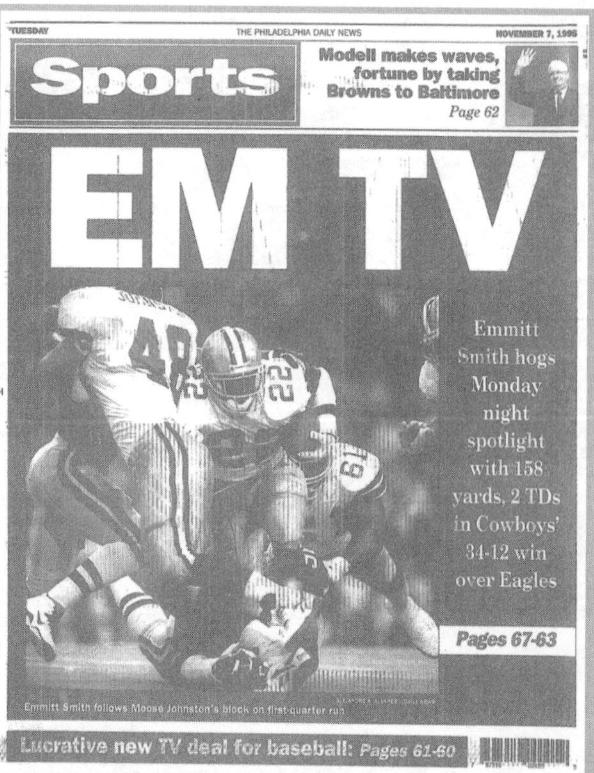

TUESDAY THE PHILADELPHIA DAILY NEWS NOVEMBER 7, 1995

Sports

Modell makes waves, fortune by taking Browns to Baltimore *Page 62*

EM TV

Emmitt Smith hogs Monday night spotlight with 158 yards, 2 TDs in Cowboys' 34-12 win over Eagles

Pages 67-63

Emmitt Smith follows Moose Johnston's block on first-quarter run

Lucrative new TV deal for baseball: *Pages 61-60*

November 6, 1995:
Philadelphia Eagles 12, Dallas Cowboys 34

MONDAY NIGHT FOOTBALL GAMES

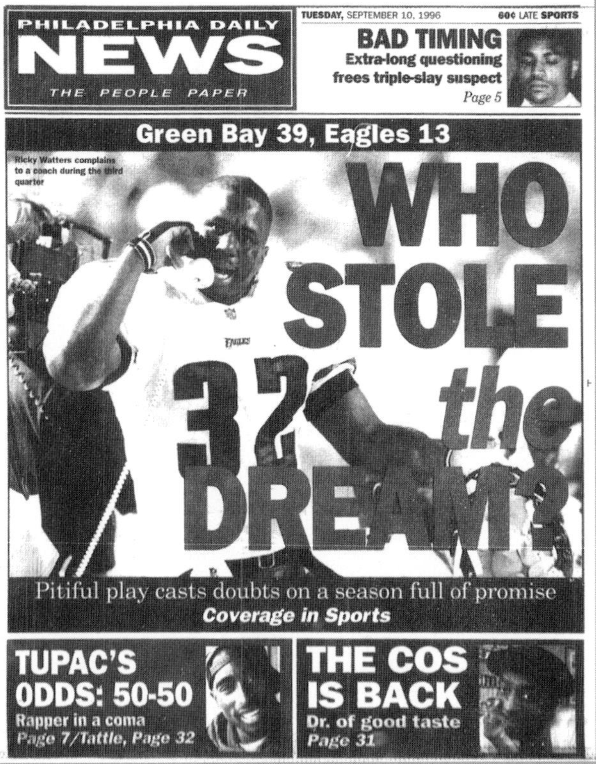
PHILADELPHIA DAILY NEWS
THE PEOPLE PAPER
TUESDAY, SEPTEMBER 10, 1996 60¢ LATE SPORTS
BAD TIMING
Extra-long questioning frees triple-slay suspect
Page 5
Green Bay 39, Eagles 13
Ricky Watters complains to a coach during the third quarter
WHO STOLE the DREAM?
Pitiful play casts doubts on a season full of promise
Coverage in Sports
TUPAC'S ODDS: 50-50
Rapper in a coma
Page 7/Tattle, Page 32
THE COS IS BACK
Dr. of good taste
Page 31

September 9, 1996:
Philadelphia Eagles 13, Green Bay Packers 39

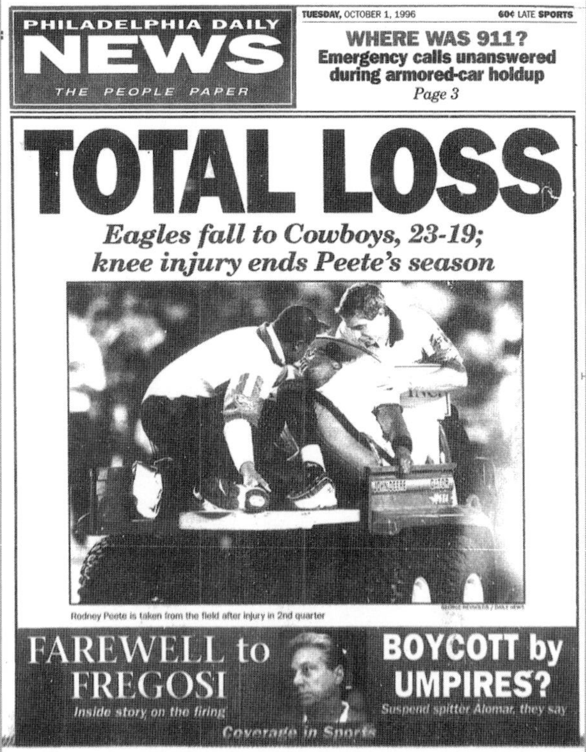
PHILADELPHIA DAILY NEWS
THE PEOPLE PAPER
TUESDAY, OCTOBER 1, 1996 60¢ LATE SPORTS
WHERE WAS 911?
Emergency calls unanswered during armored-car holdup
Page 3
TOTAL LOSS
Eagles fall to Cowboys, 23-19; knee injury ends Peete's season
Rodney Peete is taken from the field after injury in 2nd quarter
FAREWELL to FREGOSI
Inside story on the firing
BOYCOTT by UMPIRES?
Suspend spitter Alomar, they say
Coverage in Sports

September 30, 1996:
Dallas Cowboys 23, Philadelphia Eagles 19

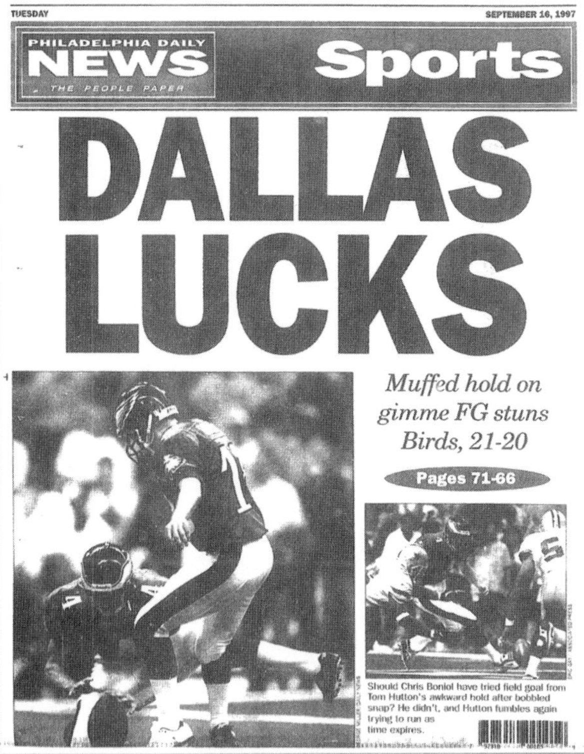
TUESDAY SEPTEMBER 16, 1997
PHILADELPHIA DAILY NEWS
THE PEOPLE PAPER
Sports
DALLAS LUCKS
Muffed hold on gimme FG stuns Birds, 21-20
Pages 71-66
Should Chris Boniol have tried field goal from Tom Hutton's awkward hold after bobbled snap? He didn't, and Hutton fumbles again trying to run as time expires.

September 15, 1997:
Philadelphia Eagles 20, Dallas Cowboys 21

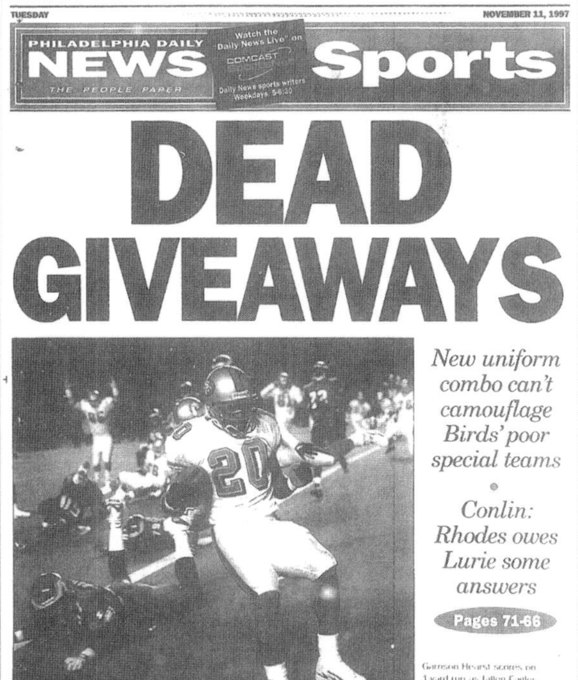
TUESDAY NOVEMBER 11, 1997
PHILADELPHIA DAILY NEWS
THE PEOPLE PAPER
Watch the Daily News Live on COMCAST
Daily News sports writers Weekdays
Sports
DEAD GIVEAWAYS
New uniform combo can't camouflage Birds' poor special teams
Conlin: Rhodes owes Lurie some answers
Pages 71-66
Garrison Hearst scores on 1-yard run as fallen Eagles defenders litter field in 49ers' 24-12 win.
NHL, Caps to deal with racial slur: Page 62

November 10, 1997:
San Francisco 49ers 24, Philadelphia Eagles 12

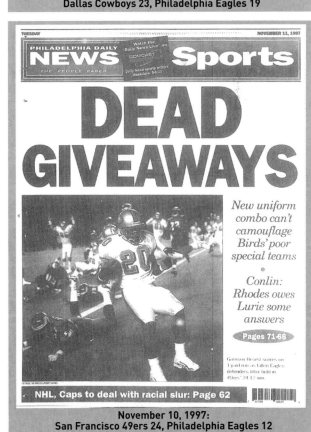

MONDAY NIGHT FOOTBALL GAMES

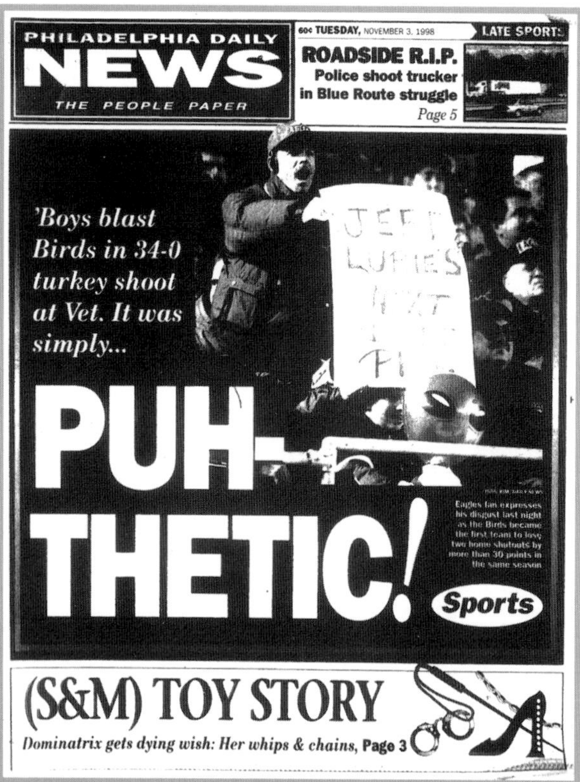

PHILADELPHIA DAILY NEWS
THE PEOPLE PAPER

60¢ TUESDAY, NOVEMBER 3, 1998 LATE SPORTS

ROADSIDE R.I.P.
Police shoot trucker in Blue Route struggle
Page 5

'Boys blast Birds in 34-0 turkey shoot at Vet. It was simply...

PUH-THETIC!

Eagles fan expresses his disgust last night as the Birds became the first team to lose two home shutouts by more than 30 points in the same season

Sports

(S&M) TOY STORY
Dominatrix gets dying wish: Her whips & chains, **Page 3**

November 2, 1998:
Dallas Cowboys 34, Philadelphia Eagles 0

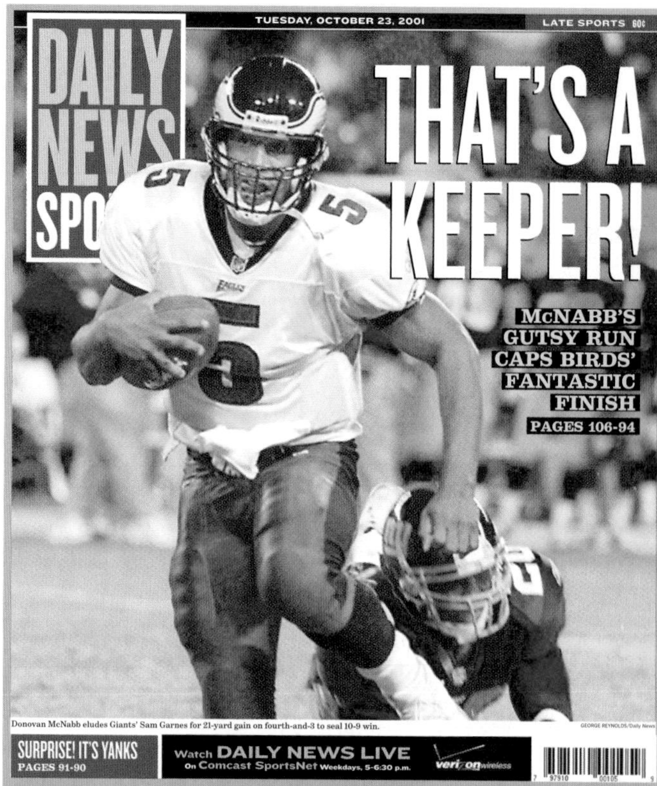

TUESDAY, OCTOBER 23, 2001 LATE SPORTS 60¢

DAILY NEWS SPORTS

THAT'S A KEEPER!

McNABB'S GUTSY RUN CAPS BIRDS' FANTASTIC FINISH
PAGES 106-94

Donovan McNabb eludes Giants' Sam Garnes for 21-yard gain on fourth-and-3 to seal 10-9 win.
GEORGE REYNOLDS/Daily News

SURPRISE! IT'S YANKS
PAGES 91-90

Watch DAILY NEWS LIVE
On Comcast SportsNet Weekdays, 5-6:30 p.m.
verizon wireless

October 22, 2001:
Philadelphia Eagles 10, New York Giants 9

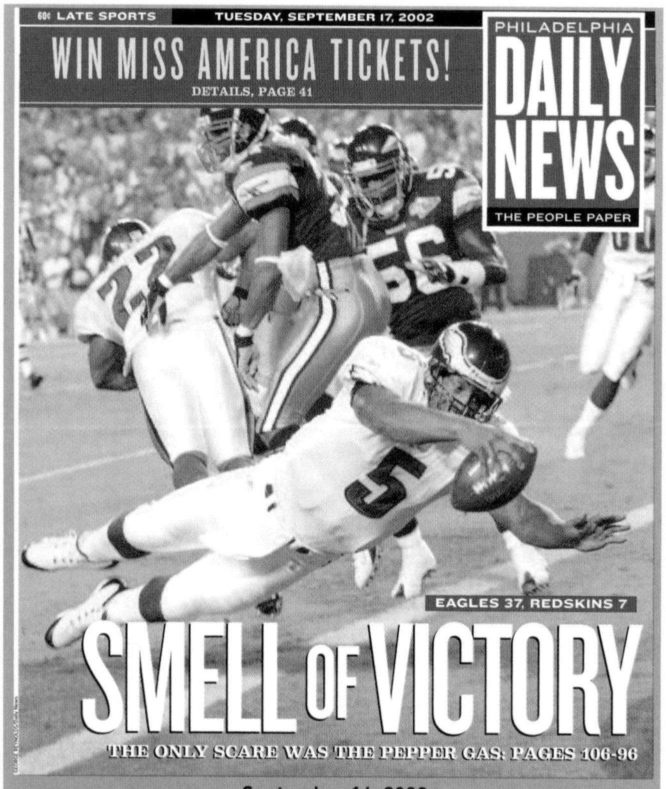

60¢ LATE SPORTS TUESDAY, SEPTEMBER 17, 2002

PHILADELPHIA DAILY NEWS
THE PEOPLE PAPER

WIN MISS AMERICA TICKETS!
DETAILS, PAGE 41

EAGLES 37, REDSKINS 7

SMELL OF VICTORY

THE ONLY SCARE WAS THE PEPPER GAS: PAGES 106-96

September 16, 2002:
Philadelphia Eagles 37, Washington Redskins 7

60¢ LATE SPORTS TUESDAY, OCTOBER 29, 2002

PHILADELPHIA DAILY NEWS
THE PEOPLE PAPER

SMASH!

EAGLES OUTCLASS GIANTS, 17-3
BIRDWATCH, PAGES 98-86

In the fourth quarter, Donovan McNabb scores the game's lone touchdown.
GEORGE REYNOLDS/Daily News

October 28, 2002:
New York Giants 3, Philadelphia Eagles 17

MONDAY NIGHT FOOTBALL GAMES

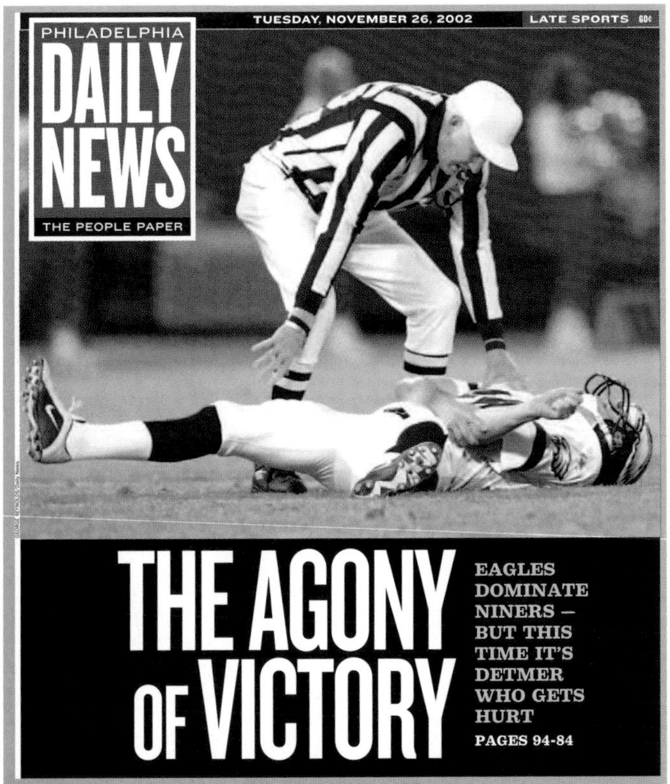
TUESDAY, NOVEMBER 26, 2002 LATE SPORTS 60¢

PHILADELPHIA DAILY NEWS THE PEOPLE PAPER

THE AGONY OF VICTORY

EAGLES DOMINATE NINERS – BUT THIS TIME IT'S DETMER WHO GETS HURT

PAGES 94-84

November 25, 2002:
Philadelphia Eagles 38, San Francisco 49ers 17

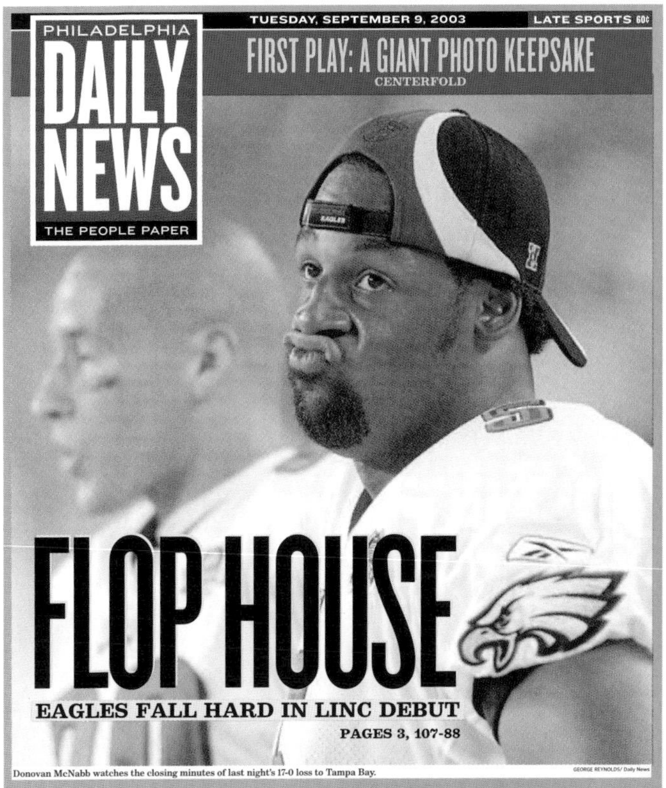
TUESDAY, SEPTEMBER 9, 2003 LATE SPORTS 60¢

PHILADELPHIA DAILY NEWS THE PEOPLE PAPER

FIRST PLAY: A GIANT PHOTO KEEPSAKE

CENTERFOLD

FLOP HOUSE

EAGLES FALL HARD IN LINC DEBUT

PAGES 3, 107-88

Donovan McNabb watches the closing minutes of last night's 17-0 loss to Tampa Bay. GEORGE REYNOLDS/ Daily News

September 9, 2003:
Tampa Bay 17, Philadelphia Eagles 0

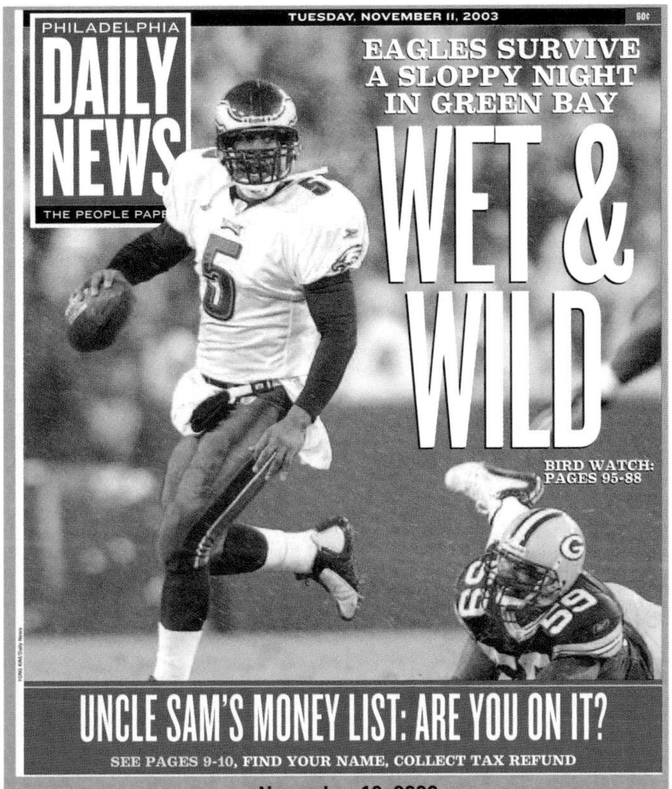
TUESDAY, NOVEMBER 11, 2003 60¢

PHILADELPHIA DAILY NEWS THE PEOPLE PAPER

EAGLES SURVIVE A SLOPPY NIGHT IN GREEN BAY

WET & WILD

BIRD WATCH: PAGES 95-88

UNCLE SAM'S MONEY LIST: ARE YOU ON IT?

SEE PAGES 9-10, FIND YOUR NAME, COLLECT TAX REFUND

November 10, 2003:
Philadelphia Eagles 17, Green Bay Packers 14

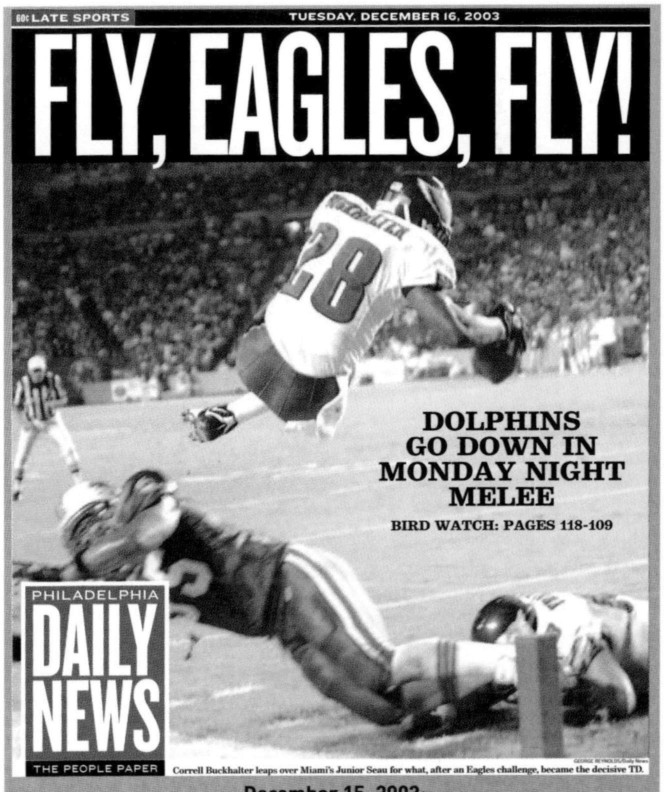
60¢ LATE SPORTS TUESDAY, DECEMBER 16, 2003

FLY, EAGLES, FLY!

DOLPHINS GO DOWN IN MONDAY NIGHT MELEE

BIRD WATCH: PAGES 118-109

PHILADELPHIA DAILY NEWS THE PEOPLE PAPER

Correll Buckhalter leaps over Miami's Junior Seau for what, after an Eagles challenge, became the decisive TD.

December 15, 2003:
Philadelphia Eagles 34, Miami Dolphins 27

MONDAY NIGHT FOOTBALL

Monday Night Football Games

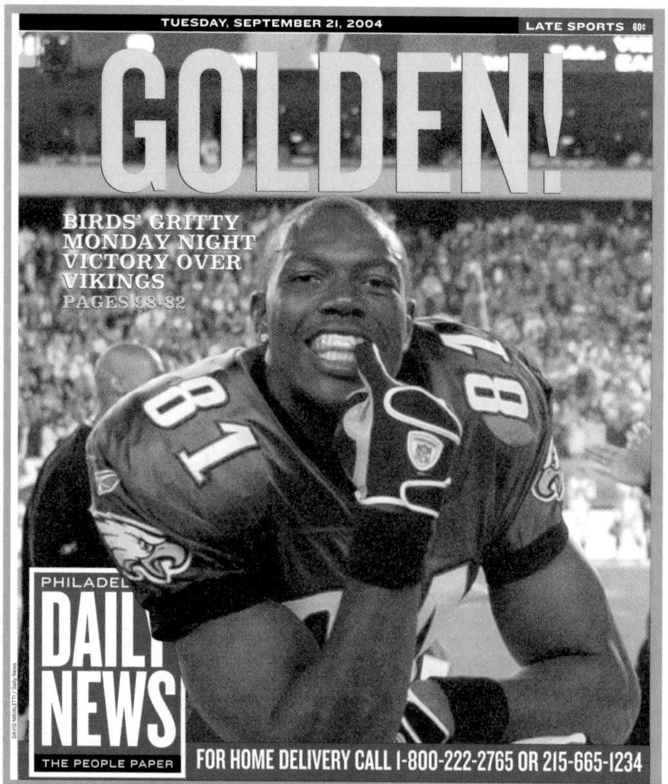
TUESDAY, SEPTEMBER 21, 2004
LATE SPORTS 60¢
GOLDEN!
BIRDS' GRITTY MONDAY NIGHT VICTORY OVER VIKINGS
PAGES 98-82
PHILADELPHIA DAILY NEWS
THE PEOPLE PAPER
FOR HOME DELIVERY CALL 1-800-222-2765 OR 215-665-1234

September 20, 2004:
Minnesota Vikings 16, Philadelphia Eagles 27

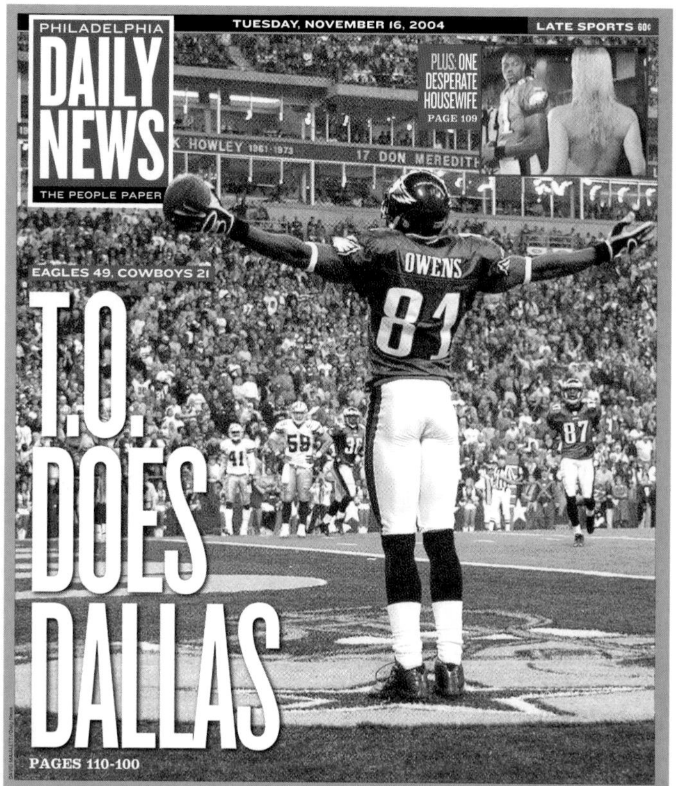
PHILADELPHIA DAILY NEWS
THE PEOPLE PAPER
TUESDAY, NOVEMBER 16, 2004
LATE SPORTS 60¢
PLUS: ONE DESPERATE HOUSEWIFE
PAGE 109
EAGLES 49, COWBOYS 21
T.O. DOES DALLAS
PAGES 110-100

November 15, 2004:
Philadelphia Eagles 49, Dallas Cowboys 21

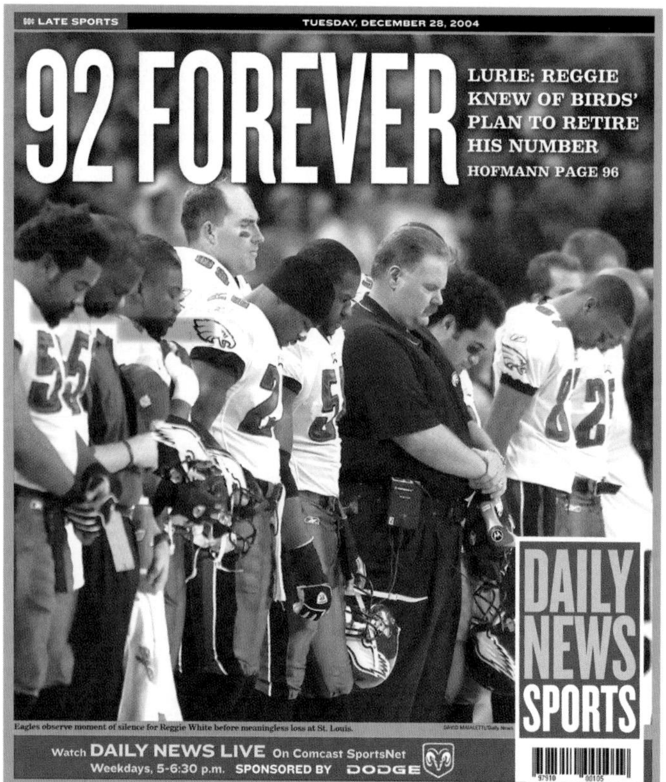
60¢ LATE SPORTS
TUESDAY, DECEMBER 28, 2004
92 FOREVER
LURIE: REGGIE KNEW OF BIRDS' PLAN TO RETIRE HIS NUMBER
HOFMANN PAGE 96
DAILY NEWS SPORTS
Eagles observe moment of silence for Reggie White before meaningless loss at St. Louis.
Watch DAILY NEWS LIVE On Comcast SportsNet
Weekdays, 5-6:30 p.m. SPONSORED BY DODGE

December 27, 2004:
Philadelphia Eagles 7 , St. Louis Rams 20

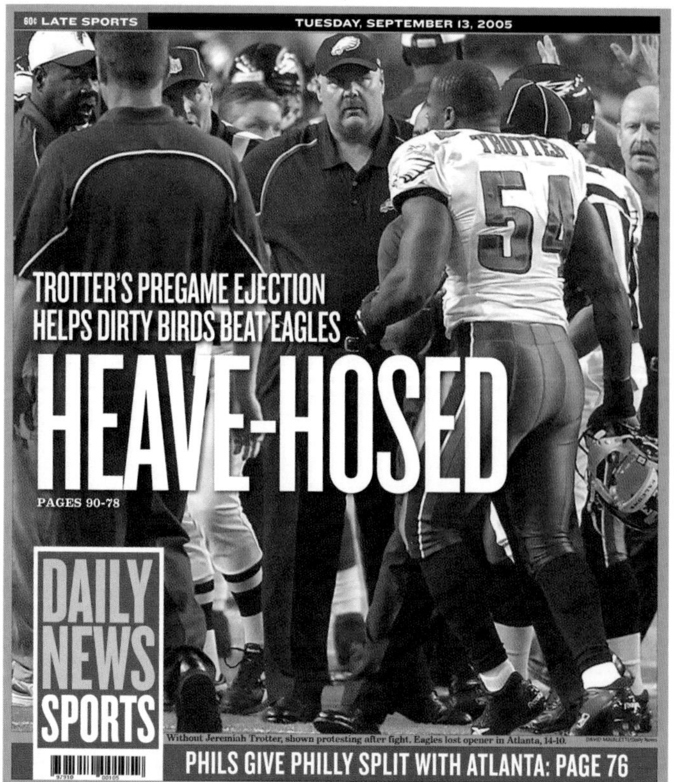
60¢ LATE SPORTS
TUESDAY, SEPTEMBER 13, 2005
TROTTER'S PREGAME EJECTION HELPS DIRTY BIRDS BEAT EAGLES
HEAVE-HOSED
PAGES 90-78
DAILY NEWS SPORTS
Without Jeremiah Trotter, shown protesting after fight, Eagles lost opener in Atlanta, 14-10.
PHILS GIVE PHILLY SPLIT WITH ATLANTA: PAGE 76

September 12, 2005:
Philadelphia Eagles 10, Atlanta Falcons 14

MONDAY NIGHT FOOTBALL GAMES

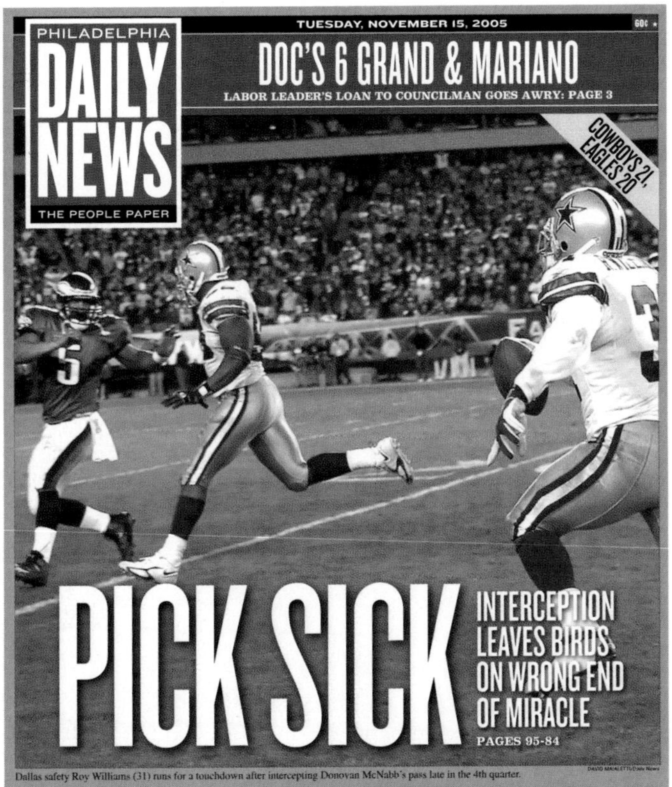
TUESDAY, NOVEMBER 15, 2005 60¢

PHILADELPHIA DAILY NEWS THE PEOPLE PAPER

DOC'S 6 GRAND & MARIANO

LABOR LEADER'S LOAN TO COUNCILMAN GOES AWRY: PAGE 3

COWBOYS 21, EAGLES 20

PICK SICK

INTERCEPTION LEAVES BIRDS ON WRONG END OF MIRACLE

PAGES 95-84

Dallas safety Roy Williams (31) runs for a touchdown after intercepting Donovan McNabb's pass late in the 4th quarter.

November 14, 2005:
Dallas Cowboys 21, Philadelphia Eagles 20

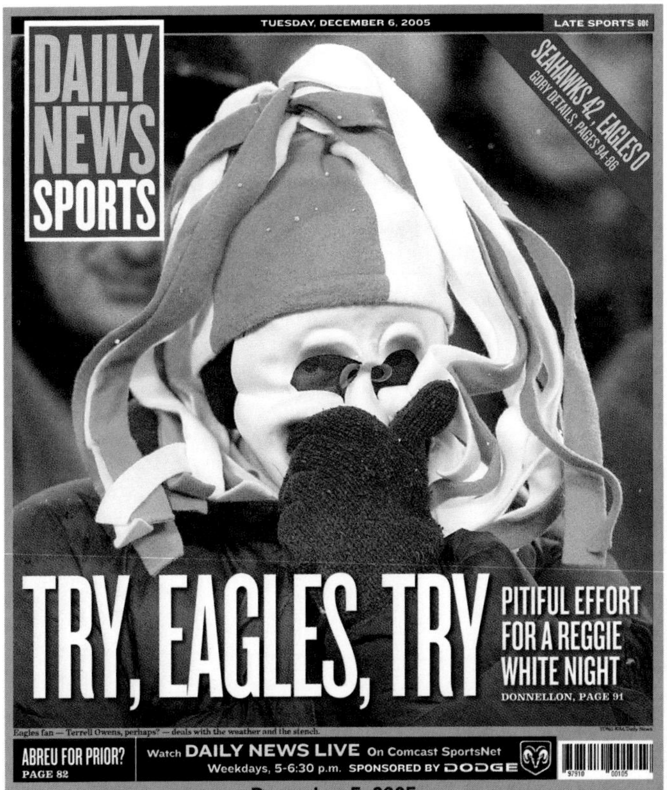
TUESDAY, DECEMBER 6, 2005 LATE SPORTS 60¢

DAILY NEWS SPORTS

SEAHAWKS 42, EAGLES 0

GORY DETAILS, PAGES 94-86

TRY, EAGLES, TRY

PITIFUL EFFORT FOR A REGGIE WHITE NIGHT

DONNELLON, PAGE 91

Eagles fan — Terrell Owens, perhaps? — deals with the weather and the stench.

ABREU FOR PRIOR? PAGE 82

Watch DAILY NEWS LIVE On Comcast SportsNet Weekdays, 5-6:30 p.m. SPONSORED BY DODGE

December 5, 2005:
Seattle Seahawks 42, Philadelphia Eagles 0

TUESDAY, OCTOBER 3, 2006 60¢

DAILY NEWS SPORTS

PHILS' NEW FAB 4 PAGE 62

EAGLES LEGENDS MEDALLIONS COUPON, PAGE 61

SMOKIN' A PACK

EAGLES KICK BUTT AFTER ROCKY FIRST HALF

BIRDWATCH: PAGES 78-66

EAGLES 31, PACKERS 9

Lar...n Ramsey (right) celebrates his interception with Jeremiah Trotter (left) and Michael Lewis.

October 2, 2006:
Green Bay Packers 9, Philadelphia Eagles 31

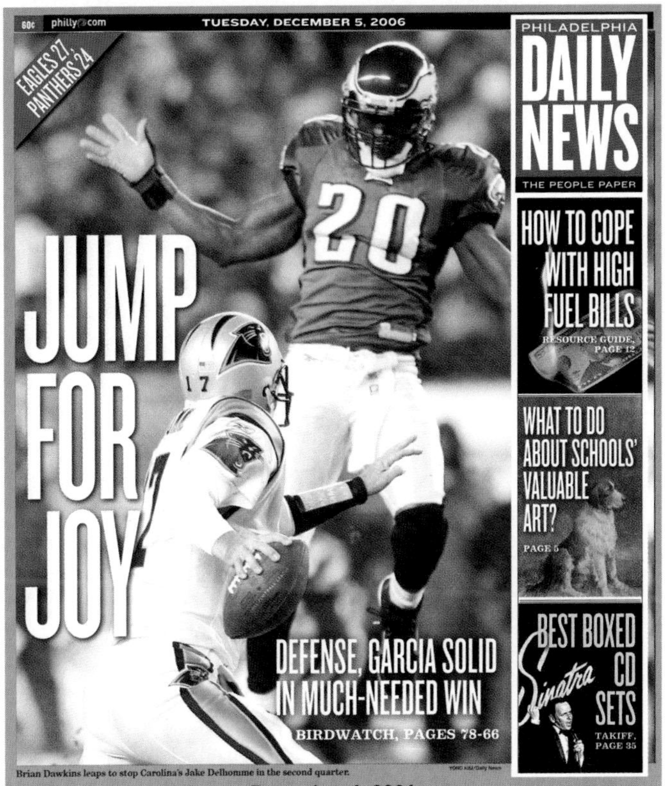
60¢ philly.com TUESDAY, DECEMBER 5, 2006

PHILADELPHIA DAILY NEWS THE PEOPLE PAPER

EAGLES 27, PANTHERS 24

JUMP FOR JOY

DEFENSE, GARCIA SOLID IN MUCH-NEEDED WIN

BIRDWATCH, PAGES 78-66

HOW TO COPE WITH HIGH FUEL BILLS

RESOURCE GUIDE, PAGE 12

WHAT TO DO ABOUT SCHOOLS' VALUABLE ART?

PAGE 5

BEST BOXED CD SETS

Sinatra

TAKIFF, PAGE 35

Brian Dawkins leaps to stop Carolina's Jake Delhomme in the second quarter.

December 4, 2006:
Carolina Panthers 24, Philadelphia Eagles 27

MONDAY NIGHT FOOTBALL

Monday Night Football Games

TUESDAY, SEPTEMBER 18, 2007 philly.com 60¢

SPRAGUE, FUMO SPLIT
PAGE 9

PHILS' SCARY WIN
PAGE 76
10G HOME-RUN PAYOFF
PAGE 77

189 COUNTS OF GULLICIDE
LONGSHOREMAN DROVE OVER BIRDS: PAGE 10

REDSKINS 20, EAGLES 12

TAILGATE UPDATE
URBAN WARRIOR, PAGE 3

PUNCHLESS EAGLES LOSE AT LINC
HOME SICK
PAGES 94-78

PHILADELPHIA DAILY NEWS
THE PEOPLE PAPER

Eagles fans in the stands had little to celebrate.

YONG KIM/Daily News

September 18, 2007:
Washington Redskins 20, Philadelphia Eagles 12
Donovan McNabb's 100th regular season start

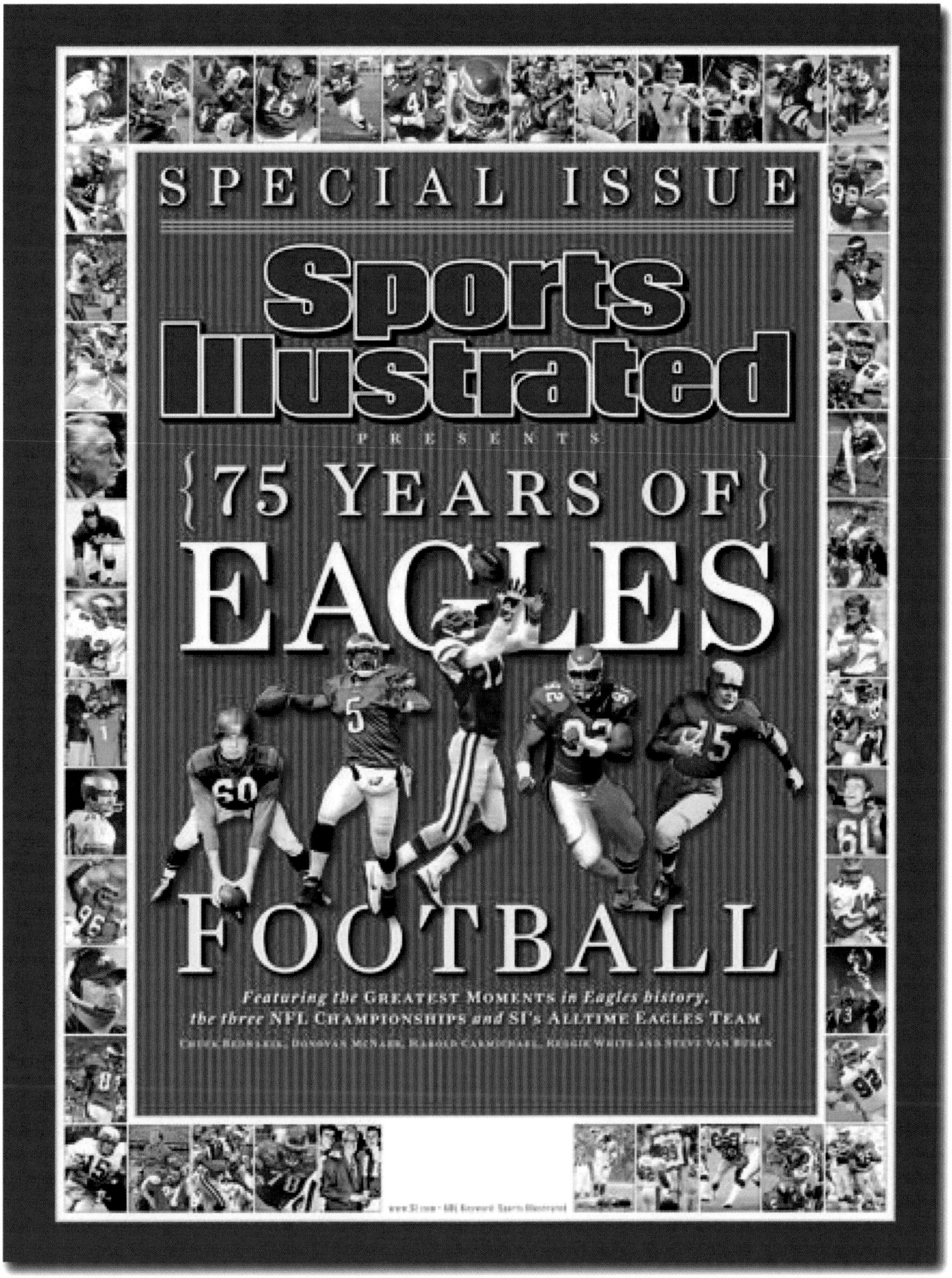
SPECIAL ISSUE
Sports Illustrated
PRESENTS
{75 YEARS OF}
EAGLES
FOOTBALL
Featuring the GREATEST MOMENTS in Eagles history,
the three NFL CHAMPIONSHIPS and SI's ALLTIME EAGLES TEAM

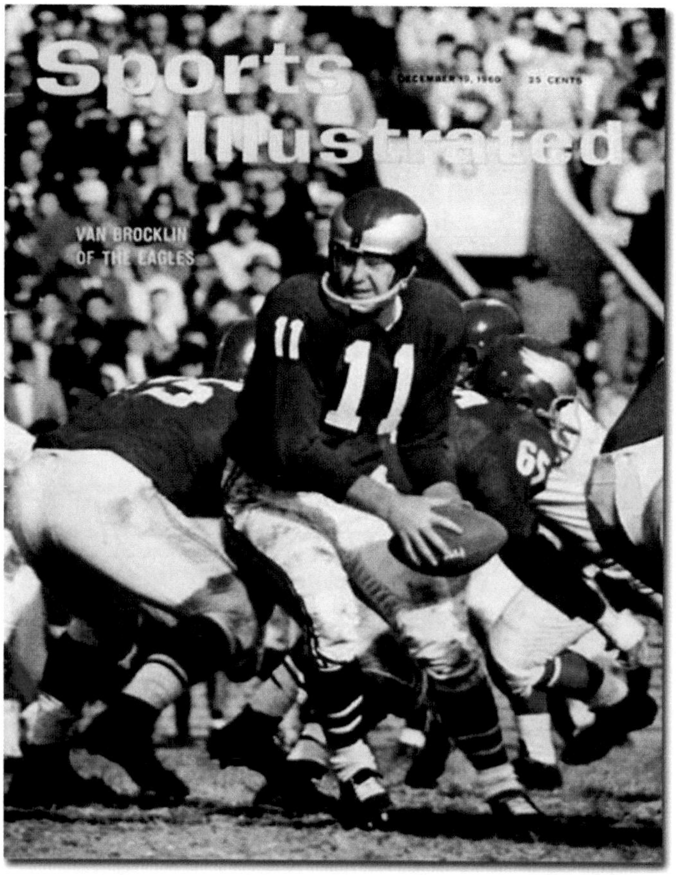
Sports Illustrated
DECEMBER 19, 1960
25 CENTS
VAN BROCKLIN
OF THE EAGLES

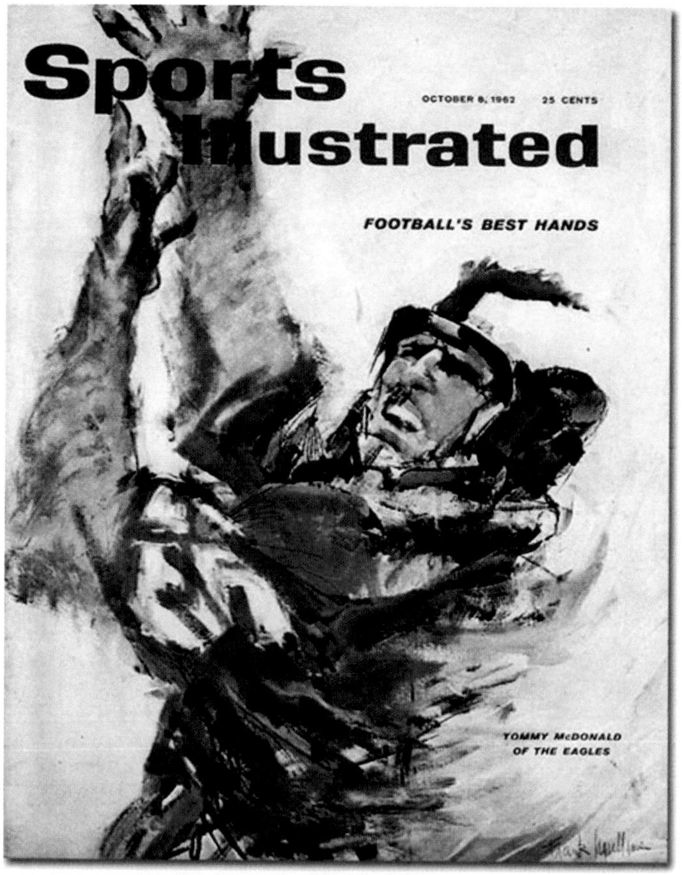
Sports Illustrated
OCTOBER 8, 1962
25 CENTS
FOOTBALL'S BEST HANDS
TOMMY McDONALD
OF THE EAGLES

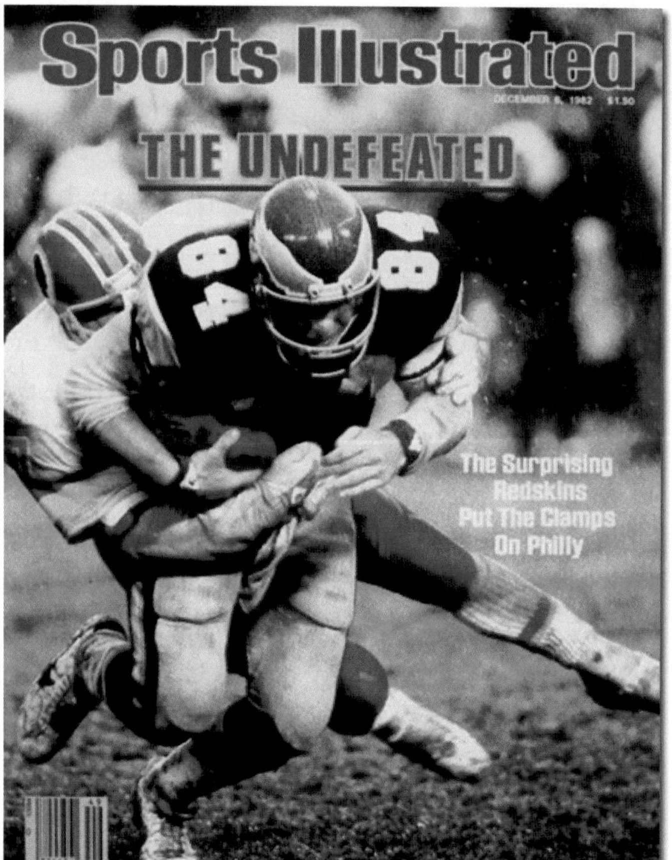
Sports Illustrated
DECEMBER 6, 1982 $1.50
THE UNDEFEATED
The Surprising
Redskins
Put The Clamps
On Philly

NFL PREVIEW ISSUE
Sports Illustrated
THE
ULTIMATE
WEAPON
PHILADELPHIA'S
RANDALL CUNNINGHAM:
THE QUARTERBACK
FOR THE '90S
DR.Z'S SUPER BOWL PICKS:
BUFFALO & CHICAGO

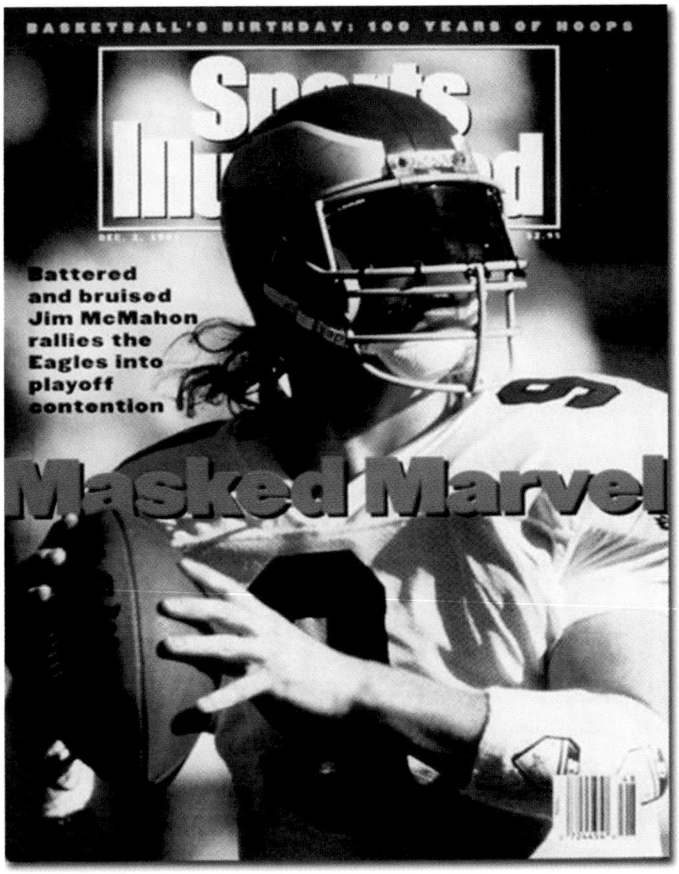
BASKETBALL'S BIRTHDAY: 100 YEARS OF HOOPS
Battered and bruised Jim McMahon rallies the Eagles into playoff contention
Masked Marvel

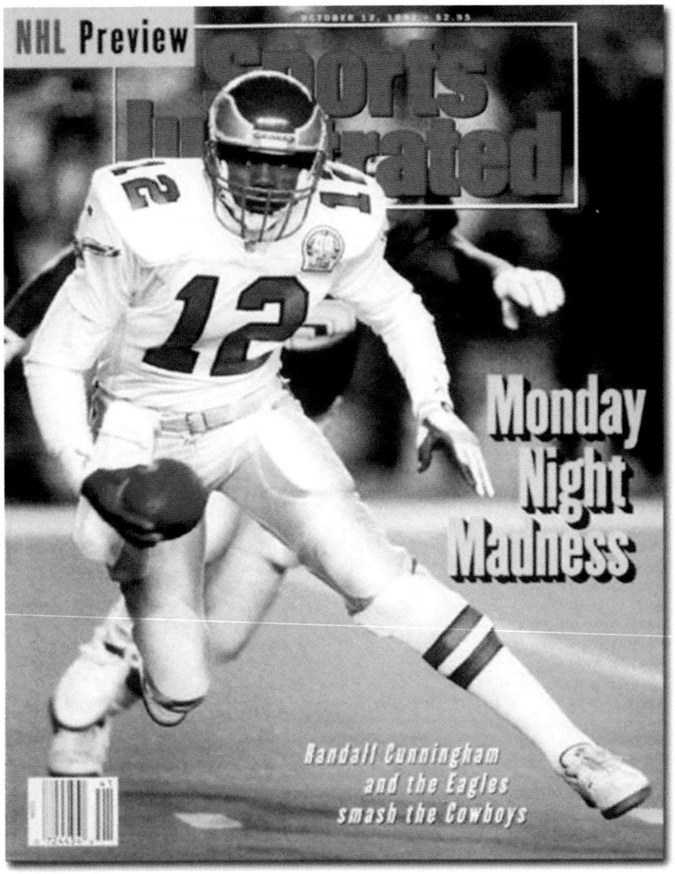
NHL Preview
Monday Night Madness
Randall Cunningham and the Eagles smash the Cowboys

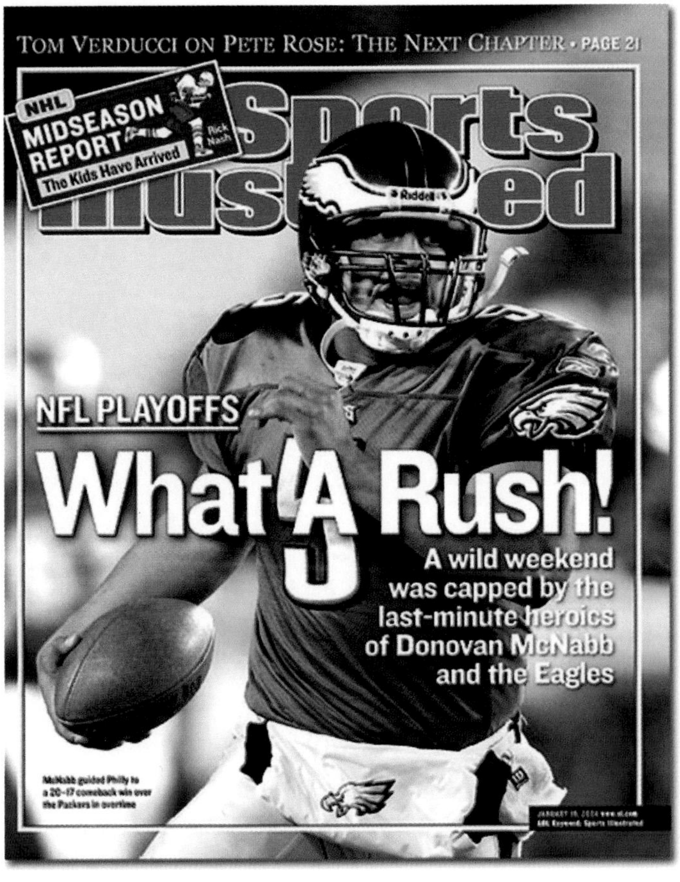
TOM VERDUCCI ON PETE ROSE: THE NEXT CHAPTER • PAGE 21
NHL MIDSEASON REPORT
The Kids Have Arrived
Rick Nash
Sports Illustrated
NFL PLAYOFFS
What A Rush!
A wild weekend was capped by the last-minute heroics of Donovan McNabb and the Eagles
McNabb guided Philly to a 20–17 comeback win over the Packers in overtime

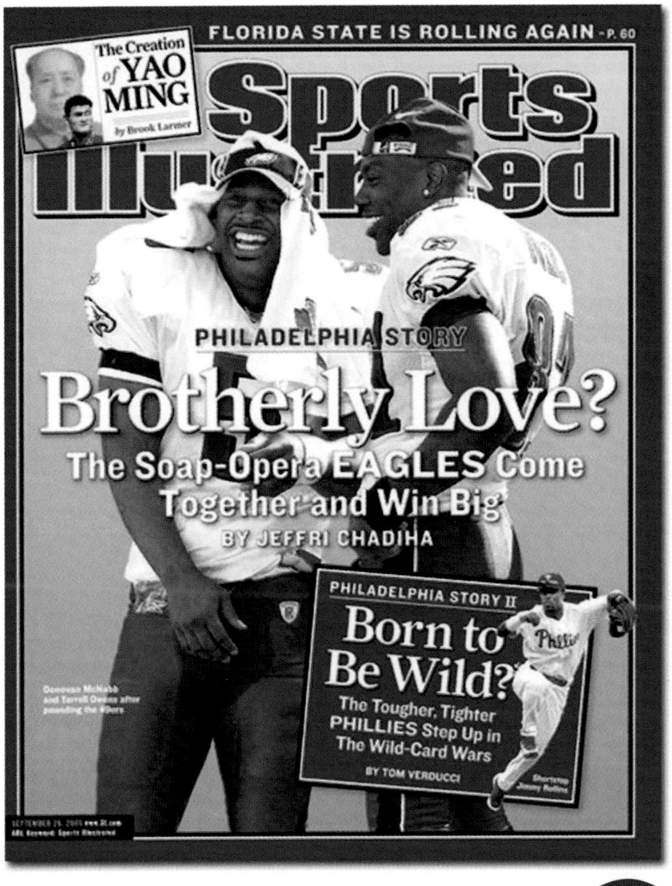
FLORIDA STATE IS ROLLING AGAIN • P. 60
The Creation of YAO MING
by Brook Larmer
Sports Illustrated
PHILADELPHIA STORY
Brotherly Love?
The Soap-Opera EAGLES Come Together and Win Big
BY JEFFRI CHADIHA
Donovan McNabb and Terrell Owens after pounding the 49ers
PHILADELPHIA STORY II
Born to Be Wild?
The Tougher, Tighter PHILLIES Step Up in The Wild-Card Wars
BY TOM VERDUCCI

WHY HOLLYWOOD LOVES THE RING | A CENTURY OF BOXING IN THE MOVIES
HILARY SWANK KNOCKS 'EM OUT
★ ONE TOUGH BABY ★
ROCKY MEETS HIS MATCH
THE STORY BEHIND MILLION DOLLAR BABY, THE GREATEST FIGHT FILM EVER | BY JOHN SCHULIAN
Sports Illustrated
Party On
The Eagles Dance into the Super Bowl
(But the Patriots Dream of Dynasty)
Remember Me?
Tiger's first PGA Tour win in 11 months may ignite a new run of dominance
BY ALAN SHIPNUCK
WHAT WOULD YOU DO?
Jermaine O'Neal explains the riot in Detroit. You'll be surprised...
BY S.L. PRICE

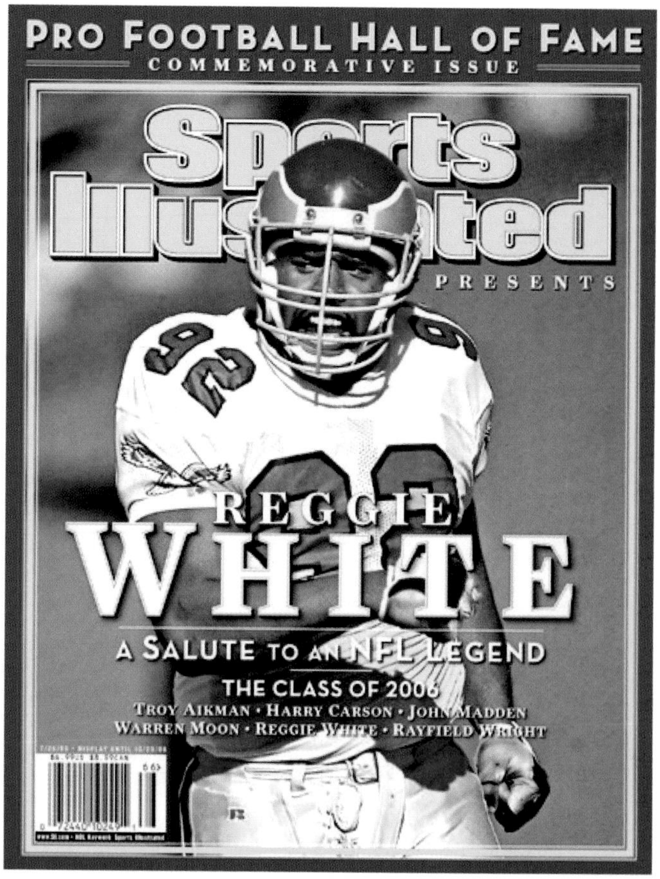
PRO FOOTBALL HALL OF FAME
COMMEMORATIVE ISSUE
Sports Illustrated
PRESENTS
REGGIE
WHITE
A SALUTE TO AN NFL LEGEND
THE CLASS OF 2006
TROY AIKMAN · HARRY CARSON · JOHN MADDEN
WARREN MOON · REGGIE WHITE · RAYFIELD WRIGHT

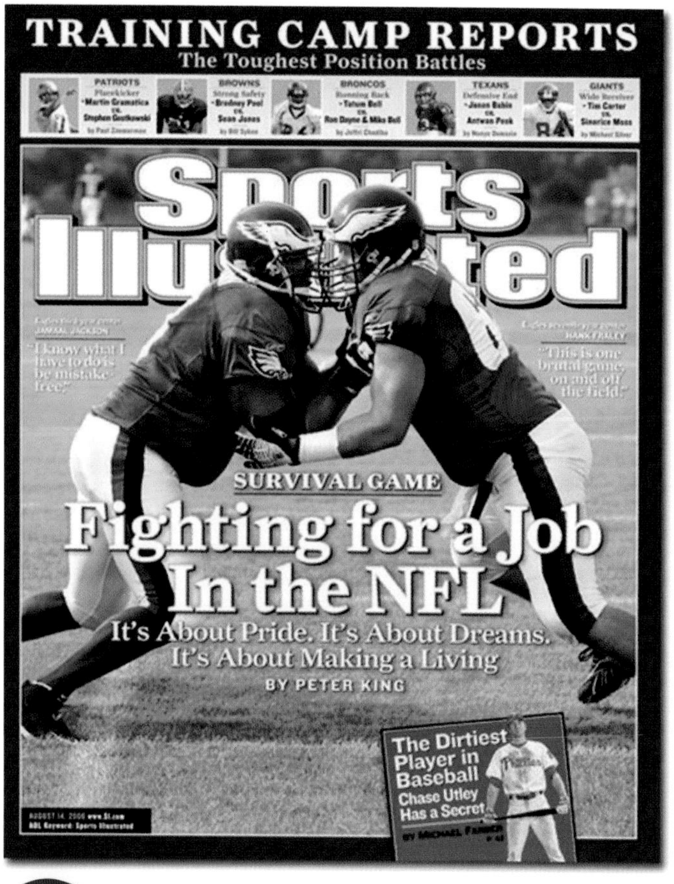
TRAINING CAMP REPORTS
The Toughest Position Battles
PATRIOTS
BROWNS
BRONCOS
TEXANS
GIANTS
Sports Illustrated
SURVIVAL GAME
Fighting for a Job In the NFL
It's About Pride. It's About Dreams. It's About Making a Living
BY PETER KING
The Dirtiest Player in Baseball
Chase Utley Has a Secret

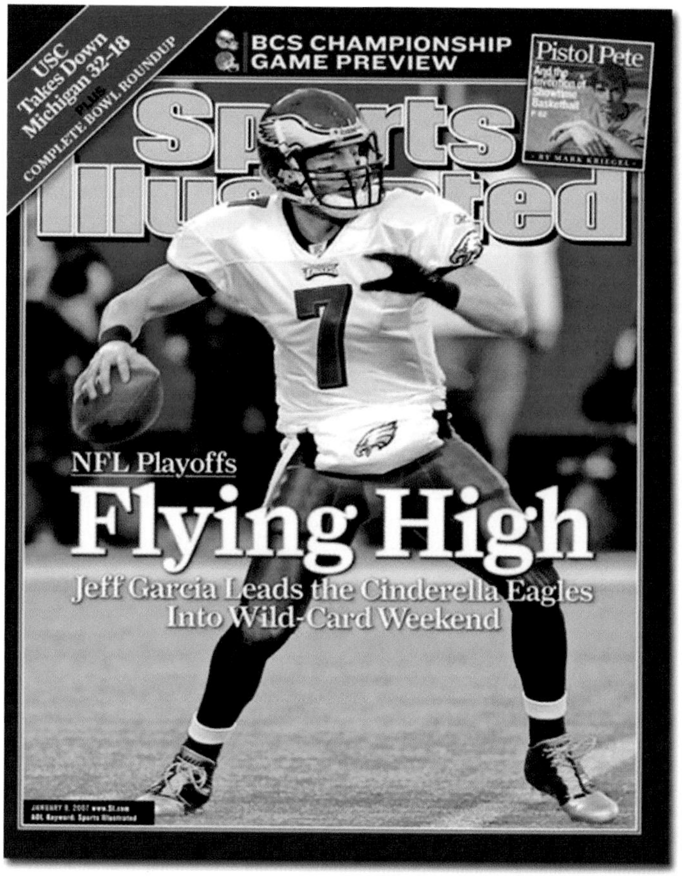
USC Takes Down Michigan 32-18
PLUS COMPLETE BOWL ROUNDUP
BCS CHAMPIONSHIP GAME PREVIEW
Pistol Pete
Sports Illustrated
NFL Playoffs
Flying High
Jeff Garcia Leads the Cinderella Eagles Into Wild-Card Weekend

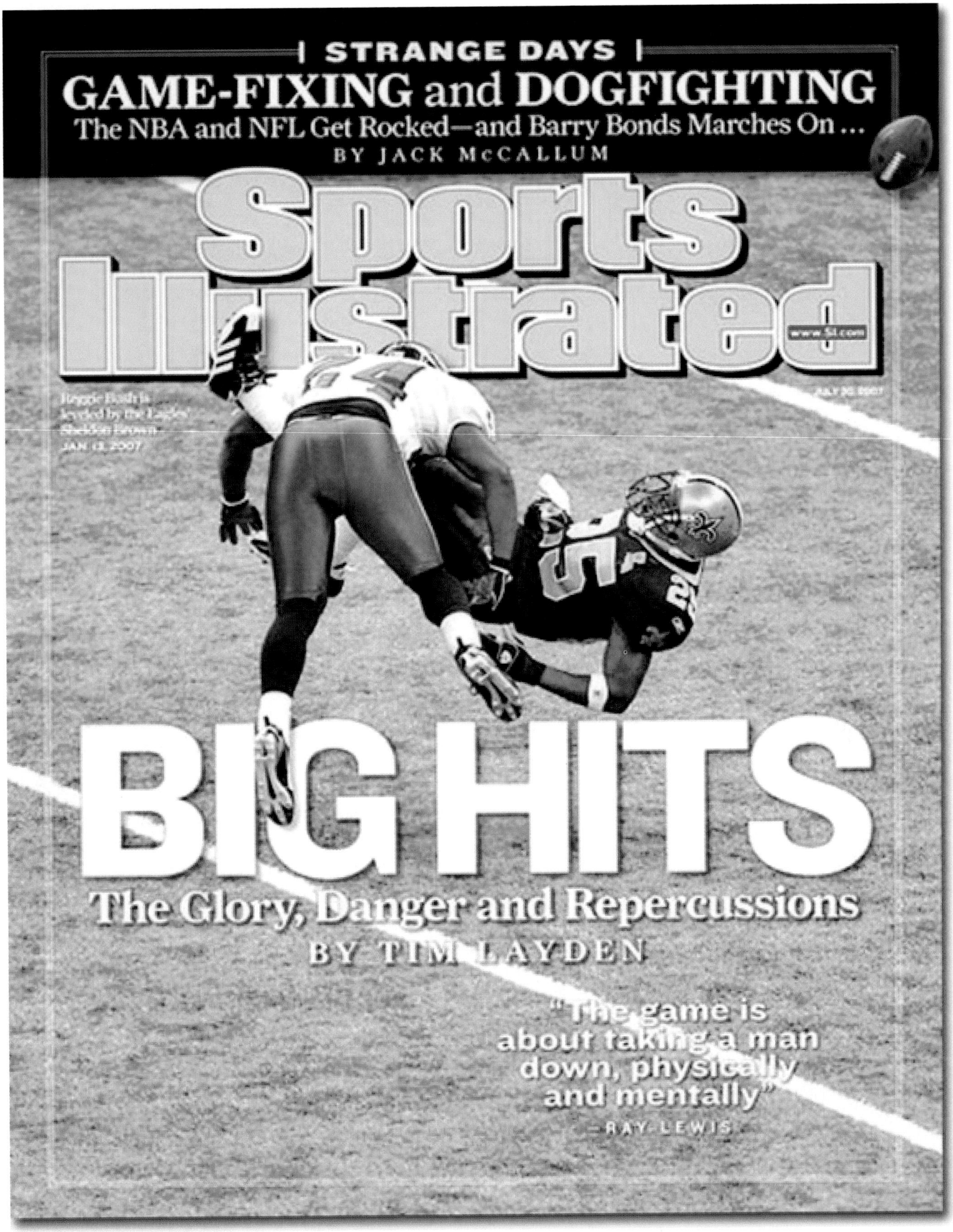
STRANGE DAYS
GAME-FIXING and DOGFIGHTING
The NBA and NFL Get Rocked—and Barry Bonds Marches On ...
BY JACK McCALLUM
Sports Illustrated
BIG HITS
The Glory, Danger and Repercussions
BY TIM LAYDEN
"The game is about taking a man down, physically and mentally"
—RAY LEWIS

Evolution of SWOOP

Ht: 6'3" Wt: 216 lbs
Pos: Center (of attention) Jersey # 00
Hatched: In the Philadelphia Zoo in December of 1995
Resides: South Philly, in the Eagles Nest
High atop Lincoln Financial Field
Diet: Smaller birds such as Cardinals, Ravens,
Falcons and Seahawks;
and of course cheesesteaks and soft pretzels.
Off the field: Swoop can be found throughout
the tri-state area at schools charity events,
birthday parties, grand openings, parades
and even weddings !

Blitz 1980's
1996 - 1999
75
1933 • SEASONS • 2007

Named by a fan through a local contest: Swoop made his first official appearance at an Eagles Pre-Season game which was on August 23rd, 1996; this game was at Veteran's Stadium against the Pittsburgh Steelers (which by the way the Eagles won 20-19). Since then Swoop has appeared at over 5000 appearances in 16 different states (including Hawaii and Puerto Rico); Canada, Mexico, and Hong Kong. Swoop has been elected to; or has represented the Philadelphia Eagles at the Pro-Bowl 8 out of his 12 seasons. In the 2000 season, Swoop made his last and final transformation to his current look for a better representation of the the team and city; but more importantly to appear more suitable to the younger fans that may have found Swoop's past look a bit too intense. It is important to have a proud and fierce looking bird for our city and team, but at the same time approachable for the children.

- EAGLES GO GREEN -

In 2003, the Philadelphia Eagles launched "Go Green," a ground-breaking campaign to better the environment. The Eagles were the first professional sports organization to implement an environmental strategy and in 2007 began to receive both local and national media attention for their efforts. The Eagles instituted recycling programs, the procurement of post-consumer recycled paper products, the purchase of renewable energy from wind and other sources, tree-planting programs, the use of organic and pesticide-free materials on playing and practice fields and the instillation of solar panels at the NovaCare Complex, the team's training facility, to offset energy costs. The Eagles are the first, and most likely only, organization to reimburse employees for purchasing wind energy, have created an Eagles Forest at Neshaminy State Park, PA where the team plants trees to offset carbon emissions caused by away-game air travel. Soon, the team will recycle cooking oils used in the kitchens at Lincoln Financial Field and at the NovaCare Complex converting the oil to biodesiel which can be used to fuel the team's field maintenance vehicles.

Go Green has dramatically reduced the organization's environmental footprint and impact on global warming by eliminating thousands of metric tons of greenhouse gases and other pollutants from being released into the earth's atmosphere. Go Green has saved hundreds of thousands of trees, the equivalent of eliminating more than seven million miles of automobile travel, or planting nearly 500,000 trees. In 2007, all 10 home games, including two preseason games, were powered on 100% clean energy and now, cups and flatware used on game day and at the NovaCare Complex are created from 100% post consumer used products, like corn and grass, that biodegrade in a landfill within 45 days.

"Go Green" is more than just a play on words for the Eagles. "Go Green" has become both a rallying cry for the football team and a good citizenship message for the community. The hope is that these efforts will educate and inspire others to improve their environmental stewardship. If every NFL team made similar efforts, and subsequently all sports and stadium businesses, the impact would be dramatic.

Go Green has produced a shift toward greener procurement practices among many NFL teams, as well as other professional sports; clean energy purchasing from wind and methane gas sources; printing of team publications on forest friendly, post-consumer recycled paper; partnerships with Pennsylvania's Department of Conservation and Natural Resources, U.S. Environmental Protection Agency, and other Philadelphia area environmental and community groups; active and comprehensive recycling at Lincoln Financial Field, the team's training facilities at the NovaCare Center, and corporate offices.

The Philadelphia Eagles are proud to have led the field in greening initiatives among professional sports teams. They are continuing to break ground in this effort by challenging themselves, their partners and their fans to take steps toward reducing their environmental impact on the planet.

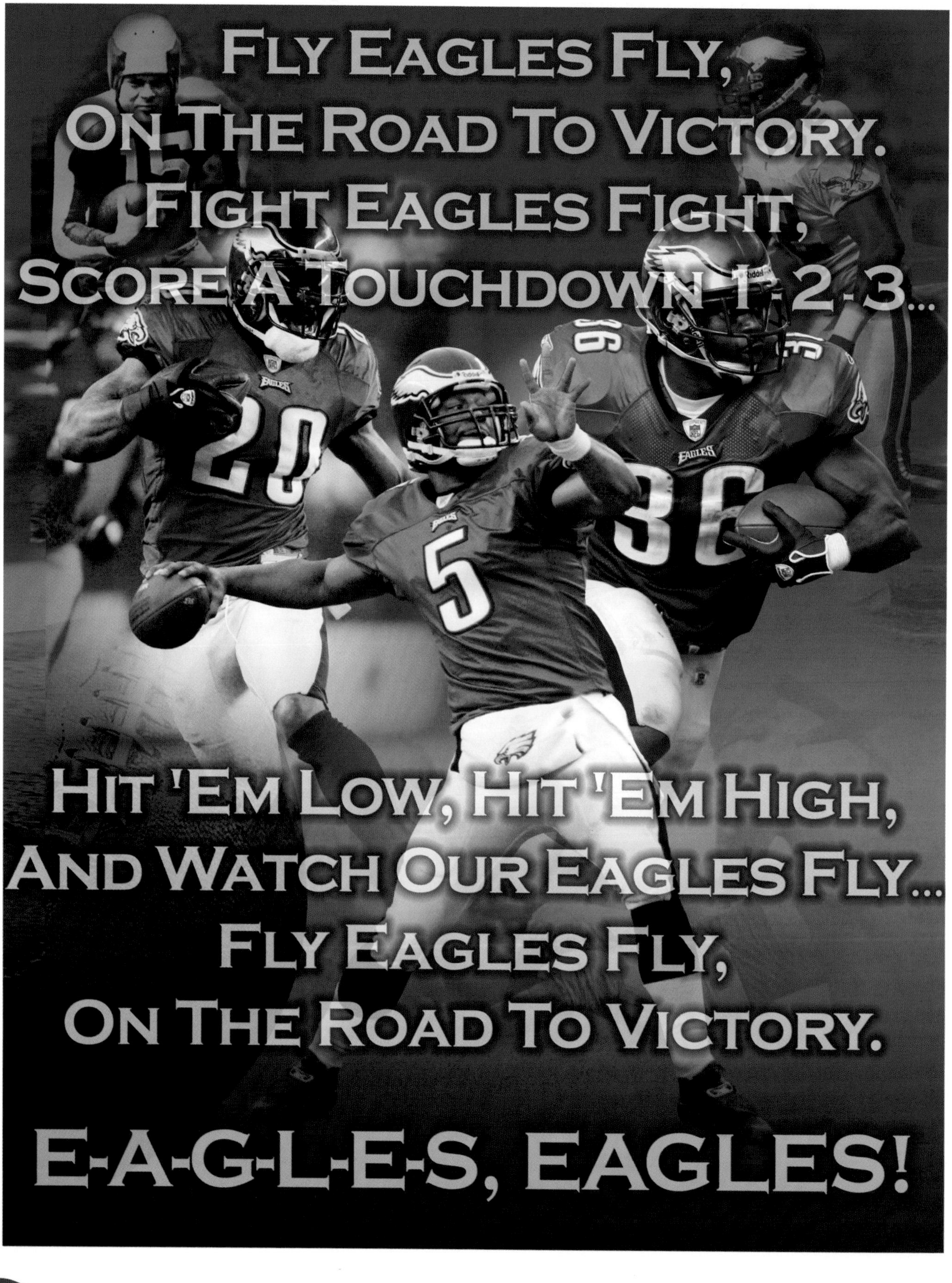
Fly Eagles Fly,
On The Road To Victory.
Fight Eagles Fight,
Score A Touchdown 1-2-3...
Hit 'Em Low, Hit 'Em High,
And Watch Our Eagles Fly...
Fly Eagles Fly,
On The Road To Victory.
E-A-G-L-E-S, EAGLES!

Philadelphia Eagles Logos

Primary Logos

1948-1968

1973 - 1995

1969 - 1972

1996 - PRESENT

Alternate Logos

1987 - 1995

1987 - 1995

1996 - PRESENT

Script Logos

1973 - 1995

1996 - PRESENT

PHILADELPHIA EAGLES LOGOS

ANNIVERSAY LOGOS

1976

2007

1992

MEMORIAL LOGO

1992

STADIUM LOGOS

1971-2002

2003

Lincoln Financial Field

2003 - PRESENT

- Eagles Youth Partnership (EYP) -

Mission – Teaming up with our community for the future of our kids.

Eagles Youth Partnership – Eagles Youth Partnership (EYP) was founded in 1995 as a 501(c)(3) public charity and serves more than 50,000 low income children in the Greater Philadelphia region each year. EYP believes that every child deserves hope, resources and opportunities. It operates multiple programs related to children's health and education that leverage the star power of the Philadelphia Eagles to improve children's lives. EYP takes its services directly to kids at their schools and in their neighborhoods. These mobile services - the Eagles Eye Mobile and Eagles Book Mobile programs – provide under-privileged children the resources they would, under normal circumstance, not have access to.

Every spring and summer, the **Eagles Book Mobile** travels to hundreds of Philadelphia area schools, libraries, recreation centers and summer camps, entertaining children with interactive storybook readings and distributing free, new books for children to keep. The Book Mobile has traveled more than 39,865 miles, distributing over 323,676 books since 2000. The program reaches 35,000 children each year. While the statistics are impressive and continuously growing, the significance of the Book Mobile runs deeper than the number of books donated. By leveraging the Eagles brand, EYP is changing children's attitudes about reading, ultimately changing their lives.

The **Eagles Eye Mobile** provides free eye exams and prescription glasses to under privileged children throughout the Philadelphia region. Since its inception in 1996, the Eye Mobile has examined more than 23,000 children in the Philadelphia region with a goal of reaching and providing comprehensive eye examinations to an additional 3,300 kids each year. Statistics show that 80 % of the children examined need and receive free prescription glasses, while 16% percent require further eye treatment and are referred to St. Christopher's Hospital for Children. The Eye Mobile functions similarly to the Book Mobile in that it gets children excited about wearing their glasses, thereby improving their chances to reach their potential.

EYP is also known for its annual playground build. Every June, the entire organization including front office staff, coaches and players volunteer one day to transform and renovate a local elementary school's grounds with a play structure, murals, mosaic benches, landscaping and a small turf field. June 4, 2008 marks the 12th annual EYP playground build. One principal summed it up with this statement, "Thank you for turning our prison into a paradise."

Eagles Youth Partnership's Strategy – Eagles Youth Partnership teams the resources of corporate and non-profit partners with the star power of the Eagles organization and its players to:

- Capture the attention of young people and inspire hope

- Improve attitudes and behavior related to learning and healthy lifestyles

- Deliver critical services to those school-aged youth who would be difficult to reach without the leverage of the football team

IN BUSINESS WORLD, BIRDS' BRAND IS SIZZLING

BY DON STEINBERG
INQUIRER STAFF WRITER - 9/12/04

All modesty aside, Eagles mania is sweeping the nation.

The team has never been more popular, Eagles officials will tell you. And the groundswell of love isn't just local. Get ready, Philadelphia: The Eagles just may be one of the premier franchises in all of sports.

"On the business side of this organization, every indicator that we look at is up," said Mark Donovan, the team's senior vice president of business operations. "We're no longer only a strong, dominating local brand. We've become a national brand."

The numbers are compelling, if you let their cumulative effect pound into your head. Of the four most-watched Monday Night Football telecasts last season - nationally - three were Eagles games, including the top-rated Monday night game: the 2003 opener vs. Tampa Bay. No other team showed up twice in that top four.

"The Eagles are a very television-attractive team. The networks like having them on their air," said Charles Coplin, the NFL's vice president of programming.

This year, the Eagles again will play on Monday Night Football three times and on Sunday Night Football once, reaching the league's maximum for prime-time games.

The Eagles' Web site had 22 million page views in August. That's about the same traffic that the site of a newspaper in a fairly large city - the St. Louis Post-Dispatch - gets.

Of the 10 best-selling jerseys at the NFL's Web site, three are Eagles: Terrell Owens, Donovan McNabb and Jevon Kearse. Owens is No. 1. No other team has two players on that list.

This month's GQ magazine features lavish pictorials of Owens and new Eagles linebacker Dhani Jones. McNabb is one of a handful of NFL players featured in multiple national TV advertising campaigns for non-sports products, including Campbell Soup, Visa, Pepsi and Lincoln Financial Group. The NFL made him national spokesman for its "Take a Player to School" program, with ads sponsored by JC Penney.

"When we found out that Donovan was going to be the spokesperson, we breathed a sigh of relief. It made our jobs a lot easier," said Brian Weston, account supervisor at the Gepetto Group, which produced the commercials and specializes in youth marketing. "For the casual fan, kids can really see him as a big brother. For the hard-core football fan, he symbolizes many of the things that a superhero does, like the ability to save the day."

Forbes magazine this month ranks the Eagles as the fifth most valuable NFL team, at $833 million, with an estimated $198 million in annual revenue.

That puts the Eagles above every team in every other sport, including the New York Yankees, which the magazine last put at $832 million. Moving into Lincoln Financial Field with a lucrative stadium-naming deal and more luxury suites made the Eagles the magazine's biggest gainer in value among NFL teams, rising by 35 percent. (Though the team's debt is among the league leaders, too.)

Eagles president Joe Banner attributes the popularity to the team itself.

"Sometimes we get criticized for not running the ball, but the truth is, most fans find it more exciting to follow a team that throws the ball a lot on offense and blitzes a lot on defense," Banner said.

It makes you wonder why the team felt it needed to launch a local advertising campaign recently to show how intense fans can be. Games at the Linc are sold out, after all, and fan loyalty doesn't need an ad campaign to be evident. Eagles games last season on Channel 29 averaged a 52 percent Nielsen share locally, meaning more than half of the households with the TV on were watching the Birds. The estimated 20,000 people at an Eagles training-camp session one day in August outnumbered attendance at several major-league baseball games.

The new TV ads, beautifully filmed and funny, with the running theme of "You Can't Script This Stuff," show diehards ranting and performing to profess their passion. They include Roy Lopez, a locksmith from Northeast Philly who displays an Eagles tattoo on his arm that he got "the year the Eagles won three games. Everyone told me to cut off my arm. Now everyone wants to kiss my arm," he says in the ad.

Lopez was among the 10,000 or so fans who traveled to Miami last season for a game against the Dolphins. "All you could hear at the game was Eagles fans," he said.

EAGLES IN THE COMMUNITY

Fan demand has allowed the Eagles this year to create what is likely the single highest-priced ticket plan in the NFL, something Donovan called "V-V-VIP" seating. Touchdown Club seats, on the 50-yard line at field level, cost $7,500 per season and are sold only in pairs. They include parking alongside the stadium, a road trip to a game in Washington, a breakfast with Banner and Eagles owner Jeffrey Lurie, and two-hour parties before every game.

"It's as high-end as high-end can get," Donovan said. "Raw bar, crab legs, top-shelf liquor, full open bar."

Mike Sheridan is a fan who bought six Touchdown Club seats this year.

"I'm going to meet Bruce Willis and Jon Bon Jovi. They're guests this week at the Touchdown Club party," he said.

So why do the Eagles need "image" commercials? It's about strengthening the brand even more.

"To continue to grow the brand and grow aspiration to be part of the brand," Donovan said. "We continue to try to get fans at a very young age and make them loyal to the Philadelphia Eagles so that 10, 20, 30 years down the road, they continue to be loyal to the Philadelphia Eagles, whether they're in Dallas, Texas, or Fort Lauderdale, Fla."

Some perspective is in order amid the hype, of course. Yes, McNabb does TV commercials - but so do Peyton Manning, Jerome Bettis, Tony Gonzalez and other NFL stars. Owens is on the cover of the new ESPN football video game - but Baltimore's Ray Lewis is on the more established John Madden game.

Eagles fans around the country gather to watch games at places such as Choppers Sports Grill in Denver and Texadelphia in Houston. But there are Green Bay Packers fan clubs in Istanbul and Okinawa.

"I have to say, the best brand in football is the Cowboys. It always has been and more than likely always will be," said Becky Wallace, editor of the Team Marketing Report, based in Chicago. "They have the highest-ranked brand every year in the NFL. They sell the most merchandise."

Banner won't mention Dallas, but he acknowledged that, if there is a kind of sports-franchise Hall of Fame, the Eagles may be only just setting foot inside.

"When you think about the legacy of the Yankees, Dodgers, Red Sox, Manchester United - and, when I was young, the Montreal Canadiens - I think we'd have to have a much longer, sustained period of success to be able to put ourselves in the class with those teams," he said. "But I do think that if you took a snapshot of this moment, right now, we're as popular as any franchise anywhere in any sport."

Sure. But let's see how they do against the Giants.

Hot TV

The top "Monday Night Football" telecasts in 2003, by national ratings:

1. Sept. 8: Tampa Bay Buccaneers at EAGLES, 13.0.

2. Sept. 15: Dallas Cowboys at New York Giants, 12.9.

3. Dec. 15: EAGLES at Miami Dolphins, 12.6.

4. Nov. 10: EAGLES at Green Bay Packers, 12.5.

Source: ABC-TV. Does not include non-Monday ABC games.

The top-selling player jerseys at the NFL's Web site:

1. Terrell Owens, EAGLES

2. Michael Vick, Atlanta

3. Chad Johnson, Cincinnati

4. Donovan McNabb, EAGLES

5. Brian Urlacher, Chicago

6. Eli Manning, N.Y. Giants

7. Priest Holmes, Kansas City

8. Roy Williams, Dallas

9. Tom Brady, New England

10. Jevon Kearse, EAGLES

Source: NFL. Includes sales from April 30 through Aug. 15 at NFLshop.com.

EAGLES AIM OUTREACH EFFORTS AT YOUTH

Eye exams and the Book Mobile are among top projects.

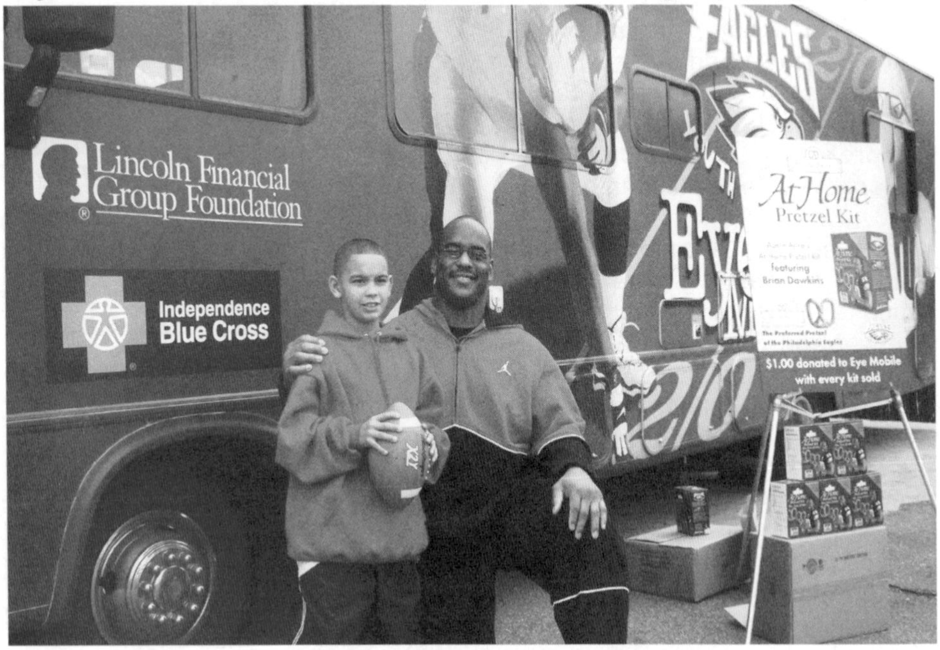

Eagles pro-bowl guard and co-founder of the Eagle Eye Mobile, Jermane Mayberry, has a catch with **a** third grader who had just completed his eye exam at the Eagles Eye Mobile.

BY MARC NARDUCCI
INQUIRER STAFF WRITER 6/01/06

More than any crunching block or all-star selection or even competing in the NFL's biggest showcase, the Super Bowl, former Eagles offensive lineman Jermane Mayberry will more likely be remembered for his vision.

Entering his second season with the New Orleans Saints, after spending nine years as an Eagle, Mayberry is legally blind in his left eye. But that didn't prevent him from seeing a better way for youngsters.

And his willingness to give back has made him a symbol of the Eagles Youth Partnership (EYP), the team's nonprofit charitable wing.

EYP is helping many disadvantaged youngsters see better, read more clearly, and simply feel good knowing that others are reaching out to them.

Next Thursday, the EYP will hit another landmark when it builds its 10th playground in the city. The entire Eagles organization - including the players and coaching staff - will be on hand to work at the event. Virtually all EYP projects are geared toward health and education for underprivileged youngsters.

Mayberry, the Eagles' first-round draft choice in 1996, donated $100,000 from his first multiyear contract to EYP. Of that, $50,000 was donated up front; four other payments of $12,500 followed. And soon after, the Eye Mobile was created.

"It's the best money I ever spent," Mayberry said in a recent phone interview.

The Eye Mobile gives free examinations and provides glasses and follow-up medical care to disadvantaged youngsters in Philadelphia and Chester.

By the end of this school year, the Eye Mobile will have examined more than 16,200 youngsters, including about 3,200 this year, according to EYP senior program manager Jennifer Stredler.

Mayberry suffers from amblyopia - an underdeveloped optic nerve - but didn't undergo his first eye exam until he was 16.

"If I had an eye exam when I was younger, this could have been prevented," Mayberry said.
Then pausing, he added, "I've been to the Super Bowl and the Pro Bowl, but nothing compares with what the Eye Mobile has accomplished."

Besides the Eye Mobile and the building of playgrounds, another popular EYP project has been its Book Mobile. From March until the end of the summer, the EYP sends out its Book Mobile, which includes an actor in full costume who reads to the youngsters. After school ends, the Book Mobile is to travel to places such as libraries, homeless shelters and summer camps.

According to the EYP, the Book Mobile reaches about 40,000 underprivileged Delaware Valley youngsters a year, each of whom receives a free book.

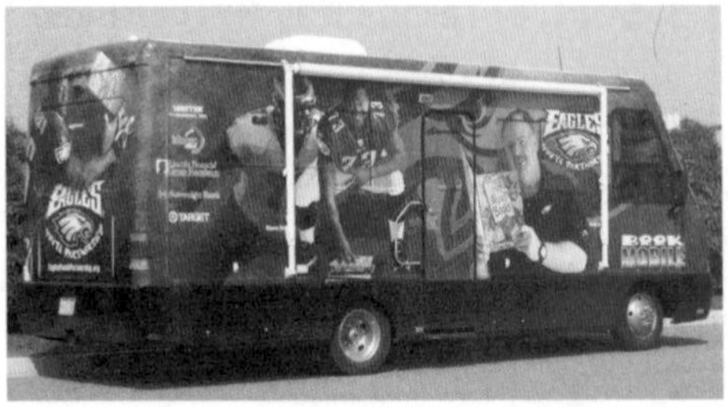

"Many times, the books we give the youngsters are the first ones they ever own," said Christina Lurie, the wife of owner Jeffrey Lurie and president of EYP.

The Eagles Youth Partnership is the brainchild of the Luries. Growing up in Boston, Jeffrey Lurie was a fanatical Red Sox fan. He saw how the Red Sox worked closely with the Jimmy Fund, the Super Bowl of charities that has done much for cancer research.

"The Jimmy Fund was a good example of a sports organization that was proactive and not just writing out checks," Jeffrey Lurie said. "When we bought the team, we wanted to make a significant impact on community service."

While the Luries had ideas, they needed somebody to implement the game plan. That person is Sarah Martinez-Helfman, the true quarterback of EYP. She has been the executive director since its inception, June 12, 1995.

"Sarah is a dynamo, and her heart is dedicated to making a difference in the greater Philadelphia area and beyond," Jeffrey Lurie said.
Martinez-Helfman is a tireless worker, whose altruistic spirit is shared by the rest of her five full-time staff members, along with other contracted workers and several interns and volunteers.

"We wanted to think outside of the box to maximize and leverage the impact we can have," Martinez-Helfman said.

The Eye Mobile is a perfect example.

The School District of Philadelphia mandates that all schools do vision screenings. The Eye Mobile examines those youngsters who fail the initial screening. Youngsters could need anything from just a pair of new glasses to surgery.

"We have so many children uninsured or underinsured, and these societal ills really stopped us from doing what we should be doing," said Diane Davis, the vision coordinator of the School District of Philadelphia. "The Eye Mobile has been wonderful because it helped so many youngsters and even if surgery is needed, if there is no other way to pay for it, the EYP handles it."

If anybody can literally see the benefits of the Eye Mobile, it's Rasheed McDuffie, a 10-year-old third grader at the Stephen Girard Elementary School in South Philadelphia.

"I got left back in the first grade because I couldn't see well," said McDuffie, who received a pair of glasses after being examined in the Eye Mobile. "It's so much better now."

On a warm spring day last month, Eagles five-time Pro Bowl safety Brian Dawkins accompanied the Eye Mobile as it visited with youngsters.

Dawkins, who wears glasses, is one of the hardest-hitting and most intimidating players in the NFL. Yet around children, his tough-guy reputation takes a major hit with the compassionate way he deals with them.

As somebody who wears glasses, Dawkins had a simple message for the youngsters.

"For some kids it can be terrifying to have to change his or her appearance and wear glasses," Dawkins said.

The message I try to give is that it's all right to wear glasses."

The Eagles have been so successful that other groups are following suit.

The Cleveland Browns hope to open an Eye Mobile in at-risk areas this fall, and members of the organization have sought out the Eagles for advice.

"The Eagles are really the model for NFL teams and have set the bar," said Renee Harvey, director of community relations for the Browns. "They have been extremely forthcoming in what they have learned, and you can't buy that kind of help they have given us."

Last year, the Eagles Youth Partnership won the inaugural Steve Patterson Sports Philanthropy Award, presented by the Robert Wood Johnson Foundation and the Sports Philanthropy Project.

"What impressed me is how the Eagles leveraged their resources in a strategic fashion that is unique," said Greg Johnson, the executive director of the Sports Philanthropy Project. "We took a look at the Eye Mobile. It's very unique to have players and a team's foundation to work so closely together."

The spirit of giving is evident in all workers. Carter Liotta is an optometrist for St. Christopher's Hospital for Children, the EYP's medical partner for the Eye Mobile. Liotta is employed by the hospital, but his job is to work each day during the school year in the Eye Mobile, examining the youngsters. He says he doesn't consider it a job.

"These kids live in a world that a lot of people never see," Liotta said. "For many, trying to get them to a doctor is a daunting prospect, but about 80 percent of the people we examine end up needing glasses."

As one of its fund-raising efforts, the Eagles will hold their annual carnival Aug. 27 at Lincoln Financial Field. Last year, the event raised more than $1 million, with the proceeds going toward EYP.

This money enables the EYP to continue the projects that have had a profound impact on the community.

"When we look at despair and have a sense that we can do something that can bring resources to children, that is powerful," said Martinez-Helfman, the EYP executive director. "That is what keeps us going and striving to do more each and every day."

The Eagles are No. 1. Forbes magazine recently named the team the fastest-growing brand in the NFL. The franchise's 75th-anniversary celebration has also provided a marketing boost.

A FORCE IN THE MARKET

The Eagles are a major success off the field as well as on it.

By Larry Eichel
INQUIRER SENIOR WRITER 9/09/07

In case you haven't noticed, it's the Eagles' 75th-anniversary season.

To passionate fans, that qualifies as a genuine historical milestone.

To the folks who run the franchise, it also qualifies as a major marketing moment, for the very reason that it's linked to something real.

The organization is making the most of it, using its corporate partners to help reach fans eager to honor the past and deepen their connections with a team that is central to the local fabric of life.

All of which helps explain why Forbes magazine recently labeled the Eagles the hottest (meaning the fastest-growing, not the most valuable) brand in the NFL.

"Branding is really trying to make people feel good about being associated with you," team president

Joe Banner said. "When you think about it that way, what we're doing [with the anniversary] is so natural, so simple. It almost takes care of itself."

For the Eagles, taking care of the anniversary means having the Lincoln Financial Group sponsor the search for the 75 greatest Eagles Fan Moments.

And having Dunkin' Donuts help identify the 75 greatest living Philadelphians - while plastering the anniversary logo on coffee cups and gift cards and sponsoring, along with Sovereign Bank, a TV show on the team's history.

And Taco Bell and KFC use plastic, 75th-anniversary cups at their restaurants.

And Miller Lite put out special-edition 75th-anniversary cans while Bud Light sells midnight-green, anniversary-logo aluminum bottles - which are certain to decorate rec rooms throughout the region for years to come.

Check out the selection of team jerseys at the Eagles Pro Shop at Lincoln Financial Field

EAGLES IN THE COMMUNITY

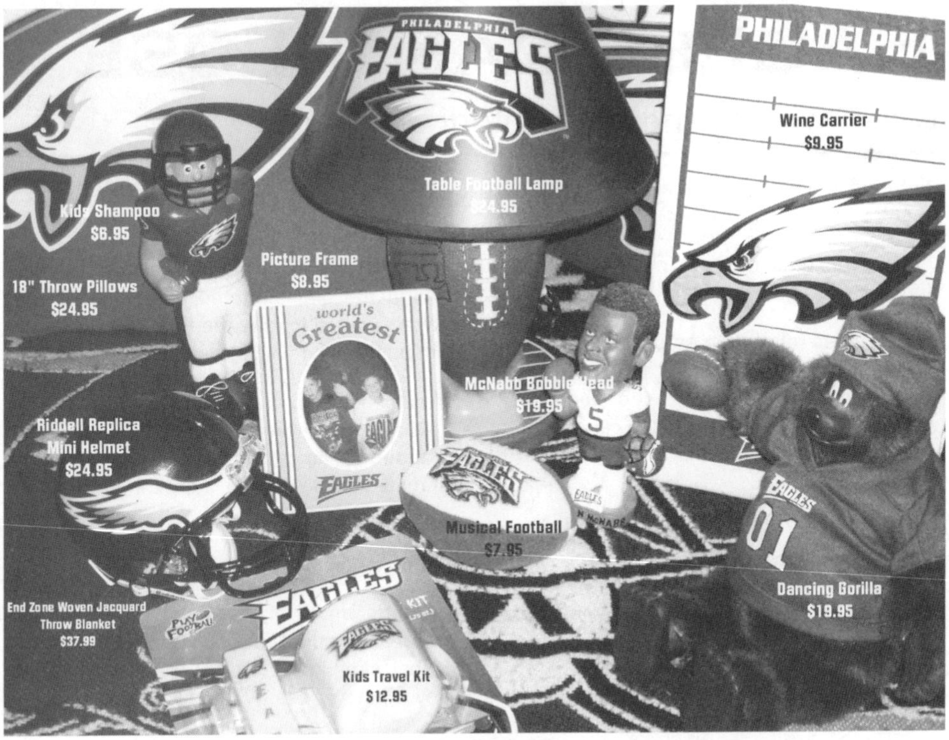

Assorted Eagles merchandise available in retail stores

Not to mention the sale of all the 75th-anniversary jerseys, T-shirts and baseball caps done in the original pale blue and gold colors. Or the various items throughout the grocery store bearing the ubiquitous logo.

"Our sponsors have exceeded our expectations in getting behind the 75th anniversary," said Mark Donovan, the team's senior vice president of business operations. "Our hope is that they'll tell us when it's over that it exceeded their expectations. Early returns are that it will."

In a league of the haves and the have-mores, the Eagles reside very much in the latter category.

According to Forbes, the franchise is the fifth most valuable in the NFL, worth more than $1 billion as of a year ago, trailing only the Redskins, Cowboys, Patriots and Texans.

The Eagles' top-of-the-line revenue stream, the team's top executives say, enhances the organization's ability to put a winning team on the field, even in a league where the salary cap restricts how much teams can spend on players.

Having all of that cash flowing in allows the Eagles to spend more than most teams on coaches, facilities and, at times, signing bonuses for key players.

"It's why we try our best to maximize our revenue," said owner Jeffrey Lurie. "It ups the odds of success on the field. In a sense, we're trying to have a business model that can give us the best chance of on-field success."

Along with their corporate sponsors, Eagles executives see themselves as the stewards of a proud, deeply entrenched brand that would, they acknowledge, surely survive in the hands of almost any leadership group.

The team's prime sponsors include Lincoln Financial, NovaCare Rehabilitation, Chrysler, Sovereign Bank, Pepsi, Anheuser-Busch, Miller Brewing, US Airways, Acme Markets, Thomas Jefferson University Hospital and GlaxoSmithKline.

New to the ranks for 2007 is SCA, a Swedish-based paper-products manufacturer with its U.S. headquarters in Philadelphia.

Team officials say that the Eagles, who consider themselves an environmentally conscious business, made the initial contact with SCA, asking about using the company's recycled paper towels, tissues and napkins at the Linc.

Soon thereafter, the Swedish company decided that a full corporate partnership might be in order.

As a result, the huge lounge on the club level on the east side of the stadium, which has never had a name sponsor, will henceforth be known as the SCA Club and Suites.

So the Eagles brand is in fine shape as the team begins its fifth season at the Linc and its 14th under Lurie's ownership.

The team raised ticket prices over the winter with hardly a peep of protest from season-ticket holders, who know full well that the region is full of fans willing to pay those prices and more.

The television ratings for Eagles games remain at a level that other major-market teams can't touch.

"We don't kid ourselves," Banner said. "We think we've done some things that have helped incrementally. But we fundamentally inherited a situation ripe for huge success, that was teed up for us to capture in this way."

ONE WAY EAGLES CAN'T LOSE

Game-day efforts show why they're ecological champs.

BY SANDY BAUERS
Inquirer Staff Writer 9/23/07

In the parking lot, the barbecue grills were sizzling.

In the locker rooms, players were taping up.

In a control room, electrical foreman Herb Keyser pressed "enter" on his keyboard.

And high above Lincoln Financial Field, 572 lights, 2,000 watts each, began sucking down enough juice to power 1,142 typical homes.
It was 6:30 p.m. Monday. Two hours before kickoff.

Major sporting events such as Eagles games are a big energy drain - and not just the emotional kind.

They can produce mountains of trash and use rivers of water, not to mention the tankers of fuel that 70,000-plus fans burn to get there.

But four years after steadily implementing ways to reduce their environmental footprint, the Eagles - though not the winningest team in the NFL - are certainly the greenest.
Maybe even the greenest in all of pro sports, NFL spokesman Brian McCarthy said.

The eco-games begin with the tickets and programs (on more than 40 tons of recycled paper a year) and end with a double trash pickup geared to send every plastic bottle off for recycling.

The Eagles purchase so much renewable energy - 30 percent of it from wind and the burning of landfill methane gases - they claim to be the biggest buyer in the state. The University of Pennsylvania, ranked 20th in the nation by the Environmental Protection Agency, may beg to differ. But Penn bases its calculation on total amount purchased, while the Eagles factor in the number of employees.

It's the equivalent of powering all 10 home games (including preseason) on wind, so the Eagles now boast they're carbon-neutral.

It didn't help Monday's game, a 20-12 loss to the Washington Redskins. But while fans were trashing the team, environmental advocates thought the Eagles were awesome.
John Hanger of Citizens for Pennsylvania's Future will give the team an eco-award next month.

"They've won some very important victories for clean air and clean water," he said.

The Eagles reimburse employees for buying wind power at home - 112 employees have taken them up on it, at a cost of about $7.25 each per month - and Hanger can't find another company in the nation that goes this far.

During the off-season, the NFL will encourage other teams to follow the Eagles' eco-lead, although McCarthy doubted any would adopt their eco-slogan: "Go Green."

Here's how it played out Monday:

8 p.m.

On the field at the 50-yard line
Linebacker Takeo Spikes, 6-foot-2 and 242 pounds, charged over from midfield, halted, turned, and then charged back, catching a short toss.

Just feet away, teensy by comparison, Eagles owner Christina Weiss Lurie smiled and chatted with friends.

In the Go Green program, she is the one calling the plays. Lurie hired Los Angeles environmental and marketing consultant Tim Sexton, who had organized Philadelphia's LiveAid concert.

The team didn't just recycle; it began buying recycled materials. Sexton produced a procurement guide for green cleaning supplies, compact fluorescent lightbulbs, bio-based paints.

After an energy audit, the team ratcheted down the field's heaters. The Eagles figure the project will save enough electricity to power 275 homes and pay for itself within two years.

Last summer, atop the Eagles' corporate headquarters, workers finished installing an array of solar panels that track the sun, producing 30 percent more power than a fixed system.

"It's important that we're successful on the field, and off the field," Lurie said optimistically. "The two sides mirror each other."

8:29 p.m.
On the field

The cheerleaders shook their pom-poms. Behind the giant inflated eagle's head, the players waited to take the field. The momentum built. The music blared. Fly, Eagles, fly...

Last week, the players drove to the game. Next month, they will fly about 1,000 miles to take on the Minnesota Vikings and release a lot more carbon dioxide, a greenhouse gas.

So they've been planting trees, which consume carbon dioxide, to offset it.

A Tufts University study has pooh-poohed the idea for individuals who pay some company they don't know to plant trees in a location they will never see. Will the trees even live?

But the Eagles have picked public spots right here. Donating $125,000 to Philadelphia's TreeVitalize program, they planted 332 oaks, cherries, plums, ginkgos and more around 25 Philadelphia public elementary schools - 16 of which had no trees. More were planted at newly renovated Franklin Square.

Eagles Forest, a 6.5-acre site at Neshaminy State Park in Bensalem, Bucks County

A major Eagles forest - hush-hush for now - is in the planning stages with the GoZero program of the national nonprofit Conservation Fund.

9:34 p.m.
The concourse

The Eagles kicked a field goal. For many fans, apparently, time for a beer. A worker for Aramark, the concession operator, picked up a cup and opened the tap.

On Monday, fans gulped their way through 88,000 cups.

All the cups were corn-based plastic, which the Eagles say takes 50 percent less petroleum to make than a regular plastic cup. And instead of taking a few centuries to break down, the cups biodegrade in as little as 50 days. (Supposedly, an Eagles employee inadvertently tested this timetable; his car's backseat will never be the same.)

These large recycling bins are located throughout the Linc, home of the Go Green program.

For the plastic water and soda bottles, the Eagles place recycling containers every 46 feet throughout the concourse. Experts who study such matters have determined that a typical person, not finding an appropriate receptacle within 23 feet, will just drop an item.

If the fans hadn't quite caught on - many stuck their biodegradable cups into the recycling containers for plastic bottles - so be it.

Likewise, out in the parking lot, bottles and cans were stacked around and on top of a recycling bin the size of a Porta-John.

By the front gates - no outside beverages may be taken in - workers would later scoop up discarded cups and cans by the shovelful and place them in the barrels the fans missed.

Paul Smits, facilities manager for Aramark, watched almost greedily, calculating the recycling potential.

"That's one of my next challenges," he said. "How can I get that?"

10:40 p.m.
SCA Americas box

It was the third quarter. The Eagles fumbled; 10-6 Redskins.

In a suite high above the field, the carpeting (with recycled fibers) was lush. The room's three TVs, like all those in the stadium, had been replaced a while back and recycled. The dinner was laid out next to biodegradable plates made partly from bamboo.

And the napkins were trash. At least two times over. Probably they were high-end paper, then newsprint, now this.

Don Lewis, a vice president with SCA Americas, fingered one appreciatively. He pointed with pride to tiny black dots in the weave. "We call those recycle verification specks."

Lewis' company supplies all the stadium's paper products. Last year, fans went through 17 tons of it, including about 1,756 miles of toilet tissue.

This year, the products are "tree-free," and SCA says its processes will save a lakeful of water, half a ton of air pollutants, 70 cubic yards of landfill space, and enough power to run 10 homes for a year.

Inside a concourse women's room at halftime, Ashley Bittle of Medford Lakes was "impressed." Kate Federico of Philadelphia said it was "smart" to take on such a globally important issue.

Sue Gettlin of Fort Washington had more immediate concerns: "I don't care what it's made of," she said of the toilet tissue. "I'm just glad it's there."

10:54 p.m.
The big screen

The player was ruled down by contact before he fumbled, but the score got worse: 13-6 Redskins. The crowd grew somber.

But No. 21 was smiling. He was up on the big screen, talking to fans. "Hey, this is William James," he said. "Carpool with your friends or take public transportation when you're headed to the game. And fill up your gas tank at night to reduce harmful vapor emissions. Be a playmaker, and Go Green."

It's one more way the Eagles are trying to get their message out, and that impressed Penn Future's Hanger.

Who better, he asked, than a sports team? "They're just so influential in our society."

12:28 a.m.
Top of the stadium

The team had lost. The fans had gone. The lights had dimmed. A machine vacuumed the field, towed by a truck that uses biodiesel. The next day, crews would spritz the turf with organic fertilizer. In the highest section of the stadium, about 100 workers pulled on latex gloves and shook out their plastic bags.

Eco-friendly tickets made from recycled paper.

Jerome Belo of Philadelphia has been working Philadelphia stadiums for 27 years. They used to put all the refuse in one bag. Now they work in pairs, the first guy picking up the recyclables.

About 1:30 a.m., three figures trudged wearily up the steps. They were with Philadelphia's Blue Mountain Recycling Co., and they had spent the night assessing. "A phenomenal job down on the concourse," said Bob Anderson, business development manager.

Since 2003, the Eagles have recycled more than 375 tons of materials. The plastic bottles will be made into new plastic bottles, carpeting or fleece clothing.

The Heineken cans go to Anheuser-Busch; they will be new cans within 60 days.

So if you're drinking a Bud Light, Anderson said with a grin, "it could be out of a Heineken can."

Meanwhile, the cleanup workers, who wouldn't be finished until after sunup, continued their bending and picking.

Just visible down on the field was one of the Eagles' banners: "Go Green. When we recycle, everybody wins."

To see a slideshow of a night at the Linc featuring the Eagles' recycling efforts, go to http://go.philly.com/greeneagles

PHILLY'S STUDENTS FIRST

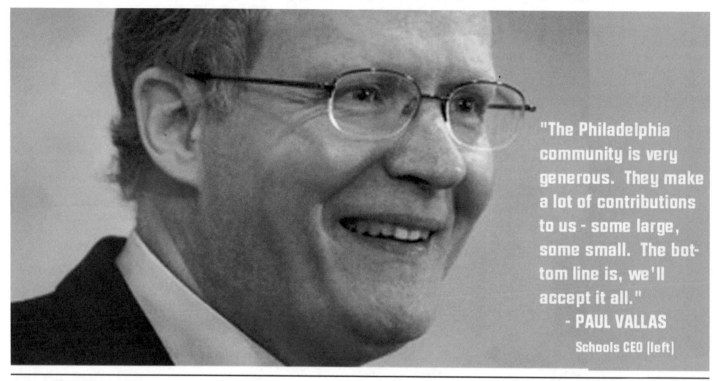

"The Philadelphia community is very generous. They make a lot of contributions to us - some large, some small. The bottom line is, we'll accept it all."
- PAUL VALLAS
Schools CEO (left)

By Mensah M. Dean
staff writer Philadelphia Daily News
5/25/05

PHILADELPHIA school officials today are expected to approve a $1.9 billon budget for the 2005-06 school year.

Not included in the plan are 400 pairs of sneakers worth $20,000. And 56,000 batteries valued at $50,000. And playground equipment, a mural and mosaic art work costing $92,400.

They're just three of the latest gifts the district has received from the corporate community, specifically from Sneaker Villa, Energizer with Office Depot and the Eagles, respectively.

In a district where an estimated 71 percent of the 185,000 students are from low-income homes, and 11,000 are homeless, such gifts are more than gravy, said district officials.

Those gifts help city, state and federal funds go further, said the officials, who have set a goal of topping last year's cumulative donations of $6 million.

"The Philadelphia community is very generous. They make a lot of contributions to us – some large, some small. The bottom line is, we'll accept it all, " said district CEO Paul Vallas.

Some schools get a big helping hand from alumni, such as Central High School, whose grads raised $4.5 million to build the school's high-tech library.

To make sure the giving reaches all 270-plus schools, School Reform Commission Chairman James Nevels has ordered the creation of Philadelphia's Children First Fund.

To be formally announced before the next school year, the tax- exempt charitable organization's mission "is to facilitate individual and organizational giving to create a permanent source of philanthropic capital to the school district."

C. Kent McGuire, dean of the Temple's College of Education, will be chairman of the fund's board, said Meghan McKeon-Mereno, manager of the district's Foundation & Business Partnerships office.

"The economic health of the entire region and the future success of our business community are directly related to what we do to help our schools today," Nevels said in 2002, shortly after taking office.

In New York City a similar effort is under way, Caroline Kennedy Schlossberg, President John F. Kennedy's daughter, is in her third year heading the office charged with wooing private dollars to public schools.

Philadelphia and New York are on the right track, said Michael Casserly, executive director of the Council of Great City Schools, a coalition of the nation's largest school systems.

"It sounds like a good idea. I suspect some corporations and foundations feel more comfortable giving to an entity like that than they do donating to the general fund of the school district," Casserly said, "Giving to the general fund makes it more likely that the donation will get lost in the overall operation."

The Eagles may not give star receiver Terrell Owens another nickel, but to the school district, the team gives plenty.

"You would be hard-pressed to find another NFL team that does as much as we have done," said Mark Donovan, the team's senior vice president.

Just how much the Eagles have donated, however, has not been tallied. But in addition to the $92,400 for a new playground at R.R. Wright Elementary School, the team has built eight other playgrounds over the years.

More than $500,000 has been invested in literacy grants to support the district's 100 Book Challenge program, and $125,000 was donated to plant trees at 24 schools. Thousands more have gone directly to teachers and for student awards.

The Eagles Eye Mobile provides free comprehensive eye exams and prescription glasses for thousands of uninsured children in the community.

And then there is the Eagles Eye Mobile. Donovan said since 1996, 14,000 Philadelphia and Chester students have received free exams. More than 75 percent actually needed prescription glasses – and got them.

"When you think of 14,000 kids, and 75 percent getting glasses." Donovan said, "this is a dedicated commitment to the kids in our school district."

The 56,000 AAA batteries were given to students who use calculators in math and science, and during last month's state standardized test.

The sneakers are going to first graders who excelled in this year's Power Hour after-school reading program.

"We are community-oriented and community-minded. Part of the philosophy of the company is, we go into communities that other businesses choose not to," said Ricky Pegram, of Sneaker Villa, a Reading-based company that moved into the Philadelphia retail market four years ago.

"We are not a business that is looking to take, take, take." Pegram added. "We have a track record of giving back. We want to take the lead, and we challenge anybody to take us upon it and be part of this."

In February, the largest gift in the history of the reform commission came in the form of a $4.3 million grant from the Broad Foundation, of Los Angeles, a philanthropic organization whose mission is to improve urban public education.

The district is using the money to attract and train principals in its leadership academy.

Mitchell & Ness, the celebrated Philadelphia-based maker of authentic professional vintage sports jerseys and accessories, gave more than it had intended last year.

Company president and CEO Peter Capolino had agreed to cover the $500 prize for the lone winner of an oratorical contest, Vallas recalled. But the field so impressed him, that Capolino ended up giving $500 to nine other students who had done well – one from each of the district's regions.

"Some are large, some are small, some are modest, some are expensive," Vallas said of the donations.

"But they are all equally appreciated."

FONDEST EAGLES MEMORIES

This book would not be complete without reliving some memories from the past. I was fortunate to have the opportunity to talk openly with many former and current Eagles players to hear what some of their fondest memories were while playing for the Eagles. Many spoke about the 1960 Championship game, others the playoffs, while others talked about their personal feelings becoming an Eagle. It was interesting to compare how different the players' memories were from some of the fans to whom I spoke.

Here is a collection of Eagles memories that I put together from former and current players, local sportscasters and, of course, the fans. In addition, I included some defining moments in Eagles history.

DECEMBER 18, 1949
(LA Memorial Coliseum, Los Angeles, CA) On the heels of their 7-0 victory in the 1948 NFL Championship Game, the Eagles returned to the title game in 1949 and topped the Rams, 14-0. Here Steve Van Buren (15), who logged an Eagles' post-season record 196 rushing yards, and Al Wistert, who would later have his #70 retired, present coach "Greasy" Neale with the game ball. Never before, nor since has an NFL team posted consecutive shutouts in championship play.

One of my fondest Eagles memories would be...
When I had the honor of sitting around a table with Eagle legends Tom Brookshier, Billy Ray Barnes, Theron Sapp, Pete Retzlaff, Tommy McDonald and Jimmy Gallagher, listening to them talk about the '60s as if it were yesterday. You could feel their closeness as they reminisced and told their stories, recalling certain plays, what happened, what didn't happen, and how they would handle things differently today. When I called some other players on the phone, I was amazed as to how cordial they were speaking with me, never rushing, always friendly and certainly accommodating. They enjoyed talking about their past and each one had a better story to tell. As I ended my conversation, almost every player with whom I spoke offered me another name and number for me to contact and obtain other memories. Some former players even called me back to ask if I had enough information. What a great feeling I had bonding with these legends. I now have a totally different outlook when I hear their names mentioned.
By: Eli Kowalski

1947
Only the second player in NFL history to top the 1,000-yard mark, Steve Van Buren rushes for a league record 1,008 yards.

What can I tell you, I'm proud to be the last football player to play both ends of the field. I had some big plays in my career like leveling New York Giants Frank Gifford, knocking the ball loose, and then Chuck Webber recovering the fumble and clinching the win for us. But nothing beats my tackle on Jim Taylor of the Green Bay Packers in the Championship game. We took over the lead on Ted Dean's 5-yard run, and then on the final drive of the game, Packers QB Bart Starr finds Jim Taylor over the middle of the field. Taylor shook off one tackler and was heading my way. From the corner of my eye I saw the clock ticking down.... 15,14,13 seconds. I thought to myself, "There is no way he is going by me." Then, I grabbed him and threw him down on the ground around the nine-yard line. I wouldn't let him get up. I looked up and saw the clock.... 5,4,3,2,1. I heard the gun sound off and the game was over and we won. "You can get up now, Jim," I told him, "this [expletive] game is over." I was so excited, I jumped in the air with my arms raised high. We actually won! We all started jumping around with excitement. What a feeling it was walking off the field at Franklin Field to the cheers of our fans.
By: Chuck Bednarik, Eagles Player 1949-62, and Hall of Fame Class of 1967

Fondest Eagles Memories

They don't get any better than the 60's Championship win! We were such a close bunch of guys, playing a game that no one expected us to win. Van Brocklin was our leader. The whole season was interesting, as we lost the first game and then came back and stole the next nine games. After the nine game winning streak, most of the starters didn't play in the loss to the Steelers. I remember I got hurt in the Cardinals game, when I was blind-sided covering a punt. I also remember our game winning drive for the Championship, having a huge block on Packers Bill Quinlan springing Ted Dean into the end zone for our final touchdown on a five-yard swept. We were a great team, but we didn't know it at the time. It's amazing how many of us are still close, some forty-seven years later. Theron Sapp and Ed Khayat were at my wedding and I still talk to many others once a month.
By: Billy Ray Barnes, Eagles Player 1957-61

One of my favorites is about our 60's Championship team. It was an honor to be member of that squad. Every game was nerve-racking; teams scored points on us and we almost came back every game. We somehow found a way to win. How can you forget Ted Dean's 58-yard kickoff return with Billy Ray Barnes making a huge block for Ted? The mere fact that we held the Packers (who were a high scoring team that year) to only thirteen points was a great accomplishment. They had a last minute drive to beat us, but Chuck Bednarik sat on Jim Taylor as the clock was winding down, and it was over. We were the champions. It was unbelievable! Then, to top off the Championship, our Head Coach Buck Shaw left and Van Brocklin retired after that season. What a year!
By: Ed Khayat, Eagles Player 1958-61, 1964-65 and Head Coach 1971-72

Our '60s Championship team was a bunch of guys who took chances and had big dreams. Looking back, we stole many games on the way to the Championship game. Who would ever think that the Eagles were going to defeat Lombardi's Green Bay Packers? I remember staying the night before the big game in a hotel room at 63rd and Walnut Streets, just getting mentally ready. The team was ready, but were the Green Bay Packers ready for us. The game was a usual come from behind win, when Ted Dean scored on a 5-yard run. All we had to do was hold them. On Green Bay's final drive, Bart Starr, the Packers' quarterback, went over the middle to find Jim Taylor, who did what he did all year and shook off a tackler. The only thing stopping him from scoring was Chuck Bednarik, who not only made the tackle, but wouldn't let Taylor get up to go meet his teammates at the line of scrimmage. As he was sitting on top of Taylor, the clock was winding down and we won! But, honestly, it was a complete team effort that got us the championship.
By: Tom Brookshier, Eagles Player 1953-61

(Franklin Field, Philadelphia) 5-foot, 9-inch, 170-pound flanker Tommy McDonald sets an Eagles' single-game receiving record with 237 yards against the New York Giants. The record would ultimately survive into the next century.

I remember this so vividly it was 1957, Bill Stribling got hurt in my rookie year in the ninth game and they put me out there in his place. I caught two touchdown passes, a 61-yarder and a 25-yarder. So the offensive coordinator Charlie Gauer comes up to me after the game and says, "I think we've found a spot for you." The rest is history!
By: Tommy McDonald, Eagles Player 1957-63 and Hall of Fame Class of 1998

NOVEMBER 20, 1960

(RFK Stadium, Washington, DC) Five TD passes and a club-record 447 passing yards by quarterback Randall Cunningham help the Eagles erase a 20-point deficit and earn a 42-37 win over the Redskins. Cunningham's effort tops the club mark of 437 yards set by Bobby Thomason in 1953.

Easy! At least, from an outstanding play perspective. Randall Cunningham on MNF-1988, takes a shot from Carl Banks of the Giants- keeps his feet, and then throws a touchdown strike to Jimmy Giles cutting across the end zone. SWEEEEEET!
By: Michael Barkann, Sportscaster Comcast Sportsnet

FONDEST EAGLES MEMORIES

FONDEST EAGLES MEMORIES

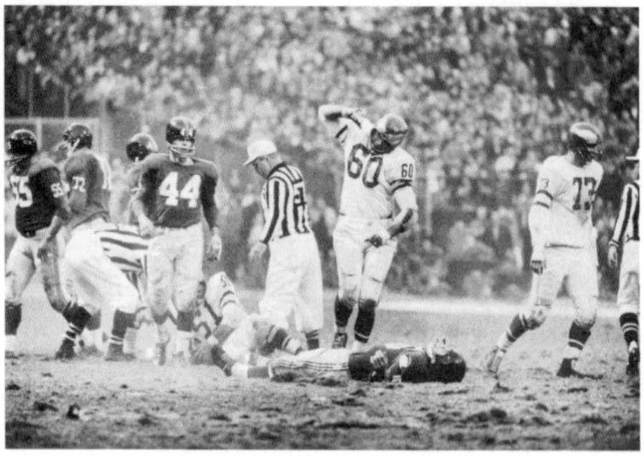

NOVEMBER 20, 1960
(Yankee Stadium, New York City, NY) In a key victory over the Giants that help propel the Eagles toward the 1960 NFL title, linebacker Chuck Bednarik forever etches his name into NFL lore. Bednarik's solid tackle of Frank Gifford causes a fumble and renders the legendary halfback unconscious. Not only is Gifford sidelined for the remainder of the game, he misses the entire 1961 season as well.

It was 1960, I remember going with my dad to my first championship game at Franklin Field. What I remember most is seeing the various Eagles players running on and off the field. However their was one player that stood out because he never came off the field, number 60 Chuck Bednarik, he played with the offense and also with the defense. The man never rested! When the Eagles won the game and championship, I recall the fans rushing onto the field (back then they were allowed) embracing Chuck. He was so big that no one could pick him up in celebration. But the image of Chuck raising his fist in the air to say we won it will always stay in the back of my mind.
By: Steve Sabol, President NFL Films

To this day, Buddy Ryan will deny it, but I was one of the few reporters who knew it to be true. The so-called BOUNTY BOWL of 1989. Luis Zendejas had kicked for Ryan and the Eagles before landing with the Cowboys. He was no buddy of Ryan's. The story goes that Ryan offered a sizeable pack of cash to the first Eagle special teamer who would run the kicker down. Thus, the "Bounty Bowl". It may have been the only thing Ryan-drafted outside linebacker Jessie Small will be remembered for. Drilling Luis he did, knocked him silly.

Word got out about the bounty. Ryan and his loyal players denied it vigorously. I put in a personal call to Zendejas. Not only did he know about the bounty, he knew it was coming. Luis told me, and our channel 3 viewers that Al Roberts, the Eagles' special team coach, had called two days before the game to warn him. In fact, Zendejas had part of the conversation on tape.
I heard it. I knew it to be true.

Bounty Bowl. Fog Bowl. The Body Bag game against the Redskins. Ryan's Eagles were one of a kind.
By: LT, Longtime Philadelphia Sports Anchor

Buddy Ryan's last year, it was the playoff game loss to the Rams on New Years Eve. I remember it was rainy game at the Vet, we just lost and I knew they (the Eagles) would blow the team up and it would never be the same for a long time. Who knew that it was also my last year as a season ticket holder.
By: Carl Henderson

1947
Led by Steve Van Buren (15) who compiles a league high 1,008 rushing yards, and by quarterback Tommy Thompson (11), the Eagles' potent offense helps Philadelphia earn the first of three straight appearances in the NFL Championship game.

One of my fondest Eagles memories would be...
About the Eagles' 1960 championship team. "They got the most out of their ability and played way over their heads, no doubt about it. I've never seen a team that had so much camaraderie. Those guys really loved each other. They fought like hell among themselves sometimes, but at the same time, they loved each other.... They weren't the best team in the league and weren't the best in their own division. But they were the best every Sunday."
By: Bill Campbell, the "Dean" of Broadcasters

Fondest Eagles Memories

DECEMBER 30, 1995

(Veterans Stadium, Philadelphia) In the highest scoring game in NFL post-season history, the Eagles soar to their first playoff win at Veterans Stadium in 15 years. Philadelphia jumps out to a 51-7 lead over Detroit and cruises to a 58-37 victory over the Lions. The Eagles' 58-point barrage marks not only a club record but the third highest output by one team in NFL playoff history.

One of my fondest Eagles memories would be...

One of my all-time favorite eagles moments does not seem to get nearly the attention it deserves. On 12/30/95, the Eagles played a game that will long stand out in my 32 plus years of covering this team. A 58-37 playoff win over the Detroit Lions at Veterans Stadium. The final score was a little misleading because the game was over at half-time and much more one-sided than a 21 point victory. The Vet had a festive atmosphere like rarely before on a New Year's Eve eve. The team advanced to play the Cowboys the following week in Dallas and in preparation, we spent a marvelous week at Dodgertown in Vero Beach. There was not only a feeling of optimism towards the cowboys game, but a general sense that the team under new head coach Ray Rhodes had turned a huge corner and was set for years to come. People seem to remember the loss in Dallas a lot more than the win that preceded it. Part of that is due to Randall's lost playbook and his inability to rally the team after Rodney Peete got hurt. Part of it is due to the east coast blizzard that forced us to stay in Dallas a couple of extra days amidst the gloating cowboys fans. As such, the memorable win over Detroit is mentioned very infrequently. I've long wondered how the rest of Ray's tenure would have turned out if key players from the '95 team like Barnett, McKenzie, Romanowski had remained. Still nothing can take away from a December day when the Eagles rocked Detroit in the playoffs and the Vet rocked along with them in an incredible party environment.

By: Tollie, Fox-29 TV Sportscaster and Radio Personality

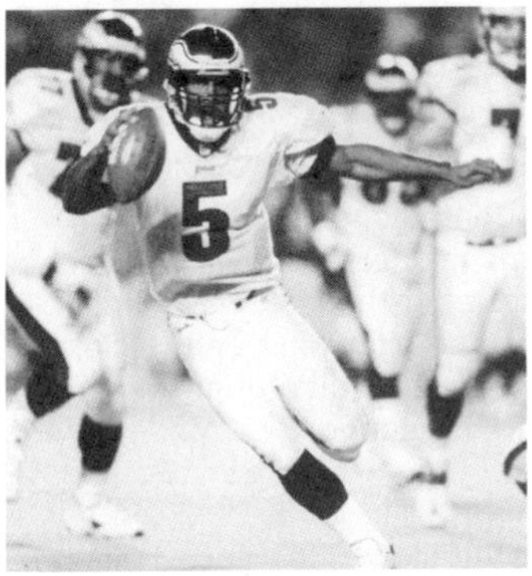

2001

Quarterback Donovan McNabb (#5) leads the Eagles to the NFC East Division crown and a pair of playoff wins that give Philadelphia a berth in the NFC Championship Game (against the Rams at St. Louis) for the first time since the 1980 season.

NOVEMBER 3, 1996

(Texas Stadium, Irving, TX) Clinging to a three-point lead with under a minute to play and with the Cowboys at the Eagles' 3-yard line, James Willis and Troy Vincent author a record setting play. Willis intercepts a pass by Troy Aikman in the end zone and returns the theft to the Dallas10. He then laterals it to Vincent, who finishes off a 104-yard interception return for a TD and a 31-21 win.

Remember Bart Oates or Brad Benson, one of the Giants offensive linemen coming up to me and wondering who was this monster that was lining up over him by the name of Reggie White. Reggie had just joined the team and was kind of underneath the radar. It was the second or third game of the year and they had no idea who he was. There was fear in their eyes like they had seen a ghost, because Reggie had picked one of them up and thrown back into Phil Simms face. They were stuttering and asking me who was number 91 (that's the number Reggie was wearing in his first year).

By: Garry Cobb, Eagles Player 1985-87 and 610 WIP Radio Sportscaster

One of my fondest Eagles memories would be...

As a Delaware Valley native since 1990, I've seen the good, (Andy Reid era) the bad (end of the Ray Rhodes era) and plenty in between. My favorite personal Eagle memory did not even take place on the field. Sunday January 23rd, 2005 at the Linc, NFC Championship against the Falcons. 2 hours prior to kick off I was the host of the pre game show on the Eagles Radio Network. I had also hosted the championship pregames at the Vet and the Linc the two previous years and had confidence in the Birds being victorious in both games. But this seemed different. The air of excitement and fanaticism was the same but the air of confidence was different in the "feel" around the stadium. Mother nature had interceded. The Linc was blanketed in a winter blizzard and it was bone chillingly cold that day. The dome-homed Falcons were coming into this winter wonderland with their potentially slick field handicapped running QB Michael Vick. My pregame show partner former Eagle great Bill Bergey exuded that superior confidence that was "in the air" that day. My premonition was proved out over the 3 plus hours preceding our little pregame show on the frozen tundra that was the Linc that day. Eagles 27-10 and it really wasn't as close as the score indicated and it was on to the until-that-time elusive Super Bowl. Sometimes the build-up is as good as the actual event!

By: Jody MacDonald, Sportscaster Sports Radio 950

FONDEST EAGLES MEMORIES

SEPTEMBER 15, 1991

(Texas Stadium, Irving, TX) Philadelphia's league-leading defense logs a club-record 11 sacks at Dallas, just one shy of the NFL mark. Defensive end Clyde Simmons, who leads the way with a team-record 4.5 sacks of Troy Aikman, is joined in the assault by Jerome Brown (99) and Reggie White (92).

December 20, 1992 home game at Veterans Stadium vs. the Redskins. Whoever wins is in the playoffs. Eagles lead 17-13, Skins have 2nd and Goal from the Eagles' 5 with two seconds left in the game. Washington Quarterback Mark Rypien drops back and flings a pass toward wide out Gary Clark. All-pro cornerback Eric Allen breaks from his coverage to deflect the pass before it can reach its target and with that the Eagles return to the playoffs with a chance to win a Super Bowl they would dedicate to the memory of their fallen teammate Jerome Brown. The quest came up short two weeks later in Dallas, but that moment provided the hope necessary.

By: John Spitzkopf

Holding that NFC Championship trophy over my head. We had been there so many times and hadn't gotten the job done. It was special that we had now earned a trip to the Super Bowl.
By: Brian Dawkins, Eagles Player 1996- current

Probably the NFC Championship game win against the Atlanta Falcons because we had been there so many times without winning it.
By: Jon Runyan, Eagles Player 2000-current

I can make this easy. I will say when the Eagles beat Atlanta in the NFC Championship game on Jan 23, 2005. From the beginning of the game until everyone left the stadium, no one sat in their seat. From Chad Lewis' multi touchdown game and arm over arm seated dance after the last one to Brian Dawkins screaming in a hoarse voice 'Hallelujah' while holding the NFC Championship trophy. There was a group of us who got rooms in the Holiday Inn the night before and I drove us all around town trying to find a place to eat. We spent most of the night in Chickies and Pete's eating. The roads were deserted as we had a brutal snowstorm to deal with that night.

It had to be close to 0 degrees with the wind-chill during the game and it felt like 85 degrees when it ended as the adrenaline just ran through all of us in the stands. Not only was it the first NFC Championship win in 24 years, it was a whitewash. Winning 27-10. Not even that close. What made the game even more special to me was watching Josh Parry come running over to his wife and brother who were sitting in the front row of the end zone I sit in. I was standing at the rail in the end zone as Josh came over. He stood up on a wood block to give his wife a hug and then to his brother. I was right next to them as this was going on. The thing that was truly awesome was the relationship that Josh and his brother had. Josh's brother had his foot amputated a few years before and had the opportunity to play in a game on special teams 'if I am correct on that' for San Jose St. This amazing heart that Josh's brother showed gave Josh the push he needed to perform well enough to make the NFL and play well for the Eagles. I can say this as Josh told me this himself in Jacksonville when I ran into them at their hotel. The emotion shown by Josh to his family made this game even more special to me. You could just feel the energy from them all. Not to mention the energy and emotion rushing through the stadium. Nothing like it!!!!! To top it all off, hearing Brian Dawkins, 'my favorite all-time Eagle' yelling in his hoarse voice 'HALLELUJAH'!!!!!!!!!!!!!!!!!!!!!!!!!!!!!!!!!!!!!

By: Shaun Young

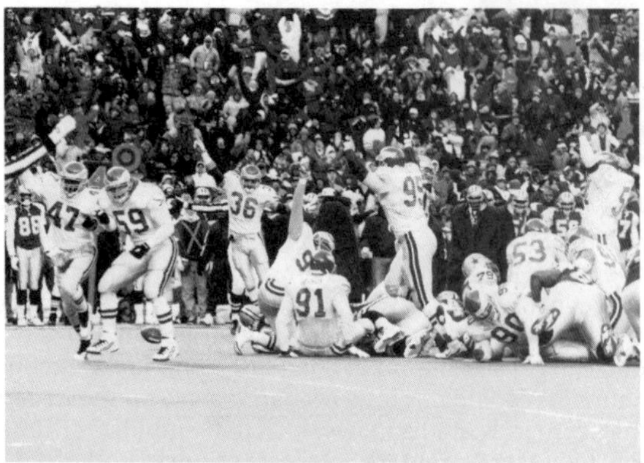

DECEMBER 10, 1995

(Veterans Stadium, Philadelphia) "The fourth-and-1-play" – with the score tied late in the 4th quarter against Dallas, the Eagles' make a dramatic stand. With the ball at their own 29, Dallas goes for it on 4th – and – 1. The Eagles subsequently stuff RB Emmitt Smith's plunge off left guard; but when officials rule that the whistle for the two-minute warning had sounded, the play is blown dead. Dallas then runs the same play again... with the same result. Minutes later, Gary Anderson's field goal gives the Eagles a win that helps propel them into the playoffs.

When the Eagles stopped Emmitt Smith 4 times on the one-yard line and took over on downs.

By: Vinnie "the crumb," 94 WYSP Radio Personality

FONDEST EAGLES MEMORIES

One of my fondest Eagles memories would be...
The day I was drafted. I can remember visiting the Eagles and immediately I wanted to be an Eagle. It was a special time for me and my family when I was drafted.
By: William Thomas, Eagles Player 1998-current

NOVEMBER 4, 1979
(Veterans Stadium, Philadelphia) An imposing wide receiver at 6 feet 8 inches tall, Harold Carmichael reached new heights in a game against Cleveland, establishing a then-NFL record mark of 106 straight games with a reception.

When I made the team in my rookie year. It was 1971 and I was so elated when I went in the training room and saw my name on the list of players who had made the team.
By: Harold Carmichael, Eagles Player 1971-83 and Eagles Director Player Development

One of my fondest Eagles memories would be...
The playoff win over New Orleans in the Superdome. We had lost Jerome Brown before that season so getting to the playoffs and getting the win was especially sweet. We were losing that game in the 4th quarter and scored 26 points in the last 11 minutes of the game.
By: Randall Cunningham, Eagles Player 1985-1996

(Franklin Field, Philadelphia) This legendary photo shows Tommy McDonald being helped to his feet after the fleet-footed Eagle had hauled in a touchdown pass from Norm Van Brocklin in the 1960 NFL Championship vs. Green Bay, McDonald's grab helped the Eagles earn a 17-13 win and the third league title in club history.

That's easy. The 1960 NFL Championship game. I still remember sitting behind the end zone at Franklin Field, Section EE, watching my hero, Tommy McDonald pull in the touchdown pass from Norm Van Brocklin and tumble into the snow. Other guys remember their first date, their first car, their first prom. Me, I remember Eagles 17, Green Bay 13.
By: Ray Didinger, NFL Films Producer, Author, Radio Personality

My sweetest moment as an Eagle occurred in the 4th and 26 game because I got a chance to redeem myself. I had missed a make able field goal in the 2nd half because of the swirling winds there in at Lincoln Financial Field. This was a playoff game and it was going to be painful if I had to go into the off-season knowing that I cost the team a playoff victory. Well it looked all was lost when Donovan connected with Freddie Mitchell on the 4th and 26. Then I went in there and made a pressurized field goal. The game went to the overtime and I got the chance to leave the stadium a winner rather leaving there as a goat. More than anybody else I appreciated that 4th and 26.
By: David Akers, Eagles Player 1999- current

One of my fondest Eagles memories would be...
When I went to an Eagles-Skins game back in 2002. I was sitting with my friend who was a Redskins fan in the lower end zone seats at Jack Kent Cooke Stadium. The "Duce" was running the ball all over the Redskins all day long. There were two huge Eagle fans several rows lower and across the aisle in Staley jerseys. Every time "Duce" touched the ball and ran for a gain, they would clap twice real quickly and then hold up two fingers - like the victory sign and chant "Duce". It almost sounded like they were booing him. Anyway, the Eagles got the ball down to around the 3-4 yard line when Staley tried to run it in. The Redskins stopped Staley just short of the one-yard line. As he got up from the pile, he trotted into the end zone shaking his head and waving his hands. Letting the fans in the stands know it's not over. The very next play was a hand off to Staley who sure enough scored! I had to sing the Eagles fight song after the touchdown along with the other guys ending with a loud. E-A-G-L-E-S, EAGLES! The Eagles skinned the Redskins 37-7.
By: Gregg Kramer

FONDEST EAGLES MEMORIES

1971-1972
Safety Bill Bradley becomes the first Eagle ever to lead the league in interceptions in consecutive years, logging 11 in 1971 and 9 more the following season.

One of my fondest Eagles memories would be...
A game that actually occurred at the Meadowlands versus the Giants in 2003. A friend of mine had invited me to go with him to the Eagles / Giants game in the Meadowlands on a very cold winter day. Needless to say we were sitting amongst a group of rabid Giants fans in our Eagles green. The game was not going in the Eagles favor and we were hearing it loudly from the Giants fans all around us. All seemed hopeless with less than 2:00 minutes left in the game, when Brian Westbrook ran back a punt 80 some odd yards to win the game. Upon completing our high fives we quickly left the Meadowlands.
By: Neil Tobin

One of my fondest Eagles memories would be...
A play that was called back but it was against a Hall Of Fame player. During my rookie year I beat the Redskins Darrell Green on a go route down there at RFK Stadium. The play went for 60 yards and it gave me confidence that I could play in the NFL.
By: Fred Barnett, Eagles Player 1990-95

NOVEMBER 10, 1985
(Veterans Stadium, Philadelphia) Eagles wide receiver Mike Quick (82) and quarterback Ron Jaworski connect on a game-winning, 99-yard touchdown pass against Atlanta. The play, which ties the NFL mark for the longest pass play in league history, is the first such one, however, to come in overtime.

We were backed up on the one-yard line against the Atlanta Falcons at the Vet. We had tried to run a deep seam route against them but Jaws and I weren't on the same page. We ran the same route the next play and Ron hit me in stride in the middle of their zone. I caught the ball and hit the jets. It was a wonderfully feeling because it was overtime and the split second I passed the safety, I knew it was over. There was no catching me. The play went for 99 yards and a touchdown. It's a record that will never been broken
By: Mike Quick, Eagles Player 1982-90 and Eagles Radio Broadcaster

One of my fondest Eagles memories would be...
We playing the Tampa Buccaneers and Trent Dilfer was their starting quarterback. I was rushing outside and up field and Trent was trying to step up in the pocket. I reached out and grabbed him with one hand by the top of his jersey. He was facing the other way and my momentum was heading up field and somehow I was able to yank him up off of his feet with one hand and sling him to the ground. It made me look like I was the strongest man in the league.
By: Hugh Douglas, Eagles Player 1998-2002, 2004 and 610 WIP Sports Radio Personality

One of my fondest Eagles memories would be...
My rookie year at the Vet against the Cowboys. I was running full speed while covering a kickoff and caught Dallas kick returner Reggie Swinton as he tried to speed to through what he thought was an opening in the coverage. I nearly killed him. I also had an interception in the game. My teammates started treating me differently after that game because they realized I could help them win. That hit and interception let me know I could play on the pro level.
By: Sheldon Brown, Eagles Player 2002- current

One of my fondest Eagles memories would be...
My greatest memory of the Eagles involves Randall Cunningham and Fred Barnett. It was probably the greatest athletic play I have ever seen. Randall went back to throw against the Buffalo Bills, at about 10 yard line. He was being rushed by two Bills pass rushers. He escaped and ducked under one while on the move, he threw one about 50-60 yards on the fly into the hands of Fred Barnett. It turned out to be a 90-yard touchdown pass.
By: Adam Poppel

FONDEST EAGLES MEMORIES

One of my fondest Eagles memories would be...
It was a Monday night game in 1974, the Cowboys were ahead in the game 10-0 and were on the verge of scoring again when Doug Dennison tried to go off tackle from the four yard line for a score, but I hit him chest high with everything I had and it was a thud. He coughed up the ball and Joe "The Bird" Lavender picked it up and ran 96 yards the other way for a score. We went on to win the game 13 to 10. It was the first time in years that we beat Dallas.
By: Bill Bergey, Eagles Player 1974-80

OCTOBER 22, 1939
(Ebbets Field, Brooklyn, NY) Long before the advent of "Monday Night Football," the Eagles and Brooklyn Dodgers took part in the first televised pro football game. NBC broadcast the game to the approximately 1,000 TV sets then in existence in Brooklyn. In this photo, Eagles end Bill Hewitt (56) hauls in a pass against two Dodger defenders.

One of my favorite Eagles memories would be...
All I have to say is Freddie Mitchell and the Eagles vs. Packers, 4th and 26. What a play!
By: Kim Sinclair, Love my Eagles!

One of my fondest Eagles memories would be...
First of all I was a free agent with a low percentage chance of making the team. I survived all the cuts and made the team. In the first regular season game against the Arizona Cardinals, I nearly fainted when I was standing on the sideline and Rich Kotite called my name. He told me to go into the game, and then in the huddle they called a play for me to carry the ball. They handed me the ball and I went off tackle for 33 yards. It seemed like the play took forever. When Hershel Walker was helping me up after the play, I had an out of body experience. It was like I was watching the game and I had trouble believing that I had really run for all that yardage. Later in the game, I scored a touchdown and I gave the ball to the referee because I wasn't all there. Thankfully Freddie Barnett got the ball back from the ref for me. The whole thing was like a dream but it was the game I proved I belonged in the NFL.
By: Vaughn Hebron, Eagles Player 1993-95, and Sportscaster Comcast Sportsnet

One of my fondest Eagles memories would be...
Well let me say this I've been a Eagles fan in and out but I must say one of the best times I've ever experience watching them had to be this. The windows were down so you could hear the entire block watching the game, it was a few years back when the Eagles were driving and then it happened... McNabb goes down and is hurt. You could hear the whole block ohhing and ahhhing, (besides other words) and it seemed all hope was gone. Now I'm a big McNabb fan so when Detmer an unknown quarterback comes into the game, well you could hear the block going "what the hell," and who is, and so on and so on.

Surprisingly he (Detmer) did well and actually got the Eagles rolling. There seemed to be an inner peace as everyone seemed to pause going WOW just maybe.... Now yes, these were the same people going "what the." It seemed like just watching a game for a few moment had everyone focusing on that instead of problems of the world and such, which kinda got me thinking at the time how incredible one sport can do this ... of course when Detmer got hurt the disbelief was back and yet again. My thing is with everything going on in the world it was nice for a few hours to have everyone on the same page and not worried about who shot who and other day-to-day problems we all face. If only all problems could be solved by watching a football game.
By: Ray, the Midas Man

One of my fondest Eagles memories would be......
It would have to be the entire 60's season. We started the season with a loss to the Cleveland Browns. Then, miraculously, we won the next nine games. What was so amazing about those nine games was that we were trailing at halftime in every game, but one, but somehow we found a way to win! Everyone knew they needed to step up and help the team. When we won the Championship against Lombardi's Green Bay Packers, it was a whole team effort. That was a great feeling and I will always remember it. I had some great years playing in Philadelphia.
By: Pete Retzlaff, Eagles Player 1956-66, and Eagles General Manager 1969-72

JANUARY 11, 1981
(Veterans Stadium, Philadelphia) Wilbert Montgomery rushes for 194 yards, including a 42-yard TD on Philadelphia's first offensive series, as the Eagles top Dallas, 20-7, in the NFC Championship Game and earn a berth in Super Bowl XV.

FONDEST EAGLES MEMORIES

One of my fondest Eagles memories would be...
So, I think it was 1961 or 62 so I was 5 or 6. My uncle Irv and my Uncle Sam had season tickets at Franklin Field. They would always take one of the nephews to a game. So I guess it was my turn. We get there. It was a December game it was freakin cold. As we are about to go in, my uncle Irv tells me to get under his trench coat, so he " sneaks" me in. I think the ticket guy knew but I thought it was the coolest thing in the world. We start walking to our seats, and we are walking and walking and walking. We were on the top row on the goal line at the open end of the Franklin Field. As we sat down I met all the regulars around them and they started their regular ritual of trading sandwiches. There was this one guy who was just silly and very funny who kept me laughing the whole game. I couldn't even begin to tell you who we were playing. The game ended and we went home. Over the years they would take me to many games, I then became a vendor first at Franklin Field and then at the VET. It was that first game and that silly guy, who I came to find out many years later, was the one and only Max Patkin.
By: Saul Braverman

One of my fondest Eagles memories would be...
We were trailing the New York Giants and hadn't really done anything that day. We preparing for a punt return and I was up at the line of scrimmage. I was responsible for faking like I was going to go for a blocked punt, then getting back downfield for and coverage guys who would try to get to Brian Westbrook. The punt was high and there was a wide receiver who was almost in Westbrook's face but he didn't signal for a fair catch, so I had to get him. I ran and hard as I could and got just a little bitty piece of his shoulder. It slowed him up enough to allow BWest to get to the sideline and the rest is history. He took it down the sideline and we won the game on that return. It turned around our season and we went on to go to the playoffs.
By: Ike Reese, Eagles Player 1998-2004

One of my fondest Eagles memories would be...
It was the first home game of the 1976 season and it was the first time I stepped onto the Vet Stadium turf for a regular season home game after sitting in the stands and watching them play for years. I had overcome some tremendous obstacles and made the team. We were hosting the New York Giants. I remember running out of the tunnel at Veterans Stadium with the crowd going crazy, then looking over my shoulder and seeing my Dad and my friends up in the stands cheering. They were so proud, I could hardly believe it. It will be a moment I will always remember because it was so special to all of us. I made a couple of big plays that day covering kickoffs and punts the on special teams. We won the game 20-7.
By: Vince Papale, Eagles Player 1976-78

DECEMBER 11, 1966
(Franklin Field, Philadelphia) Defensive back Al Nelson sets the NFL mark for the longest return of a missed field when he runs one back 100 yards for a touchdown vs. Cleveland. Five years later he would break his own record with a 101-yard effort vs. Dallas.

One of my fondest Eagles memories would be...
I have man fond memories of attending games as for a three-year stretch I attended every game home and away. I had been to four straight championship games and a Super Bowl over the last 7 years. I have been a season ticket holder for approximately 13 years. But my fondest memory as an Eagles fan was Brian Westbrook running back the punt in New York against the Giants in the fourth quarter with a couple minutes left. See, up until that point I think the score was 13-7 Giants, and the game was boring and the New York fans were obnoxious. Everyone in the stadium, myself included, knew that the Giants had the game won, the Eagles offense was defunct and the only chance they had was a big play by Westbrook. So, obviously, kick it out of bounds. Well, everyone knows what happened and we started celebrating in our seats, as that was the turning point for the game and the season.

By: Jerry D'Addesi

I will never forget the joy I felt as we celebrated at the Vet in front of the fans in the cold, after beating the Cowboys in the 1980 NFC Championship Game. It was a dream come true. We had planned, prepared and finally beat Dallas. It was special time for Mr. Tose, Coach Vermeil and all the rest of us.
By: Ron Jaworski, Eagles Player 1977-86, and TV Sportscaster

FONDEST EAGLES MEMORIES

DECEMBER 19, 1948

(Shibe Park, Philadelphia) Steve Van Buren's 5-yard TD run in the fourth quarter of the 1948 NFL title game gives the Eagles their first ever league championship. Van Buren's TD is set up when the Eagles recover a Chicago fumble at the Cardinals' 17-yard line.

My earliest memories as a 7 or 8 year old is listening to the Eagles on the radio during the 1948 or 49 season when they beat the Cardinals for the championship 7 to 0 in a snowstorm. I remember being with my father and grandfather listening to this game. My Favorite memories are of the 1960 season when I had season tickets for the grand price of $15 for students at Franklin Field. I remember well, the hit that my hero, Chuck Bednarik, put on Frank Gifford and will never forget the championship game against the Packers. Norm Van Brocklin was amazing, Pete Retzlaff was unstoppable and Bednarik was Bednarik. We sat in the upper deck at about the 20-yard line for all of the 8 games at home. There was no better place to watch a game. Every seat was a good one. Who would know that this was the last championship for so many years? The great fun was riding the subway and the subway surface cars to the game and stopping at the luncheonettes on Chestnut Street before the games to eat and talk football. It was a great time. Incidentally I met Chuck Bednarik many years later on a flight to Phoenix and talked football with while he was on his way to a NFL Golf outing. It was kind of a dream come true for a guy who is still a kid with certain old time sports heroes.

By: Larry Kagel

One of my fondest Eagles memories would be...

It was 1992 and we were trailing the New York Giants and there was a drizzling rain falling. I was about to receive the punt. All I remember was weaving side to side to beat the Giants defenders as I took that punt 87 yards for a touchdown. That return was and still is the Eagles record for the longest punt return. At the end of the run I put a move on long-time Giants and Eagles punter Sean Landeta and that play ended his season because he hurt his knee when I faked him out. After I scored, I started punching the goal post. I did it as a tribute to my father who watching the game and always wanted me to become a pro boxer.

By: Via Sikahema, Eagles Player 1992-93 and NBC 10 Sports Director

NOVEMBER 8, 1953

(Shibe Park, Philadelphia) Bobby Thomason becomes the first Eagle passer to throw for 400 yards in a game with a 437-yard effort, including 4 TDs, in a win over the Giants. Thomason's record would subsequently stand for 36 years before being topped by Randall Cunningham.

OCTOBER 17, 1954

(Griffith Stadium, Washington, DC) in a 49-21 victory over the Redskins, Eagles QB Adrian Burk ties Sid Luckman's NFL record of 7 touchdown passes in a game. By the year 2000, three other NFL passers George Blanda in '61, Y.A. Tittle in '62 and Joe Kapp in '69 would equal the mark. None, however, would surpass it.

One of my fondest Eagles memories would be...

January 11, 1981, the home Conference Championship game against the Dallas Cowboys. It was Dick Vermeil's pre-game locker room speech. He spoke about building a winning team; he thanked the coaching staff, how proud he was of everyone in this locker room. Spirits were high the weather was cold and the team was ready to defeat the Cowboys on their way to the Super Bowl. I also remember at the end of the game seeing on those policemen with dogs and horses lined up around the field. The Vet was filled with enthusiasm as the Eagles won. It truly was a special moment.

By: Jim Murray, Eagles General Manager 1969-83

FONDEST EAGLES MOMENTS

FONDEST EAGLES MEMORIES

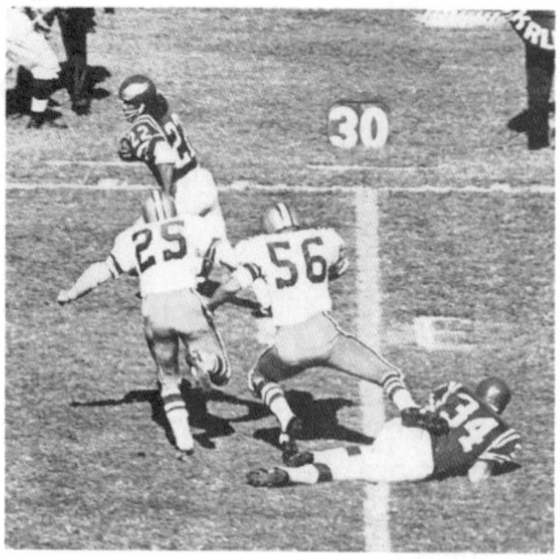

NOVEMBER 6, 1966
(Franklin Field, Philadelphia) Eagles running back and kick returner Timmy Brown (22) etches his name into the NFL record books, becoming the first player in league history to return two kickoffs for touchdowns in a single game.

APRIL 17, 1999
(New York, NY) With the second overall pick in the draft, the Eagles selected Syracuse quarterback Donovan McNabb (shown here with NFL commissioner Paul Tagliabue). On this date, McNabb joined Tim Couch (the #1 pick overall by Cleveland) and Akili Smith (chosen third by Cincinnati) in becoming only the second group of passers ever to be chosen 1-2-3 in the draft.

One of my fondest Eagles memories would be...
Nov 11, 1962, I was 9 years old and my blessed grandfather, 'Big' Nat Kleinman, took me to Franklin Field to see the Eagles play the Green Bay Packers: Horning, Taylor, Starr, Lombardi, etc. We sat on the first row of the second level (I sat on his lap) at the 50-yard line and the Packers won 49-0. I recall it also being freezing cold and wet. I was miserable. We parked miles from the stadium so we didn't have to pay for parking. I don't remember the Eagles ever coming close to a Packers player.
By: Brian "Shifty" Schiff, producer Comcast Sportsnet

DECEMBER 1, 1940
(Griffith Stadium, Washington, DC) Eagles end Don Looney sets the club's single-game record for the most receptions in a game when he grabs 14 passes against the Redskins. Perhaps more noteworthy is the fact that Looney's record still stands today.

NOVEMBER 19, 1978
(Giants Stadium, East Rutherford, NJ) "The Miracle of the Meadowlands" – With the NY Giants simply trying to run out the clock and with the Eagles seemingly headed for defeat, Philadelphia's Herman Edwards authors a miracle. Edwards scoops up a fumbled handoff from Joe Pisarcik to Larry Csonka and races 26 yards for a TD in the final 20 seconds of play. The win helps propel the Eagles into the playoffs for the first time since 1960.

Herman Edwards picks up a botched exchange between Joe Pisarcik and Larry Csonka and runs it in for a touchdown in the dwindling seconds to give the Eagles a 19-17 win over the New York Giants in the "Miracle of the Meadowlands."
By: Gary Discount

SEPTEMBER 3, 2000
(Texas Stadium, Irving, TX) Although the thermometer read 109 degrees, it was Eagles running back Duce Staley who burned the Cowboys. Staley's 201 rushing yards, the second most in club history, helped the Eagles open the 2000 NFL season with a resounding 41-14 victory.

One of my fondest Eagles memories would be...
I grew up in Philadelphia went to school at West Philly High. I always dreamed about playing for my hometown football team. It all started in 1940, as a 15 year old kid when I was able to attend the Eagles training camp at West Chester and be a water boy, catch punts during practice and run errands for the players. Then in 1947, my dreams came true when I became a member of the Philadelphia Eagles. In 1948, our QB Tommy Thompson got injured during the Redskins game. We were going to play the powerhouse Chicago Bears in the next game. I started that game and we defeated the Bears 12-7. It was the Eagles first win ever over the Bears.
By: Bill Mackrides, Eagles Player 1947-51

FONDEST EAGLES MEMORIES

I have so many, but let me tell you about one from 1953, Shibe Park. December 13th, it was the last game of the season. We were playing the dreaded Cleveland Browns. They were coming in with a perfect record winning their last eleven straight games. We all thought that they were going to "clean our clocks". The team felt they had nothing to lose. Tommy Thompson threw for 3 touchdowns and somehow the team found a way to defeat the Bears 42-27. It was an unbelievable win for the team.
By: Jim Gallagher, Eagles Public Relations Director 1949-95 and member of the Eagles Honor Roll

One of my fondest Eagles memories would be...
I had a bad two years in Washington playing for the Skins so I will always remember when I came back to the Eagles. I pulled up to the Nova Care Complex expecting to walk into the locker room with little fanfare, but I saw all of those television trucks and media people waiting for me to come in and talk. I had no idea that the city cared about me so much. It really touched me because of the way I had left. I really appreciated returning to Philly to play for the Eagles because I knew the grass wasn't greener on the other side of the street.
By: Jeremiah Trotter, Eagles Player 1998-2001 and 2004-2006

One of my fondest Eagles memories would be...
We were trailing the Giants and we hadn't been able to do much in the game. It was a high punt and I saw a Giants coverage guy getting close but I didn't want to fair catch because we needed a big play. I caught the ball and made a move to get inside that first guy who was coming from the side where we had the return set up. A slight block helped me get by him. After that, I hit the gas so I could get to the wall, which we had set up down the left sideline. I just ran as fast as I could for the end zone. I remember the play so well because it helped us win that game and turned around our season.
By: Brian Westbrook, Eagles Player 2002-current

2002
Led by an offense that set an Eagles record for points in a season (reflected in this photo of a pair of Eagles rejoicing after a score) and by one of the league's top defenses, Philadelphia wins its second straight NFC East Division title and advances to the NFC Championship Game for the second consecutive year. The 2002 season would be the team's 31st – and last – campaign at Veterans Stadium.

It was the 4th quarter of the NFC Championship game and I rolled out to my right and looked for Chad Lewis to make his cut outside. I spotted him and let the ball go. I knew if he caught it we were going to the Super Bowl. When he came down with the ball and the referees' signaled touchdown, I knew we had finally gotten over the hump and secured a place in the Super Bowl. Unfortunately, Chad hurt his foot on the play and wasn't able to play in the Super. But, it was something I will never forget because we had been to the NFC Championship game three other times and come up short. This was our time because we had all worked so hard to get there.
By: Donovan McNabb, Eagles Player 1999- current

One of my fondest Eagles memories would be...
"As a boy I suffered through the seventies with countless defeats every Sunday as the birds would find ways to lose. Most would question how they could watch this team, or worse yet become a cowboy's fan. Not I...It made me tough, as we enter the millennium waiting a home victory. For the last eight years, I live my dream as a season ticket holder, arriving six hours early to tailgate, unable to sleep the night before from anticipation of an Eagle victory, knowing full well that I bleed green if they lose again. At halftime I stand on the fifty-yard line before the greatest fans in all sports, who are misunderstood for merely booing Santa Claus and pelting Cowboy coach Jimmy Johnson with snowballs. I feel their roar as I gracefully spell out the E-A-G-L-E cheer like a twisted ballet. As they cheer sixty thousand strong, I know that they are standing before me, the greatest Eagle fan. I am ... Green Man!"
By: Tom Murphy "Green Man"

FONDEST EAGLES MEMORIES

One of my fondest Eagles memories would be...
My first ever-regular season game which was on Sept. 12th 1999 (Eagles vs. Cardinals)... I wanted to make a big splash for my first game so I set up a skydive into Veteran's Stadium. I had never skydived before and the company and I wanted to see how the costume would react to the wind after jumping out of the plane. For a month we tried to set up a practice jump in Williamstown, NJ but never had any luck setting up a practice run due to scheduling or weather. We decide to do a practice run the morning of the game (knowing that if the weather is bad we can't do the jump into the Vet anyway) So there I am 3 months fresh out of college trying to impress my new boss and co-workers and promising a skydive entrance for the home opener and I don't even know if it we can physically do the stunt.

The day was picture perfect, about 75 degrees and not a cloud in the sky; I arrived in Williamstown, NJ about 7am on game-day and we ran through two practice runs and luckily enough everything went flawlessly. The third jump that day was into the Vet; from our vantage point in the plane the Vet was the size of a cookie from about 8000 feet above it. I jumped tandem with a Pro, Doug; who had forewarned me about a possible "Crash" landing into the stadium. As we fell closer to the stadium and opened the chute we could already he the crowd and music playing even though we were still a few thousand feet above the stadium, it must have acted like a speaker with its oval shape funneling the noise upward towards us. Doug looked at the field flags and mentioned it was going to be a rough landing, Phanavision picked us up during the SWOOOOOP entrance and the crowd grew even louder as we entered the stadium. We must have landed at about 30 miles per hour, and my tail-end was the shock absorber for the both of us; thank God for adrenaline because I shot right up and cheered with the crowd even though I couldn't sit for a week! There was no better way to start of my NFL career!
By Ryan Hughes "SWOOP"

JANUARY 11, 2004
(Lincoln Financial Field, Philadelphia)

Who could ever forget the 2004 Divisional Playoffs against Green Bay. The Eagles were faced with a 4th and 26 to gain a 1st down. The game was late and the Eagles had to go for it. Donovan McNabb connected with Freddie Mitchell who made an unbelievable 28-yard catch and the first down. The Eagles would tie the score on the same drive and eventually win the game in overtime 20-17.

One of my fondest Eagles memories would be...
One of my best Eagles memories is the "4th and 26" playoff game against Green Bay. It was only the 2nd game ever where I dressed as "Andy Reid", so the people in my section at the Linc were still not sure what to make of me. Very quickly, the Eagles fell behind 14-0. Predictably, I was taking some heat.

I remember Green Bay's Coach Sherman making a gutless call to punt from his own 41 on 4th and 1. A first down would have ended the Eagles season. Instead the Packers punted into the end zone, and the Eagles had the ball at their own 20, trailing 17-14.

Obviously, the actual "4th and 26" play was a huge memory. But, the play that really sticks with me happened later that game in overtime. I announced to those seated around me that Brett Favre was really due to throw up one of his classic "trying to make too much out of nothing" interceptions. Within seconds, Favre threw up a pass that was half punt, half javelin being thrown straight into the air coming down with a dead bird (a la the old Atari "Track and Field" game). Brian Dawkins fielded it and returned it like a punt. About 10 people sitting around me starting hitting and smacking me (in a good-natured fashion) while yelling, "Andy Reid just predicted that", "the Coach guy just completely called that". I was feeling claustrophobic and euphoric at the same time.

A few plays later Akers kicked a 31-yd game winning FG in overtime and the Eagles went on to their 3rd straight NFC Championship. The rest is history (and by history, I mean, we got humiliated by the Panthers a week later).
By: Steve Odabashian, comedian/pianist and Andy Reid impersonator

First Draft Selections per Year

1936 Jay Berwanger (HB), Chicago, 1st overall
1937 Sam Francis (FB), Nebraska, 1
1938 James McDonald (HB), Ohio State, 2
1939 Davey O'Brien (QB), Texas Christian, 4
1940 George McAfee (HB), Duke, 2
1941 Art Jones (HB), Richmond (2nd round), 11
1942 Pete Kmetovic (HB), Stanford, 3
1943 Joe Muha (FB), VMI, 2
1944 Steve Van Buren, (HB), LSU, 5
1945 John Yonaker (E), Notre Dame, 9
1946 Leo Riggs (HB), Southern California, 7
1947 Neil Armstrong (E), Oklahoma A&M, 8
1948 Clyde Scott (HB), Arkansas & Naval Acad., 8
1949 Chuck Bednarik (C), Penn (Bonus Pick), 1
Frank Tripucka (QB), Notre Dame, 9
1950 Harry Grant (E), Minnesota, 14
1951 Ebert Van Buren (FB), LSU, 7
1952 John Bright (FB), Drake, 5
1953 Al Conway (HB), Army & Wm. Jewell (2nd round), 20
1954 Neil Worden (FB), Notre Dame, 9
1955 Dick Bielski (FB), Maryland, 9
1956 Bob Pellegrini (C-LB), Maryland, 4
1957 Clarence Peaks (FB), Michigan State, 7
1958 Walter Kowalczyk (FB), Michigan State, 6
1959 J.D. Smith (T), Rice (2nd round), 15
1960 Ron Burton (B), Northwestern, 9
1961 Art Baker (B), Syracuse, 14
1962 Pete Case (G), Georgia (2nd round), 27
1963 Ed Budde (T), Michigan State, 4
1964 Bob Brown (T), Nebraska, 2
1965 Ray Rissmiller (T), Georgia (2nd round), 20
1966 Randy Beisler (T), Indiana, 4
1967 Harry Jones (RB), Arkansas, 19
1968 Tim Rossovich (DE), USC, 14
1969 Leroy Keyes (RB), Purdue, 3
1970 Steve Zabel (E-LB), Oklahoma, 6
1971 Richard Harris (DE), Grambling, 5
1972 John Reaves (QB), Florida, 14
1973 Jerry Sisemore (T), Texas, 3
Charlie Young (TE), USC, 6
1974 Mitch Sutton (DT), Kansas (3rd round), 63
1975 Bill Capraun (T), Miami (7th round), 167
1976 Mike Smith (DE), Florida (4th round), 111
1977 Skip Sharp (CB), Kansas (5th round), 119
1978 Reggie Wilkes (LB), Georgia Tech (3rd rd),66
1979 Jerry Robinson (LB), UCLA, 21
1980 Roynell Young (CB), Alcorn State, 23
1981 Leonard Mitchell (DE), Houston, 27
1982 Mike Quick (WR), North Carolina St., 20
1983 Michael Haddix (FB), Mississippi St., 8
1984 Kenny Jackson (WR), Penn State, 4
1985 Kevin Allen (T), Indiana, 9
1986 Keith Byars (RB), Ohio State, 10
1987 Jerome Brown (DT), Miami, 9
1988 Keith Jackson (TE), Oklahoma, 13
1989 Jessie Small (LB), E. Kentucky (2nd round), 49
1990 Ben Smith (S), Georgia, 22
1991 Antone Davis (T), Tennessee, 8
1992 Siran Stacy (RB), Alabama (2nd round), 48
1993 Lester Holmes (G), Jackson State, 19
Leonard Renfro (DT), Colorado, 24
1994 Bernard Williams (T), Georgia, 14
1995 Mike Mamula (DE/LB), Boston College, 7
1996 Jermane Mayberry (G/T), Texas A&M ,25
1997 Jon Harris (DE), Virginia, 25
1998 Tra Thomas (T), Florida State, 11
1999 Donovan McNabb (QB), Syracuse, 2
2000 Corey Simon (DT), Florida State, 6
2001 Freddie Mitchell (WR) UCLA, 25
2002 Lito Sheppard (CB) Florida, 26
2003 Jerome McDougle (DE) Miami, 15
2004 Shawn Andrews (T/G) Arkansas, 16
2005 Mike Patterson (DT) USC, 31
2006 Brodrick Bunkley (DT) Florida State, 14
2007 Kevin Kolb (QB) Houston, (2nd round),36

ALL TIME RECORDS
- TOP 5 LEADERS -

MOST YARDS PASSING
(based on total passing yards)

Player	Years	Comp/Att	Total Yds
1.Ron Jaworski	1977-86	2088/3918	26,963
2. Donovan McNabb	1999-2007	2189/3732	225404
3. Randall Cunningham	1985-95	1874/3362	22,877
4. Norm Snead	1964-70	1154/22336	15,672
5. Tommy Thompson	1941-42, 45-50	723/1396	10,240

KICKOFF RETURN LEADERS

Name	Years	No	Yds	Avg	Lg	TDs
1. Steve Van Buren	1944-51 (8)	76	2030	26.7	NA	3
2. Irv Cross	1961-69 (6)	28	745	26.6	74	0
3. Timmy Brown	1960-67 (8)	169	4483	26.5	105t	5
4. Al Nelson	1965-73 (9)	101	2625	26.0	78	0
5. Wilbert Montgomery	1977-84 (8)	32	814	25.4	99t	1

LONGEST PASS PLAYS

Player	Game	LG
1. Ron Jaworski to Mike Quick	Nov. 10, 1985 vs. Falcons	99t*
2. Randall Cunningham to Fred Barnett	Dec. 2, 1990 at Bills	95t
3. Randall Cunningham to Herschel Walker	Sept. 4, 1994 at Giants	93
4. King Hill to Ben Hawkins	Sept. 22, 1968 vs. Giants	92t
5. Donovan McNabb to Terrell Owens	Oct. 30, 2006 at Broncos	91t
Norm Van Brocklin to Tommy McDonald	Oct. 5, 1958 vs. Giants	91t

• NFL Record

MOST TOUCHDOWN PASSES

Player	Years	TD's
1. Ron Jaworski	1977-1986	175
2. Donovan McNabb	1999-2007	171
3. Randall Cunningham	1985-1995	150
4. Norm Snead	1964-1970	111
5. Tommy Thompson	1941-1950	90

LONGEST INTERCEPTION RETURNS

Player	Game	LG
1. James Willis	*intercepted a pass 4 yds. deep in the end zone and returned it 14 yds. before lateralling to Troy Vincent, who ran 90 yds.* Nov. 3, 1996 at Cowboys - QB Troy Aikman)	104t
2. Lito Sheppard	Oct. 8, 2006 vs. Cowboys - QB Drew Bledsoe)	102t
3. Lito Sheppard	Nov. 15, 2004 at Cowboys - QB Vinny Testaverde)	101t
4. Jerry Norton	Oct. 5, 1957 vs. Giants - QB Charlie Conerly, deflected off goal post)	99t
5. Eric Allen	Oct. 3, 1993 at Jets - QB Boomer Esiason)	94t
Irv Cross	Oct. 25, 1964 at Steelers - QB Terry Nofsinger)	94t

LONGEST RUSHING PLAYS

Player	Game	LG
1. Herschel Walker	Nov. 27, 1994 at Falcons	91t
2. Wilbert Montgomery	Dec. 19, 1982 vs. Oilers	90t
3. Brian Mitchell	Dec. 1, 2000 vs. Falcons	85t
4. Leroy Harris	Nov. 25, 1979 at Packers	80
5. Bosh Pritchard	Oct. 23, 1949 vs. Redskins	77t

ALL TIME RECORDS
- TOP 5 LEADERS -

LONGEST PUNTS

Player	Game	LG
1. Randall Cunningham	Dec 3, 1989 at Giants	91
2. Joe Muha	Oct. 10, 1948 vs. Giants	82
3. Randall Cunningham	Oct. 16, 1994 at Cowboys	80
King Hill	Nov. 11, 1962 vs. Packers	80
5. Jeff Feagles	Sept. 15, 1991 at Cowboys	77

MOST SEASONS PLAYED

Player	Years	Seasons
1. Chuck Bednarik	1949-1962	14
2. Harold Carmichael	1971-1983	13
2. Frank (Bucko) Kilroy	1943-1955	13
2. Vic Sears	1941-1953	13
5. Brian Dawkins	1996-2007	12
Jerry Sisemore	1973-1984	12
Bobby Walston	1951-1962	12

LEADING RUSHERS

Player	Years	Games	Att	Yds	Avg	Lg	TDs
1. Wilbert Montgomery 1977-1984	8	100	1465	6538	4.5	90t	45
2. Steve Van Buren 1944-1951	8	83	1320	5860	4.4	70t	69
3. Duce Staley 1997-2003	7	98	1200	4807	4.0	64t	22
4. Brian Westbrook	6	85	1014	4785	4.7	71t	27
5. Randall Cunningham (QB) 1985-1995	11	122	677	4482	6.6	52t	32

MOST INTERCEPTIONS

Player	Yards	INT's	TD's
1. Bill Bradley	536	34	1
2. Eric Allen	482	34	5
3. Brian Dawkins	490	33	2
4. Herman Edwards	98	33	1
5. Wes Hopkins	241	30	1

MOST SACKS

Player	Years	Sacks
1. Reggie White	1985-92	124
2. Clyde Simmons	1986-93	76.5
3. Hugh Douglas	1998-2002, '04	54.5
4. Greg Brown	1982-86	50.5
5. Andy Harmon	1991-97	40

LONGEST FIELD GOALS

Player	Game	LG
1. Tony Franklin	Nov. 12, 1979 at Cowboys	59
2. David Akers	Sept. 14, 2003 vs. Patriots	57
3. Tom Dempsey	Dec. 12, 1971 vs. Cardinals	54
4. David Akers	Sept. 30, 2007 at Giants	53
David Akers	Oct. 24, 1999 at Dolphins	53
Roger Ruzek	Dec. 9, 1990 at Dolphins	53

MOST POINTS SCORED

Player	Years	Pts
1. David Akers	1999-2007	897
2. Bobby Walston	1951-62	881
3. Sam Baker	1964-69	475
4. Harold Carmichael	1971-83	474
5. Steve Van Buren	1944-51	464

PUNT RETURN LEADERS

(Based On Punt Return Average, min. 20 returns)

Name	Years	Yds	Avg	Lg	TDs
1. Ernie Steele	1942-48	737	16.8	80	1
2. Steve Van Buren	1944-51	473	13.9	NA	2
3. Pat McHugh	1947-51	402	13.0	NA	1
4. Brian Westbrook	2002-07	498	12.8	84t	2
5. Brian Mitchell	2000-02	1369	11.7	76t	2

ALL TIME RECORDS
- TOP 5 LEADERS -

MOST RUSHING TOUCHDOWNS

Player	Years	TD's
1. Steve Van Buren	1944-51	69
2. Wilbert Montgomery	1977-84	45
3. Randall Cunningham	1985-95	32
4. Ricky Watters	1995-97	31
5. Timmy Brown	1960-67	29

LONGEST PUNT RETURNS

Player	Game	LG
1. Vai Sikahema	Nov. 22, 1992 at Giants	87t
2. Brian Westbrook	Oct.19, 2003 at Giants	84t
3. Brian Westbrook	Dec. 21, 2003 vs. 49ers	81t
Tommy McDonald	Oct. 4, 1959 vs. Giants	81t
5. Brian Mitchell	Nov. 25, 2002 at 49ers	76t
Gregg Garrity	Nov. 30, 1986 at LA Raiders	76t

PLAY BY PLAY RADIO BROADCASTERS

1.Merrill Reese	1977-2007*	30 years
2.Byrum Saam	1940-49, 1952-1955	14 years
3.Bill Campbell	1956-1964	9 years
4.Charlie Swift	1969-1977	9 years
5.Andy Musser	1965-1968	4 years

* current play-by-play announcer

WINNING PERCENTAGE BY A COACH

Coach	Year	Pct.
1. Andy Reid	1999-2007*	.636
2. Greasy Neale	1941-50	.596
3. Rich Kotite	1991-94	.561
4. Buck Shaw	1958-60	.554
5. Jim Trimble	1952-55	.552

*current coach

MOST PRO BOWL SELECTIONS

Name	Pos	Pro Bowls	Seasons
1. Chuck Bednarik	LB	8	1951-55, 57-58, 61
2. Reggie White	DE	7	1987-93
3. Brian Dawkins	FS	6	2000, 02-03, 05-07
Pete Pihos	WR	6	1951-56
5. Donovan McNabb	QB	5	2001-05
Troy Vincent	CB	5	2000-04
Eric Allen	CB	5	1990, 92-95
Mike Quick	WR	5	1984-88
Pete Retzlaff	WR	5	1959, 61, 64-66
Maxie Baughan	LB	5	1961-62, 64-66

ROOKIE RECEIVING RECORDS

PLAYER	YEAR	RECEPTS
1. Keith Jackson (TE)	1988	81
2. Charle Young (TE)	1973	55
3. Lee Bouggess (RB)	1970	50
4. Reggie Brown	2005	43
5. Victor Bailey	1993	41
Junior Tautalatasi (RB)	1986	41

LEADING RECEIVERS

Player	Years	Total Yards	Receptions	TDs
1. Harold Carmichael	1971-83	8,978	589	79
2. Pete Retzlaff	1956-66	7,412	452	47
3. Pete Pihos	1947-55	5,619	373	61
4. Keith Byars	1986-92	3,532	371	13
5. Mike Quick	1982-90	6,464	363	61

MOST CONSECUTIVE GAMES PLAYED

Name	Games
1. Harold Carmichael (1972-1983)	162
2. Randy Logan (1973-1983)	159
3. Bobby Walston (1951-1962)	148
4. Ken Clarke (1977-1987)	139
5. Herman Edwards (1977-1985)	135

MOST SCRIMMAGE YARDS

Name	Years	Games	Touches	Yds	Avg	Yds/G	TDs
1. Harold Carmichael (WR)	1971-1983 (13)	180	598	9042	15.1	50.2	79
2. Wilbert Montgomery (RB)	1977-1984 (8)	100	1731	8985	5.2	89.9	57
3. Brian Westbrook (RB)	2002-2007 (6)	85	1361	7992	5.9	94.0	50
4. Pete Retzlaff (E)	1956-1966 (11)	132	458	7408	16.2	56.1	47
5. Duce Staley (RB)	1997-2003 (7)	98	1475	7305	5.0	74.5	32

MOST TOUCHDOWNS SCORED

Player	TDS
1. Harold Carmichael (WR)	79
2. Steve Van Buren (B)	77
3. Tommy McDonald (FL)	67
4. Pete Pihos (E)	63
5. Timmy Brown (B)	62

ALL-TIME EAGLES ROSTER

The following players have been on the Eagles' active roster for at least one regular or postseason game during the years indicated. In addition, players who spent the entire year on the injured reserve list since 1993 and thus have accrued an NFL season are also listed below.

*=players that are on the current 2007 roster r= 1987 replacement strike players

A

Abercrombie, Walter 1988 (RB)
Abiamiri, Victor 2007-p* (DE)
Absher, Dick 1972 (LB)
Adams, Gary 1969 (DB)
Adams, Keith 2002-05 (LB)
Adams, Theo 1995 (G)
Agajanian, Ben 1945 (G)
Akers, David 1999-p* (K)
2001-2002, 2004 All Pro Selection
2002-03, 2005 Pro Bowl
Alexander, David 1987-94 (C)
1991 Ed Block Courage Award
Alexander, Kermit 1972-73 (DB)
Allen, Chuck 1972 (LB)
Allen, Eric 1988-94 (CB)
1989, 1991, 1993 All Pro Selection
1990, 1992-95 Pro Bowl
1993 NFC Defensive MVP
Allen, Ian 2004 (T)
Allen, Jackie 1972 (DB)
Allen, Kevin 1985 (T)
Allert, Ty 1987-89 (LB)
Allison, Henry 1971-72 (G)
Amerson, Glen 1961 (B)
Amundson, George 1975 (RB)
Anderson, Gary 1995-96 (K)
Andrews, Leroy 1934 (B)
Andrews, Shawn 2004-p* (G)
2007 All-Pro
2007 Pro Bowl
2008 Pro Bowl
Angelo, Jim 1987 (G)
Antwine, Houston 1972 (DT)
Archer, Dave 1991-92 (QB)
Armour, Justin 1997 (WR)
Armstrong, Calvin 2005- (T)
Armstrong, Harvey 1982-84 (DT)
Armstrong, Neill 1947-51 (E)
Arnold, Jay 1937-40 (B)
Arrington, Rick 1970-73 (QB)
Aschbacher, Darrel 1959 (G)
Asher, Jamie 1999 (TE)
Atkins, Steve 1981 (FB)
Auer, Howard 1933 (T)
Auer, Jim 1987r (DE)
Autry, Darnell 1998, 2000 (RB)
Avant, Jason, 2006-p* (WR)
Ayers, Marvin 1987 (DE)

B

Bahr, Matt 1993 (K)
Bailey, Dave 1990 (DE)
Bailey, Eric 1987 (TE)
Bailey, Howard 1935 (T)
Bailey, Tom 1971-74 (B)
Bailey, Victor 1993-94 (WR)
Baisi, Albert 1947 (G)
Baker, Jason 2002 (P)
Baker, John 1962 (DE)
Baker, Keith 1985 (WR)
Baker, Ron 1980-88 (G)
Baker, Sam 1964-69 (K)
1965, 1969 Pro Bowl
Baker, Tony 1971-72 (B)
Baldinger, Brian 1992-93 (G)
Ballman, Gary 1967-72 (TE)
Banas, Stephen 1935 (B)
Banducci, Bruno 1944-45 (G)
1945 All Pro Selection
Banta, Jack 1941, 1944-45 (B)
Barber, Shawn 2002, 06 (LB)
2002 Ed Block Courage Award
Barker, Bryan 1994 (P)
Barlow, Corey 1992-94 (CB)
Barnes, Billy Ray 1957-61 (RB)
1958-60 Pro Bowl
Barnes, Larry 1978-79 (FB)
Barnes, Walter 1948-51 (G)
1951 Pro Bowl
Barnett, Fred 1990-95 (WR)
1993 Pro Bowl
1994 Ed Block Courage Award
Barnhardt, Dan 1934 (B)
Barni, Roy 1954-55 (B)
Barnum, Leonard 1940-42 (B)
Barr, Stephen 1965 (WR)
Bartholomew, Sam 1941 (B)
Bartlett, Doug 1988 (DT)
Bartley, Ephesians 1992 (LB)
Bartrum, Mike 2000-06 (TE)
2006 Pro Bowl
Basca, Nick 1941 (B)
Baskett, Hank 2006-p* (WR)
Bassi, Dick 1940 (G)
1940 All Pro Selection
Bassman, Herman 1936 (B)
Battaglia, Matt 1987r (LB)
Baughan, Maxie 1960-65 (LB)
1961, 1964-65 All Pro Selection
1961-62, 1964-66 Pro Bowl
Bauman, Alfred 1947 (T)
Bausch, Frank 1940-41 (C)
Bavaro, Mark 1993-94 (TE)
Bawel, Ed 1952, 1955-56 (B)
Baze, Winford 1937 (B)
Beach, Pat 1992 (TE)
Beals, Shawn 1988 (WR)
Beaver, Jim 1962 (G)
Beckles, Ian 1997-98 (G)
Bednarik, Chuck 1949-62 (C)/LB
1950-57, 1960-61 All Pro Selection
1951-55, 1957-58, 1961 Pro Bowl
1954 Pro Bowl MVP
Beisler, Randy 1966-68 (DE)
Bell, Eddie 1955-58 (DB)
Bell, Todd 1988-89 (LB)
Bellamy, Mike 1990 (WR)
Bellamy, Victor 1987r (CB)
Bendross, Jesse 1987r (WR)
Benson, Harry 1935 (G)
Berger, Mitch 1994 (P)
Bergey, Bill 1974-80 (LB)
1974-78 All Pro Selection
1975, 1977-79 Pro Bowl
Berry, Dan 1967 (B)
Berzinski, Willie 1956 (B)
Betterson, James 1977-78 (RB)
Bielski, Dick 1955-59 (B)
Bieniemy, Eric 1999 (RB)
Binotto, John 1942 (B)
Bishop, Blaine 2002 (S)
Bjorklund, Robert 1941 (C)
Black, Michael 1986 (T/G)
Blackmore, Richard 1979-82 (CB)
Blaine, Ed 1963-66 (G)
Blake, Jeff 2004 (QB)
Bleamer, Jeff 1975-76 (T)
Bleeker, Mel 1944-46 (B)
Blue, Lither 1980 (WR)
Blye, Ron 1969 (RB)
Boatswain, Harry 1995, 1997 (G/T)
Boedeker, William 1950 (B)
Borgren, Vince 1944 (E)
Bolden, Gary 1987r (DT)
Bonial, Chris 1997-98 (K)
Booty, John 1991-92 (DB)
Boryla, Mike 1974-76 (QB)
1976 Pro Bowl
Bostic, James 1998-99 (RB)
Bostic, Jason 1999-2000 (RB)
Bouggess, Lee 1970-73 (RB)
Bouie, Kevin 1995-96 (RB)
Bova, Tony 1943 (E)
Bowman, Kevin 1987r (WR)
Boykin, Deral 1996 (S)
Bradley, Bill 1969-76 (S)
1971-73 All Pro Selection
1972-74 Pro Bowl
Bradley, Carlos 1987r (LB)
Bradley, Stewart 2007-p* (LB)
Bradley, Harold 1958 (G)
Brady, Rickey 1995 (TE)
Bredice, John 1956 (E)
Brennan, Leo 1942 (T)
Brewer, Jack 2005 (S)
Brewer, John 1952-53 (B)
Brian, William 1935-36 (T)
Bridges, Jeremy 2003 (T/G)
Brister, Bubby 1993-94 (QB)
Britt, Rankin 1939 (E)
Brodnicki, Chuck 1934 (T)
Brooks, Barret 1995-98 (T)
Brooks, Clifford 1975-76 (DB)
Brooks, Tony 1992-93 (RB)
Brookshier, Tom 1953, 1956-61 (CB)
1959-60 All Pro Selection
1960-61 Pro Bowl

ALL-TIME EAGLES ROSTER

Broughton, Luther 1997, 1999-2000 (TE)
Brown, Aaron 1985 (LB)
Brown, Bob 1964-68 (T)
1964-68 All Pro Selection
1966-67, 1969 Pro Bowl
Brown, Cedrick 1987 (CB)
Brown, David 1987r (LB)
Brown, Deauntee 1997 (CB)
Brown, Fred 1967-69 (LB)
Brown, Greg 1981-86 (DE)
Brown, Jerome 1987-91 (DT)
1989-91 All Pro Selection
1991-92 Pro Bowl
1992 Ed Block Courage Award
Brown, Na 1999-2001 (WR)
Brown, Reggie 2005-p* (WR)
Brown, Reggie 1987r (RB)
Brown, Sheldon 2002-p* (CB)
Brown, Thomas 1980 (DE)
Brown, Tim 1960-67 (RB)
1963, 1965-66 All Pro Selection
1963-64, 1966 Pro Bowl
Brown, Willie 1966 (WR)
Brumm, Don 1970-71 (DE)
Brutley, Daryon 2003 (CB)
Brunski, Andrew 1943 (C)
Bryant, Bill 1978 (CB)
Brzezinski, Doug 1999-2003 (G)
Buckhalter, Correll 2001-p* (RB)
2003 Ed Block Courage Award
Budd, Frank 1962 (E)
Bukant, Joe 1938-40 (B)
Bulaich, Norm 1973-74 (RB)
Bull, Ron 1971 (RB)
Bunkley, Brodrick 2006-p* (DT)
Bunting, John 1972-82 (LB)
Burgess, Derrick 2001-04 (DE)
2004 Ed Block Courage Award
Burk, Adrian 1951-56 (QB)
1955 Pro Bowl
Burke, Mark 1976 (DB)
Burks, Dialleo 1996 (WR)
Burnette, Tom 1938 (B)
Burnham, Lem 1977-80 (DE)
Burnine, Hank 1956-57 (E)
Burroughs, Don 1960-64 (DB)
1960-62 All Pro Selection
Bushby, Thomas 1935 (B)
Buss, Art 1936-37 (T)
Butler, Bob 1962 (G)
Butler, John 1943, 1945 (B)
Byars, Keith 1986-92 (RB)
Byrne, Bill 1963 (G)

C

Cabrelli, Larry 1941-47 (E)
Caesar, Ivan 1993 (LB)
Caffey, Lee Roy 1963 (LB)
Cagle, Jim 1974 (DT)
Cahill, Dave 1966 (DT)
Caldwell, Mike 1998-2001 (LB)
Calhoun, Don 1982 (RB)
Callicchio, Lonny 1997 (K)
Calloway, Ernie 1969-72 (DT)
Campbell, Glenn 1935 (E)
Campbell, Marion 1956-61 (DT)
1960-61 Pro Bowl
Campbell, Stan 1959-61 (G)
Campbell, Tommy 1976 (DB)
Campfield, Billy 1978-82 (RB)
Campion, Thomas 1947 (T)
Canale, Rocco 1943-45 (G)
Carmichael, Harold 1971-83 (WR)
1973, 1979-80 All Pro Selection
1974, 1979-81 Pro Bowl
Carollo, Joe 1969-70 (T)
Carpe, Joe 1933 (T)
Carpenter, Robert 1995 (WR)
Carr, Earl 1979 (RB)
Carr, Jim 1959-63 (S)
Carroccio, Russ 1955 (G)
Carroll, Terrence 2001 (S)
Carson, Carlos 1989 (WR)
Carter, Cris 1987-89 (WR)
Carter, Joe 1933-40 (E)
1935-36, 1938 All Pro Selection
Case, Pete 1962-64 (G)
Cassady, Howard 1962 (B)
Castiglia, Jim 1941, 1945-46 (B)
Caterbone, Tom 1987r (CB)
Catlin, Tom 1959 (LB)
Cavanaugh, Matt 1986-89 (QB)
Caver, Quinton 2001-2002 (LB)
Celek, Brent 2007-p* (TE)
Cemore, Tony 1941 (G)
Ceppetelli, Gene 1968-69 (C)
Chalenski, Mike 1993-95 (DL)
Chapura, Dick 1990 (DT/G)
Cheek, Louis 1990 (T)
Cherry, Je'rod 2000 (S)
Cherundolo, Chuck 1940 (C)
Chesley, Al 1979-82 (LB)
Chesson, Wes 1973-74 (WR)
Christensen, Jeff 1984-85 (QB)
Chuy, Don 1969 (G)
Cifelli, Gus 1954 (T)
Clark, Al 1976 (CB)
Clark, Mike 1963 (K/E)
Clark, Algy 1934 (B)
Clark, Willie 1997 (CB)
Clarke, Adrien 2004 (G)
Clarke, Ken 1978-87 (DT)
Clayton, Don 1936 (T)
Clemons, Topper 1987r (RB)
Cobb, Garry 1985-87 (LB)
Cody, Bill 1972 (LB)
Colavito, Rocky 1975 (LB)
Cole, Nick 2006-p* (OL)
Cole, John 1938-40 (B)
Cole, Trent 2005-p* (DE)
2008 Pro Bowl
Coleman, Al 1972-73 (DB)
Collie, Bruce 1990-91 (G)
Colman, Wayne 1968-69 (LB)
Combs, Bill 1942 (E)
Concannon, Jack 1964-66 (QB)
Conjar, Larry 1968 (FB)
Conlin, Ray 1987r (DT)
Conner, Darion 1996-97 (DE)
Considine, Sean 2005-p* (S)
Conti, Enio 1941-45 (G)
Conwell, Joe 1986-87 (T)
Cook, Leon 1942 (T)
Cook, Rashard 1999-2000 (S)
Cooke, Ed 1958 (E)
Cooper, Evan 1984-87 (DB)
Cooper, Louis 1993 (LB)
Cooper, Richard 1996-98 (T)
Copeland, Russell 1997-98 (WR)
Cornish, Frank 1995 (C)
Cortez, Joseph 2005 (K)
Coston, Zed 1939 (C)
Cothren, Paige 1959 (B)
Cowher, Bill 1983-84 (LB)
Cowhig, Jerry 1951 (B)
Crabb, Claude 1964-65 (DB)
Craft, Russ 1946-53 (B)
1952-53 Pro Bowl
Crafts, Jerry 1997-98 (T/G)
Crawford, Charles 1986-87 (RB)
Creech, Bob 1971-72 (LB)
Creswell, Smiley 1985 (DE)
Crews, Terry 1996 (LB)
Cronin, Bill 1965 (E)
Cross, Irv 1961-65, 1969 (DB)
1965-66 Pro Bowl
Crowe, Larry 1972 (RB)
Crutchfield, Darrel 2001 (CB)
Cuba, Paul 1933-35 (T)
Culbreath, Jim 1980 (FB)
Cullars, Willie 1974 (DE)
Cumby, George 1987r (LB)
Cunningham, Dick 1973 (LB)
Cunningham, Randall 1985-95 (QB)
1988, 1990, 1992 All Pro Selection
1989-91 Pro Bowl
1988 NFL MVP
1989 Pro Bowl MVP
1990 NFL MVP
1990 NFL Offensive MVP
1990 NFC Offensive MVP
1992 NFL Comeback player of the Year
Cuppoletti, Bree 1939-40 (G)
Curcio, Mike 1981-82 (LB)
Curtis, Kevin 2007-p* (WR)
Curtis, Scott 1988 (LB)

D

D'Agostino, Frank 1956 (G)
Darby, Byron 1983-86 (DE/TE)
Darelik, Trey 2004-05 (G/T)
Darling, James 1997-2000 (LB)
Darwin, Matt 1986-90 (C)
Davis, Al 1971-72 (B)
Davis, Antone 1991-95 (T)
Davis, Bob 1942 (B)
Davis, Norm 1970 (G)
Davis, Pernell 1999-2000 (DT)
Davis, Stan 1973 (B)
Davis, Sylvester 1933 (B)
Davis, Vern 1971 (DB)
Dawkins, Brian 1996-p* (S/LB)
2001-2002, 2004, 2007 All Pro Selection
2000, 2002-03, 2005-07 Pro Bowl
Dawson, Dale 1988 (K)
Dean, Ted 1960-63 (RB)
1962 Pro Bowl

ALL-TIME EAGLES ROSTER

DeLine, Steve 1989 (K)
Dellenbach, Jeff 1999 (G/C)
Delucca, Gerry 1959 (T)
Demas, George 1933 (G)
Dempsey, Jack 1934, 1937 (T)
Dempsey, Tom 1971-74 (K)
Dennard, Mark 1984-85 (C)
Dent, Richard 1997 (DE)
DeStantis, Dan 1941 (B)
Detmer, Koy 1997- (QB)
Detmer, Ty 1996-97 (QB)
DeVaughn, Dennis 1982-83 (DB)
Dial, Alan 1989 (DB)
Dial, Benjy 1967 (QB)
Diaz-Infante, David 1999 (G)
Dickerson, Kori 2003 (TE)
DiFilippo, Dave 1941 (G)
Dimmick, Tom 1956 (T)
Dimry, Charles 1997 (DB)
Dingle, Nate 1995 (LB)
DiRenzo, Danny 1948 (P)
Dirks, Mike 1968-71 (G)
Disend, Leo 1943 (T)
Ditka, Mike 1967-68 (E)
Dixon, Al 1983 (TE)
Dixon, Floyd 1992 (WR)
Dixon, Ronnie 1995-96 (DT)
Dixon, Zach 1980 (RB)
Dobbins, Herb 1974 (T)
Dorow, Al (QB)
Dogins, Kevin 2003 (G/C)
Dorenbos, Jon 2006-p* (LS)
Dorow, Al 1957 (B)
Dorsey, Dean 1988 (K)
Doss, Noble 1947-48 (B)
Douglas, Dameane 1999-2002 (WR)
Douglas, Hugh 1998-2002, 2004 (LB/DE)
2000, 2002 All Pro Selection
2001-03 Pro Bowl
Douglas, Merrill 1962 (B)
Douglas, Otis 1946-59 (T)
Dow, Woody 1938-40 (B)
Dowda, Harry 1954-55 (B)
Doyle, Ted 1943 (T)
Drake, Joe 1985 (DT)
Drake, Troy 1995-97 (T)
Drummond, Robert 1989-91 (RB)
Duckworth, Bobby 1986 (WR)
Dudley, Paul 1963 (B)
Dumbauld, John 1987-88 (DE)
Duncan, Rick 1968 (P)
Dunek, Ken 1980 (TE)
Dunn, Jason 1996-98 (TE)
Dunstan, Bill 1973-76 (DT)
Durko, John 1944 (E)

E

Edwards, Anthony 1989-90 (WR)
Edwards, Herm 1977-85 (CB)
Ehlers, Tom 1975-77 (LB)
Eibner, John 1941-42, 1946 (T)
Eiden, Ed 1944 (B)
Elewonibi, Moe 1995 (T)
Ellis, Drew 1938-40 (T)
Ellis, Ray 1981-85 (S)
Ellstrom, Swede 1934 (B)
Emanuel, Charles 1997 (S)
Emelianchik, Pete 1967 (E)
Emmons, Carlos 2000-03 (LB)
Emmons, Franklin 1940 (B)
Ena, Justin 2002-03, 2005 (LB)
Engles, Rick 1978 (P)
Enke, Fred 1952 (B)
Ephraim, Alonzo 2003-04 (C)
Erdlitz, Richard 1942, 1945 (B)
Estes, Larry 1972 (DE)
Evans, Byron 1987-94 (LB)
1990, 1992 All Pro Selection
Evans, Donald 1988 (DE)
Evans, Mike 1968-73 (C)
Everett, Eric 1988-89 (CB)
Everett, Major 1983-85 (FB)
Everitt, Steve 1997-99 (C)

F

Fagioli, Carl 1944 (G)
Farmer, Ray 1996-98 (LB)
Farragut, Ken 1951-54 (C)
1954 Pro Bowl
Fazio, Ron 1987r (TE)
Feagles, Jeff 1990-93 (P)
Feehery, Gerry 1983-87 (C/G)
1987 Ed Block Courage Award
Feeley, A.J. 2001-03, 2006-p* (QB)
Felber, Nip 1933 (E)
Feller, Happy 1971 (K)
Fenci, Dick 1933 (E)
Ferko, Fritz 1937-38 (G)
Ferrante, Jack 1941, 1944-50 (E)
1945, 1949 All Pro Selection
Ferrara, Frank 2003 (DE)
Ferris, Neil 1952 (B)
Fiedler, Bill 1938 (G)
Fiedler, Jay 1994-95 (QB)
Finn, Mike 1994 (T)
Finneran, Brian 1999 (WR)
Fitzgerald, Mickey 1981 (FB)
Fitzkee, Scott 1979-80 (WR)
Flanigan, Jim 2003 (DT)
Flores, Mike 1991-94 (DT)
Floyd, Eric 1992-93 (G)
Fogle, DeShawn 1997 (LB)
Folsom, Steve 1981 (TE)
Fontenot, Chris 1998 (TE)
Ford, Carl 2005- (WR)
Ford, Charles 1974 (DB)
Ford, Fredric 1997 (aCB)
Foules, Elbert 1983-87 (CB)
Fox, Terry 1941, 1945 (B)
Fraham, Dick 1935 (B)
Fraley, Hank 2000-05 (C)
France, Todd 2005 (K)
Frank, Joseph 1941, 1943 (T)
Franklin, Cleveland 1977-78 (RB)
Franklin, Tony 1979-83 (K)
Franks, Dennis 1976-78 (C)
Frazier, Derrick 1993-95 (CB)
Freeman, Antonio 2002 (WR)
Freeman, Bob 1960-61 (DB)
Frey, Glenn 1936-37 (B)
Friedlund, Bob 1946 (E)
Friedman, Bob 1944 (G)
Fritts, George 1945 (T)
Fritz, Ralph 1941 (G)
Fritzsche, Jim 1983 (T/G)
Frizzell, William 1986-90, 1992-93 (S)
Fryar, Irving 1996-98 (WR)
1997-98 Pro Bowl
Fuller, Frank 1963 (T)
Fuller, James 1996 (S)
Fuller, William 1994-96 (DE)
1995 All Pro Selection
1995-97 Pro Bowl
Furio, Dominic 2004 (C)

G

Gabbard, Steve 1989 (T)
Gabriel, Roman 1973-77 (QB)
1973 NFL Comeback Player of the Year
1974 Pro Bowl
Gaither, Omar 2006-p* (LB)
Gambold, Bob 1953 (B)
Gaona, Bob 1957 (T)
Gardner, Barry 1999-202 (LB)
Garner, Charlie 1994-98 (RB)
1995 Ed Block Courage Award
Garrity, Gregg 1984-89 (WR)
Gary, Rusell 1986 (DB)
Gauer, Charlie 1943-45 (E)
Gay, Blenda 1975-76 (DE)
George, Ed 1976-78 (T)
George, Raymond 1949 (T)
Gerber, Woody 1941-42 (G)
Gerhard, Chris 1987r (S)
Gerhart, Tom 1992 (DB)
Gersbach, Carl 1970 (LB)
Ghecas, Lou 1941 (B)
Giammona, Louie 1978-82 (RB)
Giancanelli, Hal 1953-56 (B)
Giannelli, Mario 1948-51 (G)
Gibbs, Pat 1972 (DB)
Gibron, Abe 1956-57 (G)
Giddens, Frank 1981-82 (T)
Giddens, Wimpy 1938 (T)
Gilbert, Lewis 1980 (TE)
Giles, Jimmie 1987-89 (TE)
Gill, Roger 1964-65 (B)
Gilmore, Jim 1986 (T)
Ginney, Jerry 1940 (G)
Glass, Glenn 1964-65 (B)
Gloden, Fred 1941 (B)
Glover, Rich 1975 (DT)
Gocong, Chris 2007-p* (LB/DE)
Goebel, Brad 1991 (QB)
Golden, Tim 1985 (LB)
Goldston, Ralph 1952, 1954-55 (B)
Golic, Mike 1987-92 (DT)
Gollomb, Rudy 1936 (G)
Gonya, Robert 1933-34 (T)
Goode, John 1985 (TE)
Goode, Rob 1955 (B)
Goodwin, Marvin 1994 (S)
Goodwin, Ron 1963-68 (E)

ALL-TIME EAGLES ROSTER

Gordon, Lamar 2005 (RB)
Gorecki, Chuck 1987r (LB)
Gossage, Gene 1960-62 (E)
Gouveia, Kurt 1995 (LB)
Graham, Dave 1963-69 (T)
Graham, Jeff 1998 (WR)
Graham, Lyle 1941 (C)
Graham, Nick 2007-p* (CB)
Graham, Tom 1935 (G)
Grant, Bud 1951-52 (E)
Grant, Otis 1987r (WR)
Grasmanis, Paul 2000-05 (DT)
Graves, Ray 1942-43, 1946 (C)
Gray, Cecil 1990-91 (G/DT)
Gray, Jim 1967 (B)
Gray, Mel 1997 (KR)
Green, Donnie 1977 (T)
Green, Jamel 2003-04 (DE)
Green, John 1947-51 (E)
1951 Pro Bowl
Green, Roy 1991-92 (WR)
Gregg, Kelly 1999-2000 (DT)
Gregory, Ken 1962 (E)
Griffen, Don 1996 (CB)
Griffin, Jeff 1987r (CB)
Griggs, Anthony 1982-85 (LB)
Grooms, Elois 1987 (DE)
Gros, Earl 1964-66 (FB)
Grossman, Burt 1998 (DE)
Gudd, Leonard 1934 (E)
Gude, Henry 1946 (G)
Guglielmi, Ralph 1963 (QB)
Guillory, Tony 1969 (LB)
Gunn, Mark 1995-96 (DL)
Gunnels, Riley 1960-64 (T)

H
Hackney, Elmer 1940-41 (B)
Haddix, Michael 1983-88 (FB)
Haden, Nick 1986 (G)
Hager, Britt 1989-94 (LB)
Hairston, Carl 1976-83 (DE)
Hajek, Chuck 1934 (C)
Hall, Andy 2005 (QB)
Hall, Irv 1942 (B)
Hall, Rhett 1995-98 (DT/G)
1997 Ed Block Courage Award
Hallstrom, Ron 1993 (G)
Halverson, Bill 1942 (T)
Halverson, Dean 1973-76 (LB)
Hamilton, Ray 1940 (E)
Hamilton, Skip 1987 (DT)
Hamiter, Uhuru 2000-01 (DE)
Hamner, Thomas 2000 (RB)
Hampton, Dave 1976 (RB)
Hampton, William 2001 (CB)
Hankton, Karl 1998 (WR)
Hansen, Roscoe 1951 (T)
Hanson, Homer 1935 (C)
Hanson, Joselio 2006-p* (CB)
Hanson, Swede 1933-37 (B)
1933-34 All Pro Selection
Harding, Greg 1987 (DB)
Harding, Roger 1947 (C)
Hardy, Andre 1984 (RB)
Hargrove, Marvin 1990 (WR)
Harmon, Andy 1991-97 (DT)
1995 All Pro Selection
Harper, Maurice 1937-40 (C)
Harrington, Perry 1980-83 (RB)
Harris, Al 1998-2002 (CB)
Harris, Al 1989-90 (LB)
Harris, Jim 1957 (B)
Harris, Jon 1997-98 (DE)
Harris, Leroy 1979-82 (FB)
Harris, Richard 1971-73 (DE)
Harris, Rod 1990-91 (WR)
Harris, Tim 1993 (DE)
Harrison, Bob 1962-63 (LB)
Harrison, Dennis 1978-84 (DE)
1983 Pro Bowl
Harrison, Granville 1941 (E)
Harrison, Tyreo 2002-03 (LB)
Hart, Clinton 2003-04 (S)
Hart, Dick 1967-71 (G)
Hartman, Fred 1948 (T)
Harvey, Richard 1970 (DB)
Haskins, Jon 1998 (LB)
Hasselbeck, Tim 2002 (QB)
Hauck, Tim 1999-2002 (S)
Hawkins, Ben 1966-67 (WR)
Hayden, Aaron 1998 (RB)
Hayden, Ken 1942 (C)
Hayes, Ed 1970 (DB)
Hayes, Joe 1984 (WR)
Haymond, Alvin 1968 (DB)
Heath, Jo Jo 1981 (DB)
Hebron, Vaughn 1993-95 (RB)
Heck, Ralph 1963-65 (LB)
Hegamin, George 1998 (G/T)
Heller, Ron 1988-92 (T)
Henderson, Jerome 1995 (CB)
Henderson, Zac 1980 (S)
Hendrickson, Steve 1995 (LB)
Henry, Maurice 1990 (LB)
Henry, Wally 1977-82 (WR)
1980 Pro Bowl
Henson, Gary 1963 (E)
Herremans, Todd 2005-p* (T)
Herrod, Jeff 1997 (LB)
Hershey, Kirk 1941 (E)
Hertel, Rob 1980 (QB)
Hewitt, Bill 1936-39, 1943 (E)
1937-38 All Pro Selection
Hicks, Artis 2002-05 (T)
Higgins, Tom 1954-55 (T)
Higgs, Mark 1989 (RB)
Hill, Fred 1965-71 (E)
Hill, King 1961-68 (QB)
Hinkle, Jack 1941-47 (HB)
1943 All Pro Selection
Hix, Billy 1950 (E)
Hoage, Terry 1986-90 (S)
Hobbs, Bill 1969-71 (LB)
Hodges, Reggie 2005 (P)
Hogan, Mike 1976-78, 1980 (FB)
Holcomb, William 1937 (T)
Holly, Bob 1984 (QB)
Holmes, Lester 1993-96 (G)
Hood, Roderick 2003- (CB)
Hooks, Alvin 1981 (WR)
Hoover, Mel 1982-84 (WR)
Hopkins, Wes 1983-93 (S)
1984-85 All Pro Selection
1986 Pro Bowl
1988 Ed Block Courage Award
Horan, Mike 1984-85 (P)
Hord, Roy 1962 (G)
Horn, Marty 1897r (QB)
Horrell, Bill 1952 (G)
Hoss, Clark 1972 (TE)
Howard, Bob 1978-79 (CB)
Howard, Darren 2006-p* (DE)
Howell, Lane 1965-69 (T)
Hoyem, Lynn 1964-67 (G)
Hoying, Bobby 1996-98 (QB)
Hrabetin, Frank 1942 (T)
Huarte, John 1968 (QB)
Hudson, Bob 1953-55, 1957-58 (B)
Hudson, John 1991-95 (G)
Hughes, Chuck 1967-69 (WR)
Hughes, William 1937-40 (C)
Hultz, Don 1964-73 (DT)
Humbert, Dick 1941, 1945-49 (E)
1941 All Pro Selection
Humphrey, Claude 1978-81 (DE)
Hunt, Calvin 1970 (C)
Hunt, Tony 2007-p* (RB)
Hunter, Herman 1985 (RB)
Huth, Jerry 1959-60 (G)
Hutton, Tom 1995-98 (P)
Huxhold, Ken 1954-58 (G)
Huzvar, John 1952 (B)

I
Ingram, Mark 1996 (WR)
Irvin, Willie 1953 (B)

J
Jackson, Al 1994 (CB)
Jackson, Alonzo 2005 (DE)
Jackson, Bob 1960 (B)
Jackson, Don 1936 (B)
Jackson, Earnest 1985-86 (RB)
Jackson, Greg 1994-95 (FS)
Jackson, Harold 1969-72 (WR)
1972 All Pro Selection
1970, 1973 Pro Bowl
Jackson, Jamaal 2003-p* (G/O)
2007 All-Pro
Jackson, Johnny 1977 (DE)
Jackson, Keith 1988-91 (TE)
1988-90 All Pro Selection
1989-91 Pro Bowl
1988 NFL Rookie of the Year
Jackson, Kenny 1984-88, 1990-91 (WR)
Jackson, Randy 1974 (RB)
Jackson, T.J. 1966 (DB)
Jacobs, David 1987r (K)
Jacobs, Proverb 1958 (T)
James, Angelo 1987 (CB)
James, Po 1972-75 (RB)
James, William 2007-p* (CB)
Janet, Ernie 1975 (T)

ALL-TIME EAGLES ROSTER

Jarmoluk, Mike 1949-55 (T)
1952 Pro Bowl
Jarvi, Toimi 1944 (B)
Jasper, Ed 1997-98 (DT)
Jaworski, Ron 1977-86 (QB)
1981 Pro Bowl; 1980 NFL MVP
1980 NFL MVP
1985 Ed Block Courage Award
Jean-Gilles, Max 2006-p* (G)
Jefferson, Greg 1995-2000 (DE)
Jefferson, William 1942 (B)
Jelesky, Tom 1985-86 (T)
Jells, Dietrich 1998-99 (WR)
Jenkins, Izel 1988-92 (CB)
Jenkins, Justin 2005- (WR)
Jeter, Tommy 1992-95 (DT)
Jiles, Dwayne 1986-89 (LB)
Johansson, Ove 1977 (K)
Johnson, Albert 1942 (B)
Johnson, Alonozo 1986-87 (LB)
Johnson, Alvin 1948 (B)
Johnson, Bill 1998-99 (DT)
Johnson, Charles 1999-2000 (WR)
Johnson, Charlie 1977-81 (DT)
1981 All Pro Selection
1980-82 Pro Bowl
Johnson, Chris 1987r (DB)
Johnson, Dirk 2003- (P)
Johnson, Don 1953-55 (B)
Johnson, Dwight 2000 (DE)
Johnson, Eric 1977-78 (DB)
Johnson, Gene 1959-60 (B)
Johnson, Jay 1969-70 (LB)
Johnson, Jimmie 1995-98 (TE)
Johnson, Kevin 1995-96 (DT)
Johnson, Lee 2002 (P)
Johnson, Maurice 1991-94 (TE)
Johnson, Norm 1999 (K)
Johnson, Reggie 1995 (TE)
Johnson, Ron 2003 (DE)
Johnson, Ron 1985-89 (WR)
Johnson, Vaughan 1994 (LB)
Jonas, Don 1962 (B)
Jones, Chris T. 1995-97 (WR)
Jones, Dhani 2004-p* (LB)
Jones, Don 1940 (B)
Jones, Harry 1967-71 (RB)
Jones, Jimmie 1997 (DL)
Jones, Joe 1974-75 (DE)
Jones, Julian 2001-2002 (S)
Jones, Preston 1993 (QB)
Jones, Ray 1970 (DB)
Jones, Spike 1975-77 (P)
Jones, Tyrone 1989 (DB)
Jordan, Andrew 1998 (TE)
Jorgensen, Carl 1935 (T)
Joseph, James 1991-94 (RB)
Joyner, Seth 1986-93 (LB)
1991-93 All Pro Selection
1992, 1994 Pro Bowl
Jurgensen, Sonny 1957-63 (QB)
1961 All Pro Selection
1962 Pro Bowl
Justice, Winston 2006-p* (T)

K

Kab, Vyto 1982-85 (TE)
Kalu, N.D. 1997, 2001-05 (DE)
Kane, Carl 1936 (B)
Kapele, John 1962 (T)
Kaplan, Bennie 1942 (G)
Karnofsky, Sonny 1945 (B)
Kasky, Ed 1942 (T)
Kaufusi, Steve 1989-90 (DE)
Kavel, George 1934 (B)
Kearse, Jevon 2004-p* (DE)
Keeling, Ray 1938-39 (T)
Keen, Rabbit 1937-38 (B)
Kekeris, Jim 1947 (T)
Keller, Ken 1956-57 (B)
Kelley, Bob 1955-56 (C)
Kelley, Dwight 1966-72 (LB)
Kelly, Jim 1965-67 (E)
Kelly, Joe 1996 (LB)
Kemp, Jeff 1991 (QB)
Kenneally, George 1933-35 (E)
Kenney, Steve 1980-85 (G)
Kersey, Merritt 1974-75 (P)
Key, Wade 1970-80 (G/T)
Keyes, Leroy 1969-72 (DB)
Keys, Howard 1960-64 (T/C)
Khayat, Ed 1958-61, 1964-65 (DT)
Kilroy, Bucko 1943-55 (T)
1948-54 All Pro Selection
1953-55 Pro Bowl
Kimmel, Jon 1985 (LB)
Kinder, Randy 1997 (CB)
King, Don 1956 (T)
Kirchbaum, Kelly 1987r (LB)
Kirkland, Levon 2002 (LB)
Kirkman, Roger 1933-35 (B)
Kirksey, Roy 1973-74 (G)
Kish, Ben 1942-49 (B)
Klingel, John 1987-88 (DE)
Kloppenberg, Harry 1936 (T)
Kmetovic, Pete 1946 (B)
Knapper, Joe 1934 (B)
Knox, Charles 1937 (T)
Koeninger, Art 1933 (C)
Kolb, Kevin 2007-p* (QB)
Kolberg, Elmer 1939-40 (B)
Koman, Bill 1957-58 (LB)
Konecny, Mark 1988 (RB)
Kowalczyk, Walt 1958-59 (B)
Kowalkowski, Scott 1991-93 (LB)
Kramer, Kent 1971-74 (TE)
Kraynak, Rich 1983-86 (LB)
Krepfle, Keith 1975-81 (TE)
Kresky, Joe 1933-35 (G)
Krieger, Robert 1941, 1946 (E)
Kriel, Emmett 1939 (G)
Kuczynski, Bert 1946 (E)
Kullman, Mike 1987r (S)
Kupcinet, Irv 1935 (B)
Kusko, John 1936-38 (B)

L

Laack, Galen 1958 (G)
Labinjo, Mike 2004-05 (LB)
Lackman, Dick 1933-35 (B)
Lainhart, Porter 1933 (B)
Landeta, Sean 1999-2002, 2005 (P)
Landsberg, Mort 1941 (B)
Landsee, Bob 1986-87 (G/C)
Lang, Israel 1964-68 (FB)
Lankas, James 1942 (B)
Lansford, Buck 1955-57 (T)
1957 Pro Bowl
Lapham, Bill 1960 (C)
Larson, Bill 1978 (TE)
Latimer, Al 1979 (CB)
Laux, Ted 1942-4 (B)
Lavender, Joe 1973-75 (CB)
Lavergne, Damian 2003 (T)
Lavette, Robert 1987 (RB)
Lawrence, Kent 1969 (WR)
Lawrence, Reggie 1993 (WR)
Lazetich, Pete 1976-77 (DT)
Leathers, Milton 1933 (G)
LeBel, Harper 1990 (TE)
Lechthaler, Roy 1933 (G)
Ledbetter, Toy 1950, 1953-55 (B)
Lee, Amp 2000 (RB)
Lee, Bernie 1938 (B)
Lee, Byron 1986-87r (LB)
Leggett, Scott 1987r (G)
LeMaster, Frank 1974-83 (LB)
1982 Pro Bowl
Leonard, Jim 1934-37 (B)
Leshinski, Ron 1999 (TE)
Levanities, Stephen 1942 (T)
Levens, Dorsey 2002, 2004 (RB)
Lewis, Chad 1997-2005 (TE)
2001-03 Pro Bowl
2005 Ed Block Courage Award
Lewis, Greg 2003-p* (WR)
Lewis, Joe 1962 (T)
Lewis, Michael 2002- (S)
2004 All Pro Selection
2005 Pro Bowl
Leyendecker, Tex 1933 (T)
Lilly, Sammy 1989-90 (DB)
Lince, Dave 1966-67 (E)
Lindskag, Vic 1944-51 (C)
1951 All-Pro
Lio, Augie 1946 (G)
1946 All Pro Selection
Lipski, John 1933-34 (C)
Liske, Pete 1971-72 (QB)
Liter, Greg 1987r (DE)
Little, Dave 1985-89 (TE)
Lloyd, Dave 1963-70 (LB)
Lofton, James 1993 (WR)
1970 Pro Bowl
Logan, Randy 1973-83 (S)
1980 All Pro Selection
1980-81Pro Bowl
Long, Matt 1987r (C)
Looney, Don 1940 (E)
1940 All Pro Selection
Lou, Ron 1975 (C)
Louderback, Tom 1958-59 (LB)
Love, Clarence 1998 (CB)
Love, Sean 1997 (G)
Lucas, Dick 1960-63 (E)
Lueck, Bill 1975 (G)

All-Time Eagles Roster

Luft, Don 1954 (E)
Luken, Tom 1972-78 (G)
Lusk, Herb 1976-78 (RB)

M

MacAfee, Ken 1959 (E)
MacDowell, Jay 1946-51 (E)
MacMurdo, Jim 1934-37 (T)
Macioszcyk, Art 1944-47 (B)
Mack, Bill 1964 (WR)
Mackey, Kyle 1986 (QB)
Mackrides, Bill 1947-51 (B)
Magee, John 1948-55 (G)
Mahalic, Drew 1976-78 (LB)
Mahe, Reno 2003- (RB)
Mallory, John 1968 (B)
Malone, Art 1975-76 (RB)
Mamula, Mike 1995-2000 (DE)
1999 Ed Block Courage Award
Mandarino, Mike 1944-45 (G)
Manning, Roosevelt 1975 (DT)
Mansfield, Ray 1963 (C)
Mansfield, Von 1982 (DB)
Manske, Ed 1935-36 (E)
1935 All Pro Selection
Manton, Taldon 1940 (B)
Manzini, Baptiste 1944-45, 1948 (C)
Marchi, Basillio 1941-42 (C)
Mark, Greg 1990 (DE)
Maronic, Duke 1944-50 (G)
Marshall, Anthony 1998 (S)
Marshall, Keyonta 2005- (DT)
Marshall, Larry 1974-77 (KR)
Marshall, Whit 1996 (LB)
Martin, Aaron 1966-67 (DB)
Martin, Ceil 1999-2002 (FB)
2000 Ed Block Courage Award
Martin, Kelvin 1995 (WR)
Martin, Steve 1998-99 (DT)
Mass, Wayne 1972 (T)
Masters, Bob 1937-38, 1941-43 (B)
Masters, Walt 1936 (B)
Matesic, Ed 1934-35 (B)
Matson, Ollie 1964-66 (RB)
Mavraides, Menil 1954, 1957 (G)
May, Dean 1984 (QB)
Mayberry, Jermane 1996-2004 (G/T)
2002 All Pro Selection
2003 Pro Bowl
Mayes, Rufus 1979 (T)
Maynard, Les 1933 (B)
Mazzanti, Jerry 1963 (E)
McAfee, Wesley 1941 (B)
McAllister, James 1975-76 (RB)
McCants, Damerien 2005 (WR)
McChesney, Bob 1950 (E)
McClellan, Mike 1962-63 (B)
McCloskey, Mike 1987 (TE)
McCoo, Eric 2004 (RB)
McCoy, Matt 2005-p* (LB)
McCoy, Pat 2006-p* (T)
McCrary, Fred 1995 (FB)
McCullough, Hugh 1943 (B)
McCusker, Jim 1959-62
McDonal, Don 1944-45 (E)
McDonald, Lester 1940 (E)
McDonald, Tommy 1957-63 (WR)
1959-1962 All Pro Selection
1959-63 Pro Bowl
McDonough, Robert 1942-46 (G)
McDougle, Jerome 2003-p* (DE)
2006 Ed Block Courage Award
McFadden, Paul 1984-87 (K)
1984 NFC Rookie of the Year
McHale, Tom 1993-94 (G/T)
McHugh, Pat 1947-51 (B)
McIntyre, Guy 1995-96 (G)
McKeever, Marlin 1973 (LB)
McKenzie, Kevin 1998 (WR)
McKenzie, Raleigh 1995-96 (C)
McKnight, Dennis 1991 (G)
McMahon, Jim 1990-92 (QB)
1991 NFL Comeback Player of the Year
McMahon, Mike 2005 (QB)
McMillan, Erik 1993 (S)
McMillen, Dan 1987r (DE)
McMillian, Mark 1992-95 (CB)
McMullen, Billy 2003-05 (WR)
McNabb, Dexter 1995 (FB)
McNabb, Donovan 1999-p* (QB)
2001-05 Pro Bowl
2000, 2004 NFC MVP
McNeill, Tom 1971-73 (P)
McPherson, Don 1988-90 (QB)
McPherson, Forrest 1935-37 (T)
McRae, Jerrold 1979 (WR)
McTyer, Tim 1997-98 (CB)
Meadows, Ed 1958 (E)
Medved, Ron 1966-70 (DB)
Mellekas, John 1963 (DT)
Mercer, Giradie 2000 (DT)
Merkens, Guido 1987 (QB)
Meyer, Fred 1942, 1945 (E)
Meyers, John 1964-67 (T)
Miano, Rich 1991-94 (DB)
Michaels, Ed 1943-46 (G)
Michel, Mike 1978 (P/K)
Michels, John 1999 (T)
Michels, John 1953 (G)
Middlebrook, Oren 1978 (WR)
Mike-Mayer, Nick 1977-78 (K)
Mikell, Quintin 2003-p* (S)
2007 All-Pro
Millard, Keith 1993 (D/T)
Miller, Bubba 1996-2001 (C/G)
Miller, Don 1954 (B)
Miller, Tom 1942-44 (E)
Milling, Al 1942 (G)
Milon, Barnes 1934 (G)
Milons, Freddie 2002 (WR)
Mira, George 1969 (QB)
Miraldi, Dean 1982-84 (T)
Mitcham, Gene 1958 (E)
Mitchell, Brian 2000-2002 (KR)
Mitchell, Freddie 2001-04 (WR)
Mitchell, Leonard 1981-86 (DE/T)
Mitchell, Martin 1977 (DB)
Mitchell, Randall 1987r (NT)
Moats, Ryan 2005-p* (RB)
Molden, Frank 1968 (T)
Monk, Art 1995 (WR)
Monroe, Henry 1979 (CB)
Montgomery, Wilbert 1977-84 (RB)
1978-79 All Pro Selection
1979-80 Pro Bowl
Mooney, Tim 1987 (DE)
Moore, Damon 1999-2001 (S)
Moreno, Zeke 2005 (LB)
Morey, Sean 2001, 2003 (WR)
Morgan, Dennis 1975 (KR)
Morgan, Mike 1964-67 (LB)
Morris, Dwaine 1985 (DT)
Morriss, Guy 1973-83 (C)
Morse, Bobby 1987 (RB)
Mortell, Emmett 1937-39 (B)
Moseley, Mark 1970 (K)
Moselle, Dom 1954 (B)
Mrkonic, George 1953 (T)
Muha, Joe 1946-50 (B)
1948, 1950 All Pro Selection
Muhlmann, Horst 1975-77 (K)
Mulligan, George 1936 (E)
Murley, Dick 1956 (T)
Murphy, Nick 2005 (P)
Murray, Calvin 1981-82 (HB)
Murray, Eddie 1994 (K)
Murray, Francis 1339-40 (B)
Myers, Brad 1958 (B)
Myers, Jack 1948-50 (B)

N

Nacelli, Andy 1958 (E)
Nease, Mike 1987r (C/T)
Nelson, Al 1965-73 (DB)
Nelson, Dennis 1976-77 (T)
Nettles, Jim 1965-68 (DB)
Newton, Charles 1939-40 (B)
Nichols, Gerald 1993 (DT)
Niland, John 1975-76 (G)
Nipp, Maurice 1952-53, 1956 (G)
Nocera, John 1959-62 (LB)
Norby, Jack 1934 (B)
Nordquist, Mark 1968-74 (G)
Norton, Jerry 1954-58 (DB)
1958-59 Pro Bowl
Norton, Jim 1968 (T)
Nowak, Walt 1944 (E)

O

Oakes, Don 1961-62 (T)
O'Boyle, Harry 1933 (B)
O'Brien, Davey 1939-40 (QB)
1939-40 All Pro Selection
O'Brien, Ken 1993 (QB)
Obst, Henry 1933 (G)
Oden, Derrick 1993-95 (LB)
Olds, Bill 1976 (RB)
Oliver, Greg 1973-74 (RB)
Oliver, Hubie 1981-85 (FB)
O'Neal, Brian 1994 (FB)
Opperman, Jim 1975 (LB)
O'Quinn, John 1951 (E)
Oristaglio, Bob 1952 (E)
Ormsbe, Elliott 1946 (B)
Osborn, Mike 1978 (LB)

ALL-TIME EAGLES ROSTER

Osborne, Richard 1976-78 (TE)
Outlaw, John 1973-78 (DB)
Overmeyer, Bill 1972 (LB)
Owens, Don 1958-60 (T)
Owens, Terrell 2004-05 (WR)
2004 All Pro Selection
2005 Pro Bowl

P

Pacella, Dave 1984 (G/C)
Padlow, Max 1935 (E)
Pagliei, Joe 1959 (B)
Palelei, Lonnie 1999 (T/G)
Palmer, Leslie 1948 (B)
Panos, Joe 1994-97 (G)
Papale, Vince 1976-78 (WR)
Parker, Artimus 1974-76 (DB)
Parker, Rodney 1980-81 (WR)
Parmer, Jim 1948-56 (B)
Parry, Josh 2002, 04-05 (FB)
Paschka, Gordon 1943 (G)
Pastorini, Dan 1982-93 (QB)
Pate, Rupert 1942 (G)
Patterson, Mike 2005-p* (DT)
Patton, Cliff 1946-50 (G)
1949 All Pro Selection
Patton, Jerry 1974 (DT)
Payne, Ken 1978 (WR)
Peaks, Clarence 1957-63 (FB)
Pederson, Doug 1999 (QB)
Peete, Rodney 1995-98 (QB)
Pegg, Harold 1940 (C)
Pellegrini, Bob 1956, 1958-61 (LB)
Penaranda, Jairo 1985 (RB)
Peoples, Woody 1978-80 (G)
Perot, Pete 1979-84 (G)
Perrino, Mike 1987r (T)
Perry, Bruce 2004- (RB)
Perry, William 1993-94 (DT)
Peters, Floyd 1964-69 (DT)
1965, 1967-68 Pro Bowl
1967 Pro Bowl MVP
Peters, Scott 2002 (OL)
Peters, Volney 1958 (T)
Pettigrew, Gary 1966-74 (DT)
Philbin, Gerry 1973 (DE)
Phillips, Ray 1978-81 (LB)
Phillips, Ray 1987r (DE/LB)
Picard, Bob 1973-76 (WR)
Pihos, Pete 1947-55 (E)
1947-50, 1952-55 All Pro Selection
1951-56 Pro Bowl
Pilconis, Joe 1934, 1936-37 (E)
Pinder, Cyril 1968-70 (B)
Pinkston, Todd 2000-04 (WR)
Piro, Henry 1941 (E)
Pisarcik, Joe 1980-84 (QB)
Pitts, Alabama 1935 (B)
Pitts, Mike 1987-92 (DL)
Pivarnick, Joe 1936 (G)
Poage, Ray 1964-65 (E)
Pollard, Al 1951-53 (B)
Polley, Tom 1985 (LB)
Porter, Ron 1969-72 (LB)
Poth, Phil 1934 (G)
Powell, Art 1959 (WR)
Powlus, Ron 2000 (QB)
Preece, Steve 1970-72 (DB)
President, Andre 1997 (TE)
Presott, Harold 1947-49 (E)
Priestly, Robert 1942 (E)
Prisco, Nick 1933 (B)
Pritchard, Bosh 1942, 1946-51 (B)
Pritchett, Stanley 2000 (FB)
Puetz, Garry 1979 (T)
Pylman, Bob 1938-39 (T)
Pyne, Jim 2001 (C/G)

Q

Qinlan, Bill 1963 (DE)
Quick, Mike 1982-90 (WR)
1983, 1985, 1987 All Pro Selection
1984-88 Pro Bowl
1989 Ed Block Courage Award

R

Rado, George 1937-38 (E)
Ragazzo, Phil 1940-41 (T)
1941 All Pro Selection
Ramsey, Herschel 1938-40, 1945 (E)
Ramsey, Knox 1952 (G)
Ramsey, LaJuan 2006-p* (DT)
Ramsey, Nate 1963-72 (DB)
Rash, Lou 1984 (CB)
Raskowski, Leo 1935 (T)
Ratliff, Don 1975 (DE)
Rauch, John 1951 (QB)
Rayburn, Sam 2003- (DT)
Raye, Jim 1969 (DB)
Reader, Jamie 2001 (FB)
Reagan, Frank 1949-51 (B)
Reagor, Montae 2007-p* (DT)
Reaves, John 1972-75 (QB)
Recher, Dave 1965-68 (C)
Reed, J.R. 2004-05, 2007* (S)
Reed, James 1977 (LB)
Reed, Michael 1998 (FB)
Reed, Taft 1967 (B)
Reese, Henry 1935-39 (C/LB)
Reese, Ike 1998-2004 (LB)
2004 All Pro Selection
2005 Pro Bowl
Reeves, Ken 1985-89 (T)
Reeves, Marion 1974 (DB)
Reichenbach, Mike 1984-89 (LB)
Reichow, Jerry 1960 (E)
Reid, Allen 1987 (RB)
Reid, Mike 1993-95 (S)
Reilly, Kevin 1973-74 (LB)
Renfro, Leonard 1993-94 (DT)
Renfro, Will 1961 (E)
Repko, Jay 1987r (TE)
Restic, Joe 1952 (E)
Retzlaff, Pete 1956-66 (TE)
1958, 1964-66 All Pro Selection
1959, 1961, 1964-66 Pro Bowl
1965 NFL MVP
Reutt, Ray 1943 (E)
Ricca, Jim 1955-56 (T)
Richards, Bobby 1962-65 (DE)
Richardson, Jess 1953-61 (DT)
1960 All Pro Selection
1960 Pro Bowl
Richardson, Paul 1993 (WR)
Richmond, Greg 2005- (LB)
Riffle, Dick 1938-40 (B)
Riley, Lee 1956, 1958-59 (DB)
Rimington, Dave 1988-89 (C)
Ringo, Jim 1964-67 (C)
1964, 1966 All Pro Selection;
1965-66, 1968 Pro Bowl
Rissmiller, Ray 1966 (T)
Ritchie, Jon 2003-04 (FB)
Robb, Joe 1959-60 (DE)
Roberts, John 1933-34 (B)
Robinson, Burle 1935 (E)
Robinson, Jacque 1987 (FB)
Robinson, Jerry 1979-84 (LB)
1980-81, 1983 All Pro Selection
1982 Pro Bowl
Robinson, Wayne 1952-56 (LB)
1955 All Pro Selection
1955-56 Pro Bowl
Rocca, Sav 2007-p* (P)
Rodgers, Stefan 2006-p* (G)
Roffler, William 1954 (B)
Rogalla, John 1945 (B)
Rogas, Dan 1952 (G)
Romanowski, Bill 1994-95 (LB)
Romero, Ray 1951 (G)
Roper, Dedrick 2005- (LB)
Roper, John 1993 (LB)
Rose, Ken 1990-94 (LB)
Ross, Alvin 1987r (FB)
Ross, Oliver 1999 (T)
Rossovich, Tim 1968-71 (LB)
1970 Pro Bowl
Rossum, Allen 1998-99 (KR/CB)
Roton, Herbert 1937 (E)
Roussel, Tom 1973 (LB)
Rowan, Everitt 1933 (E)
Rowe, Robert 1935 (B)
Royals, Mark 1987r (P)
Rucker, Keith 1996 (DT)
Rudolph, Joe 1995 (G)
Runager, Max 1979-83, 1989 (P)
Runyan, Jon 2000-p* (T)
2003 Pro Bowl
Russell, Booker 1981 (FB)
Russell, James 1936-37 (T)
Russell, Laf 1933 (B)
Russell, Rusty 1984 (T)
Ruzek, Roger 1989-93 (K)
Ryan, Pat 1991 (QB)
Ryan, Rocky 1956-58 (E)
Ryczek, Paul 1987r (C)
Rypien, Mark 1996 (QB)

S

Sader, Steve 1943 (B)
Saidock, Tom 1957 (T)
Sampleton, Lawrence 1982-84 (TE)
Samson, Michael 1996 (DT)
Sanders, John 1977-79 (DB)
Sanders, John 1943, 1945 (G)
Sanders, Thomas 1990-91 (RB)

ALL-TIME EAGLES ROSTER

Sandifer, Dan 1950-51 (DB)
Sapp, Theron 1959-63 (B)
Savirsky, George 1948-49 (T)
Saxon, James 1995 (FB)
Scarpati, Joe 1964-69, 1971 (S)
Schad, Mike 1989-93 (G)
Schaefer, Don 1956 (B)
Schau, Ryan 1999-2001 (G/T)
Schmidt, Ted 1938-40 (C)
Schnelker, Bob 1953 (E)
Schneller, Bill 1940 (B)
Schobel, Matt 2006-p* (TE)
Schrader, Jim 1962-64 (C)
Schreiber, Adam 1986-88 (C/G)
Schuehle, Jake 1939 (B)
Schultz, Eberle 1940, 1943 (G)
1943 All Pro Selection
Schulz, Jody 1983-87 (LB)
1986 Ed Block Courage Award
Sciarra, John 1978-83 (DB)
Sciullo, Steve 2004 (G)
Scott, Clyde 1949-52 (B)
Scott, Gari 2000-01 (WR)
Scott, Tom 1953-58 (DE)
1955-56 All Pro Selection
1958-59 Pro Bowl
Scotti, Ben 1962-63 (CB)
Seals, Leon 1992 (DT/G)
Sears, Vic 1941-53 (T)
1943, 1945, 1949-50, 1952 All Pro Selection
Seay, Mark 1996-97 (WR)
Sebastian, Mike 1935 (B)
Selby, Rob 1991-94 (G)
Shann, Bob 1965-67 (B)
Sharkey, Ed 1954-55 (T)
Shaub, Harry 1935 (G)
Shaw, Ricky 1989-90 (LB)
Sheppard, Lito 2002-p* (CB)
2004 All Pro Selection
2005, 2007 Pro Bowl
Sherman, Al 1943-47 (B)
Sherman, Health 1989-93 (RB)
Shires, Marshall 1945 (T)
Shonk, John 1941 (E)
Short, Jason 2004- (LB)
Shuler, Mickey 1990-91 (TE)
Siano, Mike 1987r (WR)
Sikahema, Vai 1992-93 (KR)
1992 All Pro Selection
Simerson, John 1957-58 (C)
Simmons, Clyde 1986-93 (DE)
1991-92 All Pro Selection
1992-93 Pro Bowl
Simon, Corey 2000-04 (DT)
2001 All Pro Selection
2004 Pro Bowl
Simoneau, Mark 2003-05 (LB)
Sinceno, Kaseem 1998-99 (TE)
Singletary, Reggie 1986-90 (DT/G)
Sisemore, Jerry 1973-84 (T)
1980, 1982 Pro Bowl
Sistrunk, Manny 1976-79 (DT)
Skaggs, Jim 1963-72 (G)
Skladany, Leo 1949 (E)
Skladany, Tom 1983 (P)
Slater, Mark 1979-83 (C)
Slay, Henry 1998 (DT)
Slechta, Jeremy 2002 (DT)
Small, Jessie 1989-91 (LB)
Small, Torrance 1999-2000 (WR)
Smalls, Fred 1987r (LB)
Smart, Rod 2001 (RB)
Smeja, Rudy 1946 (E)
Smith, Ben 1990-93 (DB)
Smith, Charles 1974-81 (WR)
Smith, Darrin 1997 (LB)
Smith, Daryle 1990-92 (T)
Smith, Ed 1999 (TE)
Smith, J.D. 1959-63 (T)
1962 Pro Bowl
Smith, Jack 1945 (T)
Smith, Jackie 1971 (DB)
Smith, John 1942 (T)
Smith, L.J. 2003-p* (TE)
Smith, Milton 1945 (E)
Smith, Otis 1991-94 (CB)
Smith, Phil 1986 (WR)
Smith, Ralph 1963-64 (E)
Smith, Ray 1933 (C)
Smith, Rich 1933 (C)
Smith, Robert 1956 (B)
Smith, Ron 1981-83 (WR)
Smith, Steve 1971-74 (T)
Smith, Tony 1999 (WR)
Smothers, Howard 1995 (G)
Smukler, Dave 1936-39 (B)
Snead, Norm 1964-70 (QB)
1966 Pro Bowl
Snyder, Lum 1952-55, 1958 (T)
1952-55 All Pro Selection
1954-55 Pro Bowl
Sodaski, John 1972-73 (LB)
Soloman, Freddie 1995-98 (WR)
Solt, Ron 1988-91 (G)
1990 Ed Block Courage Award
Somers, George 1939-40 (T)
Spach, Stephen 2005 (TE)
Spagnola, John 1979-87 (TE)
1984 Ed Block Courage Award
Spikes, Takeo 2007-p* (LB)
Spillers, Ray 1937 (T)
Stackpool, John 1942 (B)
Stacy, Siran 1992 (RB)
Stafford, Dick 1962-63 (E)
Staley, Duce 1997-2003 (RB)
2001 Ed Block Courage Award
Steele, Ernie 1942-48 (B)
1943 All Pro Selection
Steere, Dick 1951 (T)
Steinbach, Laurence 1933 (T)
Steinke, Gil 1945-48 (B)
Stetz, Bill 1967 (G)
Stevens, Don 1952, 1954 (B)
Stevens, Matt 1997-98 (S)
Stevens, Pete 1936 (C)
Stevens, Richard 1970-74 (T)
Steward, Dean 1943 (B)
Stewart, Tony 2001-02 (TE)
Stickel, Walt 1950-51 (T)
Stockton, Herschel 1937-38 (G)
Storm, Edward 1934-35 (B)
Strauthers, Tom 1983-86 (DE)
Stribling, Bill 1955-57 (E)
Strickland, Donald 2005- (CB)
Striegel, Bill 1959 (G)
Stringer, Bob 1952-53 (B)
Stubbs, Dan 1995 (DE)
Sturgeon, Cecil 1941 (T)
Strum, Jerry 1972 (C)
Suffridge, Bob 1941-45 (G)
1941 All Pro Selection
Sugar, Leo 1961 (DE)
1961 All Pro Selection
Sullivan, Tom 1972-77 (RB)
Supulski, Leonard 1942 (E)
Sutton, Joe 1950-52 (B)
Sutton, Mitch 1974-75 (DT)
Swift, Justin 1999 (TE)
Sydner, Jeff 1992-94 (WR)
Szafaryn, Len 1957-58 (T)
Szymanski, Frank 1948 (C)

T

Talcott, Dan 1947 (T)
Taliaferro, George 1955 (B)
Tamburello, Ben 1987-90 (C/G)
Tapeh, Thomas 2004-p* (F B)
Tarasovic, George 1963-65 (DE)
Tarver, John 1975 (RB)
Taseff, Carl 1961 (DB)
Tautalatasi, Taivale 1986-88 (RB)
Tautolo, Terry 1976-79 (LB)
Taylor, Bobby 1995-2003 (CB)
2002 All Pro Selection
2003 Pro Bowl
1998 Ed Block Courage Award
Teltschik, John 1986-90 (P)
Thacker, Alvin 1941 (G)
Thomas, Hollis 1996-05(DT)
Thomas, Johnny 1996 (CB)
Thomas, Juqua 2005-p* (DE)
Thomas, Markus 1993 (RB)
Thomas, William 1991-99 (LB)
1995 All Pro Selection
1996-97 Pro Bowl
Thomas, William "Tra" 1998-p* (T)
2002, 2004 All Pro Selection
2002-03, 2005 Pro Bowl
Thomason, Bobby 1952-57 (QB)
1954, 1956-57 Pro Bowl
Thomason, Stumpy 1935-36 (B)
Thomason, Jeff 2000-2002, 2004 (TE)
Thoms, Art 1977 (DE)
Thompson, Broderick 1993-94 (T)
Thompson, Don 1964 (E)
Thompson, Russ 1940 (T)
Thompson, Tommy 1941-42, 1945-50 (QB)
1942, 1948-49, All Pro Selection
Thorton, Richard 1933 (B)
Thrash, James 2001-03 (WR)
Thrower, Jim 1970-72 (DB)
Thurbon, Robert 1943 (B)
Timpson, Michael 1997 (WR)
Tinsley, Scott 1987r (QB)
Togafau, Pago 2007* (LB)
Tom, Mel 1967-73 (DE)
Tomasetti, Lou 1940-41 (B)

ALL-TIME EAGLES ROSTER

Toney, Anthony 1986-90 (FB)
Torrey, Bob 1980 (FB)
Townsend, Greg 1994 (DE)
Tracey, John 1961 (DE)
Tremble, Greg 1995 (DB)
Tripucka, Frank 1949 (QB)
Trost, Milton 1940 (T)
Trotter, Jeremiah 1998-2001, 2004-06 (LB)
2000 All Pro Selection
2001-02, 2005-06 Pro Bowl
Troup, Bill 1975 (QB)
Tupper, Jeff 1986 (DE)
Turnbow, Guy 1933-34 (T)
Turner, Kevin 1995-99 (FB)
1996 Ed Block Courage Award
Turral, Willie 1987r (RB)
Tuten, Rick 1989 (P)
Tyrell, Joe 1952 (G)

U
Ulmer, Michael 1987 (QB)
Unutoa, Morris 1996-98 (C)
Upersa, Tuufuli 1971 (G)

V
Valentine, Zach 1982-83 (LB)
Van Brocklin, Norm 1958-60 (QB)
1960 All Pro Selection
1959-61 Pro Bowl
1960 NFL MVP
Van Buren, Ebert 1951-53 (B)
Van Buren, Steve 1944-51 (RB)
1944-50 All Pro Selection
Van Dyke, Alex 1999-2000 (WR)
Van Dyke, Bruce 1966 (G)
Vasys, Arunas 1966-68 (LB)
Vick, Roger 1990 (RB)
Vincent, Troy 1996-2003 (CB)
2002 All Pro Selection
2000-04 Pro Bowl
von Oelhoffen, Kimo 2007* (DT)

W
Wagner, Steve 1980-81 (S)
Wainwright, Frank 1995 (TE)
Walik, Billy 1970-72 (WR)
Walker, Adam 1996 (FB)
Walker, Corey 1997-98 (RB)
Walker, Darwin 2000- (DT/G)
Walker, Herschel 1992-94 (RB)
Wallace, Al 1997-99 (DE/LB)
Walston, Bobby 1951-62 (E/K)
1951 All Pro Selection
1961-62 Pro Bowl
1951 NFL Rookie of the Year
Walters, Pete 1987r (G)
Walters, Stan 1975-83 (T)
1979 All Pro Selection
1979-80 Pro Bowl
Walton, John 1976-79 (QB)
Ward, Jim 1971-72 (QB)
Ware, Matt 2004-05 (CB)
Warren, Busit 1945 (B)
Warren, Chris 2000 (RB)
Waters, Andre 1984-93 (S/LB)
1993 Ed Block Courage Award
Waters, Mike 1986 (FB)
Watkins, Foster 1940-41 (B)
Watkins, Larry 1970-72 (B)
Watson, Edwin 1999 (RB)
Watson, Tim 1997 (S)
Watters, Ricky 1995-97 (RB)
1996-97 Pro Bowl
Waynes, Nate 2003-04 (LB)
Wear, Robert 1942 (C)
Weatherall, Jim 1955-57 (T)
1956-57 Pro Bowl
Weaver, Jed 1999 (TE)
Weber, Chuck 1959-61 (LB)
Weedon, Don 1947 (G)
Wegert, Ted 1955-56 (B)
Weiner, Albert 1934 (B)
Weinstock, Isadore 1935 (B)
Welbourn, John 1999-2003 (G/T)
Weldon, Casey 1992 (QB)
Wells, Billy 1958 (B)
Wells, Harold 1965-68 (LB)
Wendlick, Joseph 1940 (B)
Wenzel, Jeff 1987r (T)
West, Ed 1995-96 (TE)
West, Hodges 1941 (T)
West, Troy 1987 (SS)
Westbrook, Brian 2002-p* (RB)
2005 Pro Bowl
2008 Pro Bowl
Whalen, Jim 1971 (TE)
Wheeler, Mark 1999 (DT/G)
Whire, John 1933 (B)
White, Allison 1939 (T)
White, Reggie 1985-92 (DE)
1986-92 All Pro Selection
1987-93 Pro Bowl
1987 Pro Bowl MVP
1987, 1991 NFL Defensive MVP
1987, 1991 NFC Defensive MVP
Whiting, Brandon 1998-2003 (DL)
Whitmore, David 1995 (S)
Whittingham, Fred 1966, 1971 (LB)
Wilburn, Barry 1995-96 (S)
Wilcox, John 1960 (T)
Wilkes, Reggie 1978-85 (LB)
Wilkins, Jeff 1994 (K)
Will, Erwin 1965 (DT)
Willey, Norm 1950-57 (DE)
1953-55 All Pro Selection
1955-56 Pro Bowl
Williams, Ben 1999 (DT)
Williams, Bernard 1994 (T)
Williams, Bobbie 2000-03 (G)
Williams, Boyd 1947 (C)
Williams, Byron 1983 (WR)
Williams, Calvin 1990-96 (WR)
Williams, Charlie 1978 (CB)
Williams, Clyde 1935 (T)
Williams, Henry 1989 (WR)
Williams, Jerry 1953-54 (B)
Williams, Joel 1983-85 (LB)
Williams, Michael 1983-84 (RB)
Williams, Roger 1973 (DB)
Williams, Ted 1973 (B)
Williams, Tex 1942 (G)
Williams, Tyrone 1999-2000 (DE)
Willis, James 1995-98 (LB)
Willson, Osborne 1933-35 (G)
Wilson, Bill 1938 (E)
Wilson, Bernard 1979-86 (S)
Wilson, Harry 1967-70 (B)
Wilson, Jerry 1959-60 (E)
Winfield, Vern 1972-73 (G)
Wink, Dean 1967-68 (DT)
Wirgowski, Dennis 1973 (DE)
Wistert, Al 1943-51 (T)
1944-51 All Pro Selection
1951 Pro Bowl
Witherspoon, Derrick 1995-97 (RB)
Wittenborn, John 1960-62 (G)
Wojciechowicz, Alex 1946-50 (C)
Wolfe, Hugh 1940 (B)
Woltman, Clem 1938-40 (T)
Woodard, Marc 1994-96 (LB)
Woodeshick, Tom 1963-71 (RB)
1968-69 All Pro Selection
1969 Pro Bowl
Woodruff, Lee 1933 (B)
Woodruff, Tony 1982-84 (WR)
Woodson, Sean 1998 (S)
Worden, Neil 1954, 1957 (RB)
Woulfe, Mike 1962 (LB)
Wright, Gordon 1967 (G)
Wright, Sylvester 1995-96 (LB)
Wukits, Al 1943 (C)
Wyatt, Antwuan 1997 (WR)
Wydo, Frank 1952-57 (T)
1953 All Pro Selection
Wyhonic, John 1946-47 (G)
Wynn, Dexter 2004-06 (CB)
Wynn, William 1973-76 (DE)

Y
Young, Adrian 1968-72 (LB)
Young, Charles 1973-6 (TE)
1973-75 All Pro Selection
1974-76 Pro Bowl
1973 NFC Rookie of the Year
Young, Glen 1983 (WR)
Young, Michael 1993 (WR)
Young, Roynell 1980-88 (CB)
1981 All Pro Selection
1982 Pro Bowl
Young, Scott 2005-p* (G)
Youngelman, Sid 1956-58 (T)
Yovicsin, John 1944 (E)

Z
Zabel, Steve 1970-74 (LB)
Zandofsky, Mike 1997 (G)
Zendejas, Luis 1988-89 (K)
Ziegler, Frank 1949-53 (B)
Zilly, John 1952 (E)
Zimmerman, Don 1972-76 (WR)
Zimmerman, Roy 1942-46 (B)
1943-44 All Pro Selection
Zizak, Vince 1934-37 (T)
Zomalt, Eric 1994-96 (S)
Zordich, Mike 1994-98 (S)
Zyntell, James 1933-35 (G)

EAGLES NICKNAMES

Ben	Agajanian	**Bootin' Ben**
David	Akers	**Green Akers**
David	Alexander	**Doughboy**
Eric	Allen	**The Flea**
Gary	Anderson	**Mr. Automatic**
Shawn	Andrews	**The Big Kid**
Neill	Armstrong	**Bird**
Walter	Barnes	**Piggy**
Billy	Barnes	**Bullet**
Fred	Barnett	**Arkansas**
Len	Barnum	**Feets**
Herman	Bassman	**Reds**
Chuck	Bednarik	**Concrete Charlie**
Todd	Bell	**Taco**
Bill	Bergey	**Bubba**
Ron	Blye	**Bye Bye**
Gary	Bolden	**The Mule**
Bill	Bradley	**Dollar**
Jerome	Brown	**Freight Train**
Aaron	Brown	**Chunky**
Jerome	Brown	**Freight Train**
Bob	Brown	**Boomer**
Reggie	Brown	**Downtown**
Don	Brumm	**Boomer**
Bill	Bryant	**Boone**
Correll	Buckhalter	**Buck**
Joe	Bukant	**Buckin**
Norm	Bulaich	**Big Boo**
John	Bunting	**Frito Bandito**
Adrian	Burk	**Abe**
Don	Burroughs	**Blade**
Tom	Bushby	**TomTom**
Keith	Byars	**Tank**
Glenn	Campbell	**Flash**
Tommy	Campbell	**Turk**
Marion	Campbell	**Swamp Fox**
Harold	Carmichael	**Hoagie**
Jim	Carr	**Gummy**
Cris	Carter	**Groucho**
Howard	Cassady	**Hopalong**
Dick	Chapura	**Tank**
Ken	Clarke	**Air**
Mike	Clarke	**Onside**
Trent	Cole	**The Hunter**
John	Coley	**King**
Brian	Dawkins	**Wolverine**
Richard	Dent	**The Colonel**
Mike	Ditka	**Iron Mike**
Elwood	Dow	**Rowdy**
Bill	Dunstan	**Popeye**
Marv	Ellstrom	**Swede**
Bryon	Evans	**B&E**
James	Feller	**Happy**
John	Ferko	**Fritz**
Jack	Ferrante	**Black Jack**
Neil	Ferris	**Wheel**
Eric	Floyd	**Pinky**
Hank	Fraley	**Honey Buns**
Bob	Freeman	**Goose**
Glenn	Frey	**Wackie**
Irving	Fryar	**Rev**
Greg	Garrity	**The Trashman**
Hal	Giancanelli	**Skippy**
Marion	Gianelli	**Yo Yo**
Carl	Hairston	**Big Daddy**
Thomas	Hanson	**Swede**
Maurice	Harper	**Moose**
Al	Harris	**Cheeseburger**
Dennis	Harrison	**Big Foot**
Alvin	Haymond	**Juggie**
Vaughn	Hebron	**Pretty Boy**
Bill	Hewitt	**Stinky**
Stuart	Hill	**King**
William	Holcomb	**Tex**
William	Hughes	**Boss**
John	Huzvar	**Jumbo**
Keith	Jackson	**Kjax**
Mike	Jarmoluk	**Big Mike**
Ed	Jasper	**Troup**
Ron	Jaworski	**Jaws**
Izell	Jenkins	**Toast**
Vaughan	Johnson	**Meat**
Carl	Jorgenson	**Bud**
Seth	Joyner	**Zeth**
Christian	Jurgensen	**Sonny**
Jevon	Kearse	**The Freak**
Allen	Keen	**Rabbit**
Ken	Keller	**Killer**
Bob	Kelley	**Whitey**
George	Kenneally	**Gus**

EAGLES NICKNAMES

Steve	Kennet	**Red Man**
Wade	Key	**Buck**
Howard	Keys	**Sonny**
Levon	Kirkland	**Captain Kirk**
Roger	Kirkman	**Red**
Scott	Kowalkowski	**Red**
Rich	Kraynak	**Conan**
Joe	Kresky	**Mink**
Emmett	Kriel	**Sally**
Joe	Lavender	**Big Bird**
Anthonia	Lee	**Amp**
Dorsey	Levens	**Horse**
Greg	Lewis	**G-Lew**
Charles	Leyendecker	**Tex**
John	Lipski	**Bull**
John	Magee	**Hog Jaw**
Ray	Mansfield	**The Old Ranger**
Kelvin	Martin	**Kmart**
Ed	Matesic	**Lefty**
Ollie	Matson	**Messiah**
Guy	McIntyre	**Angus**
Dennis	McKnight	**Conan**
Mark	McMillian	**Little Mac**
Donovan	McNabb	**Five**
Forrest	McPherson	**Aimee**
Ed	Meadows	**Country**
John	Mellekas	**Golden Greek**
Ed	Menske	**Eggs**
Keith	Millard	**Moamar**
Stephen	Miller	**Bubba**
Freddie	Mitchell	**FredEx**
Frank	Molden	**Bruno**
Art	Monk	**Money**
Eddie	Murray	**Money**
Al	Nelson	**Pete**
Davey	O'Brien	**Slingshot**
Terrell	Owens	**T.O.**
Artimus	Parker	**T Bone**
Clarence	Peaks	**High**
Edwin	Perot	**Petey**
William	Perry	**Refrigerator**
Pete	Pihos	**Golden Greek**
Todd	Pinkston	**Pinky**
Edwin	Pitts	**Alabama**
Joe	Pivernick	**Butch**
Art	Powell	**King Pin**
Abisha	Pritchard	**Bosh**
Mike	Quick	**Silk**
George	Rado	**Mousie**
Mike	Reichenback	**Rock 'em Back**
Andy	Reid	**BigRed**
Pete	Retzlaff	**The Baron**
John	Roberts	**The Ripper**
William	Roffler	**Bud**
Herbert	Roton	**Bummie**
Everitt	Rowan	**Deb**
James	Russell	**Casey**
Lafayette	Russell	**Reb**
David	Ryan	**Buddy**
John	Ryan	**Rocky**
Clyde	Scott	**Smackover**
Mike	Sebastian	**The Sharon Express**
Lawrence	Shaw	**Buck**
Health	Sherman	**Wolfman**
Fred	Smalls	**Boom Boom**
Dave	Smukler	**Dynamite**
Norman	Snead	**Stormin**
Ken	Snyder	**Lum**
Ray	Spillers	**Brush**
Duce	Staley	**Buddy Lee**
Herschel	Stockton	**Mule**
Tom	Sullivan	**Silky**
William	Thomas	**Tra**
Clarence	Thomason	**Stumpy**
Jeremiah	Trotter	**Axeman**
Rick	Tuten	**Bootin**
Norm	Van Brocklin	**The Dutchman**
Bobby	Walston	**The Sheriff**
Andre	Waters	**Muddy**
Albert	Weiner	**Reds**
Brian	Westbrook	**B West**
Reggie	White	**Minister of Defense**
Norm	Willey	**Wild Man**
Clyde	Williams	**Weenie**
Henry	Willimas	**Gizmo**
Osborne	Willson	**Diddie**
Al	Wistert	**Big Ox**
Neil	Worden	**Bull**
Charles	Young	**Tree**
James	Zyntell	**Iggy**

LAST TIME THE TEAM...

WON IN OVERTIME
By Eagles: 10/24/04 Eagles win at Cleveland, 34-31
By Opponent: 9/17/06 Giants win at Philadelphia, 30-24

WON BY SCORING IN THE LAST TWO MINUTES OF REGULATION
By Eagles: 9/25/05 Eagles win vs. Oakland, 23-20 (last score at 0:09)
By Opponent: 10/21/07 Bears win at Philadelphia, 19-16 (last score at 0:09)

TIED GAME BY SCORING IN THE LAST TWO MINUTES OF REGULATION
By Eagles: 12/11/05 Eagles loss vs. NY Giants, 26-23 ot (tied game at 1:52)
By Opponent: 10/15/06 Giants win at Philadelphia, 30-24 ot (tied game at 0:10)

WON ON NATIONAL TELEVISION
By Eagles: 12/16/07 Eagles win at Dallas, 10-6
By Opponent: 11/25/07 Patriots win at New England, 31-28

WON IN PRIME TIME
By Eagles: 12/4/06 Eagles win vs. Carolina, 27-24
By Opponent: 11/25/07 Patriots win at New England, 31-28

SHUTOUT
By Eagles: 12/1/1996 Win vs. Giants at PhiladeLphia, 24-0
By Opponent: 12/5/05 Seahawks win at Philadelphia, 42-0

WON BY 20-OR-MORE POINTS
By Eagles: 9/23/07 Eagles win vs. Detroit, 56-21
By Opponent: 11/4/07 Cowboys win at Philadelphia, 38-17

WON AFTER TRAILING BY 20-OR-MORE POINTS
By Eagles: 10/3/1993 Eagles win at NY Jets, 35-30
(Jets ahead 21-0 in 2nd quarter)
By Opponent: 9/12/1999 Cardinals win at Philadelphia, 25-24
(Eagles ahead 21-0 in 1st quarter)

HELD A 28-OR-MORE POINT LEAD
By Eagles: 9/23/07 Eagles win vs. Detroit, 56-21 (35)
By Opponent: 11/4/07 Cowboys win at Philadelphia, 38-10 (28)

HELD A 21-OR-MORE POINT LEAD
By Eagles: 9/23/07 Eagles win vs. Detroit, 56-21 (35)
By Opponent: 11/4/07 Cowboys win at Philadelphia, 38-17 (21)

HELD A 14-OR-MORE POINT LEAD
By Eagles: 12/23/07 Eagles win at New Orleans, 38-23 (15)
By Opponent: 11/4/07 Cowboys win at Philadelphia, 38-17 (21)

SCORED 20-OR-MORE POINTS IN A QUARTER
By Eagles: 12/23/07 Eagles win at New Orleans, 38-23 (21 points, 1st Q)
By Opponent: 12/5/05 Seahawks win at Philadelphia, 42-0 (21 points, 2nd Q)

SCORED 20-OR-MORE POINTS IN A HALF
By Eagles: 12/23/07 Eagles win at New Orleans, 38-23 (24 points, 1st half)
By Opponent: 12/2/07 Seahawks win at Philadelphia, 28-24 (21 points, 1st half)

HELD OPPONENT WITHOUT A TOUCHDOWN
By Eagles: 12/30/07 Eagles win vs. Buffalo, 17-9 (3 FGs)
By Opponent: 9/17/06 Redskins win at Philadelphia, 20-12 (4 FGs)

TOUCHDOWNS SCORED BY OFFENSE AND DEFENSE
By Eagles: 12/17/06 Eagles win at NY Giants, 36-22 (4 offense, 1 defense)
By Opponent: 11/25/07 Patriots win at New England, 31-28 (3 offense, 1 defense)

TOUCHDOWNS SCORED BY OFFENSE, DEFENSE AND SPECIAL TEAMS
By Eagles: 12/24/1994 Eagles loss at Cincinnati, 33-30
(1 offense, 1 defense, 1 special teams)
By Opponent: 11/19/06 Titans win at Philadelphia, 31-13
(2 offense, 1 defense, 1 special teams)

TOUCHDOWN SCORED ON FIRST DRIVE
By Eagles: 12/23/07 Eagles win at New Orleans, 38-23
By Opponent: 12/23/07 Eagles win at New Orleans, 38-23

SAFETY SCORED
By Eagles: 12/7/03 Cowboys center Matt Lehr errant snap goes out of end zone at Philadelphia
By Opponent: 1/19/02 Sean Landeta runs out of the back of the end zone at Chicago [playoffs]
9/9/1996 Rodney Peete sacked in end zone by Reggie White and Santana Dotson at Green Bay

SUCCESSFUL TWO POINT CONVERSION
By Eagles: 12/17/06 L.J. Smith pass from Jeff Garcia at NY Giants
By Opponent: 10/17/04 Keary Colbert pass from Jake Delhomme vs. Carolina

FAILED TWO POINT CONVERSION ATTEMPT
By Eagles: 11/11/07 Pass failed from Donovan McNabb to Matt Schobel
By Opponent: 11/11/07 Pass failed Jason Campbell to Antwan Randle El

FUMBLE RECOVERED FOR TOUCHDOWN
By Eagles: 12/30/07 Kevin Curtis recovered a Reggie Brown fumble in the endzone vs. Bills
By Opponent: 9/30/07 Kavika Mitchell recovered a Donovan McNabb fumble and returned it 17 yards at NY Giants

TOUCHDOWN OFF OF FAKE FIELD GOAL
By Eagles: 12/24/1989 Cris Carter 22-yard pass from Roger Ruzek vs. Phoenix
By Opponent: 12/20/1998 Holder Eric Bjornson 7-yard run at Dallas

TOUCHDOWN OFF OF FAKE PUNT
By Eagles: 9/29/02 Brian Dawkins 57 yard pass from Brian Mitchell vs. Houston
By Opponent: (could not find an instance when it occurred)

NO TURNOVERS
By Eagles: 10/28/07 Eagles win at Minnesota, 23-16
By Opponent: 12/30/07 Eagles win vs. Buffalo, 17-9

TOUCHDOWN DRIVE OF 10-OR-MORE PLAYS
By Eagles: 12/30/07 Eagles win vs. Buffalo, 17-9
(12 plays; Brent Celek 2-yd. pass from Donovan McNabb)
By Opponent: 11/25/07 Patriots win at New England, 31-28
(10 plays; Laurence Maroney 4-yd. run)

TOUCHDOWN DRIVE OF 80-OR-MORE YARDS
By Eagles: 12/23/07 Eagles win at New Orleans, 38-23 (98 yards; Greg Lewis 9-yd. pass from Donovan McNabb)
By Opponent: 11/11/07 Eagles win at Washington, 33-25 (92 yards; James Thrash 12-yd. pass from Jason Campbell)

TOUCHDOWN DRIVE OF FIVE-OR-MORE MINUTES
By Eagles: 12/30/07 Eagles win vs. Buffalo, 17-9 (5:59; Brent Celek 2-yd. pass from Donovan McNabb)
By Opponent: 11/25/07 Patriots win at New England, 31-28 (5:03; Heath Evans 1-yd. run)

LAST TIME THE OFFENSE...

500-or-More Total Net Yards of Offense
By Eagles: 9/23/07 Eagles win vs. Detroit, 56-21
(536; 173 rushing, 363 passing)
By Opponent: 10/30/05 Eagles loss at Denver, 49-21
(564; 255 rushing, 309 passing)

400-or-More Total Net Yards of Offense
By Eagles: 12/23/07 Eagles win at New Orleans, 38-23
(435, 184 rushing, 251 passing)
By Opponent: 11/25/07 Patriots win at New England, 31-28
(410; 48 rushing, 362 passing)

300-or More Net Yards Rushing by Team
By Eagles: 9/3/2000 Eagles win at Dallas, 41-14 (306)
By Opponent: 9/25/1960 Browns win at Philadephia, 41-24 (329)

200-or-More Net Yards Rushing by Team
By Eagles: 11/18/07 Eagles win vs. Miami, 17-7 (202)
By Opponent: 12/10/2006 Redskins loss at Washington, 21-19 (210)

Individual 200-Yard Rushing Game
By Eagles: 9/3/2000 Duce Staley (26-201-1TD) at Dallas
By Opponent: 12/28/2002 Tiki Barber (32-203-0TDs) at New York

Individual 150-Yard Rushing Game
By Eagles: 10/20/2002 Duce Staley (24-152-0TDs) vs. Tampa Bay
By Opponent: 12/10/2006 Ladell Betts (33-171-0TDs) at Washington

Individual 100-Yard Rushing Game
By Eagles: 12/23/07 Brian Westbrook (17-100-0TDs) at New Orleans
By Opponent: 12/30/07 Marshawn Lynch (22-105-0TDs) vs. Buffalo

Two 100-Yard Rushers in the Same Game
By Eagles: 10/28/02 Duce Staley (24-126-0TDs)
& Donovan McNabb (8-107-1TD) vs. NY Giants
By Opponent: 10/30/05 Mike Anderson
(21-126-1TD) and Tatum Bell (14-107-2TDs) at Denver

Consecutive 100-Yard Rushing Games
By Eagles: 11/11/07-11/18/07 Brian Westbrook (20-100-1TD) at Washington;
Brian Westbrook (32-148-0TDs) vs. Miami
By Opponent: 11/19/06 - 11/26/06 Travis Henry (18-143-1TD) vs. Ten.;
Joseph Addai (24-171-4TDs) at Ind.

Combined 200-Yard Rushing by Two Players
By Eagles: 10/28/02 237 by Duce Staley (24-126-0TDs)
& Donovan McNabb (8-107-1TD) vs. NY Giants
By Opponent: 12/10/06 209 by Ladell Betts (33-171-0TDs)
& Jason campbell (4-38-0TDs) at Washington

Individual with 30-or-More Carries
By Eagles: 11/18/07 Brian Westbrook
(32-148-0TDs) vs. Miami
By Opponent: 11/11/07 Clinton Portis
(30-137-0TDs) at Washington

Individual with 25-or-More Carries
By Eagles: 11/18/07 Brian Westbrook
(32-148-0TDs) vs. Miami
By Opponent: 11/11/07 Clinton Portis
(30-137-0TDs) at Washington

Rushing Play of 80-or-More Yards
By Eagles: 10/1/00 85t by Brian Mitchell vs. Atlanta
By Opponent: 9/30/01 80 by Troy Hambrick vs. Dallas

Rushing Play of 60-or-More Yards
By Eagles: 9/24/06 71t by Brian Westbrook at San Francisco
By Opponent: 11/19/06 70t by Travis Henry vs. Tennessee

Rushing Play of 40-or-More Yards
By Eagles: 12/23/07 40 by Donovan McNabb at New Orleans
By Opponent: 12/30/07 56 by Marshawn Lynch vs. Buffalo

Individual with Two-or-More Rushing Touchdowns
By Eagles: 9/23/07 Brian Westbrook
(14-110-2TDs) vs. Detroit
By Opponent: 12/23/07 Aaron Stecker
(13-49-2TDs) at New Orleans

400 Net Yards Passing by Team
By Eagles: 9/18/05 Eagles win vs. San Francisco, 42-3 (443)
By Opponent: 11/4/07 Cowboys win at Philadelphia, 38-17 (434)

300 Net Yards Passing by Team
By Eagles: 12/30/07 Eagles win vs. Buffalo, 17-9
By Opponent: 11/25/07 Patriots win at New England, 31-28 (362)

Individual with 50-or-More Pass Attempts
By Eagles: 10/23/05 Donovan McNabb
(54-35-287-2-1TD) vs. San Diego
By Opponent: 11/25/07 Tom Brady
(54-34-380-0-1TD) at New England

Individual with 40-or-More Pass Attempts
By Eagles: 12/30/07 Donovan McNabb
(41-29-345-1TD) vs. Buffalo
By Opponent: 12/23/07 Drew Brees
(45-30-289-1-0TDs) at New Orleans

Individual with 30-or-More Pass Completions
By Eagles: 10/23/05 Donovan McNabb
(54-35-287-2-1TD) vs. San Diego
By Opponent: 12/23/07 Drew Brees
(45-30-289-1-0TDs) at New Orleans

Individual with 25-or-More Pass Completions
By Eagles: 12/30/07 Donovan McNabb
(41-29-345-1TD) vs. Buffalo
By Opponent: 12/23/07 Drew Brees
(45-30-289-1-0TDs) at New Orleans

LAST TIME THE OFFENSE...

No Sacks Allowed
By Eagles: 11/18/07 Eagles win vs. Miami, 17-7
(19 attempts - A.J. Feeley & 11 attempts - Donovan McNabb)
By Opponent: 12/30/07 Eagles win vs. Buffalo, 17-9
(30 attempts - Donovan McNabb)

Individual 300-Yard Passing Game
By Eagles: 12/30/07 Donovan McNabb
(41-29-345-1 TD) vs. Buffalo
By Opponent: 11/25/07 Tom Brady
(54-34-380-0-1 TD) at New England

Consecutive 300-Yard Passing Games
By Eagles: 9/10/06 - 9/17/06 Donovan McNabb (35-24-314-1-3TDs) at Houston; McNabb (45-27-350-0-2TDs) vs. NY Giants
By Opponent: 12/2/90 - 12/9/90 Jim Kelly (32-19-334-1-3TDs) at Buffalo; Dan Marino (54-27-365-0-2TDs) at Miami

Individual with Four-or-More Touchdown Passes
By Eagles: 11/11/07 Donovan McNabb
(28-20-251-0-4TDs) at Washington
By Opponent: 10/30/05 Jake Plummer
(35-22-309-0-4TDs) at Denver

Individual with Three-or-More Touchdown Passes
By Eagles: 12/23/07 Donovan McNabb
(35-24-263-0-3TDs) at New Orleans
By Opponent: 11/11/07 Jason Campbell (34-23-215-0-3TDs) at Washington

Individual with 10-or-more Receptions
By Eagles: 11/4/07 Brian Westbrook (14-90-0TDs) vs. Dallas
By Opponent: 11/25/07 Wes Welker (13-149-0 TDs) at New England

Individual with 150-Yard Receiving Game
By Eagles: 9/23/07 Kevin Curtis (11-221-3TDs) vs. Detroit
By Opponent: 11/4/07 Terrell Owens (10-174-1TD) vs. Dallas

Individual with 100-Yard Receiving Game
By Eagles: 12/2/07 Kevin Curtis (6-111-1TD) vs. Seattle
By Opponent: 12/16/07 Jason Witten (8-113-0TD) at Dallas

Two 100-Yard Receivers in the Same Game
By Eagles: 9/23/07 Kevin Curtis (11-221-3TDs) & Brian Westbrook (5-111-1TD) vs. Detroit
By Opponent: 9/17/06 Amani Toomer
(12-137-2TDs) & Plaxico Burress (6-114-1TD) vs. NY Giants

Consecutive 100-Yard Receiving Games
By Eagles: 10/15/06 - 10/22/06 Reggie Brown (6-121-1TD) at New Orleans; Brian Westbrook (7-113-1TD) at Tampa Bay
By Opponent: 12/9/07 - 12/16/07 Plaxico Burress (7-136-1TD) vs. NY Giants; Jason Witten (8-113-0TDs) at Dallas

Pass Play of 80-or-More Yards
By Eagles: 12/31/06 89t, A.J. Feeley to Hank Baskett vs. Atlanta
By Opponent: 9/23/07 91t, Jon Kitna to Roy Williams vs. Detroit

Pass Play of 60-or-More Yards
By Eagles: 10/14/07 75t, Donovan McNabb to Kevin Curtis at NY Jets
By Opponent: 9/23/07 91t, Jon Kitna to Roy Williams vs. Detroit

Pass Play of 40-or-More Yards
By Eagles: 12/30/07 40, Donovan McNabb to Greg Lewis vs. Buffalo
By Opponent: 12/23/07 52, Drew Brees to Devery Henderson at New Orleans

Individual with Three-or-More Touchdown Receptions
By Eagles: 9/23/07 Kevin Curtis (11-221-3TDs) vs. Detroit
By Opponent: 10/3/1993 Johnny Mitchell (7-146-3TDs) at NY Jets

Individual with Two-or-More Touchdown Receptions
By Eagles: 11/25/07 Greg Lewis (4-88-2TDs) at New England
By Opponent: 11/11/07 James Thrash (5-85-2TDs) at Washington

Led Team in Both Rushing and Receiving Yards in the Same Game
By Eagles: 11/11/07 Brian Westbrook
(18-81-0TDs rushing, 9-63-0TDs receiving) at Dallas
By Opponent: 12/4/06 DeAngelo Hall
(17-74-0TDs rushing, 7-101-1TD receiving) vs. Carolina

100-Yard Rusher & Receiver in the Same Game
By Eagles: 10/14/07 Brian Westbrook
(20-120-0TDs rus.) & Kevin Curtis
(5-121-1TD rec.) at NY Jets
By Opponent: 12/11/05 Tiki Barber
(32-124-0TDs) & Jeremy Shockey (10-107-0TDs) vs. NY Giants

100-Yard Rusher, 100-Yard Receiver & 300-Yard Passer in the Same Game
By Eagles: 9/23/07 Brian Westbrook (14-110-2TDs rush. & 5-111-1TD rec.) & Kevin Curtis (11-221-3TDs rec.) vs. Detroit
Donovan McNabb
(26-21-381-0-4TDs) vs. Detroit
By Opponent: 12/11/05 Tiki Barber
(32-124-0TDs), Jeremy Shockey (10-107-0TDs) & Eli Manning (44-28-312-3-1TD) vs. NY Giants

Individual with at Least One Rushing and One Receiving Touchdown in the Same Game
By Eagles: 11/11/07 Brian Westbrook
(20-100-1TD rushing, 5-83-2TDs receiving) at Washington
By Opponent: 11/7/04 Hines Ward
(1-16-1TD rushing, 2-32-1TD receiving) at Pittsburgh

Individual with at Least One Rushing Touchdown and One Touchdown Pass in the Same Game
By Eagles: 10/8/06 Donovan McNabb
(33-18-354-0-2TDs passing, 1-1-1TD rushing) vs. Dallas
By Opponent: 12/11/05 Eli Manning
(44-28-312-3-1TD passing, 4-8-1TD rushing) vs. NY Giants

LAST TIME THE DEFENSE...

HELD OPPONENT UNDER 200 YARDS TOTAL OFFENSE
By Eagles: 11/18/07 Eagles win vs. Miami, 17-7
(186; 77 rushing, 109 passing)
By Opponent: 9/30/07 Giants win at New York, 16-3
(190; 114 rushing, 76 passing)

HELD OPPONENT UNDER 300 YARDS TOTAL OFFENSE
By Eagles: 12/30/07 Eagles win vs. Buffalo, 17-9
(271; 138 rushing, 133 passing)
By Opponent: 12/10/06 Redskins loss at Washington, 21-19
(263; 99 rushing, 164 passing)

HELD OPPONENT UNDER 50 YARDS RUSHING
By Eagles: 11/25/07 Patriots win at New England, 31-28 (48)
By Opponent: 12/31/06 Eagles win vs. Atlanta, 24-27 (43)

HELD OPPONENT UNDER 75 YARDS RUSHING
By Eagles: 12/23/07 Eagles win at New Orleans, 38-23 (65)
By Opponent: 12/30/07 Eagles win vs. Buffalo, 17-9 (69)

HELD OPPONENT UNDER 100 YARDS RUSHING
By Eagles: 12/16/07 Eagles win at Dallas, 10-6 (53)
By Opponent: 12/30/07 Eagles win vs. Buffalo, 17-9 (69)

HELD OPPONENT UNDER 100 NET YARDS PASSING
By Eagles: 11/19/06 Eagles loss vs. Tennessee, 31-13 (84)
By Opponent: 9/30/07 Giants win at New York, 3-16 (76)

HELD OPPONENT UNDER 150 NET YARDS PASSING
By Eagles: 12/30/07 Eagles win vs. Buffalo, 17-9 (133)
By Opponent: 9/30/07 Giants win at New York, 3-16 (76)

HELD OPPONENT UNDER 200 NET YARDS PASSING
By Eagles: 12/30/07 Eagles win vs. Buffalo, 17-9 (133)
By Opponent: 12/16/07 Eagles win at Dallas, 10-6 (181)

INTERCEPTION RETURN FOR A TOUCHDOWN
By Eagles: 12/17/06 Trent Cole, 19 yards (QB Eli Manning) at NY Giants
By Opponent: 11/25/07 Asante Samuel, 40 yards (QB A.J. Feeley) at New England

INDIVIDUAL WITH THREE-OR-MORE INTERCEPTIONS
By Eagles: 10/23/66 Joe Scarpati (1-Earl Morrall, 2-Gary Wood) at NY Giants
By Opponent: 12/2/07 Lofa Tatupu (3-A.J. Feeley) vs. Seattle

INDIVIDUAL WITH TWO-OR-MORE INTERCEPTIONS
By Eagles: 10/8/06 Lito Sheppard (2-Drew Bledsoe) vs. Dallas
By Opponent: 12/2/07 Lofa Tatupu (3-A.J. Feeley) vs. Seattle

SEVEN-OR-MORE SACKS BY TEAM
By Eagles: 9/23/07 Eagles win vs. Detroit, 56-21 (9)
By Opponent: 9/30/07 Giants win at New York, 3-16 (12)

SIX-OR-MORE SACKS BY TEAM
By Eagles: 9/23/07 Eagles win vs. Detroit, 56-21 (9)
By Opponent: 9/30/07 Giants win at New York, 3-16 (12)

FIVE-OR-MORE SACKS BY TEAM
By Eagles: 9/23/07 Eagles win vs. Detroit, 56-21 (9)
By Opponent: 9/30/07 Giants win at New York, 3-16 (12)

INDIVIDUAL WITH THREE-OR MORE SACKS
By Eagles: 9/23/07 Trent Cole (3.0 of Jon Kitna) vs. Detroit
By Opponent: 9/30/07 Osi Yumenyiora
(6.0 of Donovan McNabb) at NY Giants

INDIVIDUAL WITH TWO-OR MORE SACKS
By Eagles: 12/9/07 T. Cole (2.0 sacks of Eli Manning) vs. NY Giants
By Opponent: 9/30/07 Osi Yumenyiora (6.0 of Donovan McNabb) at NY Giants

LAST TIME THE SPECIAL TEAMS...

KICKOFF RETURN FOR A TOUCHDOWN
By Eagles: 11/4/01 Brian Mitchell, 94 yards at Arizona
By Opponent: 10/2/05 Dante Hall, 96 yards at Kansas City

KICKOFF RETURN FOR A TOUCHDOWN TO START A GAME
By Eagles: 11/4/01 Brian Mitchell, 94 yards at Arizona
By Opponent: 10/12/03 Randal Williams, 37 yards at Dallas

PUNT RETURN FOR A TOUCHDOWN
By Eagles: 12/21/03 Brian Westbrook, 81 yards vs. San Francisco
By Opponent: 11/18/07 Ted Ginn Jr., 87 yards vs. Miami

BLOCKED PUNT RECOVERED FOR TOUCHDOWN
By Eagles: 11/22/92 Ken Rose returned Sean Landeta's blocked punt (blocked by Rose) 3 yards at NY Giants
By Opponent: 11/10/96 Gabe Northern returned Tom Hutton's blocked punt (blocked by Northern) 18 yards vs. Buffalo

BLOCKED PUNT
By Eagles: 11/28/04 Jevon Kearse blocked Jeff Feagles' punt at NY Giants
By Opponent: 11/20/05 David Tyree blocked Reggie Hodges' punt at NY Giants

BLOCKED PAT
By Eagles: 10/30/88 Reggie White blocked a PAT attempt by Greg Davis vs. Atlanta
By Opponent: 12/19/04 Greg Ellis blocked a PAT attempt by David Akers vs. Dallas

MISSED (NOT BLOCKED) PAT
By Eagles: 9/25/05 Mark Simoneau vs. Oakland
By Opponent: 11/11/07 Shawn Suisham at Washington

BLOCKED FIELD GOAL
By Eagles: 10/23/05 Quintin Mikell blocked a 40-yard attempt by Nate Kaeding vs. San Diego
By Opponent: 10/2/05 Eric Hicks blocked a 40-yard attempt by Todd France at Kansas City

INDIVIDUAL WITH FIVE-OR MORE FIELD GOALS
By Eagles: 11/18/01 David Akers (5-5) at Dallas
By Opponent: 12/3/00 Al Del Greco (5-5) vs. Tennessee

INDIVIDUAL WITH FOUR-OR MORE FIELD GOALS
By Eagles: 9/17/07 David Akers (4-4) vs. Washington
By Opponent: 10/21/07 Robbie Gould (4-5) vs. Chicago

INDIVIDUAL WITH THREE-OR MORE FIELD GOALS
By Eagles: 10/28/07 David Akers (3-4) at Minnesota
By Opponent: 12/30/07 Ryan Lindell (3-3) vs. Buffalo

SUCCESSFUL ONSIDES KICK
By Eagles: 11/25/07 David Akers kick recovered by Eagles Hank Baskett (2nd Q)
By Opponent: 10/8/07 Ryan Longwell kick recovered by Vikings Heath Farwell at Minnesota (1st Q)

FAILED ONSIDES KICK ATTEMPT
By Eagles: 10/29/06 David Akers kick recovered by Jaguars Daryl Smith at Philadelphia (4th Q)
By Opponent: 9/24/06 Joe Nedney kick recovered by Greg Lewis at San Francisco (4th Q)

OVER THE PAST 75 YEARS - THE EAGLES...

BEST SEASON, WIN PERCENTAGE
1949 Won 12, Lost 1, Percentage .923

BEST SEASON, WIN TOTAL
2004 13 wins, 3 losses

WORST SEASON
1936 Won 1, Lost 11, Percentage .083

LONGEST WINNING STREAK
9 (10/19/03 - 12/15/03)
9 (9/30/60 - 12/4/60)

LONGEST WINNING STREAK AT HOME
13 (12/12/47 - 12/11/49)

LONGEST LOSING STREAK AT HOME
8 (9/20/36 - 9/21/37)

LONGEST WINNING STREAK ON ROAD
9 (10/19/03 - 10/24/04)
9 (11/12/00 - 12/16/01)

LONGEST LOSING STREAK ON ROAD
13 (10/15/39 - 12/1/40)

LONGEST LOSING STREAK
14 (9/20/36 - 9/21/37)

MOST CONSECUTIVE WINS - START OF SEASON
7 in 2004

MOST CONSECUTIVE WINS - END OF SEASON
8 in 1949 (Reg. Season)

MOST CONSECUTIVE LOSSES -
Start of Season - 11 in 1968

MOST CONSECUTIVE LOSSES -
End of Season - 11 in 1936

TOTAL SHUTOUTS BY EAGLES
35 last vs. NYG, 12/1/96

MOST SHUTOUTS IN A SEASON
4 in 1934 and 1948

MOST CONSECUTIVE GAMES - SCORED POINTS
126 (11/8/42 - 12/8/53)

MOST CONSECUTIVE GAMES - SCORED TOUCHDOWN
88 (11/8/42 - 11/26/50)

LARGEST COMEBACK VICTORY BY EAGLES
28-24 vs. Chicago Cardinals
at Metropolitan Stadium, October 25, 1959 (came back from 24-0 deficit in 3rd qtr.)

28-24 vs. Washington Redskins
at Griffith Stadium, October 27, 1946
(came back from 24-0 deficit at halftime)

LARGEST COMEBACK VS. EAGLES
28-23 vs. Minnesota Vikings
at Veterans Stadium, December 1, 1985
(came back from 23-0 deficit in 4th QTR

AUTOGRAPHS

AUTOGRAPHS

AUTOGRAPHS

AUTOGRAPHS